BLACK MAN
OF THE NILE

BLACK MAN OF THE NILE AND HIS FAMILY

Published 1989, by
BLACK CLASSIC PRESS

with the permission of the author. We are indebted to Malik Azeez for preparing the Select Bibliography, Noni Faruq for preparing the Name and Subject Index, and graphic artist extraordinaire, Tony Browder, for our cover.

©1970,1972 Yosef ben-Jochannan
all rights reserved
Originally published by Alkebul-lan Books Associates

Printed by BCP Digital Printing, *a division of Black Classic Press*

Library of Congress Catalog Card Number 88-61274
ISBN: 0-933121-26-1

Founded in 1978, Black Classic Press specializes in bringing to light obscure and significant works by and about people of African descent. If our books are not available in your area, ask your local bookseller to order them. For our current list of titles, visit our website at http://www.blackclassic.com or write:

Black Classic Press
c/o List
P.O. Box 13414
Baltimore, MD 21203

BLACK MAN
OF THE NILE

AND
HIS
FAMILY

By Dr. Yosef A.A. ben-Jochannan

DEDICATED TO MY DAUGHTER COLLETTE DENISE [Makeda] AND SON KWAME
EDWIN, BOTH OF WHOM REPRESENT THE FUTURE AFRICAN PEOPLES EVERY-
WHERE; ALSO, TO MISS LARUE HEARD WHO PASSED ON TO AN UNTIMELY DEATH
IN 1969 C. E. AT AGE 24 AFTER HAVING WON THE PULITZER PRIZE WITH OTHERS
FOR HER STORY ON THE "Detroit Riot" OF 1968. SHE WAS AN INSPIRATION TO
YOUNG BLACK WOMANHOOD EVERYWHERE.

Works available by Dr. Ben

African Origins of the Major Western Religions. 1970*, 1991. 363 pp. (paper $24.95, ISBN 0933121-29-6). First published in 1970, this work continues to be instructive and fresh. Dr. Ben critically examines the history, beliefs, and myths that are the foundation of Judaism, Christianity, and Islam. He highlights the often overlooked African influences and roots of these religions. The Black Classic Press edition is a facsimile edition, with an added index and extended bibliography.

Black Man of the Nile. 1972*, 1989. 381 pp. illus. bibl. (paper $24.95, ISBN 0933121-26-1). In a masterful and unique manner, Dr. Ben uses Black Man of the Nile to challenge and expose "Europeanized" African history. He reveals distortion after distortion made in the long record of African contributions to world civilization. Once these distortions are exposed, he attacks them with a vengeance, and provides a spellbinding corrective lesson. Of all the works published by Dr. Ben, this one remains a treasured all-time favorite. Readers continue to demand this work.

A Chronology of the Bible: Challenge to the standard version. Yosef ben-Jochannan.* 1972, 1995. 24 pp.(paper $4.00, ISBN 0-933121-28-8). Chronology documents the African origins of Judaism, Christianity, and Islam. Dr. Ben traces some of the significant influences, developments, and people that have shaped and provided the foundation for the holy books used in these religions.

Abu Simbel to Ghizeh. 1987*, 1989. 350 pp. illus. gloss. (paper $22.00, ISBN 0933121-27-X). This tour guide is an alternative to guides written for and by Europeans. Dr. Ben draws from his many years of travel, study, and living in Egypt to provide a useful history and guide to ancient Egyptian/African monuments, cultural sites, and prominent people. Although it is intended for readers who plan to travel to Egypt, this guide is helpful to anyone who wants to gain a better understanding of ancient African history.

Africa: Mother of Western Civilization. 1971*, 1988. 750 pp. illus. bibl. (paper $34.95, ISBN 0933121-25-3). Dr. Ben examines the African foundations of Western civilization. In lecture essay format, he identifies and corrects myths about the inferiority and primitiveness of the indigenous African peoples and their descendants. He mentions many authorities on Africa and their works and proves how they are racist in intent. Dr. Ben is often humorous, and always critical of traditional Western scholarship and values.

We The Black Jews. 1983*, 1993. 408 pp. (paper $24.95, ISBN 0933121-40-7). Dr. Ben destroys the myth of a "white Jewish race" and the bigotry that has denied the existence of an African Jewish culture. He establishes the legitimacy of contemporary Black Jewish culture in Africa and the diaspora, and predates its origin before ancient Nile Valley civilizations. This work provides insight and historical relevance to the current discussion of Jewish and Black cultural relationships.

To order, send a check or money order to:

Black Classic Press
P.O. Box 13414
Baltimore, MD 21203-3414

Credit Card Orders Call—1-800-476-8870
Please have your credit card available.
Include $3.00 for the first book ordered, $1.00 for each additional title.

* *indicates first year published*

Content

LIST OF ILLUSTRATIONS:

PREFACE

In this volume facts of African history which have been for so long purposefully withheld from the public shall be revealed and carefully explained. Africa [Alkebu-lan] will be seen from eyes which are different to the Henry Morton Stanley and Dr. David Livingston's drama; the salvation through Jesus Christ view-point; the Tarzan and Jane atmosphere; the "Great White Father" paternalism; and last, but not least, it will not include "the lazy Africans who did nothing in Africa before slavery," and "developed nothing or created nothing historically" propaganda angle of the "Christian missionaries." These age-old stereotyped racist conceptions about the Africans shall not appear in this book.

The culture of the indigenous peoples of Africa [Alkebu-lan] was copied and adopted extensively by the so-called "Modern" or "Western Man" [Caucasian, or White Man]. Much of "Western Man's" culture also came from an Africa, which once held the central focal point of learning of all forms; where man himself has so far proven to have originated; at least, where the oldest forms of man have been unearthed [discovered]; also man as he is known today. This Africa, correctly Alkebu-lan, will be reviewed from firsthand information recorded during the periods when the Africans were the teachers of the world, and since.

Bearing in mind what has just been stated, a statement of the main purpose for this work is now being entered into, since so many other books on Africa [Alkebu-lan] and her peoples are being "manufactured" in such abundance these days. Remember however, that this work cannot cover every minute detail dealing with Africa's history; neither can it cover all areas of African history which each reader believes to be the most important development in Africa, nor can the material selection satisfy everyone.

Some of the major and most pivotal occurrences which contributed to the earliest African High-Cultures, from prehistoric times to the final days of the West African Kingdoms and Empires, shall be reviewed.

No attempt is being made to claim that this work is based upon an UNBIASED presentation of the subject, as in the case of so many other works on the history and High-Culture of Africa. In fact, many such authors find themselves wrapped up in their own prejudices which they too often incorporate into their works.

What does this work seeks to accomplish which others before it have not yet achieved?

Simply the following: It is an honest effort to present Africa's history, some aspects
of it, from an African's [Black man's] point of view; an understanding of how a Black
man and his fellow Black men [Africans] see their "Mother Continent" - Africa [Alkebu-
lan]. Not only how the African sees his history, from his point of view, but also how he
sees those who are most responsible for Africa's present deplorable conditions and the
degradation which her children still suffer at the hands of Europeans and European-
Americans; and most importantly, how a Black man and his fellow Black men view
those who have been most responsible for the deliberate suppression and distortion of
"TRUE" African history. An interpretation of history such as this may assist the reader to better understand the present social disruptions in progress in Africa and everywhere else the African [Black man] and his descendants reside.

This work is also an attempt to create in the young African, African-American
[Black person], and all other youthful people, a sense of pride in his or her great African heritage. For "HERITAGE" is that something which all other people are reminded
of daily. And, since this work is being produced in the United States of America, it is
specifically directed to those who have criminally demasculinized, denuded, and otherwise debased the Africans of their CULTURAL, ECONOMIC, POLITICAL, SCIENTIFIC,
SPIRITUAL, and all other forms of their heritage and human decency. Religion and the
European and European-American colonialists, for over the past three to four-hundred
years, shall be shown to be two of the basic causes of Africa's downfall. Of course
there is no attempt made to dismiss from guilt those Africans [Blacks] who contributed
in the past, and in the present, to the criminal conspiracy of genocide against their own
African brothers and sisters for their own selfish economic gains.

The writing style, which contains numerous redundancies, repetitions and emphases
[according to the average "Western" reader], is more closely African than it is European or European-American, and as such may be a new experience. While the reader
may find other works more journalistically excellent than this, the objective of this
work is to present AFRICAN ORIGINS OF EUROPEAN CIVILIZATION in a manner where-
by scholars can find substantial use for it in their research; as much as the layman can
for general information. This work is also presented to reach the mind of those young
peoples and adults who are in search of another face of "TRUTH" about mankind in Africa [Alkebu-lan]; those who are not too prejudice to be able to see "TRUTH" other than
in terms of skin pigmentation.

xii

Still another objective of this work is its presentation of pertinent data needed in the African peoples' RE-IDENTIFICATION with their great ancestral heritage. For the BLACK PEOPLES have maintained that:

> IF THE EUROPEAN JEWS CAN FIGHT FOR AN ARID PIECE OF DESERT; THE IRISH FOR A SMALL EMERALD ISLAND; THE BRITISH FOR A BARREN ISLAND OF MISERY; PROTESTANT ANGLO-SAXON AMERICAN FOR THEIR STOLEN "INDIAN" EM- PIRE; WHY SHOULD THE BLACK MAN [the African, African- Caribbean, and African-American] NOT FIGHT FOR THE RICHEST PIECE OF REAL ESTATE ON THE PLANET EARTH - HIS ORIGIN- AL HOMELAND - "MOTHER AFRICA" [Alkebu-lan] ?

He must, though the struggle seems at times insurmountable. For IT IS IN THE DOING OF THE IMPOSSIBLE which made the Blacks and Africa great for hundreds of centuries and IT IS ONLY BY THE RECAPTURING AND RECREATION OF NEW VALUES BY THE BLACK MAN will he free his mind, then his body, and lastly - his power. The Black man must, therefore, return to his temples in Ethiopia and Egypt and read his age-old reminders, which emphatically states to him and the world these prophetic words:

" MAN KNOW YOURSELF. "

These words were said by Black men to Black men of religions now called "PAGANISM" and "HEATHENISM" thousands of years before their adoption by Hebrews [Jews], Chris- tians, and Muslims who followed them. They said them in their luxurious GRAND LODGES, in man's first known religions, and in man's first peep into the universe. [See Sir E. A. Wallis Budge's, BOOK OF THE DEAD; also his, OSIRIS].

The Black man [indigenous African and his descendants] must once more write about himself, his cultures, and his continent [Alkebu-lan, Africa, Ethiopia, Libya, etc.]. For no one cares about another's history to the point where he can feel the emotional values of the inheritors. Moreover, when a man's history is written by his master's religion or economic philosophy, such history is always distorted to suit the MASTER-SLAVE re- lationship, which is the only possible result from such an enforced union. Such paternal- ism does not have to be vindictive. The mere fact of the relationship's existence forces one to feel, in fact, superior to the other. And if the history of such a union is of very long duration, many of the captured begin to accept their status of inferiority. They then allow themselves to be renamed accordingly. With their new NAME a new psycology na- turally develops; and with the new mind, a new docility.... This was done to the "NEGRO.'

The major desired accomplishment this volume seeks to achieve, is to provide anthropological research in the ancient heritage of the Africans and their descendants all over the world. This is to be, for the first time, in a manner and writing which persons of average ability and understanding can digest. For this reason the parenthesis or bracket is generously used throughout this volume. Equally, certain words have been repetitiously used by intent; so is a number of statements and questionable phrases which one erroneously uses under the belief that their authenticity [correctness] is "SACRED" and have been sanctioned by "GOD." Of course "GOD" is dependent upon one's own religious belief. If "GOD" is Hebrew [misnomered "Jew"], he is according to the Holy Torah; if Christian, he is according to the Christian Holy Bible [all versions]; and if Muslim [or Muslim], he is according to the Holy Koran. All of the three mentioned religious interpretations of a GOD or GODS are accepted in America or Europe by either group, at least to some extent. But if the GOD [or GODS] be RA, KRISHNA, DAMBALLAH QUE DO [of West Africa], or any other than the three acceptable to the so-called"Western" or "Modern man," then such a God [or Gods] is relegated to obscenity and paganism. Yet in this society it is fashionable to say:

"AMERICA WAS FOUNDED ON THE BASIC BELIEF OF
FREEDOM OF WORSHIP.

Such"...freedom of worship..." is always with a proviso. That is, providing one's GOD is the Christians' Jesus Christ, Hebrews' Jehovah [Yvh], and maybe the Muslims' Al'lah.

The Africans and their descendants, including many of those who live in the Western Hemisphere, also have GODS which to them are as SACRED as those of Asia and Europe. Therefore, until European-Americans and Europeans are ready to accept these "TRUTHS," the "American Dilemma" shall be the ultimate reaction. No man forever allows his MOTHER, which is the LAND OF HIS ORIGIN, to be constantly subjected to all sorts of vilification without one day rising to the challenge; even if it means his eventual annihilation , for that has been man's historical behavior.

It must be remembered, however:

A MAN WITHOUT THE KNOWLEDGE OF WHERE HE HAS
BEEN, KNOWS NOT WHERE HE IS, OR WHERE HE IS GOING.

The African [Black man] refuses to be such a man any longer; if ever he was.

Note: Due to the many requests made by students, professional associates, and close friends who consider publication of the information revealed in this volume of urgent im-

xiv

portance, I have released this preliminary edition of a much more extensive seven volume work. The major work will follow as soon as funds for the publication of same are available to me, as I have been so far unsuccessful in obtaining any publisher; most of them claiming that they are unable to publish it because [a], they have no consultants who are competent to check the historical accuracy, [b] it would require financing beyond their ability, [c] there is no market for this type of "Black history" at this time, etc.

The seven volumes contain more than three-thousand dates and events in Alkebulan's history, set in chronological order. It covers the period from 1,750,000 B.C.E. to 1966 C.E. More than thirty [30] years of research and writing have been given to this work.

It should be noted, however, that the process used in producing this volume made the low price possible. And since material content is the major objective of "SCHOLAR-LY WORK, not graphic elaborateness, other works of equal interest and major research into the Black man's history shall be produced by the same method employed in this volume in order that students, researchers, and other interested persons can have them as soon as possible, and at reasonable prices.

This work would not be possible without the special assistance I received from Miss Doris Mosley and Mr. George E. Simmonds. Miss Mosley for her critical examination with respect to its presentation and contents; and Mr. Simmonds for his checking of the authenticity of the documentation and historical facts.

Constructive criticism of this work is welcome.

Reprinted from the First Edition [1969 – 1971 C.E.]
1st through 5th impression.

FOREWORD

A portion of AFRICAN HISTORY, not "NEGRO HISTORY," is presented in a different light in this work as stated before. The African peoples are not labeled with European names: such as - "BUSHMAN, HAMITE, BANTU, DANAKILL, FUZZY WUZZY,
PYGMY. NEGRO," and other European colonialist superlatives.[1] These designations
have been forced upon the Africans by their European conquerors and slave owners.[2]
They represent one of the means by which Africans were kept apart from each other, on
the basis of each being some sort of a "SEPARATE RACE"[3] or "ETHNIC GROUP." It is
like saying that DARK-SKINNED ITALIANS, GREEKS, SPANIARDS, FRENCHMEN, AND
SLAVIC PEOPLES are made-up of "DIFFERENT RACES" than their BLONDE and much
more LIGHT-SKINNED brothers and sisters of northern Europe, which it will be shown
that such designations were not coincidental. They were planned, as evidenced in the
case of the word "NEGRO" being applied to a special group of African peoples.[0] This
word has no historic origin or bearing before the enslavement of the Africans by European and European-American slavers during the early 16th century C.E. [A.D.].[4]

What was or is. to be gained by the designation of the Africans into "SEPARATE
RACES" by the European invaders and colonizers? It was, and still is, a means to divide the Africans and remove them from their CULTURAL, SCIENTIFIC, POLITICAL,
SPIRITUAL. and ANCESTRAL heritage, thereby enabling the colonialist slave masters
from Europe to claim them and force their own concepts of MORALITY, LAW, ECONO-
MICS, POLITICS, ANCESTRAL VALUES, etc., upon the Africans' mind.[5] For, without
one's consciousness of the past. one remains a virtual SLAVE to the whims of his MAS-
TER. As a result of this type of damaging characterizations the author has included a set
of new terms common to the African peoples, all of which are defined, redefined, and explained from an African point of view. The "NEGRO" is an example of such a phenomenon.
The "BLACK MAN" [African] is the opposite of the "NEGRO." He is a MAN who has retained his self-consciousness and self-respect for his past, or one who has regained it
after being forced to accept "NEGRO" status, due to no fault of his own.

---

[a]. See Moll's map - AFRICA, p. 401 this volume, with respect to the mythological
country - "NEGROLAND" - created for West Africa by European colonialists, imperial-
ists and "Christian missionaries." who enslaved the peoples of Alkebu-lan from the 16th
century C.E. to the present time.

In order to present a balanced view of the African, this work also highlights adverse comments and sayings against him. Even inflamatory comments by Professor
M.D.W. Jeffreys, one of the Black man's worst critics, are presented.[6] Other patern-
alists and believers in a "SUPERIOR WHITE RACE" are equally given exposure. This
method of presentation is seldom used, but it always proves to the best for the student
to reach his [or her] own conclusions upon the presentation of data reflecting both sides
of a question or issue. As such, much of what was generally believed to have started
by the ancient Hebrews and other "BIBLE PEOPLES" will be shown to have existed
thousands of years before the first Hebrew, "ABRAHAM," was born.[7]

This work also exposes unfounded and unscientific concepts constantly parroted by
most religious bigots and their supporters who say that:

> "...THE NEGRO [Black man] GOT HIS COLOR BECAUSE OF HAM
> WATCHING HIS FATHER'S NAKEDNESS...,"[8] etc.

But, Ham's parents could not have been "WHITE," since they were from, and of, a
BLACK or BROWN-SKINNED nation of people [Palestine, later Israel] who had lived
for four-hundred [400] years in "NEGRO [Black] EGYPT" - the Hebrews ["Jews"]. Even
today the world's most traditional or ORTHODOX Hebrews are the Yemenites, most of
whom are now in Israel; and the Beta Israel or Falasa [or Falasha], the BLACKEST of
the world's "JEWS," most of whom are still living in the biblical:

> "...LAND OF MILK AND HONEY TO THE SOUTH...CUSH
> [Kush, modern Ethiopia].[9]

Lastly, the chapter on the earliest known "MAN" or "MAN-LIKE" fossils is presented in detail, in order that the reader can see how deep the roots of all mankind is
imbeded in Alkebu-lan [Africa]. And that it is not around the Tigris and Euphrates valleys as it was erroneously, sometimes maliciously, presented by "EDUCATORS" who
are considered to be "AUTHORITIES" on the origin of the original man, which so many
have labled "ADAM."

The MAPS, GRAPHS, and CHARTS in this work have been carefully arranged to
provide the necessary ease required in research, which so many other books have not

---

. Practically none was of so-called "CAUCASIAN STOCK," and none of "SEMITIC
STOCK," until the creation of the Noah and the Flood mythical drama in the BOOK OF
GENESIS of the Hebrew Holy Torah. There is not a single one in the Africans BOOK OF
THE DEAD that preceded the Hebrew and Christian bibles by thousands of years.

attempted to do. They will also reveal certain origins of the misconceptions which still remain notoriously prevalent today. This will include the word "NEGRO," which alleged-ly "DESCRIBES THE BLACK PEOPLE" of the mythical country the European colonizers called "NEGROLAND."[10] Some of these maps are collectors items, and very seldom re-vealed in other works. Many of them date back to the days of 450 B.C.E., when the South Atlantic Ocean was still the "ETHIOPIAN OCEAN," and the Mediterranean Sea was still the EGYPTIAN SEA. Of course, the SAHARA[a] was then considered by the Euro-peans of that era to be a "LARGE LAKE" or "OCEAN;"[11] and the NILE RIVER ran across the Sahara to the Ethiopian Ocean [east to west]. Therefore, one can readily see that much of what has been written about Africa [Alkebu-lan] in those days of the ancient Europeans, and still being peddled as FACTS, forms the basis of most of the present prejudices of so-called "MODERN MAN" about Africa and her indigenous peoples. This is especially "TRUE" about those Africans inland from the Mediterranean Sea, who most Europeans and European-Americans prefer to call "AFRICANS SOUTH OF THE SAHARA."[12] The reader will notice that the indigenous peoples of Africa are BLACK - and of various shades. This is "TRUE," regardless of the names and classifications any-one gives them, just as much as DARK-SKINNED Europeans and European-Americans re-gardless of the names they are, or were, being called today or yesteryears. Thus: A Greek in southern Europe with his DARK SKIN is equally a European as a Swede with his BLONDE [White] SKIN. Equally, an indigenous BLACK-SKINNED or BROWN-SKINNED Egyptian is as much an African as a South African from any part of southern Africa - the so-called "BANTU" or "NEGRO" - with his equally BLACK SKIN.

------

a. The term "SAHARA DESERT" is incorrect. The word "SAHARA" or "ZAARA" by it-self means "GREAT DESERT."
     One should remember that only names used by Africans relative to themselves and things African are honored in this volume. For example: There is no such person as a "PYGMY." This RACIST term was the result of the enslavement and colonization of African peoples by European and European-American imperialists, so-called "Christian Missionaries, entreprenuers, explorers, adventurers, big game hunters, and plain masters of genocide, who exterminated more than one-hundred million [100,000,000] African people between 1503 to 1865 C.E. [A.D.] all over the planet EARTH. The cor-rect name of the so-called "PYGMY" is "TWA." This principle is followed scrupulously throughout this volume.

PREFACE

The general response to BLACK MAN OF THE NILE has been so overwhelming that its re-editing, revision, and enlargement became necessary. Due to certain demands resulting from responses by students, faculty members, and the general reading public, for further information on the areas of the NILE VALLEY HIGH-CULTURES the following supplementary chapters - IX, QUESTIONS AND ANSWERS; X, THE MOTHER OF GOD, and also the SPECIAL BIBLIOGRAPHY were added.

The extended or SPECIAL BIBILIOGRAPHY has been added for the benefit of everyone, but mainly for the FACULTY MEMBERS of various colleges and other institutions of learning who have constantly requested certain materials to cover many areas already mentioned throughout the original volume [1st Edition] to a greater degree, particularly in the areas that exposed certain myths in the BOOK OF GENESIS and BOOK OF EXODUS of the Hebrew ["Jewish"] Holy Torah or Christian Old Testament, also to some extent in the Christian New Testament and Muslim Holy Quran [Koran], with re - gards to the RACIST PRESENTATION of Jesus Christ to support European and European-American versions of JUDAEO-CHRISTIAN GREEK-CENTRIC WHITE STUDIES schools of HIGHER LEARNING.[0] The addition of the extra information is primarily geared towards presenting both student and faculty with a very much wider scope and insight into the current obsession of certain so-called "WHITE LIBERAL AFRICANIST HISTORIANS" HAMITICISM and SEMITICISM relative to Africa and her indigenous northern and eastern peoples [sons and daughters]. Of course the "CAUCASIAN" North and East Africa SYNDROME is equally affected by the additional documentation and citation of materials generally suppressed, along with the extended or SPECIAL BIBLIOGRAPHY, and with the addition of other works in each chapter's BIBLIOGRAPHY.

Many "WHITE LIBERAL" and "ORTHODOX" Africanist professors and others who are overtly "...INTERESTED IN THE PROGRESS OF THE NEGRO PEOPLE...," have complained about the presentation of the material contents that are solely complimen - tary to Alkebu-lan [Africa] and her indigenous sons and daughters, which include their

---

[0]. Note that this added information does not in any manner or form negate the work in the author's other book, AFRICAN ORIGINS OF THE MAJOR "WESTERN RELIGIONS" [Judaism, Christianity, and Islam], Alkebu-lan Books Associates, New York, 1971.

descendants everywhere, without showing that the opposite exists. It must be stated here and now, if this was not sufficiently expressed in the PREFACE and FOREWORD of the First Edition of this work, that:

> THERE IS NO INTENT ON THE AUTHOR'S PART TO SHOW ANY OTHER SIDE THAN THAT OF THE AFRICAN PEOPLES "GREATEST HERITAGE" THROUGHOUT ALL OF THE PAGES OF THIS VOLUME, AND THE FORMER, AS ALL OTHERS, EVEN THOUGH THERE ARE COUNTLESS INSTANCES WHERE AFRICANS AND EUROPEANS, EQUALLY EUROPEAN-AMERICANS AND ASIANS, ARE VERY HIGHLY AND DESERVINGLY PRAISED.

Why? Because of the vast majority of the existing and new works by so-called "ORTHODOX" and "LIBERAL" White Africanists and "INTERGRATIONISTS" have never ceased projecting derogatory presentations about African peoples in their teaching and writing, all of which they have carried and extended into "BLACK STUDIES" and "AFRICAN STUDIES." Thus, they still refer to African peoples as "PRIMITIVE, PAGAN, UNCIVILIZED, CANNIBAL, UNDERDEVELOPED, AFRICAN RACES, TRIBES, " and a host of other derogatory superlatives they have reserved exclusively for usage with respect to Africans only; these metioned being but a very few of the words and terms in their very specialized vocabulary for "NEGROES, AFRICANS SOUTH OF THE SAHARA, BANTUS, NIGGERS, " etc. Moreso; because people who still call themselves "CHRISTIAN MISSION - ARIES" have never ceased in their obsession of imposing their type of "GOD" upon African people, at the same instance being purposefully disrespectful and abusive to the African "GOD" or "GODS" they have not already co-opted and/or projected in their own so-called "WESTERN RELIGIONS" - Judaism, Christianity, and to a somewhat minor extent Islam; all of them forgetting that the indigenous Africans of the Nile Valleys and Great Lakes regions of North, East, and Central Africa, CREATED and DEVELOPED the PHILOSOPHICAL CONCEPTS of a GOD-HEAD all three of the so-called "WESTERN RELIGIONS" used, and still use, CONCEPTS which they cannot survive without.

The area of RELIGION, being the most difficult and fearsome to handle in European-America's selfrighteous society which feels no guilt for its committal of genocide against the people of North America, the enslavement and dehumanization of the people of Alkebulan [followed by their physical and mental colonization], must be shown to have had its origin in the earliest stages of the same African peoples' HIGH-CULTURES all over the continent of Alkebu-lan [AFRICA] before the so-called "SEMITE" or "CAUCASIAN" was known in the prehistory or history of mankind. It had to be shown that it was from the

xx

same African people ["Negroes" or whatever else] that JUDAISM, CHRISTIANITY, and ISLAM [the so-called "Western Religions"] got their "GODS" and "SAINTS," equally their "RELIGIOUS PHILOSOPHY," stories about "RESURRECTION. ANCESTOR WORSHIP [saints and prophets], VIRGIN BIRTH , HEREAFTER [heavens], HELL [punishment chambers], and a host of other myths, allegories, and teachings which not one of them can do without today in the 20th century C.E.; all of which are still evident in the Africans BOOK OF THE COMING FORTH BY DAY [Egyptian Book Of The Dead] and PAPYRUS OF ANI, PYRAMID TEXTS, COFFIN TEXTS, and various other papyri that were stolen from Africa and suppressed throughout Europe's and European-America's educational institutions - both secular and religious.

The arrangements of the new materials follow no set standard by the author of this volume other than before. However, even though they do not represent all of the questions asked, they are never-the-less those which have had the most requests. Of course there are others which the author could have included, but the cost of any further enlargement of this volume would have placed the price of the end product beyond the maximum financial budget established, thus making it impossible to keep an honest price for the completed work.

The cost for the conventional indexing is beyond the budget means at this time, thus the very highly specialized extra documentation covering the major target areas according to requests from students, faculty members, and the general reading public which all of the author's works have served for the past thirty-four [34] years of his writing on Africa and her sons and daughters, strictly from an AFRICAN POINT OF VIEW. As each edition comes forth, this area of the mechanics of a book shall be that much more expanded to have the format of other works, only if this is what the students, faculty members, and the general reading public the author serves decide it shall be.

The author and the publisher - ALKEBU-LAN BOOKS ASSOCIATES, all concerned of African birth and/or origin, remain open-minded to as many suggestions anyone may have for further constructive improvement of any of the many books they have so far jointly and individually produced and published, and about to be published in the very near future, relative to ALKEBU-LAN'S people.

This REVISED, ENLARGED, and RE-EDITED edition of BLACK MAN OF THE NILE, originally the first of the "African-American Heritage Series," has been totally coordinated with the three [3] other works of the "Series" - AFRICAN ORIGIN OF THE MAJOR

WESTERN RELIGIONS, AFRICA: MOTHER OF "WESTERN CIVILIZATION," and THE BLACK MAN'S NORTH and EAST AFRICA; all of them by the same author, the latter co-authored with Alkebu-lan Books Associate's research director - Mr. George E. Simmonds [Chairman of African, African-American, and African-Caribbean Studies, at Harlem Preparatory School of New York, New York].

Except for the added QUESTIONS AND ANSWERS, MOTHER OF GOD, SPECIAL BIBLIOGRAPHY, FOOTNOTES, PICTURES, and a few minor grammatical corrections throughout the text, this volume remains exactly the same in its African orientation as the FIRST EDITION and its five [5] different impressions. Holders or purchasers of the FIRST EDITION need not hesitate to use their copy in fear of its AUTHENTICITY, as not one solitary FACT has been changed; to the contrary - each FACT has been further' supported by further documentation.

The incorporation of ALKEBU-LAN BOOKS ASSOCIATES into a subsidiary of ALKEBU-LAN FOUNDATION, Inc., an all African people [BLACK] communal coopera-tive venture, on 1 July, 1971, rendered added support and quality to the output and speed of this volume, and should be of greater dimension for future publications. ALKEBU-LAN BOOKS ASSOCIATES can now publish the works of other African [BLACK] authors geared to HISTORY and HIGH-CULTURE in the field of the social and physical sciences, authors who could not otherwise get their works published. The EDITORIAL STAFF that we have been able to assemble among our own members includes licensed teachers, a lawyer, an economists, a few students, Muslims, Israelites ["Jews"], Christians, fe-males and males, etc., all of whom shall add to the already HIGH calibre of our publi-cations, but most of all prevent whatever typographical deficiency that showed up in the FIRST EDITION of this volume due to the author having to be his own editor.

In general BLACK MAN OF THE NILE, and all of the other works by Alkebu-lan Books Associates, will continue as a catalyst in presenting the African peoples of the entire world, those of "MOTHER AFRICA " [Alkebu-lan] in particular, as the indigenous originators of every HIGH-CULTURE in all of the geo-political areas [North, South, East, West, and Central] of mankind's original "GARDEN OF EDEN" - ALKEBU-LAN [Africa, according to the Greeks and Romans of ancient times]. These works shall con-tinue exposing those individuals, societies, and institutions formerly and presently en-gaged in the cultural and physical GENOCIDE directed against African peoples anywhere, and pinpoint areas of learning and materials still being used in order to maintain the alleged "SUPERIORITY" of the so-called "CAUCASIAN, SEMITE and HAMITE RACES OVER THE NEGRO RACE." They shall continue exposing the so-called "SEMITIC" professors attempt at removing the indigenous Africans, irregardless of whatever names they are called, from NORTH and EAST AFRICA'S prehistory and history and replacing them with "SEMITES, CAUCASOIDS, CAUCASIANS, HAMITES, NILOTS," etc. In so doing, at the same instance presenting all forms of documentation in support of HISTORICAL FACTS which show that ALL OF THE INDIGENOUS AFRICANS OF THE ENTIRE BLUE AND WHITE NILE, as elsewhere throughout Alkebu-lan [Africa], were responsible for everything created and developed by African peoples that became the "GREATEST CIVILIZATION [High-Culture] OF ANTIQUITY," whether in Ta-Merry [Kimit, Sais, Mizrain, Egypt, etc.], Zimbabwe [southern "Rhodesia"], Khart Haddas [The New Town or Carthage], Itiopi [Cush or Ethiopia, "Abyssinia, " etc.], Meröwe [Meröe], Puanit [Punt - areas of today's Kenya, Somalia, and Tanzania], Monomotapa [all of today's "Union of South Africa], Zaire or Kongo [Congo or Congoland], Ghana, Melle [Mali], Benin, Edoh, et al [the major West African Empires], etc., ALKEBU-LAN in general.

FOREWORD

This enlarged and revised edition of BLACK MAN OF THE NILE is superb and masterful in its areas of research; and makes the reading of the pages following that educationally exciting. The updating of the existing data and the added information, will be looked upon by scholars and laymen alike as a work to be long cherished and placed among the masterpieces [books] that depict the greatness that was, and still is, Alkebu-lan [Africa].

Having worked very closely with the author, and knowing that no time nor effort was spared in making this the informative work that it is, I highly recommend it for both academic and secular studies as a MUST. It should be on the shelf of every library in the world where it can have universal usage. For it will certainly help everyone to better understand the great contributions made by the Africans along the Nile River Valley - from Uganda in Central Africa to Egypt at the Mediterranean Sea in North Africa.

One can observe the many unfamiliar African names and terminologies that generally appear in Dr. ben-Jochannan's works, and as found in this Revised Edition, and wonder what fired his reasoning for their re-introduction. It will become very evident that he is interested in giving to the reader many of the ancient names and terminologies used before those of which most of us have become best acquainted. A superb example is the ancient name "ALKEBU-LAN," which is the name the ancient Moors and Ethiopians themselves called the continent that is today known to us as "AFRICA." The names - "KIMIT, SAIS, KHAM, HAM, MIZRAIN," as is "TA-MERRY," are only some of the names that "EGYPT" was known by; all of which Dr. ben-Jochannan has brought to our knowledge in documents and bibliographical materials of which we did not know exist.

The CHRONOLOGIES of the Egyptian kings or phraraohs are of very extensive research and excellent scholarship, and represent the best I have witnessed in any work by a historian on Africa's HISTORY, PREHISTORY, and CIVILIZATIONS. No other historian to date, of which I am aware, has done so much in pointing out the LIES and INJUSTICES perpetuated against Africa and African peoples historically as Dr. ben-Jochannan has so vividly done. The RACIAL PREJUDICE against the so-called "NEGRO RACE" that cluttered the works of such world renown scholars, writers, and historians as M.D.W. Jeffreys and James Henry Breasted have been brought to the forefront in his writings, equally as he has with many others of much recent acclaim. He exposed the RACISM in their

works which blacks have used for generations as "AUTHORITATIVE NEGRO HISTORY."
In so doing, he pointed out areas of anti-Negro hysteria in the current works by the so-
called "WHITE LIBERAL AFRICANISTS," most of which we were not aware of before
the exposure of such information·

The "STOLEN LEGACY" from the Blacks of the Nile Valleys and Great Lakes
High-Cultures being taught in European and European and European-American [WHITE]
schools of elementary and advanced levels as "GREEK PHILOSOPHY" is thoroughly exposed in this book. In reading these revelations one becomes extremely shocked and utterly dumb-founded when faced with the TRUTH contain in them about the so-called
"GREEK PHILOSOPHERS", all of whom received their initial education·in "PHILOSO-
PHY" in Egypt and Nubia, Northeast Africa· Those who did not received their initial
education from the indigenous Africans of these two Nile Valley African nations got
theirs from others who studied under said Africans or in countries where the Africans'
Mysteries System had established subordinate Lodges of the OSIRICA - which was
centered in the Grand Lodge at Luxor, Nubia.

The information in this book has brought to light the "TRUE" role of the "BLACK
MAN [Negro or whatever else he is called] OF THE NILE AND HIS FAMILY." It deals
specifically with that part of the BLACK MAN'S High-Culture that commanded a major
role in "CIVILIZING" the "MOTHER NATION OF THE EUROPEANS" - GREECE. Dr.
ben-Jochannan did not spare any documentation, as he more than adequately recorded
and documented the words and pictures used to present this historic revelation.

As an instructor, lecturer, and writer in AFRICAN, AFRICAN-AMERICAN, and
AFRICAN-CARIBBEAN CULTURE AND HISTORY, this book certainly bears very
heavily on my own teaching and course outline at present, and it will continue in the
same manner for some time in the future.

We ought to be thankful that there is a writer like Dr. ben-Jochannan in our midst
to tell the "TRUTH" about AFRICAN [black] PEOPLES without fear of powerful publishers and other controllers of the written word in print as taught by "WHITE LIBERAL
AUTHORITIES ON AFRICA [Alkebu-lan] " and her SONS and DAUGHTERS. But, in spite
of of the so-called "AUTHORITIES ON AFRICA" and "AFRICANS" in White academic
circles; it is a book like this one by Dr. ben-Jochannan which will continue revealing
TRUE LIGHT to African peoples about OUR GREAT AND MOST GLORIOUS PAST .

George E. Simmonds: Instructor of African,
African-American, and African-Caribbean
Studies, Harlem Preparatory School of N.Y.

MAP
Of AFRICA.
1688C.E.

A FRIC A, by the Ancients, was called *Olympia, Hesperia, Oceania, Coryphe, Ammonis, Ortygia,* and *Æthiopia.* By the *Greeks* and *Romans, Lybia* and *Africa.* By the *Æthiopians* and *Moors, Alkebu-lan.*

Note: The European colonialists, from the 15th through 19th century, C.E. refused to accept their ignorance of Africa's interior and made all sorts of map with waterways, mountains, nations and peoples which did not exist on the continent.

THERE A PEOPLE NOW FORGOTTEN DISCOVERED WHILE
OTHERS WERE YET BARBARIANS, THE ELEMENTS OF THE
ARTS AND SCIENCES. A RACE OF MEN NOW REJECTED FOR
THEIR SABLE SKIN AND FRIZZLED HAIR, FOUNDED ON THE
STUDY OF THE LAWS OF NATURE THOSE CIVIL AND RE-
LIGIOUS SYSTEMS WHICH STILL GOVERN THE UNIVERSE.

From Count C. F. Volney's
RUINS OF EMPIRE, 1789
[Preface of Ist Edition].

Left: Pharaoh Akhenaton or Amen-hoteo IV, the "FIRST CHRIST" whom many have also called "THE FATHER OF THE TRINITARIAN CONCEPT." Note the so-called "NEGROID CHARACTERISTICS" of this African that were, and still are, common in most Africans today.

Right: Pharaoh Djoser's ("Cheops") statue; a tribute to the so-called "NE-GROID CHARACTERISTICS" of the Nile Valley Africans. The pharaoh, who com-missioned the renowned African archi-tect, Imhotep, to design and build the "WORLD'S FIRST BUILDING OF STONE" - the Step Pyramid at Sakhara (Saqqara).

See other pictures and statues of the Africans shown above in other chapters of this volume for contrast with the so-called "NEGROES" of Nubia and those called "BANTUS," etc., in the southern limits of the continent of Alkebu-lan.

2

INTRODUCTION TO CHAPTER I

The author begins this chapter by presenting one of the most famous of the indigenous Africans of ancient Ta-Merry [Kimit, Sais, Egypt, etc.] and the Nile Valleys in general, who, according to a certain WHITE LIBERAL AFRICANSIT and EGYPTOLOGIST, was "...ill-formed..." and presented a picture of "...physical monstrosity...." This conclusion the so-called "AUTHORITY" drew from the "...thick lips" and "hatchet face..." appearance of the Africans. However, we will notice that the two Africans on page 2, as previously shown, represented the same type "PHYSICAL" [facial or racial] description of the vast majority of the pharaohs [kings] who were indigenous to Alkebu-lan [Africa]. But, it is Pharaoh Amenhotep IV [otherwise known as Akhenaten or Ikhnaton, etc.] who is the center of focus at this point, as is his family shown on pages 7, 8, and 203 of this volume. The specific interest with reference to this pharaoh resulted from the following article on pages 5 and 6 of this chapter, all of which appeared in THE NEW YORK TIMES [9 January 1972] by Donald Janson, who allegedly developed his story from a conversation he had with Ray Winfield Smith, an archaeologist of the Museum of the University of Pennsylvania.

We will notice the strikingly different presentation of Queen Nefertiti on the "RECONSTRUCTION OF THE WALL AT KARNAK TEMPLE" in the following article and that shown on page 5. We will also notice that the Queen is shown somewhat artistically elongated as her husband, Pharaoh Akhenaten, on page 7. Both presentations represented the asthetic style of art used in Ta-Merry [Egypt] during the reign of both the Pharaoh and his Queen.

The following article being referred to is a prime example of the type of callously RACIST HYPOTHESIS still being projected by certain "ACADEMICIANS" and "AUTHORITIES ON AFRICA" as "SCHOLARSHIP;" particularly relating to Ta-Merry, Nubia, and other indigenous African nations of the Nile Valleys, the Great Lakes regions, and of North and East Africa generally. It is "SCHOLARS" such as this one, who have for years prejudiced the mind of the "average" European and European-American [WHITE PEOPLE] against the facial [RACIAL] appearance of the indigenous African and African-American [BLACK PEOPLE] everywhere.

"THICK LIPS, BROAD NOSES, WOOLLY [kinky] HAIR," and "BURNT [black] SKIN" are distinctly so-called "RACIAL CHARACTERISTICS" most of the ancients of Hellas [Pyrrhus or Greece] and Rome, along with many others from other parts of

Europe and Asia, used in their own works to describe the "COLCHIANS, EGYPTIANS, ETHIOPIANS, NUBIANS, MEROITES, PUANITS," and other indigenous peoples of North and East Alkebu-lan [Africa]. Those living in southern Europe for centuries before Christ[0], with whom they came in contact, were also described. Even Herodotus, the Europeans' and European-Americans' "FATHER OF HISTORY," used the same type of "RACIAL" or "PHYSICAL" description of the indigenous Africans in his own work - THE HISTORIES, especially in Book II, which this author has quoted numerous times in his various books listed in the first part of this volume under "OTHER WORKS BY THE AUTHOR."

This most timely article's contents have corroborated the FACT that RACISM is as much a part of European-American WHITE STUDIES and SCHOLARSHIP in the year 1972 C.E. [A.D.] as it was at the height of the chattel slave system from c. 1619 or 1620 to 1865 C.E. Also, RACISM will never cease in any meaningful way to include any group of the indigenous Africans of the past or their descendants [BLACKS] as the equal of European-Americans and their descendants [WHITES] covering the slave periods in the United States of America's dream - "DEMOCRACY." As such, it is an opportunity of the last dimension to have been able to add the article to this chapter, which had been written over two [2] years before.

It there was any doubt that the "PHYSICA CHARACTERISTICS" [race] of the so-called "NEGROES" are still considered "ABNORMALITIES" in the eyes of the so-called "ORTHODOX" and "LIBERAL WHITE AFRICANIST AUTHORITY ON AFRICA [on any and all parts of Africa and its indigenous people].....the RACIST proclamations and hypotheses in this article should dispel such a notion. This is the reason the entire article is presented without any editing whatsoever. Hoping that your curiosity led you to read the full text of the article, the author of this volume wonders if you have reached the same conclusion from the picture that Pharaoh Akhenaten's "ABNORMALITIES" were due to his "...THICK LIPS..." and other NORMALITIES common to indigenous African peoples here in the United States of America and all of their ancestors of the entire continent of Alkebu-lan ["Africa," according to the Greeks and Romans].

---

[0]. Jesus Christ, the Christians' God, was also described as having "HAIR LIKE LAMB'S WOOL" in the Holy Bible [New Testament; all versions], and He was allegedly the son of two [2] "SEMITES - JOSEPH AND MARY," both of whom were Israelites whose ancestors were "SLAVES" of the indigenous Africans of Ta-Merry and Ta-Nehisi.

Carvings Give Nefertiti Big Role

By DONALD JANSON
Special to The New York Times

PHILADELPHIA, Jan. 8 — History has short-changed Queen Nefertiti of ancient Egypt's Golden Age by stressing only her beauty, Ray Winfield Smith, an archeologist, believes.

The young queen may well have wielded the major religious, political and economic power of the day, he said in an interview.

If so, the comely Nefertiti was influential in establishing what was probably the world's first single-god religion, the worship of the sun disk Aten.

She may also have guided a change to greater naturalism in Egyptian art.

Both developments of the mid-14th century B.C. have been attributed to her husband, the eccentric King Akhenaten (or Ikhnaton). But Mr. Smith said his studies in Egypt for the last five years point to a far loftier role for Nefertiti than ever before accorded her.

She may not only have been the brains in the family, he said, but may also have done without the aid of the king in conceiving their six daughters.

Carvings Analyzed

Mr. Smith based his observations on his analysis of carvings of some 35,000 stones of a temple to Aten that the youthful pharaoh had built at Karnak in the Egyptian capital of Thebes early in his 17-year reign.

The archeologist, a research associate at the University Museum of the University of Pennsylvania here, headed a team that has used photographs and computers to reconstruct in pictures enough of the temple's scattered sandstone wall blocks so inscriptions and decorations can be seen and studied in proper relationship to each other rather than in fragments. Sponsors of the project include the museum, the Smithsonian Institution, and the Department of Antiquities of the United Arab Republic.

The temple was razed by a successor of Akhenaten after it stood for only two decades. The Smith team found individual blocks in museums and in private hands throughout Europe and in the United States. Many others had been stacked by excavators in storehouses in Karnak or in the open at

University of Pennsylvania

Reconstruction of wall at Karnak Temple, using the few available sandstone blocks, shows two figures—both Nefertiti—making an offering to Aten, sun disk god.

Culver

Queen Nefertiti

Luxor. Since the demolition of the temple, many of these had been used as foundations and fill in monuments built in

Thebes by rulers who did not share Akhenaten's monotheistic view of religion.

Massive Jigsaw Puzzle

Mr. Smith, just back from Egypt to publish a book on his findings, said the 35,000 pieces of the massive jigsaw puzzle his team put together amounted to only 15 per cent of the original structure but enough to establish Nefertiti's pre-eminence in her day.

Images of the queen rather than the king dominated the temple carvings. An entire courtyard was devoted exclusively to her. Never before had a temple in the country's capital so emphasized a woman over the king, Mr. Smith said.

A century earlier a queen had ruled Egypt, but she (Hatshepsut) disguised her sex by calling herself the king and wearing a beard. Nefertiti, whose name means "the beautiful one has come" retained her femininity.

Each Egyptian king was a god as well as secular ruler, but the temple drawings showed that Nefertiti matched her husband in religious stature. She was revered as a goddess. Depictions of the holiest of ritualistic ceremonies of the time, the offering of a treasured object to Aten, show twice as many gold statues of Nefertiti used in the ceremonies as statues of her husband.

Egyptians addressed prayers to Nefertiti. No other queen, Mr. Smith said, was accorded divinity while her husband lived. The loftiness of her role, he said, was not known before the pieces of the temple puzzle were put together.

Additional Evidence

Mr. Smith said supplementary evidence of Nefertiti's standing can be found at Tell el Amarna, 240 miles down the Nile from Thebes, where Akhenaten built a new capital. An inscription on a stone boundary panel reports that the queen had an idea of her own about building the city. Never before in Egyptian history, the archeologist said, had there been a recorded concession that a queen expressed ideas different from those of her husband.

Mr. Smith said his interpretation of the evidence was that the tributes to Nefertiti at Karnak were not the result of the initiative of an admiring husband but flowed from her own dominant personality.

He noted that existing literature gives the revolutionary god-king credit for the religious and cultural innovations of the day and for a powerful personality and intellect. But he said this was done without proof.

He pointed out that panels and statues of Akhenaten found at the temple depicted him as "a physical monstrosity," with a long narrow face, thick lips, hatchet chin, thin neck, vestigial breast development, wide hips, thick thighs and spindly legs, apparently the result of glandular trouble.

Syndrome Cited

Persons born with such a syndrome, he said, are not likely to be particularly intelligent and tend to be easily influenced. He believes Nefertiti held strong sway over him and her subjects from the time they married as teen-agers till the young Pharaoh died in his 30's after a reign of 17 years.

5

In wall carvings the six incesses were almost always own with their mother. Mr. nith said it would have been istomary to show them with e king some of the time if : had been the predominant gure historians have credited m with being.

He said that because some ople with Akhenaten's physi-il abnormalities are sterile, ere has been speculation that hers sired the children attrib-:ed to him.

No matter how forceful her personality, Mr. Smith said, Nefertiti had no desire to em-barrass her husband. When pic-tured together on stones of the temple "she always brought up the rear."

Subtle Power Base

"Whatever power she wielded was probably wielded subtly," he said.

The influence of neither was strong enough to perpetuate monotheism much beyond their

reign. The previous prolifera-tion of gods returned to favor under succeeding pharaohs, the Aten temple was razed and its pictorial testament to the his-tory of the day was hidden from view.

More of the temple building blocks will be turned up, Mr. Smith said, but never enough for a physical reconstruction of the vast structure.

Nevertheless, he said, re-searchers will henceforth have his team's large pictorial panels,

some incorporating as many as 30 stone blocks, available for study instead of separate in-dividual stones that showed only part of the picture.

Mr. Smith reported on how computers were used to put the panels together in a 1970 article in National Geographic. Many of the integrated panels and his analysis of the stories they tell will be contained in his forthcoming book.

One should readily understand why this chapter is of such major importance to the understanding of WHO WERE/ARE THE AFRICAN peoples of the PAST, PRESENT, and of course the FUTURE. For, we are certain to find that the Africans who were, are, or will be, indigenous to the continent the Romans and Greeks misnamed "AFRICA," did or do not all, nor will they all, ever have so-called "NEGRO" or "NEGROID" character-istics such as Queen Nefertiti's Pharaoh and husband - Amenhotep IV [Akhenaten]. But, "THICK LIPS, WOOLLY HAIR, BROAD NOSES," and "BURNT SKIN," have never sepa-rated the indigenous Africans before European and European-American "SCHOLARS" and "ACADEMICIANS" created "RACE." For these two Africans are no exception to all of the others from SOUTH to NORTH and WEST to EAST, Alkebu-lan [Africa]. Their FACIAL TYPES are as common in one area as they are in any other. RACISM, hope-fully, will never be added to the already herculean tasks the African people face in their RECONSTRUCTION.

We need to take another long look at both Pharaoh Djoser and Pharaoh Akhenaten on page 2, also other pharaohs shown in Chapter IV of this volume, and see if all of them were not equally "ABNORMAL" from the point of reference of this "AUTHORITY ON AFRICA" [Egypt specifically] hypothesis. On page 185 of Chapter IV in this volume the alledged "ABNORMALITY" which Pharaoh Akhenaten had can be best observed in its much more advance stage in the face of Pharaoh Djoser. On many other pages through-out this volume the "ABNORMALITY" has definitely reached EPIDEMIC proportion - THICK LIPS, BROAD NOSES, WOOLLY [kinky] HAIR, and BURNT [black] SKIN. "Ne-groes" and "Niggers" are all over Egypt's and other Nile Valleys' High-Cultures history and geneaology.

One need not only use the "RECONSTRUCTION OF [the] WALL AT KARMAK TEMPLE" that was collected in bits by Mr. Smith and projected with fill-ins from a RACIST point of view. The actual photograph of a FRIEZE from Tell el-Amarna with-

6

out artistic "RECONSTRUCTION" below allows the reader to examine the alledged "AB-
NORMALITIES" shared by Queen Nefertiti, as much as her husband - Pharaoh **Akhenaten**.
if this is what they were. We must, in examining this FRIEZE, remember that **FACTS**
will always survive RACIST MYTHS and WISHFUL HYPOTHESES.

Pharaoh Akhenaton and Queen Nefertiti presenting offerings to Aton (the Sun God).

The frieze above is taken from a painting on one of the walls of the Temple of Abu S Simbel, Nubia. On the left is the Goddess Hathor: on the right is the Goddess Isis: in the center stands the wife of Pharaoh Akhenaten - Queen Nefertiti. This section of the Temple was consecrated to the favorite wife of Pharaoh Rameses II.

Note that this is another style used by the ancient Africans of Egypt in depicting their personalities of royal stature. Here they and the Hieroglyphic figures are shown extremely elongated. Maybe Mr. Smith could find some kind of "ABNORMALITY" caused by this extreme manner of showing Queen Nefertiti, who in this presentation seems to have a greater amount of the "ILL FORMED" attributes than her husband did in the scene presented by Mr. Smith - shown on page 5 of this chapter.

It is rather strange that the contemporaries of Pharaoh Akhenaten and Queen Nefertiti did not mention that any of the two of them suffered from any unusual physical disturbance. As usual, it takes the racist and religiously bigoted "AUTHORITIES ON AFRICA" to find all sorts of RACIAL DEFECTS in anyone who had or have "THICK LIPS BROAD NOSE WOOLLY HAIR " and "BURNT SKIN" like those who taught or civilized the earliest Greeks and Haribu ["Jews"].

8

King Nar-mer, Cairo Museum, Egypt (Africa)

Pharaoh Mena or Nar-mer (Herodotus' Menes), 1st of the Dynastic Kings of Egypt, 1st Dynasty, c. 3200 B.C.E., seemed to have been as "ABNORMAL" as Akhenaton.

9

Pharaoh Amenophis III and Queen Teja at the FEAST OF HEBSED, from the tomb of Cheruef at Luxor (Thebes). Note the various royal guests' so-called "ethnic" composition ."SEMITES" and "NEGROES" were present, as shown at the bottom frieze.

10

The type of RACISM manifested in the previous article we have just dealt with has already brought forward the only result it could have generated - its usual companion - RELIGIOUS BIGOTRY. Thus, we find a follow-up article on Mr. Smith's RACIST HYPOTHESIS by one Steve Harvey of the NEW YORK POST, dated Wednesday, January 26, 1972 [page 21], in which he is expanding the alledged conflict that occurred between Pharaoh Rameses II and his fellow African of Ta-Merry [Kimit, Sais, Egypt, etc.] named Moses into a case of "... PARANOIA..." on the part of Rameses II for chasing the African "Jews" out of his kingdom but not of Moses for starting the entire conflict when he murdered Rameses II soldier on an alledged "...COMMAND FROM JEHOVAH ..." - the God of the Haribu ["Israelites or Jews"]. The article, which follows below, speaks for itself

21   NEW YORK POST, WEDNESDAY, JANUARY 26, 1972

Nefertiti Ruled in Her Digs

By STEVE HARVEY

The most liberated woman of her time in Egypt was unquestionably Nefertiti.

In fact, she may have been even more powerful than the man of her house, archeologists from the University of Pennsylvania theorize.

Using a computer to reconstruct Egyptian ruins, the archeologists discovered that her pharaoh King Akhenaten, built three temples—and two apparently were for her.

"This emphasis on a woman," they added, "is unparalleled in Egyptian history." Such power endowed to a woman in ancient Egypt would have been unusual indeed.

Pharaoh Had Status

It is difficult today to comprehend just how great a hold the pharaoh had on ancient Egypt.

He was, in the first place, god—the son of the sun Ra).

He did not die. He merely united with the sun. The death notice of the assassinated ruler, Amenemhat I, begins: "Year 30, third month of the inundation season, Day 7. The god mounted to his horizon . . ."

The Egyptians, like other primitive peoples, were constantly aware of outside forces which they could not control by any physical means: Winds, floods, rains, droughts.

So they sought answers through religious means: through their pharaoh. He was their protector.

Religious Duty

Although one might sympathize at first glance with the millions of Egyptians who labored under the blazing sun to build a pyramid or fight a war for the pharaoh, they apparently felt thankful; they were paying tribute to their god.

His personal name was so sacred that it was dangerous to utter. Thus, he called by the impersonal title of "pharoah" — meaning "great house." A comparable example would be to refer to President Nixon as "White House."

The kings were, of course, susceptible to human problems. Rameses II, the pharaoh reputedly in power when Moses was born, may have been suffering from a toothache when he ordered the massacre of the newborn males of the Jews.

Two professors of dentistry recently concluded from X-rays that Rameses had "an extreme case of destructive periodontal disease — badly abcessed teeth."

His subjects would do almost anything for the pharaoh. But alas, they knew nothing of root canals during Rameses' time.   (LAT)

One must conclude from the above article that King Saul of Israel must have had a double case of "TOOTHACHE" when he ordered that genocide be committed against the AMALAKITES, JEBUSITES, MOABITES, PARAZITES, and other peoples of very small kingdoms of Western Asia [the so-called "Middle East" or "Asia Minor"] during the Israelites' ["Jews"] establishment of their own nation on the ruins and graves of

11

those mentioned. Maybe it   to be assumed that "JEHOVAH", the God of the Jews, told

the Israelites to MURDER and COMMIT GENOCIDE in His name, but the Egyptians

[Africans or "Negroes"] whose God was RA were not told. For the biblical highlights of

this story see CHRONICLES Chapter I and II of the Holy Torah [Five Books of Moses

or Old Testament of the Christians].

Obviously, since Moses disappeared in EXODUS as fast as he came about in the

same SECOND BOOK OF MOSES, or HOLY TORAH, the current dental "AUTHORITIES"

cannot equally examine his remains, particularly his mouth and teeth, to find out if

this African also had...

> "AN EXTREME CASE OF DESTRUCTIVE PERIODONTAL
> DISEASE - BADLY ABCESSED TEETH."

Is it possible that Pnaraoh Akhenaten's...

> "LONG NARROW FACE THICK LIPS AND HATCHET
> CHIN..."

in Mr. Smith's hypothesis resulted from the same "DISEASE"?

These two articles will no doubt become, if they have not already, FACTS in the

mind of most who read them. But, what other purpose than to create an atmosphere of

RACISM and RELIGIOUS BIGOTRY directed against the people of present-day Egypt,

and Africans as a whole, do these articles serve? This author cannot see any other ra-

tionale for them at this time when the Europeans, European-Americans, and Asians of

modern Egypt and Israel are fighting over the spoils left by African and Asian peoples,

who in no way whatsoever can prove that they are related to them more so than any

other person can claim heritage of this region of the ancient world. They may be satis-

fying to many priests. rabbis. ministers, and inmans, and other protectors of the world

and morality for Jehovah, Jesus Cnrist. and Al'lah against those of us who may be label-

ed "PAGANS" and "HEATHENS." But, in them we are being asked to accept, subtly of

course, RACISM and RELIGIOUS BIGOTRY in Judaism, Christianity, and Islam against

the indigenous peoples of Africa: yet, all three of these religions were founded upon the

teachings and philosophies of the Africans of the Nile Valleys' religions, as projected

in the BOOK OF THE COMING FORTH BY DAY [Egyptian Book Of Tne Dead, and Papy-

rus Of Ani]. However, if this type of CULTURAL GENOCIDE against the indigenous

African peoples' history and heritage is allowed to continue unchecked and unchallenged,

we will certainly have to deal with the following RACIST and RELIGIOUSLY BIGOTED

propaganda by the Babylonian Talmudist "SCHOLARS" of 6th century C.E. Europe once

12

again: these men wrote the following interpretation of the story about Noah and his sons in the BOOK OF GENESIS [First Book Of Moses] in the Hebrew or "Jewish" Holy Torah. Noah was allegedly speaking to his son Ham - the "ANCESTOR OF THE NEGROES: "

> Now I cannot beget the fourth son whose children I
> would have ordered to serve you and your brothers! There-
> fore it must be Canaan, your first born, whom they enslave.
> And since you have disabled me...doing ugly things in black-
> ness of night, Canaan's children shall be born ugly and black!
> Moreover, because you twisted your head around to see my
> nakedness, your grandchildren's hair shall be twisted into
> kinks, and their eyes red; again because your lips jested at
> my misfortune, theirs shall swell; and because you neglected
> my nakedness, they shall go naked, and their male members
> shall be shamefully elongated! Men of this race are called
> Negroes, their forefather Canaan commanded them to love
> theft and fornication, to be banded together in hatred of their
> masters and never to tell the truth." ·

It should not suprise anyone to find out that lately the "WHITE LIBERAL AFRICAN-IST" historians and egyptologists have turned upon their "WHITE SEMITES" whom they were claiming. for over two centuries, occupied Egypt and were the masters of the "NEGRO SLAVES FROM NUBIA. " The reason for this turn about face is that BLACK and AFRICAN STUDIES, headed by knowledgeable African and African-American educators and administrators. are bringing to the forefront WORKS. PAPYRI, and other evidence of FACTS that show these articles as hypothetical works of a purely RACIST and RELIGIOUSLY BIGOTED nature without credibility. And indigenous Africans [Ethiopians, "Negroes, Bantus, Africans South of the Sahara. " Blacks, etc] were the originators of much of what is presently called "WESTERN CIVILIZATION" and "JUDAEO-CHRISTIAN RELIGION" today throughout the United States of America, Great Britain, Europe, and all other areas controlled by these powerful nations that operate on the basis of MIGHT MAKES RIGHT.

A very partial list of the usually surpressed bibliographical works which these answers are based on follows: these of course do not exclude others throughout the entire volume:

---

[0] See Robert Graves and Robert Pattai's HEBREW MYTHS, New York, 1964, p. 121;
also a similar article in the OLD TESTAMENT OF THE HOLY BIBLE [Aonfraternity
Version]. Guild Press. New York [1952, 1955, 1961], footnote comments by Rev. Joseph
Grispino, S. M. L. commenting on the alleged RACIAL references by Noah: and Y. ben-
Jochannan's AFRICA: MOTHER OF "WESTERN CIVILIZATION " Alkebu-lan Books Asso-
ciates. New York 1971.

Count C.F. Volney, RUINS OF EMPIRE.

G.G.M. James, STOLEN LEGACY.

J.J. Jackson, INTRODUCTION TO AFRICAN CIVILIZATION.

S. Lane-Poole, THE MOORS IN SPAIN.

Sir J. Frazier, THE GOLDEN BOUGH [13 vols.].

F.W. Snowden, BLACKS IN ANTIQUITY: A GRECO-ROMAN EXPERIENCE.

G. Massey, EGYPT THE LIGHT OF THE WORLD.

Sir E. A. Wallis Budge, THE BOOK OF THE DEAD AND THE PAPYRUS OF ANI
            ------------, HISTORY OF EGYPT [8 vols.].

Baron V. Denon, JOURNEY TO EGYPT AND ASSYRIA.

S. Griffith, NEGATIVE CONFESSION.

     -------, COFFIN TEXT.

     ------, PYRAMID TEXT.

J. Soaanes, COAST OF THE BARBARY.

E.B. Sandford, MEDITERRANEAN WORLD.

Y. ben-Jochannan, AFRICA: MOTHER OF "WESTERN CIVILIZATION."

     -------------, AFRICAN ORIGINS OF THE MAJOR "WESTERN RELIGIONS."

G. Maspero, HISTORY OF EGYPT AND ASSYRIA [8 vols.].

Mrs. S. Erskine, THE VANISHED CITIES OF NORTHERN AFRICA.

When one speaks about proof, with respect to the THICK LIPS, BROAD NOSES, WOOLLY HAIR, AND BURNT SKIN of the ancient Africans of the Nile Valleys and Great Lakes, it does not mean that all of the Africans of these areas had such physical appearance. The following mummies on page 15 are only a few of the hundreds in the possession of museums throughout the world. These five [5] are of different physical types; yet, they were only a handful in terms of the vast majority of the pharaohs, queens, and other members of the nobility we find mummified in so many tombs, mastabas, and pyramids of the Nile Valleys and Great Lakes regions. Because of the constant conquest by Asians and Europeans over the lower Nile Valley indigenous African people and their nations, it was virtually impossible to keep the population PURE of anything with regards to the worthless term "RACE." The reader may select whatever "RACIAL" or "ETHNIC" type he or she feels is most appropriate for any of the mummies shown, remembering of course that the term "SEMITIC" relates to language.

14

A FEW OF THE MUMMIES OF ROYALTY   from Elliot Smith,
"The Royal Mummies," Cairo; Catalogue General des An-
tiquites Egyptiennes, 1912. (Condition subject to changes).

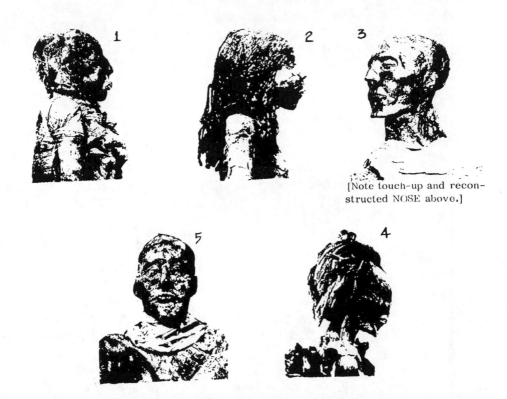

[Note touch-up and recon-
structed NOSE above.]

The above mummies are presently housed in the Egyptian Museum, Cairo,

Egypt (Africa). They represent many of the various facial types that inhabited

Egypt before and after the Dynastic periods. Many of the so-called "NEGROID

TYPES" are eventually coming to the focus of the general public, but it is the

TYPES like number 3 that receive most of the projection in European and

European-American works we are always having to use constantly.

KEY
1. Queen Taiouhrit, 2 Queen Notmit, 3 Pharaoh Seti I, 4 Queen Anhapou, and
5 Pharaoh Rameses III.

15

A HISTO-GEOPOLITICAL GRAPH OF ALKEBU-LAN
4,241 B.C.E. - 1600 C.E.
by
yosef ben-jochannan

Date BCE		Name, Description of Kingdom & Empires, Events, Personalities, Religions, etc.		Date BCE
4241	Saharan culture Tasilli rock paint- ings. Ti- assti art.	Introduction of the world's first Calendar in Egypt and other parts of the Nile Valley.		4241
3500		Tasian Period: The "Prehistoric Epoch") & 1st Dynasty forerunners.	Predynastic Nubian kingdom	3500
3000		Beginning of the Tasian and 1st Dynasty Periods.	Dynastic Nubia Upper Egypt, et.	3000
2500		2,780 . End of the IInd Dynasty. Be- ginning of the Pyramid Age (Old King- dom Era).	Twa mi-	2500
2000		2,100. Beginning of the Middle Kingdom (XIth Dynasty).	gra- tions back to the south (the so- called "Pygmies, Bushmen" and "Hoten-	2000
1500	African migra- tion began.	c1,675. Hyksos (Asians) invasion Hyksos Empire begins. XVth Dy- nasty. (They were chased from Egypt in 1,555 by the Thebans)	tots," etc.)	1500
1000	African Sava- settlers moved to Niger and Se- negal rivers delta	1,090 . New Kingdom (Tanite Period). Beginning of the XVIIIth Dynasty. 718 Late Epoch. Beginning of the Eth- iopian Period. XXIV - XXVIth Dynasties (Saite Period).	PreRowzwis migration to the south.	1000
500	...can mi- ...tion.	526 Beginning of the Persians defeat of Egyptians. Late Epoch. Ethiopians drive. from Lower ... beginning		500

[continued on following page]

Date BCE	Name, Description of Kingdom, Empires, , Events, Personalities, Religions,etc.			Date BCE

500

Beginning of the Ghana Empire. Earliest date according to traditional records

of XVIIIth Dynasty Greeks invasion. Rule of the Ptolemys begin. The XXXIst Dynasty

Expansion of the Ethiopian Empire

Rozwis invasion of the Zimbabwe Empire

500

100

100

50 B.C.E. Roman general Paulnius in Ghana; 30 B.C.E. Flaccus.

47 or 30 BCE Romans defeated Greeks, XXXIII Dynasty beginnings.

0 BCE

0 BCE

0 CE

0 CE

100

Kingdom of Monomotapa began

100

200

200

Beginning of Ghana Empire according to Europeans

300

Beginning of the Zulu Kingdom

300

400

400

500

500

End of Roman Empire in North Africa

600

Ngonis attack on Monomotapa Empire & States

600

Ending of the Roman Empire in North Africa in 640 CE after defeat by Muslim invaders. Arab masters of North Africa

Beginning of the Great Mani-Kongo Empire under Kongolo.

700

700

African Moors invaded Iberian Peninsula under command of General Tarikh. Arab Moors joined African Moors in Spain, Portugal and France.

Founding of the Zulu Empire began out of the Monomotapa Empire & States

800

800

900

900

1000

1000

[continued on following page]

17

[continued from page 17]

Date CE	Name, Description of Kingdom, Empires, Events, Personalities, Religions, etc.	Date CE
1000	1024 CE Tarsina Abdallah Mohammed drove the Jews from Ghana into the Ashanti Kingdom. 1.076 CE Khoumbi (Ghana City or Djene) destroyed by Al-mahodes or Almoravids from Morocco. 1086 CE, Oct. 23 Beginning of Senegal Empire at defeat of King Alfonso of Sevile, Spain in the Battle Of Zalaca. Moorish Empire extended from Spain to the Senegal River in West Africa. Africans of North	1000
1100	Almahodes (Almoravids) began Empire under Ibn Tumert. End of the Senegal Empire - 1186 CE	1100
1200	Beginning of the Melle (Mali) Kingdom by Sundiata (Mari Jata) in 1230 CE: Beginning of the Melle Empire by Sundiata in 1238 CE 1260 Manalukes seized Egypt's rule 1286 CE, end of the Almohade Empire	1200
1300	1332-1359 CE Civil War. Sulayman and Magham ruled Melle jointly. One in the South, other in the East. 1390 CE Melle (Mali) Empire ended with Mansa Musa IInd on the Throne. Musa ruled from 1374 CE.	1300
1400	Songhai (Songhay) Kingdom revolted. 1464 CE Sonni Ali Ber (Ali Kolon) mounted Songhai's throne. 1488 CE Sonni Ali founded the Songhai Empire.	1400
1500	1531-1549 CE Civil War in Songhai Empire between Askia Ismail and Askia Ishak I divided country and rule. 1591 CE Moroccan military forces invaded and destroyed Songhai during the reign of Askia Ishak IInd (1582-1581 CE).	1500
1600		1600

18

It is of very deep significance to begin the identification of the Africans by citing certain major quotations about them. There could be no better way to start than with the writings of an Englishman named Thomas Hodgkin, former Secretary of the Oxford University Delegacy for Extra-Mural Studies and a Fellow of Bailliol College, Oxford. The quotation from Mr. Hodgkin stems from an article that appeared in THE HIGHWAY, February 1952, pp. 169-170, under the title - "National Movements In West Africa." He wrote:

> It is no doubt flattering to our vanity to imagine that the peoples of Africa were 'primitive' and 'barbarous' before the penetration of the Europeans, and that it was we who have "civilized" them. But it is a theory that lacks historical foun - dation. The Empire of Ghana flourished in what is now French West Africa during the dark ages of Western Europe. By the fifteenth century there was a university at Timbuktu. The Ashantis of the Gold Coast and the Yorubas of Nigeria possess- ed highly organized and complex civilizations long before their territories were brought under British political control. The thesis that Africa is what Western European missionaries, traders, technicians and administrators have made it is com- forting [to Western Europeans] but invalid. The eruption of Western European colonizers into Africa - with all the effects of their religion and their schools, their Gin and their cotton goods and their systems of administration is only an event, though a very important event, in the history of the African peoples.
>
> If, therefore, we wish to understand the national move - ments that have emerged in Africa - and have reached their most mature and advanced stage in West Africa - we have to begin by trying to rid our minds of the European preconcep- tions that influence our thinking on this subject. This is not easy, since most of the available material on African affairs is presented from a European standpoint - either by imperial historians [who are interested in the record of European pene- tration into Africa], or by colonial administrators [who are interested in the pattern of instructions imposed by European governments upon African societies], or by anthropologists [who are often] though not always, mainly interested in the forms of social organizations surviving in the simplest Afri- can communities, considered in isolation from political de- velopments in the world around them. We shall probably have to wait a little while for the real history of Africa to be written by African scholars for an African reading public.

The last sentence by Mr. Hodgkin, which this author has carefully underlined, is the

key to BLACK and AFRICAN studies courses everywhere. But, an author of African
origin selects to paraphrase Mr. Hodgkin in the following manner:

> When "AFRICAN SCHOLARS" interpret their own
> African history from an African perspective, for an
> African reading public everywhere, including the United
> States of America, then, and only then, shall we have
> TRUE AFRICAN HISTORY.

Mr. Hodgkin's revelations were brought to light on somewhat of an official basis.
His response was to certain allegations made by Sir Hugh Clifford, former Governor
of Britain's West African colony, which the British had ren med "GOLD COAST
CROWN COLONY"[1] [presently the Republic of Ghana].

Writing in BLACKWOOD'S MAGAZINE, January 1918, and having very much to
say about the Africans of the "Gold Coast," Sir Clifford had stated:

> Much the most notable achievement that can be placed
> to his credit is his invention, without the assistance of ex-
> traneous influence, of the democratic system of government
> and State socialism, which are the basic principles upon
> which his tribal policy is founded. Recent innovations, as I
> have indicated, tend seriously to undermine this system;
> and it is interesting to note that while European political
> theorists are apparently working their way back to a state
> of things closely resembling that which the TWI-speaking
> peoples long ago evolved for themselves, the latter are
> displaying an inclination to discard them as immediate and
> inevitable accomplishment of their first real and solid ad-
> vance towards a higher standard of civilization.

The vast majority of the TWI people are located around the nations of Liberia,
Ghana, Guinea, and other West African nations within the same general area[2] of the
Gulf of Guinea and the former Ethiopian [Atlantic] Ocean.

These are two most privileged first-hand accounts of great African High-Cultures
[civilizations] on the part of two men who were in position to know the "TRUTH." But,
this work is dealing primarily with man's cultural and historical development, which in
this case are the Africans.' Therefore there are those who, for various reasons, do not
credit Africa's sons and daughters with being human, much less being able to produce
human culture, civil traits, and societies, which all amounts to what is presently called
"CIVILIZATION." This type of characterization has been perpetuated by certain learned
men or scholars, otherwise called academicians, such as one professor M.D.W.
Jeffreys. This "learned" professor's works, but more specifically his personal views

20

about indigenous African peoples and their descendants everywhere, were published in the September 1951 issue of the WEST AFRICAN REVIEW under the title ... "The Negro Enigma." It revealed a profound disregard for documentation, a picture of racist propaganda, and displayed an extraordinary gift for creating stereotypes. He wrote:

> The Negro is divided linguistically into main groups. The Sudanic speaking Negroes of West Africa and the Bantu speaking Negroes[0] of the Congo, East and South Africa. All are of one race and are remarkably uniform in appearance.

> The Black Belt, anthropologically speaking, is that area on the earth's surface that comprises the dark-skinned races. Excluding the American Negroes who were brought there by Europeans. The Black Belt extends from Africa; via India, to Melanesia and Australia. In this great arc the position of the Negro is the enigma. At the two ends, or horns, are the people who are Negroes, but in the centre there are none. The centre is occupied by a dark-skinned race, the Hindu, but he offers no difficulty. He belongs to the same race as the "European," namely the Caucasians - the inhabitants of Europe - and the dark-skinned Caucasians, the inhabitants of North Africa, Asia Minor and India.

Although Professor Jeffreys, at this juncture, had established his RACIST hypothesis, he continued to expand his "LIGHT" and "DARK-SKINNED" Caucasianism to the point where he eliminated everyone of the indigenous Africans - the so-called "SUDANIC" and "BANTU -SPEAKING NEGROES" - from all of North and East Africa, and purified the area with a new population of "DARK-SKINNED CAUCASIANS." Thus he questioned:

> How comes it then that east and west India is flanked by Negroes? That is the puzzle: i.e. that there are Oceanic and African Negroes separated from each other by Arabia, India and Malaya? Let us view the problem from another angle. The Caucasians come from an old human stock - a stock that is today called Modern Man. Modern Man goes back a long way in time. The Swanscombe skull found in Great Britain is dated 250,000 years and is our stock, not Negro. The skeletal remains dug up by the Leakeys in East Africa are us, not Negro. Boskop man, found in the Cape, is dated 50,000 years and falls into our group not that of the Negro.

What is meant by "BANTU-SPEAKING NEGROES"? There is no language in any part of Africa by that name. This RACIST classification is partly responsible for much of the conclusion in Seligman's, RACES OF AFRICA, New York, 1930, etc.

There are no Negro skulls of antiquity - the oldest known
is about 6000 B.C. The two Grimaldi skulls, one of a woman
and the other a boy, are not Negro skulls. They merely show
Negro features.

So the enigma deepens: all evidence points to the Negro
being a comparatively recent race and here is the old Caucasian race in a continuous stretch from Britain to India and yet
on the other side of India are Negroes.

Professor Jeffreys constantly placed great emphasis on the word "NEGRO," ten
[10] times in two [2] paragraphs he used it, indicating each time the extent of his Negrophobia and the obsession that drove him in that direction. But, still not satisfied
with his obvious state of confusion and deep ..RACISM.. Jeffreys reached his climax
when he wrote:

Now in Africa there is continuous evidence, unlike anywhere else on the globe, of man's uninterrupted occupation of
the earth for close on a million years. Africa is thus today accepted by many scientists as the cradle of the human species.
Thus, in Africa from the Old Stone Age to modern time, Modern Man is the tool maker. No where is the Negro, unlike the
Bushman, associated with any of these stone-age cultures.

One can readily see why Professor Jeffreys had so many problems in finding
why most "...scientists..." concluded that the "Negroes"' homeland, "AFRICA,"
around the Great Lakes regions and the Nile Valley [from Tanzania in central East
Africa to the Mediterranean Sea at North Africa], is THE CRADLE OF HUMAN [be
they black, white, brown, yellow, red, or whatever else] CIVILIZATION. This is
more so TRUE even though he failed to note that the indigenous Africans, not only
"DARK-SKINNED," but also "BLACK," which he preferred to call "NEGROES," were
included on his side of the anthropological and geneaological [RACIAL] scale among
his "LIGHT" and "DARK-SKINNED CAUCASIANS." For he included among them the
Cushites [Ethiopians], Nubians [Sudanese], Agikuyu [Kenyans], Egyptians [presently
Africans, Arabized-Africans, Arabs and a combination of African-Asian-European
mixture of people - if this description is adequate for human beings] , Masais, and
others renamed "BANTUS" around Tanzania to Monomotapa [South Africa], who reside
along the more than 4100 mile length and breadth of the Nile Valley [from Uganda in
central Africa to Egypt at the Mediterranean Sea].[3] Moreover, he also included the
Rozwis, descendants of the builders of the stone structures of the Great Zimbabwe

22

[notoriously renamed "SOUTHERN RHODESIA" in honour of the "ADOLPH HITLER" of colonial Africa, who murdered more Africans than Hanan and Hitler combined murdered European Jews], and the Swazis and Sethos of Monomotapa [South Africa],[4] in order to lay claim to Tanzania's fossil-man - "ZINJANTHROPUS BOISIE," Monomotapa's "BOSKOP MAN," and Zimbabwe's "BROKEN HILL MAN," as members, or forerunners, of his "DARK-SKINNED CAUCASIAN RACE."

Professor Jeffreys was able, somewhat, to camouflage his racially impregnated non-scientific jargon by virtue of the QUOTATION MARKS. But, he should have realized that in this case he was only proving that his "LIGHT" and "DARK-SKINNED CAUCASIANS" especially the "LIGHT" ones, had no historical past into antiquity and ancient cultural greatness - i.e. - "WESTERN CIVILIZATION" - without the inclusion of a vast number of indigenous Africans he selected to label "NEGROES" and "BANTUS," including Africans descended from others who were most responsible for the early education of the FIRST and GREATEST of the "LIGHT-SKINNED CAUCASIAN RACE" - the people of Hellas, otherwise known as the "GREEKS." It is, therefore, regrettable it appears that this "learned" professor must have not read very much about the early Greeks physical description of the "...BLACK, BROAD NOSE THICK LIPS, and WOOLLY-HAIRED EGYPTIANS, COLCHIANS, NUBIANS, and ETHIOPIANS,"[5] who taught the earliest "LIGHT-SKINNED CAUCASIANS" - from whom he sprang. As such, it is understandable why he had to claim some of his "SUDANIC" and "BANTU-SPEAKING NEGROES" as his "DARK-SKINNED CAUCASIAN" relatives of his ancient past, while rejecting them as the cousins they are at the present 20th century C.E.

It is very much apparent that professor Jeffreys must have forgotten more than the history of how, and from who, the earliest Europeans - Greeks and Romans - received their education. He also overlooked the FACT that Greek and Roman life [culture or civilization] had been patterned by the training the Greeks and Romans received in Africa from the Africans - the so-called "NEGROES" and "BANTUS" included; and, from the Greeks and Romans all of Europe's other civil compacts developed;[6] thus it is clearly shown that from this African "SUDANIC" and "BANTU" background his so-called "MODERN MAN" originated.[7] This is recorded evidence, written by the professor's own earliest "LIGHT-SKINNED CAUCASIANS" - both Greeks and Romans. But, maybe professor Jeffreys would prefer to revise what the earliest Greeks and Romans wrote about their apprenticeship under the indigenous Africans, "NEGROES" and "BAN-

TUS," to suit his own RACISM and PREJUDICES he demonstrated in his writings. The professor's hypothesis on his "MODERN MAN" is endorsed by thousands of RACIST educators and authorities on Africa and African peoples of the "CAUCASIAN RACE;" all of whom demand that they be recognized by African peoples everywhere as the "SOLE AUTHORITY" on everything African. Yet, all of them have equally failed to explain what is meant by "NEGRO FEATURES" in the "TWO GRIMALDI SKULLS" found in Monomotapa [southern Africa].

Before further and much more extensive research is undertaken in this area one needs the privilege of hearing a few comments from a slightly opposite point of view by another "LIGHT-SKINNED CAUCASIAN" writer on this subject , Sir Harry H. Johnston, as he wrote in his work - A HISTORY OF THE COLONISATION OF AFRICA, p. 2:

> There are certain anatomical differences between the existing Negroes of Asia and Oceania on the one hand and the Negroes of Modern Africa on the other. Whether the African Negro was the first human colonizer of Africa, or was preceded by more brutish or more generalized type, such as the Galley-Hill man, is not yet known to us. But from the little we possess in the way of fossil human remains and other evidence it seems probable that every region of Africa, even Algeria and Egypt, once possessed a Negro population. In Mauretania [Morocco to Tripolitania] these ancient Negroes were partly driven out by prehistoric Caucasian invaders and partly absorbed by intermarriage, the mixture resulting in the darkened complexions of the North African people.[8] In Egypt a dwarfish type of Negro seems to have inhabited the Nile delta some 10,000 years ago; and big black Negroes formed the population of Upper Nubia and Dongola as late as about 4000 years ago.[9]

One has to note that Johnston was very careful to overlook the ABSORPTION of the so-called "NEGROES" in southern Europe, western Europe, and Great Britain. He seemed to have forgotten that as late as 711 C.E. "...BIG BLACK NEGROES.." were being "...ABSORBED..." by the thousands throughout Iberia and southern France, from there into other parts of Europe, and finally into the British Isles - including England, Scotland, Wales , and Ireland.

Neither in Sir Harry H. Johnston's analysis or in professor M.D.W. Jeffreys' wide and sweeping unscientific statements. can one find the necessity for determining why proof of the Africans', also called "NEGROES, '" origin in Africa is so utterly important, unless it is to justify all of the ruthless RACIAL PREJUDICE and BIGOTRY being still de-

24

monstrated daily by the overwhelming majority of Professor Jeffreys' "LIGHT-
SKINNED CAUCASIAN" educators and writers against their defenseless African victims for over the past four hundred years [c. 1503 - 1972 C.E. or A.D.]. One must
be reminded of the FACT that Sir Harry H. Johnston's conclusions relied heavily upon
the theories expounded by Sir Arthur Keith and W.L.H. Duckworth. Therefore, as
was to be expected, each compounded the others prejudiced misinformation. It seems
that the compilation of errors was accomplished in too many instances in the writings
of these two men - Sir Harry and Professor Jeffreys. However, as a "HISTORIAN" or
"ANTHROPOLOGIST " Professor Jeffreys must be separated, somewhat, from Sir
Harry. For all evidence points to the FACT that Sir Harry based some of his conclusions, appearently not very much, upon certain scientific analysis [he claimed] which
came partly from his own historical data and the actual examination of certain human
remains ["fossils"]. He, then, let the "FACTS," distorted as they were, and still are,
prevail as he saw them. On the other hand, Professor Jeffreys presented no apparent
evidence, scientific or otherwise, to support any of his conclusions in the entire article. Nowhere in the professor's theories has he submitted any statistical data necessary for "SCHOLARSHIP CREDIBILITY." Yet, no one should slightly dispel Professor
Jeffrey's apparently RACIST and UNSCIENTIFIC conclusions. No! To dispel them solely on the basis that they are without scientific evidence or historical facts would not
be sufficient. Historical evidence through data and scientific facts to the contrary,
using substantially varied sources of "AUTHORITATIVE WORKS," must be presented.
Due to an abundance of creditable materials on AFRICAN HISTORY and HIGH-CULTURE,
it will not be difficult to accomplish this goal. This GOAL is reached throughout the entire text of this volume.

Before referring to certain other "UNIVERSALLY RECOGNIZED EUROPEAN
AND EUROPEAN-AMERICAN WRITERS, HISTORIANS, AND GENERAL SCHOLARS
ON AFRICAN STUDIES," one must again refer to Sir Harry H. Johnston - who earned
the Hon. Sc.D. at Cambridge University "...FOR HIS EXTENSIVE SCIENTIFIC AND
HISTORICAL EXPLORATIONS AND RESEARCH ON THE SUBJECT OF AFRICA..," etc.
He once wrote:

> The successor and supplanter of Homo primigenius in
> Western Europe was a generalized type of Homo sapiens, re-
> presented by the negroid strain has never been completely
> eliminated in these lands.

H. G. Wells in his book, A SHORT HISTORY OF THE WORLD, p. 59, apparently supporting Sir Harry H. Johnston's position, wrote:

> **Three** main regions and three main kinds of wandering
> and imperfectly settled people there were in those remote
> days of the first civilizations in Sumeria and early Egypt.
> Away in the forests of Europe were the blonde Nordic peoples,
> hunters and herdsmen, a <u>lowly race</u>. The primitive civiliza-
> tions saw very little of this race before 1500 B.C. [10]

It should be quite obvious to everyone that while those who cherish Professor Jeffreys outlook on history, and who would remove every trace of the indigenous Africans [the so-called "SUDANIC" and "BANTU-SPEAKING NEGROES"] from North, East, and even certain parts of South Africa [Alkebu-lan], cannot even remove the pronounced "NEGROID [African] STRAIN" in themselves and other fellow European and European-American peoples, especially of the Mediterranean Europeans' physcial appearance, nor from the LIGHTEST BLONDE of Professor M.D.W. Jeffreys' LIGHT-SKINNED CAUCASIAN RACE - the Nordic peoples. Within this same scope of logical reasoning the grandson of the Victorian scientist of world fame - Sir Charles Darwin, himself honoured and also named [Sir] Charles Darwin, a scientist of note in his own rights, wrote an article titled - THE NEXT MIILION YEARS - in which he stated that:

> "...the average skin color of the human race will get darker and,
> furthermore, economic and military power in Africa and Asia will
> wrest the leadership from Europe...."

The late C.P. Snow, in his comments on Sir Charles Darwin's statements, wrote in JOHN O'LONDON'S WEEKLY the following :

> It means, incidentally, that the racial discrimination which
> has been the least creditable feature of the period of white hegem-
> ony is not wicked ; it is worse than wicked, it is criminally fool-
> ish.

One must return to Professor M.D.W. Jeffreys' remarks, since he seemed to have been the champion and most quoted social [cultural] anthropologist of those who would remove all "NEGRO" [indigenous African] "PEOPLES" from North and East Africa's ancient and present history and High-Culture [civilization]. It is to be equally noted that the professor was also contradicted by Sir Harry H. Johnston on the theory of "...THE INDIANS..." [indigenous people of India, southern Asia] also being "DARK-SKINNED CAUCASIANS." Sir Harry H. Johnston wrote in THE WEST AFRICAN RE-VIEW, p. 3, September, 1951, the following:

There is a strong underlying Negroid element in the mass of the Indian population, and in the southernmost part of the great peninsula there are forest tribes of dark-skinned and strikingly Negro physiognomy, with frizzled or woolly hair. There is a negroid element in gentle Burmese; and in the Adaman Islands - geologically little more than a depressed peninsula of Further India - the dwarfish people are absolute Negroes of the Asiatic type... In the more eastern among the Malay islands - especially in Burn, Jilolo and Timor - the interior tribes are of obvious Negro stock. Still more marked is the case of New Guinea, and most of all in the Bismarch archipelago and northern Solomon Islands. In these last resemblance of the natives to the average Negro of Africa is most striking, although the distance is something like 8000 miles. Negro affinities extend east of the Solomon archipelago to Fiji and Hawaii, and south of New Caledonia, Ismania and New Zealand. On the other hand, Africa for many thousand years has been obviously the chief domain of the Negro.[11]

It is not strange that Sir Harry H. Johnston could not see the obvious "NEGROID ELEMENT IN THE MASS OF THE ..." European and British..."POPULATION IN THE SOUTHERNMOST PART OF THE GREAT..." Mediterranean Sea coast of Europe where the Africans even became emperors, and from whence thousands of African "NEGROES" were exported into Britain to pacify "...BRITONS WHO WERE NOT EVEN FIT TO BE SLAVES." One will better understand the position of Sir Harry H. Johnston in the above article, as he wrote it for THE WEST AFRICAN REVIEW, p. 3, September 1951, for a European reading public on the African continent.

Those who have had the privilege of traveling in the areas of the world mentioned by Sir Harry H. Johnston and Professor M.D.W. Jeffreys, also in Europe and Great Britain [including Ireland, Scotland, Wales,and England], and here in the United States Of America, have seen the evidence of Sir Harry's statement. Such proof is most definitely opposed to professor Jeffreys. Moreover, history reminds mankind of the role the Africans ["NEGROES" etc.] played in Persia during the period of the civilization of the Kingdom of Elam [a "CIVILIZATION", High-Culture ,which the indigenous Africans established in Persia of antiquity]. It seems that Professor Jeffreys had also forgotten that the Ganges River in India got its name from the famous Ethiopian, General Ganges, who captured and ruled that area with thousands of Ethiopian ["NEGRO"] troops. Maybe

---

.He also failed to mention is that there is also a "...strong underlying Negroid element in the mass of the ..." southern and western European and European-American "population," which was ignored by most European-American academicians.

the ETHIOPIANS are also to be considered amongst Professor Jeffreys' "DARK-SKINNED CAUCASIANS!" They are also part and parcel of the ancient peoples who once ruled UPPER, MIDDLE, and LOWER EGYPT [Ta-Merry, Kimit, Sais, etc.], and much of the so-called "MIDDLE EAST," India, Persia, and Arabia, also Palestine [Israel]. If so, then the peoples of the entire Nile Valley, up to Uganda, should be equally considered and designated as such. [12] [See Joel B. Rogers' WORLD'S GREAT MEN OF COLOR, vol. I; J.J. Jackson's INTRODUCTION TO AFRICAN CIVILIZATION; Sir E.A. Wallis Budge's NUBIA AND ETHIOPIA; Count C.F. Volney's RUINS OF EMPIRE; E. B. Sandford's MEDITERRANEAN WORLD; Y. ben-Jochannan's AFRICA: MOTHER OF "WESTERN CIVILIZATION"].

The so-called "NEGROES" have become such a "DILEMMA" to the "LIGHT-SKINNED CAUCASIANS" [Modern Man] of Professor Jeffreys, that now practically every university in the Americas and Europe has become over-indulgent in the studies of African ["Negro"] history and High-Culture. Of course this trend would have been a blessing if the materials on hand in most of them were of good quality. And, providing the documents of quality amongst the mass-produced editorialized history books would be used in the preparation of current and future teachers in AFRICAN and BLACK studies. But, how can the administrators of famous European and European-American universities and other institutions of "higher learning," whose main goal appears to be the perpetuation of their own archaic teaching about Africa and her peoples, wrong or right, come in contact with teachers or professors who are versed in AFRICAN STUDIES; who are free of "CHRISTIAN MISSIONARY PATERNALISM," and void of the "TARZAN AND JANE" or "HENRY MORTON STANLEY'S DARKEST AFRICA" syndrome? To have expected Europeans and/or European-Americans of any economic persuasion whatso-ever [capitalists, communists, socialists, etc.] , and of any religious affiliation [Jews, Christian, Muslim, etc.], before the mid-nineteenth century C.E. to teach "BLACK HISTORY" from a point of African or African-American interpretation, when in fact BLACK PEOPLE ["Negroes"] everywhere were beginning to surface their violent revo-lution to rid themselves of all controls by the same European and European-American "EDUCATORS," would be nothing more than an exercise in futility and wishful thinking. [13]

In conjunction with the above remarks, we find one of the "AUTHORITIES ON AFRI-CA" and her "PEOPLES" - the "learned" Professor C.P. Groves in his four volume work, THE PLANTING OF CHRISTIANITY IN AFRICA, vol. I, p. 1, writing the follow-

28

ing:

> "...it is the paradox of this vast continent" [Africa] "that while sharing in the earliest history of the human race, it was yet not opened up until the late nineteenth century."

Professor Groves' assertion that Africa "...YET WAS NOT OPENED UP..," etc., is typically the same position held by most of Professor Jeffreys' "LIGHT-SKINNED CAUCASIAN" academicians, especially those who prefer to be called "WHITE LIBERAL" on the subject of Africa and the indigenous Africans. For the openly professed "WHITE LIBERAL AFRICANIST" European and European-American educators and authors still find it extremely difficult to write or speak in defense of the indigenous Africans and Africa without first asserting their own feeling of SUPERIORITY in the background. This practice of paternalism, common among all missionaries and colonialist settlers, is the order of the day throughout Professor Groves' declarations in his books. Africa's isolation, if ever such was the case, was the right of its indigenous peoples. But the TRUTH is that there has never been a period in man's history when Africa "...WAS NOT YET OPENED-UP..." to all. It seems that any place where a European or European-American has never been is UNDISCOVERED, CLOSED, SECRETIVE, DANGEROUS, PRIMITIVE, and "...NOT OPENED-UP...." However, the first of their appearance at any place inhabited by people other than their own "ETHNIC GROUP" suddenly becomes SAFE, DISCOVERED, "OPENED-UP," and all that is worthy of their God's grace.

Not only was Africa "...OPENED-UP..." to all of mankind, including Europeans, Africa carried her "CIVILIZING " [cultural] influences into Europe by way of her ancient and glorious sons and daughters of Egypt, Nubia, Ethiopia,[14] Libya, Carthage, Numidia, and other nations before there was a JESUS CHRIST, muchless CHRISTIANITY for Groves to be able to PLANT it in Africa. Africa, once again, during the beginnings of the Chritian Era [711 C.E. or A.D.], sent her sons from the northwest - the MOORS.[0] As late as the closing of the 15th Century C.E., when the last of the African or "Negro" MOORS were finally driven out of Granada, Spain, indigenous Africans were still "CIVILIZING" Professor Groves' "CHRISTIAN EUROPEANS", Jeffreys' "LIGHT-

---

[0]. Note that there were three [3] types of MOORS referred to in the history of African, [the so-called "NEGRO"] rule in Spain from 711 to 1485 C.E. Thus; the BLACKAMOORS, many of whom went to southern Ireland with the Spaniards; the MOORS, and the ARABIAN MOORS from Arabia; the first two [2] were of indigenous African or so-called "NEGRO STOCK."

SKINNED CAUCASIAN RACE," within their own homeland - the continent called EUROPE. Of course the indigenous Africans of West Africa and Central Africa, the so-called "TRUE NEGRO," also engaged in the "CIVILIZING" of the Europeans and Britons through their UNIVERSITY OF SANKHORE in the City of Tombut or Timbuktu, Melle [Mali], and through other types of educational contact. [15]

As for the Africans [the so-called "Negroes"] being indigenous to Ta-Merry [Egypt] there is abundant evidence that they were there from the first prehistoric days of Nile Valley culture; not as "SLAVES," as most European and European-American writers prefer one to believe, but as the originators of the first Ta-Merrian [Egyptian] High-Culture ["civilization"], and as the FIRST KINGS [pharaohs]. [16] The Blacks, or Ethiopians as they were called by the earliest Europeans of Greece and Rome, were in Egypt before the "STONE-AGE CULTURE," at least. The Europeans who came there met them in power. [17] Finally, the indigenous Africans of the LOWER and CENTRAL Valley, North, and East Africa, subsequently became enslaved by invading Asians, and then Europeans. [18] The late Sir E.A. Wallis Budge, formerly Keeper of Egyptian and Assyrian Antiquities of the British Museum, in his "AUTHORITATIVE" book, EGYPT, p. 42, with regards to this point, wrote:

> There is no evidence that the Egyptians of the New Stone
> Age had invented the art of writing, but there is abundant proof
> that they could draw pictures of the symbols of their totems and
> sacred animals and objects. These symbols are found painted
> on pots at Makadah and are supported on standards fixed in the
> prehistoric period, and they form the oldest Egyptian hiero-
> glyphs known. They are very important as showing that the ear-
> liest attempts to write in Egypt was made by native African
> Egyptians.

Sir E.A. Wallis Budge's conclusion must be given serious recognition, as his works are universally recognized among Europeans and European-Americans; and he was rated..."ONE OF THE BEST EGYPTOLOGISTS OF ALL TIME." It was typical of Budge not to show any fear that the Africans being BLACK, or "NEGROES," should have been the first to teach all of mankind [including the Greeks and Romans] civil government, or that they were the first to inhabit the entire Nile Valley, [19] all of this having preceded his works he wrote at the turn of the 20th century C.E.

Since you are about to embark upon an expedition into the inner reaches of AFRICAN STUDIES, you must be extraordinarily clear on at least one major point from the outset That is, NAMES. For example: "HAMITE" and "SEMITE," equally "CAUCASIAN," are

30

terms which have been created and developed by European and European-American orthodox and liberal "scholars" from Hebrew [Jewish] RACIST and BIGOTED religious mythology found in the FIVE BOOKS OF MOSES, otherwise known as the Holy Torah [the Christian Holy Bible's Old Testament]. They have no authoritative relationship to Africa's indigenous peoples. Using them as "AFRICAN NAMES" would be tantamount to calling the Arabs "INDIGENOUS AFRICANS" because they have dominated certain areas of North and East Africa for the past 1327 years.[20] For no where in the records of Africa's glorious history, written by indigenous African historians, is there any mention of "HAMITES," and of course "SEMITES" or even "CAUCASIANS," before their Hebrew and Christian European and European-American advocates created them for EUROPEAN and WHITE STUDIES. Equally before, and after, the arrival of the Western Europeans in West Africa there was no word in any of Africa's many languages and dialects which could be translated into any European language to mean "NEGRO," this word having stemed from the ridiculous word "NEGROLAND" shown on maps like that on page 401 of this volume by H. Moll, titled AFRICA 1729. Yet, there is ample proof that for more than 1,000,000 years the BLACK MAN has occupied the entire continent of Alkebu-lan [Africa]. And, at no time during this history and prehistory has he ever called himself, nor any member of his family, "SEMITE, HAMITE, CAUCASIAN" or "NEGRO." The ancient Africans ["Negroes" or otherwise] of Egypt[0] were BLACK when the Asians called Haribus [Hebrews or Israelites later] arrived in Egypt with Abraham [c. 1640 B.C.E.], and before Abraham [the first Haribu or Hebrew] was born. The Africans certainly needed no Haribu mythological and secular classification [the Biblical story of HAM][00] to establish their African identity. Labels or names such as "NEGROES, SEMITES, HAMITES," etc., are only tools of subterfuge on the part of the RACIST ideology inherent in what today is being called "WESTERN CIVILIZATION." Their usage amounts to a vicious crime against humanity, and a malicious attempt to eradicate the contributions of an entire segment of mankind - the so-called "NEGROES" - in practical-

---

[0]. Among the many names it was called were: Ta-Merry, Mizrair, Mizrain, Sais, Cham, Pearl of the Nile, Land of the Pharaohs, Land of the Nile, etc., Egypt being the last of them, a name given this African land through Hebrew mythology from Noah and the "Great Flood" drama in the Book of Genesis - the FIRST BOOK OF MOSES of the Hebrew ["Jewish"] Holy Torah.

[00]. The same "...AUTHORITIES..." declared that "...the Negroes [meaning the African peoples] are inferior to the Caucasians, Semites, Hamites," and even the "Caucasoids" and "Negroids."

ly each and every school of learning in Europe, the Americas, and other areas of the world under the control of colonialist-minded Europeans and European-Americans [capitalists, feudalists, communists, socialists, liberals, and whatever else there may be].

Professor J.C.deGraft-Johnson in his book, AFRICAN GLORY,[21] p. 9, commenting on egyptologists E. Meyer and H.R. Hall's conclusions on the entrance of the so-called "NEGRO" into Dynastic Egypt, from about 5869 to 3315 B.C.E. supported the position of the usual RACIST European and European-American writers, historians, and general educators [see Dr. Donald Wiedner's hypothetical map on p. 45 of this volume] who would like to remove each and every trace of the Africans ["Negroes", etc.] from all of northern Africa's history. He wrote the following:

> All authorities, however, agree that the Dynastic Egyptians invaded Egypt during or before the fourth millennium B.C. They populated and ruled the narrow valley of the Desert Nile as far south as the First Cataract. They also ruled and populated the broad delta to the shores of the Mediterranean.
> To the south of the First Cataract were people of mixed origin - Egyptians, Hamites, and Negroes of the Nubian race, beyond the Second Cataract the population of the Nile Valley, while Dynastic Egyptian rule lasted, was entirely Negro.

Anyone can readily see that Professor deGraft-Johnson, himself an African, had fallen for the "HAMITIC" and "NEGRO"[22] jargon within the unscientific language of his colleagues who taught him at European universities. Not only did he use the RACIST and RELIGIOUSLY BIGOTED colloquialisms common to his profession, but he also introduced another stereotype classification of the same type of terminology, namely, "NUBIAN RACE." Yet, there is no doubt that Professor deGraft-Johnson was once considered "...ONE OF THE BEST KNOWN AFRICAN HISTORIANS OF MODERN TIMES ON WEST AFRICAN HIGH-CULTURES [civilizations] AND CULTURAL ANTHROPOLO - GY..." by orthodox and liberal Europeans and European-Americans. However, he too has been unable to project his researches beyond the bias which his European and British teachers have directed against African [BLACK] people in their attempt to remove the Black Man and his family [the so-called "NEGROES"] from the history and heritage of ancient Egypt and other parts of North and East Africa through certain very well contrived manipulations of the English language [semantics]. As a result, he degraded the African people, while at the same instance trying to remove the slanders and insults

32

by their slave masters under which they suffered for so many generations. He had fall-
en victim to the concept of "FOLLOW THE MASTER" even when he, as researcher,
should have known that before the 17th Century C.E. the word "NEGRO" did not appear
anywhere in writings relating to the indigenous African people - Egyptians, Nubians,
and others included.

Certainly there were no "NEGROES" in Dynastic Egypt. "NEGROES" never existed
in Africa until they were placed there by European and European-American historians,
palaeontologists, ethnologists, and anthropologists,[23] just as "INDIANS" were created
by the same "AUTHORITIES" for the Americas. It is, therefore, quite difficult to distinguish who were the "NEGROES" in African history, when so many Africans are
labeled practically everything else throughout the so-called "prehistoric" and "historic"
periods by European and European-American "EDUCATORS." For example: To say
that the ELAMITES [Africans or Blacks] who settled in Persia were "NEGROES" would
be ridiculous. Yet, these were the same African people as the African-Americans of
today and the indigenous Egyptians, Nubians, Meroites, and Ethiopians of yesteryears.[24]
The difference is that historians, writing in ancient times, did not record the indigenous
[original] Africans as "NEGROES, CAUCASIANS, SEMITES, HAMITES," etc. These
RACIST and RELIGIOUSLY BIGOTED names, nor anything resembling them, were not
existence then. This contention is best highlighted in one of Egypt's most famous his-
torical documents dealing with the question of the BLACKS ["Negroes"] in Ta-Merry
[Egypt] thousands of years before the current Arabized-Africans who now control North
Africa; and before the ancient Semitized-Hyksos Asians [Egypt's first foreigners]. Thus
it is shown that Usertsen II,[25] the fifth pharaoh of the XXIInd Dynasty, c. 870 - 847
B.C.E., conqueror of certain parts of Ta-Nehisi [Nubia, Zeti, or Sudan], set-up a
Stelae at Samªah for the purpose of barring the Nubians [the so-called "NEGROES"]
whom he had defeated in battle. It also indicated that he had driven them out of a certain section of Egypt, that is the Nubians, not the BLACKS - or he would have driven
most of the entire population of Ta-Merry [Egypt] into Ta-Nehisi [Nubia]. And, that he
too was not of solely indigenous African-Egyptian origin. The inscription, as translated into English from the original Hieroglyph, states the following:

> I am the king [my] word is performed. My hand performs what
> my mind conceives....I attack my attacker..... The man who re-
> treats is a vile coward; he who is defeated on his own land is no man.
> Thus is the Nubians. He falls down at a word of command, when at-

tacked he runs away - when pursued he shows his back in flight. The
Nubians have no courage, they are weak and timid, their hearts are
contemptible. I have seen them, I am not mistaken about them. I
seized their women, I took their goods, I stopped up their wells, I
slew their bulls, I reaped their crops, I burnt their houses. I am
speaking the truth....My son who maintains this boundary is indeed
my son; he who allows it to be thrust back is no son of mine, and I
never got him. I have set up a statue of myself here, not only for
your benefit, but also that you should do battle for it.

There are many fundamental points brought out in this inscription which bears directly upon the current "COLOR QUESTION" about "NEGROES IN ANCIENT EGYPT;"
also pr of [on the positive side] that "BLACK AFRICANS" were in Africa before the
"LIGHT-SKINNED CAUCASIANS" of Professor M.D.W. Jeffreys, "HAMITES" of C.G.
Seligman, and "SEMITES" of Dr. Donald Wiedner. The following is a BREAK DOWN of
the FACTS highlighted in the inscription:

1.   The word "NEGROES" was not mentioned in any part of the story. Yet the so-
called "Modern European" and "European-American" writers, historians, egyptologists, ethnologists, and other "orthodox" and "liberal" educators, have insisted that the
"NUBIANS WERE NEGROES," and use this inscription as proof of their contention. They
further state that the Egyptians were "CAUCASIANS, CAUCASOIDS, SEMITES," and
even "HAMITES," also using this inscription for proof. Again, nothing in this inscription indicates that the Nubians or Egyptians were "WHITE" or "BLACK," or for that
matter any COLOR.

2.   Nubia was a part of Egypt during many periods of Egyptian rule over that land
before the reign of Pharaoh Usertsen II. Equally, Egypt was a part of Nubia at various
periods when ruled by the Nubians [Blacks, Negroes, or whatever else anyone desires
to call those African Nile Valley peoples from the First Cataract and further south],
making it totally impossible for any of the two groups to have remained purely anything
separate of the other if ever they once were.

3.   "NUBIANS" has been used to designate the indigenous Africans [Blacks or
Sudanese] of the geo-political boundary of the African land directly south of Egypt.
"SEMITES, CAUCASIANS, HAMITES" or WHITES, was not mentioned, and neither can
be assumed with any sense of honesty.

4.   The typical slurs thrown against all losers in battle during that period in
history were being used by one African geo-political grouping against another; in this
case against the Nubians or UPPER Egyptians by Africans from further north. This was
seen when the "DARK-SKINNED" Greeks belittled the "BLONDE" or "LIGHT-SKINNED"
northern Europeans of Sweden; yet both are still called "CAUCASIANS," equally the
Britons whom the Romans said were " TOO DUMB EVEN TO MAKE SLAVES OF THEM."[26]

5.   The Nubians, the so-called "NEGROES", are described as having produced a
High-Culture or society [civilization] worthy of being ravaged. This bear witness to the

34

distortions about the Nubians High-Culture which certain "ACADEMICIANS" continue writing. All of them stating that "...THE NUBIANS [generally shown as Negroes] WERE IN EGYPT ONLY AS SLAVES OF THE EGYPTIANS." Of course they called the Egyptian Africans - "SEMITES, CAUCASIANS, CAUCASOIDS," and even "HAMITES."

6.   The land conquered, NUBIA or Ta-Nehisi and Zeti, is described as belonging to the "NUBIANS;" not of the NEGROES! The ancients knew not anything of this word. All of the Nile Valley [Blue and White] people were of the same roots or origin in Central Africa; just as Zinjanthropus boisie shown in Chapter II following.

7.   The value of BLACK WOMANHOOD was held in very high esteem, to the point where she was PREFERRED BOOTY. For thousands of years wars have been fought over and about her; the indigenous African men of Egypt being no exception, neither the Asians and Europeans who came later on, to this unwritten rule; as she became the MOTHER of countless millions of Asia and Europe's FINEST.

8.   It exposed the LIES told in the early European-style "CHRISTIAN MISSIONARY WRITINGS," most of which stated that the so-called "...NATIVES, BANTUS," or "NE-GROES" [Blacks] "DID NOT PRODUCE ANY CIVILIZATION IN AFRICA BEFORE THE EUROPEAN CHRISTIAN MISSIONARIES ARRIVED" [in Africa].[27] Unfortunately such stories are still being perpetuated by the same group today.

Of course the above comments by the so-called "CHRISTIAN MISSIONARIES" were, and still are, very easy to contradict, as Africans were "...FATHERS OF THE NORTH AFRICAN CHURCH...", and also "...POPES OF THE ROMAN CATHOLIC CHURCH" for centuries prior to the arrival of the first WHITE [Caucasian] MAN in West Africa,[28] many of whom established dogmas which are being used by the world of Christendom.

Going back further into the past, it is also revealed that Pepi I, also called MERIRA [third pharaoh of the VIth Dynasty, c. 2440 - 2270 B.C.E.], cooperated with the Nubian pharaohs. He joined them in a very highly successful adventure in the capture of the Ha-ribu people [Black, Brown, Yellow, etc.] and their homeland Palestine [later on Israel]. This was long before the XIIth Dynasty, c. 2000 - 1767 B.C.E., when there were serious conflicts between Nubia and her sister nation, Ta-Merry or Egypt, which eventually caused Pharaoh Usertsen III to attack Nubia, and finally to capture her. This is further proof that the BLACKS were prominent and honored people in Egyptian life, even up until Pharaoh Usertsen III.[29] Other documents showed the BLACKS as the original rulers of Egypt as long as human beings occupied that land before the Christian Era and since.

---

0. See J.C. deGraft-Johnson's, AFRICAN GLORY; J.A. ROGERS,' WORLD'S GREAT MEN OF COLOR; Harmack's, MISSION AND EXPANSION; J. Soames' COAST OF THE BARBARY; Mrs. S. Erskine's, THE VANISHED CITIES OF NORTH AFRICA; St. Augustine's, CONFESSIONS; St. Augustine's, ON CHRISTIAN DOCTRINES; Tertullian's,

These FACTS are best detailed in the following works: Sir E.A. Wallis Budge's, BOOK
OF THE DEAD AND PAPYRUS OF ANI; Count C.F. Volney's, RUINS OF EMPIRE;
J.A. Rogers', WORLD'S GREAT MEN OF COLOR; Herodotus', THE HISTORIES; G.G.
M. James', STOLEN LEGACY; and, Y. ben-Jochannan's, AFRICA: MOTHER OF
"WESTERN CIVILIZATION."

With respect to calling the Africans, and things African, other than by names established by the indigenous African [or Ethiopian] people, we even find Herodotus [the
Greek citizen, who originally came from the Egyptian colony of Ionia] describing the
building of the world's largest statue, the SPHINX OF GHIZEH, as having been "...
built by Pharaoh Kheops." Why did Herodotus call Pharaoh Khufu by the name -
KHEOPS [Cheops]? For the same reason that MENA, who Herodotus called "MENES,"
one of the two independent kings or pharaohs that ruled Egypt just before the Dynastic
Periods, was not addressed by his indigenous Ta-Merry, Kimit or Sais [Egyptian]
language name - "AHA" or "NARMER". Why did Herodotus, the "FATHER OF EURO-
PEAN HISTORY," refer to these indigenous African pharaohs of Ta-Merry other than
by their Alkebu-lan [African] names? Because of the following reasons, and many more,
too many to be listed here:

1.   The Greeks of Herodotus' era could not pronounce certain indigenous African
words of the Nile Valley Africans of Egypt, their Hieroglyphic forms or language being
to complex for the Europeans at this period in history for the average man on the street.
This was true of the languages used by other Nile Valley Africans.

2.   Herodotus received his basic and advanced education from the indigenous
Egyptians ["Negroes"] while he was studying the seven liberal arts and science in the
Mysteries System in Egypt. He had to translate his new knowledge to the understanding
of his fellow Greek citizens in terminology and sounds which they could comprehend.
Also, there were not sufficient Greek characters in the Greek alphabet to produce cer-
tain indigenous African sounds in Greek word construction [Greek language].

3.   There are facts known to men who study, so-called "egyptologists, about ancient Egypt which the Egyptians of Herodotus' era kept secret from him. It must be understood that certain secrets of Egyptian society could not be revealed to Herodotus -
who was a native of Ionia and a citizen of Greece [a foreigner]. Like today, friendly
foreigners are not openly trusted with all of the secrets of any government [here in the
United States of America included] where they are guests in the process of receiving
their education and indoctrination. Egyptians were no exception to this human behavioral trait; especially in this case, where these Africans were the teachers of the Greeks -
including Herodotus, a Greek citizen.

Recall that Sir Ernest A. Wallis Budge wrote the following English translation about

36

the "...PEOPLE OF IGNOBLE BIRTH WHO CAME FROM EASTERN PARTS...," during the reign of Pharaoh Timaus and invaded Ta-Merry [Kimit or Egypt]. Sir Ernest was quoting the "Jewish" historian Flavius Josephus, who lived around c. 37 - 95 C.E. He further stated that the invaders were "...ARYANS." He did not mention that they were "ARABS SEMITES" or HAMITES." as some European-American and European-American "educators" have insinuated. [See Sir E.A. Wallis Budge's EGYPT, p. 94]. The "ARYANS" were also known as "HYKSOS" or "SHEPHERD KINGS." This revelation, of course, brings back memory of the battle that was fought against the Hyksos invaders by Prince SeqenenRa III. As a result of said battle this Prince, of the so-called "BLACK BELT." lost his life. His mummy, which is to date in the Cairo Museum, Egypt, shows the effects of his agonizing death. His lower jawbone was broken, skull fractured, and brains were protruded. His tounge is bitten through and a dagger is thrusted above one of the eyes. This occurred during c. 1580 B.C.E.; the same year Crown Prince Ahmes I, son of Pharaoh SeqenenRa III , became pharaoh after his father's death. It was also Pharaoh Ahmes I who finally drove the "ARYANS" from Ta-Merry [Egypt] into Palestine, and beseiged the Hebrew City of Sharukhana. This is the same city mentioned in the BOOK OF JOSHUA I: xi, 6, of the so-called FIVE BOOKS OF MOSES or HEBREW ["Jewish"] HOLY TORAH. as "SHARUHEN."[0]

History reveals that the "LIGHT-SKINNED CAUCASIANS" did not really established themselves in Ta-Merry [Egypt] until the entrance of Alexander II ["the great"], the son of Philip II of Macedon, as conqueror, very late in the year c 332 B.C.E. At the same instance. one has to remember that Alexander's successes in the many battles he fought in order to capture Ta-Merry were highly dependent upon the indigenous Africans of Ta-Merry and Ta-Nehisi who hated their existing foreign rulers from Persia. Because of their apparent mutual hatred for the Persian [brown people] invaders, the Egyptians [black people] joined with the Macedonian-Greeks [white people] in the expulsion of their common enemy, only to become slaves of the new invaders from southern Europe. This period marked the beginning of the "LIGHT-SKINNED CAUCASIAN" [European] rule in Ta-Merry.[30] It was also the end to indigenous Ethiopian [African, "Negro, Bantu, African South of the Sahara," etc.] rule in Ta-Merry, and to some extent Ta-Nehisi.

---

[0]. Note that the Bible, or Holy Book, Torah, Quran, etc., of both Hebrews and Christians, and including the Muslims, are also sources of material of the indigenous Africans' history. They are part and parcel of today's "BLACK STUDIES," or should be.

Alexander's death brought back to Egypt the same murderous rule of a type the equally ruthless Aryans or Hyksos employed before they were driven out by Pharaoh Ahmes I. For example: From the line of the Ptolemies [descendants of General Soter, who declared himself "Pharaoh of all Egypt," and renamed himself "Ptolemy I"], the inheritors of Macedonian-Greek colonialism in Egypt by means of Alexander's death, were to become... the dictators of Egypt for the benefit of Arrhidaeus [the second son of Philip II of Macedon or Macedonia - Alexander's brother] and his family. Instead, the Ptolemies [I - XIII, including the Cleopatras - I - VIII] usurped their authority. They instituted the worse "BLOOD BATH" in Egypt's more than forty-thousand [40,000] years of recorded history. This was the Macedonian-Greeks major contribution to the Egyptian throne. The Ptolemies ruthlessness also started the end to Dynastic and Pharonic Ta-Merry [Egypt]. The following highlights cite in capsule form the history of the Ptolemies in Egypt:

CHRONOLOGY OF THE GREEK-EGYPTIAN "BLOOD BATH" IN
EGYPT [Kimit, Ta-Merry, etc.]

1.   In c. 332 B.C.E. Alexander II [Alexander "the great"] died and General Soter proclaimed himself..."PHARAOH OF ALL EGYPT." He was the ruler who ordered the secret works of the "MYSTERIES SYSTEM" of Egypt seized by Aristotle and other Greek and Macedonian-Greek looters. The works which Aristotle and his fellow looters did not personally steal from the Grand Lodge and other libraries and archives and personally kept for themselves were burnt or carried off to Greece. The balance became the nucleus of which Aristotle used to start the second museum and library in the City of Alexandria.[0] Indigenous African priests [professors] were kept and forced to teach the Greeks and other Europeans from southern Europe, but no indigenous students were allowed in.

2.   Ptolemy II [Philadelphus, son of Ptolemy I and his African Queen] was the Pharaoh who started the building of the "PHARAOH'S LIGHTHOUSE," one of the WONDERS OF THE WORLD.During this period the Greeks and Hebrews translated their Egyptian works into what is presently called the "HEBREW TORAH" [Old Testament of the Christian Bible - all versions] into Greek. Manetho's [the Egyptian High-Priest of African-European parentage, Priest of the Mysteries System] works that divided Egyptian history and High-Culture into "DYNASTIES," titled HISTORY OF EGYPT, was published. This was the only real creative period of the so-called "LIGHT-SKINNED CAUCASIANS" imperialist colonial rule over the indigenous Africans of Egypt.[31]

3.   The beginning of the disintegration of Macedonian-Greek rule in Egypt. Also, the last days of the Ptolemies untold murderous intrigues. The Royal Family against itself; beginning with Ptolemy IX overthrow of his brother - Ptolemy VIII.

---

[0]. This name existed in Egypt before Alexander "the great" arrival. It existed when Egypt was still called Ta-Merry,Kimit,and Sais by the indigenous Africans.

4.   Ptolemy X murdered his wife - Cleopatra Bernice.

5.   Ptolemy XII chased his sister, Cleopatra VIII, off the throne. He saw to it that Pompey, his guardian, was murdered just a few days after the Battle of Pharsalia.

6.   Julius Caesar reinstated Cleopatra VIII, the daughter of Ptolemy XIII, on her throne in c. 47 or 30 B.C.E.[0]

7.   Ptolemy XII was murdered , through drowning, at the hands of his sister - Cleopatra VIII.

8.   Ptolemy XIII was appointed co-Regent with Cleopatra VIII. She immediately thereafter planned and aided in his execution.

9.   Julius Caesar appointed Ptolemy XIV, Caesarion [Caesar's own son with Cleopatra VIII], to rule jointly as co-Regent with his mother.

10.   Cleopatra VIII committed suicide after being discovered in a plot with Marcus Antonius [Marc Anthony] to dispose of the Caesar.

11.   Octavianus, later called Agustus Caesar, defeated Marcus Antonius in the Battle of Actium during c. 30 B.C.E. At this juncture, the end to the so-called "Pharonic Period of the Greeks" ["Modern Man" - the first of the "light-skinned Caucasians" of Professor Jeffreys] came. Egypt was subsequently reduced to a common "Province" [colony] "of the Roman Empire." The glory which was once Egypt was gone forever. The indigenous African peoples [Blacks, Negroes, Ethiopians, Bantus, or whatever] of Egypt were never able to recapture their homeland, the vast majority of them having been driven south into Ta-Nehisi [Zeti or Sudan], Ethiopia, and other parts of Alkebu-lan [Africa].

The preceding information contains sufficient pertinent background material to enter into current studies on the history of "MOTHER AFRICA" [Alkebu-lan]. However, it is much more advantageous to look somewhat deeper into Africa's past, so that once and for all time the "NEGROPHOBES" and their "NEGROPHOBIA" can be placed in their final resting place in history.

H.G. Wells in his book, A SHORT HISTORY OF THE WORLD, pp. 49 - 50, wrote:

> We have to remember that the human races[0] can all inter-
> breed freely and that they separate, mingle and reunite as clouds
> do. Human races do not branch out like trees with branches that
> never come together again. It is a thing we need to bear constant-
> ly in mind, this remingling of races at any opportunity. It will
> save us from many cruel delusions and prejudices if we do so.

---

[0] Historians continue to argue over these two dates with respect to Cleopatra's return to her throne of the command of Julius Caesar. They claimed that it was c. 47 B.C.E. that Egypt was actually captured and the Queen returned to her throne. Others differ.

> People will use such a word as race in the lowest manner, and
> base the most preposterous generalization upon it. They will
> speak of a "British" race or "European" race. But nearly all
> the European nations are confused mixtures of brownish, dark-
> white and Mongolian elements. [0]

We must note that Wells was able to see, somewhat, beyond the narrow path of

total "WHITE RACISM," as he pointed out some of its fallacies, [32] even though he for-

got to mention that millions of indigenous Africans, the so-called "NEGROES," resided

and intermarried [amalgamated] with Europeans from before the turn of the Christian

Era, and ever since.

Was it not a very sad day indeed when the originators of the disgusting term -

"RACE" - introduced it to mankind as a "SCIENTIFIC EXPLANATION" for the apparent

physical, mostly facial, variations between the various so-called "ETHNIC" groupings

within the human family? Between the terms - "RACE" and "RELIGION" - mankind has

created the abyss which will certainly help to destroy civil living itself. [33] This will cer-

tainly come to pass, should sanity fail to prevail over the pathological RACISTS and RE-

LIGIOUS BIGOTS who write history for their colleagues - the conquerors - to gloat over,

while the conquered languish in cultural deprivation and physical torture until death

[through genocide] finally makes its long awaited appearance.

AFRICA today is still being systematically RAPED spiritually, materially, econo-

mically, politically, and otherwise; in part, due to the causes and effects of the results

of "RACE" and "INSTITUTIONALIZED RELIGION." Not only was Africa RAPED during

the advent of the coming of the self-proclaimed Spanish and Portuguese "CHRISTIAN

MISSIONARIES" [the earliest slave traders from Europe, and later on from the United

States of America] to West, South, East, and Central Africa, but also as a direct re-

sult of the combined malady of chattle slavery inflicted upon her by the Europeans and

the Arabs; the latter who started at her northern and eastern shores over three-

hundred [300] years before the European-Spaniards in c 1503 C.E. Between both of these

evils another was compounded, the so-called "EUROPEAN CHRISTIAN MISSIONARIES"

[most of whom knew very little, and cared less, about Christianity] began their stomp-

ing out of Africa's indigenous religions which they were not able to co-opt as they had

---

[0]. This statement has been the crux of so-called "MODERN" historians rejection of
Wells' work. But, even Wells could not mention that the Europeans are also of "BLACK"
or "NEGRO" elements [ancestry].

40

done with JUDAISM and CHRISTIANITY, equally of the offspring of the two - ISLAM.
However, their attempts at the destruction of the indigenous African religions caused
bedlam to break loose in Africa,[34] the end result being the metaphysical disarrangement
of many Africans mind up to and including the 20th Century C.E. Add to this dilemma
the vast majority of the Africans forced conversion to European and European-American
style "CHRISTIANITY" and Asian "ISLAM," from the 7th Century C.E. [640 C.E. or
18 A.H.] through the present day [1972 C.E. or 1350 A.H.], and you have what is more
commonly referred to as "...THE DISENCHANTED, DISORGANIZED, DENUDED, AND
DEHUMANIZED...AFRICAN BODY WITH A EUROPEAN...[or Asian]...MENTALITY."
Such a "BODY" is also otherwise called a "NEGRO." Thereby - the "WEST INDIAN
NEGRO, AMERICAN NEGRO, AFRICAN NEGRO, OUR NEGRO," and a host of other
classifications of "NEGROES."

Dr. Lothrop S. Stoddard in his book, THE RISING TIDE OF COLOR, p. 90, stated
the following:

> From the First glance we see that, in the Negro, we are in
> the presence of a being differing profoundly not merely from the
> white man but also from those human types which we discovered
> in our surveys of the brown and yellow worlds. The black man is,
> indeed, sharply differentiated from the other branches of mankind.
> His outstanding qualities is super-abundant animal vitality. In this
> he easily surpasses other races. To it he owes his intense emo-
> tionalism. To it, again, is due his extreme fecundity,[35] the Negro
> being the quickest of the breeders. This abounding vitality shows
> in many other ways, such as the Negro's ability to survive harsh
> conditions of slavery under which other races have succumb. Last-
> ly, in the ethnic crossings, the Negro strikingly displays his pre-
> potency, for black blood, once entering a human stock, seems never
> really bred out again.[36]

One can only wonder what made a man, who held the highest degree that could be
conferred in an institution of higher learning, lavished such stereotype cliches and
racist ignorance in his public utterances, such as you have just witnessed in Dr. Stod -
dard's conclusion on his so-called..."NEGRO." Due to such utterances, however,
one can readily understand why there is no such fear among Europeans and European-
American males of the African, African-American,and African-Caribbean [BLACK]
males. For it is declarations, such as Dr. Stoddard's, which WHITE LIBERAL and
ORTHODOX American Society is nourished upon daily. This is especially TRUE throughout the most formative years of the educational experiences in the life of WHITE AMERI-

41

CAN YOUNGSTERS in their churches, synagogues, mosques, schools, places of employment, and all other avenues of their daily lives; from their cradles to their graves, most of which is due to their most basic fear in adult life that SOMEDAY BIG BLACK NEGROES [African-Americans] WILL TAKE OVER PURE WHITE FEMALES OF THE UNITED STATES OF AMERICA AND EUROPE . Of course, the "FREED NEGROES" are all "OVERSEXED ANIMALS," a kind of NEARLY-MAN or MAN-LIKE APES with extreme sexual progenitive ability and "...EXTREM FECUNDITY," according to Stoddard.

One must also understand that the European Hebrews ancestors [misnomered Jews][37] claimed to have survived BONDAGE under the Africans in Ta-Merry [Egypt]; equally the English under their fellow Europeans from Rome - including the period when the indigenous Africans, Septimus Severus and his son Caracalla, were the emperors of the Roman Empire of the East and West. Did the Europeans under the rule of these two "NEGROES," Septimus Scverus and Caracalla, not survived their conquerors wrath because of "...THEIR ABILITY OF EXTREME FECUNDITY..." according to Dr. Stoddard's theory? If one is not to conclude such was the case, then it is necessary to have some sort of scientific facts submitted to prove the outright lies, distortion of evidence, and unscientific conclusions, about the so-called "Negroes" by Dr. Stoddard, Dr. H.H. Breasted, Sir H.H. Johnston, Dr. D. Wiedner, Professor M.D. W. Jeffreys, and others [past and present] of like "scholarship" and "authority." But, in these days of the super-human "Modern Man" [the "LIGHT-SKINNED CAUCASIAN"] and his herrenvolk philosophy that...

THE WHITE MAN MUST ALWAYS REIGN SUPREME...
it is obviously apparent that the RACIST THEORY of men such as Dr. Stoddard and Professor Jeffreys shall continue to be the basis upon which Africa's sons and daughters shall forever be prosecuted and persecuted.[38] Let one not forget that Aristotle said:

THAT WHICH IS NOT GREEK IS BARBARIAN.[39]
Today Aristotle's RACISM is heard as:

THAT WHICH IS NOT MODERN MAN OR LIGHT-SKINNED CAUCASIAN
[European, European-American, White, Semite, Hamite, Judaeo-Christian, Indo-European Aryan, Nordic, Alpine, and even Mediterranean] IS OVERSEXED, CANNIBALISTIC, AND SUBHUMAN..., etc., etc.

In most European and European-American "ORTHODOX" and "LIBERAL" historians' works the Africans are not given credit for being "SUB-HUMAN." The United

States of America's Federal Constitution was one such document, which for generations after generations of "...FREEDOM-LOVING PEOPLE IN A LAND OF THE FREE AND THE HOME OF THE BRAVE..." did not recognize its "NEGRO [African-American or Black] SLAVES" as human beings.[40] And it would seem that most White Americans were not, and are not now, willing to move from their nation's former official position on their so-called "NEGROES...THREE-FIFTHS [$^3/_5$ ths] OF A MAN..." status.

Sir Ernest A. Wallis Budge's, EGYPT, pp. 21 - 22, states that:

> THE HISTORIC NATIVE OF EGYPT, BOTH IN THE OLD
> AND NEW Stone Ages, WAS AFRICAN.[41]

Sir Ernest continued further in his work:

> There are many things in the manners and customs and religions of
> the historic Egyptians, that is to say, of the workers on the land,
> that suggest that the original home of her prehistoric ancestors was
> a country in the neighborhood of Uganda and Punt.

The above citations certainly nullify Professor Jeffreys' geographic line of his "light-skinned Caucasian" theory, as described on Dr. Donald L. Wiedner's hypothetical map on page 45 following. For he included the indigenous peoples of Africa, particularly those of Kenya, Punt [the areas of present-day Somalia],and Uganda [at the time including parts of today's Tanzania], in his "CAUCASIAN RACE" group, in order to lay claim of a CAUCASIAN ORIGIN to Zinjanthropus boisie [42] the oldest fossil-man known to date, and reviewed in Chapter II of this volume. It must be noted that there are two [2] Nile Valleys. One starts in Uganda, the other in Ethiopia; while both becomes one after passing through Upper Sudan before it meets Upper Egypt and empties into the Mediterranean Sea. Also that the Nile Valleys High-Cultures [civilizations] travelled from SOUTH to NORTH, as the river flows; not NORTH to SOUTH [up hill] as once falsely taught by so-called "ORTHODOX" and "LIBERAL WHITE AFRICANIST HISTORIANS" and "AUTHORITIES" on Africa of Europe and European-America, particularly in the United States of America's institutions of learning - both secular and religious.

No attempt seemed to have been made to find out why southern Europeans such as Italians, Greeks, Spaniards, Slavic peoples, Portuguese, and Frenchmen, are generally "DARK-SKINNED."[43] Further, no questions are being asked about any of the Europeans of Sweden, Norway, Denmark, and Germany who have definitely described...

"NEGROID PHYSICAL CHARACTERISTICS."[44]

Yet if an African has a POINTED NOSE, THIN LIPS, and LIGHT SKIN [pigment] all sorts of theories as to his or her being "NOT OF NEGRO ORIGIN" are brought forward. Why? What purpose can such information serve, other than to project the RACIST PHILOSOPHY of the inquirer against a helpless BLACK victim of more than four-hundred [400] years of persecution, enslavement, and genocide?

One can only examine certain facts to find the answer to the "WHY" asked in the previous paragraph. In so doing the following becomes evident:

[a]. Michaelangelo painted his European version of the Christian God - JESUS CHRIST - to look like the image of any northern Italian one could have found during his lifetime. He and his Pope created what is today the official white , blue - eyed, and golden-haired picture of Christendom's God-head. His selection was a natural one, as he too was a part of the image he projected as "JESUS CHRIST AND THE DICIPLES" at "THE LAST SUPPER" [Seder]. He thereby made his GOD in his OWN IMAGE, COLOR, and PHYSICAL APPEARANCE - a WHITE MAN, a NORTHERN ITALIAN, a EUROPEAN, a "LIGHT-SKINNED CAUCASIAN" of the type spoken of by Professor M. D. W. Jeffreys and Dr. D. L. Wiedner in this chapter. Yet chapters IX and X of this volume show a historical analysis that refute the Michaelangelo's Christian Holy Family color spectrum.

[b]. The statue of ISIS and OSIRIS,[45] depicting the indigenous African [Black or "Negro"] Goddess and God of Ta-Merry [Egypt], has been imitated and projected as the "BLACK MADONNA AND CHILD." Yet the "CHILD - Jesus Christ," grows up to be a WHITE MAN with LONG CURLY GOLDEN HAIR, BLUE EYES, and KEEN [straight] FEATURES - called CAUCASOID. Also, his mother, MARY, turns out to suit the image and color of her European female worshippers. But ISIS and OSIRIS statue still remains BLACK, the same as the original MADONNA AND CHILD statues all over Europe; even in St. Peter's Church in Rome. They remain in their original indigenous BLACK [Negro or African] SPLENDOUR.[46]

[c]. There is a deliberate attempt to remove every trace of BLACKNESS from the African-Moors, thereby making all the BLACK people who conquered and ruled Spain, Portugal and parts of southern France from Africa - "Arabs;" conveniently forget or ignore the fact that there were two cultural groups of "MOORS" that entered Europe [the Iberian Peninsula] from Africa.[47] The first of the two groups were the indigenous Africans under the command of a fellow African Muslim - General Tarikh - for whom the ROCK OF GIBRALTAR [Gibral Tarikh or Rock of Tarikh] is named.[48] WHY? Dr. Goebels [Adolph Hitler's Nazi Propaganda Minister] provided the answer quite vividly in his attempt to "ARYANIZE" Europe; not CAUCASIANIZE it. Adolph Hitler, himself, echoed it much more succinctly in his book titled - MEIN KAMPF; Professor M.D.W. Jeffreys answered it in his work - THE NEGRO ENIGMA - cited before; the dictators of South Africa and their concetration camps ["Native Reserves"][49] of the "APARTHEID" philosophy answered it; the late George L. Rockwell and his successors of the self-styled Fuehrer's American Nazi-type WHITE NATIONALIST organization's propaganda, and other equally super patriotic Americans and their "PURE WHITE" nationalist organizations continuously answer it in much more sophisticated RACIST jargon, just as

44

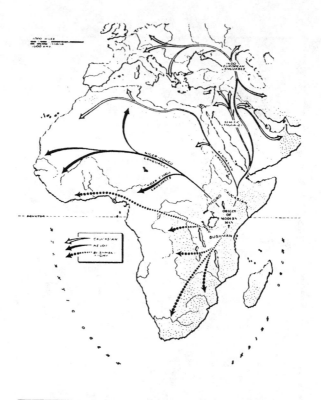

ETHNOGRAPHY OF AFRICA BEFORE 300 B.C. (HYPOTHESIS)

The above map is extracted from Donald L. Wiedner, A HISTORY OF AFRICA SOUTH OF THE SAHARA, Vintage Book [Alfred A. Knof, Inc., and Random House], New York, 1962. Note the stereotype attempt by this <u>White Liberal Africanist</u> AUTHORITY ON AFRICA AND AFRICAN PEOPLE to remove all of his "NEGROES" from North and East Africa. He has made the indigenous people of the East and North "CAUCASIAN:" even those of Northwest Africa. Wiedner followed the same RACIST pattern of M.D.W. Jeffreys' "NEGRO ENIGMA." By a few strokes of the pen and some artistic geography he was able to manipulate even the so-called "NEGRO NUBIANS" into full-blooded "CAUCASIAN" stock. All of the indigenous Africans of Ethiopia, Kenya, Uganda, Northeast Zaire [Congo or Kongo], Sudan, Egypt, Numidia, Libya, Morocco, Spanish Sahara, Mauretania [Mauritania], and even certain parts of the Senegal River basin became "CAUCASIAN." It is to be carefully noted that even the "SEMITE" and "INDO-EUROPEAN" came out of Alkebu-lan [Africa]. What ever happened to the Garden of Eden at the Tigris and Euphrates rivers? Wiedner's NEGROPHOBIA even made him produce a NEGRO-LESS Congo, Nigeria, Ghana, Burundi, Cameroon, and Angola - all of these areas being given to the so-called "PYGMY." When one considers that this "AUTHORITY ON AFRICA" is dealing with a period no earlier than 300 B.C. the RACIST "HYPOTHESIS" becomes that much more meaningful; ye, he is no different to all of the other WHITE LIBERALS.

45

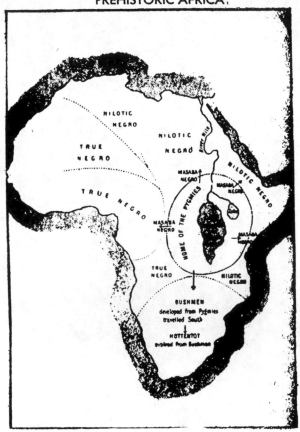

Compared with the Map on page 45 by Dr. D. L. Wiedner, the above map, extracted
from Albert Churchward's [M.D., British archaeologist and palaeontologist of world
fame], ORIGIN AND EVOLUTION OF FREEMASONRY, London, 1920, is totally in
contradiction. Dr. Churchward attributed the entire continent of Alkebu-lan [Africa] to
the so-called "PYGMY" and "NEGRO" - "True, Nilotic", and "Masaba." Even the so-
called "BUSHMEN" and "HOTTENTOT" came from the same source in Alkebu-lan where
all of mankind originated, including the so-called "CAUCASIAN," thus making the dis-
credited theory of the Wiedners, Jeffreys', Stoddards, and Junods appear to be that
much more RACIST than they would have normally observed. Is it not strange that all
of the so-called "ORTHODOX" and "LIBERAL WHITE AUTHORITY ON AFRICA AND
AFRICAN PEOPLE" are so far apart on whether or not the indigenous Africans were
the first to settle all over the continent of Africa, including the North and the East?

46

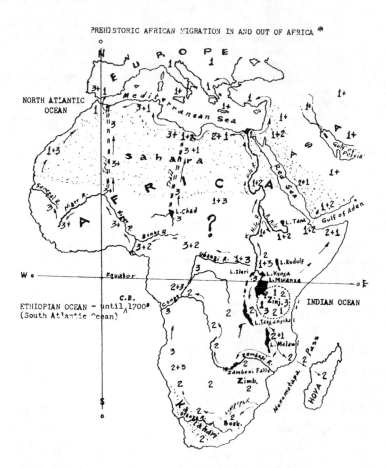

Among the many names Alkebu-lan [the "mother of mankind" or "garden of eden"] was called are the following: "ETHIOPIA, CORPHYE, ORTEGIA, LIBYA," and "AFRICA" -the latest of all. "ALKEBU-LAN" is the oldest, and the only one of indigenous origin. It was used by the Moors, Nubians, Numidians, Khart-Haddans [Carthagenians], and Ethiopians. "AFRICA," the current misnomer adopted by almost everyone today, was given to this continent by the ancient Greeks and Romans.

KEY TO MAP

1] Nile Valley African; 2] South bound African; 3] West bound African. Note that the dotted circle area is locate around the same vicinity of the OLDUVAI GORGE in Tanzania [Tanganyika], which has been so far proven to be mankind's oldest home - a kind of true "GARDEN OF EDEN." Zinjanthropus boisie, 1,750,000 + years old, shown on pp. 83 - 84 of this chapter, was unearthed at this area of East Alkebu-lan. The above map is a pictorial hypothetical illustration of the author of this volume "BELIEF" [not proof] of how the earliest people of Alkebu-lan migrated all over their original continent and spread out to other lands of the planet EARTH. This HYPOTHETICAL MAP was developed by the author in 1969 C.E. [or A.D.] for and exhibit in Ghana, West Africa.

47

King Leopold II of the Belgians and Henry Morton Stanley planted it in GENOCIDE in Zaire [KONGO]. It is more commonly called in its ugliest form..."WHITE SUPREMACY." It is the greatest murderer of the last four-hundred [400] years. It is the beginning to an END; the END being the impending holocaust between the "NON-WHITE" peoples of Africa and Asia, and elsewhere, against the "WHITE" peoples of Europe, Great Britain, and the United States of America, only because those who control the world's military power to date decided some "GOD" or the other commissioned them to control all of mankind on the planet EARTH.[50] In order to accomplish this END certain groups must be marked for extermination [genocide] - BLACKS [the so-called "Negroes"] being the selected victims.

Let us also examine the work of one of Europe's "AUTHORITIES" on the intermingling and amalgamation of the ancient peoples of Africa, Asia, and Europe, and see what he has to say on this question. Thus, we read the late Sir Harry H. Johnston's conclusion in his book, A HISTORY OF THE CIVILIZATION OF AFRICA, p. 48:

> ....These are the only recorded attempts of the Romans to reach the Sudan across the Sahara desert; but that intercourse had been going on for hundreds, if not thousands, of years between the Libyans and Hamites[0] of Northern and North-Eastern Africa on the one hand, and the Negroids and Negroes of the Lake Chad and Benue regions and of the chole Niger basin on the other, there can be little doubt, from a variety of evidence.[51]

We have noted that the ancient Libyans were "BLACK," Africans; even Professor Jeffreys admitted this fact. Lebu, later renamed "LIBYA" by the Greeks, is still a part of Africa; always the nation on the western border of Ta-Merry [Egypt]. Where did the "HAMITES" come from? Is he saying that the Hebrew Holy Torah [Old Testament of the Christian Holy Bible, any version] is lying when it claimed that:

MOSES LED THE HEBREW PEOPLES OUT OF EGYPT?

Sir Harry obviously got his theory quite mixed-up with the biblical allegories and mythology of the Book of Genesis, dealing with the RACISM in Noah and his sons story, according to Chapter I, p. 13 of this volume.

The latter conclusion arrived at by Sir Harry H. Johnston on the number of Romans who penetrated the Sahara and the Savanahs to reach the Niger basin of Alkebu-lan [Africa], and of course the Africans [the so-called "Negroes"] who traveled in the opposite direction, is phenomenal. However, such crossings had been made before by General

---

[0]. This racist term is best analyzed in Y. ben-Jochannan and G.E. Simmonds, THE BLACK MAN'S NORTH and EAST AFRICA, Alkebu-lan Books Associates, New York, 1971, Chapt. I, pp. 67-77; also Y. ben-Jochannan, AFRICA: MOTHER OF "WESTERN CIVILIZATION, New York, 1971, p. 57.

Setenius Flaccus in the year c. 50 B.C.E., and in the year c. 30 B.C.E. by a military explorer - Julius Maternus reached the area around Lake Tchad in Central-West Africa, and proceded down to Bornu in the areas of today's northern Nigeria. Both Flaccus and Maternus were Romans of European [White] origin. These two men had accompanied African caravans, and traveled along well established trade routes by said Africans[52] whom many "Western historians" [the so-called "White liberal Africanists] now labeled "Negroes" in their obsession to repopulate ancient North and East Alkebu-lan [Africa] with races called "CAUCASIAN, HAMITIC, SEMITIC, and INDO-EUROPEAN ARYAN."

The social and commercial intercourse between the ancient indigenous West, Central West, and North Africans [Blacks, Negroes, or whatever else] and Romans [Whites, Caucasians, or whatever else] were so extensive that it was impossible to avoid free inter-breeding and sexual amalgamation between the various African, Asian, and European peoples, this being especially true of the entire Mediterranean lands, since the color of one's skin was never a factor in those days; neither was the physical appearance of one's face - the asthetic "good" or "bad looks" of a person.
It was not because either of these two reasons, if for any other, that so many Africans became "GREAT" and "NOTED GENERALS OF THE ROMAN EMPIRE;" a few also having become "EMPERORS OF ROME."[53] However, the indigenous Africans were never recorded as being "NEGROES," because the term was unknown to the ancients of Africa, Asia, and Europe. They were called "ETHIOPIANS, LIBYANS, NUBIANS, BLACKS, AFRICANUS, AFER," and a host of other names; but NEVER "NEGROES." Even the indigenous Africans as far SOUTH as the Niger River basin were never called "NEGROES" until sometimes after European colonialist entreprenuers and their Christian missionary companions arrived there late in the 17th century C.E.[0] At least they could have been called "NIGERS" or "NIGGERS," which would have had a very logical semantical basis with respect to the Niger River of West Africa. But, the FACT is that IT DID NOT HAPPEN THAT WAY. The word "N.E.G.R.O" in no way whatsoever has any right of attachment to any segment of the indigenous peoples of North, South, East or Central Alkebu-lan. It is a name forced upon African peoples by their one-time European slave masters, and adopted by their European-American counterparts. It is a name which self-respecting Africans despise and reject, even some "NE-

_____

[0]. See Richard B. Moore's, THE NAME NEGRO, ITS ORIGIN AND EVIL USE, New York, 1954.

GROES."

One has to remember that Rome nor Hellas [Pyrrhus or Greece] were not cultural centers of a particular HOMOGENEOUS group of people. They were the homelands of so-called "RACES" or "ETHNIC GROUPS" from many nations and two continents - Africa and Asia, the vast majority being Europeans. For example: Saul [Paul] was a Roman citizen, yet he was a Haribu [Hebrew or "Jew"]; Seneca, the philosopher of politics, was from Spain - a Spaniard; Septimus Severus, who became Emperor of Rome, was an indigenous African from Khart-Haddas [Carthage], and appeared like any of the African-Greeks and African-Romans shown on page xxx of this volume.[54] Emperor Septimus Severus' son, Caracalla, was also Emperor of Rome - succeeding his father, and was of African [black] and Asian [brown] parentage. Of course these are only two of the noted thousands of Africans of Rome who made history during the Christian Era. But there were countless others through ordinary marriages and common-law relationships that resulted in thousands upon thousands of offspring between Europeans, Asians, and Africans in Rome and Greece before and after the Christian Era; a condition which later came to Egypt and other parts of North Africa. With regards to this historical FACT an English "AUTHORITY" on this area - Jane Soames - in her book, THE COAST OF BARBARY, pp. 30 - 31, wrote:

> At the height of Roman power in North Africa the population of Italy was actually declining and there was never any vast number of Roman colonists in the racial sense of the word. The Romans knew nothing of those modern emotions which are to us so powerful and omnipresent that we can hardly imagine a civilisation from which they should be absent; She had neither colour prejudice nor religous intolerance in the days of the Republic. The Christian martyrs of the early church suffered because they were felt to be a menace to the State, propagating doctrines subversive to good order and discipline: they were regarded as the Communists of their day. But highly cultivated Roman opinion considered all religions to be essentially the diverse manifestations of one great truth, and had no conception of that white heat of missionizing zeal which would put whole populations of unbelievers to the sword or send men to the scaffold and the fire for the sake of a disputed theological definition.

Jane Soames' remarks should have been sufficient proof in refuting some of the anti-Black propaganda that was so common in history books of the past two-hundred [200] years, and those still being written by so-called "WHITE LIBERAL AFRICANISTS" dealing with African, African-American, and African-Caribbean peoples and their

50

"MOTHERLAND - ALKEBU-LAN ." But, she continued further in another paragraph in the same book:

> ...All that part of the make-up of men's minds [religious bigotry]
> came later, as did the acute sense of differentiation of race and
> consequent antagonism which may be summed up in the phrase
> "colour bar."

On page 45 she opened up tremendous insight on the indigenous African ["Negro", etc.]

who ruled Great Britain sometime around c. 193 to c. 211 C.E., and stated that:

> ...It is peculiar interest to remember that this amazing career
> terminated in Great Britain. Faithful to his life-long preoccupa-
> tion with military matters, Septimus Severus, spent the last
> three years of his reign in Britain reorganizing and strengthen-
> ing the defenses ot its northern frontier.He was accompanied by
> his son, Caracalla, who succeeded him, and it is said that so long
> a sojourn in one of the most distant and barbarous of the provinces
> was in part due to an attempt to keep that son away from the dele-
> terious and corrupting influence of the court [in Rome].[0]

It was that heavy task in "...THE MOST DISTANT AND BARBAROUS OF THE

PROVINCES..." [Great Britain] on Emperor Septimus Severus which finally caused

him to lose his own life in England. He died in York, during the month of February,

c. 211 C.E. Of course England's adverse climate also proved too much for this African,

who was definitely more at home in the hot temperature of his native North Africa than

he was in cold, foggy and misty England.

R.G. Collingwood in his book, ROMAN BRITAIN, along with many other "WESTERN"

historians, supported Jane Soames conclusions. The FACTS of history, and the PHY-

SICAL results that are still visible in the peoples of Mediterranean Europe, especially

Turkey, Italy, Greece, Spain, and even Portugal on the Atlantic Ocean, further support-

ed, and still support, her conclusions physically and visually.[55]

The entire world of Christendom owes its greatest successes to many indigenous

Africans; not only for their contributions before the advent of the Christian Era, but in-

cluding the Christian Era. In this regard, one must remember that"...THE FIRST

MARTYRS OF CHRISTENDOM..." were indigenous Africans, the very "FIRST" being

NAMPHAMO.[56] Namphamo was born in Numidia, an African nation that occupied much

of the area presently known as Libya and Algeria. The names- TERTULLIAN, CYPRIAN,

---

[0.] Words in brackets [ ] by the author of this volume for clarity only.

and AUGUSTINE - are other "GREAT PATRONS" and "SAINTS" [ancestors] of Christendom.[57] All were indigenous Africans [otherwise called "Negroes" by many] to whom Christians of today must, and still, give honour and praise in their churches. Professor C.P. Groves in his book, THE PLANTING OF CHRISTIANITY IN AFRICA, [4 vols.], introduced this point as he questioned:

WHO WERE THE THREE "...FATHERS OF CHRISTENDOM"?
They were Africans, euphemistically given the name "NEGROES" by their fellow African brothers and sisters slavemasters from Europe in the 17th century C.E. Thus, they are according to Mrs. Stewart Erskine in her book, THE VANISHED CITIES OF NORTHERN AFRICA, p. 80:

> The three great names that bring honour to the African Church
> are Tertullian, the first of the Church writers who made Latin the
> language of Christianity,[58] Cyprian, Bishop and martyr; and Augustine,[0] one of the most famous of the "Fathers of the Church."

The strength and depth of the personality of one of these indigenous African "Fathers of the Church" is felt in his work. For example, he once wrote:

> Surely a glance at the wide world shows that it is daily being
> more cultivated and better peopled than before. All places are now
> accessible, well known, open to commerce. Delightful farms have
> now blotted out every trace of the dreadful wastes; cultivated fields
> have overcome woods; flocks and herds have driven out wild beasts;
> sandy spots are sown; rocks are planted; bogs are drained. Large
> cities now occupy land hardly tenanted before cottages. Islands are
> no longer dreaded; houses, people, civil rule, civilisation, are
> everywhere.

The above quotation is taken from Tertullian's, De ANIMA, XXX [as translated from the original Latin text by Harnach in his MISSION AND EXPANSION, vol. III, p. 275]. This quotation also shows that Tertullian was deeply concerned and involved in interpreting the economic life of the common man under Roman colonialism in his own African community. His involvement in such religious significance as a North African Christian, indicate that he was keenly aware of the socio-political ramifications of the economy of Roman colonial North Africa during his lifetime. Also, that he saw no separation between the North African or Roman Christian Church and the Roman Province

---

[0]. Augustine's "CONFESSIONS" left no doubt about his indigenous African origin; equally of his parents - Patricus [his father] and Monica [his mother], the latter also being a "saint" [ancestor, or ancestral spirit] as her son.

[his homeland - Carthage or Khart-Haddas] had become; thereby his religious interpretation of colonial economics was moulded to the extent that he was able to produce
the type of insight that was so very unusual in the CHRISTIAN DOCTRINES of his era;
DOCTRINES which the Roman Church-State had altered from its original development
when the Christian Church existed only in North and East Africa, and before its teachings crossed over the Mediterranean Sea into Europe.

What has been learned so far from the data presented and reviewed that is not common knowledge to most Americans?:

[a]. That it should be obvious, by now, the Africans were involved with Europeans
who were the most instrumental in making Europe what it is today;

[b]. that they too helped, and in many instances led, in laying the foundation for
Europeans to build upon until the present 20th Century C.E.;

[c]. that the ancient indigenous Africans were responsible for many of the basic
tenets of present-day Christendom, just as they were in the past;

[d]. that Africans were not "CIVILIZED" by anyone other than themselves;

[e]. and, that "CHRISTIANITY" is nothing new to the indigenous Africans, they
having worked with it before in its original home - Egypt, North Africa, over two-
hundred [200] years before the Romans and Greeks of Europe. Of course;

[f]. that they sired just as many EUROPEANS bearing the name "CAUCASIANS,"
as did European equally sired as many AFRICANS having been labeled "NEGROES;"[59]

[g]. that RACISM is the decease of a sick and fearful "MODERN MAN;"

[h]. that the BLACK MAN'S [the indigenous African and his descendants] history
in Alkebu-lan [Africa] existed for as long as mankind itself exists; and

[i]. that no amount of wishful hypotheses can change these FACTS, regardless of
the so-called "WHITE LIBERAL AUTHORITIES ON NEGRO HISTORY" in their "INSTI-
TUTIONS OF HIGHER LEARNING" who remain in Europe and the Americas, particularly in the United States of America, and try to decide, as usual, everything for their
"NATIVES OF AFRICA SOUTH OF THE SAHARA - BLACK AFRICA."

What influences overshadowed the contributions of the early Africans of Christendom?[60] What happened to remove the Africans [Ethiopians, Blacks, "Negroes," or
whatever else they may be called] from their leadership they once held in Christendom?
Part of the answer is that there were many causes which changed the course of African
leadership in the Christian Church of North Africa and Southern Europe, especially
Rome. They go back very far indeed, even before the advent of the proclamation of the

"BIRTH OF JESUS CHRIST."[61] From the indigenous Africans whom the Europeans call-
ed "Carthagenians" defeat of the Romans during the Ist and IInd so-called "PUNIC
WARS,"[62] which should have been settled by the Africans defeat by the Romans in the
IIIrd and final "PUNIC WAR"[0]

Historians, such as Dr. Lothrop S. Stoddard, who seemed to have suffered from
extreme cases of "NEGROPHOBIA" in their works, also helped. For example: Dr.
Stoddard wrote in his book, THE RISING TIDE OF COLOUR, p. 68, added proof to support the Africans fall among their European Christian counterparts thusly:

> Of course Christianity has made distinct progress in the Dark
> continent. The natives of the South African Union are predominantly
> Christianized. In east-central Africa Christianity has also gained
> many converts, particularly in Uganda, while on the West African
> Guinea coast Christian missions have long been established and have
> generally succeeded in keeping Islam away from the Seaboard.

Before completing Dr. Stoddard's major premise, which shows that his type of
"TRUE CHRISTIANITY" was similar to that of Dr. Goebels of Nazi Germany and Dr.
Verwoerd of the Union of South Africa, one must recall that the history of the Christian
Church, from its infancy, shows that Christianity was in North, East, and West Africa
before the birth of the first Western European Christian, muchless Dr. Stoddard.[63]
And , what he and his fellow Europeans and European-Americans brought to Africa were
WHITE SUPREMACY, CHATTEL SLAVERY, and COLONIALISM under the disguise of
a Europeanized version of Christianity. Dr. Stoddard continued on pages 96 and 97:

> ...   Certainly, all white men, whether professing Christians or not,
> should welcome the success of missionary efforts in Africa. The de-
> grading fetishism and demonology which sum up the native pagan cults
> cannot stand, and all Negroes will some day be either Christian or
> Moslems. In so far as he is Christianized, the Negro's savage in-
> stincts will be restrained and he will be disposed to acquiece in white
> tutelage. In so far as he is Islamized, the Negro warlike propensi-
> ties will be inflamed, and he will be used as the tool of Arab Pan-
> Islamism seeking to drive the white man from Africa and make the
> continent his very own.[00]

It is very necessary to analyze certain aspects of the good doctor's "NEGROPHO-

---

[0]. This war, as the other two before it, was fought between predominantly indigenous
Africans [the so-called "Negroes"] of Khart-Haddas [which the European renamed "Car-
thage"] and Europeans called Romans; thus it was the Roman - Khart-Haddan War or
Khart-Haddan-Roman War.

[00]. See Stoddard's FLASHING TIDES OF COLOUR for his extreme position in this area.

54

BIA," and the apparently RACIST cancer that obsessed his mind. However, Dr. Stoddard's arrogance, in his NEGROPHOBIA, was typical of the White Christian Missionaries of his days; and as stated before, including most of the present 20th century confessants of the Christian faith.

The following points of contention are obvious in the writings of Dr. Stoddard:

1]. He began on the usual White Racist note that AFRICA IS SOME KIND OF A FANTASTICALLY MYTHICAL "DARK CONTINENT." Of course this was to make his readers imagine that CANNIBALS were creeping all over Africa eating each other until the Europeans arrived with their self-style colonialist Christianity; something like the "BOGEY MAN" or "COMMUNIST COSPIRACY" one calls upon today to frighten people into joining anti-SIN movements designed to stop "CRIME [niggers] IN THE STREET."

2]. He assumed that "ISLAM" and its teachings would have only brought out the "SAVAGE INSTINCTS [in the] NEGROES." And of course SAVAGERY is only relegated to all non-whites and non-pretenders of European - type Christianity. This means that the SLAVE TRADE, which was condoned and supported in Rome by many Popes through their Bishops, starting with Pope Martin V and Pope Alexander VI,[64] and in the citadels of Protestant colonialist nations, was not "SAVAGE;" nor were "...THE FOUNDING FATHERS OF THE UNITED STATES OF AMERICA" who sold Africans as they sold molasses [including the first President of the United States of America - George Washington][0] and exterminated the indigenous peoples they labeled "INDIANS" and "SAVAGES." Even King Leopold II[65] and Adolph Hitler, accordingly, were not "SAVAGES", because they were "ALL WHITE MEN" of the type Dr. Stoddard appealed to. One is expected to assume that those named could not possibly be "SAVAGES," solely on the flimsy basis that they were "WHITE MEN" of the type Professor Jeffreys called "LIGHT-SKINNED CAUCASIANS," and of course those of Dr. Stoddard's.

3]. "...THE DEGRADING FETISHISM AND DEMONOLOGY..." which Dr. Stoddard seemed to abhor are being practised by the Africans [natives] to date. But those who accept his religiousity have never stopped to question what right he had to challenge the Africans religious practices in their own homeland - Alkebu-lan [Africa]. He failed to remember that "...THE AFRICANS RIGHT TO BE WRONG [in their own homeland, "mother Africa"] IS SACRED."[00]

4]. He appealed to any ...WHITE MAN..., when he wrote: "CERTAINLY ALL WHITE MEN, WHETHER PROFESSING CHRISTIANS OR NOT, SHOULD WELCOME THE SUCCESS OF THE MISSIONARY EFFORT IN AFRICA." Here again Dr. Stoddard realy display-

---

[0]. George Washington, as President of the United States of America, also as a British subject, owned one of the largest slave farms in the history of chattel slavery anywhere in the world; not even in his last will and testimony, as Thomas Jefferson - the so-called "LIBERTARIAN," did he free his "NIGGER SLAVES." This African-Americans of the 20th century C.E. remember in "NEGRO HISTORY WEEK," particularly on February 22nd each year.

[00]. Stoddard was very easy in the above book with regards to the so-called "NEGROES." A look at one of his other works, FLASHING TIDES OF COLOUR, should prove much more interesting in the height of the RACISM he reached.

ed RACISM at at its highest. Not only RACISM, but the ONLY TRUE PURPOSE of his professed interest in Christianizing the so-called "NEGROES" of the "DARK CON-TINENT." One can readily see that European-style "CHRISTIANITY" was, and still is, the weapon which he, as so many others, used to accomplish his colonialist aspirations. With this type of historical background, is it surprising that over the entire world European and European-American so-called "CHRISTIAN MISSIONARIES" are being slaughtered and persecuted daily?[66]

As it has been mentioned before, Dr. Stoddard was only expressing the prevailing sentiments about Africans and other "non-white peoples." Yet in support of Stoddard's RACIST THEORY we find Henri Junod writing in his book, BA-RANGA, p. 482 [as quoted by Raymond Michelet], similarly with respect to the African races, stated:

> I speak of resignation. It is necessary to the Blacks, for dispite all that has been written on the fundamental axiom of the absolute equality of mankind, they are an inferior race, a race made to serve.

However, is it suprising that so many professed "LIBERAL" and "INTELLECTUAL WHITE AFRICANIST" in "Negro" and "Coloured [certainly not BLACK] CIRCLES" of today still consider Junod "...AN OBJECTIVE PROTESTANT ETHNOGRAPHER"? But what kind of OBJECTIVITY did Junod displayed in the following statement about the African peoples when he wrote that:

"...THEY ARE AN INFERIOR RACE, A RACE MADE

TO SERVE."

Maybe Jesus Christ, the Christians' God-head, or one of his prophets, came to Junod in a GRAND DREAM, since this has been the way most of religion's RACIST EDICTS came - by MASTERFUL DREAM. The angel in-charge of MASTERFUL DREAMS must have told Junod that Blacks, whom he too preferred to call "NEGROES," were made by his CAUCASIANIZED-EUROPEAN Jesus Christ [God] to "...SERVE..." the White man. But, this type of expression by the Junods and Jeffreys, also the "modern" Wiedners and Smiths who continue in their footsteps, have been the basis upon which so-called "NEGRO HISTORY" was written in the past. It was so yesterday, and it is still taught in the same manner today by so-called "ORTHODOX" and "WHITE LIBERAL AFRICAN-IST HISTORIANS". This is the major reason why "AFRICAN STUDIES," also called "BLACK STUDIES," is today the challenge to most European-American WHITE STUDIES "educators" in the field of history, ethnology, anthropology, palaeontology, etc., on the issue of RACE. For most of what they have taught as "TRUTHS" with regards to the history of peoples other than those labeled "CAUCASIAN" they must now discard, par-

56

ticularly that which they have written about African-Americans, their so-called "AMERICAN NEGROES," the same being true for their "NEGROES" everywhere else.

Once again it becomes necessary to reflect a bit, and of course return to the origin of Christianity to see upon what basis the early White Christian Missionaries of Europe, and later on European-America, got the idea that "JESUS CHRIST," the Christian God, ordained them to convert BLACKS [African peoples] of different religions. In so doing it is necessary to read a quotation from a Roman Catholic monk, who was at the time of his writing living off the spoils of Alkebu-lan - just as his leaders and other European colonialist "Christians" were living and still live today. This man was the often-quoted "CHRISTIAN WRITER - SALVIANUS" [Salvian or Sylvian]. He wrote, as he questioned:

> Where are there more abundant treasures than with the Africans? Where can we find more prosperous commerce - shops better stocked? The Prophet Ezekiel said of Tyre "Thou has filled thy treasury with gold and silver by the extent of thy commerce," but I say of Africa that her commerce enriched so much taht not only were her treasuries filled, but she seemed able to fill those of the whole universe. ... Carthage, formerly the Rival of Rome as regards power and warlike quality, was she not afterward her rival in splendor? And in imposing majesty? Carthage, the Rome of Africa, held in her bosom all the treasures of the State; here was the seat of government and all the instituters of the State; here there were schools for the liberal arts, audiences for philosophers, chairs for professors of all languages and for every branch of law.

Quite a summary of achievements for people who were, and are, only fit "... TO SERVE...," according to Henry Junod's BaRANGA, p. 482.

Anyone familiar with the cultural "RAPE OF AFRICA" knows that the Whites, European colonialist Christian Missionaries including, involved in the PARTITION OF AFRICA from 1830 to 1900 C.E. even dared to suggest that the Holy Temples of the ancient Monomotapa Empire's seat of government, Zimbabwe [presently misnamed "Rhodesia" by the English colonialist invaders and settlers], must have been " BUILT BY THE GREEKS, ROMANS, OR SHIPWRECKED EUROPEAN MARINERS." But none of them suggested, or in anyway whatsoever pointed to, one bit of evidence to substantiate any of their conclusions, RACIST as they were. All that was fixed is that "... IT COULD NOT HAVE BEEN THE WORK OF THE NATIVES...," etc. The "NATIVES," of course, being another name or title for the so-called "BANTUS, NE-

GROES, BLACK AFRICANS, AFRICANS SOUTH OF THE SAHARA", and other such
colonialist labels tagged to the indigenous African peoples by their enslavers and economic exploiters. But subsequently Dr. Gertrude Gaton-Thompson [accomplished
British anthropologist] , and a few other members of her professional discipline, laid
the ridiculous disclaimers above to rest in her timely book, THE ZIMBABWE CUL-
TURE. [67] She was very shortly followed by numerous other anthropologists and historians, all of whom went to the area of the "HOLY OF HOLIES" of the Rozwis peoples
shown on page 289 of this volume. The "HOLY OF HOLIES" of Zimbabwe had been renamed "AFRICAN ACROPOLIS" by the European colonialists who first came upon, or
read of, Zimbabwe - its African name; this African name not being suitable for the
use of "CIVILIZED WHITE MEN AND WOMEN." Of course the only "CIVILIZED
PEOPLE" are Europeans and European-Americans. At least this was, and still is,
the prevailing sentiment expressed by the vast majority of European-Americans. For
millions of White Americans are being taught this each and every day in many different ways in their synagogues, churches, schools, and other institutions of learning,
Black Americans being subjected to the same teachings in the same institutions they
must also attend in "WHITE STUDIES" settings - this due to the constant process of
their de-Africanization and European-Americanization which has never ceased or
paused from the first day during their enslavement on the White man's slave plantations
and elsewhere.

One can see the parallel in the following quotations from Stanley Lane-Poole's
book, THE MOORS IN SPAIN. He wrote:

> The misguided Spaniards knew not what they were doing....
> The 'infidels' were ordered to abandon their native and picturesque
> c ostumes, to assume the hats and breeches of the Christians, to
> give up bathing and adopt the dirt of the conquerors, to renounce
> their language, their customs and ceremonies, even their names.

One can hardly imagine how the Africans could be considered "UNCIVILIZED,"
when it was known by almost every European historian of the Middle-Ages and ancient
times that the Africans ["Negroes," Blacks, etc.] even introduced the "COMMON
BATH" to the Europeans, beginning with Spain, Southern France and Portugal; which
was as late as 711 C.E. Stanley Lane-Poole explained how those Europeans of Spain
also demanded that the Africans from Morocco [the Mauritania Empire] "...GIVE UP
BATHING...." He continued:

It is stated that no less than three million of Moors were banished between the fall of Granada[0] and the first decade of the seventeenth century...But the Spaniards did not understand that they had killed their golden geese. For centuries Spain had been the centre of civilization, the seat of arts and sciences, of learning and every form of refined enlightenment. No country in Europe had so far approached the cultivated dominion of the Moors. The Moors wer banished, and for a while Christian Spain shone like the moon, with a borrowed light; when came the eclipse, and in the darkness Spain has grovelled ever since. The true memorial of the Moors is seen in the desolate tracts of utter barrenness, where once the Moslem grew luxuriant vines, olives and yellow ears of corn; in a stupid ignorant population where once art and learning flourished, in the general stagnation and degradation of a people which has hopelessly fallen in the scale of nations and has deserved its humiliation.

The amazing phenomena about the African-Moors [Moroccans] in Spain is that they extended their rule for two-hundred [200] years [to c. 1485 C.E.] in Granada, when in all other areas of Spain the Asian [Arab] Moors had been driven out by the European Christian Spaniards in c. 1285 C.E. The African-Moors, the first to enter Spain in c. 711 C.E., were the last to leave in c. 1485 C.E.

It must be remembered that Spain was captured by General Tarikh [an African of the Muslim religion] quite a while before the coming of the Arab-Moors [also Muslims] to Spain.[68] History shows that General Tarikh was a "BLACK MAN" [African, Negro, Bantu, etc.].[69] He was the first "MOOR" to capture the first part of the Iberian Peninsula - Mons Calpe. He accomplished this fete in c. 711 C.E.[70] He had also fought against the Asian or Arab-Muslims [Brown people] from Arabia in c. 680 C.E. or 58 A.H.; before his own capture by them, and his conversion to the faith of Islam [the religion of the Arabs and other Muslims].

With the African-Moors, and Asian or Arab-Moors that followed them in Spain, the inter and intra-Muslim-Jewish-Christian marriages and concubine relationships that preceeded the conversion of Jews and Christians to the Muslim Faith [ISLAM] be-

---

[0]. Granada fell to the Christian Europeans from the Muslim Africans - MOORS - in 1485 C.E.; just seven short years before the African or Moorish family of Spain by the name of Ninos, son - Don Pietro Olonzo Nino, formerly an Admiral of the Spanish Navy, was given command of the Santa Maria, tho Flag Ship of the seven ships in the expedition commandered by Admirante Cristobal Colon [Christopher Columbus] in the Spaniards thrust to find a shorter route to India to feed the starving peoples of Western Europe. See Stanley Lane-Poole's, THE MOORS IN SPAIN; J.A. Rogers, AFRICA'S GIFT TO AMERICA; and , ONE HUNDRED AMAZING FACTS ABOUT THE NEGRO.

came totally wide-spread, just as it was to be expected when any conqueror enters any conquered people's homeland. In simple words, the BLACK-SKINNED Africans and BROWN-SKINNED Asians inter-bred and amalgamated sexually [cohabited freely]with the WHITE-SKINNED European [Spanish, Portuguese, Southern French] population they met in every inch of the Iberian Peninsula. This was the same as the ancient indigenous BLACK-SKINNED Africans [Ethiopians] had done with the Maltese, Sicilians, Romans, and Hellenites during the so-called Ist and IInd Punic Wars [Khart-Haddan Roman Wars], and with the Britons [or English, Irish, Scotts, and Welch] during the reign of the African Emperor;of Rome - Septimus Serverus and his son Caracalla⁷ᴸ that entered this area of Europe; equally as Europeans did with their enslaved Africans, and the so-called "American Negroes" [African-Americans or Blacks],during the PARTITION OF AFRICA in c. 1830 - 1884 C.E., and before - during the SLAVE TRADE to the Americas from c. 1503 - 1865 C.E. that was initiated by the Right Reverend Bishop Bartolome deLas Casas.

There has been a jump of almost 700 to 1000 years ahead of the basic point in this chapter. This had to be done, because it was necessary to look around into all of the relative matters to reach the above and following historical conclusions. If this were always done most, if not all, of the illconceived and emotionally-based RACIST HYPOTHETICAL conclusions by "learned Negrophobes" could have been stopped, and the peoples of the world would have been that less confused on the matter of their contempt for each other solely on the shaky grounds of "RACE, COLOUR, RELIGION, GEOGRAPHIC BOUNDARIES," or for whatever other reasons man and woman superficially discriminate against their brother and sister human beings.

Professor James Henry Breasted in his book, ANCIENT RECORDS OF EGYPT, vol. I, p. 358, wrote the following:

> This nobleman of Aswan on the Middle Nile was sent by Pepi II - late third millenium B.C.[0] on two imperial expeditions southward into Nubian lands of Wawat and Irthet, thus preparing the way for later conquests. His inscriptions survive.

The professor was dealing with the building of the early Egyptian Empire, indicating the contact which existed between the indigenous Africans of Ta-Merry [Egypt] and those of Ta-Nehisi [Nubia], both of whom descendants are today called "Semitic" and

---

[0]. VIth Dynasty, c. 2420 - 2458 B.C.E.

"Negroid Stock" by Breasted and his fellow European-Americans and their European counterparts or "AUTHORITIES." But there were never "NEGRO," or "NEGROID," peoples;[72] thus no "NEGROLAND" as shown on the map on page 401 of this volume. Such names which European and European-American writers, historians, and other "scholars" continue to call the indigenous African peoples were never used in ancient times, the ancients being totally ignorant of them. Some African and African-American writers and historians also know that neither term is acceptable to most people of African origin. Yet, they too continue to use them as the means of least resistance to the criticism from those powers that control the economic livelihood of Black peoples - the WHITE "academic community" not excluded.

Professor Breasted, in vol. 2, pp. 486 - 487 of the above work, also noted that:

> From very early times the Egyptians also traded with Punt,
> which may be placed at the southern extreme of the Red Sea and
> the north coast of Modern Somalia. One great expedition ordered
> by Queen Hatshepsut [1490 - 1468 B.C., by Gardiner's conjectur-
> al dating] is marvelously recorded in the queen's temple at Deir-
> el-Bahri.[73] Here, together with many inscriptions, are depicted
> scenes of Punt, a "portrait" of the chief of Punt and another of his
> wife, who resides upon a donkey: the earliest pictorial records of
> Africa "South of the Sahara," together with an explicit list of "the
> loading of the ships very heavily with marvels of the country of
> Punt."[74] Hatshepsut's coeval, Tuthmosis III [1490 - 1436, by
> conjectural dating], continued the trade.

Breasted, following the lead of his European counterparts, could not give the honour of KING or PHARAOH to the head of the nation of Punt as he did for the nation of Ta-Merry [Egypt], instead the African "South of the Sahara" had to be a "CHIEF." At least, it is quite obvious that the Africans of Punt must have had the basic necessities of life that were very badly needed by the Africans "North of the Sahara" - the peole of Ta-Merry. To have had extensive trade with Punt, it meant that the Ta-Merrians [Egyptians] must have respected and honoured the friendship of their fellow Africans at their South.[75]

The errors, or willful distortions, of Africa's history were not only written by European and European-American writers and historians during, and since, the Afri-can Slave Trade . Herodotus, the first of the "European"[0] historians, also engaged in

---

[0]. Note that Herodotus was not in fact a Greek. He was a "Greek citizen" of Ionian birth. At the time of his birth Ionia was a colony of Egypt. See G.G.M. James, STOLEN LEGACY, New York, 1945.

injecting his own Europeanized version and values into African history while describing what he believed to have been "...Ethiopian [Kushite or Cushite] customs of worship." Thus he wrote [according to an English translation by Aubrey Selincourt titled, HERODOTUS', THE HISTORIES]:

> After crossing the lake one comes again to the stream of the Nile, which flows into it. At this point one must land and travel along the bank of the river for forty days, because sharp rocks, some showing above the water and many just avast, make the river impracticable for boats. After the forty days journey on land one takes another boat and in twelve days reaches a big city named Meroe, said to be the capital city of the Ethiopians.[75] The inhabitants worship Zeus and Dionysus of the Gods, holding them in great honor. There is an oracle of Zeus there, and they make war according to its pronouncements, taking from it both the occasion and the object of their various expeditions.

Herodotus, obviously, did not make any attempt to verify this aspect of the information about the religion of the Ethiopians, the same as "Modern Man" with respect to Africa and other Africans at the present time. He went on further to suggest that:

> .....the Ethiopians worship the Gods of the Greeks, Zeus and Dionysus...,

as shown above. But Herodotus did not stop there, continuing, he stated that he...

> could not enter into Ethiopia...[due to the fact that]...the Nile was not navigable...[from the point where]...the streams of the Nile, which flows into it....

In other words, Herodotus made his conclusions in this respect solely on hearsay evidence. Yet, thousands upon thousands of European and European-American ["Western"] historians and other writers wrote millions of volumes echoing Herodotus description of the Ethiopians' religion as TRUTH, in the process ignoring Ethiopian historians who constantly protested the inaccuracy of such reportings. This continued until the present twentieth century C.E. before "Westerners" accepted that the Ethiopians have never worshipped "Zeus" nor "Dionysus" in Ethiopia; but, instead, the ancient Greeks adopted many mythological GODS and GODDESSES under Greek names - these two included.

There is another aspect to the "NEGROPHOBIA" among present day historians, who project their own WHITE SUPREMACY, those who will stop at nothing in destroying the image of any African man or woman whenever they have failed to establish his or her non-existance in ancient North, East, and even South Africa. Their theory is,

62

IF YOU CANNOT CONVINCE PEOPLE THAT THE "negroes" DID NOT EXIST AT ALL IN A PARTICULAR SOCIETY, then say that EVERYONE OF THEM HAD A WHITE [European or European-American] MOTHER AND/OR FATHER, etc. [77] And, if neither of the two does not accomplish the desired goal they counter with, HE [or SHE , the indigenous African, "negro,"] RULED AS A DESPOT, HE MURDERED UNSCRUPU-LOUSLY, HE DID NOT TREAT HIS OWN PEOPLE [other indigenous Africans] AS HE SHOULD..., etc. This type of behavioral pattern presented itself as far back as the charges made against the African [Negro] Emperor of Rome [including, Spain, France, Portugal, Carthage, Ireland, Scottland, Wales, and England] - Septimus Severus. This African Emperor of Rome supposedly started...

> the persecution of the Christians and their institutions...[the Roman Catholic Church and its "mother Church" - the North African Church, from Ta-Merry to Khart-Haddas]...during the year 193 A.D.

Yet, other "Western" historians blamed his son, Caracalla, who succeeded him at his death. [78]

The above type of propaganda leveled against the "greatest of the three [3] African emperors of Rome" is a very feeble RACIST and RELIGIOUSLY BIGOTED attempt by European and European-American-controlled Christendom's self-appointed PRO-TECTORS OF THE WORLD FOR JESUS CHRIST to besmirch his character. One can see that the late Emperor Septimus Severus is still being tried other than for his role as the head of the Roman State or Empire. He is still being tried because of the "BLACKNESS OF HIS SKIN. "[79] Of course, this rationale does not hold true for the Christian Church historians of that period, the IInd Century C.E. or A.D. For it is only from the past two centuries [18th - present] that the White protagonists of the "FAITH" started to imply that"...Emperor Severus was a despotic ruler...," solely on the basis of his African [Ethiopian, "negro" or racial] origin.

If the first part of the BIG LIE technique is deflated the other parts remain dis-credited also, without further comments. However, it must be remembered that the Church of Rome, in its own official history, stated that:

> On July 19, A.D. 180., Felicitas and Perpetua were martyred by the soldiers of Emperor Septimus Severus. [80]

Of course it is assumed by church historians and theologians, all of whom continue to project this aspect of "NEGROPHOBIA," that their readers will not remember the date when the African Emperor, Septimus Severus, mounted the throne of Rome, which did not occur until three [3] years after the death of Felicitas, Perpetua, and Nymphamo - the alleged "FIRST CHRISTIAN MARTYRS."[81] Strange as it may seem, these "FIRST CHRISTIAN MARTYRS" were also indigenous African women - so-called "Negroes, Bantus, Africans South of the Sahara," even "niggers," etc.; not "Semites, Hamites, Caucasians," or "Indo-European Aryans."

One may enquire why so much time is being spent on the role of the Church of Rome with respect to the history of the BLACK MAN, the indigenous African? The answer is strictly fundamental. Thus, The Roman Catholic Church [Church of Rome], the first European Church, through her "Christian Missionaries" in consort with the imperial colonialist governments of Portugal, Spain, France, and Great Britain, along with many other European governments of the same type, were equal partners, and were equally responsible for the early destruction of many African High-Cultures [civilizations], and the distortion of their history. This was not only true of North Africa, but of West, South, East, and Central Africa. The Protestant Church is definitely not exempted, the only difference being that the Protestants entered after the Roman Catholics and Arab Muslims had already begun[82] their own JIHADS [Holy and economic wars]. And of course in this role the Roman Church, the Protestant Church, the Muslim Mosque, and the Jewish Synagogue indirectly, equally assumed and reaped enormous economic benefits during the earlier periods from the persecution of the Africans and their churches and other religious institutions in North Africa, and up to the present day throughout most of Africa [Alkebu-lan], especially where Portugal, Spain, France, Belgian, and Italian rule or influence still continue in Africa,[83] not to mention Arab-controlled African lands where the same continues unchecked.

Completing the rationale on the "greatest African [black or "Negro"] Emperor of the Roman Empire," which included Spain, Portugal, France, Ireland, Scottland, Wales, and England, once again it becomes necessary to quote from the work of another author and "AUTHORITY" on this phase of history - Jane Soames', THE COAST OF BARBARY, p. 47:

> Just as Gibbon started from the presumption which was in reality
> a prejudice and based all his work upon it, so today we will tend to em-
> phasize those elements contributing to the death of Rome which march
> with our own preoccupations and appear to bear out the contemporary
> economic, social, religious, and racial theories which happen to appeal

64

to us. There is, however, general agreement upon the fact that Rome was not murdered, but died of a mortal disease the symptoms of which were apparent long before the final crisis set in, and the African Emperor Septimus Severus was probably not far wrong in the palliative he adopted to stave off the evil day. His preoccupation with the efficiency of the army, quite apart from personal considerations, arose from instinctive knowledge that without it all was lost.

Current White supremists, many of whom call themselves "CHRISTIAN THEOLO-GIAN," do not sum-up the beginning of the fall of the Roman Empire under its African ["Negro"] Emperor with the rationale of Jane Soannes. They insist that it was due to some sort of a :

"...MYSTERIOUS FORCE FROM JESUS CHRIST THAT CRUSHED THE ROMAN EMPIRE AND ITS DEVILISH AFRICAN EMPEROR."[84]

How many times have this last quotation of religious jargon been preached in the pulpits of so many "CHRISTIAN CHURCHES"? How many times people of African origin were the audience listening and digesting this line of African character assasination? Countless number of times. Yet, this type of RACISM and RELIGIOUS BIGOTRY directed against African people continue on and on as:

"...THE WORD OF GOD AND HIS MINISTRY...."

Of course since GOD [Jehovah of the Jews, Jesus Christ of the Christians, and Al'lah of the Muslims, all of the so-called "Western religions"], himself, suposedly, placed it into the mind of his earthly representatives - PRIESTS, RABBIS, MINISTERS, IMANS, through inspirations and/or dreams, thus their pronouncements are not even questionable. All of these "men of the cloth" [clergymen] have established themselves in the position where they are above being questioned by their faithful followers. But to the enquiring mind this type of malicious stereotype characterization of any African group cannot be allowed to stand unchallenged in the 20th Century C.E. For no longer can the TRUE HISTORY of Africa and the indigenous Africans remain distorted just to save the sanctity of certain past, and present, RACIST and RELIGIOUSLY BIGOTED "Church Fathers" from exposure, which has for too long become necessary.

The traditional misinformation in Church history - Roman Catholic, Protestant, and Jewish alike, espouses all sorts of propaganda which too many "Negroes" and "Coloured people," not Blacks, repeat like parrots without question. The "Negroes," as the "Coloured people," pay large sums of monies on Friday nights, Saturdays, and most certainly on Sundays, to hear certain priests, ministers, and rabbis, known as

65

"men of the cloth," tell them how much less than human the "natives of africa" are, but extoll the greatness of the "Europeans of Europe and the United States of America" who have continuously made journeys to Africa as "entrprenuers" and "Christian Missionaries."[85] The real irony of this tradegy comes when a "NEGRO" or "COLOURED" minister stands before an all "Negro" congregation and tells them:[86]

YOUR HEARTS HAVE GOT TO BE WHITE AS SNOW BEFORE YOU
CAN ENTER THE GATES OF THE KINGDOM OF HEAVEN.

One's imagination must stretch very far indeed to see a"Negro" with a WHITE HEART AS SNOW. Maybe this too is possible under current RACIST Christian teachings, since one must assume that such teachers got the words directly from Jesus Christ [God] through "INSPIRED DREAMS" to pass on to their DREAMLESS congragations. At least, this is the impression given by these men who enter into areas they know very little or absolutely nothing about; most of them knowing the various versions of every bible, but not the slightest of anything about the history of the development of such books or the materials therein. Nor are they aware of the development of the institutions that manufacture said works, or the history of the peoples mentioned in the bibles they so galantly champion, beginning with the Haribu of Africa and Yaweh[0] against the Egyptians of Africa and Ra.[00]

One is to expect that the above revelations will cause certain viloent reactions by many who feel that their religion, even their God, is being attacked. Their religious leaders have kept them in total ignorance of Church [Jewish, Christian, or Islamic] history, and for a very good reason. Why? Because these "men of the cloth", for the most part, cannot explain their religion's involvement in colonialism and the slave trade in Africa, the Caribbeans, the Americas, Asia, and Europe with any sense of Godliness. They cannot explain why there are no pictures of BLACK, BROWN, YELLOW or RED angels, nor of disciples sitting at the table of the "LAST SUPPER" with the blonde-white and blue-eyed Jesus Christ, nor any in Jewish books, when in fact Pales-

---

[0]. The Haribu [later called Israelites, Hebrews, and today "Jews"] or "WANDERING PEOPLE" - nomads and their God-head Yaweh or Jehovah of the FIVE BOOKS OF MOSES or Old Testament.

[00]. The first God on record - the SUN or RA, the GOD of the religion of the indigenous Africans of Ta-Merry [Egypt] that formed the basis of many of the Judaeo-Christian and Islamic teachings, era of today.

66

tine [Israel] was, during Jesus Christ's lifetime, a Hebrew or Jewish country that was not the White man's homeland. Not only is Jesus Christ blonde, but all of his disciples are equally blonde with blue eyes and golden hair. At least, if they were somewhat tan from the red hot scorching sun of the Israeli desert, and not like their Falasha brothers and sisters on pages 68 - 70 there could have been some grounds for acceptance of this Caucasian image. But today the Africans, African-Americans, and other peoples whose heritage and homeland are as much grounded in Palestine as Europe's White Jews, the so-called "Semites" not excluded, are asking:

WHY HAVE I BEEN EXCLUDED FROM THIS, MY HERITAGE, BY YOU [whites], FOR SO MANY THOUSAND YEARS?

What will the answer be? Who will give the answer? Who is ready to tell the "TRUTH," and nothing bu the "TRUTH," to the Africans and their descendants and pay the conseq-quence?[87]

In looking at the picture of the Falasha youngsters shown on page 68, along with the European-Israeli in their midst, what significant difference is there between them and the so-called "NEGRO JEWS" in the United States of America except RACIAL IGNORANCE on the part of certain preachers of the purity of the so-called "SEMITES." It would seem that the Falasha shown on page 70 with his European Israelite teacher could have been easily mistaken for any "NEGRO" on the streets of Harlem or South Bronx, New York City. But the Israelites of Harlem on the top section of the same page shown in prayer to the same God-head the Falasha youngsters also adore are the rejected ones, solely on the basis that they cannot prove their "JEWISHNESS." Whatever "JEWISHNESS" is, it is obviously nothing related to color or facial characteristics, as somewhere among all of them the original HARIBU [Hebrew or Jew] is to be found in the ancient ruins of Palestine or modern Israel. Thus, to say that either of the Israelites, the BLACK ones that is, ancestors are only related back to "King David", and not for the others from Europe, is to assume that the ancient Haribus from the time of the first Haribu, ABRAHAM, were Caucasian or White people. Yet, after the ancient Haribus had suffered slavery under the indigenous Africans for more than 400 years it would have been impossible for them to leave Ta-Merry [Egypt] as they came in -"WHITE." Obviously, the ancient Haribus were not as RACIST as their more "modern" descendants of European-America, otherwise Moses and Solomon would not have married or cohabited with Ethiopian ["Negro"] women.

67

Falasha Jews From Ethiopia Studying in Israel

Their Tribe Practices Judaism According to Law of Moses

By HARRY GILROY
Special to The New York Times.

KFAR BATYA, Israel, Feb. 25 —Twelve young Falasha Jews, who might be taken as living proof of the legend that today's Ethiopians descend from Solomon and the Queen of Sheba, are studying at this children's village.

They come from a tribe, numbering 50,000, scattered over Ethiopia. The tribe is called Falasha, which in the Amharic tongue means "stranger." Its members practice Judaism according to the law of Moses, but have no tradition about later feasts such as Hanukkah and Purim.

The youngsters are here for two years of training. They are in a beautiful farm school adjoining Raanana on the Sharon plain—established and operated by the Women's Mizrachi Organization of America. Hadassah, the American Women Zionists, is aiding the project through Youth Aliyah, to which it contributes.

There are ten boys and two girls in the Falasha group. The other children of Kfar Batya have made them welcome.

Bible Read in Amharic

Details about the Falasha were supplied by the director of Kfar Batya. He is a stocky young man named Leonard Rauchwerger, a native of Vienna who had to flee medical school there because of Hitler. He subsequently was drafted while at the City College of New York and as a G. I. student at the Hebrew University of Jerusalem ran into the Arab-Israeli war.

Mr. Rauchwerger sent a Falasha lad for the oldest boy and girl. The boy came first, a tall 16-year-old who gave his name as Isazah Adomic. He said he had learned English at a military school in Addis Ababa.

Isazah Adomic, 16-year-old leader of Falasha youngsters studying at Kfar Batya in Israel, serves Malka Avraham. Another Falasha student and an Israeli friend await their turns.

The girl was 15. She said her name was Malka (Hebrew for Queen) Avraham. Mr. Rauchwerger said she was translating from her native name of Negus, which is the royal title.

Isazah said they had read the Bible in a dialect of the Amharic tongue. It was the custom of his people, he said, for all the men and women of the tribe to gather for prayers. Some of the tribe were priests.

The older pair were soon joined by several younger boys and also by a ring of curious but friendly white boys. The Falasha said they liked what they had seen of Israel—the farm work, food and soccer games at Kfar Batya —and that Hebrew was a hard language. One wrote rapidly in Amharic. It was translated —

they were having a good time and liked their companions.

The Falasha tribe practiced the ancient rite of animal sacrifice up to twenty years ago, according to Zvi Weiss of the Youth Aliyah Department of the Jewish Agency for Palestine. He said that the Falasha contend they are descendants of Israelites who went to Ethiopia when Sheba returned from her stay with Solomon. The Queen, according to their legend, had a son Menelik by Solomon.

There are other theories about the origin of the Falasha. One is that they were Ethiopian converts to Judaism at some ancient time. Another is that they are the descendants of a Hebrew mercenary army that fled southward along the Nile when their

Egyptian employer was overthrown. A third idea is that they emigrated from the Arabian peninsula, either in Biblical times or after the rise of Islam.

Reports of Jewish tribes in Africa have been noted by historians and travelers many times in the last thousand years. But the Falasha themselves apparently did not know that Judaism still existed outside Ethiopia.

Prof. Joseph Halevy of France visited the Falasha in the Eighteen Sixties. In 1904 Dr. Jacob Faitlovitch, Professor Halevy's pupil, went to visit them and thereafter devoted his life to bringing them back into the world communion of Judaism. His work resulted in the coming of Falasha students to Israel and in the development of Hebrew education in Ethiopia.

68

In religious high school, integration is the rule and girls attend classes along with the boys. Compulsory education for all is the rule in Israel.

Their ancestry goes back to time of King David

The above heading is the title of an article written by Noah ben-Horin about the Black Israelites from Ethiopia studying and living in Israel today. Why are these Nile Valley Africans acceptable in Israel and the equally" NE-GROID" Israelites ("Jews") of the United States of America are not? RACE is the only answer.

At prayer. Members of the choir, wearing prayer shawls, await signal. Other Negro Jewish communities are set up in Philadelphia, Brooklyn, Pittsburgh, Chicago and Youngstown, Ohio.

Alphabet lessons. Children of the Commandment Keepers Congregation are taught Hebrew.

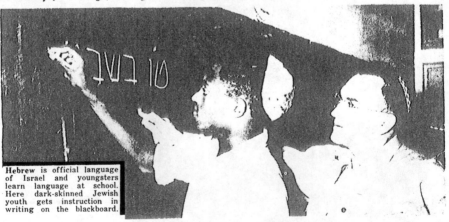

Hebrew is official language of Israel and youngsters learn language at school. Here dark-skinned Jewish youth gets instruction in writing on the blackboard.

The above are all Africans and Europeans of African parentage. Some of statues, and some from pottery. [See Y. ben-Jochannan and G. E. Simmonds, THE BLACK MAN'S NORTH AND EAST AFRICA, Alkebu-lan Books Assoc., N.Y. 1971]

1. Bronze bust of a "Negro" Roman, from G. Calaza, "Expression of Art in a Roman Commercial City : Ostia," Journal Of Roman Studies V [1915], 165-167, fig. 41.

2. Marble head of "Negro" Roman found at Agora, Trajonic period. ["The Excavation of the Athenian Agora Twelfth Season," by H. A. Thompson, 1947].

3. Pharaoh Taharqa from Ethiopia, XXV th Dynasty of Egypt [Ta-Merry].

4. "Negro'Greek of the 4th Century B.C.E.

5. "Negro" Roman ambassador of the Flavian period. [Rome, Villa Albani, 209, Deutsches Archaologisches Instituto, Rome].

6. Sphinx Of Ghizeh, Ta-Merry [according to a painting by Baron Viviant Denon, "Travels In Egypt and Assyria," France, 1895].

8. Pharaoh Aspelta of Ta-Merry.

7. Pharaoh Amenohat III of Ta-Merry, the so-called "NEGRO PHARAOH."

9. Faience Vace of "Negro" Cypriot, late 7th Century B.C.E., with bearded bar-barian. [British Museum, A7 8-6 2D].

10. Roman Emperor Caracalla, son of Roman Emperor Septimus Severus, Rome, 193 A.D. Both of African origin – father of African birth, Carthage; son of Syrian mother.

[All of the above are of African birth or origin; some with Asian or European lineage. See F.W. Snowden, BLACKS IN ANTIQUITY: A GRECO-ROMAN EXPERIENCE, Cambridge, Mass., 1970; J.A. Rogers, WORLD'S GREAT MEN OF COLOR, vol. I., New York, 1954; Y. ben-Jochannan, AFRICA: MOTHER OF "WESTERN CIVI-LIZATION, New York, 1971; G.G.M. James, STOLEN LEGACY]

CHAPTER I BIBLIOGRAPHY

Sir E.A. Wallis Budge, EGYPT, London, 1895

H.G. Wells, A SHORT HISTORY OF THE WORLD, London, 1927

Dr. L. Stoddard, THE RISING TIDE OF COLOUR, New York, 1930 [London]

-------, CLASHING TIDES OF COLOUR, London, 1935 [New York]

C.P. Groves, THE PLANTING OF CHRISTIANITY, 3 vols., New York, 1927

R.G. Collingwood, ROMAN BRITAIN

Tertullian's De ANIMA XXX [transl. by Harnach in his MISSION AND EXPANSION]

R. Michelet, BaRANGA [quotations from Henri Junod]

Herodotus, THE HISTORIES [transl. by Aubrey deSelincourt], New York, 1954

HOLY BIBLE [any version]

G.G.M. James, STOLEN LEGACY, New York, 1954

R.B. Moore, THE WORD NEGRO, ITS ORIGIN AND EVIL USE, New York, 1954

Flavius Josephus, EGYPT

W. Whiston, THE LIFE AND WORKS OF FLAVIUS JOSEPHUS, New York, 1960

S. Lane-Poole, THE MOORS IN SPAIN, New York, 1886

G. Caton-Thompson, THE ZIMBABWE CULTURE, Oxford, 1931

J.H. Breasted, ANCIENT RECORDS OF EGYPT, 4 vols., Chicago, 1906

J. Soames Nickerson, THE COAST OF BARBARY, New York, 1954

--------- , A SHORT HISTORY OF NORTH AFRICA, New York, 1961

Sir H.H. Johnston, A HISTORY OF CIVILIZATION IN AFRICA, London, 1920

Sir C. Darwin, Jr., THE NEXT MILLION YEARS, London, 1945

M.D.W. Jeffreys, "The Negro Enigma" [in: WEST AFRICAN REVIEW, Sept., 1951]

J.C. deGraft-Johnson, AFRICAN GLORY, London, 1954

Mrs. Stewart Erskine, THE VANISHED CITIES OF NORTHERN AFRICA, London

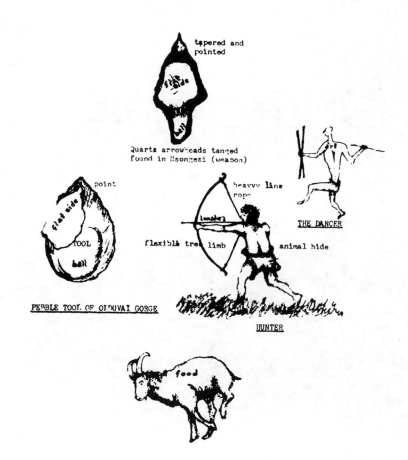

tapered and
pointed

Quartz arrowheads tanged
found in Nsongezi (weapon)

point

flat side

TOOL

ball

PEBBLE TOOL OF OLDUVAI GORGE

heavy line
rope

timber

flexible tree limb   animal hide

HUNTER

THE DANCER

food

EARLY MAN of the NILE VALLEY
(c1,750,000 BCE - ?)

73

Top: The elegance of prehistoric African art unearthed
in southern Africa presently located in the Pretoria Mu
seum, approximately 30,000 years old. Cut by Flint Stone
tools by prehistoric indigenous Africans.

Bottom: Reconstruction of a Stone Age indigenous African skull. Such Africans lived during the same period as
the artist who made the carving above. (See: J. A. Rogers,
AFRICA'S GIFT TO AMERICA, p. 7; also, SEX AND RACE, vol.
I, pp. 26, 35).

The prehistoric art of Africa was continuous, as one can readily see in
the following statement:"10,000 B.C.E. a Grimaldi"(indigenous south African)
sculptor in Monomotapa"(South Africa)"carved the first known statue of a human body." Europeans misnamed it "VENUS OF WILLENDORF." It was confiscated
from Africa and placed in the Museum of Vienna, Austria (Europe).[2]

74

GLOSSAR

Acheulian: Later of the two stages of the Chelles-Acheul culture, characterized by hand axes named after St. Acheul, France.

Acheulio-Levalloisian: A Culture recognized in the Somali area. It includes Acheulian-type hand axes and flake tools by the Levalloisian.

Africa: A Greek and Roman name given to the continent originally called Alkebu-lan by its indigenous peoples. Other names which the early Europeans used for this continent are: Corphye, Amonis, Ortegyia, Ethiopia, Libya, Oceania, etc.

Alkebu-lan: Ancient name of Africa by the Moors and Ethiopians.

Atlanthropus mauritanicus: possibly the same species as Pithecanthropus erectus, generally located in the Algerian region of North Africa and Casablanca areas.

Australopithecinae: relatives of the family Hominidae, or sub-family, to the earliest known upright-walking, tool-making hominids, generally located around the regions of South and East Africa.

Austratopithecines: Members of the Australopithecinae sub-family.

Australopithecus: Genus of the sub-family Australopithecinae. There are two species, africanus and robustus.

Auxumite Period: Period of the Kingdom of Axum in Ethiopia, founded in 18 C. E., presently the religious City of Ethiopia, formerly the ancient capital.

Bantu: A misnomer Europeans use for the African peoples from the Sudan down to the tip of Southern Africa. Allegedly to distinguish between African groups. Like the word "Negro", which has no scientific basis to justify its usage; It too stems from the slave period.

Boskopoid: Ancient South African (so-called "Bushmen") skulls. First of the type recognized in a skull from Boskop, South Africa. Bushman is a European word. It is used to single out a specific group of Africans. This group is the same as other African groups. However, the difference among Africans is the same as the difference among Europeans.

Capsian: Mesolithic culture of North Africa characterized by microliths; named after Gafsa in Tunisia.

Capsian, Kenya: Culture known around the Kenya Rift Valley, similar to the Capsian of Gafsa.

Carbon-14 dating: Method of dating material containing carbon, based on the rate of radioactive decay of the isotope carbon-14. A system used in the dating of fossils.

Chellean: A lesser stage of the earlier Chelles-Acheul culture, characterized by crude hand axes; named after Chelles, France.

Chellean Man: A skull from Bed II, Olduvai Gorge, Tanganyika, accompanied by Chellean type hand axes.

Chelles-Acheul: Lower Paleolithic hand-ax culture of Africa, Asia, Europe; named after Chelles and St. Acheul, France.

Civilization: People who live in a civil compact. High-Culture is a better word.

Colchians: An African people, once located in the Near and Middle-east. "Extremely black in color, and with very wooly hair," according to Herodotus' report on his trip to Egypt in the early 450 B. C. E.

Doian: Culture of southern Somali region, having deposits of microliths and pottery, named after the word "doi," in the Somali language, it describes orange-colored sand.

Dolichocephalic: Long, narrow skull with cranial index rating of less than 75%.

Earlier Stone Age: E. S. A. Cultures ending at the Chelles-Acheul and African equivalent of the Lower-Paleolithic of Europe.

Elmenteitan: Culture from the Kenya Rift Valley to the Upper Kenya Capsian, characterized by long double-edge blades.

Eyasi Man: Fragmentary skulls from Lake Eyasi Tanganyika, similar to "Rhodesian Man." Zimbabwe is the name of this country; thus "Zimbabwe Man."

Fetishism: Relating to African art. A misnomer taken from the African town of Fete, which was the name of an existing African metropolis in what was called "Gold

Coast" (presently Ghana) by the Portuguese in the 16th Century C. E.

First Intermediate Period: Period between the Earlier Stone Age and the Middle Stone Age in Africa 40,000 years ago, plus or minus.

Frontal Bone: Bone forming the front of the skull or forehead.

Gamblian: Fourth pluvial period in East Africa, dating from the Upper Pleistocene named after deposits on the farm of a Mr. Gamble in the Kenya Rift Valley.

Gerontomorphic: Exaggerated or "masculine" features of a skull stoids as seen in the Zimbabwe and Zambia regions.

Hamitic: Supposedly an African,or Black people. From the word Ham in the Hebrew Bible. The origin changes with each professor's prejudice.

Hominidae: Family that includes the Australopithecines; extinct in much later forms of man.

Hominids: Upright-walking, toolmaking members of the family Hominidae.

Hominae: Sub-family of the family Hominade, but excluding the Australopithinecines.

Homo erectus: Alternative name for Pithecanthropus erectus—For example: Java Man and similar.

Homo habilis: A hominid from Olduvai, similar to Australopithecus.

Homo neanderthalensis: Neanderthal Man of the early Upper Pleistocene of Africa, Asia,and Europe,

Homo rhodesiensis: Rhodesian Man of the early Upper Pleistocene of Africa, represented by a skull from Broken Hill, Zambia.

Homo sapiens: Man as we know him today.

Homo soloensis: Solo Man of the early Upper Pleistocene of Java, very similar to Rhodesian Man. Note that the correct name is "Zimbabwe Man."

Hyrax Hill: Earliest known variation of the Stone Bowl Culture; named after a site in the Kenya Rift Valley near Nakuru.

Kanam stage: First Pleistocene faunal stage of East Africa, dated back to the lower Pleistocene; named after a site on the Kavirondo Gulf of Lake "Victoria," Kenya.

Kanjeran pluvial: Third pluvial period in East Africa; dated to the later part of the Middle Pleistocene; a site on the Kavirondo Gulf of Lake "Victoria," Kenya.

Khartoum Mesolithic: Culture of fishing on the banks of the Nile at Khartoum, specifically noted by its bone harpoons and "wavy-line" pottery.

Khoisan people: The so-called "Bushmen" and "Hottentots" who speak click-like sounding languages, generally having a yellowish tinted skin tone.

Kumasian pluvial: Second pluvial period in East Africa; dated to the Middle Pleistocene; named after deposits of a former "Lake Kamasia" near the Kamasian escarpment of the Kenya Rift Valley.

Kush: Kingdom of the Sudan, extending into Ethiopia, dominant during the twenty-fifth Dynasty of Egypt. Around the period of 350 C. E., with the fall of Meröe, the term Kush (Cush) disappeared from universal usage. However, it is still being used to represent present-day Ethiopian cultural heritage, as well as **her** ancient recordings in the "KEBRA NEGAST" [Book Of The Chronicles Of Ethiopia].

Kushites (Meröeites): Peoples of Ethiopia and Sudan during certain periods. Generally of ancient days before the Christian era (B. C. E.) and two to three hundred (200—300) years beyond the turn of the Christian era (C. E.). Present day Southern Sudan and Ethiopia's peoples are typical of the Kushites (Cushites).

Lanet culture: Associated with ironworking dating back to the sixteenth century C. E., named after a site in the Kenya Rift Valley near Nakuru.

Laterite: Alternative name for Ferricrete.

Later Stone Age: L. S. A. A stage following the Second Intermediate Period in Africa, beginning about 8000 B. C. E., characterized by microlithic cultures.

Lower Egypt: The area of Egypt along the Mediterranean Sea, and inland.

Lunate: Small crescent-shaped implement used for barbs on arrows.

Magosian: Culture of the Second Intermediate Period, characterized by microliths, named after Magosi, a water hole in the eastern area of Uganda.

Makalian: First postpluvial wet phase lasting from about 5,500 B. C. E. to about 2,500 B. C. E., named after the Makalia River in the Kenya Rift Valley.

Mauritania: An African nation at the Northwest coast of Africa.

"Meganthropus africanus": Name given to a jaw fragment from Laetolil, Lake Eyasi, Tanganyika, considered to belong to the Australopithecus africanus groupings.

Meroitic: Period of the kingdom of Meröe (Sudan) on the Nile, about 400 B. C. E. to 300 B. C. E., associated with ironwork development.

Mesolithic: Stage following the Paleolithic. Generally applied to a settled way of life often based on fishing; the term stands for Middle Stone Age, however, not equivalent to the M. S. A. of Africa.

Middle Egypt: The area of Egypt between the Upper and Lower areas.

Middle Stone Age: Abbreviated M. S. A., a stage following the First Intermediate Period in Africa; beginning about 40,000 B. C. E., symbolized by cultures with varied types of flake tools.

Monomotapa: The ancient empire of south and south-east Africa from about 1200 to 1700 B. C. E.

Moors: African Muslims from Mauretania and Morocco mixed with Arab Muslim invaders from Arabia. Also Africans of any place who were Muslims when the Portuguese invaders entered Africa in the 15th Century C. E.

Nachikufan: Later Stone Age culture first recognized at the Nachikufu caves, Zambia, associated with rock paintings.

Nakuran: Second postpluvial wet phase beginning about 850 B. C. E., named after Nakuru in the Kenya Rift Valley.

Negro: A name given the African (Black) people by their European and European-American slave masters.

"Negroland": A mythical area in West Africa designated as such by the European slavers and colonialists during the 16th and 17th centuries.

Nilotic: A European term for Africans of the Nile Valley. Like other words used to describe "ethnic characteristics," it too falls very short of accuracy. There are Africans all over Africa who match this classification.

Nubia: An African state at the Southern border of Egypt. Presently Sudan.

Oldowan: Earliest known culture, prior to the Chelles-Acheul, symbolized by "pebble tools"; named after Olduvai Gorge, Tanganyika.

Omo-Kanam stage: First faunal stage recognized in the Pleistocene of East Africa, dated to the Lower Pleistocene named after sites in the Omo Valley, southern Ethiopia and Kanam in western Kenya.

Paranthropus: Genus of Australopithecines, generally called Australopithecus robustus.

Parietats: Bones on either side of the skull, behind the frontal bone and above the temporal bones.

Pebble culture: Equivalent to the Oldowan culture, prior to the Chelles-Acheul.

Pebble tool: Chopping tool of a crude type made by removing a few flakes to form a cutting edge at one end of a pebble.

Pedomorphic: "Feminine" of infantile features retained by the adult.

Pehecanthropus: Genus of extinct men including two species from Java, one from Peking, "Chellean Man" from Olduvai, and "Atlanthropus" of North Africa—otherwise called Homo erectus.

Pleistocene: First period of the Quaternary era, which started about 2 million years B. C. E., ending about 8000 B. C. E.

Pliocene: Last period of the Tertiary era, spanning a period of about 4 million (4,000,000) to 2 million (2,000,000) B. C. E.

Pluvial: Period when the rainfall was greater than it is at present during a specific length of time.

Polyhedral stones: Stone spheres with facets, common in Acheulian and later cultures.

80

Pongidae: Family including the apes or pongids.

Potassium-argon dating: An absolute method of dating rocks which are rich in potassium, based on the rate of disintegration of potassium-40 into calcium-40 and argon-40, generally applied to rocks more than about 400,000 years old.

Pre-"Zinjanthropus": A hominid from Bed I of the Olduvai Gorge, named "Homo habilis."

Primitive: A term which is supposed to designate the earliest stage of development.

Prognathism: Protrusion of the upper jaw, characterized by certain indigenous African types.

Race: The mythical non-scientific classification of mankind into allegedly "distinct groups."

(Rhodesian) Zimbabwian* Man (Homo rhodesiensis): Named after a skull from Broken Hill, Zambia, dating back to the period of the Upper Pleistocene. (African equivalent of Neanderthal Man).

(Rhodesioids) Zimbaboids*: Type of man-like Zimbabwian (Rhodesian)* Man, noted for his heavy brow ridges and other gerontomorphic features.

Sabeans: Inhabitants of western Arabia who migrated to the Kingdom of Axum in the Empire of Ethiopia just before the turn of the first Century C. E.

Saldanha Man: One of the Zimbaboids (Rhodesioids), located at Hopefield, near Saldanha Bay, Cape Province, Monomotapa (South Africa).

Sangoan: Early Middle Stone Age culture of the forested and steppe country of central Africa named after Sango Bay of Lake Victoria.

Second Intermediate Period: Period between the Middle Stone Age and the Later Stone Age in Africa, covering a scale of about 10,000 to 6,500 B. C. E.

---

*Cecil Rhodes, the man in whose honor the name of this fossil appears was a master of genocide, a slave merchant, and racist of the enth degree. To the Africans of Southern and South-eastern Africa in the 1800's he represented the same type of impetuous maniac Adolph Hitler represents to world Jewry. These fossils should be renamed by African educators—"ZIMBABWE."

Shaheinab Neolithic: Earliest culture with evidence of domesticated animals in eastern Africa characterized by stone gouges, bone axheads, and pottery; named after a site on the Nile approximately thirty (30) miles north of Khartoum.

Shemitic : People who allegedly originated from a Character in the Hebrew Bible called "Sem" or "Shem."*

Stone Bowl culture: Culture of the Kenya Rift Valley characterized by stone bowls; noted by its early Neolithic and later Iron Age variants.

Swanscombe skull: A fragmentary skull from Swanscombe, Kent, England, similar to the Steinheim skull.

Upper Egypt: The area of Egypt along the northern border of Sudan (Nubia). Beginning between the 2nd and 3rd Cataract, ending somewhere in modern Ethiopia.

Zimbabwe: One of Africa's wonders. An ancient masonry structure of great engineering. It was the center of the Great Monomotapa Empire, which stretched from what is today called "Mozambique" to the tip of Southern Africa. Europeans and European-Americans tried to date this High-Culture back to 1500 C. E. only. African historians, on the other hand, dated it back to the pre-Christian era (B. C. or B. C. E). Oral tradition of the area indicates that it existed at least 100 B. C. E. or earlier. Archaeological findings have proven that many indigenous civilizations in this area were developed to the point that iron smelting had become common by 43,000 years ago. (See page 289 of this volume].

---

*See page 599 of Y. ben-Jochannan, AFRICA: MOTHER OF "WESTERN CIVILIZATION," New York, 1971, for a detailed analysis of this RELIGIOUSLY BIGOTED myth as it relates to Africa and her peoples; also page 30 of Y. ben-Jochannan and G. E. Simmonds, THE BLACK MAN'S NORTH and EAST AFRICA, New York, 1971.

Fossils Trace Man Back 600,000 Years In Gorge in Africa

LEOPOLDVILLE, Belgian Congo, Aug. 23 (Reuters)— Human fossils about 600,000 years old—possibly the earliest known trace of man—have been found in Tanganyika.

Dr. Louis S. B. Leakey, a prominent anthropologist, said that his wife, also an anthropologist, had found the fossils among animal remains in th Oldoway Gorge in Tanganyika, July 17.

Dr. Leakey, 56 years old, a British expert on East African anthropology, has searched for many years to prove his belief that man originated in Africa. He is curator of the Corydon Museum of Natural History in Nairobi, Kenya.

Dr. Leakey reported his wife's find to the Pan-African Congress of Prehistory here yesterday. Sixty delegates from fifteen countries, including the United States, are at the congress.

Crude tools were found with the fossils, suggesting some form of human culture, Dr.

Palate and teeth of "boise" (below) compared with those of an Australian indiginous man (so-called"aborigine").

Leakey said. He said a reconstruction of the bones showed a skull that was estimated to date from the second half of the Pleistocene geological era 600.000 years ago.

N.Y.Times.Aug.24,1959

National Geographic Magazine, Sept. 1960, has a picture of one skull, and quotes Prof. Leakey as saying that it was that of the first tool-making human; and that the discoveries "strongly support Charles Darwin's prophecy that Africa would prove to have been the birthplace of mankind."

Prof. Leakey has since discovered a still older skull "considerably more than 600,000 years old." With it were other human relics, one of them a child. (New York Times, Feb. 25, 1961).

N. Y. Times, Aug. 24, 1959.

The age of the skulls is now set at 1,750,000 years. (*New York Times,* July 23, 1961.)

Side view of skull

External construction of skull and face.

Front view of skull

Left: Reconstruction of the Rhodesian Man-with the original skull

The skull was found at Broken Hill Rhodesia, almost in the heart of Africa with 160 feet of packed above it.

RECONSTRUCTION OF FOSSIL-MAN[1]

(Top) Reconstruction of
Zinjanthropus boisie
(African fossil-man)

(Top) A sculptured at-
tempt at reconstructing
Neanderthal man (Euro-
pean fossil-man).

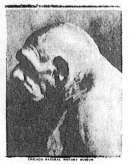

Full figure attempt
by
Maurice Wilson

(Bottom) Skull of Zin-
janthropus boisie un-
earthed in Bed I of Ol
Olduvai Gorge, Tangan-
yika, by Dr's. L.S. &
M. Leakey.

(Bottom) An attempt in
paint. Both by Maurice
Wilson.

ACKNOWLEDGMENTS

British Museum (Natural History), Department of Anthropology

American Museum of Natural History, New York

Chicago Museum of Natural History

BBC School Publications

Leonard Grant of the National Geographic Society.

Note: Note the RACIST attempt to make the African fossil-man
appear to be of "CAUCASIAN" or "SEMITIC" origin. Why was
Zinjanthropus boisie not shown with the so-called "NEGROID"
characteristics generally attributed to the so-called "BAN-
TU", "NEGRO", or "AFRICAN SOUTH OF THE SAHARA" of Africa.

84

PREHISTORIC MAN: A COMPARISON IN TWO PERIODS

(BETWEEN THE MIDDLE AND LOWER PLEISTOCENES)

MIDDLE PLEISTOCENE

Australopithecus	Ubeidiya, and the Jordan Valley area.
Robustus	Kromdraai
	c. 400,000 B. C. E.
	Swartkrans
Africanus	Sterkfontein area
	Makapan
	Taung
Robustus ("Meganthropus")	Djetis beds, Java c. 500,000 B. C. E.

LOWER PLEISTOCENE

Australopithecus	Lake Chad region
Robustus ("Zinjanthropus boisie")	Olduvai Gorge c. 1,750,000 B. C. E.
Australopithecus ("Homo habilis")	Olduvai Gorge
Africanus	Laetolil

There is very strong evidence that the Australopethicines evolved in the regions of the northeast forest of Alkebu-lan [Africa], along the equatorial line. Also, that they formerly spread from the forest area into the wide open plains. In their new environment conditions forced them to assume and adopt an erect posture and to use their hands in certain experiments with tools;[2] although they were not tools as man knows them today. It was also from this region that they first migrated to southern Alkebulan and to Asia.[3]

CLASSIFICATION OF MAN

First or Prime Stage:

Australopithecus ("Paranthropus, "Meganthropus," "Zinjanthropus," and maybe Homo havilis are included). There are two species, Africanus and robustus, from approximately 1,750,000 years to 500,000 years ago. Lower Pleistocene is North Africa (Sahara) and the early Middle Pleistocene around the Kalahari Desert (South Africa), Palestine and Java.

Second or Intermediate Stage:

Pithecanthropus (Homo erectus), Modjokertensis, and erectus, c. 500,000 years in Java. Germany (Heidelberg jaw), Peking (Pithecanthropus pekinensis), Tanzania, East Africa (Olduvai Bed II), and Algeria ("Atlanthropus"), c. 450,000 years (around the Mindel Glaciation period). In Morocco, up to c. 250,000 years.

Third or Final Stage:

Homo "sapiens-Neandertheloid" dating to their ancestors in England and Germany (Swanscombe and Steinheim), c. 250,000 years (during the Second Inter-glacial period).

Homo neanderthelensis generally found in North Africa, Asia and Europe, c. 70,000 to 40,000 years.

"Rhodesioids" (Homo Soloensis and Homo Rhodensiensis found in

---

*The student must realize that the existing conflict between religious theology and evolutionary scientific knowledge with respect to this type of data is just cause for constant re-examination of the Book of Genesis (First Book of Moses) in the Hebrew Holy Torah (Christian Old Testament).

Africa and Java, c. 35,000 years.

Homo sapiens, Combe Capelle, exclusively in Europe, c. 30,000—
35,000 years.

Florisbad, South Africa, c. 40,000 years;

Niah, c. 40,000; Kanjera, East Africa, unknown but generally given as
about c. 50,000 to 55,000 years.

A Short Chronology of the History of Palaeontology in Africa

1863 C. E.   During the late 19th Century (1863) certain Europeans, such as
Boucher de Perthes, became aware of the missing link between man
and the so-called "lower primates."[4] Africa at that time was not considered to be of importance as a source of such fossil deposits, since
the African was not considered to be "human."[5] As a result, only
European and Asian fossils (man) were sought out for the possible
link between the so-called "Modern Man" and his original ancestors.
[Note: "Modern Man" is used here in the same sense as Professor
Jeffreys' terminology. It did not take into account all of mankind in
the world. The reference was to Europeans, and some Asians].

For centuries after Boucher de Perthes found half of a jawbone and
some stone tools of a **Pre-historic man,** not far from Abbeville in the
Moulin-Quignon quarry of France, it was believed that "ancient man"
stemmed from South-western Europe only. From this hypothesis
succeeding European and European-American anthropologists and
archaeologists pursued their research with contempt for any sugges-
tion that excavations for **fossil-man** should also be made in Africa and

87

or Asia.

1924 It was, however, not until 1924 that Dart discovered a skull which he called—"Australopithecus," having found it in Australia.[6] Because of Dart's find some researchers in the field turned their attention outside of Europe for a possible link between so-called "Modern Man" and his originators which did not include any part of Alkebu-lan.

1937 During 1937 in Java a Dutch geologist named Von Koenigswald found a fossil which he named "JAVA MAN." It was a complete skull, many thousands of years older than de Perthes' "Jawbone" find of 1863.

1856 The first skull (top half) that really caused alarm in European scientific circles was found in 1856 by workmen working in the Feldhofer Cave, between Dusseldorf and Elberfeld Germany, at the side of a ravine called Neanderthal. This discovery fell into the hands of one Dr. Fühlrett, who named it "Neanderthal Man" in recognition of the place where it was discovered. A description of this fossil was published in detail in a German scientific review under the name of the world renowned palaeontologist, Schaaffhausen.

1866 C. E. By 1865 the mad rush for further discoveries of prehistoric man was in full force. The high point was reached when Sir Charles Darwin published his book – THE ORIGIN OF MAN. Following Darwin was Huxley, Darwin's faithful follower, who established that the "Neanderthal skull was definitely the top-half of a human cranium." But he also claimed that it was "...much more primate in character than contemporary man..." of his era. Huxley's conclusion, one should recall, brought forward the intemperate vituperations of Bishop B. Wilberforce (an ultra-orthodox type Adam and Eve advocate of the Christian faith); the good Bishop proclaiming that he "...would rather be a perfected ape than a degenerate Adam..."[7] This comment, of course, seemed to have affected Huxley, as in latter years when the controversy increased he wrote of the same cranium being of a creature clearly "...intermediate between man and ape.." without any new theoretical reason given. Subsequently Huxley reversed himself completely. He went so far as to question if the cranium had any possibility whatsoever of being the intermediary link between "Modern Man" and his ancestors.

Huxley's confusion is to be understood when one considers the social and political climate raised by Bishop Wilberforce and his fellow religious bigots, who feared that their livelihood would have been taken away - had it been proven that the cranium was in fact "...MAN'S INTERMEDIARY LINK TO AN APELIKE ANCESTOR." At this juncture it must be noted that Darwin used the term "APE-LIKE;" not "APE."[8]

The confusion, as well as the persecution of all palaeontologists and their associates by the anti-scientific clergy, continued. However, the collection of human fossil remains also continued and accumulated into large numbers. A few are chronologically listed as follows, according to the date of their discovery.[9]

1864	A fossil-head was discovered and displayed before the British Museum Association. It is also identical with that of the Neanderthal. Yet, it was discovered in England.
1866	At La Naulette, not very far from the City of Liege in Belgium, a lower jaw of a much more ancient ["primitive"] appearance was discovered in an excavation in a cave.
1866	In 1866 in a cave at Spy, near Namur, two Belgian geologists - de Puydt and Lohest, discovered the skeletal remains of three men. Two of these skulls were almost intact, including some of their limb bones. These human remains were also mixed with some animal bones of the Mousterian period, giving rise to the dating of the age of the remains.
1908	The discovery of the complete skeleton of the "Neanderthal Man" by three abbes in France, and its analytical explanation by the palaeontologist Marcellin Boule made "Modern Man" understand the true nature of man in scientific terms for the first time. However, this did not change the narrow prejudices of the Europeans to look for fossils in Alkebu-lan as they were doing in Europe and Asia. For, Asia had by now become an acceptable area of research. A cranium with most of its jaw intact, similar to Neanderthal, was found in southern France.

1900	It was not until 1900 that Europeans and European-Americans engaged with the study of palaeontology decided to turn their attention towards Alkebu-lan [Africa] for possible discoveries. As such, they decided to look in Egypt, being that Egypt was closest to Europe. And for reasons that they would only find further remains of Europeans, whom they believed once wandered into Alkebu-lan from Europe before the Hyksos[10] and other periods prior to them.
1910	In 1910 the first two of more than forty different human-type skulls and limbs of fossil-man were discovered in Egypt. They were named "parapithecus fardi" and "propliopithesus hacekelli; the latter being a chimpanzee-like skull with jaw. They also have teeth that are extremely similar to "Modern Man," as observed at the turn of the twentieth century C.E.
1913	During 1913, by sheer accident, Homo capenses ["Boskop Man"] was discovered [unearthed] in Monomotapa [South Africa].[11] This discovery upset the entire RACIST and NON-SCIENTIFIC approach of European scientists towards Alkebu-lan and the indigenous African peoples. For it was then proven that ancient man, or man's link [fossil-man], was not exclusive to the regions of the shores along the Mediterranean Sea or Asia. That all over the Planet Earth such fossils were available. From this point of leverage the drive for further fossils in Alkebu-lan [Africa] advanced. As a result the following incomplete, but most representative of the available outstanding list of fossil-human and proto-human found in Alkebu-lan to date is copiled:[12]

1. **Parapithecus frasi,** Egypt 1910, unearthed by Max Schlosser. An African ape of more than 35 million years.

2. **Propliopithecus haeckelli,** Egypt 1910, unearthed by Max Schlosser. An African ape found at Fayoun, bigger than Parapithecus frasi, and related.

3. Homo capenses (Boskop Man) Monomotapa (South Africa), 1913.

4. Olduvai skeleton (Tanganyika, East Africa), 1914.

5. Homo **rhodesiensis** (Zambia), 1921 (colonial ''Northern Rhodesia).

6. **Australopihecus africanus** (Botswana, South Africa, Colonial Bechuanaland), 1924.

7. **Willey's Kopje skeletons** (Kenya, East Africa), 1927.

8. The **Elmenteita skeletons** (Kenya, East Africa), 1927.

9. **Parc Epic skull remains** (Ethiopia, East Africa), 1928.

10. The **Asselar skeleton** (Western Sudan, the Sahara, Colonial French Soudan), 1928.

11. The **Gamble's Cave skeletons** (Kenya, East Africa), 1928—1929.

12. **Proconsul africanus** (skeletal remains, Kenya, East Africa), 1931—48. An ape of about 20 million years ago, unearthed by Dr. Mary Leakey (a British archaeologist—just as her equally famous husband, Louis Leakey).[13] However, proconsul africanus, like parapithecus, belong to the most human-type ape found in Kenya. "Linnopithecus' molars" are strikingly similar to those of present day human.

13. **Homo Kanmensia** (Kenya, East Africa), 1932.

14. The **Kanjera skulls** (Kenya, East Africa), 1932.

15. The **Homo shell Mound skeletons** (Kenya, East Africa), 1932.

16. The **Rabat skull** (Morocco, North Africa), 1933.

17. **Africanthropus njarasensia** (Tanganyika, East Africa), 1936.

18. **Australopithecus transvaalensis** (Zulu Nation, colonial "Transvaal"—Monomotapa, South Africa), 1936.

19. **Plesianthropus transvaalensis** (Zulu Nation, colonial "Transvaal," Monomotapa, South Africa), 1936.

20. **Paranthropus robustus** (Zulu Nation, colonial "Transvaal," Monomotapa, South Africa), 1938.

21. **Tangier skull fragments** (Morocco, North Africa), 1939.

22. **Meganthropus africanus** (Tanganyika, East Africa), 1948.

23. **Paranthropus crassidens** (Zulu Nation, colonial "Transvaal," Monomotapa, South Africa), 1948.

24. **Telanthropus capensis** (Zulu Nation, colonial "Transvaal," Monomotapa, South Africa), 1949.

25. **Atlanthropus mauritanicus** (Algeria, North Africa), 1955—56.

26. **Zinjanthropus** (Tanganyika, East Africa), July 17, 1959; unearthed by Dr. Mary Leakey and Dr. Louis Leakey in Olduvai Gorge. Among the first of the tool-making hominids. Man's most possible prehistoric relative to date.

27. **Pre-Zinjanthropus** (Homo habilis), same as Zinjanthropus. Unearthed from the lowest bed of the Olduvai Gorge by Dr's. Louis and Mary Leakey. Rated at 1.8 million years old by the University of California new potassium-argon method test.[14]

28. **Chellean Man.** A skull found in the Olduvai Gorge in Tanganyika.[15] Named from the earlier Chellean Stage of the Lower Paleolithic Chelles-Acheul culture. It has a brain case larger than the Pithecanthropus from Peking, but not Homo Sapien. Approximately 500,000 years old.

29. **Pitecanthropine skull.** Of the Olduvai Gorge (Tanganyika, East Africa); found in various years.

30. **Skull fragments of the Acheulian industry from Kajera** (Western Kenya, East Africa) are still puzzling scientists as to their likeness to 20th century C. E.

man. Approximately 55,000 to 60,000 years old. Possibly the earliest of the true Homo sapiens in the world.

The pioneers and the pre-historians of East African archaeological findings were men such as E. J. Wayland, who used Uganda as the first East African area to gain attention. He was at the time Director of Uganda's Geological Survey soon after the first World War. He worked primarily on the cultural succession and past climatic changes of Africa; identifying the "Kafuan" pebble culture (presently descredited as being of human workmanship). His "Sangoan" and "Magosian" are names he selected from sites on the Kafu River, Sango Bay, on Mwanza Nyanza (colonial Lake Victoria) shores, including a water-hole called "MAGOSI" - in Karamoja [See ANNUAL RE-PORTS OF THE GEOLOGICAL SURVEY OF UGANDA and other journals by T. P. O'Brien 1939 for discoveries by E. J. Wayland].

A European Boer [Afrikaaner] settler in Monomotapa [South Africa], Professor C. Van Rist Lowe, in 1952, published the first detailed account of Africa's cultural sequence. It was basically concerned with Nsongezi on the Kagera River, the most ancient of the prehistoric site known in Uganda to date. However, the first European to visit this site was E. J. Wayland in 1930. Geologist W. W. Bishop and archaeologist M. Posmansky have also made extensive examination and rendered equally exhaustive interpretations of Uganda's archaeological past.

During 1926 a cultural anthropologist, and self-trained archaeologist, Dr. Louis S. B. Leakey began the first scientifically systematic investigation of the Stone Age Cultures of Kenya, East Africa.[0] His first archaeological expedition was in 1926 in the Nairraha-Nakura Lake Basin of the Rift Valley, where he noted the climatical changes and effects shown in his works. He was assisted by E. J. Wayland, and later on by the Swedish geologist E. Nilsson - who was on his own investigation of Kenya's Rift Valley.

In 1893 a geologist named J. W. Gregory noted that a formation of a large lake in the Rift Valley must have been in existence for thousands of years, accounting for the vast deposits of DIATOMITE accumulated in the Kamasian escarpment west of

[0]. Dr. Leakey was born in Kenya of English "Christian Missionary" parents. He was educated at Cambridge University, England. He became Curator of CORYNDOM MUSEUM, Nairobi, Kenya, which position he held until 1961.

Lake Bamngo and elsewhere. He also dated the Kamasian Lake to the Niocene period. However, Dr. Louis S.B. Leakey's hand axes were found imbeded in the lake deposite, thereby giving rise to its Pleistocene age.

In 1931 Dr. Leakey's book, THE STONE AGE CULTURES OF KENYA COLONY, was published. In this work the "blade-and-burin Culture, hand-axe Culture, flake-Culture," and the so-called "Mesolithic" and "Neolithic industries," were given full recognition. Within a period of five years Dr. Leakey had unearthed skeletal remains older than any other man had seen before. These remains were unearthed at Kanam and Kanjera in Western Kenya. [See L.S.B. Leakey, THE STONE AGE RACES OF KENYA, 1935].[0]

In 1913 the late Dr. Hans Reck, a German geologist, unearthed a skeleton at Olduvai Gorge, which was to him contemporary with the Middle Pleistocene deposits. Later on he found burial mounds in the Ngorongoro Crater, which also contained Skeletons, stone bowls, and beads, but no Stone-Age implements. In 1931 Dr. Leakey visited the Olduvai Gorge, and revisited it in 1932, at which time he found his astonishing skeletal remains. This discovery is to date only surpassed by his later findings in Tanzania [Tanganyika], East Africa. From here on it was a field-day for archaeologists and anthropologists: beginning with the 1935 L. Kohl-Larsen find of "fragments of a highly humanized skull" near the shores of Lake Eyasi, not too far from the Olduvai Gorge - from which H. Weinert created his new genus for "Africanthropus" [a name which soon after lost acknowledgement]. The "Eyasi Man," as the find was later called, was regarded as a relative of the "Rhodesia [Zimbabwe] Man" - a fossil found at Broken Hill in 1921 by African and European miners in the area.

In 1929-31 Seton-Karr found the "Acheulio-Sevallvisian" artifacts, which is the most ancient collection of its kind from the so-called "HORN" [located at approximately 90 mile southeast from Berbera, Somalia, at an area named "Issutugan," formerly called "British Somaliland," presently the Somali Republic]. C. Barrington found similar collections in Northeast Africa during 1931. In the same year A.T. Curle found some artifacts on the Hargeisa Plateau. [See Sonia Cole, THE PREHISTORY OF EAST AFRICA; also, Y. Gordon Childe, MAN MAKES HIMSELF].

---

[0]. Dr. Leakey was born in Kenya, East Africa, of British "Christian Missionary" parents. He was educated at Cambridge University, England. He became CURATOR OF CORYNDOM MUSEUM, Nairobi, Kenya, which position he held until 1961.

With respect to all of the scientists mentioned, and those not mentioned, it is still the Leakeys - Drs. Mary and Louis - who have made the most significant inroad on the "average man," so far as "prehistoric man" is concerned. Their unearthing of "ZIN-JANTHROPUS boisie" on July 17, 1959, on the slopes of Bed I of the Olduvai Gorge, Tanzania, East Africa, at a site known as "F. L. K.," has been to date the most outstanding find in the link of man [as we know him today] and his prehistoric ancestors of thousands, also millions, of years ago; the type of "MAN" Sir Charles Darwin Sr., the Victorian scientist, spoke about; superior in its MANLIKE qualities to "Rhodesia[0] [Zimbabwe] Man" in every respect.

It is in BED I [which contains VILLAFRANCHIAN FAUNA, as well as the AUSTRA-LOPITHECENES and the PEBBLE CULTURE which they produced] that Dr. Leakey found his "ZINJANTHROPUS" and "HOMO HABILIS" entombed at its base. One can only imagine the extent of the work that was necessary to collect the fragmented fossils, and the subsequent reconstruction to replace them in their original form, considering the expansion and contraction caused by the bentonitic clay in which the remains were trapped for so many thousands of years at a level exceeding more than twenty-one [21] feet below the top of Bed I. This substance, "bentonictic clay," is approximately forty [40] to forty-two [42] feet thick at the point of contact. Luckily the bones were not dis-torted in anyway; even the fragile pieces of the nasals were recovered in almost perfect condition.

Of course pre-Zinjanthropus type fossils were unearthed later on by the Leakeys [Louis and Mary], to which much of Zinjanthropus' glory must pass. The latter fossils appear to have been much more intelligent by far.[16] Note that this prehistoric fossil's name stems from "ZENJ BAR," an early name the Persian and Arabian invaders call-ed the East Coast of Africa. Thereby: "Zinjanthropus," or "MAN OF ZENJ BAR," "BLACK COAST MAN." "Boisie," at the end, is in honour of the financial sponsor of

---

[0]. It must be carefully noted that the name "RHODESIA MAN" is a grave insult to the African peoples; as CECIL RHODES, for whom the African land called "RHODESIA" was named, was to the African peoples as Adolph Hitler of Nazi Germany was to the European Jews. The correct name of the area is "ZIMBABWE," the name the African people named it before the first European arrived in Southeast Africa [Alkebu-lan]. This fossil-man should have been named "ZIMBABWE MAN." This is the only name this author will officially use for it, irrespective of the hypothetical maps shown by the RACIST European and European-American historians who have removed every trace of the so-called "NEGRO" and "BANTU" from even Southeast Alkebu-lan.

94

the many fossil searches in the area. Thus the name, "ZINJANTHROPUS BOISIE."

Although the Leakeys find is not the end to the link between man of the twentieth century C.E. [A.D.] and his most ancient ancestors, it is the evidence [so far] that sets Alkebu-lan [Africa] as the apparent home of man's origin - the so-called "GARDEN OF EDEN." Of course not the "GARDEN OF EDEN" spoken of in the Hebrew and Christian "Holy Books" [Torah or Old Testament] with the usual "FIG TREE" and "FORBID-EN FRUIT," etc. It is the "GARDEN OF EDEN" of man's evolution from prehistoric to historic HOMO SAPIENS.[17]

Note that the GLOSSARY at the beginning of this chapter is meant to familiarize the reader with the terminologies used in this chapter. It is student and general reader's advantage to secure an adequate dictionary for explanations of the anthropological, arch-aeological, and palaeontological name of fossil-man generally. One should find this type of follow-up study extremely beneficial to the overall understanding of the scientific disciplines already named. It will also help one to better understand one's own involve-ment in the universe as to the "GOD" and "EVOLUTION" arguments between scientists and theologians with respect to the origin of mankind.

Following on pages 96 and 97 the maps and charts shown are for the express pur-pose of highlighting the scenes or sites where fossil-man or fossil-men have been un-earthed in Alkebu-lan. In view of these locations, where Boskop Man, Zimbabwe [Rho-desia] Man, Broken Hill Man, Zinjanthropus boisie, and all of the other fossil finds, were located and unearthed, can one honestly conclude that Professor M.D.W. Jeffreys' claim that said finds are in fact "CAUCASIANS" or "MODERN MAN," which he also called "US," was rational? Equally, in looking back at the hypothetical maps by Dr. Wiedner, Dr. Churchward, and ben-Jochannan, can anyone equate either of them to the facts presented on the maps and graphs on pages 96 and 97? If so, ask yourself; why is it that "BLACK STUDIES" and "AFRICAN STUDIES" do not face the issues pre-sented here as RACISTLY oriented with respect to their presentation by certain so-called "ORTHODOX" and "LIBERAL WHITE AFRICANIST HISTORIANS, EGYPTOLO-GISTS, ANTHROPOLOGISTS," etc.

The bottom graph on page 97 shows a hypothetical chronology of the evolution of fossil-man to man, from LEMURS to HOMO SAPIENS. The arguments on ADAM AND EVE to "Modern Man" [all of mankind], a religious hypothesis, is equally as specula-tive; thus both of these theories remain solely BELIEFS , NOT FACTS.

KEY

A. Tropical Rain Forest
1. Mediterranean-type vegetation
2. Desert
3. Steppe & Semi-Desert
4. Highland Forest
5. Savanna (Savannah)
6. Woodland & Savanna
7. South vegetation

MAJOR VEGETATION ZONES

KEY

Diagonally crosshatched areas are highlands. (Locations "a" through "l" are the same as the map below).

0   300   1000
      Scale

HIGHLANDS MORE THAN 5,000 ft.
ABOVE SEA LEVEL

KEY

* 1. Broken Hill
* 2. Diredawa
* 3. Singna
* 4. Springbak (Tulnplaats)
* 5. Boskop
* 6. Hopefield
* 7. Tulnplaats
* 8. Vaal River region
* 9. Asselar
* 10. Mechta-el-Arbi
* 11. Rabat
* 12. Hau Fteah
* 13. Ngorongoro Crater

FOSIL FIELD MAIN SITES

KEY TO FOSSIL FIELD MAIN SITES ABOVE

[a] Gamble's Cave; [b] Olduvai and Eyasi; [c] Kanam and Kanjera; [d] Cape Flats and Fish Hoek; [e] Matjes River and Tzitzikama; [f] Florisbad; [g] Taung; [h] Sterkfrontein; [i] Makapansgat; [j] Sidi Abderrahman; [k] Ternifine; [l] Afalou-bou Rhummel.

The maps above are intended to give approximate locations of the sites and terrain. The highlands range from 5,000 to 19,000 plus feet elevation. They are drawn to the scale of 3/4" equal 1000 miles, unless otherwise shown - which reduced in the shooting of the pages for reproduction.

96

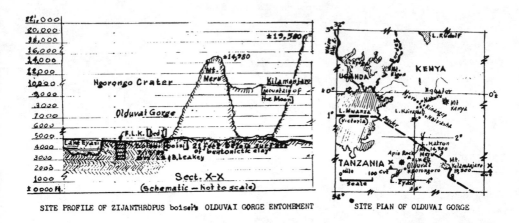

SITE PROFILE OF ZIJANTHROPUS boisei's OLDUVAI GORGE ENTOMEMENT   SITE PLAN OF OLDUVAI GORGE

Periods	TERTIARY				QUATENARY		Periods
Epochs	EOCENE	OLIGOCENE	MIOCENE	PLIOCENE	PLEISTOCENE	LATE-PRESENT	Comments
+ Lemurs	Lemurs	Lemurs	Lemurs	Lemurs	Lemurs	+ *
	Monkeys	Monkeys	Monkeys	Monkeys	Monkeys	+
	* Gibbons	Gibbons	Gibbons	Gibbons	Gibbons	1
		Orang-utan	Orang-utan	Orang-utan	Orang-utan	2
			Chimpanzee	Chimpanzee	Chimpanzee	3
		Gorilla	Gorilla	Gorilla		4 5
		Ape	Ape-Man Apelike-Man 1	Apelike-Man 2	Apelike-Man 4 (Missing transition between Ape-men and man) Man	

ZINJANTHROPUS boisei & 20th CENTURY C.E. MAN's EVOLUTION

PERIOD COMMENTS   PERIOD COMMENTS

+ Notharctus (a prehistoric lemuroid primate).

* Propliopithecus (a prehistoric ape).

✦ Drycpithecus (an ape with man-like characteristics and traits).

1 Pithecanthropus (commonly called "apeman").

2 Eoanthropus (so-called "dawn man").

3 Homo heidelbergensis.

4 Homo neanerthalensis .

5 Zinjanthropus boisi and other prehistoric Homo Sapiens, and man.

43,000 - YEAR-OLD MINE
discovered in Swaziland *

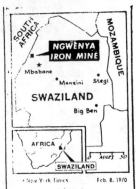

New York Times   Feb. 8, 1970

Special to The New York Times

JOHANNESBURG, South Africa, Feb. 7—South African archeologists have reported discovering the world's oldest mine. The mine, in an iron-ore mountain in neighboring Swaziland, is 43,000 years old, according to radio-carbon dating

It was discovered by Adrian Boshier, field research officer for the Museum of Man and Science in Johannesburg. Mr. Boshier made his discovery at Bomvu Ridge in the Ngwenya (Crocodile) mountain range in Swaziland.

He discovered caverns extending into the mountain and stone-age mining tools, indicating that, prehistoric man had been there mining hematite—a source of iron.

The early miners had excavated for hematite rich in specularite—one of the most prized pigments and cosmetics of ancient times, he said.

Mr. Boshier was joined by another young archeologist, Peter Beaumont, who excavated deeper. Mr. Beaumont found samples of charcoal from old fires. The samples were sent to radio carbon dating laboratories at Yale and Groningen

One can only wonder how soon it will be, if it has not yet happened, when some deciple of the Jeffreys' and Weidners lay claim to the above mine being the work of shipwrecked Caucasians or Semites as they did with respect to the RUINS OF ZIMBABWE. Of course it will be said that 'THE BANTUS [Negroes] HAD NOTHING WHATSOEVER TO DO WITH ITS OPERATION.' But as in all of their other denials of the indigenous African creations and development done below or "SOUTH OF THE SAHARA," this too will equal the Grimaldi skulls, Boskop Man and Zinjantropus boisie disclaimers.

> This accomplishment brings the greatest honor to the black
> race and merits, from the view point, all our attention. In the 16th
> Century, the Songhay land awoke. A marvelous growth of civiliza-
> tion mounted there in the heart of the Black continent....And this
> civilization was not imposed by circumstances, nor by an invader,
> as is often the case even in our own day. It was desired, called
> forth, introduced and perpetuated by a man of the Black race.

The above quotation was taken from Felix DuBois' [distinguish French authority of
African origin] major work, TIMBUCTOO THE MYSTERIOUS,[1] in which he was describing West African societies and High-Cultures [civilizations].

> When Arab merchants came to the Sudan, about 1000 A.D.,
> they already found a well-arranged system of commerce. When
> the Arabs first visited Negroland[2] by the Western route in the 8th
> and 9th centuries of our era, they found the black kings of Ghana
> in the height of their prosperity.

The comments we have just read were by the wife of the colonial imperialist who
designed and developed the theory of "INDIRECT RULE," Captain [Lord] Lugard, her
name - Lady Flora Shaw Lugard, prior to her marriage a newspaper writer for the
London Times.

> The virile peoples of the Western Sudan have always been
> distinguished for commercial enterprise, masterful ardour, and
> aptitude for the art of government. From the happy combination
> of these qualities there sprang a number of political States to
> which the grandoise style of empire is often loosely assigned.
> None, however, can challenge the fairness of its application to
> the great Mandingo Kingdom which is known as the empire of
> Mali or Mande, and is sometimes called the Mellestine.

The above comments were extracted from E.W. Bovill's, CARAVANS OF OLD
SAHARA, p. 67. Note that this work has since been revised under the title, THE
GOLDEN TRADE OF THE MOORS.

> For mine owne part, when I hear the Africans evil spoken
> of, I will affume my selfe to be one of Granada: and when I per-

---

"NEGROLAND," the word underscored in Lady Lugard's comments about Ghana, was a
creation of the imagination of the colonialist Europeans before Lady Lugard's era. It
was incorporated on maps by Europeans such as her husband. Captain [Lord] Lugard,
like Cecil Rhodes and King Leopold II of the Belgians, was responsible for the murder
of millions of Africans in South and West Africa. These men committed a type of genocide in Africa that was not equaled even by Adolph Hitler and his Nazis at the height of
their massacre of the European Jews. It is conservatively estimated that between them
they had killed more than 100 million Africans in their quest for control of the natural
resources of the Africans in their own continent - Alkebu-lan [AFRICA].

ceive the nation of Granada to be discommended, then I professe myselfe, to be an African.

The beauty of the Old English in which the above was written took nothing away from the manner in which Leo Africanus described his beloved Granada, Spain, and praised his African origin, as demonstrated in his book - THE HISTORY AND DESCRIPTION OF AFRICA [translated into English by John Pory, and edited by Dr. R. Brown, Hakluyt Society, London, England].[3]

> Forced to defend themselves against raids and eager to break the coastal monopoly on the import of European goods, notably firearms, the Fons of Dahomey broke through in the sea in 1724. They became a power with whom the Europeans had to reckon and soon learned to respect.

The above was written by Archibald Dazell in his book, HISTORY OF DAHOMEY, London, 1793, p. 60. Dazell was governor of the English trading station and castle at Cape Coast. He also spent four years at Quidah, where he came into personal contact with the newly rising nation of Dahomey [originally called DanHomey or DanHome].

> In Kilwa there are many strong houses several stories hing. They are built of stone and mortar and plastered with various designs. As soon as the town had been taken without opposition, the Vicar-General and some of the Franciscan fathers came ashore carrying two crosses in procession and singing the TEDEUM. They went to the palace, and there the cross was put down and the Grand-Captain prayed. Then everyone started to plunder the town of all its merchandise and provisions. Two days later d'Almeida fired the town, destroying, as the account in deBarros explains," the greater part of this city of abomination.

The above comments were extracted from Basil Davidson's book, THE AFRICAN PAST, p. 136; it dealt with the city of Kilwa, which is still located on Africa's East Coast. Note that the so-called "Christian missionaries," particularly the priests, and a "VICAR-GENERAL", acted in this case as the only true HEATHENS and UNCIVILIZED PEOPLE; or are we to assume that it is a CHRISTIAN ACT to "PLUNDER" and STEAL as long as the victims are not "European-style Christians"? What a touching Christian happening that must have been; "...THE FRANCISCAN FATHERS CAME ASHORE CARRYING TWO CROSSES" and led the pirates in prayer, as "...EVERYONE [of the civilized Modern Men] STARTED TO PLUNDER THE [uncivilized Africans] TOWN OF ALL ITS MERCHANDISE AND PROVISIONS." This is a befitting story of the type of "CIVILIZING" and "CHRISTIANIZING" that the "Christian Missionaries" did in all of the conquered African nations, and to a great extent still do.

100

Tnere is another habitation of Moores two Caliver shot from the Castle, poore and misserable, which live by serving the Portugals. The women performe there the offices of Tillage and Husbandry; as also do the Moores. They pay their tithes to the Dominicans Church. The fortress was built in 1505 by Pero da Nhaya, with consent of the Moorish King Zufe, a man blinde of both his eyes [in both senses, externall and internall; religious and politike] who too late repenting, thought to supplant it with trecherie, which they returned upon himselfe and slew him. In old times they had petty Moorish Kings on the coast, few of which remaine by reason of the Portugal Captaynes succeeding in their places, and in their amitie and commerce with the Quitene King of these countries.

The above remarks are from a Dominican Priest, Joa dos Santos, first-hand confession in his book, ETHIOPIA ORIENTAL, as translated into English in Purchas,' HIS PILGRIMS [reprinted in Glassgow, 1905], Vol. 9; also in J. Pinkerton's, A GENERAL COLLECTION OF THE MOST INTERESTING VOYAGES AND TRAVELS, Vol. 16, London, 1814.

In the remarks we have noted that the word "MOORS" or "MOORES" is used to represent all Africans of the Muslim [Moslem] religion - also called Islam. That Father Joa dos Santos, who wrote the earliest reports known on Central Africa by a European, himself a Dominican Priest of the Roman Cat' 'ic Church, first visited Alkebu-lan's East Coast in 1596 C.E.; and served in Sofala until 1590 C.E. He made extensive travels to Zambezi and Tete, also Monomotapa [at the seat of government in Zimbabwe - the Portugals called it Zimboae]. Upon his return to Portugal he remained for approximately ten [10] years; some European writers contend that it was eleven [11] years. He returned to Alkebu-lan, which he seemed not able to resist, where he wrote his ETHIOPIA ORIENTAL in 1609 C.E., and published it in Evora, and was later translated into English. The Muslim inhabitants of Alkebu-lan, all of them, were called MOORES before dos Santos. Yet, the majority of these peoples of East Alkebu-lan were later called "SWAHILIS" by European colonialist historians and the so-called "Christian Missionaries." They did likewise during the same period dos Santos wrote his work, in which one can see a Roman Catholic priest first-hand recording of how his church's representatives engaged in the RAPE of the African peoples and Africa [Alkebu-lan]. This is only one aspect of the many reasons why this author labored so much on the history of the "PLANTING OF CHRISTIANITY" - European style - in Alkebu-lan earlier in this work.

I the Emperor Monomotapa, think fit and pleased to give to
his majesty all the mines of gold, copper, iron, lead and pewter
which may be in my empire, so long as the King of Portugal, to
whom I give the said mines, shall maintain me in my position...."

The above quotation was allegedly written by the Monotuepa [Monomotapa] on 1
August, 1607 C.E. through a Portuguese named Simoes to the King of Portugal. Diogo
Simoes was at the time KEEPER OF THE ARCHIVES AND CHRONICLER OF INDIA
under Portuguese colonial rule. He was followed in his post by another Portuguese,
Antonio Bocarro, whose work was translated into English in Theal's, RECORDS OF
SOUTH EASTERN AFRICA, Vol. 3, 1900. This part of the work dealt with at least one
aspect of the manner in which Portugal and her colonialist exploiters [followed by
other Europeans and European-Americans later] otherwise called "EXPLORERS" and
"DISCOVERERS," got fabulously wealthy by way of gun powder and the use of the
"CHRISTIAN RELIGION" - European style [including its priests and layity].

Speaking about "archives;" the following data from the British Museum Archives
should prove quite an interesting point on which to examine certain "TRUTHS" - as
stated in the Hebrew [Jewish] Torah and Christian Bible. It is a document that was
surrendered to the Museum by the late "...world famous egyptologist... " Sir Ernest
A. Wallis Budge, who became the work's first editor. Note the striking similarity that
exists between the papyrus titled "THE TEACHINGS OF AMEN-EM-EOPE" and the
"PROVERBS OF SOLOMON" [in the so-called "Canonical Books"].

Before reading excerps from these two works the reader must remember that King
Solomon of Israel was not known to have written any literary work before mounting the
Hebrew throne during the year c. 970 B.C.E. - which was during the period of the XXI
st Dynasty of Ta-Merrian [Egyptian] rule. The papyrus, on the otherhand, was found to
have been written during c. 1000 B.C.E., at least 31 years before Solomon mounted
the throne of Israel [Palestine] - and before he was credited with writing the "PRO-
VERBS."

The following revelations should be of no supprise to anyone who has studied the
religious history of the Haribu [Hebrew or "Jewish"] peoples from the time of Abraham
to the beginning of the so-called "Christian Era." Those who have done research in this
area are fully aware of the fact that the basic "MOSAIC LAWS" [Commandments and
Diety concepts] came from the training Moses, himself an African of Ta-Merry [Egypt],
received in the LAWS OF THE MYSTERIES SYSTEM while he was a boy, and later as a
102

grown man in Alkebu-lan [Africa]. This is according to the oldest documents about the Hebrew religion, as recorded by Moses himself in his own BOOK OF EXODUS, one of the so-called "FIVE BOOKS OF MOSES" of "HOLY TORAH," otherwise known as the Christian OLD TESTAMENT - any version.

THE COMPARATIVE WORKS [4]

ISRAEL (Asia-Minor)	EGYPT (North-Africa)
PROVERBS XXII. 17-XXIII. 14;	THE TEACHINGS OF AMEN-EM-OPE
The "teachings of King Solomon" of Israel	Pharoah of Egypt

1. Incline thine ear, and hear my words,
   And apply thine heart to apprehend;
   For it is pleasant if thou keep them in thy belly,
   That thy may be fixed like a peg upon thy lips.

1a. Give thine ear, and hear what I say,
   And apply thine heart to apprehend;
   It is good for thee to place them in thine heart,
   Let them rest in the casket of thy belly.
   That they may act as a peg upon thy tongue.

2. Have I not written for thee thirty sayings
   Of counsels and knowledge!
   That thou mayest make known truth to him that speaketh.

2a. Consider these thirty chapters;
   They delight, they instruct.
   Knowledge how to answer him that speaketh,
   And how to carry back a report to one that sent him.

3. Rob not the poor for he is poor,
   Neither oppress the lowly in the gate.

3a. Beware of robbing the poor,
   And of oppressing the afflicted.

4. Associate not with a passionate man,
   Nor go with a wrathful man,
   Lest thou learn his ways
   And get a snare to thy soul.

4a. Associate not with a passionate man,
   Nor approach him for conversations;
   Leap not to cleave to such a one,
   That the terror carry thee not away

5. A man who is skillful in his business
   Shall stand before Kings.

5a. A scribe who is skillful in his business
   Findeth himself worthy to be a courtier.

The above comparisons are but a choice few of the selected sayings of the entire so-called "PROVERBS OF KING SOLOMON" of Israel, which have been earmarked for cross reference. However, the entire PSALMS ["Songs of Solomon"], and all of the HOLY TORAH generally, are full of direct copies of works written WORD-FOR-WORD as their African [Egyptian, Nubian, Ethiopian, Meroite, etc.] sayings and teachings. This should not be supprising to anyone, since Moses and most of the earliest Haribus [Hebrews or Israelites later on] in GENESIS and EXODUS were all Africans. They were all born in Ta-Merry,[5] Ethiopia [the Falashas], and Ta-Nehisi [Nubia]. Even the theory of "MONOTEISM," the belief of "ONE GOD" above all others, was taught in Ta-Nehisi [Nubia], Ta-Merry [Egypt], and Itiopi [Ethiopia] before the birth of Moses by the Pharaoh Akhenaten [Amen-hotep IV], c. 1370-1352 B.C.E. Moses did not live until the reign of Pharaoh Rameses I, c. 1340-1320 B.C.E. or Seti I, c. 1318-1298 B.C.E. For it was during the period of the reign of Pharaoh Rameses II, c. 1298-1232 B.C.E., at which time Moses was allegedly more than "NINETY [90] YEARS OLD," that one is to hear of Moses receiving the so-called "TEN COMMANDMENTS" from the Haribu God - "JEHOVAH, ON MOUNT SINAI."

These literal translations are extracted from very much older versions and less complex conservative texts than the presently revised versions of the Hebrew Holy Torah [Christian Old Testament]. Professor W.O.E. Oesterley had been given the greatest amount of credit by leading scholars in this field, with respect to his first-hand research and revelations on this particular point in literature, which influenced other noted historians and theologians to equally observe and examine the mythology of certain alleged "HEBREW ORIGINS." Besides the works of Professor Oesterley, the following specialized bibliography on the "COMPARATIVE WORKS" [Solomon and Amen-em-eope] should be of particular benefit to the researcher and student who desire to delve deeper into this area of biblical history and mythology:

Griffith, THE WORLD'S BEST LITERATURE, 1897
Esman, DIE LITERATUR der AGYPTER, 1897
Griffith, Ranke [in: Gressman], Sange, DAR WEISBEITSBUCH des AMEN-EN-EOPE, 1925. [English translation: "Amen-em-eope Teachings"]
Blackman's Essay in "THE PSALMISTS," [edited by D.C. Simpson], 1926
ben-Jochannan, Y. AFRICAN ORIGIN OF THE MAJOR "WESTERN RELIGIONS," 1971
Hooke, S.H. [ed.], MYTH AND RITUAL, 1933
Blackman's English Translation of Die LITERATUR der AGYPTER, 1923
Cook, S.A. THE RELIGION OF ANCIENT PALESTINE IN THE LIGHT OF ARCHAE-OLOGY, 1930
Buchler, DIE TOBIADEN und die ONIADEN, 1899
Cowley, JEWISH DOCUMENTS OF THE TIME OF EZRE, 1919
"ARAMAIC PAPRI OF THE FIFTH CENTURY B.C., 1923
Peet, EGYPT AND THE OLD TESTAMENT, 1922
Osterly and Robinson, A SHORT HISTORY OF ISRAEL, 1934
Jack, J.W. THE DATE OF THE EXODUS, 1925
Breasted, J.H. ANCIENT RECORDS OF EGYPT: THE HISTORICAL DOCUMENTS, 1905
-------- THE DAWN OF CONCIENCE, 1934
Smith, H.W. MAN AND HIS GODS, 1953
Frazier, Sir J. THE GOLDEN BOUGH, [13 vols.], 1922
Wallis Budge, Sir E.A. THE BOOK OF THE DEAD, 1895
------------ OSIRIS, 1920

As we continue our safari into the annals of Alkebu-lan's colonial past we find Sir John Harris explaining Cecil Rhodes' economic motives in the following manner:

> "It was the scintilating gleam of gold in the rock-strewn ground of Matableland that forced Sir Starr Jamason's hand and compelled him to invade the Matabele from Fort Victoria," and adds, " the effect of this impact upon the backward peoples has always been acutely violent; coupled with bloodshed and cruelty upon an atrocious scale."[6]

The above remarks were extracted from Sir John Harris,' SLAVERY OR SACRED TRUST?, p. 68, a work that reveals quite a lot of the ghastly acts of genocide committed by the European slavers and colonialist settlers against the indigenous African peoples [the so-called"UNCIVILIZED HEATHEN NATIVES"] for over three hundred years.

Sir Godfrey Higgins, Premier and Minister of Native Affairs of Rhodesia, addressing the COLONIAL OVERSEAS LEAGUE in London, England, 12 July, 1934, stated:

> It is time for the people in England to realize that the white man in Africa is not prepared and never will be prepared to accept the African as an equal, socially or politically.

Strange as it may seem, the RACIST colonialists, other imperialist murderers, and masters of genocide, who took turn in exterminating the indigenous African peoples, often debased each other in the process. In the following quotation from William Polmer's, CECIL RHODES, p. 73, with respect to his conversation with Boer President Kruger's estimation of Rhodes; he wrote:

> "Rhodes was one of the most unscrupulous characters that ever lived;...No matter how debase, no matter how contemptible; be it lying, bribery or treachery, all and every means were welcomed subjects."

If an African historian or any other kind of recorder had written this type of indictment against the Adolph Hitler of Alkebu-lan, Cecil Rhodes, it would have been rejected as a piece of unscholarly nonsense. But the same Cecil Rhodes is the man for whom the "RHODES SCHOLARSHIP" is named. This type of infamy is equivalent to naming a fellowship 'THE ADOLPH EICHMAN SCHOLARSHIP' and offering it to Jewish students. Shamefully enough African and other BLACK students often accept "RHODES SCHOLARSHIP."

Sir Godfrey Higgins, already mentioned, had continued further with his expressed RACISM during a much later speech on 30 March, 1938, to his fellow White colonialist settlers at Bulawayo, Zimbabwe [so-called "Rhodesia"].[7] He referred to the White

settlers community as:

> ..... An island of white in a sea of black, with the white artisans
> and tradesmen forming the shores and the white professional
> classes the highlands. Was the native to be allowed to erode the
> shore and gradually attack the highlands? To permit this would
> mean that the leaven of civilization would be removed and that
> the blacks would inevitably revert to barbarism, because the
> ancient control, such as tribal authority, had gone never to re-
> turn, leaving only the white man's law, religion and example.
> While there was yet time and space, the country must be divid-
> ed into separate white and black areas.
> In the white areas the natives would be welcomed, but on
> the understanding that he merely assist and not compete with the
> white man. Native education should be by missions and not by
> the State till natives had a background of Christianity.

Sir Godfrey Higgins' position of the early 1900's still expresses the general feel-

ings common among the White man in Africa, and to a great extent in the United States

of America, to date; and of course, the same holds true with respect to the so-called

"Christian Missionaries, who will like to continue selling their European and European-

American version of economic capitalism and religious bigotry as "CHRISTIANITY."

The contempt for the Africans - "THE NATIVES" - [black-skinned peoples] became so

intense that certain White "Jewish" writers specializing on the so-called "Ghetto" or

"Inner-City" blacks, themselves not too long removed from servitude and the RACIAL

SCORN of their fellow Europeans and European-Americans [the Christians, and others],

have endorsed the following by G.C. Seligman, written in 1924:

> ..... It would be very wide of the mark to say that the history of
> Africa South of the Sahara is no more than the story of the per-
> meation through the ages, in different degrees and at various
> times, of the Negro and Bushman aboriginals by Hamitic blood
> and culture.

One should be able to observe that the type of theories like that stated above by

Seligman are those that created the type of RACIST and RELGIOUSLY BIGOTED posi-

tion by Sir Godfrey Higgins in 1938, and Adolph Hitler earlier in 1936 C.E. Such reck-

lessly loose remarks were still the order of the day, and they still linger on in the

works of the Professor Jeffreys, Dr. Wiedners, and others of their projection at pre-

sent -the latter part of the 20th Century C.E. What is "HAMITIC BLOOD"? Is it pos-

sible that the Black Peoples of Alkebu-lan sprung up from a 'MYTHICAL JEWISH AN-

106

CESTOR' by the name of "HAM"? And, that the story shown on page 12 of this volume, relative to the origin of the "NEGROES," is still the prevalent view of the African peoples that frighten the President of the United States of America on "BUSSING", and the White Jews of Forrest Hills, New York City, on "PUBLIC HOUSING"? The unquestionable fact is that African [BLACK] peoples existed thousands upon thousands' of years before the first Haribu [Hebrew or "Jew"] - Abraham was ever heard of. African societies ["civlizations"] or High-Cultures existed an equal amount of time before the story of "...ADAM AND EVE" and the "...CREATION OF THE WORLD..." by the Haribu God - Jehovah in the BOOK OF GENESIS [the First Book Of Moses, Holy Torah, or Old Testament of the Christians]. Source materials on this point are almost limitless; therefore, no one, who attended school, should be ignorant of them. At least, no professor of history or cultural [social] anthropology should be ignorant of the existence of these FACTS, though, it may be economically, socially or politically more feasible to support the "BIG LIE" than to teach the "TRUTH" about the indigenous Africans and Africa [Alkebu-lan] - the so-called "NEGRO" or BLACK AFRICAN and his or her continent.

In all of the vileness perpetuated against Alkebu-lan ["Mother Africa"] and her indigenous peoples [North, South, East, West, and Central, every last inch of Alkebu-lan], a few voices in White ["Caucasian"] Europe and European-America , the United States of America particularly, still managed to speak in praise of Alkebu-lan's GLORY, such as James Montgomery's poems of 1841 C.E. , one in which he wrote:

> Unutterable mysteries of fate
> Involve, O Africa!, Thy future state
> Dim through the night of these tempestuous years
> A Sabbath dawn o'er Africa appears;
> Then shall her neck from Europe's yoke be freed,
> And healing arts to be hideous arms succeed;
> at home fraternal bonds her tribes shall bind,
> Commerce abroad espouse them with mankind.

Ancient and modern European and Asian "greats" who worshipped and praised Africa and the Africans did so orally, as well as in their writings. Some samples of their writings follow.

Pleny quoted an ancient Greek saying in his book, ROMAN HISTORY, written sometime between the years c. 23 and c. 79 C.E. , thus:

> ... EX AFRICA SEMPER ALIQUID NOVI...

The English traslation of the above quotation:

"Out of Africa comes something always new."

Always, of late, we speak of what the Arabs and Islam gave to the indigenous Africans; here we see the reverse, as we read an ancient Arabian saying:

"HE WHO HAS DRUNK FROM THE WATERS OF AFRICA
WILL DRINK AGAIN.

In a similar light we see the world noted literary great of Great Britain, Sir William Shakespeare, saying the following in his HENRY IV, v. III:

" I SPEAK OF AFRICA AND GOLDEN JOYS."

The honoured English physician and author, Sir Thomas Browne, 1605-1682 C.E., wrote the following:

"THERE IS AFRICA AND HER PRODIGIES IN US."

Sir Thomas' comments were stretched somewhat by the following from Dr. Victor Robinson, author of CIBA SYMPOSIA, 1940, who felt obliged to say:

It is one of the paradoxes of history that Africa, the Mother of Civilisation, remained for over two thousand years the Dark Continent.[8] To the moderns Africa was the region where ivory was sought for Europe, and slaves for America. In the time of Johathan Swift [1667 - 1745], as the satirist informs us, geographers in drawing African maps would fill in the gaps with savage pictures. Where towns should have been they placed elephants.

"WHERE TOWN SHOULD HAVE BEEN THEY PLACED ELEPHANTS;" and WHERE INDIGENOUS AFRICANS WERE, and ARE, THEY PLACED "SEMITES, HAMITES, CAUCASIANS, BANTUS, NEGROES, HOTTENTOTS, BUSHMEN," and a host of other creations to satisfy their RELIGIOUS BIGOTRY and RACIST HYPOTHESIS. But the writer of the book, HISTORY OF NATIONS, Vol. 18, p. 1, 1906, saw Alkebu-lan in the following manner, as he wrote:

The African continent is no recent discovery; it is not a new word like America or Australia... While yet Europe was the home of wandering barbarians one of the most wonderful civilizations on record had begun to work its destiny on the banks of the Nile....

The crux of the de-NEGROZATION or de-AFRICANIZATION of North and East Africa by so-called "White Liberal" and "White Orthodox" AUTHORITIES ON AFRICA AND AFRICANS is shown in its major projection in the underscored quotation above. This is one of the many reasons why BLACK STUDIES and AFRICAN STUDIES must remain under the control of European and European-American [White or Caucasian] AU-

THORITY, and books of the early 19th Century C.E. and before prasing Africa and her sons and daughters must be suppressed in favor of the moderated RACIST works by so-called "WHITE LIBERAL AFRICANISTS" who pretend to be the friend of their so-called "NEGROES;" allegedly,on the premise that "...THEY TOO SUFFERED LIKE THE NE-GROS" and "...BELONG TO A MINORITY." But,the Africans are not deceived by any of these statements by any group, be they a MINORITY or the MAJORITY of White America.

Count C.F. Volney, who visited Ta-Merry [Egypt, Kimit, Sais, Pearl of the Nile, etc.] in c. 1787 C.E., unlike those Orthodox and Modern Liberal AFRICANISTS, wrote that the Greek citizen of Ionian birth - Herodotus, the "father of European history," solved for him the problem of why the people [Africans, Niggers, Negroes," etc.] of Egypt were so "...BLACK AND WOOLLY-HAIRED...;" and especially the Great Sphinx of Ghizeh [Giza] - the SUPREME SYMBOL OF WORSHIP AND POWER. Reflecting on how he, on his trip, met the State of Egypt in its reduced image and grandeur, the Count wrote:

> To think that a race of black men who are today our slaves
> and object of our contempt is the same one to whom we owe our
> arts, sciences and even the very use of speech.

It is needless to underline any part of the above for specific emphasis; but, the reader should understand why the works of Count Volney, and others like him, are sup-pressed throughout the United States of America, thus they cannot be taught.

Of the indigenous Blacks of Alkebu-lan, Africa, Count Volney saw in the ruins of the Colossal Monuments in Upper Egypt [once a part of Lower Ta-Nehisi or Nubia, also called Zeti], he wrote the account of praises to the Africans shown on the first page of this Chapter.[9] [See VOLNEY'S RUINS OF EMPIRE, pp. 16 - 17, c. 1890; also OEUVRES, vol. 2, pp. 65 - 68, c. 1825].

Two other respected European scholars of Volney's era, who saw the Sphinx of Ghizeh, Baron Viviant Denon and Gustav Flaubert, expressed similar opinions. In par-ticular Denon, who made a first-hand sketch of the Sphinx in c. 1798 C.E., as shown page 111, wrote that:

> THE CHARACTER IS AFRICAN...THE LIPS ARE THICK...
> ART MUST HAVE BEEN AT A HIGH PITCH WHEN THIS MONUMENT
> WAS EXECUTED.

[From Baron Viviant Denon, TRAVELS IN UPPER AND LOWER EGYPT, vol. I, p. 115, - 1910].

Gustave Flaubert indentified the Sphinx' African group in 1849 when he noted that:

IT IS CERATINLY ETHIOPIAN. THE LIPS ARE THICK...," etc.

Flaubert's comment was extracted from his book, NOTES de VOYAGE, p. 115 [1910]; Baron Denon's first-hand sketch of the Sphinx appears on pages   and   of this volume. It is to be noted that the "BLACK" and "THICK LIPS," also "WOOLLY HAIR" and "BROAD NOSE," ascribed to the early Egyptians, Nubians, Ethiopians, and other North and East Africans[10], were commonly used by the ancients of Europe and Asia in describing all of the indigenous peoples of North and East Africa, just as they did for others who came from the West, South, and Central parts.

In the year 1910 C.E. a German scholar and explorer named Leo Frobenius furthered Count C.F. Volney's work, as he influenced the recording of Alkebu-lan history by subsequent European scholars who took a completely new posture because of his own deep researches and writings on, and about, the African peoples. In his most basic work, UND AFRIKA SPRACH [English translation: The Voice of Africa, or Africa Speaks], Leo Frobenius urged his fellow colleagues to:

LET THERE BE LIGHT!
LIGHT IN AFRICA. IN THAT PORTION OF THE GLOBE·TO WHICH
THE STALWART ANGLO-SAXON STANLEY GAVE THE NAME
'DARK' AND 'DARKEST'. LIGHT UPON THE PEOPLE OF THAT
CONTINENT WHOSE CHILDREN WE ARE ACCUSTOMED TO RE-
GARD AS TYPES OF NATURAL SERVILITY WITH NO RECORDED
HISTORY. [BUT] THE SPELL HAS BEEN BROKEN. THE BURIED
TREASURES OF ANTIQUITY AGAIN REVISIT THE SUN.

On Leo Frobenius' comment this chapter can be brought to its conclusion, even though it has barely touched the surface of the overwhelming amount of data dealing with praises for ALKEBU-LAN [Africa] and her sons and daughters [children]. However, the data in the following chapters will more than explain many of the other laudatory comments which cannot be dwelt upon in this volume because of space and time. Of course, there is an equal amount of adverse comments against Alkebu-lan and her indigenous sons and daughters down through the ages. However, the general public has only heard the adverse comments in the past, not knowing that the opposite exists, or caring one iota about the cultural genocide that the Africans suffer at the hands of Europeans and European-Americans [irrespective of religious affiliation, economic circumstance, or political attachment] over the last three to four hundred years; from the vicious SLAVE TRADE of c.1503 - 1865 C.E., and the wantom PARTITION OF ALKEBU-LAN to the BERLIN COFERENCE - c. 1830 - 1884 C.E.

The Sphinx of Gizeh as it appeared to Baron Denon in 1798 C.E., from one of his own drawings he made first hand. Note the relative indigenous African characteristics - nose, lips, etc. This was the way it appeared before Napoleon's soldiers blew its face assunder in distaste of its "Negroid looks."This took place during France's invasion of Egypt.

Note: Why was this picture witheld from students and the general public?

Akhet Khufu
[Horizon of khufu]

The Sphinx as it appears in 1970; showing the temple and dream-stele.

*[Partial English translation]

"The Great King, Monomotapa. Very powerful and rich in gold. Several kings are tributary to him. His territory comprises Lower Ethiopia....His empire is very large and has a cicuit of 2,400 miles. His court is at Zimboae. There are women in his guard...He has a great number of them in his army which give great help to the men. He also has a great number of elephants. His subjects are black, brave and swift runners, and he has very fast horses. Idolators, sorcerers, and thieves are severely punished."

BIBLIOGRAPHY FOR CHAPTER III

Dazells, Archibald, HISTORY OF DAHOMEY, London, 1793.

dos Santos, Joa, "Ethiopia Oriental" (In: Purchas, HIS PILGRIMS, vol. 9, Glassgow, 1905

Pinkerton, J., A GENERAL COLLECTION OF THE BEST AND MOST INTERESTING VOYAGES AND TRAVELS, vol. 16, London, 1814.

Theal, G. M. RECORDS OF SOUTH EASTERN AFRICA, vol. III, 1900.

Pleny, ROMAN HISTORY

Flaubert, NOTES de VOYAGE, 1910

DuBois, Felix, TIMBUCTOO THE MYSTERIOUS

Bovills, E. W., CARAVANS OF OLD SAHARA

Lugard, Lady Flora S., A TROPICAL DEPENDENCY

Africanus, Leo, A HISTORY AND DESCRIPTION OF AFRICA., (translated by John Pory to English; edited by Dr. R. Brown, Hakluyt Society).

Davidson, Basil, THE AFRICAN PAST, New York, 1964.

Wallis Budge, Sir E. A., BOOK OF THE DEAD, New York, 1959

--------, THE TEACHINGS OF AMEN-EM-EOPE, (Papyrus collections. Written about 1001 B. C. E. or earlier).

Harris, Sir John, SLAVERY OR SACRED TRUST

Polmer, William, CECIL RHODES

Shakespeare, William, HENRY IV, London

Robinson, Dr. Victor, CIBA SYMPOSIUM

Volney, Count C., RUINS OF EMPIRE, 1789 (Latest edition 1950)

Denon, Baron, TRAVELS IN LOWER AND UPPER EGYPT, vol. I, 1803

Frobenius, Leo, UND AFRICA SPRACH

Chapter IV: <u>ANOTHER LOOK AT NUBIA, MEROE, EGYPT, ETHIOPIA, ETC.</u>

<u>Introduction</u>

> Nubia. The lands of the south of Egypt were inhabited by less
> civilized people who were good soldiers. They were rich in
> gold, good quality stone, hard wood, and large cattle. They
> formed the gateway to central Africa, whence came ivory,
> strange animals and pygmies.

The above quotation is taken from the ENCYCLOPEDIA OF EGYPTIAN CIVILIZA-

TION, p. 191, under the heading of "NUBIA." This RACIST proclamation is typical of

most "ACADEMICIANS'"works on Egypt, with respect to other areas of Alkebu-lan

[Africa]. It was rehatched by the General Editor, Georges Posener [professor at the

Colege de France], with the assistance of Serge Saumeron and Jean Yoyette, et al, and

published by Tudor Publishing Company, New York. Of course, this "ENCYCLOPEDIA'

displays pictures and inscriptions from the tombs [pyramids, etc.] of many pharaohs

and viceroys, dipicts the Nubians only as "TRIBUTE BEARERS" and "SLAVES" for the

Ta-Merrians [Egyptians], but never the relationship is shown in the reverse - the Ta-

Merrians equally being "TRIBUTE BEARERS" and "SLAVES" for the Ta-Nehisians

[Nubians]. It ignores the latter aspect totally and purposefully, while at the same time

adding to the further suppression of pertinent evidence showing the commonality be-

tween the Nile Valleys [Blue and White] indigenous people and their High-Cultures

[civilizations] that came about before the creation of "ADAM AND EVE" and the Hebrew

God - Jehovah by Moses, and indigenous African of Ta-Merry. Yet, the editors could

not avoid showing pictures that depicted the Ta-Nehisians [Nubians or Zetis] being

equally dressed as the Ta-Merrians, better jeweled, knowledgeable of the wheel and

the chariot bounded, and oviously in control of greater material wealth than their north-

ern neighbors and fellow Africans, the Ta-Merrians [Egyptians] of the same period.

To imply that only certain basic NATURAL MATERIALS, of course produced by

the so-called "PYGMIES," came to Ta-Merry from her SOUTHERN NEIGHBOURS is

not only prejudicial to the "TRUTH;" it is a deliberate attempt at injecting and project-

ing European and European-American WHITE CAUCASIANISM and SEMITICISM, in

other words - RACISM, under the disguise of "ACADEMIC SCHOLARSHIP," into the

history of the ancient indigenous peoples of the continent of Alkebu-lan [Africa] - the

so-called "NEGROES, BANTUS, AFRICANS SOUTH OF THE SAHARA, BLACK AFRI-

CANS," of which they were totally unaware.

114

In the first place, where along the entire more than 4100 miles long Nile River Valley can anyone of the European and European-American "AUTHORITIES ON AFRICA" pinpoint the ancient "DIVIDING LINE" or "BOUNDARY" between Ta-Merry and Ta-Nehisi before the IVth Dynasty, c. 2680 - 2565 B.C.E., also for Meröe and Itiopi [Ethiopia, sometimes called Kush]? Obviously, such a "LINE," as established in the mind of the many hundreds of "White Liberal" and "Orthodox AUTHORITIES ON AFRICA," and "THINGS AFRICAN," is as numerous in location as there are volumes of books and treatises dealing with this subject area. And, to expect that they will cease establishing new ones because of the protest in this work, or other works of this kind, would be hopeless wishful thinking to the enth degree on the part of the believer. The present "DEMARCATION" at the Second Cataract as a beginning point for Ta-Nehisi [Nubia or Zeti] is totally rediculous, and without foundation, when in fact the "NOME OF ELEPHANTINE" [Aswan] was always mentioned by the ancients of Ta-Merry, and other Nile Valley people, as being the "TERRITORY OF THE TA-NEHISIANS." For, it was not until very much later in history before it was observed that the FIRST PHA-RAOH of the FIRST DYNASTIC PERIOD, Pharaoh Aha or Narmer, also called Mena [Herodotus' Menes], came from UPPER TA-NEHISI [Nubia] and unified LOWER TA-NEHISI with UPPER and LOWER TA-MERRY [Egypt, around the Delta region]. This HISTORICAL FACT caused the "egyptologists" and other so-called "White Liberal Africanists" to impose their "FIRST CATARACT BOUNDARY LINE" between Ta-Merry and Ta-Nehisi south of the First Cataract to justify their own RACIST hypothesis of an all "CAUCASIAN" and "SEMITIC" North and East Africa, especially Ta-Merry. But, this type of RACISM is related directly to the type of material one reads in the ENCYCLOPEDIA OF EGYPTIAN CIVILIZATION, which was originally published in the French language as the "DICTIONNARIE de la CIVILISATION EGYPTIENNE [edited by Fernand Hazan], Paris, 1959.

The European and European-American historians and egyptologists of the "CAUCASIAN" and/or "SEMITIC" schools have conveniently forgotten that COMMERCIAL, as well as SOCIAL and SEXUAL, intercourse among all of the indigenous Nile Valley [Blue and White] Africans were commonplace before the first of the so-called "WHITE CAU-

Note: Ancient Egypt was called "KIMIT, SAIS, PEARL OF THE NILE," etc. before it was given its present misnomer in the Haribu mythology about Noah and his sons in the story of the Book of Genesis. The original African name for Nubia is Ta-Nehisi or Zeti ‽.

115

CASIAN, SEMITE" or "HAMITE", otherwise called "HYKSOS" or "SHEPHERED KINGS OF BEDUINA, from Asia, arrived in Northeast Alkebu-lan, at Ta-Merry, about 1675 B.C.E., at which time the indigenous Africans ["Negroes, Bantus, Pygmies," or whatever else] had already developed most of their Nile Valley High-Cultures, and were in the the midst of their XIVth Dynasty in Ta-Merry, Ta-Nehisi, and Ethiopia.

Unfortunately, for the past two hundred [200] years or more "ORTHODOX HISTORY," as written by European and European-American writers and academicians, have been related primarily to WARS and the NOBILITY that caused them, very little ever being stated in the cause of the so-called "COMMON" or "LITTLE MAN." But, it was the ROYALTY of Ta-Nehisi, along with the common people North of the First Cataract, that the people of Ta-Merry and its NOBILITY had to fight for the second time in their history during the IInd Dynasty, c. 2800 B.C.E. The proof of this historical event is recorded in a fragmented inscription that is presently misnormered the "HERAKONPO-LIS STONE." It is an appearent depiction of Pharaoh Khasekhenui "KNEELING ON A NUBIAN PRISONER." But, there is a similar type inscription that came down to us from the IVth Dynasty, c. 2720 B.C.E., showing Pharaoh[0] Sneferu, allegedly, "DE-STROYING NUBIA," this being the so-called "PALERMO STONE."

If one is to assume that the indigenous Africans of Ta-Merry [Blacks and Brown people] were "SUPERIOR RACIALLY" to their indigenous sisters and brothers of Ta-Nehisi [Blacks and Browns, fellow Africans] because of their military victories in the above mentioned wars **detailed** in the inscriptions; then, this logic must equally hold true that the European-American Caucasians of the United States of America [WHITE] are of a 'SUPERIOR RACE' to the Germans and Italians of Caucasian Europe[00] they defeated in World War I [1914-1918 C.E.] and World War II [1936-1945 C.E.]. But, the same "INFERIOR" Africans of Ta-Nehisi were the people who actually opened up and worked the DIORITE QUARIES, and made all of the CAST and CARVED STONE FIGURES for most of Ta-Merry's colossal monuments, also their own - such as for ABU SIMBEL and TUMAS during the IVth Dynasty, c. 2723-2563 B.C.E. They were the same "IN-

---

[0]. The word PHARAOH means "GREAT HOUSE" in Hieroglyph. It also means "KING," as it was used as the symbol or title of the HEAD OF STATE OF TA-MERRY. The first usage is literal, the second is representative of the meaning of the symbol of a "Great House."

[00]. Both of these Axis Power partners were members of the 'INDO-EUROPEAN ARYAN MASTER RACE.'

116

FERIORS" from whom the Ta-Merrian "SUPERIORS" stole "...200,000 SHEEP AND
CATTLE...[and]...CAPTURED 7000 PRISONERS..." during the Ta-Merry - Ta-
Nehisi Wars of the IIIrd Dynasty, c. 2720 B.C.E., during the reign of Pharaoh Snefe-
ru. [0]

There are many samples of unused DIORITE INSCRIPTIONS found at two quaries
by certain egyptologists, and others, from Europe, European-America, and Asia,
which they stole from the Nile Valley indigenous Africans. This desecration of the
graves by said people, most of whom call themselves religious names as "Christians,
Jews, Muslims," etc., continues , as the robbers remove from Alkebu-lan all of her
treasures year after year. Many others called "anthropologists" and "egyptologists"
have stolen countless numbers of African artifacts that find their way into the public
and private museum collections of some of Europe's, England's, and the United States
of America's most distinguished citizens or subjects, all with the blessing of the religious heads of each of the so-called "Western Religions" - Judaism, Christianity, and
Islam. " But, not one of the robbers and grave snatchers paid one solitary penny, or received any consent whatsoever, for the removal and confiscation of said treasures [the
properties of the indigenous Africans and their descendants of the Harlems of the world
today] from their legitimate owners possession. This role the Nubian Africans, Ta-
Nehisians, suposedly played for the Egyptian Africans, Ta-Merrians; both of them -
the Ta-Nehisians and the Ta-Merrians - Black members of the so-called "NEGRO" or
"NEGROID RACE, " which allegedly extended until the reign of the last pharaoh of the
VIth Dynasty, c. ? - 2270 B.C.E., whose inscription bear his name - "MERNERE. "
The latter artifact and inscription was unearthed at an area around the First Cataract ,
where the so-called "BOUNDARY LINE" between Ta-Merry and Ta-Nehisi, allegedly,
had been pushed southwards by the military forces from the NORTH - Upper Egypt.
However, quarrying activities further SOUTH in Ta-Nehisi proved that the so-called

---

[0]. At this juncture it must be remembered that the first Pharaoh of the Ist Dynasty,
AHA or Narmer, also known as Mena [Herodotus' "Menes"], was born in the "LAND TO
THE SOUTH OF TA-MERRY" or "TA-NEHISI, " later called "ZETI" or "NUBIA. " That
Aha, Narmer or Mena, also captured Ta-Merry with military forces from the SOUTH
[as far up the Nile Valley as Central - East Africa, around the Great Lakes regions.
Pharaoh Narmer is shown on page 9 of this volume.
[00]. For the most popular comments on this episode see the "PALERMO STONE INSCRIP-
TION" in Yearby P. Armstrong's book, THE PALERMO STONE, London, 1910; and
James Henry Breasted's, RECORDS OF ANCIENT EGYPT, Chicago, 1920.

"INFERIOR RACE" [the Nubians or Ta-Nehisians] was involved in such production long before the northern reaches of their own homeland were annexed by the Ta-Merrians after many wars of conquest. Inscriptions from points still farther SOUTH referred to much later wars in which the Ta-Nehisians lost more of Ta-Nehisi's territory to the Ta-Merrians, to the point of having the Lords of Medja, Irtet, and Wawat surrender to the Ta-Merrians military control over their country.

From many more inscriptions, which still exist in private and public collections, we can still note the struggles put up by the "...GREAT SOLDIERS..." of Ta-Nehisi in defense of their homeland. One of the foremost descriptions dealing with these wars was written in the so-called "INSCRIPTION OF UNI" [Governor of Northern Ta-Nehisi], which was distorted by "White Liberal Africanist ORTHODOX historians" to appear that parts of Northern Ta-Nehisi [Nubia or Zeti] were in Southern Ta-Merry [Kimit, Sais, Egypt]. It also mentioned many of the projects at Abydos which the Ta-Merrians undertook during the reign of the Viceroy [Overlord] Uni for his Pharaoh - Mernere. These projects included the continuation of the largest BOAT BUILDING INDUSTRY on the entire Nile River 4,100 miles length [from Uganda in Central East Alkebu-lan to the Mediterranean Sea], which Uni met when he arrived in Ta-Nehisi. The "BEST WOODS FROM WAWAT WERE USED" for this industry, brought to the site of construction on the canals the Ta-Nehisians built by diverting the Nile River for irrigation and shipping before their conquest by the Ta-Merrians. These canals were also used to ship materials, finished products, and craftsmen DOWN North to Ta-Merry. Natural materials and their manufactured by-products, and the craftsmen that produced them, were also brought from points farther UP South for this industry. They came from Ta-Nehisi's Yam, Irtet, Medju, and Ka'at, from Itiopi, and to the southeast at Puanit - the most eastern point of the continent of Alkebu-lan. The boats were of a type which the Ta-Merrians were in-capable of building at this early period in their High-Culture, c. 2423 - 2242 B.C.E. The purpose of such extremely large boats was to transport the colossal hand-carved and uncarved granite and dorite blocks and stones DOWN north on the Nile River from Ta-Nehisi to Ta-Merry for the construction and errection of the stelae and pyramid of Pharaoh Mernere, and for many other pharaohs before and after him. It is surely during this Dynasty, the VIth, c. 2565 - 2420 B.C.E., that the Ta-Nehisians truly became the conquered victims of the Ta-Merrians, who forced them to surrender most of their individuality in their High-Culture and adopt every aspect of the cultural values of their fel-
118

low Africans from the North. However, being that the Hyksos - the so-called "WHITE SEMITES" or "SHEPHERD KINGS FROM BEDUINA," did not arrive in Ta-Merry until the XIVth to XVIth Dynasty, c. 1675-1600 B.C.E., neither the "WHITE CAUCASIANS" nor "MACEDONIAN-GREEKS" until the ending of the XXXth Dynasty, c. 332 B.C.E. - which they caused by their defeat of the Persian interloopers; as such, one can definitely state that the indigenous Africans of Ta-Nehisi and Ta-Merry were still of the same people "RACIALLY," though at various times they differed somewhat "POLITICALLY." The beginning of their political separation, not RACIAL separation, actually began around the IIIrd Dynasty, c. 2780 - 2680 B.C.E., and not before.

A much broader and intricate detailing of the data in this INTRODUCTION is given in the following chronologies, graps, charts, and pictures of this chapter. In them, most of the information outlined on a general basis above are shown in detail, and are documented, with respect to their socio-political and histographical perspectives. Along with the details are the BIOGRAPHICAL MATERIALS and GLOSSARY presented for the student, professor, researcher, and general reader's convenience and clearer understanding of the otherwise complex data.

History will yet show that the following information is but a very minute part of the "GLORIOUS TRUTH" that was once the common "HIGH-CULTURE" of the entire Nile Valleys [Blue and White], and all of the other "HIGH-CULTURES" of Alkebu-lan ["MOTHER AFRICA"]. It will show that the FIRST indigenous Africans of the LOWER NILE VALLEY, around the Delta region, came from Central Africa - "AFRICA SOUTH OF THE SAHARA" as it is misnomered by "European and European-American "AFRICANISTS." It may also prove that the ORIGINAL HOME OF ALL OF MANKIND was in the same area where the oldest FOSSIL-MAN, Zinjanthropus boisie,[0] known to date evolved, in Tanzania [Central EAST ALKEBU-LAN].

OSIRIS, SON OF THE GODDESS ISIS

119

Achaemendis	The ancient ruling house of Persia that dominated a large area of the "Near East" from the 6th through 4th century prior to the Christian Era [period] B.C.E.
Acheulian	The height of the handaxe development in Lower and Middle Palaeolithic context.
Alkebu-lan	The most ancient name the indigenous people called their continent before the Greeks and Romans renamed it "AFRICA."
Barbarian	A name given to the prehistoric culture of the indigenous Africans of the Nile Valley around the so-called "BADARI" in Middle Ta-Merry.
Chronological	K = King; Y = Year; M = Month; D = Day; ? = Unknown Date; c. or ca. = Approximate Date; B.C.E. = Before the Christian Era or B.C., C.F. = Christian Era or A.D.
Demotic	Hieratic writing of the indigenous Africans of the ancient High-Cultures most simplified form. It was very common in the latest periods of Dynastic Ta-Merry.
Dynasty	Rulers by succession within a common line, as determined by High-Priest Manetho around c. 280 B.C.E., during the so-called "XXXIInd Dynasty."
Erg	An area of piled-up shifted sand in the desert.
Gerzean	The earliest of the predynastic cultures of the indigenous Africans of LOWER and UPPER Nile Valley that amalgamated with the Amratian. The earliest of the indigenous African predynastic cultures of Ta-Merry and Ta-Nehisi, sometime between c. 4000 and 3400 B.C.E., to form the late predynastic cultures down to the Ist Dynasty [sometime around c. 3200 - 3100 B.C.E.].
Handaxe	Tool of the Lower Palaeolithic period made of flint stone core and expertly chipped on both flat faces into a triangular form.
Hieratic	Cursive form of writing developed for the indigenous African languages called "HIEROGLYPHICS."
Hieroglyphics	The most ancient form of writing for communication originated and developed by Nile Valley Africans of Itiopi, Ta-Nehisi, Meröe, Punt, Ta-Merry, Kush, and others.
Levalloisian	Flake-tool industry of the Middle Palaeolithic period.
Mastaba	A funerary building that was generally connected to the main pyramids

built during the early dynastic periods of Ta-Nehisi and Ta-Merry. Unlike the pyramids, they are generally flat-topped and rectangular in design. They contained the chapel and covered burial chamber for use as a mortuary.

Mesolithic — Middle Stone Age. The period between the three Stone Ages, sometimes called the "TRANSITIONARY PERIOD."

Neolithic — Old Term for the New Stone Age; allegedly, the period when "... THE USE OF METAL BECAME COMMON IN THE NILE VALLEY."

Palaeolithic — Old Stone Age. Allegedly, the period of man's earliest cultures; from hunting to planting, etc. In the Frigid Zone it was from the Ice Age.

Papyrus — Papyrus [cyperus papyrus], a writing material. PAPYROS or Greek paper, from PAPURO - the Egyptian Africans' "ROYAL PAPER." A VOLUMEN or BOOK covered with writing, etc. The native plant of the Nile Valley marshes and adjacent areas of the Nile River. From the pit of this plant the ancient Nile Valley Africans made the world's first paper.

Obelisk — A tapered stone slab errected upright, with inscriptions about the Gods, Goddesses, pharaohs, and events of history; generally cut from red granite in Elephantine [Aswan], Ta-Nehisi, during the pre-dynastic and dynastic periods.

Pharaoh — A king of Ta-Merry, Ta-Nehisi, Meroe, Itiopi, Lebu, Kush, and other Nile Valley nations of the dynastic periods. The original meaning in Hieroglyph is "GREAT HOUSE" or "MAIN HOUSE."

Pleistocene — Earlier of the two Eras of the Quaternary Period; generally associated with the Ice Age.

Piocene — The latest Era of the Tertiary Period.

Pylon — A gateway with sloping sides that create the appearance of a truncated pyramid. A general form of construction beginning around the New Kingdom Period of the indigenous Africans of the Lower Nile regions.

Quaternary Period — The geological period that began with the end of the Tertiary Period and continued to the present 20th Century C.E. "THE AGE OF MAN;" combining both the Pleistocene and Holocene Eras or Periods.

Race — A nebulous term with respect to the ancient Egyptians, or any other group of people; - thus, "PURE RACE," etc. Allegedly the physical differences between one group of people and another, originally between one specie and another. This term has as many descriptions and interpretations as there are people who use it.

Stele or Stela	Stone slab placed vertically and bearing inscriptions commemorating the deceased or in celebration of an event; common among the ancient indigenous African High-Cultures of the Nile Valleys and Great Lakes regions.
Tertiary Period	Geological time-period following the "AGE OF REPTILES" that allegedly preceded the Quaternary Period; consisting of the Palaecene, Eocene, Oligocene, Miocene, and Pilocene periods or eras.
Ushabti	Funerary practices of the ancient indigenous Africans of the Lower Nile Valley High-Cultures. Generally a mummiform modle of a servant of a pharaoh or noble man intomb for the purpose of performing certain magical duties for his master during their stay in the "NETHER WORLD" [Heaven].

In the above inscription ANI is witnessing the "WEIGHING OF HIS HEART," preparatory to his entering the Nether World [Heaven]. This scene is extracted from THE BOOK OF THE COMING FORTH BY DAY [Egyptian Book Of The Dead, as translated into English by Sir E.A. Wallis Budge, London, 1895] and THE PAPYRUS OF ANI. The deceased, ANI, is shown at the extreme left being led by the God - ANUBIS.

FIG. 118.

The First or " The Maatit Boat."

From photo by Emil Brugsch-Bay. Original found at Meir is now at Gizeh. [?] only boat which has preserved its original rigging. Dates from eleventh [?] twelfth Dynasty. The dead man is sitting in his cabin wrapped in his cloak.

A similar scene is duplicated many times in the Papyrus Of Ani and the Book Of The Coming Forth By Day, where Ani is shown in the "BOAT OF AMENTA" traveling across the treacherous waters of the "UNDER WORLD" on his way to be received by Ra, who was to make him another of the GODS of Ta-Merry. [See Dr. Albert Churchward's ORIGIN AND EVOLUTION OF RELIGION, London, 1924, p. xxx].

Amuletic figures of Egyptian gods and goddesses.

HORUS I.—THE DIFFERENT NAMES OR ATTRIBUTES OF HORUS AND AMSU, THE RISEN HORUS OR HORUS IN SPIRIT

Horus—The first Man-God
Horus—I. U. or I. A. U. = Jesus.
Horus—The Light of the World.
Horus—God of Life.
Horus—God of the Four Quarters, N. E. S. W.

Horus—The Mighty One of the Teshert Crown.
Horus—In the Resurrection.
Horus—The Child-suckling.
Horus—The Great Spirit.
Horus—The Seven Powers of.

124

Horus—God of the Pole Star.
Horus—God of Light.
Horus—Creator of Himself and Heir of Eternity.
Horus—Child of Isis.
Horus—King of the North and South.
Horus—Guide of the Northern Horizon.
Horus—In Spirit (Amsu).
Horus—Guardian of Sut.
Horus—Lord of Dawn and Evening Twilight.

Horus—Lord of the Northern and Southern Horizon.
Horus—Fettering Sut (or binding or chaining Satan).
Horus—Prince of the Emerald Stone.
Horus of the Triangle.
Horus—The Great One — The Mighty One.
Horus—The Great Chief of the Hammer or Axe.
Horus—Lord of Tattu.
Horus—The Blind.
Horus—The Tears of.
Horus—The Followers of.
Horus—The Feet of.
Horus—The Divine Healer.
Horus—The Master.
Horus—In the Tank of Flame (Baptiser with Fire).
Horus—The Good Shepherd with the Crook upon His Shoulder.
Horus—With Four Followers on the Mount.
Horus—With the Seven Great Spirits on the Mount.
Horus—As the Fisher.
Horus—As the Lamb.
Horus—As the Lion.
Horus—Of Twelve Years.
Horus—With the Tat (Cross).
Horus—Made a man at 30 years in his Baptism.
Horus—The Healer in the Mountain.
Horus—The Exorciser of Evil Spirits, as the Word.
Horus—Who gives the Waters of Life.
Horus—In the Bush of Thorns (as Unbu).
Horus—The Just and True.
Horus—The Bridegroom with the Bride in Sothis.

Horus—Of the Two Horizons.
Horus—As Hawk or Vulture or Eagle Hawk.
Horus—As Young Ear of Corn.
Horus—As Her-Shef or Khnemu—He who is on his Lake.
Horus—The Anointed Son of the Father.
Horus—The Red Calf (Type of Horus the Child).
Horus—In the Tree.
Horus—On the Cross.
Horus—As "I am the Resurrection and the Life."
Horus—Prince of Peace.
Horus—Who descends into Hades.
Horus—Lord of the Two Eyes or Double Vision.
Horus—The Manifesting Son of God.
Horus—As Child of the Virgin.
Horus—The Sower of Good Seed (and Sut the Destroyer).
Horus—Carried off by Sut to the Summit of the Mount Hetep.
Horus—Contending with Sut on the Mount.
Horus—One of Five Brethren.
Horus—The Brother of Sut, the betrayer.
Horus—Baptised with water by Anup.
Horus—Who exalted His Father in every Sacred Place.
Horus—The Weeper.
Horus—The Lifted Serpent.
Horus—In the Bosom of Ra (his Father).
Horus—The Avenger.
Horus—He who comes with Peace.
Horus—The Afflicted One.
Horus—The Lord of Resurrection from the House of Death.
Horus—As the type of Eternal Life.
Horus—The Child Teacher in the Temple (as Iu-em-Hetep).
Horus—As Ma-Kheru (the Witness unto Truth).
Horus—As the Lily.
Horus—Who came to fulfil the Law.
Horus—Walking the Water.
Horus—The Raiser of the Dead.
Horus—One with his Father.
Horus—Entering the Mount at Sunset to hold Converse with his Father.
Horus—Transfigured on the Mount.

Horus had two mothers : Isis, the Virgin, who conceived him, and Nephthysis, who nursed him.
He was brought forth singly and as one of five brothers.
Jesus had two mothers : Mary the Virgin, who conceived him, and Mary, the wife of Cleophas, who brought him forth as one of her children.
He was brought forth singly and as one of five brethren.
Horus was the Son of Seb, his father on earth.
Jesus was the son of Joseph, the father on earth.
Horus was with his mother, the Virgin, until 12 years old, when he was transformed into the beloved son of God, as the only begotten of the Father in heaven.
Jesus remained with his mother, the Virgin, up to the age of 12 years, when he left her " to be about his Father's business."
From 12 to 30 years of age there is no record in the life of Horus.

From 12 to 30 years of age there is no record in the life of Jesus:
Horus at 30 years of age became adult in his baptism by Anup:

Jesus at 30 years of age was made a man of in his baptism by John the Baptist:
Horus, in his baptism, made his transformation into the beloved son and only begotten of the Father—the holy spirit, represented by a bird.
Jesus, in his baptism, is hailed from heaven as the beloved son and only begotten
of the Father, God—the holy spirit that is represented by a dove.

The ancient Egyptian code of morals, as may be seen from chap. cxxv., was the grandest and most comprehensive of those now known to have existed amongst any nation.

The " Recension," no doubt, was drawn up by the priests of On or Heliopolis (Moses was one of them), and it contains the views held by the priests of the colleges of that very ancient city.

---

[6]. All of the above comments with respect to the Gods and Goddesses, also the comments on Horus, were extracted from Dr. Albert Churchward's book, SIGNS AND SYM-
BOLS OF PRIMORDIAL MAN, pp. 421 , 422 and 423. One should not forget to examine
the Judaeo-Christian-Islamic "Holy Works" for another look at their origin in the above.
For we have seen that AMEN is still carried in them, the God of the Africans of Egypt,
which the Jews and Christians claimed to be : "SO BE IT." But, AMEN - RA was the
God that Moses knew before YAWEH or JEHOVAH. AMEN - RA preceded all of the so-
called "Western religions" - Judaism, Christianity, and Islam." Before the creation of
ADAM AND EVE, THE GARDEN OF EDEN, even before JEHOVAH and the TRINITY.
All of this can be found in the BOOK OF THE COMING FORTH BY DAY.

Dates in parenthesis [3987-1978, etc.] are for references, showing the extent to which the so-called "AUTHORITIES ON EGYPT" and other African High-Cultures [civilizations] disagree with each others, according to listings on pages 131 - 137 of this chapter.

The dates used in the chronologies with reference to the pre-Christian periods are alleged to have been taken from the indigenous African High-Priest of Ta-Merry, Manetho, calcualtions. Certain dates have been calculated by this author whenever the originals have become obscured or missing for one reason or another. All of the dates must be considered to be approximate, for there was no such thing as "BEFORE THE CHRISTIAN ERA" or "BEFORE CHRIST" as a period of time-reference known to the ancients of Manetho's lifetime; thus, the circa sign - ca. or c. - should prefix each date relating to these periods, at least until the beginning of the so-called "XXXIst DYNASTY" [c. 332 B.C.E. or 332 B.C., etc.].

The period between the PALAEOLITHIC [Old Stone Age, c. 6000 B.C.E.] and the NEOLITHIC [New Stone Age, c. 3200 B.C.E.], or immediate PREDYNASTIC ERA, is quite obscure with regard to dates. There are hundreds of hypotheses dealing with this period, none of which this writer can say with any sense of honesty should be adhered to at this juncture in the BLACK EXPERIENCE.

The "HYKSOS" [Shepherd Kings of Deduina] are made to appear as "WHITE SEMITES" by most European and European-American anthropologists and historians of the anti-Negro NORTH and EAST Africa schools. Nothing can be said of the "HYK-

During 1,750 [the XIIIth Dynasty] BCE Civil
Strife racked Princess Sebeknefrue to the point
where hordes of Nomads (called Hyksos) invaded
and colonized Egypt from 1,700 BCE to 1,600 B.CE
when Ahmose I (Pharoah of Egypt) and the Emperor of
Ethiopia joined forces and drive the
Hyksos from
Egypt.

EGYPT & LIBYA
1,700-1,600 B.CE.
HYKSOS INVASION & OCCUPATION

SOS" in any regards to COLOR, RACE or ETHNIC ORIGIN, other than they came to
Ta-Merry [Egypt] and Lower Ta-Nehisi [Nubia], Northeast Alkebu-lan ["Mother Africa'], sometime between the XIVth and XVIIth Dynasties, c. 1675 - 1600 B.C.E., as
demonstrated on the map on the previous page. The Africans [the indigenous people
of Ta-Merry and Ta-Nehisi] the "HYKSOS" met in Ta-Merry and Ta-Nehisi were the
same as those described over one thousand years later by the first European-Asian
historian, Herodotus - the Greek citizen of Ionian birth [at the time a colony of Ta-
Merry], in about c. 457 - 450 B.C.E. Herodotus, in his book - THE HISTORIES,
wrote that:

> "THE COLCHIANS, ETHIOPIANS, AND EGYPTIANS HAVE
> THICK LIPS, BROAD NOSE, WOOLLY HAIR, AND THEY
> ARE BURNT OF SKIN.

You will note that this "RACIAL" description by Herodotus is only applied to the "AFRI-
CANS SOUTH OF THE SAHARA" and the "NUBIANS" [Ta-Nehisians or. Zitis] by so-
called "White Liberal" and "Orthodox AFRICANISTS and other "Westerners" [Euro-
pean and European-American] who make it their business to establish themselves as
the sole "AUTHORITY ON EGYPT" and all other parts of "AFRICA", and her "PEOPLE."
    The so-called "PTOLEMAIC PERIOD," or "XXXIInd DYNASTY," began with
Alexander II ["the great"] and his best general. The actual beginning was Alexander's
death in c. 327 B.C.E., at which time all of his generals who were serving him as
governors of his conquered territories declared themselves KING of whatever land they
governed. General Soter, the Governor of Ta-Merry [Egypt, Kimit, Sais, etc.], declared himself "KING [Pharaoh] OF ALL EGYPT, SOTER I, which he later changed to
"PTOLEMY I, PHARAOH OF ALL EGYPT." He was the original member of the Ptolemies - IInd to XVth, XXXIInd Dynasty [includin the Cleopatras - Ist to VIIIth [some
historians only listed the VIth]. The original Queen-Mother was an indigenous Ethi
opian [African or "Negro"]. Ethiopian was the term most of the ancient Europeans,
particularly the Greeks and Romans, called all of the people of Alkebu-lan [Africa] they
came in contact with. A very good detailing of this FACT is thoroughly demonstrated
in Frank W. Snowden's book, BLACKS IN ANTIQUITY: A GRECO-ROMAN EXPERIENCE,
Belknap Press [Harvard University], Cambridge, 1970, which also shows pictures of
Greeks and Romans that are no different from the so-called "NEGROES, BANTUS,"
and "NIGGERS" of today.
    In order to gain control of the Suez Canal the French government permitted the
corrupted Khedive Ismail to borrow more money than he could repay, money which he
used to pay bills for prostitution and gambling in Paris, France, and other citadels
of Europe. The money was not directed towards the good and welfare of the Egyptian
people or their government. [See G. Douin, HISTORIE du RIGNE du KHEDIVE ISMAIL,
Cairo, 1937; W. Hallberg, THE SUEZ CANAL: ITS HISTORY AND DIPLOMATIC IM-
PORTANCE, New York, 1933].
    British military forces under the command of General [Sir] Ganet Wolsely, who
had been deployed to Cyprus and Malta by the imperial government of Great Britain on
20 July, 1882 C.E. in anticipation of the invasion of French imperial and colonial Egypt,
attacked French military garrisons under the command of General Napoleon Boneparte
on 16 August, 1882 C.E. and started the defeat of France in Egypt. [See Spencer Childers, THE LIFE...OF HUGH CHILDERS, London, 1901, vol. II; R. Robinson and J.
Gallagher with A. Denny, AFRICA AND THE VICTORIANS - THE CLIMAX OF IM-
PERIALISM, New York, 1968; J.L. Garvin, THE LIFE OF JOSEPH CHAMBERLAIN,
London, vol. I; J. Chamberlain, A POLITICAL MEMOIR, 1880-1882, ed. by C.D.

Howard, London, 1935; H.L. Hoskins, BRITISH ROUTES TO INDIA, London, 1928;
C.W. Hallberg, THE SUEZ CANAL: ITS HISTORY AND DIPLOMATIC IMPORTANCE,
New York, 1931].

The period when the British imperial and colonial government in London, England, ended its DIRECT and INDIRECT colonialist hold on Ta-Nehisi [Nubia] and Ta-
Merry [Egypt], particularly Egypt, commenced its NEO-COLONIAL masterminding
of its puppets - King Farouk et al. Britain's removal of its military apparatus for colonial control in 1952 C.E. was not a victory for the indigenous Africans of Egypt nor
their Arab colonizers who had ruled the Africans from before the French came as
conquerors. In fact, the turn-over of government passed from European Englishmen to
Europeanized-Arabs and a few Arabian-Arabs and Islamized-Africans; Egyptians of
solely indigenous African origin found themselves still under colonial "MASTERS OF
THEIR DESTINY;" a "DESTINY" in which they still do not have a SOLITARY WORD in
the decision as to where they are, and where they are to go next, the same being very
much true for the indigenous Africans of the Sudan.

Throughout the CHRONOLOGICAL ORDER the student will find dates which may
conflict with certain other aspects of the general texts. This condition is unavoidable
at this time due to the missing chapters of the history of the ancient indigenous Africans of Ta-Merry, Ta-Nehisi, Meroe, and Itiopi, also other High-Cultures that developed along the entire Nile Valleys [Blue and White] and the Great Lakes regions of
Central East Africa [Alkebu-lan]. These short-comings are related to thousands upon
thousands of years of Nile Valley history and High-Culture which the foreign invaders
from Asia and Europe have made confusing by their destruction of some of the most
important records of the indigenous Africans. The invaders most responsible for said
CULTURAL GENOCIDE were the Hyksos, Assyrians, Macedonian-Greeks, Greeks,
Romans, Arabs, Ottoman Turks, French, and British, in the order listed, their acts
of barbarity and human degradation having lasted over a period of approximately 3,627
years. Another major reason, and the much more current one, is the injection of the
"AUTHORITIES ON EGYPT", or "EGYPTOLOGISTS," from Europe and European-
America, each finding it necessary to remove every trace of the indigenous Africans
they have labeled "NEGROES, BANTUS, AFRICANS SOUTH OF THE SAHARA, BUSH-
MEN, HOTTENTOTS, PYGMIES, SAVANAH NATIVES," and a host of other names
created by them, from the history and High-Culture of North and East Alkebu-lan [Afri-
ca]. Thus, their have replaced the indigenous people of Nothern and Eastern Alkebu-
lan with "MORE CIVILIZED HAMITIC, CAUCASIAN, SEMITIC, INDO-EUROPEAN
CAUCASIAN ARYAN, and SEMITES who RULED THE GREAT EMPIRES OF WEST
AFRICA" - which were basically populated by "LESS CIVILIZED MANDINGOES...,"
etc., as witnessed in E.V. Bovil's book - CARAVAN OF OLD SAHARA, London, 1934
[presently published as THE GOLDEN TRADE OF THE MOORS, London, 1968, second
edition]. Are the following Africans of the Nile River Valley [Ethiopia] "SEMITIC, NI-
LOTIC, HAMITIC, NEGROID, BANTU, CAUCASIAN," or WHAT?

DIVISIONS OF THE 4,100 B. C. E. NILE YEAR CALENDAR USED BY THE INDIGENOUS AFRICAN HIGH-PRIESTS FOR THEIR CALCULATIONS OF THE PERIODS OF THEIR HISTORY.

Akhet, season of inundation.

Peret, springtime, appearance of crops.

Shemu, summer.

1. Thoth. **or** *tepy*
January
I

5. Tybi.
May
I

9. Pachons.
September
I

2. Paophi.
February
II

6. Mechir.
June
II

10. Payni.
October
II

3. Hathor.
March
III

7. Phamenoth.
July
III

11. Epiphi.
November
III

4. Choiak.
April
IIII

8. Pharmouthi.
August
IIII

12. Mesore
December
IIII

12 Months, 365 1/4 Days, 3 Seasons of 4 Months each: AKHET (Season of Inundation), PERET (Springtime), and SHENU (Summer).

This is the same type of calendar used by High-Priest Manetho in his calculations of the DYNASTIC PERIODS in the CHRONOLOGY and NUMEROLOGICAL CHARTS in his work, HISTORY OF EGYPT, c. 280 B.C.E. It should be remembered that there was a calendar that preceded this one – the STELAR CALENDAR of the PREDYNASTIC KINGDOMS.

The above calendar is used for references throughout the CHRONOLOGIES.

130

DATES OF EGYPTIAN DYNASTIES BY EUROPEAN "AUTHORITIES IN EGYPTOLOGY" COMPARED TO MANETHO'S ORIGINAL WORKS

Period or DYNASTY	Manetho (280 B.C) DATE	Champollion-Figeac (?AD) DATE	Lepsius (1858AD) DATE	Brugsh (1877AD) DATE	Mariette (?AD) DATE
	First Book				
I	9K, 253Y	5,867*	3,892*	4,400*	5,004*
II	9K, 302Y	5,615	3,639	4,133	4,751
III	9K, 214Y	5,318	3,338	3,966	4,449
IV	8K, 284Y	5,121	3,124	3,733	4,235
V	9K, 248Y	4,673	2,840	3,566	3,951
VI	6K, 203Y	4,225	2,744	3,300	3,703
VII	70K, 0Y, 70D	4,222	2,592	3,100	3,500
VIII	27K, 146Y	4,147	2,522	?	3,500
IX	19K, 409Y	4,047	2,674**	?	3,358
X	10K, 185Y	3,947	2,565**	?	3,249
XI	192K, 2300Y, 70D	3,762	2,423	?	3,064
XII	7K, 160Y	3,703	2,380	?	2,851
XIII	?	3,417	2,136	2,235	?
XIV	76K, 184Y	3,004	2,167	?	2,398
XV	?	2,520	2,101	?	2,214
XVI	32K, 518Y	2,270	1,842	?	?
XVII	86K, 151Y	2,082	1,684	?	?
VIII	16K, 263Y	1,822	1,581	1,700	1,703
	Second Book				
XIX	7K, 209Y	1,473	1,443	1,400	1,462
XX	12K, 135Y	1,279	1,269	1,200	1,288
XXI	7K, 130Y	1,101	1,091	1,100	1,110
XXII	9K, 126Y	971	961	966	980
XXIII	4K, 28Y	851	787	766	810
XXIV	1K, 6Y	762	729	733	721
XXV	3K, 40Y	718	716	700	715
XXVI	9K, 150Y, 6M	674	685	666	665
XXVII	8K, 124Y, 4M	524	525	527	527
XXVIII	1K, 6Y	404	525	?	406
XXIX	4K, 20Y, 4M	398	399	399	399
XXX	3K, 38Y	377	378	378	378
	Third Book				
XXXI***	?????????	399	340	340	340

The student will notice that the chronological dates given above by four different "AUTHORITIES" and/or "EGYPTOLOGISTS" do not, for the most part, coin-

---

* Note that the "AUTHORITIES" disagree as much as 1,000 years difference.
** These dates only prove the extent to which Lepsius was confused in his work.
*** Manetho did not complete this Dynasty's listing; he died before its termination in approximately 324 C.E. He actually did not list it as a "Dynasty."

cide with the original calculated dates established by High-Priest Manetho in his CHRO-
NOLOGY OF DYNASTIC EGYPT, NUBIA, MERÖE, ITIOPI, PUANIT, and LEBU, which
he developed and recorded in his three major works he wrote during the 3rd Century,
c. 280 B.C.E. However, there are many instances where this writer may also differ
somewhat from Manetho's dates,[0] but, only in certain areas where the original figures
Manetho listed have become obscured, and in other instances where his documents
have been tampered with or destroyed by the ravagers of invading armies from Europe
with their "Christian Missionaries," and of course where the missing documents have
been plagiarized by Arab Muslims during their JIHADS [religious wars] across North
Africa about the 7th [18 A.H.] through [870 A.H] century C.E. or A.D. Yet, much of
Manetho's original documentary works have to be taken from the volumes of many of
his followers and disciples down through the ages, such as the Hebrew or Jewish historian Flavius Josephus [Ist Century C.E.], the African Christian chronographer Julius
Africanus [c. 220 C.E.], and the European Christian Eusebius [c. 320 C.E.], only to
mention just a few who copied from the originator of Ta-Merrian [Egyptian] and other
Nile Valley Africans HISTORY and HIGH-CULTURE. For this salvation, it is in the
works of Syncellus [also called "GEORGE"] - c. 800 C.E., titled HISTORY OF THE
WORLD FROM CREATION TO DIOCLETION, that we are to find the best recordings of
High-Priest Manetho's originally documented HISTORY and CHRONOLOGY of the Nile
Valleys [Blue and White, the Atbara River Valley included] High-Cultures of the so-
called "PRE-CHRISTIAN ERA" [B.C.E. or B.C.].

   Who was the indigenous African scholar and historian of the Nile Valley's PEARLS -
Ta-Merry, Ta-Nehisi, Meroe, Itiopi, etc. - we are discussing? The late indigenous
African of African-European parentage known by the name - "MANETHO." He was born
of an African mother of Ta-Merry and a European father of Macedonian-Greek origin
in the Sebennytos area of the town of Samanud in Lower Egypt [Ta-Merry]. Although extremely proficient in his mother's language, HIEROGLYPH, he was obliged to write all
of his works in the Greek language of his father, the Greeks and Macedonians being the

---

[0]. If space permitted the following "AUTHORITIES" conflicting chronologies on Dynastic
Ta-Merry, etc., would have been included: J. H. Breasted, G. Maspero, F.W. Petrie
[father of archaeology], Sir E.A. Wallis Budge, Sir A. Gardner, W.B. Emery, and
W.J. Arkell; these, of course, were the most flagrant of the thousands who altered or
otherwise showed distorted views of Manetho's masterpiece he produced more than
2,251 years ago [c. 280 B.C.E.].

imperial colonizers of Ta-Merry [Egypt] at the time of his birth and death, which was during the period some of us recklessly call the "XXXIst DYNASTY" and/or "XXXIInd DYNASTY," c. 332 - 47 or 30 B.C.E.

Of the eight works [books or volumes] Manetho wrote on "RELIGIOUS DOCTRINES, MORALS, MANUFACTURE OF INCENSE, RITUAL AND FESTIVALS, still, it is his AEGYPTICA [History of Egypt] in approximately c. 280 B.C.E. that is considered "...THE GREATEST." The BOOK OF SOTHIS is also attributed to his scholarship and genius, even though they are those of European and European-American "scholarship" who questioned his authorship of said work. However, from him Aristotle, and others who are called 'ARISTOLEAN PHILOSOPHERS," learned much of what we are attributing to them in our courses in "WHITE STUDIES" or "WESTERN CIVILIZATIONS."

It cannot be over-emphasized here [in anyway whatsoever] that the so-called "XXXIst" through "XXXIVth" DYNASTIES, c. 332 B.C.E. - 640 C.E., were nothing more than the figments of the imagination of their creators - the so-called "AUTHORITIES ON AFRICA" and "AFRICANS" of European and European-American scholarship. These last three "DYNASTIES," if that they may be called by a grave stretch of the imagination, are the result of the confusion the earliest European and European-American archaeologists, anthropologists, historians, and general educators suffered in deciphering the documents in HIEROGLYPHS unearthed in the many temples, pyramids, and other structures the indigenous Africans of the Nile Valley, most of which have been plundered to the ultimate by vulterous-acting European, European-American, and Asian so-called "ENTREPRENUERS" or"PROSPECTORS" who have practically drained Alkebulan of most of her artifacts to the point where her sons and dauthers must now go to the MUSEUMS and LIBRARIES of foreign lands - Europe, Great Britain, and the Americas - to learn about her "GREAT AND GLORIOUS PAST."

We note that there is approximately 2,677 years difference between the Ist Dynasty - c. 5,867 B.C. listing by Jean Champollion-Pigeac and the Ist Dynasty - c. 3,200 B.C. established by High-Priest Manetho of the Egyptian Mysteries System Manetho's list resulted from calculating procedures he developed from the OSIRICA'S teachings at the Grand Lodge of Luxor [Thebes] and other temples "SECRET ORDER" of the Nile Valley. C.R. Lepsius' Ist Dynasty, c. 3,592 B.C., came closest, but he was still 692 years away from Manetho's calculations, as he too overlooked the fact that Manetho's NILE YEARS were not based upon any relationship to the so-called "CHRISTIAN CALENDAR'S SOLAR

YEAR" system developed hundreds of years after the proclamation of the "BIRTH" and "DEATH OF JESUS CHRIST."[0] A second point in this particular issue was that Manetho's NILE YEAR consisted of at least 365 1/4 days, with 1/4 day correction each 7th year, etc., very much unlike the current ROMANIZED CALENDAR from Europe we are still using with its 365 days corrected each 4th year by the addition of 1 day.

As to the Macedonian-Greeks having a "DYNASTY," equally the Greeks that later usurped the Macedonian imperial throne in the colonies, and of course the Romans, as indicated on pages 336-346 of Sir Ernest A. Wallis Budge's book, THE NILE, London, 1895, these four so-called "AUTHRORITIES ON EGYPT" or "EGYPTOLOGISTS have utterly failed to mention any of them - the "XXXIInd" through"XXXIIIrd" - in any of their works known to this writer and student of Alkebu-lan's history and High-Culture, par-ticularly that of Ta-Merry, Ta-Nehisi, Meröe, Itiopi, Puanit, Lebu, Khart-Haddas, Numidia, and other nations along the Nile River and the Great Lakes regions.

Mention of the period of the so-called "CHIEF-KINGS OF THE MACEDONIAN GREEK" - the XXXIst and XXXIInd, c. 332 - 47 or 30 B.C.E., is already a fact in this work. It is being considered because it was during the colonization of Ta-Merry, North Alkebu-lan, by the foreigners from Europe that Manetho was forced to write his HISTORY, CHRONOLOGY, and other "SECRETS" of the reigns of Ta merry and other Nile Valley's PHARAOHS [Kings] and QUEENS, which he divided into PERIODS called "DYNASTIES" or "DYNASTIC REIGNS."

All of the dates shown on the previous pages with respect to Manetho were further complicated by certain very basic calendar changes made by the Roman Emperor Jus-tinian and his scribes, which they committed in their attempt to stomp out the religion of RA - the indigenous Africans of the Nile Valley SUN DIETY, the "FIRST GOD-HEAD" ever to be worshipped by man through different names and titles. The confusion worsen-ed when the Arab Muslims invasions and JIHADS stretched across North and East Afri-ca from the Arabian Peninsula in Western Asia, over Ta-Merry in particular, at the time in the year 640 C.E. or 18 A.H. [the year after the Hegira of Hejira]. The Arab Muslims were on their course of total destruction of anything they felt was not in the in-terest of AL'LAH [their God] and Mohamet ibn Abdullah [their Holy Prophet]. This they

[0]The validity of "JESUS CHRIST'S BIRTH" and "DEATH" is not supported or contested here in this chapter. References to either event are for the convenience of the time-period used in "Western Societies," and for no other reason. See page 130 of this chap-ter for a review of the NILE YEAR CALENDAR used by High-Priest Manetho.

accomplished by burning and plundering everything within their path in a SCORCH EARTH policy that lasted for many centuries.

From the period marked by the XIVth to XVIIth dynasties, or the so-called "HYKSOS EPOC" [era], c. 1675 - 1600 B.C.E., of which European and European-American "AUTHORITIES" manufactured into their hypothesis of "WHITE SEMITES" from Asia, we can certainly say that the confusion between egyptologists and "WHITE LIBERAL AFRICANISTS," with respect to their chronological dates, lessened some-what. This was the period upon which they have based their claim to indigenous Alkebu-lan origin, in the process denying the same right of claim by the indigenous Africans of Ta-Merry which they prefer to call "NEGROES, BANTUS, PYGMIES, HOTTENTOTS, BUSHMEN, TROPICAL AFRICANS, BLACK AFRICANS, NATIVES, AFRICANS SOUTH OF THE SAHARA," and plain old simple "NIGGERS." All of these names they created in disciplines known as "ANTHROPOLOGY, PALAEONTOLOGY, EGYPTOLOGY, ARCHAEOLOGY," and a host of other "OLOGIES" too numerous to mention here.

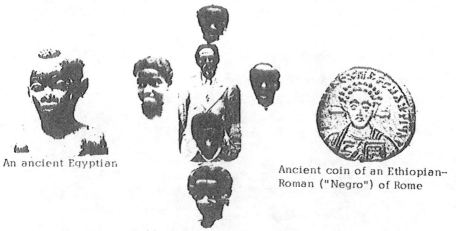

An ancient Egyptian

Ancient coin of an Ethiopian-Roman ("Negro") of Rome

Rabbi Abraham and Falasa ("Jewish") students of Gon-dar, Ethiopia (East Africa)

The name EGYPT was assigned to this North African country through Haribu religious mythology dealing with the HOLY TORAH'S (Old Testament) story about Noah and his sons, one allegedly named Egypt having founded this African nation of the Nile Valley. Apart from this mythological source there is no other to verify it, but Ta-Merry (Egypt) existed for thousands upon thousands of years before the Haribu and their God - YAWEH or JEHOVAH.

CHRONOLOGICAL CLASSIFICATIONS & DATES OF EGYPTIAN, NUBIAN, MERÖEAN, THEBAN and ITIOPIAN HIGH-CULTURES

ERA	DESCRIPTION	DATE B.C.E.	
	Lower Palaeolithic Period......................250,000 -		?
	Middle Palaeolithic [Old Stone] Period...........100,000 -		?
Prehistoric Era	Neolithic [New Stone] Period:.....................6000-		?
	Tasian Period:..		?
	Badarian Period:...		?
	Predynastic Period:...............................6000-3200		
Old Kingdom	Archaic Period: Ist & IInd Dynasty......3200-2780	(4400-4266)*	
	Great Pyramid Age:		
	IIIrd - VIth Dynasties.................2780-2270	(4266-3100)	
	VIIth-Xth Dynasties..................2270-2100	(3100-2533)	
Middle Kingdom	XIth-XIVth Dynasties.................2100-1675	(2520-2500)	
Hyksos Era	Hyksos invaders from Asia in Africa:		
	XVth-XVIIth Dynasties. 1675-1600	(2500-2333)	
New Kingdom	Theban Period:		
	XVIIIth-XXth Dynasties...............1600-1090	(1700-1333)	
	Tanite & Bubasite Period:		
	XXIst-XXIIIrd Dynasties..............1090-718	(1133-733)	
Itiopian Era	Kushite & Saite Period:		
	XXIVth-XXVIth Dynasties...............718-527	(733-666)	
Late Kingdom	Old Persian & Mendesian Period:		
	XXVIIth-XXXIst Dynasties..............527-332	(666-336)	
	Persian invaders from Asia in Africa.		
Ptolemaic Era	Macedonian-Greeks Period:		
	XXXIInd Dynasty ?....................332-47-30	(332-30)	
	Macedonian-Greeks from Europe in Africa.		
Greco-Roman Era	Roman Colonial Period:		
	XXXIIIrd Dynasty (so-called)?........47 or 30 B.C.E. - 324 C.E.		
Byzantine & Coptic Era	Greco-Roman-African Period:		
	XXXIVth Dynasty (so-called)?..................324- 640 C.E.		
	Institutionalized Religion & Wars in Egypt.		

*Bracketed dates given to show comparisons by European and European-American "AUTHORITIES ON EGYPT" and AFRICA generally.

Arab Jihad Muslims	Islamic Period: Arabs from Asia in Africa.........................640-1798

French Imperialism	French Imperial Period: Frenchmen from Europe in Africa...................1798-1882

British Imperialism	British Imperial Period: British subjects from Britain in Africa.............. 1882-1952

European Imperialism Ended	Arab, Arab-European Period: Britain returned Egypt to Arab invaders descendants..1952-1958 Farouk et al control of Arab-African population

Arab Republic	First "REPUBLIC" founded: Sudanese colonel Naguib overthrow of Farouk et al...1958-1958 Colonel Nasser removed Naguib, Asian Arab control.

Pan-Arab Asian Era	Pan-Arab Period: President Nasser's Pan-Arabism....................1958-1961 Egypt removed from Pan-African position.

Arab Unity State	Pan-Arab "REPUBLIC" Period: United Arab Republic (African-Asian Arab State).....1961-1968 Pan-Arab African-Asian State failed.

Arab Republic	Second "REPUBLIC" Period: Egypt returned to single state status..............1968-1971

Pan-Arab State	Second "PAN-ARAB STATE" Period: President Nasser died; Suddath President..........1971-Present Suddath returned Egypt to Asian-African State.

The following chronological dates and events have been detailed from the above outline of the various periods of Nile Valley High-Cultures, especially those of Ta-Merry (Egypt), Ta-Nehisi (Nubia), Meröe, Lebu (Libya). Itiopi (Ethiopia and/or Cush), Puanit (Punt) and others along the entire length of the Blue and White Nile, the Atbara, and the Great Lakes regions of Alkebu-lan (Africa). The GREAT LAKES and NILE VALLEYS map before the extended chronology allows the student to be able to make cross-references with respect to the modern and ancient "BOUNDARIES" of Nile Valleys' High-C ures.

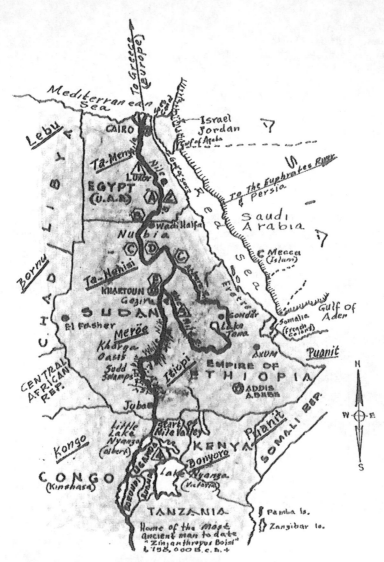

THE NILE VALLEYS AND GREAT LAKES REGION
1969 C.E.
Key

Cataracts: A, B, and C
Dams: ⚠Asiut ⚠ Aswan ⚠ Sennar
⚠ Nyanza (Owens) Falls
[4,100 + statute miles, south to north]

138

Date BCE	Period	Monarch, etc.
?250,000-100,000	Lower Palaeolithic Period. Hand-axes 100 feet and 50 feet Nile Terraces. Imigrants from central East Africa's Great Lakes region ("AFRICANS SOUTH OF THE SAHA-RA," the so-called "NEGROES").	
?100,000-25,000	Middle Palaeolithic Period. Hand-axes Levallosian flakes 10 feet Nile Terraces.	
? 25,000-12,000	Upper Palaeolithic Period.	Sebilian I, Builder of the first Silt Terraces.
? 12,000-8,000		Sebilian II.
? 8,000-6,000		Sebilian III.

PREDYNASTIC PERIODS

Lower Ta-Merry (North)	Period	Ta-Nehisi (South)
? 4,400-4,400	Fayum "A". Imigrants from Puanit, Itiopi, Meroe and Ta-Nehisi.	Imigrants from central and East Africa.
? 4,000-3,800	Halwan (El Omari). Merendeh and Tasian Culture.	Tasian Culture.
? 3,800-3,600	Fayum "B"	Badarian Culture (Khartoum).
? 3,600-3,500	Early Predynastic imigrants from Ta-Nehisi and Meroe, etc.	Early Predynastic (Amratian).
3,500-3,400	Middle Predynastic or Gerzean Period.	Middle Predyanstic or Gerzean Period.
3,400-3,200	Late Predyanstic or Gerzean Period up to Pharaoh Aha.*	Late Predynastic or Gerzean Period.
3,200-3,200	First Dynasty - Ta-Merry united.	

*NARMER [or Mena] SUTEN NET = 𓈖𓏏 = *suten net,* "King of the North and South.'

CHIEF-KINGS or PHARAOHS of the OLD KINGDOM and ARCHAIC PERIOD
(3200-2780 BCE, Ist-Xth Dynasties)
Aha to Nefer-ka-ari-Ra

Date BCE	Period	Monarch
3200-2980	Ist Dynasty (From Ta-Nehisi, or Nubia, the SOUTH)	Aha to Qeb Aha, Teta, Arteø, Ata, Hesep-ti, Mer-ba-pen, Semen-Ptah, Qebh.

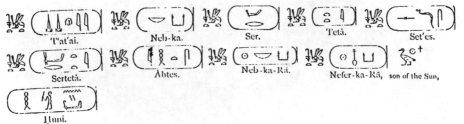

Mená.   Tetá.   Áteθ.   Áta.   Hesep-ti.   Mer-ba-pen.

Semen-Ptah.   Qebh.

2980-2780	IInd Dynasty (From Tinis or Tanis, the SOUTH)	Neter-baiu to Nefer-ka-seker. Neter-baiu, Ka-kau, Ba-en-meter, Uat'-nes, Senta, Per-ab-sen, Nefer-ka-Ra Nefer-ka-seker, Het'efa.

Neter-baiu.   Ka-kau.   Ba-en-neter.   Uat'-nes.   Sentá.

$\substack{\text{}}$ = suten net,

Per-áb-sen.   Nefer-ka-Ra.*   Nefer-ka-seker.   Het'efa.

"King of the North and South."

2780-2680	IIIrd Dynasty (From Memphis, the SOUTH)*	T'at'ai to Humi. T'at'ai, Neb-ka, Ser or Djoser, Nefer-ka-Ra(Son of the Sun,** Set'es),Serteta, Ahtes, Neb-ka-Ra, Humi.

T'at'ai.   Neb-ka.   Ser.   Tetá.   Set'es.

Sertetá.   Ahtes.   Neb-ka-Rá.   Nefer-ka-Rá, son of the Sun,

Humi.

---

*The first of the GREAT PYRAMIDS was built during this dynastic period by Djoser.

Date BCE	Period	Monarch
2680-2565	IVth Dynasty (From Memphis, the SOUTH). Continuation of the Great Pyramid Age .	Seneteru to I-em-hetep. Seneferu, Khufu (Xufu), Khafra, (Xa-f-Ra), Men-kau-Ra, Tet-f-Ra, Shepeses-ka-f-Ra, Sebek-ka-Ra, I-em-hetep.

Seneferu.   xufu. (Cheops.)   xā-f-Rā. (Chephren.)   Men-kau-Rā. (Mycerinus.)   Teţ-f-Rā.

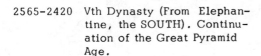

Shepses-ka-f.   Sebek-ka-Rā.   I-em-hetep.

2565-2420	Vth Dynasty (From Elephantine, the SOUTH). Continuation of the Great Pyramid Age.	Usr-ka-f to Unas. Usr-ka-f, Sah-u-Ra, Nefer-ka-ari-Ra (SOS, Kahaa), Nefer-f-Ra (SOS, Shepses-ka-Ra), Nefer-xa-Ra (SOS, Heru-a-ka-u), Usr-en-Ra (SOS, An), Men-kau-Heru, Tet-ka-Ra (SOS, Assa), Unas.

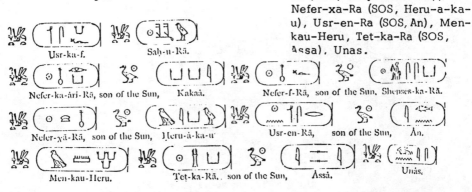

Usr-ka-f.   Sah-u-Rā.

Nefer-ka-āri-Rā, son of the Sun,   Kakaā.   Nefer-f-Rā, son of the Sun, Shepses-ka-Rā.

Nefer-xā-Rā, son of the Sun, Heru-ā-ka-u   Usr-en-Rā, son of the Sun,   An.

Men-kau-Heru.   Tet-ka-Rā,. son of the Sun,   Assā.   Unās.

2420-2270	VIth Dynasty (From Memphis, the SOUTH). Continuation of the Great Pyramid Age.	Teta to Men-ka-Ra. Teta (Teta-mer-en-Ptah, or Teta the Beloved of Ptah), Usr-ka-Ra (SOS, Ati), Meri-Ra (SOS, Pepi I), Mer-en-Ra (SOS, Heru-em-sa-f), Nefer-ka-Ra (SOS, Pepi II), Ra-mer-en-se, Neter-ka-Ra (SOS, Netaqerti).

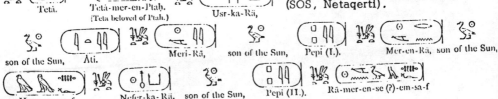

Tetā.   Teta-mer-en-Ptah. (Teta beloved of Ptah.)   Usr-ka-Rā,

son of the Sun,   Ati.   Meri-Rā, son of the Sun,   Pepi (I.).   Mer-en-Rā, son of the Sun,

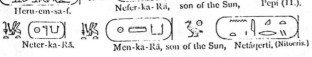

Heru-em-sa-f.   Nefer-ka-Rā, son of the Sun,   Pepi (II.).   Rā-mer-en-se (?)-em-sa-f

Neter-ka-Rā.   Men-ka-Rā, son of the Sun,   Netāqerti. (Nitocris.)

141

Date BCE	Period	Monarch
2270-2100	VIIth – Xth Dynasties. Beginning of the INTER-MEDIATE PERIOD. (From Memphis, the SOUTH) – VIIth–VIIIth. (From Heracleopolis , the NORTH) – IXth-Xth. MIDDLE KINGDOM CHIEFS.	Neter-ka to Nefer-ka-ari-Ra. Nefer-ka, Nefer-seh..., Ab (Aba), Nefer-kau-Ra, Xaroi, Nefer-ka-Ra, Nefer-ka-Ra-Nebi, Tet-ka-Ra-maa, Nefer-ka-Ra-Xentu, Senefer-Ra, Nefer-ka-Ra-t-rer-1, Mer-en-Heru, Se-nefer-ka-Ra, Nefer-ka-ka-Heru, Nefer-ka-Ra-Pepi-senb, Nefer-ka-Ra-annu, Nefer-kau-Ra, Nefer-kau-Heru, Nefer-ka-ari-Ra.

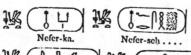

Nefer-ka.   Nefer-seh....

Ab.   Nefer-kau-Rā.   xaroi.   Nefer-ka-Rā.

Nefer-ka-Rā-Nebi.   Tet-ka-Rā-maā....   Nefer-ka-Rā-xentu.   Mer-en-Heru.

Senefer-ka.   Or   Se-nefer-ka-Rā.   Ka-en-Rā.   Nefer-ka-Rā-t-rer-1 (?).

Nefer-ka-Heru.   Nefer-ka-Rā-Pepi-senb   Nefer-ka-Rā-ānnu.   Nefer-kau-Rā.

Nefer-kau-Heru.   Nefer-ka-ari-Rā.

CHIEF-KINGS of the MIDDLE KINGDOM (FIRST DYNASTIC INTERMEDIATE PERIOD)

2100-2000	2152-1675 XIth-XIVth Dynasties Antef to Tet-xeru-Ra	
2100-2000	XIth Dynasty (From Thebes, the SOUTH).	Erpa (Hereditary Prince) to Se-anx-ka-ka. Antef, Men-tu-hetep, Antef II, Antef III, Antef IV or Neter Antef (Beautiful God of Antef), Son of the Sun Antef (SOS, Anaa), Nub-xeper-Ra (SOS, Antuf), Aha-Heru-Ra-apu-maat (SOS, Antuf-aa), Aha-renpit-Ra-aput-maat (SOS, Antef-aa), Tet-Ra-her-her-maat (SOS, Antef), Senefer-ka-Ra..., Usr-en-Ra, Neb-nem-Ra (SOS, Menou-hetep I), Se-Ra-Meno-hetep II, Neb-hetep-Ra (SOS,

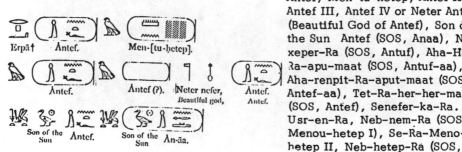

Erpāt   Antef.   Men-[tu-hetep].

Antef.   Antef (?).   Neter nefer,   Antef.   Antef.
Beautiful god,

Son of the Sun   Antef.   Son of the Sun   An-āa.

142

Date BCE	Period	Monarch

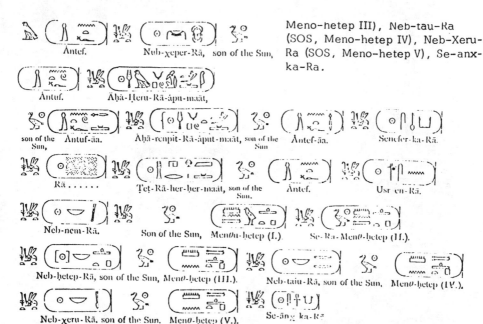

Meno-hetep III), Neb-tau-Ra (SOS, Meno-hetep IV), Neb-Xeru-Ra (SOS, Meno-hetep V), Se-anx-ka-Ra.

Ántef.

Nub-χeper-Rā, son of the Sun,

Ántuf.

Áḥā-Ḥeru-Rā-áput-maāt,

son of the Sun, Ántuf-āa. Áḥā-renpit-Rā-áput-maāt, son of the Sun Ántef-āa. Senefer-ka-Rā.

Rā...... Teṭ-Rā-her-her-maāt, son of the Sun. Ántef. Usr-en-Rā.

Neb-nem-Rā. Son of the Sun, Menθu-hetep (I.). Se-Rā-Menθ-hetep (II.).

Neb-hetep-Rā, son of the Sun, Menθ-hetep (III.). Neb-taiu-Rā, son of the Sun, Menθ-hetep (IV.).

Neb-χeru-Rā, son of the Sun. Menθ-hetep (V.). Se-ān χ ka-Rā

2000-1785 XIIth Dynasty (From Thebes, the SOUTH)

Sehetep-ab-Ra to Sebek-neferu-Ra.

Sehetep-ab-Ra (SOS, Amen-em-hat I), Xeper-ha-Ra (SOS, Usertsen I), Nub-kau-Ra (SOS, Amen-em-hat II), Xeper-xa-Ra (SOS, Usertsen II), Xa-kau-Ra (SOS, Usersten III), Maat-en-Ra (SOS, Amen-em-hat III), Maa-xeru-Ra (SOS, Amen-em-hat IV), Sebek-neferu-Ra.

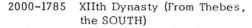
Sehetep-ab-Rā, son of the Sun, Amen-em-hat (I.).

χeper-ka-Rā, son of the Sun, Usertsen (I.).

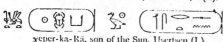
Nub-kau-Rā, son of the Sun, Amen-em-ḥat (II.).

χeper-χā-Rā, son of the Sun, Usertsen (II.).

χā-kau-Rā, son of the Sun, Usertsen (III.).

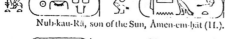
Maāt-en-Rā, son of the Sun, Amen-em-ḥāt (III.).

Maā-χeru-Rā, son of the Sun, Amen-em-ḥāt (IV.).

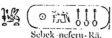
Sebek-neferu-Rā.

143

1785- ?   XIIIth Dynasty (From Thebes,
            the SOUTH)

Xu-taiu-Ra to Xerp-
-uah-xa-Ra (SOS,
Ra-hatep)
Xu-taiu-Ra, Xerp-ka-Ra,...em-
hat, Sehetep-ab-Ra, Auf-na,
Seanx-ab-Ra (SOS, Ameni-Antef-
Amen-em-hat), Semen-ka-Ra,
Sehetep-ab-Ra,...*ka, Net'em-
ab-Ra,Sebek [hetep]-Ra, Ren....
Set'ef....Ra, Ra-xerp-xu-tau
Sebek-hetep I, Semenx-ka-Ra
(SOS, Mer-menfitu),Xerp-seuat'-
Ra (SOS, Sebek-hetep II), Xa-
sexem-Ra (SOS, Nefer-hetep),
Ra-het....se (SOS, Het-Heru-
se), Xa-nefer-Ra (SOS, Sebek-
hetep III), Xa-hetep-Ra (SOS,
Sebek-hetep IV), Uah-ab-Ra-aa-
ab, Xaa-xeru-Ra, Neb-f-aa-mer-
Ra, Nefer-ab-Ra, Xa-anx-Ra
(SOS, Sebek-hetep V), Mer-xerp-
Ra, Men-xau-Ra (SOS, Anab),
Xerp-uat-Ra (SOS, Sebek-em-sa-
f I), Xerp-seser-taiu-Ra (SOS,
Sebek-em-sa-f II), Sesusr-taiu-
Ra, Xerp-Uast-Ra, Xerp-uah-xa-
Ra (SOS, Ra-hetep).

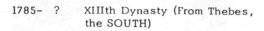

yu-taiu-Ra.   xerp-ka-Ra.   .... em-hat.

Sehetep-ab-Ra.   Auf-na.   Seanx-ab-Ra,

son of the Sun, Ameni-Antef-Amen-em-hat.   Semen-ka-Ra

Sehetep-ab-Ra.   .... ka..

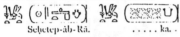

Net'em-ab-Ra.   Sebek-[hete]p-Ra.

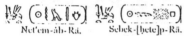

Ren......   Set'ef .... Ra.

Ra-xerp(?)-xu-taiu Sebek-hetep (I.).   Semenx-ka-Ra,

son of the Sun, Mer-menfitu.   xerp-seuat'-taiu-Ra,

son of the Sun, Sebek-hetep (II.).   xa-sexem-Ra,

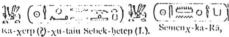

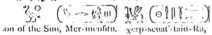

son of the Sun, Nefer-hetep.   Ra-het .... se, son of the Sun, Het-Heru-se   xa-nefer-Ra, son of the Sun.

Sebek-hetep (III.).   xa-hetep-Ra, son of the Sun, Sebek-hetep (IV.).   Uah-ab-Ra-aa-ab.

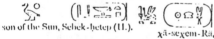

xaa-xeru-Ra.   Neb-f-a(?)a-mer-Ra.   Nefer-ab-Ra.   xa-anx-Ra, son of the Sun,

Sebek-hetep (V.).   Mer-xerp-Ra.   Men-xau-Ra, son of the Sun,   Anab,   xerp-uat'-xau-Ra,

son of the Sun, Sebek-em-sa-f (I.).   xerp-seset-taiu-Ra, son of the Sebek-em-sa-f (II.). Sesusr-taiu-Ra,
Sun,

xerp (?)-Uast-Ra.   xerp-uah-xa-Ra, son of the Sun,   Ra-hetep.

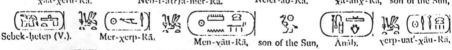

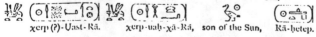

Date BCE	Period	Monarch
? -1675	XIVth Dynasty (From Thebes, the SOUTH)	Ner-neter-Ra to Tet-xeru-Ra

Ner-nefer-Ra (SOS, Ai), Mer-hetep-Ra (SOS, Ana), Sean-xensehtu-Ra, Mer-xerp-Ra-an-ren, Seuat-en-Ra, Xa-ka-Ra, Seheb-Ra, Mer-t-efa-Ra, Sta-ka-Ra, Neb-t-efa-Ra, Uben-Ra, Her-ab-Ra, Neb-sen-Ra, Seuah-en-Ra, Sexeper-en-Ra, Tet-xeru-Ra.

Mer-nefer-Rä, son of the Sun, Ai.

 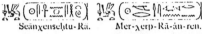

Mer-hetep-Rä, son of the Sun, Anä.

Seanxensehtu-Ra.   Mer-xerp-Rä-än-ren.

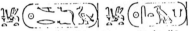 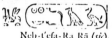

Seuat'-en-Rä.   xä-ka-Rä.   Ka-meri-Rä   neter nefer   Mer-kau-Rä.   Seheb-Rä

 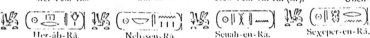

Mer-t'efa-Rä.   Sta-ka-Rä.   Neb-t'efa-Ra Rä (sic).   Uben-Rä.

Her-äb-Rä.   Neb-sen-Rä.   Seuah-en-Rä.   Sexeper-en-Rä.

CHIEF-KINGS OF THE FIRST NON-AFRICAN INVADERS - THE HYKSOS OF ASIA PERIOD
(1675-1555: XVth - XVIIth Dynasties)
Aa-peh-Set to Aah-mes-se-pa-ari

1675-1600	XVth Dynasty (From Asia)	Aa-peh-Set (SOS, Nub-Set...) to Apepa.

Aa-peh-Set (SOS, Nub-Set... ....Banan, Abeh.. -en-xepe Apepa.

Neter nefer Beautiful god,   Aa-äb-taiu-Rä,   son of the Sun,   Apepä.

or neter nefer Aa-qenen-Rä.

1600-1600	XVIth Dynasty (From Asia)	Neter neter* Aa-ab-taiu-Ra (SOS, Apepa or Neter nefer* As-qenen-Ra).

Aa-peh-peh-Set, son of the Sun, Nub-Set (?).

Abeh(?)-en-xepeś.   Apepä.   .... Bänän.

Date BCE	Period	Monarch

1600-1555   XVIIth Dynasty (From Asia)

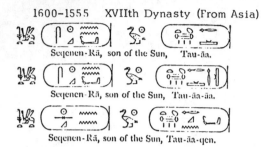

Seqenen-Rā, son of the Sun,   Tau-āa.

Seqenen-Rā, son of the Sun,   Tau-āa-āa.

Seqenen-Rā, son of the Sun,   Tau-āa-qen.

Uat'-xeper-Rā, son of the Sun,   Kames.   Suten ḥemt   Āaḥ-ḥetep.   Āaḥ-mes-se-pa-āri.
Royal wife.

Seqenen-Ra (SOS,
Tau-aa) to Aah-mes-
se-pa-ari.
Seqenen-Ra (SOS, Tau-aa),
Seqenen-Ra (SOS, Tau-aa-aa),
Seqenen-Rā (SOS, Tua-aa-qen),
Uat'-xeper-Ra (SOS, Khamose
or Kames), Sutep hemt** Aah-
hetep, Aah-mes-se-pa-ari.

CHIEF-KINGS OF THE NEW KINGDOM
(1580-1085: XVIIIth-XXIst Dynasties)
Neb-peh-peh-Ra to Men-mat-Ra setep-
en-Ra.

1555-1340   XVIIIth Dynasty (From Thebes,
the SOUTH)

Neb-peh-peh-Rā, son of the Sun,   Āaḥmes.
(Amasis I.)

Neter ḥemt   Āaḥ-mes-nefert-āri.
Divine wife.

Ser-ka-Rā, son of the Sun,   Amen-ḥetep.
(Amenophis I.)

Āa-xeper-ka-Rā, son of the Sun,   Teḥuti-mes.
(Thothmes I.)

Āa-xeper-en-Rā,   son of the
Sun,   Nefer-xau-Teḥuti-mes.
(Thothmes II.)

Ahmose I to Ser-
xeperu-Ra (SOS,
Amen-meri-en Heru-
en-heb).
Neb-peh-peh-Ra (SOS, Ahmose I),
Neter hemt Aah-mes-nefert-ari,
Ser-ka-Ra (SOS, Amen-hetep or
Amenophis I),Aa-xeper-ka-Ra
(SOS, Tehuti-mes or Thutmose I),
Aa-xeper-en-Ra (SOS, Nefer-xau-
Tehuti or Thutmose II), Mat-ka-Ra
(SOS,Hatshep-sut-xnem-Amen or
Queen-King Hatshepsut),Men-
xeper-Ra (SOS, Tehuti-mes or
Thutmose III), As-xeperu-Ra (SOS,
Amen-hetep neterheq Annu or
Amenophis II),Men-xeperu-Ra
(SOS, Tehuti-mes xa-xau or
Thutmose IV), Neb-mat-Ra (SOS,
Amen-hetep heq-Usat or Ameno-
phis III), Suten hemt Øi*, Nefer-
xerperu-Ra (SOS,Amen-hetep neter
heq Uast or Amenophis IV, also
Xu-en-Aten), Suten hemt urt**

---

*Beautiful God = Neter nefer   **Royal Wife = Sutep hemt   *** Divine wife =
Neter hemt. All of these will repeat ; they should be remembered.

146

Date BCE	Period	Monarch

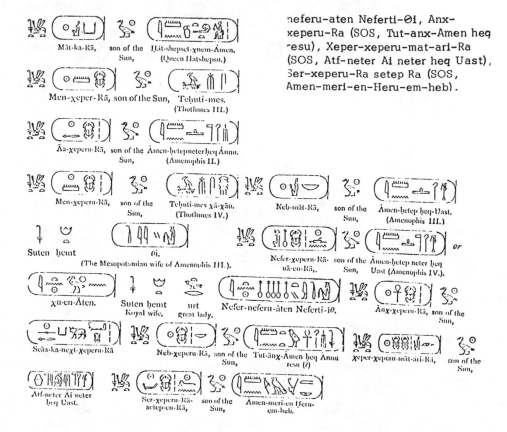

Māt-ka-Rā,	son of the Sun,	Ḥāt-shepset-χnem-Ámen. (Queen Hatshepsu.)
Men-χeper-Rā,	son of the Sun,	Teḥuti-mes. (Thothmes III.)
Āa-χeperu-Rā,	son of the Sun,	Ámen-ḥetepneterḥeq Ánnu. (Amenophis II.)
Men-χeperu-Rā,	son of the Sun,	Teḥuti-mes χā-χāu. (Thothmes IV.)
Neb-māt-Rā,	son of the Sun,	Ámen-ḥetep ḥeq-Uast. (Amenophis III.)
Suten ḥemt	Ói. (The Mesopotamian wife of Amenophis III.)	
Nefer-χeperu-Rā-uā-en-Rā,.	son of the Sun,	Ámen-ḥetep neter ḥeq Uast (Amenophis IV.).
χu-en-Áten.	Suten ḥemt Royal wife,	urt great lady.
Nefer-neferu-āten Neferti-íô.		
Ánχ-χeperu-Rā,	son of the Sun,	
Seāa-ka-neχt-χeperu-Rā		
Neb-χeperu-Rā,	son of the Sun,	Tut-ānχ-Ámen ḥeq Ánnu resu (?)
Χeper-χeperu-māt-ari-Rā,	son of the Sun,	
Atf-neter Ai neter ḥeq Uast.		
Ser-χeperu-Rā-setep-en-Rā,	son of the Sun,	Ámen-meri-en Ḥeru-em-heb.

neferu–aten Neferti–Θi, Anx-xeperu–Ra (SOS, Tut-anx-Amen heq resu), Xeper-xeperu-mat-ari–Ra (SOS, Atf-neter Ai neter heq Uast), Ser-xeperu-Ra setep Ra (SOS, Amen-meri-en-Heru-em-heb).

| 1340–1232 | XIXth Dynasty (From Thebes, the SOUTH) | Men-pehtet-Ra (SOS, Ra-nessu or Rameses I) to Usr-xau-Ra setep en-Ra meri-Ameri (SOS, Ra-meri Amen-merer Set-next or Set-Next). Men-pehtet-Ra (SOS, Rameses I), Men-mat-Ra (SOS, Ptah-meri-en-Seti or Seti I), Usr-mat-Ra setep-en-Ra (SOS, Ra-nessu-meri-Amen |

Men-peḥtet-Rā,	son of the Sun,	Rā-messu. (Rameses I.)
Men-māt-Rā,	son of the Sun,	Ptaḥ-meri-en-Seti. (Seti I.)

---

*Amenophis' wife from Mesopotania he married for political reasons; joining of political bond of friendship between Ta-Merry and Mesopotania (Africa and Asia). **Sten hemt = Royal wife; urt = Great lady. ****Allegedly the Pharaoh who chased Moses and the Haribu out of Ta-Merry (Egypt) during the EXODUS.

Date BCE	Period	Monarch

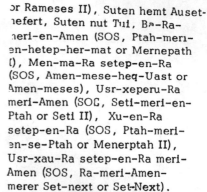

or Rameses II), Suten hemt Auset-
nefert, Suten nut Tui, Ba-Ra-
meri-en-Amen (SOS, Ptah-meri-
en-hetep-her-mat or Mernepath
I), Men-ma-Ra setep-en-Ra
(SOS, Amen-mese-heq-Uast or
Amen-meses), Usr-xeperu-Ra
meri-Amen (SOS, Seti-meri-en-
Ptah or Seti II), Xu-en-Ra
setep-en-Ra (SOS, Ptah-meri-
en-se-Ptah or Menerptah II),
Usr-xau-Ra setep-en-Ra meri-
Amen (SOS, Ra-meri-Amen-
merer Set-next or Set-Next).

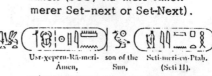

1232-1085 XXth Dynasty (From Thebes,
the SOUTH)

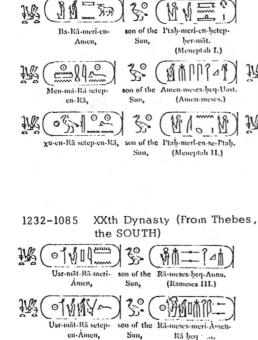

Usr-mat-Ra-meri-
Amen (SOS, Rameses
III) to Men-mat-Ra
setep-Ra (SOS, Ra-
meses XIII).

Usr-mat-Ra-meri-Amen (SOS,
Ra-meses-heq-Annu or Rameses
III), Usr-mat-Ra-setep-en-Amen
(SOS, Ra-meses-meri-Amen-Ra
heq mat or Rameses IV), Usr-
mat-Ra s-xeper-en-Ra(SOS, Ra-
mes-meri-Amen-Amen suten-f or
Rameses V), Ra-Amen-mat-meri-
neb (SOS, Ra-Amen-meses neter
heq Annu or Rameses VI), Ra-
usr-Amen-meri-setep-en-Ra
(SOS, Ra-Amen-neses-ta neter-
heq-Annu or Rameses VII), Ra-

Lord of the land = Neb-ta. Lord of two crowns = Neb xau.   Royal wife = Suten
hemt.   Called the "COMMONER PHARAOH"

| Dat<u>e</u> BCE | <u>Period</u> | <u>Monarch</u> |

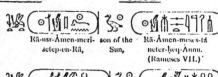

Rā-usr-Amen-meri-   son of the   Rā-Åmen-meses-tá
setep-en-Rā,   Sun,   neter-heq-Ånnu.
                                   (Rameses VII.)

Rā-māt-usr-xu-en-   son of the   Rā-Ámen-meses-meri-
Ámen,   Sun,   Åmen.
                                 (Rameses VIII.)

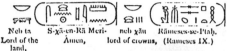

Neb ta   S-xā-en-Rā Meri-   neb xāu   Rameses-se-Ptah.
Lord of the   Åmen,   lord of crowns, (Rameses IX.)
land,

Nefer-kau-Rā   son of the   Rā-meses-merer-Åmen-
setep-en-Rā,   Sun,   xā-Uast (?).
                            (Rameses X.)

Rā-xeper-māt setep-   son of the   Rā-mes suten (?) Åmen.
en-Rā,   Sun,   (Rameses XI.)

Usr-māt-Rā setep-   son of the   Åmen mer-Rā-meses.
nu-Rā.   Sun,   (Rameses XII.)

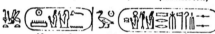

Men-māt-Rā   son of the   Rā-meses-merer-Åmen xā
setep-en-Rā,   Sun,   Uast (?) neter heq Ånnu.
                          (Rameses XIII.)

1085-950   XXIst Dynasty (From Tanis, the NORTH)

Rā-neter-xeper setep-en-   son of the   Se-Mentu meri-Rā.
Åmen,   Sun,   (Se-Mentu.)

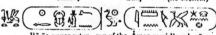

Rā-āa-xeper setep-   son of the   Åmen-meri Pa-seb-xā-nu.
en-Mentu,   Sun,   (Pasebxānu I.)

Åa-seh-Rā   son of the Sun, ...

Setep-en-Mentu-Rā,   son of the   Meri-Mentu-Åmen-
                     Sun,   en-āpt.
                                 (Amenenmapt.)

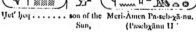

Het' heq ......   son of the   Meri-Åmen Pa-seb-xā-nu.
                 Sun,   (Pasebxānu II)

mat-usr-xu-en-Amen (SOS, Ra-Amen-meses-meri-Amen or Rameses VIII), Neb-ta* S-xa-en-Ra-Meri-Amen neb xau** Rameses-se Ptah or Rameses IX, Nefer-kau-Ra setep-en-Ra (SOS, Ra-meses-merer-Amen-xa-Uast or Rameses X), Ra-xeper-mat-setep-en-Ra (SOS, Ra-meses suten Amen or Rameses XI), Usr-mat-Ra setep-nu-Ra (SOS, Amen mer-Ra-meses or Rameses XII), Men-mat-Ra setep-en-Ra (SOS, Ra-meses-merer-Amen xa Uast neter heq Annu or Rameses XIII).

Ra-neter-xeper setep-Amen (SOS, Se-Mentu meri-Ra; to Het'heq....... (SOS, Meri-Amen Pa-seb-xa-nu)
Ra-neter-xeper setep-Amen (SOS, Se-Mentu meri-Ra or Se-Mentu), Ra-neter-xeper setep-en-Amen (SOS, Se-Metu meri-Ra or Se-Mentu), Ra-aa-xeper setep-en-Mentu (SOS, Amen-meri Pa-seb-xa-nu or Pasebxanu I), Aa-seh-Ra (SOS,.....), Setep-en-Mentu-Ra (SOS, Meri-Mentu-Amen-em-apt or Amenenmapt), Het'heq.... (SOS, Meri-Amen Pa-seb-xa-nu or Pasebxanu II).

Date BCE	Period	Monarch

XXIst Dynasty (From Thebes, the SOUTH)

Neter-hen-hetep en-
Amen to Suten hemt
Mat-ka-Ra.

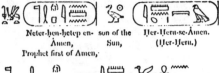

Neter-ben-hetep en-   son of the   Her-Heru-se-Amen.
Amen,   Sun,   (Her-Heru.)
Prophet first of Amen,·

Neter-hen-hetep en-Amen or
Prophet First of Amen (SOS, Her-
Heru-se-Amen or Her-Heru),
Neter he hetep em Amen Pa-anx
or Prophet First of Amen Pa-anx,
Pai-net'em I, Xeper-xa-Ra-
setep-en-Amen(SOS, Amen-meri-
Pai-net'em II),Suten nut Hent-
tau, Prophet First of Amen or
Masahero, Prophet First Men-
xeper-Ra Child Royal Amen-meri
Pat-net'em, Neter hen hetep en
Amen-Ra or Pai-net''em III or
Prophet First of Amen-Ra, Suten
hemt Mat-ka-Rå.

Neter ben hetep   en   Amen   Pa - ānχ
Prophet   first   of   Amen   Pa - ānχ.

Pai-net'em (I).   xeper-xā-Rā setep-   son of the
en-Amen,   Sun,

Amen-meri-Pai-   Suten   mut   Hent-taiu.
net'em (II).   Royal mother.   Hent - taiu.

Prophet first of Amen,   Masahero.   Prophet first, Men-χeper-Rā, child Royal, Amen-meri Pai-net'em.   Neter hen hetep
                                                                                                          Prophet   first

en   Amen-Rā, Pai-net'em (III.)   Suten ḥemt Māt-ka-Rā.
of   Amen-Rā.   Royal wife.

950-772   **XXIInd Dynasty (From Bubastis,* the NORTH)**

Xeper-sexet-Ra to
Usr-mat-Ra setep
-en-Amen.

Xeper-sexet-Rā   son of the   Amen-meri-Shashanq.
setep-en-Rā,   Sun,   (Shashanq I.)

Xeper-sexet-Ra or Setep-en-Ra
(SOS, Amen-meri-Shashanq or
Shashanq I), Xeper-sexet-Ra or
Setep-en-Ra (SOS, Amen-meri
Usarken or Osorkon I), Het'-Ra-
setep-en-Amen (SOS, Amen-meri
Auset-meri or Takeleth I), Ra-
usr-mat setep-en-Amen (SOS,
Amen-meri Usarken or Osorkon
II), Xeper-sexem-Ra setep-en-
Amen (SOS, Amen-meri Shashanq
or Shashanq II), Het'-xeperu-Ra
setep-en-Ra (SOS, Amen-Ra-meri

xerp-xeper-Rā   son of the   Amen-meri Uasirken.
setep-en-Rā,   Sun,   (Osorkon I.)

Het'-Rā-setep-en-Amen   son of the   Amen-meri Auset-meri
neter ḥeq Uast,   Sun,   θekeleθ.
                                 ('Takeleth I.)

Rā-usr-māt setep-en-   son of the   Amen-meri Uasirken.
Amen,   Sun,   (Osorkon II.)

---

*Ancient Libya was called"LEBU, LIBU", and "LIBUS" by the indigenous Africans.
Her inhabitants were called "BUBASITES, TANITES, MASHWAHAS" or "MESHWESH

150

xeper-sexem-Rā son of the Amen-meri Shash[anq].
setep-en-Amen, Sun,   (Shashanq II.)

or Takeleth II), Usr-mat-Ra setep-en-Ra (SOS, Amen-meri-se Bast Shashanq or Shashanq III), Usr-mat-Ra setep-en-Amen (SOS, Amen-meri Pa-mai).

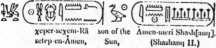

Het'-xeperu-Rā son of the Amen-Rā-meri Auset-meri
setep-en-Rā, Sun,   θekelet.
                (Takeleth.)

Usr-mät-Rā son of the Amen meri-se-Bast Shasha[n]q.
setep-en-Rā, Sun,   (Shashanq III.)

Usr-mät-Rā setep- son of the Amen-meri Pa-mái.
en-Amen,   Sun,   (Pa-mai.)

772-718   XXIIIrd Dynasty (From Tanis, the NORTH)

Se-her-áb-Rā, son of the Sun, Petä-se-Bast.

Se-her-ab-Ra (SOS, Peta-se-Bast), and, Aa-xeper-Ra setep-en-Amen (SOS, Ra-Amen-meri Jasarkena or Osorkon III).

Aa-xeper-Rā son of the Rā-Amen-meri Uasarkenā.
setep- en-Amen, Sun,   (Osorkon III.)

718-718   XXIVth Dynasty (From Tanis, the NORTH)

Uah-ka-Rā, son of the Sun, Bakenrenf.

Uah-ka-Ra to Amen-meri P-anxi.
Uah-ka-Ra (SOS, Bakenrenf),

718-717   (From Itiopi,
        the SOUTH)

Suten Kasta or King Kashta, Men-xeper-Ra (SOS, P-anxi or Piankhi), Amen-meri P-anxi or Piankhi.

Suten Kasta.
King Kashta.   Men-xeper-Rā, son of the Sun, P-änxi.   Amen-meri P-änxi, son of the Sun,

P-änxi.

717-653   XXVth Dynasty (From Itiopi, the SOUTH)

Nefer-ka-Ra (SOS, Shabaka or Sabacon) to Neter nefer* Usr - mat-Ra setep-en- Amen** Amenrut.
Nefer-ka-Ra (SOS, Shabaka or

Neteru-xu (?)-uā-Ptah-xeper-setep-en-Rā-Amen-äri-mät (?).

*God beautiful. ** Lord of two lands (Ethiopia or Itiopi and Ta-Merry or Egypt).

Date BCE	Period	Monarch

Nefer-ka-Ra, son of the Sun,   Shabaka.
(Sabaco.)

Sabacon), Tet-kau-Ra (SOS, Shabataka), Ra-nefer-tem-xu (SOS, Tahrq or Tirhakah), Neter nefer Usr-mat-Ra setep-en-Amen Amernrupt.

Tet-kau-Ra, son of the Sun,   Shabataka.

Ra-nefer-tem-xu, son of the Sun,   Tahrq.
(Tirhakah.)

Neter nefer   Usr-mat-Ra setep-   lord of two   Amenruf.
God beautiful,   en-Amen,   lands,

653-527   **XXVIth Dynasty (From Sais, the NORTH)**

Uah-ab-Ra to Anx-ha-en-Ra

Uah-ab-Ra (SOS, Psemoek or Psammetichus I), Nem-ab-Ra (SOS, Nekau or Necho I), Nefer-ab-Ra (SOS, Psemoek or Psammetichus II), Haa-ab-Ra or Apries), Xnem-ab-Ra (SOS, Ahmes-se-net or Amasis II), Anx-ka-en-Ra (SOS, Psemoek or Psammetichus III).

Uah-ab-Ra, son of the Sun,   Psemoek.
(Psammetichus I.,

Nem-ab-Ra,   son of the Sun,   Nekau.
(Necho II.)

Nefer-ab-Ra, son of the Sun,   Psemoek.
(Psammetichus II.)

Haa-ab-Ra,   son of the Sun,   Uah-ab-Ra.
(Apries.)

xnem-ab-Ra, son of the Sun,   Ahmes-se-net.
(Amasis II.)

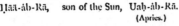

Anx-ka-en-Ra, son of the Sun,   Psemoek.
(Psammetichus III.)

CHIEF - KINGS OF THE LATE KINGDOM
Second invaders from Asia –Foreigners.
(527-332: XXVIIth-XXXIst Dynasties)
Mesue-Ra to ?

527-404   **XXXVIIth Dynasty (From Persia, Asia, the Foreigners)**

Meuse-Ra to Ra-meri –Amen

Meuse-Ra (SOS, Kembaoet or Cambyses), Settu-Ra (SOS, Antariusha or Darius Hystapes),

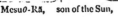

Mesuo-Ra,   son of the Sun,   Kembaoet.
(Cambyses.)

Date BCE	Period	Monarch

Settu-Rā.   son of the Sun,   Āntariusha.
                                (Darius Hystaspes.)

Lord of two lands Xshaiarsha or
Xerxes "the great," Artaxshashas
or Xerxes Artaxerxes, Ra-meri-
Amen (SOS, Anoeriutsha or Darius
Xerxes).

Lord of two
lands,   xshaiarsha.
              (Xerxes the Great.)

Artaxshashas.
(Artaxerxes.)

Rā-meri-Āmen, son of the Sun,   Anoerirutsha.
                                (Darius Xerxes.)

| 404-399 | XXVIIIth Dynasty (From Persia, Asia, Foreigners) | Semen-en-Ptah-Mentu-setep (SOS, Xabbesha). |

Senen-en-Ptah-Mentu-   son of the   (Xabbesha.)
setep,   Sun,

| 399-378 | XXIXth Dynasty (From Mendes, Asia, FOREIGNERS) | Ba-en-Ra neteru-meri to Ra-usr-Ptah-setep-en. Ba-en-Ra neteru-meri (SOS, Psemut), Xnem-mat-Ra (SOS, Haker), Ra-usr-Ptah-setep-en (SOS, Psemut). |

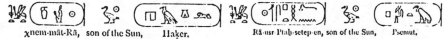

Ba-en-Rā neteru-   son of the   Niafāaurut.
meri,   Sun,

xnem-māt-Rā, son of the Sun,   Haker.   Rā-usr-Ptah-setep-en, son of the Sun,   Psemut.

| 378- 341 | XXXth Dynasty (From Thebes, the SOUTH)* | S-net'em-ab-Ra or setep-em-Amen (SOS, Next-Heru-hebt-meri-Amen or Nectanebus I) and , Xeper-ka-Ra (SOS, Next-neb-f or Nectanebus II). |

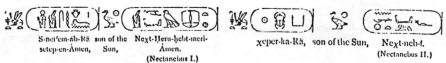

S-net'em-ab-Rā son of the   Next-Heru-hebt-meri-   xeper-ka-Rā, son of the Sun,   Next-neb-f.
setep-en-Amen, Sun,   Amen.   (Nectanebus II.)
                             (Nectanebus I.)

* Last of the indigenous African Pharaohs who ruled Ta-Merry (Egypt).

CHIEF-KINGS OF THE SECOND NON-AFRICAN
INVADERS - THE PERSIANS FROM ASIA

341 - 332   XXXIst Dynasty (From Persia)   Records of these
             Asia, Foreigners)   kings have been
          (Alexander "the great" captured Egypt in 332 BCE)   uncovered to date.

CHIEF-KINGS OF THE THIRD NON-AFRICAN
INVADERS - MACEDONIAN-GREEKS FROM
EUROPE - Alexander to the Ptolemies, etc.
(332-30: XXXIInd-XXXIIIrd Dynasties, so-called)
Setep-en-Ra-meri Amen to Ra se neb Xaa*
Kiseres anx Auset meri**

332 - 305   "XXXIInd Dynasty" (From   Setep-en-Ra-meri-
             Macedonia, Europe)   Amen (SOS, Alek-
                                            santres or Alexander

332 - 323   Alexander ("The Great")   "the great") to Ra-
                                             qa-ab-setep-en-Amen
                                             (SOS, Aleksantres or
                                             Alexander IV).

Setep-en-Ra-meri-Amen (SOS, Aleksantres or Alexander "the great"),
neb-taiu Setep-en-Ra-meri-Amen
(SOS, Phiuliupas or Philip Aridaeus),
and, Ra-qa-ab-setep-en-Amen (SOS,
Aleksantres or Alexander IV).

Setep-en-Rā-meri-   son of the   Aleksantres
Amen,   sun,   (Alexander the Great.)

neb taiu Setep-en Rā- son of the   Phiuliupuas
meri-Amen,   Sun,   (Philip Aridaeus.)

Rā-qa-ab-setep-en-Amen, son of the   Aleksantres.
                      Sun.   (Alexander IV.)

305-47 or 30   "XXXIIIrd Dynasty" From   Setep-en-Ra-meri-
                  Macedonia, Europe,   Amen (SOS, Ptulmis
                  Foreigners   or Ptolemy I, also
                                            Soter I) to Ra se neb
                                            Xaa Kiseres anx t'etta
                                            Ptah Auset meri.

Setep-en-Rā-meri-   son of the   Ptulmis
Amen,   Sun,   (Ptolemy I, Soter I.)

Setep-en-Ra-meri-Amen (SOS,
Ptulmis or Ptolemy I, Soter I), Neter +
nut Bareniket or Bernice I, Ra-usr-
ka-meri Amen (SOS, Ptulmis or
Ptolemy II or Philadelphus), Sutenet
set suten sent hemt neb taiu Arsanat,
Suten set suten sent Pilatra or

Neter inut,   Bareniket.
Divine Mother   (Berenice I.)

---

*Son of the Sun, Lord of diadens, **Ceasar, living for ever, of Ptah and Isis
beloved. +Divine mother.

Date B.C.E.	Period	Monarch

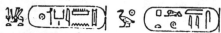

Rā-usr-ka-meri Åmen, son of the Sun, Ptulnis
(Ptolemy II. Philadelphus.)

Sutenet set suten sent suten hemt neb taiu   Årsanat
Royal daughter, royal sister, royal wife, lady of the two lands (Arsinoë)

Suten   set   suten sent   Pilatra.
Royal daughter,   royal sister   (Philotera).

Neteru-senu-uā-en-Rā-setep-Åmen-χerp (?)-en-ānχ, son of the Son,

Ptualmis ānχ t'etta Ptah meri
Ptolemy (III. Energetes I.), living for ever, beloved of Ptah.

Ḥeqt   nebt   taiu,   - Bārenikat
Princess, lady of the two lands,   (Berenice II.)

Neteru-menχ-uā-[en]-Ptah-setep-en-Rā-usr-ka-Åmen-χerp (?)-ānχ,

son of the Sun   Ptualmis ānχ t'etta Åuset meri
Ptolemy (IV. Philopator,) living for ever, beloved of Isis.

Suten set suten   sent   ḥemt   urt   nebt   taiu
Royal daughter, royal sister, wife, great lady, lady of the two lands.

Arsinai.
Arsinoë (III., wife of Philopator I.)

Neteru-meri-uā-en-Ptah-setep-Rā-usr-ka-Åmen-χerp-ānχ.

son of the Sun   Ptualmis ānχ t'etta Ptah meri.
Ptolemy (V. Epiphanes) living for ever, beloved of Ptah.

Ptolemy VI. Eupator, wanting.

Philotera, Neteru-senu-ua-en-Ra-setep-Amen-xerp... -en-anx (SOS, Ptualimis anx t'etta Ptah meri Ptolemy III or Euergetes), Heqt nebt taiu Barenikat or Bernice II, Neteru-menx-ua- [en]-Ptah-setep-en-Ra-usr-ka-Amen-xerp... - anx (SOS, Ptualmis anx t'etta Auset meri Ptolemy IV, Philopator, living for ever, beloved of Isis), Suten set suten sent urt nebt taiu, Arsinai or Arsinøe III (wife of Philopator I), Neteru-meri-ua-en-Ptah-setep-Ra-usr-ka-Amen-xerp-anx (SOS, Ptualmis anx t'etta Ptah meri or Ptolemy V, Epiphanes - living for ever beloved of Ptah), Ptolemy VI or Eupator, Suten set sen hemt Qlauapetrat or Cleopatra (Royal daughter, sister, wife), Ne Neteru-xu...-ua-Ptah-setep-en-Ra-Amen-ari-mat-... (SOS, Ptualmis anx t'etta Ptah meri Ptolemy VII or Philometor I), Sutenet set suten hemt suten neb taiu or Qlauapetrat (Cleopatra II, wife of Philometor I), Ptolemy VIII or Philopator II, Neteru-xu-...ua-en-Ptah-setep-en-Ra-ari-mat xerp anx (SOS, Ptualmis anx t'etta Ptah meri or Ptolemy IX, Euergetes II), Suten net (King of North and South, Lord of two lands) Neter-menx-mat-s-meri-net-ua-Ptah-xerp...-setep-en-Ra-Amen-ari-mat, Ra-se-neb xau Ptualmis t'etta Ptah meri or Ptolemy X (Soter II or Philometor II), Suten net (King of the North and South) Neteru-menx-ua-Ptah-setep-Ra-Amen-ari-mat-senen-Ptah-anx-en (SOS, Ptualmis t'etu-nef Aleksentres anx t'etta Ptah meri Ptolemy XI (Is he Alexander, living for ever, beloved of Ptah), Heqt neb taiu Erpa-ur-qebh-Baaarenekat or Bernice III, Ptolemy XII or Alexander II, P-neter-n-ua-

Date B.C.E.	Period	Monarch

Suten set   sen   ḥemt   Qlauapetrat.
Royal daughter, sister, wife,   (Cleopatra I).

son of the Sun.   Ptualmis ānχ t'etta Ptah meri.
Ptolemy (VII. Philometor I.), living for ever, beloved of Ptah.

Sutenet set   suten sent ḥemt   suten   mut   neb   taiu
Royal daughter, royal sister, wife, royal mother, lady of the two lands,

Qlauapetrat.   Neteru-χu (?) uā-en-Ptah-setep-en-Rā-Amen-āri-māt χerp ānχ
(Cleopatra II. wife of Philometor I.).

Ptolemy VIII. Philopator II. wanting.

son of the Sun.   Ptualmis ānχ t'etta Ptah meri.   Suten net   lord of   two lands,
Ptolemy (IX. Euergetes II.), living for ever, beloved of Ptah.   King of North and South,

Neteru-menχ-māt-s-meri-net-uā-Ptah-χerp (?)-setep-en-Rā-   Rā-se neb χāu   Ptualmis ānχ t'etta Ptah meri.
Amen-āri-māt.   Son of the Sun, lord of   Ptolemy X. (Soter II. Philometor II.).
                                          diadems,

Suten net,   Neteru-menχ-uā-Ptah-setep-en-Rā-Amen-āri-māt-   on of the   Ptualmis t'etu-nef Aleksentres ānχ t'etta Ptah meri
King of North and   senen-Ptah-ānχ-en,   Sun.   Ptolemy (XI.) called is he Alexander, living for ever,
South,   beloved of Ptah.

Ḥeqt   neb taiu   Erpā-ur-qebḥ-Rāaarencḳāt.   P-neter-n-uā-enti-nehem-Ptah-setep-en-āri-māt-en-
Princess, lady of two lands,   Berenice (III.)   Rā-Amen-χerp-ānχ

Ptolemy XII. (Alexander II.), wanting.

son of the Sun.   Ptualmis ānχ t'etta Ptah Auset meri.   Neb taiu   Qlapetrat t'ettu-nes Trapenet.
Ptolemy (XIII.), living for ever, beloved of Isis and Ptah.   Lady of two lands,   Cleopatra (V.), called is she Tryphaena.

Ḥeqt   taiu   Qluapeter.   Suten net   neb   taiu   Ptualmis.
Queen of two lands,   Cleopatra (VI.)   King of North and   lord of   two lands,   Ptolemy (XIV.)
                                South,

Rā   se   neb   χāā   Kiseres ānχ t'etta Ptah Auset meri
son of the   lord of   Cæsar, living for ever, of Ptah and
Sun,   diadems,   Isis beloved.

enti-nehem-Ptah-setep-en-ari-mat-en-Ra-Amen-xerp-anx (SOS, Ptualmis anx t'etta Ptah Auset meri or Ptolemy XIII), Neb taiu Qlapetrat t'ettu-nes Trapenet or Cleopatra V (Is she Tryphaena), Heqt taiu Qluapeter or Cleopatra VI, Suten net neb taiu Ptualmis or Ptolemy XIV (Ra se neb xaa Kiseres anx t'etta Ptah Auset meri Caesar).

156

Date BCE	Period	Monarch

FOURTH NON-AFRICAN INVADERS - THE ROMAN EMPERORS OF COLONIAL TA-MERRY (Egypt)
The so-called "XXXIVth Dynasty"
(30 BCE - 324 CE. Chaos & Rape)
Suten net neb taiu Autegreter to Autegreter Caesar

30 - 0 B.C.E.

"XXXIVth Dynasty" (From Rome, Europe, Foreigners)

Suten net taiu Autegreter (Autocrator) to Autocrator Caesar (Taksas netx-Decius). Suten net neb taiu Auterqreter (Autocrator)*, Ra se neb xau Kiseres anx Ptah Auset meri Caesar Augustus, Suten net neb taiu Autegreter Ra se (SOS, neb xau, or Tebaris Kiseris anx t'etta).

Autocrator Caesar

Taksas netx.
Decius . . . . .

Suten net King of North and South,	neb lord of	taiu two lands,	Auteqreter Autocrator,	Ra se Sun's son,	neb xau lord of crowns.	Kiseres anx t'etta Ptah Auset meri Caesar (Augustus), living for ever, of Ptah and Isis beloved.

0 - 0 Christian Era or C.E. or A.D. New calendar issued hundreds of years beyond this point under the edict of the Roman Emperor Justinian. From this juncture we are changing from NILE YEARS," SOLAR YEARS," LUNAR YEARS, etc. to the present calendar system, thus abondoning the MASONICAL CALCULATIONS used by the ancient indigenous Africans of the Nile Valley of North and East Africa.

0 - 324

"XXXIVth Dynasty" (From Rome,Europe, Foreigners)

Heq hequ Autekreter Ptah Auset-meri (SOS, Qais Kaiseres Kermenis or Gaius * Caesar Germanicus) to Auteqreter Caesar.

Heq hequ Autekreter Ptah Auset-meri King of kings, Autocrator, of Ptah and Isis beloved,	son of the Sun.	Qais Kaiseres Kermeniqis. Gaius (Caligula) Caesar Germanicus.

Neruas netx Nerva	Autukreter Kiseres Autocrator Caesar,	son of the Sun,

---

*Due to the very long list of names of the Roman Emperors and Viceroys or Governors of the so-called "XXXIVth DYNASTY" the author found in necessary to list only those mentioned in the general body of the text throughout all of the chapters. They are those who have influenced the course of Nile Valley High-Culture up to a point just beyond the proclaimed "BIRTH OF JESUS CHRIST" - the "Nativity." Other works by the author show all of them as they relate to the texts.

QUICK REFERENCE CHRONOLOGY OF THE DYNASTIC REIGN
OF THE MOST NOTED PHARAOHS AND QUEENS OF TA-MERRY,
TA-NEHISI, MERÖE, ITIOPI, LEBU & PUANIT

Date B.C.E.	Name	Origin	Date B.C.E.	Name	Origin
	Ist Dynasty		1970-1936	Senwosret I	Thebes
3200-2980	Aha or Narmer	Thebes	1938-1904	Amenohat II	
			1906-1888	Senwosret II	
	IInd Dynasty		1888-1850	Senwosret III	
2980-2900	Neter-baiu	Tanis	1850-1800	Amenohat III	
			1800-1792	Amenohat IV	
	IIIrd Dynasty			XIIIth Dynasty	
2720-2700	Djoser, Humi	Memphis	1785- ?	Xu-taiu-Ra,	Thebes
				Semen-ka-Ra,	
	IVth Dynasty			Sebek-hetep I,	
2680-2565	Sneferu, Khufu,	Memphis		Xa-hetep-Ra,	
	Khafra, Men-kau-Ra			Xerp-uah-xa-Ra	
	Vth Dynasty			XIVth Dynasty	
2565-2420	Nefer-f-Ra,	Elephan-	? -1675	Ner-nefer-	Thebes
	Tet-kau-Ra,	tine		Ra, Tet-xeru-	
	Unas.			Ra	
	VIth Dynasty			XVth Dynasty	Asia [FA]
2420-2270	Teta, Usr-ka-Ra,	Memphis	1675-1600	Aa-peh-Set,	
	Pepi I, Mernere.			Apepa	
	VIIth, VIIIth, IXth			XVIth Dynasty	
	& Xth Dynasties		1600-1600	Aa-ab-taiu-Ra	
2270-2100	Nefer-ka, Ab,	Memphis		Ra	
	Nefer-ka-Ra,	& On		XVIIth Dynasty	
	Nefer-ka-ari-Ra		1600-1580	Seqenen-Ra,	Asia [FA]
				Kamose	
	XIth Dynasty				
2150-2090	Antef II	Thebes		XVIIIth Dynasty	
2090-2085	Antéf III		1580-1558	Ahmose I	Thebes
2085-2065	Mentuhotep I		1557-1530	Amenhotep I	
2065-2060	Mentuhotep II		1530-1515	Thutmose I	
2060-2015	Mentuhotep III		1515-1505	Thutmose II	
2015-2005	Mentuhotep IV		1515-1484	Hatshepsut	
2005-2000	Mentuhotep V			the "Queen King"	
	XIIth Dynasty		1504-1450	Thutmose III	
2000-1979	Amenehat I	Thebes			

*Place of birth of the Pharaoh or Queen: FA = Foreigner from Asia. FE = Foreigner from Europe. All of the others are from Alkebu-lan (Africa), as designated.

158

Date B.C.E.	Name	Origin
1450-1415	Amenhotep II	Thebes
1415-1405	Thutmose IV	
1405-1370	Amenhotep III & Queen Tiyi	
1370-1352	Amenhotep IV & Queen Nefer-ti-ti	
? -1349	Tut-ankh-Amen	
	XIXth Dynasty	
1340-1320	Haremheb	Thebes
1320-1318	Rameses I	
1318-1298	Seti I	
1298-1232	Rameses II	
	XXth Dynasty	
1232-1224	Merneptah	Thebes
1200-1198	Setinekht	
1198-1168	Rameses III, the "COMMONER"	
	XXIst Dynasty	
1085-950	Ra-neter-xeper	Thebes
	XXIInd Dynasty	
950-925	Sheshonq	Bubastis
925-893	Osorkon I	
893-870	Takhlet I	
870-847	Osorkon II	
847-823	Takhlet II	
823-772	Sheshonq II	
	XXIIIrd Dynasty	
772-718	Se-her-ab-Ra, Ra-setep-Amen	Tanis
	XXIVth Dynasty	
718-718	Kashta,	Tanis
	Piankhi	Itiopi
	XXVth Dynasty	
718-716	Piankhi	Itiopi
716-701	Shabakha (Shabacom)	
701-690	Shabatakha	

Date B.C.E.	Name	Origin
690-664	Taharkha (Taharqa)	
664-653	Tanutemun	
	XXVIth Dynasty	
663-609	Psenthek I	Sais
609-594	Necho (Neku)	
594-588	Psemthek II	
588-568	Apries	
568-527	Amasis	
	XXVIIth Dynasty	
527-404	Cambyses, Darius	Asia [FA]
	XXVIIIth Dynasty	
409-399	Semen-en-Ptah-mentu-setep	Asia [FA]
	XXIXth Dynasty	
399-378	Ba-en-Ra neteru-meri	Asia [FA]
	XXXth Dynasty	
378-360	Nectanebos I	Asia
360-341	Nectanebos II	[FA]
	XXXIst Dynasty	
341-332	These rulers UNKNOWN	Asia [FA]
	XXXIInd Dynasty	Europe [FE]
332-323	Alexander II ("the great")	
	XXXIIIrd Dynasty	
323-283	Soter I (Ptolemy I)	Europe [FE]
283-244	Ptolemy II-XIII,	
244-30	Cleopatra VIII (last Queen)	
	XXXIVth Dynasty	
BCE 30-324 CE	Suten net Au Autocrator, Caesar Augustus, Tiberias, etc.	Europe [FE]

CHRONOLOGY OF NILE VALLEY HIGH-CULTURES
COLONIZATION PERIODS

[Ta-Merry under Ta-Nehisi colonial rule]

Viceroy or Governor (Rep. of Ta-Nehisi)	Date & Period B.C.E.	Pharaoh or Queen Monarch

Ist Dynasty [From Thebes]

Aha	3200 - ?	Aha (Narmer or Menes)

[Ta-Nehisi under Upper Ta-Merry colonial rule]
(Rep. of Ta-Merry) XVIIIth Dynasty - From Thebes or Luxor

Thure	1550 - 1528	Amenhotep I & Thutmose I
Seni	1528 - 1503	Thutmose I & II
Nehi	1503 - 1450	Hatshepsut & Thutmose III
Wesesersetet	1450 - 1417	Amenhotep II
Amenophis	1417 - 1402	Thutmose IX & Amenhotep III
Mermose	1402 - 1365	Amenhotep III
Thutmose	1373 - 1357	Amenhotep IV
Huy-Amenhotep	1357 - 1349	Tutankhamen

XIXth Dynasty - From Thebes or Luxor

Passer I	1346 - 1315	Ay & Horemheb
Amenemopet	1320 - 1298	Seti I & Rameses I
Hekanakht	1298 - 1232	Rameses II

XXth Dynasty - From Thebes or Luxor

Passer II	1298 - 1232	Rameses II
Sethauw	1298 - 1232	Rameses II
Messuwy	1232 - 1224	Mernepatah & Seti II
Seti II	?	Siptah
Hori I	?	Siptah & Setinekht
Hori II	?	Rameses III & IV
Wetawuat	?	Rameses VI & VIII
Ramesesenakht	?	Rameses IX
Pa-Nehisi	?	Rameses XI
Herihor	?	Rameses XI
Piankhi (Piankhy)	?	Herihor

Ta-Nehisi & Itiopi Imperial Rule Over Ta-Merry

(Rep. of Ta-Nehisi) XXIVth Dynasty - From Ta-Nehisi

Kashta	706 - 751	Kashta
Piankhy (Piankhi)	751 - 716	Piankhi

Ta-Nehisi & Ta-Merry under rule
of Itiopi colonial expansionists

(Rep. of Itiopi, Lord of Two Lands, N. & S.)	Date & Period B.C.E.	Pharaoh or Queen Monarch

XXVth Dynasty – From Itiopi or Ethiopia

Shabaka (Sabacon)	716 – 701	Shabaka
Shabataka	701 – 690	Shabataka
Taharqa	690 – 664	Taharqa
Tanwetamani (Tanutemun)	664 – 653	Tanwetamani

Itiopi imperial rule over Ta-Nehisi
and Ta-Merry ended by Persians.

The following CHRONOLOGY is exactly the same as it appeared in the First
Edition. There have been very few technological changes. The author found it necessary to combine various aspects of all of the chronologies dealing with the indigenous African peoples of the Nile Valley and Great Lakes regions to show
the commonality of the High-Cultures they developed from the beginning of
their migrations to the NORTH – Ta-Nehisi, Ta-Merry, Itiopi, Puanit, Lebu,
Hata, Khart-Haddas, Meroe, Numidia, etc.

It will be noticed that there are many periods in the above chronology for
which no coverage of a particular VICEROY or MONARCH is given. Such periods
are marked by the confusing lack of information for anyone to draw a definite
conclusion as to just where the "BOUNDARY" of either of these countries actually began or ended. There were many periods in which overlapping-reign
existed, to the extent that the cultures of the Nile Valleys and Great Lakes regions appeared to be the co-equal of other indigenous cultures all over the continent of Alkebu-lan (Africa).

Because of the above cross-references one can better understand why it was
impossibe for the Africans of Ta-Nehisi and Ta-Merry to have developed completely separate High-Cultures that had no common origin. However, the following chronologies deal with the OVER-LAPPING pharaohs, monarchs, and countries.

A CHRONOLOGY OF
NOTED RULERS OF KUSH UNDER EGYTIAN IMPERIALISM

Governor or Viceroy	Date B.C.E	Monarch or Pharaoh
XVth Dynasty		
Thure	1550 - 1528	Amenhotep I & Thutmose I
Seni	1528 - 1503	Thutmose I & II
Nehi	1503 - 1450	Hatshepsut & Thutmose III
Wesesersatet	1450 - 1417	Amenhotep II
Amenophis	1417 - 1402	Thutmose IX & Amenhotep III
Mermose	1402 - 1365	Amenhotep III
Thutmose	1373 - 1357	Amenhotep IV
Huy-Amenhotep	1357 - 1349	Tutankhamun
XIXth Dynasty		
Paser I	1346 - 1315	Ay & Horemheb
Amenemopet	1320 - 1298	Seti I & Ramses I
Hekanakht	1298 - 1232	Ramses II
Passer II	1298 - 1232	Ramses II
Sethauw	1298 - 1232	Ramses II
XXth Dynasty		
Messuwy	1232 - 1224	Merneptah & Seti II
Seti	?	Siptah
Hori I	?	Siptah & Setinekht
Hori II	?	Ramses III & IV
Wetawuat	?	Ramses VI & VIII
Ramessenakht	?	Ramses IX
Pa-nehesi	?	Ramses XI
Herihor	?	Ramses XI
XXVth Dynasty		
Piankhy (Pianki)		Herihor

GREAT MONARCHS OF KUSH (Cush)
[538 - 308 B.C.E.]

Date B.C.E	Monarch	Date B.C.E.	Monarch
538 - 533	Analma'aye	483-418	Talakhamani
533 - 513	Amani-natake-lebte	418 - 398	Aman-nete-yerike

Date B.C.E.	Monarch	Date B.C.E.	Monarch
513 - 503	Korkamani	398 - 397	Baškakeren
503 - 478	Amani-astabarqa	397 - 362	Harisiotet
478 - 458	Sisaspiqa	362 - 342	?
458 - 453	Nasakhma	342 - 328	Akhratan
453 - 423	Malewiebamani	328 - 308	Nastasen

GREAT MONARCHS OF MERÓE
&
ITIOPI
[706 B.C.E. - 350 C.E.]

No.	Name	Date	No.	Name	Date
1.	Kashta	706-751	27.	Arakakami	295-275
2.	Piankhy (Piankhi)	751-716	28.	Amanislo	275-260
3.	Shabato	716-701	29.	Queen Bartare	260-250
4.	Shebitku	701-690	30.	Amani...takha	250-235
5.	Taharqa	690-664	31.	Arnekhamani	235-218
6.	Tanwetamani	664-653	32.	Arqamani	218-200
7.	Atlanersa	653-643	33.	Tabirqa	200-185
8.	Senkamanisken	643-623	34.	...iwal (awal)	185-170
9.	Antamani	623-593	35.	Queen Shanckiakhete	170-160
10.	Aspelta	593-568	36.	(Unknown King)	160-145
11.	Malenaqen	568-555	37.	Naqrinsan	145-120
12.	Amtalqa	555-542	38.	Tanyidamani	120-100
13.	Analmaye	542-538	39.	....khale	100- 80
14.	Amani-nataki-lebte	538-519	40.	....amani	80- 65
15.	Karkamani	519-510	41.	Amanikhabale	65- 41
16.	Amaniqstabarqa	510-487	42.	Queen Amanishabhete	41- 23
17.	Siaspign	487-468	43.	Netakamani	
18.	Malewiebamani	463-435	44.	Queen Amaritare	
19.	Tallakhamani	435-431	45.	Sherkarer	12 - 17
20.	Amani-nete-yerike	431-405	46.	Pisakar	17 - 35
21.	Baskakeren	405-404	47.	Amanitaraqide	35 - 45
22.	Harsiotef	404-369	48.	Amanitenmemide	45 - 62
23.	(Unknown King)	367-350	49.	Queen Amanikhastashan	62 - 85
24.	Akhnatan	350-335	50.	Tarokeniwal	85 -103
25.	Nastasen	335-310	51.	Amanikhalika	103 - 108
26.	Amanibakhi	310-295	52.	Aritenyesbekhe	108 - 132

No.	Name	Date	No.	Name	Date
53.	Aqrakamani	132 - 137	60.	Teritnide	228 - 246
54.	Adeqetali	137 - 146	61.	Aretnide	246 - 246
55.	Takideamani	146 - 165	62.	Teqerideamani	246 - 266
56.	...reqerem	165 - 184	63.	Tamelerdpamani	266 - 283
57.	(Unknown)	184 - 194	64.	Yesbekheamani	283 - 300
58.	Teritedabhatey	194 - 209	65.	Lakhideamani	300 - 308
59.	Aryesbekhe	209 - 228	66.	Malegerebar	308 - 320

MAJOR EVENTS OF MODERN TA-NEHISI (Sudan) & MEROE ? - 350
[350 - 1956 C.E.]

Date C.E.	Event
? - 350	Fall of Meröe or Meröwe; the beginning of Christian rule.
? - 550	Conversion of Ta-Nehisi and Meroe to Christianity by military force.
641 - ?	Muslim invasion of Ta-Nehisi; the JIHADS (religious wars) exterminated Nile Valley civilization and people. Africans forced to join Islam.
1484 - 1790	Reign of the Fungs. The Fung Kingdom greets Ta-Nehisi.
1820 - 1821	Mohammad Ali of Egypt (originally of Albania?] captured Ta-Nehisi (Nubia, Ziti, or modern Sudan); the extension of the Ottoman-Turks empire and influence in Alkebu-lan.
13 Sept. - 1882	Battle of Tel-el-Keber.
1882 - 1883	British military forces occupied Egypt and Sudan; beginning of the so-called "CONDOMINIUM" between Egypt and Great Britain.
1884 - 1898	El Madhi Rebellion; the beginning of the British-Madhi Wars for the conquest of Sudan.
12 Jan. 1885	El Mahdi killed General ["Chinese"] Gordon, commander of all British and Egyptian forces in the war against Sudan
2 Sept. 1898	Battle of Omdurman was fought; beginning of the so-called British and Sudanese "CONDOMINIUM" under varied pretexts, with Great Britain always in command.
1899 - 1956	British imperialism and colonialism negated in Sudan: end to "CONDOMINIUM" and colonialism.

Dealing with Ta-Merry, Ta-Nehisi, Meröe, Itiopi, Kush, and Puanit as if they were distinctly separate nations of the Nile Valley at anytime during the first four DYNASTIES, c. 3200 - 2565 B.C.E., is completely erroneous. This must be taken into consideration even though European-American "EDUCATORS" [who have established themselves as "THE SOLE AUTHORITY" on all of the Nile Valley High-Cultures in their own RACIST interpretation of this area of Alkebu-lan's history, which developed from the early half of the 19th century C.E.] purposfully ignored this fact. Most of them have attributed this aspect of their folley to the misinterpretation of the INSCRIPTION on the so-called "PALERMO STONE" by the late professor James Henry Breasted, founder of the Oriental Institute of the University of Chicago, Illinois. Yet, it is this professor's version of said document that most "MODERN WHITE LIBERAL AFRICANISTS" use for this aspect of Ta-Nehisian [Zetian, Nubian, or Sudanese] and Ta-Merrian [Egyptian] history.[0] The same professor Breasted, the United States of America's "FIRST RECOGNIZED AUTHORITY ON EGYPT," was the "Noted Academician" who wrote the following "SCHOLARLY" comments about the SUPERIORITY of "...THE GREAT WHITE RACE..." in his book, THE CONQUEST OF CIVILIZATION, pp. 112 - 113:

> The population of the Great Northwest Quadrant, from the Stone Age onward, has been a race of white men of varying physical type. The evolution of civilization has been the achievement of this Great White Race. In the territory adjoining the Northwest Quadrant there are only two other clearly differentiated races, the Mongoloid and the Negroid. On the *east* of the Northwest Quadrant the secluded plateaus of High Asia developed a type of man with straight and wiry hair, round head, almost beardless face, and yellow skin—a man whom we call Mongoloid. The migrations of these yellow men out of High Asia eventually diffused them in all directions, but they did not reach the Northwest Quadrant until long after civilization was already highly developed. Nor did they themselves develop a civilization until long after it was far advanced in the Northwest Quadrant (see remarks on China, p. 114). On the *south* of the Northwest Quadrant lay the teeming black world of Africa, separated from the Great White Race by an impassable desert barrier, the Sahara, which forms so large a part of the Southern Flatlands. Isolated thus and at the same time unfitted by ages of tropical life for any

0. See James Henry Breasted, ANCIENT RECORDS OF EGYPT, Chicago, Ill., 1906, vol. I, Sect. 146.

effective intrusion among the White Race, the negro and ne-groid peoples remained without any influence on the develop-ment of early civilization. We may then exclude both of these external races—the straight-haired, round-headed, yellow-skin-ned Mongoloids on the east, and the wooly-haired, long-headed, dark-skinned Negroids on the south—from any share in the origins or subsequent development of civilization.[1]

The Great White Race itself, which dominated the North-west Quadrant, includes and always included a considerable range of types from the fair-haired, long-headed, so-called "Nordics" of the Northern Flatland, through the round-headed Alpine or "Armenoid" peoples of the Highland Zone in the middle, to the dark-haired, long-headed "Mediterranean Race" of the Southern Flatland. To this type belonged the Egyptians (notwithstanding their tanned skins), doubtless also the Sem-ites, and of course the great bulk of the populations of Greece, Italy and Spain, long loosely called "Aryan" because of their speech, which of course has no necessary connection with race.

[1] The exceptions which may be made on behalf of the Mongoloids in later European History do not concern us in this book.

How could professor Breasted [himself a full-fledge member of "THE GREAT WHITE RACE," and thinking as he did in the above honestly see the commonality be-tween his "MEDITERRANEAN RACE" of Egypt and his "NEGRO" and "NEGROID PEOPLE of Nubia, who REMAINED WITHOUT ANY INFLUENCE OF THE DEVELOP-MENT OF EARLY CIVILIZATION..."? This projected and paraphrased citation of pro-fessor Breasted's RACISM is best observed in the underlined sentences above. Breast-ed's contempt for his "...NEGRO AND NEGROID PEOPLES..." even made him for-get to capitalize the word "NEGRO", as he did the word "WHITE." Of course Breasted's citation is an example of the type of "ORTHODOX ACADEMIC AUTHORITY" and "SCHOLARSHIP" African, African-American, and African-Caribbean writers and pro-fessors are expected to endorse in their own works dealing with the HISTORY and HIGH-CULTURE of the indigenous Africans [their own ancestors] of the Nile Valleys and Great Lakes regions, not to mention the others of the entire northern limits above the Sahara. But, let it not be mistaken, professor Breasted's declaration is still the 'GOD INSPIRED HOLY WORDS' with respect to Alkebu-lan, particularly Ta-Merry and Ta-Nehisi, so far as the "MODERN WHITE LIBERAL AFRICANISTS" who teach and write for "AFRICAN" and "BLACK STUDIES" departments throughout the academic com-

Words in brackets [ ], and inserted between quoted materials, are of the author of this volume for clarity only.

munity.

Leaving Breasted's NEGROPHOBIA for a while; it must be stated, quite emphatically, that it is the INSCRIPTION on a stone fragment from Hierakonpolis dealing with a
battle that was fought between the military forces of Pharaoh Khasekhemui of Ta-Merry
and Pharaoh Djer[0] of Ta-Nehisi [whose name is not mentioned in most of the works related to this story] they have proclaimed was a conflict between the "SEMITIC EGYP-
TIANS" and their "LESS CIVILIZED NEGRO [Nubian] NEIGHBOURS TO THE SOUTH" -
both, allegedly, being of TWO DISTINCTLY DIFFERENT RACES; at least, this is what
"orthodox" and "liberal Africanists" would have us believe.

From the two INSCRIPTIONS mentioned above the "White Liberal Africanist
AUTHORITIES" have established their hypothesis that:"...SOUTH OF THE FIRST
CATARACT..." [from at least during the IInd Dynasty - c. 2800-2780 B.C.E.] EGYPT
AND NUBIA WERE TWO DISTINCTLY SEPARATE NATIONS RACIALLY." The major
premise of these allegedly "AUTHORITATIVE" declarations on the part of the "AFRI-
CANISTS" and "EGYPTOLOGISTS" is that:

> [the]...inscription on the Hierakonpolis fragment shows the sign
> Zeti...[𓊃]...over the head of the kneeling [Pharaoh][00] Khasek-
> hemui on a prisoner.

J.E. Quibell and W.F. Green in their article, "Hierakonpolis II," [in: EGYPTIAN
RESEARCH ACCOUNT, London, 1902], mentioned the above theory many years before
professor Breasted passed off his own ORTHODOX WHITE RACIST interpretation of
the INSCRIPTION on the so-called "Palermo Stone" to his fellow European-American
"EDUCATORS" from his citadel at the University of Chicago, Illinois, where he also
developed much of the "SEMITIC, HAMITIC," and "CAUCASIAN," North and East Africa syndrome currently taught by his disciples and others who still control much of the
written information related to Africa's history and High-Culture.

Professor Breasted's version of the INSCRIPTION on the "Palermo Stone," obviously, tried to prove the same alleged FACT, if such we may call the above remarks,

---

[0]. Note the commonality of the language construction of the name "DJER" in Nubian or
Ta-Nehisian hieroglyph and the name "DJOSER" in Egyptian or Ta-Merrian hieroglyph.
The common development of both nations High-Culture caused the carry-over each
maintained after their eventual separation after the VIth Dynasty.

[00]. Words in brackets [ ] above have been inserted by the author of this volume for the
sake of clarity mainly. The hieroglyphic inscription is the manner in which the word -
"ZETI" was written.

through the hypothesis that Pharaoh Sneferu of the IVth Dynasty - c. 2720-? B.C.E.
war against his fellow indigenous Africans of Ta-Nehisi [the "LAND OF THE SOUTH-
ERNERS"] extended beyond the First Cataract; and, that the withdrawal of the Ta-
Merrians back to this alleged "BOUNDARY LINE" [created by the First Cataract]
meant that they considered this NATURAL BARRIER the "DIVIDING LINE" between
their two countries - Ta-Merry and Ta-Nehisi. But, the professor failed to mention
that the Ta-Merrians [blacks, browns, or Egyptians] had already established "BATTLE
LINES!" [not "boundary line"] beyond their own possibility of supplying them against the
almost equally powerful Ta-Nehisians [blacks, browns, or Nubians] of this period in the
history of both national groupings. Since the professor did not emphasize the fact that
the Ta-Merrians made it a point to capture"...7000 prisoners...[and confiscate at
least]...200,000 cattle and sheep..." from the Ta-Nehisians during the battle in question; could he not have also overlooked the fact that the main purpose of the battle was
ECONOMICS, the Ta-Merrians wanting to plunder and ravage the much more materially prosperous Ta-Nehisians land at the south of Ta-Merry, and not for "RACIAL"
reasons as he and others before him [not to mention those after him] have continuously
implied? Equally, he must have forgotten that the "FIRST UNIFIER" of what turned out
to be DYNASTIC EGYPT was a "SOUTHERNER FROM NUBIA" named "AHA" or "NAR-
MER", on some inscriptions "MENA" [Herodotus' "Menes"]? This aspect of Nile Valley
HISTORY and HIGH-CULTURE began on the FIRST day of the FIRST Daynasty - c. 3200
B.C.E., according to the chronological calculations of the High-Priest of Egypt's Mysteries System, Manetho, at approximately the year c. 280 B.C.E. during the so-called
"XXXIInd DYNASTY." But, is it not equally a fact that "...the Monarchs and Lords of
two lands..." [Nubia and Egypt], also Lebu, Meröe, Itiopi, and Puanit were related in
every manner possible - including RACIALLY?

The usually self-proclaimed European-American "WHITE ORTHODOX" and "LIBER-
AL AFRICANIST AUTHORITY ON EGYPT" has carefully forgotten that the vast majority
of the PHARAOHS OF EGYPT, those who did not come from far-off Asia and Europe as
invaders and conquerors [beginning with the XIVth Dynasty, c. 1675 B.C.E., and after]
came from the "SOUTH," at least from Egypt's SOUTH, which was very much NORTH
of the First Cataract at that period in Nile Valley HISTORY and HIGH-CULTURE. The
Egyptians, or Ta-Merrians, entire LITERATURE - both secular and religious [if
separable], is replete with documentary INSCRIPTIONS relating to their "SOUTHERN
168

ORIGIN;" and, even their "GODS" they said:

CAME FROM THE SOURCE OF THE NILE..., HAPI
[the Nile God], AT THE MOUNTAIN OF THE MOON.

One must remember that the "...SOURCE OF HAPI..." [the Nile River] is still the
same place in Central East Africa [around Uganda, Kenya, Zaire or Congo, Tanzania,
and other areas around the Great Lakes], at the foot of the "MOUNTAIN OF THE MOON"
[today's Kilamanjaro, in the Kenda-based language called KiSwahili], as recorded in
THE BOOK OF THE COMING FORTH BY DAY [Egyptian Book of the Dead, and the
Papyrus Of Ani, written about c. 4000 B.C.E.]. The other two "SOURCES OF THE
NILE" are both in the so-called "Ethiopian Highlands." The BLUE NILE, which begins
at Lake Tana, and the Atbara River that commences North of the lake, along with the
White Nile, all three joins at Atbara [Nubia, Ta-Nehisi, Zeti or Sudan] to form what is
called the "NILE."

What the "ORTHODOX AUTHORITIES ON AFRICA" purposefully ignore is that the
military expeditions by the Ta-Merrians into Ta-Nehisian lands were the "cause celebre"
that created their imaginary "BOUNDARY LINE" around the regions of the FIRST
CATARACT which allegedly took place during the IVth Dynasty, c. 2268-2258 B.C.E.
They have carefully forgotten that Ta-Nehisi was, in FACT, the center of Ta-Merry's
building materials industry, and its supply of professional craftsmen from the beginning
of its predynastic existence, which was hundreds of years before the so-called "HYKSOS
SEMITES" from Asia arrived as conquerors in Alkebu-lan about c. 1675 B.C.E., and
many hundreds more before the "WHITE CAUCASIAN INDO-EUROPEAN MACEDONIAN-
GREEKS" from Europe in c. 332 B.C.E. The Macedonian-Greek conquerors being referred to were the same people that ravaged and plundered the libraries and other repositories of the indigenous Africans works in art, science, religion, law, etc., on the
orders of General Soter and Aristotle - who placed his own name on many of the documents he stole from the Lodges and temples of the Nile Valley Africans' Mysteries
System at Luxor. Luxor, today called "THEBES," was originally located in Ta-Nehisi
before the imaginary "BOUNDARY [border] LINE" that allegedly "...DIVIDED NUBIA
FROM EGYPT..." was carried southwards through military conquest at a very much
later period in Nile Valley history. For example: All of the IVth Dynasty, c. 2723 -
2663 B.C.E., diorite quaries at the west of Abu Simbel and Tumas produced most of the
materials used in the construction of the statues for Ta-Merrian ROYAL PYRAMIDS and

MASTABAS, including the colossal TEMPLE OF ABU SIMBEL built by Pharaoh Rameses II[0] of the XIXth Dynasty, c. 1298 - 1232 B.C.E., shown on page 184 of this volume. European and European-American treasure-seekers and archaeologists have unearthed, discovered or found, INSCRIBED, SCULPTURED, and PAINTED stones by the thousands with the name and title of countless pharaohs and other royal members dealing with religious and secular history, and other aspects of Nile Valley High-Culture; some of them specifically related to pharaohs Khufu and Dedefre of the IInd Dynasty, c. 2680 B.C.E., also to Sa'hure - the second pharaoh of the Vth Dynasty, c. 2565 - 2420 B.C.E.; all of them are still waiting to be transported to Ta-Merry. Others have found INSCRIPTIONS that were designed for the tomb and temple of pharaohs Teti and Pepi I of the VIth Dynasty, c. 2420 - 2258 B.C.E., at Tumas.

The following comments or the CHRONOLOGIES [which began on page 136 of the inter and intra relationships between the High-Cultures of the Nile Valleys [blue and white] and Great Lakes regions pinpoint many of the inaccuracies caused by the distortions of countless INSCRIPTIONS of Alkebu-lan's history we have been, and will be, examining; and to a very great extent they will also expose how the "AUTHORITIES ON AFRICA" and "AFRICAN PEOPLES" continue perpetuating RACISM and RELIGIOUS BIGOTRY of an alleged NORTH and EAST Africa that was, and still is, "SEMITIC" and/or "CAUCASIAN," but never "NEGRO, NEGROID" or "BANTU," according to the countless distorted hypotheses they have attributed to the INSCRIPTIONS.

Upon what justifiable basis did the RACIST conclusions already drawn from the INSCRIPTIONS on the "Palermo Stone" and "Hierakonpolis Fragments" apply to the chronologies? The chronologies previously shown and those to follow, among other graphs, charts, and pictures, certainly indicate that the Ta-Nehisians resisted Ta-Merrian imperial colonialism to the point of defeating the Ta-Merrians on many occasions, forced them out of Ta-Nehisi, and following this became this became themselves imperial colonizers of Ta-Merry again and again. These FACTS are very seldom mentioned by the self-appointed "AUTHORITIES ON AFRICA" in their "SEMITIC" and "CAUCASIAN" North and East Africa syndrome.

It is obvious that whatever is responsible for mankind in Alkebu-lan [Africa] equal-

---

[0]. The PHARAOH of Ta-Merry [Egypt] charged with chasing Moses and his fellow African Haribus out of Northern Africa's Egyptian Delta to North Africa's Mount Sinai in what is called the "EXODUS."

ly created all sorts of the same physical types of indigenous Africans of Ta-Merry, Ta-Nehisi, Itiopi, Merŏe, and elsewhere throughout the entire Nile Valleys and Great Lakes regions before the "AUTHORITIES" from Europe and European-America arrived on the scene with their textbooks and hypotheses and moved the frontier of Ta-Merry SOUTHWRADS in order to sustain their "NEGRO-LESS" North and East Africa where only "WHITE" and "BLACK CAUCASIANS, WHITE SEMITES," and "BLACK" or "BROWN HAMITES," also an occasional "NILOT," occupied before the "NEGROES WERE BROUGHT THERE AS SLAVES FROM NUBIA." When the White "ORTHODOX" and "LIBERAL AFRICANIST AUTHORITIES" accomplished their re-population of the Nile Valley and North Africa to suit their RACIST NEGROPHOBIA, mentally that is, were they not aware of the two most noted INSCRIPTIONS dealing with the quarrying activities of Mernere, the last pharaoh of the VIth Dynasty, c. 2420-2258 B.C.E., found near the First Cataract, which explained that Pharaoh Mernere's armies came from very much farther "NORTH"?

The INSCRIPTIONS dealing with the submission of a few Ta-Nehisian minor "...PRINCES AND LORDS OF MEDJA, IRTET, AND WAWAT..." to Pharaoh Mernere, frequently cited in most of the "AUTHORITIES" works, did not indicate in any way whatsoever that the "...PRINCES AND LORDS...," captured SOUTH OF THE FIRST CATARACT," proved that their nation's "BOUNDARY LINE" with Ta-merry began at that point, as implied by the late professor James Henry Breasted[0] and so many others of the so-called "AUTHORITIES ON AFRICA" of European-American and European origin.

The military occupation of Ta-Nehisi by the Ta-Merrians of the MIDDLE KING-DOM PERIOD, c. 2150 - 1580 B.C.E., all of whom European and European-American White "Liberal Africanists" labeled "C GROUP PEOPLE," was in fact no unusual situation as most egyptologists would like us to believe. This is obvious, as the chronologies have shown that the people of the LOWER and UPPER Nile River Valley [blue and white] were part and parcel of the original unitary High-Culture which completely fragmentized itself about the period of the IVth Dynasty, c. 2680-2565 B.C.E. They were from all over the entire more than 4,100 miles length of the Nile River Valley. Their arrival in the LOWER LANDS began with the migrations from SOUTH-Central Alkebu-lan NORTH to the Mediterranean Sea, as they traveled with the flow of the Nile.

For example: Was it not the OPE from the SOUTH whom the Greeks renamed

"THEBANS" [because they originally came from the City of Thebes, ancient Luxor]
that took control of the entire Fayum region, which included Memphis and Herakleoplis
up until the IXth and Xth Dynasties, c. 2100 - 2052 B.C.E. ? The FACT is that these
SOUTHERNERS actually ruled all of NORTHERN Ta-Nehisi and most of SOUTHERN
Ta-Merry before they finally assumed military and political command over the Royal
Thrones of the entire SOUTH and NORTH [the two lands]. Their innitial campaign control extended in a NORTHERN course all the way to Asyut. The second NORTHERN
drive took them to the SOUTHERN limits of the Delta. The third and final thrust led
them all the way across the Delta to the seashore of the SOUTHERN Mediterranean
Sea [Ta-Merry's NORTH]. These indigenous Africans of the XIth Dynasty, c. 2150 -
2000 B.C.E., were actually "...THE POWER BEHIND THE THRONE..." of the IInd
through XIth Dynasties, c. 3200 - 2100 B.C.E.; this fact is explicitly cited in the
chronologies. "Western educators" [irrespective of their areas of discipline] could not
in the past, and cannot now, tell themselves this, because of the fact that they are
fully aware the origin of the "OPE" is without a doubt the Great Lakes region of the
beginning of the Nile River Valley in Central Alkebu-lan - which of course qualified
them as "AFRICANS SOUTH OF THE SAHARA, NEGROES," and/or "BANTUS."[0] These
indigenous Africans, founders of the LUXOR DYNASTY [later Theban Dynasty] - the XIth
Dynasty, control is obvious all the way to the UPPER land [SOUTH] at the FIRST
CATARACT where there still exist INSCRIPTIONS relative to Pharaoh Meri-ib-Re of
the XIth Dynasty, c. 2242-2200 B.C.E. One of these INSCRIPTIONS even referred to
the "OPE" control all the way to the LOWER land [NORTH] to the city of Heraklioplis
near Memphis - the capital of Ta-Merry at this period in Nile Valley history. In the
same set of INSCRIPTIONS there are references to Prince Antef's [a distant predecess-
or of the XIth Dynasty Pharaoh Antef I, c. 2160-2150 B.C.E.] expedition during the
FIRST INTERMEDIATE PERIOD [VIth - Xth Dynasties, c. 2258-2052 B.C.E.] to secure
the SOUTHERNERS control of the "...SOUTHERN GATEWAY..." North of the First

---

[0]. See pages   -   for the hypothetical movement of ancient man before Ta-Merry,
as portrayed by the PREHISTORIC MAP of Africa by Dr. Albert Churchward, also his
two other works - SIGNS AND SYMBOLS OF PRIMORDIAL MAN, and THE ORIGIN AND
EVOLUTION OF THE HUMAN RACE. Include the other hypothetical maps by Dr.
Wiedner and Y. ben-Jochannan; re-examine the oldest fossil-man and his origin.
[00]. Note that the topographical NORTH of Ta-Merry [Egypt] is the LOWER land of the
entire Nile Valley.

Cataract.

The FACT that the indigenous Africans of the Nile Valley were just ONE COM-
MON STOCK OF PEOPLE, who at various periods in their history found it necessary
to wage war against each others for economic and geopolitical gains, may be observed
in the INSCRIPTION on a fragmented stone taken from the "Gebelein temple" of Pharaoh Mentohotep II of the XIth Dynasty. This pharaoh is depicted in a position suggestive
of "...SMITING FOUR ARMIES...." These "...FOUR ENEMIES..." represented the
"FOUR" physical types common to the area of the LOWER Nile Valley during the XIth
Dynasty - EGYPTIANS, NUBIANS, ITIOPIANS, and FOREIGNERS who came from Asia
and Europe only for education and visits up to this period. One will note that the latter
two [foreigners] European and European-American "AUTHORITIES" have labeled
"WHITE" and "BLACK SEMITES, HAMITES," also "BLACK" and "WHITE CAUCA-
SIANS." Pharaoh Mentuhotep II successor, Pharaoh Mentuhotep III of the same Dynasty,
c. 2060-2010 B.C.E., is also recorded on another rock INSCRIPTION with respect to
his own expedition when he crossed the Nile River near the First Cataract with "...
SHIPS TO WAWAT...[during the]...FORTY-FIRST NILE YEAR OF...[his]...REIGN."
The interaction between the NORTH [Ta-Merry] and SOUTH [Ta-Nehisi], sometimes
including Meröe and Itiopi, had become so intense that Pharaoh Mentuhotep III was
forced to restore the military office and title of "KEEPER OF THE DOOR OF THE
SOUTH," a title still symbolically used in modern masonic orders by the office of the
" JUNIOR WARDEN," who is the "PROTECTOR OF THE SOUTHERN DOOR" or
"COLUMNS." These areas of intercourse between NORTHERNERS and SOUTHERNERS
are so glaringly clear in the INSCRIPTIONS left by the indigenous Africans of the Nile
Valley High-Cultures, that even the so-called "SEMITIC SCHOOL" of "WHITE LIBERAL
AFRICANISTS" of almost every type of discipline have concluded that:

> "THE PRINCELY FAMILY OF AMENEMHAT[0] THE VIZER OF
> [Pharaoh] MENTUHOTEP III [c. 2060-2010 B.C.] HAD NUBIAN
> BLOOD IN HIS VEINS."

The above extract is taken from an article by H. Junker, "The first appearance
of the negroes in history,"[JOURNAL OF EGYPTIAN ARCHAEOLOGY, vii, 124];and
one by H.E. Winlock, "Neb-hetep-Re Mentu-hotep of the XIth Dynasty,"[JOURNAL OF
EGYPTIAN ARCHAEOLOGY, xxvi, 116-19]. This type of RACIST interpretation came
by way of the willful distortion and plagiarization of the INSCRIPTIONS taken from the
Egyptian documents in a collection called the "PETROGRAD PAPYRUS 1116. Like all

of the others removed from Ta-Merry, not a single indigenous African to whom such documents belong authorized their removal from Alkebu-lan [Africa].

The issue of "...NUBIAN [negro] ...BLOOD IN HIS VEINS..." is the basic reason why so many European and European-American educators cannot honestly IN-TERPRET, WRITE or TEACH any aspect of Africa's history and High-Culture, the Nile Valley's in particular, to the satisfaction of any self-respecting BLACK woman, man or child anywhere who is aware of his or her GLORIOUS AFRICAN HERITAGE.

By what type of remote genealogical method of conception did Pharaoh Amenem-hat[0] of the XIIth Dynasty, c. 2000-1785 B.C.E., received "...NUBIAN ["negro"]... BLOOD IN HIS VEINS..." and not Pharaoh Aha or Narmer [Mene or Mena] of the Ist Dynasty, c. 2780-2680 B.C.E.? Pharaoh Akhenaten [Amen-hotep IVth] of the XIIIth Dynasty, c. 1785 - ? B.C.E.? architect and God of medicine Imhotep of the IIIrd Dy-nasty for Pharaoh Djoser? or even the statue of Isis and the infant Horus [Black Madon-na and Child]? By the RACIST and RELIGIOUSLY BIGOTED anti-NEGRO and anti-BLACK process in which Africa's history, North and East especially, is being taught and written by European-American "educators" who continue spewing WHITE CHRIS-TIAN "RACIAL PURITY" and "JUDAIC PURITY IN WHITE SEMITISM" in the form of the "GOD'S CHOSEN PEOPLE" propaganda. All of this is consistent with their member-ship in the "SUPERIOR GREAT WHITE RACE" professor Breatsed, Dr. Junod, pro-fessor Groves, and others under the disguise of "WHITE LIBERAL AFRICANISM" have assured them, equally applied to the "SEMITIC EGYPTIANS." Such teachings find these "EDUCATORS" following the others that preceded them in what they have common-ly described as "ACADEMIC SCHOLARSHIP AND DISCIPLINE," the indigenous Africans and their descendants, of course, being unable to receive or deal with such "GODLY INSPIRATION" and "RECOGNITION" of their own HISTORY and HIGH-CULTURES.

How coud it have been possible for any indigenous group of the Nile Valley African people to have remained "PURE" anything, "WHITE CAUCASIAN, HAMITE, SEMITE, or "CAUCASOID" particularly, if that they were, and did not become totally whatever else their neighbours at their immediate SOUTH [Ta-Nehisians, Meröites, Itiopians] were, particularly when there were no PHYSICAL or MENTAL barriers between them, plus the FACT of the many times their armies overran each others homeland and con-

---

[0]. A picture of this pharaoh appears on page 199 of this volume.

sistently RAPED each others women? It could only happen in the textbooks and other academic scholarship works of European-American, European, and British "AFRI-CANISTS" of "liberal" and "orthodox" vintage. Unfortunately, very little of this type of RACIST propaganda and RELIGIOUS BIGOTRY is being challenged in BLACK or AFRICAN studies courses, as too many of said departments depend upon the same people who are preaching such CULTURAL GENOCIDE for all forms of grants and scholarships, not to mention annual budgets.

One must certainly feel totally frustrated about the entire basis upon which this aspect of Alkebu-lan's history has been presented so far to students in AFRICAN and BLACK STUDIES courses by so-called White Liberal Africanists; but, mostly by Black professors who know different, and still ape said "AUTHORITIES ON AFRICA" and "AFRICAN PEOPLES" everywhere. For, one too often finds that even W.M. Flanders Petrie, "the father of archaeology" and "one of the first of the egyptologists," some years ago, claimed that:

> "...THERE ARE DEFINITE CONNECTIONS BETWEEN ANCIENT
> EGYPT AND SOUTHERN RUSIA, MORE PARTICULARLY WITH
> THE CAUCASUS."

Petrie's comments above, as presented in ANTIQUITY, XV [1941], p. 384, were typical of the WHITE RACISM of the late 1800's and early 1900's, and such was the order of every branch of human bahavior in "Western civilization." Margaret A. Murray, writing in her own work, ANCIENT EGYPT, London, 1916, p. 115, detailed the entire hypothesis by Petrie, which she endorsed in its entirety. From these events, and many more which this writer has brought to your attention, one should be able to see and understand why the self-proclaimed "AUTHORITIES ON EGYPT" and "NUBIA," all of whom are Europeans and European-Americans, cannot be expected to have the confidence and endorsement or title of respectibility on anything African, by Africans, and people of African origin anywhere.

Of course, the language and/or dialects used among the Nile Valley indigenous African people were common from the Nile's most SOUTHERN beginnings in Central Alkebulan to its most NORTHERN endings at the SOUTHERN shores of the Mediterranean Sea. The proof is that they used the same common writing and language to communicate during their many periods of conquest and rule over each others nation. These historical FACTS have been carefully edited-out from WHITE STUDIES courses which everyone must learn, and in many cases have been purposely suppressed by "ACADEMICIANS." For example: The titles of the PHARAOHS and QUEENS of Itiopi, Puanit, Meröe, Kush [sometimes part of Itiopi or Ethiopia in various periods in history], Ta-Nehisi, and Ta-Merry were similar, and in many respects they were the same. The following are exact titles for both Ta-Nehisi and Ta-Merry:

> WIFE OF THE GOD.... The widow of the deceased Pharaoh, whom the current one succeded, being the recepient of said title from her husband's role as the "GOD OSIRIS," which he became by virtue of his death and resurrection into the Nether World [which the Greeks called the "UNDERWORLD"] and diefication with OSIRIS.

In the following we can see the second role that the queen played in her. role as the wife of a particular pharaoh, mother of his children, daughter, or even sister. In this case the pharaoh had to be alive; thus, her title:

> LADY OF TWO LANDS = The heires who became the "Great Wife of the living pharaoh."

Another example of the commonality of the Nile Valley indigenous languages and related dialects used by the Africans of the LOWER LANDS[0] can be seen in the titles Queen [Pharaoh][00] Hat-shep-sut used in her marriages to her oldest brother - Thumose II, and youngest brother - Thutmose III [possibly her own son or step-son], at various periods of her reign over Ta-Merry during the XIIIth Dynasty, c. 1515 - 1484 B.C.E. These factors were rapidly changed after various wars had ensued between the Nile Valley Africans.

By the ending of the NEW KINGDOM PERIOD, XIIIth - XXXth Dynasties, c. 1580 - 1050 B.C.E., the entire nation of Ta-Nehisi had become the colonial territory of Ta-Merry, including all of the territories SOUTH of the Fourth Cataract. The development of superior military arms by the NORTHERNERS of Ta-Merry made the difference. But,

---

[0]. This writer and student of Nile Valley HISTORY and HIGH-CULTURE realize that there needs to be a greater in-depth study of the Africans of ancient Alkebu-lan along the entire Nile Valleys [blue and white] from an AFRICAN POINT OF VIEW AND INTERPRETATION, using no European or European-American source as "AUTHORITY." It is frustrating to know that there is no such work being undertaken at this present juncture, late as it is, as most BLACK STUDIES and AFRICAN STUDIES professors of African origin are totally engaged in works mostly related to "SLAVERY AND WEST AFRICA," as if the only credibility in their BLACKNESS lies in how much they can regurgitate about the "BLACK EXPERIENCE" from a standpoint of latent anti-SLAVERY militancy.
[00]. Hat-shep-sut became the "FIRST QUEEN" to be recognized as a KING or PHARAOH. She presented herself at all times as a PHARAOH, even to the point of appearing in her pictures with a BEARD and the CLOTHING of a pharaoh.

176

the expansion of the NORTH on the SOUTH was as inevitable as the invasion of Cueta, North Alkebu-lan [Africa], by French military forces from France [Southwest Europe] in 1830 C.E. The underlying reality was the threat of starvation on the part of the NORTHERNERS [Egyptians and French in either case].In the Dynastic Periods of the Ta-Merrians their basic economic needs and natural resources, also their skilled artisans, etc.,came from Ta-Nehisi to their SOUTH. The same type of situation equally held true for theEuropeans of France to the NORTH [Europe] of Cueta [Africa]: as the French, who had nothing that resembled the abundance of the natural resources the Africans of Cueta to their SOUTH appeared to have enjoyed [which was very much more than the indigenous Africans needed for their own economic requirements], had to conquer them. The invasion of the SOUTHENERS by the NORTHENERS was not from the standpoint of anything called "PREDESTINATION". In each case it was due to the practical geopolitics of governments and the economic realities that bred wars down through the centuries of "MAN'S INHUMANITY TO MAN." In either case the invaded SOUTHE.RNERS were looted of their natural resources, their women raped, their God or Gods and temples of worship sacriligiously abused, and they found themselves colonially occupied to protect the constant flow of their produce to the homeland of the NORTHERNERS. Along with their natural resources, their professionals and technicians were carried off to the NORTH to build new metropolis which later on stole many more of their unskilled workers for a cheap labour, and ever so often said market developed into full-fledge "SLAVE LABOUR" situations exclusively. Was this not the case of the Ta-Merrians and the Ta-Nehisians, just as it were with the Greeks and Romans, British and European-Americans, European-Americans of the South and North of the United States of America, Germans and French [repeatedly], Khart-Haddans or Carthagenians and Romans, African-Moors and Iberians? This author sees it both ways with respect to the history of these two nations of Alkebu-lan - Ta-Merry [Egypt] and Ta-Nehisi [Nubia].

In ending this very brief INTRODUCTION to some of the chronologies of Ta-Nehisi, Ta-Merry, Itiopi, Kush, Meröe, Puanit, and other nations of the Nile Valleys and Great Lakes regions of Alkebu-lan, one needs to point out that there are recordings of countless events of a historical nature that took place between the invading Asians, the so-called "HYKSOS SEMITES" - of the XIVth-XVIIth Dynasties [c. 1675-1600 B.C.E.], found at what was once considered "ALL THE WAY DOWN SOUTH AT LUXOR" [later

Thebes, originally part of Nubia]. They refer to the tyranical treatment of the Ta-
Merrians under Pharaoh Khamose [Kames], the last pharaoh of the XVIIth Dynasty, c.
1600-1555 B.C.E., during the period in which the NORTHERNERS of Ta-Merry were
appealing to the SOUTHERNERS of Ta-Nehisi, Meröe, Kush, and Itiopi [the last three
nations located below the "SOUTHERN BOUNDARIES OF THE FOURTH CATARACT at
the period of the appeal] to assist them in their last battle against the "HYKSOS TY-
RANTS." This historical FACT is equally highlighted in M. Hammand's, "Découverte
stéle du roi Kamose," [CHRONIQUE d'EGYPTE, xxx, 1955, pp. 198-208]; and A. H.
Gardiner's," The defeat of the Hyksos by Kamose: the Carnavon tablet, No. 1,"
[JOURNAL OF EGYPTIAN ARCHAEOLOGY, iii, 95-110]. Later findings included an
INSCRIPTION on a rock at Toski, which show that Pharaoh Khamose's successor, Pharaoh Ahmes [the first pharaoh of the XVIIIth Dynasty, c. 1555-1340 B.C.E.], was
planning an invasion of the "SOUTHERN LANDS" beyond the Fourth Cataract, which did
not take place. The latest aspects of Ta-Merry and Ta-Nehisi's military encounters
can be best appreciated in an article by F.L. Griffith, "Oxford excavations in Nubia,"
[LIVERPOOL ANNALS OF ARCHAEOLOGY and ANTHROPOLOGY, London, 1921, p.6].

What we have, or should have, observed is at least one main point in our safari
into these chronologies with respect to the "BOUNDARIES BETWEEN TA-MERRY AND
TA-NEHISI" is; there was NONE in the true sense of the term's usage in the international parlance of the 20th century C.E. For, it was not until Pharaoh Thutmosis I of the
XVIIIth Dynasty, c. 1350-1550 B.C.E., the successor of Pharaoh Amenophis [Amenho-
tep I , c. 1557-1530 B.C.E.], who was the real conqueror of the NORTHERN section
of Ta-Nehisi, that any such reference had been noted on a "ROCK INSCRIPTION" at
Tangur in Batn el Hagar, which he had done in "...THE SECOND NILE YEAR [of his]
GLORIOUS REIGN." Near the Third Cataract another INSCRIPTION on a granite boulder at a place called Thumbus provides us with a reference to Pharaoh Thutmosis' naval
engagement at the Dongola Reach of the fertile lands NORTHERN beginnings in Kush.
The Dongola Reach INSCRIPTION, as shown on the following page in Hieroglyph, is the
very FIRST of its kind which, with a little stretch of the imagination, could be said to
have been a "BOUNDARY MARK" or "LINE" in the truest sense of the usage of the
term in modern parlance. Never-the-less, the White "liberal" and "orthodox"
AUTHORITIES OF AFRICA", particularly Ta-Merry [Egypt] and Ta-Nehisi [Nubia],
have invented many more for their "NEGRO-LESS" North and East Africa.
178

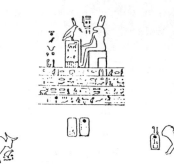

BOUNDARY INSCRIPTION AT KURGUS
Errected by Pharaoh Thutmosis I, c. 1530-1520 B.C E. (successor of Pharaoh Amenophis I), final conqueror of Ta-Nehisi, done in the 2nd Nile Year of his reign, c. 1528 B.C.E., on a granite boulder, relating to his victory over the Ta-Nehisians.

In the final analysis it is the African or African-American and African-Caribbean [BLACK] writer who must do his or her research into the background of the hundreds of thousands of INSCRIPTIONS on papyri, stone fragments, walls of tombs and temples, and other structures, in order that the pattern of the RACIST and RELIGIOUSLY BIGOTED interpretations of said INSCRIPTIONS can be edited out of future textbooks on Africa and African peoples everywhere. The texbooks in question specifically relate to the RACIST hypothesis of a "CAUCASIAN, SEMITIC," and/or "HAMITIC NORTH AND EAST AFRICA" where there was never a "NEGRO, NIGGER, BANTU, BLACK AFRICAN, AFRICAN SOUTH OF THE SAHARA, FOREST NEGRO," UNTIL "THEY WERE BROUGHT THERE AS SLAVES FOR THE EGYPTIANS. Of course, such textbooks writers have conveniently overlooked the writings of Herodotus, Eusebus, Polybus, Julius Africanus, Terrence Afer, St. Augustine, Josephus, and thousands more, all of whom referred to the Africans of Egypt [originally Ta-Merry, Kimit, Sais, etc.] and other Nile Valley nations "...THICK LIPS, BROAD NOSE, WOOLLY HAIR, BURNT SKIN...," etc. But, if the EDUCATORS of African origin should write their own INTERPRETATIONS of their own HISTORY and HERITAGE, using their own African AUTHORITIES as the sole point of reference, then, and only then, will one see that the self-appointed European and European-American "LIBERAL" and "ORTHODOX AUTHORITIES ON AFRICA" and "AFRICAN PEOPLE" for the RACIST and RELIGIOUS BIGOT most of them are; thus their RACISM and RELIGIOUS BIGOTRY can be hastily

179

removed from the "RESPECTABILITY OF ACADEMIC SCHOLARSHIP," an HONOUR which they have notoriously cc-opted due to the negligence of African and African-American EDUCATORS - Writers, historians, anthropologists, sociologists, and whatever else there may be. Yet this writer is quite clear to the FACT that the same self-appointed "AUTHORITIES ON BLACK PEOPLE" are the ones who, for the most part, control most of the funds which are necessary for grants that will make works of the type of BLACK [African or African-American and African-Caribbean] INTERPRETA-TIONS necessary and meaningful. But, there is no excuse of any worth which will continue to ponder the defeatest attitude that BLACK PEOPLE, sons and daughters of "Mother Africa" [Alkebu-lan], cannot produce their own DOCUMENTARY HISTORY of their own past GLORY and HERITAGE, as they do their own MISFORTUNE - which of course include the bestial SLAVE TRADE initiated by the Right Reverend Bishop Bartolome de LasCasas of the Roman Catholic Church in the year c. 1503 or 1506 C.E. Any such type of DEFEATIST attitude has for too long smothered the brain cells of the BLACK COMMUNITIES of the America, the United States of America particularly; all of this being especially true in the sacred halls of the "NEGRO CHURCH;" and as such, it has tolerated [?] an indigenous African of Ta-Merry [Egypt] named MOSES to take honour for his wrongdoings in violating "LAW AND ORDER" in his own country in his commission of "MURDER" against a fellow indigenous African. But, African-Americans [Negroes and Blacks] berate the protector of said "LAWS," including that which say to the Africans thousands of years before the birth of Abraham [the first Haribu or "Jew"] - "YOU SHALL NOT KILL" [taken from the "Negative Confessions" that preceded Abraham and Moses by thousands of years], Pharaoh Rameses II, because most African-American are not aware of the FACT that Moses, as Rameses II and themselves, was an African; nor, that the BOOK OF EXODUS drama dealing with the "JEWISH PASSOVER" is an African story of people who had been in Africa [Alkebu-lan] for at least 400 years as "SLAVES" - according to the biblical texts. And, if they were in FACT "SLAVES " FOR THE AFRICANS OF EGYPT," the people Herodotus and others described in their works; what happened to their WOMEN? Did they not suffered the same fate as the African WOMEN in the United States of America when the slave masters were desireous of RAPING them sexually? NO! Not in the mind of those who are made to believe that NORTH and EAST Africa, Egypt particularly, was never inhabitted by anyone that looked like them - the so-called "NEGRO." This is the same reason they do not know anything about the following INSCRIPTIONS, all of which were supposed to have been SEMITIC.
180

TOP SECTION OF THE GRANITE STELA OF PHARAOH
PIANKHI, XXIVth - XXVth Dynasties, c. 751-716 BC,
AT JEBAL BARKAL [Holy Mountain], TA-NEHISI::::::

The above INSCRIPTION depicts the dethroned King Menareth (leading his horse),

Osorkon IV and other princes of Ta-Merry as slaves in submission and bearing

tributes for the "LION OF THE SOUTH" (Ta-Nehisi, Meröe, Kush, Itiopi, Puanit).

It was errected in the 21st NILE YEAR of Pharaoh Piankhi's reign, c. 730 B.C.E.,

and found near the GREAT TEMPLE OF AMEN-RĒ in 1862 C.E.; presently housed

in the Cairo Museum, Cairo, Egypt, North Africa (The United Arab Republic).

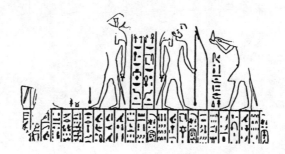

DAMAGED INSCRIPTION ON THE GREAY ALTAR OF THE GREAT
TEMPLE OF AMEN-RĒ SHOWING PHARAOH TAHAKHA (Taharqa)
"WITHIN THE HOLY MOUNTAIN" [Jebel Barkal], c. 678 BCE.

The colossal figures errected in the front of this temple are in excess of the great-

ness of those errected by Pharaoh Rameses II, XIXth Dynasty, c. 1298-1232 B.C.E.,

at Abu Simbel; both of them in Ta-Nehisi, and of the craftsmanship of the SOUTH.

Note similarity of HIEROGLYPH to that of Ta-Merry (Cham, Sais, Kimit, Egypt).

The "BOUNDARY LINES" shown on
this map are reflections of the FACTS
stated in the chronologies and historical
data just presented. They also relate to
the conflicting presentation by the self-
appointed "AUTHORITIES ON AFRICA" with
respect to the alleged "RACIAL DIFFERENCES
BETWEEN THE EGYPTIANS AND THE NUBIANS"
we read so much about, all of which were supposed to have developed as a direct result of
the physical and geographical barriers between
Egypt at the NORTH and Nubia at the SOUTH.

This map is followed by others that relate
to both Nubia and Egypt, along with
Meröe, Itiopi, Kush and Puanit as
they relate to a UNITARY HIGH-
CULTURE (civilization) that fragmented into various HIGH-CULTURES
beginning with the turn of the IInd Dynastic Period, c. 2980 B.C.E., and culminated with the VIth Dynastic Period, c.
2258 B.C.E. The student, as well
as the general reader, should re-
examine the text in conjunction
with the topography of this map.

THE UPPER & LOWER NILE, c. 751-332 B.C.E.

182

NILE VALLEYS AFRICANS; NOT ONE A "NEGRO"

KEY

1. Ta-Nehisi (Nubia)

2. Ta-Merry (Egypt)

3. Itiopi (Ethiopia)

4. Ta-Nehisi (Meroe)

5. Ta-Merry (Kimit)

6. Ta-Nehisi (Nubia)

7. Bunyoro (Uganda)

8. Puanit (Kenya, etc.)

Any of the above indigenous Africans of centuries ago and the present can be seen by the millions all over the continent of Alkebu-lan, "MOTHER AFRICA".

The great colossal statue of the TEMPLE OF ABU SIMBEL in Ta-Nehisi (Zeti or Nubia, modern Sudan) bear witness to the glory that was the High-Culture of the land to the SOUTH of Ta-Merry. It was in this land that the ancient Africans of the High-Culture at the end of the Lower Nile Valley found their

Temple of Abu Simbel — Nubia

glorious beginning. Here in Ta-Nehisi the colossal STONES were cut and carved out of the marble, granite, and dorite quarries. All of this was completed hundreds upon hundreds of years before the arrival of the first European conquerors – the Macedonian-Greeks under Alexander II ("the great") and general Soter. It was scenes such as this that made the earliest of the Greeks come to Ta-Merry [Alkebu-lan] and all of the other High-Cultures of the Lower Nile included, to learn architecture, engineering, mathematics, astronomy, medicine, history, philosophy, astrology, numerology, agriculture, and all of the other disciplines they engaged in from before and after their first student, Homer, graduated in the teachings of the Nile Valley indigenous Africans' MYSTERIES SYSTEM that was centered in the OSIRICA at Luxor [today's Thebes]. They were the Africans whose descendants are now called "NEGROES" and "BANTUS."

184

THE FOUR MOST GLORIOUS PHAROAHS AND PYRAMID BUILDERS
of the
"GREAT PYRAMID AGE" *
(IIIrd through Vth Dynasty, c. 2780-2420 BCE)

Pharaoh Djoser, IIIrd Dynasty,
c.2780 - 2680. The STEP
PYRAMID OF SAKHARA . First
of the COLOSSAL PYRAMIDS.

Pharaoh Khufu, IVth Dynasty,
c. 2680 -2258, PYRAMID OF
GHIZA (147m high).

Pharaoh Khafra, IVth Dynasty,
c. 2680 - 2258, PYRAMID OF
GHIZA (143m high). Last of the
COLOSSAL PYRAMID builders.

Pharaoh Men-kau-Ra, IVth
Dynasty, c. 2780 - 2258,
PYRAMID OF GHIZA (66.40m
high). First of the MODERATE
PYRAMIDS.

*Other major Pharaohs who built PYRAMIDS of moderate size were: Sahure,
Nusere and Unas of the IVth Dynasty; also Pepi I of the VIth Dynasty. Although
there are many other very noted ones, these Pharaohs are mentioned more than
all of the others by "WESTERN" historians, egyptologists, anthropologists, and
other writers who call themselves "WHITE LIBERAL AFRICANISTS."
 Pharaoh Djoser's "NOSE" and "LIPS" are quite typical of the description of the
Africans of Ta-Merry, Ta-Nehisi, Itiopi, Meröwe and Puanit, and of course of
the Europeans and Asians along the eastern shores of the Mediterranean Sea –
the Colchians, Hittites, Jebusites, etc, all of whom Josephus, Eusebius, Polybus and Herodotus mentioned in their historical works. Of course this is not
the type of Egyptians generally spoken of in the institutions of education
throughout the United States of America (religious or secular). If he is an example of a "SEMITE," the Harlems of the world are certainly "SEMITIC!"

Reconstruction of funerary buildings by Jean-Philippe Lauer, Paris, France. Main PYRAMID dimensions: L=431'0" x W= 344'0" x H=200'0". Height of exterior wall enclosure, 33'0".

Southern Elevation of the Step Pyramid of Sakhara (Saqqara)

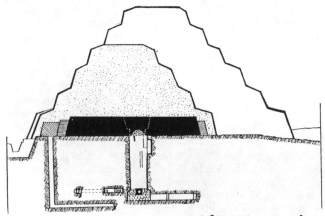

Cross Section of Step Pyramid [Cut West-East]
View South to North

186

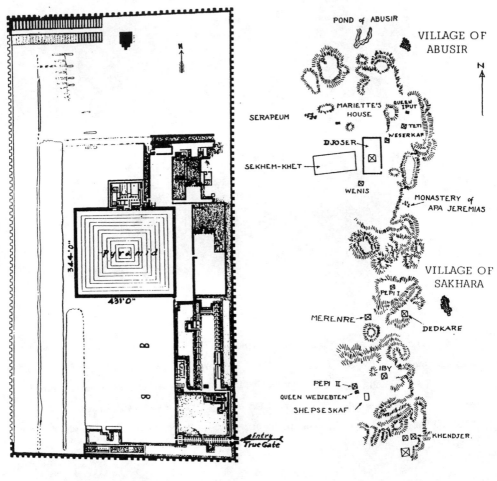

POND of ABUSIR

VILLAGE OF
ABUSIR

N

MARIETTE'S
HOUSE

QUEEN
IPUT

SERAPEUM

TETI

WESERKAF

DJOSER

SEKHEM-KHET

MONASTERY of
APA JEREMIAS

WENIS

VILLAGE OF
SAKHARA

PEPI I

MERENRE

DEDKARE

IBY

PEPI II

QUEEN WEDJEBTEN

SHEPSESKAF

KHENDJER

344'0"

Pyramid

431'0"

B

8

Entry
True Gate

N

STEP PYRAMID
of Pharaoh Djoser, c. 2780,
IIIrd Dynasty, B.C.E.

GENERAL AREA SITE PLAN
of the
PYRAMID FIELD OF SAKHARA

15 miles south of the center of Cairo, Egypt (NORTH AFRICA), the cemetery
of Sakhara (Saqqara) stand's eclipsed by the towering colossal STEP PYRAMID
built by the architect and builder for Pharaoh Djoser, IMHOTEP, with its
graciously beautiful temples and Serapecum (subterranean cemetery of the
Apis – Sacred Bull); the first stone building in history. 545 meters long (from
south to north) and 277 meters wide (from east to west), 14 Bastion gates (13
simulated, only one "True Gate") – a recreation of Pharaoh Djoser's Palace
at Memphis.
The "SOUTHERN TOMB" [a misnomer by egyptologists] has a pit of 7 meters

RUINS OF THE TEMPLE OF THE STEP PYRAMID
OF SAKHARA

On page 190 there is a picture of the indigenous African architect and builder who designed and built the STEP PYRAMID and its compliments. On preceding pages there are other views and plans of the PYRAMID'S cross-section, elevation, and reconstructed scheme. On page 187 there is an AREA SITE PLAN and FLOOR PLAN of the PYRAMID. Other related drawings and pictures are to be found throughout this chapter and others of this volume.

---

square and 28 meters deep. Below is a granite block finished room that measures 1.6 meters square. Its galleries are decorated with blue faience tiles from Ta-Nehisi. One of the walls has three simulated doors carved with the name, figure and titles of Pharaoh Djoser. Over the subteranean passage is a massive rectangular shaped superstructure with a concave roof measuring 84 meters long and 12 meters wide, and contains a chapel . Along the passageway one of the walls was fully decorated with a frieze of cobras on the limestone masonry.

Temple of Luxor — Upper-Egypt

The temple with fluted columns at Saqqâra.

Note the highly specialized type of architecture in the above ruins of the Temple of the Grand Lodge of Luxor [Thebes] and those designed much earlier by Imhotep – the architect of Pharaoh Djoser in the IIIrd Dynasty, c. 2780-2680 B.C.E. It is also noted that the Greeks copied their mushroom and fluted columns from these Nile Valley African structures they observed when they came to the MYSTERIES SYSTEM to be taught by the indigenous Africans who are now being called "SEMITES, HAMITES, CAUCASIANS," and "NILOTS."

IMHOTEP
[Bronze Statue, Paris Museum, Paris, France]
Physician, Prime Minister, Grand Vizer, Poet, Magician, Architect and Builder
of the STEP PYRAMID OF SAKHARA   for Pharaoh Djoser‚ IIIrd Dynasty, 2780 BCE.

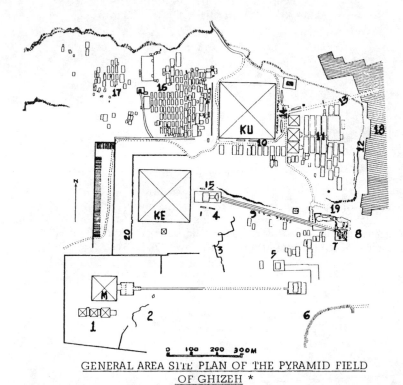

GENERAL AREA SITE PLAN OF THE PYRAMID FIELD
OF GHIZEH *

1. Funerary Temple

2. Men-kau-Rē Quarry

3. Rock-cut Tombs

4. Boat Pitts

5. Tomb of Khemt-ka-
   wes

6. Valley Temple of
   Men-kau-Rē

8. Temple of Great Sphinx

9. Cause Way

10. Boat Pitt of Khu-fu

11. Eastern Cemetery

12. Rock-cut Tombs

13. Cause Way

14. Funerary Temple

15. Funerary Temple of
    Khaf-Ra

16. Western Cemetery

17. Office of Pyramid
    Studies

18. Village

20. Rock-cut Tombs

*Like most of the archaeological sites of the Nile Valleys (Blue and White),
there are many ways to spell the names of different ones. The correct spelling
of this shrine is as shown above, but the following is also a most common way
in which it is also written - "GIZA." You will also note that many of the pharaohs (kings) names are written in different manners than you may be accoustomed
to seeing.

191

"GREAT PYRAMIDS OF GHIZEH"
(Akhet Khufu, Horizon of Pharaoh Khufu)

(A view from the South)

Left: Pyramid of Khufu ("Cheops"), 147m high; Center: Pyramid of Khafra (Cheph-ren), 143m high; Right: Men-kau-Ra ("Mycerinus"), 66.40m high. The three (3) small Pyramids in the foreground are of Queens of the IVth Dynasty - c.? - 2258 B.C.E. [Encyclopedia of Egyptian Civilization, p. 195].

DIMENSIONS FOR PYRAMID OF KHUFU

L = 756'0" x W = 760'0" x H = 481'0". Angle created from base to extreme top: 51° 50'. Total mass: 3,277,000 Cubic Feet.

CROSS-SECTION THROUGH PYRAMID OF KHUFU
[Cut South-North Line]

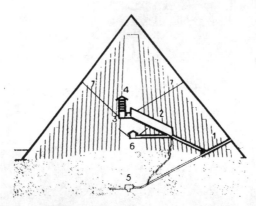

1. Entrance corridor leading to funerary chambers. 2, Grand Gallery. 3, Funerary chamber with royal sarcophagus. 4, Pressure releasing compartments for ceiling of tomb chamber. 5 and 6, First and Second tomb chambers, discarded. 7, Ventilation shafts. [From a drawing by L. Borchardt,"Encyclopedia of Egyptian Civilization].

The dimensions of the other two (2) Pyramids above appear in various other places of this volume. The magnitude of the type of construction the indigenous Africans of the Nile Valley engaged...., thousands upon thousands of years before the creation of the Greek nation -"WETSERN CIVILIZATION," is shown above.

CEMETERY PYRAMIDS and CANDACES
of Meroe and Ta-Nehisi

[Photo: Museum of Fine Arts, Boston, Mass.]

Foreground: SOUTHERN MECROPOLIS - IIIrd Century B.C.E.
Background: NORTHERN MECROPOLIS - IVth Century B.C.E. to C.E.

COLOSSAL Step Pyramid of Sakhara, by Pharaoh Djoser, IIIrd Dynasty; architect and builder Imhotep.

MEDIUM Pyramid of Ghiza, by Pharaoh Snefru, IVth Dynasty.

One will notice that the PYRAMIDS got larger, and to the point of becoming COLOSSAL, as the indigenous Africans High-Cultures [civilizations] of the Nile Valleys [blue and white] traveled farther NORTH from their SOUTHERN origin. Obviously, the different types of construction materials the indigenous Africans employed in the above pyramids were not in any sense "MUD AND STRAW BRICKS" after the IIIrd Dynasty, c. 2780 B.C.E.; they were GIGANTIC STONES up until the IVth Dynasty, c. 2680 B.C.E. Even as late as the IIIrd to Ist century B.C.E. the indigenous Nile Valley Africans were still building their homes of the NETHER WORLD [pyramids or tombs] in the manner typically of their Great Lakes origin around Central East Africa.

Note that the IIIrd Dynasty STEP PYRAMID of Pharaoh Djoser [Zozer] and his architect - IMHOTEP- influenced the dominant design of pyramids all through the VIth Dynasty; this we can readily notice in the MEDIUM PYRAMID of Pharaoh Snefru above.

GREAT SPHINX OF GHIZEH

Showing the inscribed marble"Dream Stela"of Pharaoh Thutmose IV and marble

Altar in foreground. Note that its face was blown assunder by General Napoleoɪ

Boneparte's officers cannon fire practice in 1798 C.E., because the general dis

approved of its African - "NEGROID" - facial characteristics. See on the spot

drawing of this colossal statue by Baron Viviat Denon on page 111 of this chap-

ter. Baron Denon accompanied Boneparte and French military forces in their at-

tempt at colonizing all of Northeast Africa. They were defeated by the British.

194

THE LOWER NILE BEFORE PALESTINE AND GREECE.
BEFORE NATIONAL BOUNDARIES: EGYPT - NUBIA.

ENLARGED PYRAMID
FIELDS

* There was no established BOUNDARY LINE between Ta-Merry (Egypt), Ta-Nehisi (Nubia), Merŏe (Merowe), Lebu (Libya), Itiopi (Ethiopia), Kush, Punt (Puanit), and other Nile Valley High-Cultures before the IIIrd to IVth Dynasty, c. 2780 - 2270 B.C.E. The concept of "NATIONAL BOUNDARY" was not employed to the extent in which we use it today in modern geopolitics and international law. Thus, the BORDERS of each country moved NORTH and SOUTH, EAST and WEST, as the armies or cultural influence of one cultural group moved to suit NATIONAL needs; to a great extent this is still happening.

195

The TA-MERRIAN EMPIRE

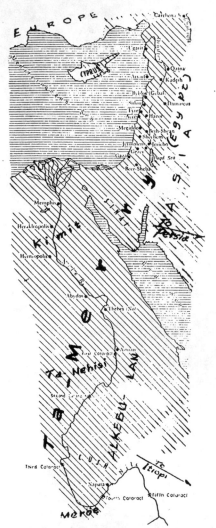

During this period in history the Empire of Ta-Merry (Egypt) extended as far EAST as the banks of the Tigris and Euphrates rivers, as far NORTH as Colchis and Hellas (Pyrrhus or Greece), as far WEST as Lebu (Libya), and as far SOUTH as the GATES OF ITIOPI (Ethiopia). The "SPHERE OF INFLUENCE" generated by the indigenous Africans of Ta-Merry, and other Nile Valley nations , conquest of these Asian and European lands also created reverse cultural CARRY-OVERS on the Nile Valley High-Cultures (civilizations). Yet, this period followed another in which the armies of the Africans of North and East Africa also entered Persia (Iran) and India, all the way to the Ganges River, as stated elsewhere in the texts.

You will note that Ta-Nehisi (Nubia) and Meröe are shown as part of the EMPIRE OF TA-MERRY; but one must not loose sight of the fact that indigenous Africans from all of the Nile Valley High-Cultures became pharaohs of the same EMPIRE during this period. The student must relate this historical period to the various chapters in the FIVE BOOKS OF MOSES (Holy Torah or Old Testament) in order to separate allegory from actual FACTS.

196

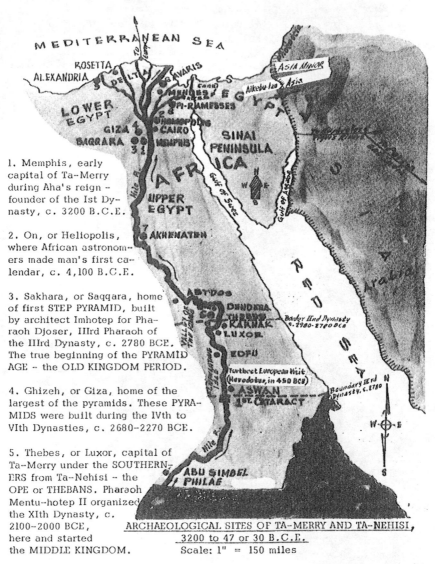

1. Memphis, early
capital of Ta-Merry
during Aha's reign --
founder of the Ist Dy-
nasty, c. 3200 B.C.E.

2. On, or Heliopolis,
where African astronom-
ers made man's first ca--
lendar, c. 4,100 B.C.E.

3. Sakhara, or Saqqara, home
of first STEP PYRAMID, built
by architect Imhotep for Pharaoh Djoser, IIIrd Pharaoh of
the IIIrd Dynasty, c. 2780 BCE.
The true beginning of the PYRAMID
AGE -- the OLD KINGDOM PERIOD.

4. Ghizeh, or Giza, home of the
largest of the pyramids. These PYRA-
MIDS were built during the IVth to
VIth Dynasties, c. 2680-2270 BCE.

5. Thebes, or Luxor, capital of
Ta-Merry under the SOUTHERN-
ERS from Ta-Nehisi -- the
OPE or THEBANS. Pharaoh
Mentu--hotep II organized
the XIth Dynasty, c.
2100-2000 BCE,
here and started
the MIDDLE KINGDOM.

ARCHAEOLOGICAL SITES OF TA-MERRY AND TA-NEHISI,
3200 to 47 or 30 B.C.E.
Scale: 1" = 150 miles

6. Avaris, capital of the first foreigners from outside of Alkebu-lan (Africa) to
invade, capture and occupy any part of the continent; in this case Ta-Merry
(Egypt) and part of LOWER (north) Ta-Nehisi, the Hyksos or so-called "SEMITES."
Beginning of the SECOND INTERMEDIATE PERIOD, XIVth - XVIth Dynasties, c.
1675 - 1600 B.C.E. The last of them were driven out in c. 1567 B.C.E.

7. City named for Pharaoh Amen-hotep IV.

8. Pi-Rameses became capital of Ta-Merry in XIXth Dynasty, c. 1340 B.C.E.
197

Right: A "TYPICAL" African of the type commonly found all along the Nile Valley (Blue and White) to the present day, 1972).

Left: Pharaoh Neb-Maat-Ra, mighty ruler and builder of the the 17th Pyramid.

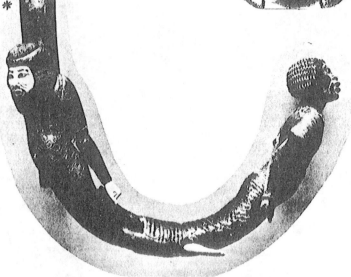

Handle of Pharaoh Tut-ankh-Amen's WALKING STICK

---

*Ceremonial staff or Walking Stick with curved end (turned upside-down) used by Pharaoh Tut-ankh-Amen of the XVIIIth Dynasty, c. ? - 1349 B.C.E., in official state functions. On the left of the curve is a "...BEARDED SEMITE...;at the right a "...NEGRO." Note that these men were both "...PRISONERS." The insert at the extreme left is an enlarged image of the profile of the "SEMITE" or "SYRIAN PRISONER;" the "NEGRO" or "NUBIAN PRISONER" is at the right. The Walking Stick was stolen from the tomb of Pharaoh Tut-ankh-Amen and kept in the Cairo Museum, Cairo, Egypt (Ta-Merry, Alkebu-lan or Africa).

** The same comparison made between the "SEMITE" and the "NEGRO" above is also applicable to all of the Pharaohs of Ta-Merry prior to the arrival of the so-called "HYKSOS SEMITES" from Asia around c. 1675 B.C.E. (XVth Dynasty); this being equally true for the so-called "INDO-EUROPEAN ARAYANS" from Persia in c. 525 B.C.E. (XXVIIth Dynasty), and the Macedonian-Greeks who followed the Persians in c.332 B.C.E. (the so-called "XXXIIIrd Dynasty). If this is not true,

Sketch of the Head of A Royal Egyptian
(F.W. Petrie Coll.)

Bronze Statue of IMHOTEP
(Paris Museum Coll.)

Sketch of Pharaoh AKHENATEN
(Berlin Museum Coll.)

Pharaoh AMONEMHAT III
XIIth Dynasty
(Cairo Museum)

then, what is the so-called "RACIAL DIFFERENCES" between Pharaoh Djoser and the Nubian ("NEGRO") and Assyrian ("SEMITE") shown on the preceding page of this volume [sculptor's model of Pharaoh Djoser, Metropolitan Museum of Art, New York City, New York]? The same must certainly hold true for countless other Pharaohs of Ta-Merry and Ta-Nehisi, including the three shown before on page 203,

ISIS and the Infant HORUS,
BLACK MADONNA & CHILD
(F.W. Petrie Coll.)

along with the others on the following pages, all of whom may not have had
"THICK LIPS" and "FLAT" or "BROAD NOSE", these being the attributes which
every African is expected to have to be a "NEGRO" according to the RACIST
teachings in WHITE STUDIES courses which every student in public an private
schools (secular and religious) must take. Note that this is the exact Pharaoh
who made the change of building pyramids out of MUD BRICKS and substituted

GREAT SPHINX OF GHIZEH

Showing its original Nile Valley African facial chracteristics as it appeared to Baron Viviant Denon, who drew this picture, before its face was marred in 1798 C.E. This statue, the world's largest, was built by the indigenous Africans of the Nile Valley more than five hundred (500) years before the "HYKSOS SEMITES" and one thousand nine-hundred (1,900) years before the "MACEDONIAN-GREEK CAUCASIANS" arrival in Ta-Merry (Egypt).

---

extremely large stones, at a period of at least 1,140 years before the arrival of the first Haribu, Abraham, and his family in Ta-Merry , North Africa, about c. 1640 B.C.E., and many hundreds of years more before the "EXODUS OF THE ISRAELITES" allegedly took place in c. 1298 to 1232 B.C.E., which was after the Haribu ("Jews") were supposed to have "...BUILT THE PYRAMIDS OUT OF BRICKS MADE FROM MUD AND STRAW...," etc. Strangely enough, the building of pyramids out of STRAW AND MUD BRICKS was discontinued in Ta-Merry before the arrival of the Haribu to Africa by hundreds of years.

In the final analysis, all of the four Pharaohs of the "GREAT PYRAMID AGE" show similar facial characteristics to the type of Nile Valley Africans Herodotus described: "...THICK LIPS, BROAD NOSE, WOOLLY HAIR...," etc. Only one, the Asian or "SEMITE" on one of the previous pages, is not also "BURNT SKINNED." [Herodotus' HISTORIES, Book II, c. 450 to 457 B.C.E.; W. Amistead, A TRIBUTE TO THE NEGRO, London, 1845; F. W. Snowden, BLACKS IN ANTIQUITY: A GRECO-ROMAN EXPERIENCE, Cambridge, Mass., 1970; Y. ben-Jochannan, AFRICA: MOTHER OF "WESTERN CIVILIZATION," New York, 1971; J. A. Rogers, WORLD'S GREAT MEN OF COLOR, New York, 1945; G.C.M. James, STOLEN LEGACY, New York, 1954; J. J. Jackson, INTRODUCTION TO AFRICAN CIVILIZTION, New York, 1970; E. M. Sandford, THE MEDITERRANEAN WORLD, New York, 1934].

The scene above is from a painting in TOMB 63 of Ta-Merry (Egypt). Like many others on the wall, it shows Assyrian (Syrian) subjects and tribute-bearers bringing quiver, vessels, ointment, and other material goods for the African Pharaoh. Note one of the gifts is a little child; probably a "SEMITE?"

The wall-painting above would be designated one of 'NEGRO SLAVES FROM NUBIA PAYING TRIBUTE TO THEIR EGYPTIAN RULER' if the people were Nubians. Since the people are designated "SEMITIC," the nomenclature - "SLAVES" - does not apply. Why is this so? The answer, RACISM and RELIGIOUS BIGOTRY.

202

Daughter of Pharaoh Akhenaton

Queen Tiyi, mother of
Pharaoh Akhenaton

Pharaoh Amen-ophis III,
father of Pharaoh Akhenaton

Pharaoh Tek-Amen of Ta-Nehisi
and Ta-Merry, c. 30 B.C.E.
[from the SOUTH].

Queen Nefertiti, beloved wife
of Pharaoh Akhenaton

Pharaoh Ra-mer-ka Amen-tarit
of Ta-Nehisi and Ta-Merry, c.
100 B.C.E. [from the SOUTH].

[See Pharaoh Akhenaton, or Amen-hotep IV, on page 199]

The above personalities of Ta-Merry and Ta-Nehisi are generally shown in their

Greco-Roman versions and not as they appear here. It is to be noted that there

are numerous of these, and others which have been painted and sculpted in va-

rious periods to suit the artists and sculptors projection of the ruling group. The

indigenous Africans of the Nile Valley made their personalities to have their own

physical appearance; the foreigners from Asia and Europe made them in their

own image, thus, the reason for the vast differences in each period of time.

203

This chapter would not have been complete without the author citing certain basic chronological data of Judaeo-Christian-Islamic and Greek religious histography, all of which had their origin in the teachings of the OSIRICA of the Grand Lodges and religious societies of the indigenous Africans of the continent of Alkebu-lan [Africa, Lebus, Ethiopia, etc.], particularly among the TWA or BAHUTU people [the so-called "Pygmies"] of central East Alkebu-lan and those along the Nile River [blue and white] Valleys, and more specifically those of Ta-Merry, Ta-Nehisi, Meröe, Itiopi, and Puanit.

There are many calculations in the following information of which the reader is about to be introduced. They may be quite difficult to understand in the case of the average reader or freshman student who has never before had any background in the HIGHER DEGREES of the Mysteries - such as the ODD FELLOWS, FREE MASONS, MECHANICS, KNIGHTS OF COLUMBUS, ROYAL ORDER OF ELKS, and other "SECRET ORDERS" commonly in practice throughout the so-called "Western World" [Great Britain, Europe, European-America, and the Caribbean Islands], all having been patterned after the teachings of the OSIRICA that was centered in the Grand Lodge of Luxor [Thebes]. Said teachings, which included philosophy and religion, are revealed [somewhat] in the BOOK OF THE COMING FORTH BY DAY [Egyptian Book Of The Dead and The Papyrus Of Ani], PYRAMID TEXTS, COFFIN TEXTS, NEGATIVE CONFESSIONS, and a host of other works left by the ancient indigenous Africans of the Nile Valley High-Cultures in their temples and tombs, also on the walls, columns, ceilings and floors of other structures they built. These were only a few of the teachings of the FELLOW CRAFTSMEN, many of whom descendants are called "NEGROES, BANTUS, AFRICANS SOUTH OF THE SAHARA, PYGMIES," etc., and are barred from European and European-American versions of what is left of the MYSTERIES SYSTEM their ancestors created and developed thousands of years before the origin of Judaism, Christianity, Islam, and Greek mythology. The "SECRETS" we are about to examine were introduced for the FIRST TIME by the indigenous Africans of the Nile Valleys and Great Lakes regions of Alkebu-lan thousands of NILE YEARS[0] before the birth and establishment of the Asian and European nations known as SUMNER, PERSIA, BABYLON, PALESTINE [later Israel], PYRRHUS [later Hellas and Greece], and ROME, muchless before the advent of what is called "WESTERN CIVILIZATION" - made up of nations whose people are today called "ANGLO-SAXON CAUCASIANS, INDO-

---

[0] One NILE YEAR = 365 1/4 days. See Nile Year Calendar on page 215, this volume.

EUROPEAN ARYANS, SEMITES," and even "HAMITES." These calculations arose from the teachings that even predated the alleged "CREATION OF THE WORLD" by the Haribu ["Jewish"] God - "JEHOVAH" or "YAWEH" - by thousands of years, and equally many thousands more before the "BIRTH OF MOSES" [another mythical Nile Valley African of the Haribu Holy Bible, the Torah or Five Books of Moses] and his invention - "THE FIRST MAN, ADAM," for his "GARDEN OF EDEN" somewhere along the Tigris and Euphrates rivers of Southern Asia; of course, all of this happened before the unearthing of the oldest known fossil-man in the entire world - ZINJANTHROUPUS boisie of central East Alkebu-lan [Africa], who is only more than 1,750,000 years older than Moses' ADAM.

The NUMEROLOGY involved in the building of numerous temples, pyramids, colossal statues, dams, canals, stelae, measurements from Earth to other Planets and Stars, cosmology, astrology, various branches of science, medicine, philosophy, etc., along the entire length of the Blue Nile and White Nile valleys, also the Great Lakes regions down to the tip of Monomotapa [Southern Alkebu-lan], formed much of the basic formulae and other calculations employed in the following data to be presented, due mostly to the complexity of the mathematics of this ancient science created and developed by the indigenous Africans in the LODGES OF THE OSIRICA that maintained its major or prime SEAT OF LEARNING at Luxor [later called Thebes]. LUXOR, the HOLY OF HOLIES that was originally part of Ta-Nehisi [Nubia or Zeti] before the IInd Dynasty, is the same CENTER OF MAJOR LEARNING mentioned here. But, it is entirely impossible to make the CALCULATIONS any clearer than they are shown in this very much condensed and simplified INTRODUCTION TO THE NUMEROLOGY OF THE LUNAR, SOLAR, NILE, TROPICAL, SIARCDIS, AND SOTHIS YEAR CALENDAR SYSTEM for calculating TIME-PERIODS OF THE PRE-CHRISTIAN[0] and CHRISTIAN ERA. [00]

The discrimination applied in the selection of the data, personalities, and historical periods involved are of course subject to quite a lot of constructive and distructive criticisms, as many members of various disciplines related to this one probably would have preferred that other materials and sources of their own choosing would have been used. However, any other method of selection would have been impossible at this time, being that the nature of the overall text of this volume had to be complimented in this chapter.

---

[0] Before the "BIRTH" and "DEATH" of the Christians God-head, JESUS CHRIST, B.C.E.
[00] Since the "DEATH" of the Christians God-head, JESUS CHRIST, C.E.

Yet, a much more extensive and detailed treatment of the ancient Nile Valley NUMER-OLOGY and MATHEMATICAL SYSTEM, with respect to the NILE VALLEY MYSTERIES SYSTEM'S OSIRICA, has been entered into by the author in his SEVEN-VOLUMES work being edited at present for possible publication in the very near future, a work of more than twenty-eight [28] years of research and preparation, titled, AFRICA [Alkebu-lan] IN HISTORY: A CHRONOLOGY, c. 1,750,000 B.C.E. - 1971 C.E., containing at least 4,000 pages - with countless maps, graphs, charts, and pictures.

Now we enter into the MATHEMATICAL CALCULATIONS developed by the indigenous Africans of the Great Lakes and Nile Valleys, many of which formed the basis of the works attributed to certain mythological Greeks, most of whom there are no records of their birth, life, nor death.

THE TRIANGLE OF THE PYRAMID FIELD - MAN'S EARLIEST
NUMEROLOGICAL and MATHEMATICAL CHALLENGE BEGAN
[African TRIG and MATH before Pythagoras & Euclid]

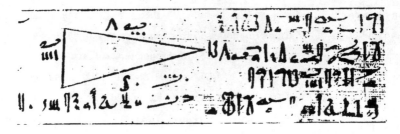

[British Museum, London, England]

The above triangular field contains mathematical calculations that solved the area of the TRI-LEG or HOUSE OF AMENTA [Pyramid or House of Heaven, the Nether World]. It was developed in the predynastic era, but the problem was solved in the IVth Century B.C.E., which was during the ending of the XXXth Dynasty [c.341 B.C.E.].

The indigenous Africans of the Nile Valley, who came from points farther SOUTH along the Great Lakes regions of Central Alkebu-lan, not only solved the TRIANGLE or PYRAMID FIELD in such an early stage in man's beginning into the reaches of scientific intellect before the origin of "WESTERN CIVILIZATION" [Greek society]; they also SQUARED THE CIRCLE by using an equation of the GEOMETRICAL EQUIVALENT OF EIGHT/NINTH [8/9] OF THE LENGTH OF THE DIAMETER and reached the CONSTANT NUMBER 3.16. It is almost the exact NUMBER and FIGURE adopted by the Greeks for
206

the SIXTEENTH LETTER of their alphabet: Ⲡ , ⲡ , pi or pe, which corresponds to the further modification by the English alphabet's P or p. It is a SYMBOL which designates THE RATIO OF THE CIRCUMFERENCE OF A CIRCLE TO ITS DIAMETER or = 3.14159265+. The Nile Valley Africans also solved the AREA of all of the objects they used in the building and development of their earliest High-Cultures [civilizations]. Their GEOMETRICIANS and TRIGOMETRICIANS had also began to challenge much more complex mathematical and scientific problems. They all started, never-the-less, from the most basic MATHEMATICAL FORMULAE of the MASONIFIED NUMEROLOGY of the OSIRICA'S MYSTERIES SYSTEM, as shown in the following examples:

<u>MASONIC MATHEMATICAL HIEROGLYPHIC CALCULATIONS</u>

[Whole Numbers]

$$\text{I} = \text{I}, \cap = \text{I0}, \text{Ⲝ} = \text{I00}$$
$$\text{Ⲭ} = \text{I,000} \quad \text{Ⲅ} = \text{I0,000}$$

Note that the large numbers were written with the highest figure first and those following in similar sequence. For example: 1,321 is written:

$$\text{I,000} + \text{I00} + \text{I00} + \text{I00} + \text{I0} + \text{I0} + \text{I} = \text{Ⲭ ℮ ℮ ℮ ∩∩I}$$

[Fractions]

2/5 was written: $I/3 + I/5 =$ ⲓⲓⲓ ∩ⲓⲓⲓⲓⲓ

Although the Nile Valley Africans had many set SYMBOLS for certain MIXED NUMBERS, most were written with a NUMERATOR of ONE [I or 1] over a DENOMINA-TOR.

The above calculations, as thousands more that the Africans developed, represent a very early stage of development of their MATHEMATHICAL AWARENESS of the FUNCTION OF NUMBERS and their EQUIVALENT MEANING AND APPLICATION TO MATERIAL USAGE AND THE SPIRITUAL THOUGHT-PROCESSES; all of this they ac-complished before the "DAWN OF WESTERN CIVILIZATION."

In order to MULTIPLY they employed the same WHOLE NUMBERS process used in the ADDITION we used above, except that they also had a duplication series. They did this by doubling the MULTIPLICAND as many times as were necessary. For ex-ample: To multiply the whole numbers, 15 × 13, they did the following:

[Multiplication]

I	I5
2	30
4	6Q
8	120

By adding the left column and then the corresponding numbers of the right

column they arrived at the answer:

$$I + 4 + 8 \qquad I5 + 60 + I20$$

Both added together they got:

$$I3 \times I5 = I95.$$

The main reason for much of the complexities in the above method of calculation
was the fact that the Nile Valley and Great Lakes Africans had not yet developed a
figure beyond the number EIGHT [8] at this early period in their history. One must
remember that we are dealing with a period that extended far into the past before the
first of the so-called "SEMITES FROM ASIA" - the Hyksos - arrived in Alkebu-lan
[Africa], Ta-Merry [Egypt] to be exact, which was at the end of the XIVth Dynasty, c.
1675 B.C.E. The period we are dealing with was hundreds of years before the first
literate Greek of historical records recorded his first word, in his first book - Homer
and his ILLYAD.

Is it not strange that we are not taught any of the above facts in courses related to
the history of mathematics in institutions specializing in WHITE STUDIES, such as
PUBLIC and PRIVATE SCHOOLS [secular and religious] throughout the United States
of America, Europe, Great Britain, and all of the colonies controlled by European and
European-American powers that be? Why is this so? Because these FACTS could not
be told and those who are in control of "RACIAL PURITY" and the protection of the
"CHOSEN PEOPLE" still retain the myth about Moses, Pythogoras, Aristotle, Plato,
and Euclid, only to mention a few of the so-called "GREAT THINKERS OF THE WEST-
ERN WORLD," being the progenitors of the OSIRICA'S MYSTERIES all of them learnt

208

when they were students in Ta-Merry and Ta-Nehisi under "...THICK LIPS, BROAD NOSE, WOOLLY HAIR, AND BURNT SKIN..." Ethiopians [the ancient name for what is today called "Negroes" and "Bantus"].

For an adequate extension of information beyond this point, with respect to the direct calculations of HIGHER MATHEMATICS developed from this level by the indigenous Africans of the Nile Valleys and Great Lakes High-Cultures [civilizations], the following works should be consulted: G.G.M. James', STOLEN LEGACY, New York, 1945; W. Amisted's, A TRIBUTE TO THE NEGRO, London, 1845; J.J. Jackson's, INTRODUCTION TO AFRICAN CIVILIZATION, New York, 1971; Y. ben-Jochannan's, AFRICA: MOTHER OF "WESTERN CIVILIZATION," New York, 1971; B.L. Latrik's, THE AFRICANS BEFORE THE FOREIGNERS IN EGYPT, London, 1798; Count C.F. Volney's, RUINS OF EMPIRE, Paris, 1800; Sir E.A. Wallis Budge's, BOOK OF THE DEAD, and, PAPYRUS OF ANI, London, 1895. All of these works will also provide the general reader, researcher, and student with added references to much more extensive and detailed data dealing with the NUMEROLOGY and MASONIFIED MATHEMATICS of the OSIRICA'S teachings.

MASONIC CHRONOLOGICAL CALCULATIONS OF THE GRAND LODGE OF LUXOR [Thebes]: THE MYSTERIES.

Working from a formula based upon TALISMANIC NUMEROLOGY we have the following: The numerical value of CUBIC DACTYLES, A, of the TALISMANIC NUMBER, G, the TALISMANIC NUMBER, D, and the SQUARE ROOT OF THE SUM OF THE SQUARES OF THE LENGTH and the HEIGHT OF THE "ARK" is equal to the mathematical calculation:

$$\sqrt{\ell^2 + a^x} = 2.915475947\,22650235 + = D.$$

By substituting NUMBERS for DAYS we arrive at the length of ONE [1] SIDEREAL or SOTHIS YEAR, which is equal to:

one/third (1/3) part of A + D' + $[x^2 \delta\, D]$ = $0^{d\cdot}3239093$ + $1095^{d\cdot}445115$ = $1095^{d\cdot}7690243$. ∴. $365^d\,6^h\,9'\,7''\ldots 9023770+$.

In the above formula the following values were used: d = Days, h = Hours,

' = Minutes, and " = Seconds. The complexity of the development of this formula requires many pages of detailed information for a minute simplification in order that the
average reader could fully comprehend its truest value. The question that would necessary follow such a disclosure is: Why was it mentioned here? Because the author
would like the general reader, as the average student of African history and High-
Culture, to see the extent to which the early indigenous Africans of the Great Lakes
and Nile Valleys MATHEMATICAL SCIENCE NUMEROLOGY*as a science, and the religious purposes it serve in terms of PHILOSOPHICAL DIMENSIONS, all of which can
be observed in the works that came out of the OSIRICA that was centered in the Grand
Lodge of Luxor.

The "ARK" mentioned in the above formula is exactly the same as the "STONE
CHEST" which is detailed in the BOOK OF THE COMING FORTH BY DAY,** which the
ancient Haribu [misnomered "Jews"] learnt in Ta-Merry and Ta-Nehisi, then co-opted
and plagiarized in their own version they called the "ARK OF THE COVENANT;" this
they have presented in the so-called "FIVE BOOKS OF MOSES" [Holy Torah or Christian Old Testament, any version]. We will uncover this type of dramatic information
in many of the older books on this subject area, especially when we deal with readings
like the following in the Holy Torah's SECOND BOOK OF MOSES, otherwise known as
EXODUS, Chapter xxv, verses 10 - 12, where it is stated:

> "And they shall make an Ark of Shitten wood: two
> cubits and a half shall be the length thereof, and a cubit
> and a half the breadth thereof, and a cubit and a half the
> height thereof....And you shall cast four rings of gold
> for it, and put them in the four corners thereof, and two
> rings shall be on the one side of it, and two rings on the
> other side of it."

*An adaptation of the Geochronological ana Monumental Section Dating,at-
tributed to the works of the African High-Priest Manetho, in NILE YEARS. Thus:
Sethos = 1322 B.C.E., Amenopath 19, and Rameses 1. The Africans of Ta-Merry,
Ta-Nehisi, Itiopi, Lebu, Puanit, etc. NILE YEAR calendar was based upon the
RISE and FALL of the Nile River; whereas the Haribu and many other Asians
based their upon LUNAR or MOON YEARS from the Patriarchial birth of Abraham
in Ur, Chaldea; other Asians upon the SIARADIC YEARS - according to the "DIAL
OF AHAZ." Added are: TROPICAL YEARS and SIDEREAL or SOTHIS YEARS.
* Also known as the Egyptain BOOK OF THE DEAD, as translated into the English language by Sir E.A. Wallis Budge, London, 1895, along with its accompany-
ing work, THE PAPYRUS OF ANI, from the Africans original writing - HIEROGLYPH.

The Ark of the Covenant[0]

The Ark of the Covenant, built and set up by Moses in the wilderness, according to the Sacred volume—and which has not been seen—is precisely similar in all measurements to the " Stone Chest " still to be seen in the King's Chamber of the Great Pyra-

mid, and which is undoubtedly the original, although the contents are gone.   According to the *Ritual* it should have contained the " Coffined One," and we know that miniatures of this used to be carried around the Egyptian temples at Memphis on stated occasions during their religious rites.

[0]. From Dr. A. Churchward's SIGNS AND SYMBOLS OF PRIMORDIAL MAN, London, 1920, p. 296.

The standard "CUBIT" used by the indigenous Nile Valley Africans was equal to 1.72091 English feet. This is tranfered to the Hebrew LUNAR SCALE by using the following values of the formula: $\ell = 2.5$, $a = 1.5$, $\beta = 2$, $\delta = X$, with the power of X raised up to its maximum strength; thus we have:

$$\frac{1.72091 \times 354 \times 360}{365.24224 \times 360} = 1.667 \frac{1314229248}{1314872064} \text{ foot.}$$

In liberating the NUMERICAL values of the latent records in the first class the TALISMANIC NUMBER or LETTER, G , is applicable. It represents the SEVENTH [7th] part of the sum of SEVEN [7] CUBIC LUNAR DACTYLE in the solid generated by the THREE [3] DIMENSIONS (cube) of the African STONE CHEST [the Haribu version is called "ARK OF THE COVENANT"]. The conversion of this into a WHOLE NUMBER [or unity] of CUBIC DACTYLES OF THE SOLAR SCALE is definitely prescribed.

The MASONIC or MYSTERIES SYSTEM THEORUM for reducing a MIXED NUMBER into a DEFINITE NUMBER is to add UNITY to the WHOLE NUMBER as the fractional part exceeds a HALF [1/2]. The formula formed by this ingenious African theorum is as follows:

$$\frac{(24^3 \ell a^2)}{7} + 7 = 11109.57 \text{ LUNAR} = 10776.28 \text{ SOLAR DACTYLES,}$$

which amounts to TWO [2] TALISMANIC NUMBERS:

11110 = A, and 10776 = G.

In order to relate the ancient Asian and African-Asian Israelite CHIEF-KINGS chronologically to their Nile Valley African cousins of Ta-Merry and Ta-Nehisi, Itiopi, Puanit, Lebu and the central Great Lakes regions included, we must first establish a common period of reign of at least ONE [1] monarch or histo-religious figure on each side of this extended family's genealogical tree. Thus, we have:

THE MANETHONIAN NILE LISTS

The Dynastic Sections	The measures of the pyramid and cataclysmal sections in metric noctas	The measures of the cataclysmal sections in metric noctas	Durations of the Cataclysmal Sections	Durations of the Egyptian Sections	The Patriarchs, and the years of time intervening between their births only.	The Samaritan numbers	The Septuagint numbers	The Hebrew numbers
	Metric noctas.	Metric noctas	Nilo years.	Nilo years.		Sacred years.	lunar years.	Nilo years.
XIX.	 209	....	204	....	Terah	70	170	70
XVIII.	{.... 263 / Amos 25 B}	25 B	262	....	Nahor	79	170	29
				....	Serug	130	130	30
XVII.	.... 151 B	2×151 B	....	151B	Reu	132	132	32
XVI.	.... 518 B	2×518 B	....	518B	Peleg......	130	130	30
XV.	 284	....	284	....	Eber	134	134	34
XIV.	.... 181 B	181 B	....	184B	Salah	130	130	30
XIII.	.... 453 B	453 B	....	453B	(Cainan II.)	109	130	160
XII.	 160	....	160	....	Arphaxad ..	135	135	35
XI.	{.. 2×16 / .... 43 B}	43 B	16 / 43 B	(43 B)	Shem......	100	100	100
					Sums ..	1140	1370	400
X.	.... 185 B	185 B	....	185B	Noah......	500	500	500
IX.	.... 409 B	409 B	....	409B	Lamech	53	188	182
VIII.	.... 146 B	146 B	....	146B	Methusaloh.	67	187	187
VII.	.... 0·2 B	0·2 B	....	....	Enoch ...	65	165	65
VI.	 203	....	197	....	Jared......	162	262	162
V.	 248	....	218	....	Mahallaleel.	65	165	65
IV.	 284	....	284	....	Cainan I. ..	70	170	70
III.	 214	....	214	....	Enos	90	100	90
II.	 302	....	302	....	Seth	105	205	105
I.	 253	....	203	....	Adam	130	230	130
	2)4523·2 / 2261·6	2)2740·2 B / 1370·1 B			Sums ..	1307	2262	1556
					Post-Noachid section ..	1140	1370	400
					Ante-Noachid section ..	1307	2262	1556
		2447	2016		Sums total..	2447	3632	2016

The above CHRONOLOGY was calculated by Hakekyan Bey with a series of special NUMEROLOGICAL NUMBERS and MASONIFIED FORMULAE he adopted from High-Priest Manetho's calculations of the Nile Valley indigenous African pharaohs GEOPHISI-CAL CALENDAR and CHRONOLOGY of their DYNASTIC REIGN, from the Ist through the XXXth Dynasty [c. 3200 - 322 B.C.E.]. Note that the last of the African Pharaohs did not rule beyond Ta-Merry's military occupation by the Persians.

In examining the above "MANETHONIAN LISTS" one will certainly question the difference between a TROPICAL YEAR and the MENOPHREAN ERA. Because of this the author of this volume has shown the method of calculating both below:

The longest TROPICAL YEAR in MEAN SOLAR DAYS =

$$T = \frac{2300 \times 354}{2300 - \frac{354}{5}}.$$

The length of the TROPICAL YEAR of the MENOPHREAN ERA =

$$T - \frac{354}{5}.$$

It is also noted that Manetho could not have developed a CHRONOLOGICAL

CHART for "ADAM," since the ancient Africans of the Nile Valley and Great Lakes

regions did not have such a character in any aspect of their mythology or religion,

muchless their history and High-Culture. For this reason, and many more we have

observed so far, the above LISTS are misleading.

At this juncture in our safari into the inner reaches of the Nile Valleys and Great
Lakes Africans intellect, it is necessary to reflect on the major point of concern, that
is: the treatment of the ancient AFRICAN HARIBU ["Jews"] of Ta-Merry and Ta-Nehisi
as "A SEPARATE RACE" than their former "SLAVE MASTERS" - the indigenous AFRI-
CAN WORSHIPERS OF RA, as taught by most European and European-American educators bearing the name "WHITE PEOPLE," which of course includes "SEMITES." But,
there are countless numbers of "BLACK, BROWN, YELLOW," and "RED-SKINNED"
Haribu or Israelites ["Hebrews" or "Jews"] available to be seen in the present state of
Israel today. The FACT that the non-WHITES among the "JEWS" in Israel are suppressed and dehumanized by their fellow "WHITE JEWS", also called "SEMITES," from the
United Sattes of America, Great Britain, and Western Europe, those who in FACT control Israel, does not in any way shape or fashion negate their right to claim ancestry
with the original "JEW," Abraham. Thus, the alleged "JEWISHNESS" which one is
supposed to "INHERIT FROM A JEWISH MOTHER" is a RACIST and RELIGIOUSLY
BIGOTED myth without the least bit of BIBLICAL TRUTH, especially if we are to
notice that the "JEWISH WOMAN," as the "JEWISH NATION," has been RAPED by
every conquering army that occupied ancient Palestine and Israel down through the
centuries. Did the "JEWISH WOMAN" [BLACK, WHITE, BROWN, YELLOW, RED, or
whatever else there may be] not suffer the same fate during her "ENSLAVEMENT" to
the Africans of Ta-Merry [Egypt] and Ta-Nehisi [Nubia], North Alkébu-lan [Africa]?
Or, are we to assume that "JEWISH SLAVERY" was different to "NEGRO SLAVERY"?

214

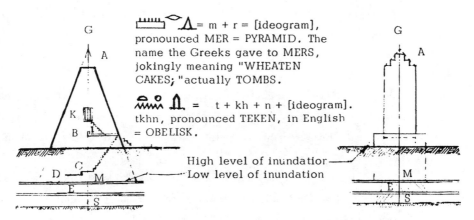

= m + r = [ideogram], pronounced MER = PYRAMID. The name the Greeks gave to MERS, jokingly meaning "WHEATEN CAKES; "actually TOMBS.

= t + kh + n + [ideogram]. tkhn, pronounced TEKEN, in English = OBELISK.

High level of inundation
Low level of inundation

MASONIC CHRONOLOGICAL SCHEME OF TA-MERRY

The Masonic Scheme of F. Josephus.			The Masonic Scheme of Theophilus.			Geochronological and Monumental Section of Manetho.			The Political Section.		
18. Sethosis, who is Ramesses.			Sethus and Rhamesses.			Sethos. B.C. 1322.			Ramses...... 51 Sethos.		
	Nilo yrs.	m.		Nile yrs.	m.		Nile yrs.			Nile yrs.	
17. Amenophis	19	0	Amenophis	19	6	Amenophath	19			+20	
16. Armesses-miamou	66	0	Sethos ....(1 3)	1	0	Ramesses	1				
15. Ramesses	1	4	Armeus	4	2						
14. Armais .... (4 7)	4	1	Sethos-miamnu	6	0	Armeses	5	Armeses	5		
13. Akencheres ....:.	12	3				Acherrhes...........	12	Acherrhea ..	12		
12. Akencheres	12	5	Chencheres.........	30	1	Chebres.............	12	Chebres ..	12		
11. Rathosis	9	0	Athoris	12	3	Rathos	6	Rathos	6		
10. Akenchres	12	1	(A queen)	10	3	Acherrhes...........	32	Acherrhes ..	32		
9. Horus ......(36 7)	36	5	Oras.........	35	5	Horus	37	Horus	37		
8. Amenophis	30	10	Dam-phenophis	30	10	Amenophis	31	Tothmes, r...	40		
7. Thmosis (Tothmes II.)	9	8	Tuthmosis	9	8	Tuthmosis...........	9				
6. Mephramouthosis	25	10	Methramuuthosis	20	10	Misphragmathosis	26	Misaphris, r.	30		
5. Mephres	12	9	Mephres	12	9	Misaphis	13				
4. Amessis	21	9	Amesse ......(21 9)	21	1	Amersis............	22	Amersis, r. ..	22		
3. Amenophis	20	7	Amenophis	20	7	Amenophthis	24	Chebros	24		
2. Chebron	13	0	Chebron	13	0	Chebros.............	13	Amos, r.	37		
1. Tethmosis (Tothmes I.)	25	4	Amasis	25	4	Amos .... (24)	--				
Sum. 333 -66-10 = -47	0 0		+25 4-13 = +12	273 4	8						
Date of Exodus 286	0			286	0	B.C. 1708 286			286		

Note: Specific dating of the above references to the so-called "EXODUS FROM EGYPT" was never mentioned by High-Priest Manetho in any of his EIGHT [8] works. They were attributed to him by conjecture in the works of Josephus, Theophilus, and others that followed them to the present date.

Era and Monarch	Post Menophrean Era, in NILE YEARS	Post Menphrean Era, in LUNAR YEARS	Post Dionysia Era, Christ Bi in NILE YEARS
Death of Alexander II =	1000.000 =	1030.000 =	321.625

Using Alexander II ["the great"] invasion of Ta-Merry in c. 332 B.C.E. as a point of reference, we find that the ruler of Israel at twenty-nine [29] NILE YEARS later was King Simon I. He reigned over Israel from c. 303 B.C.E., following the death of his father King Eleazer, who died in the twenty-third [23rd] year of his pontificate. Simon I was succeded by King Onias I in c. 324 B.C.E. This would place King Onias I assuming the throne of Israel at approximately eight [8] years after the invasion of Ta-Merry by Alexander II, and a little less than three [3] years following Alexander's death in c. 327 B.C.E.

We could have used the ASTRONOMICAL CANON OF PTOLEMAEUS OF PELUSIUM [Theon of Alexandria's version] of the ECCLESIASTICAL account in relating the above dates. His interpretation of them was the FIRST established for the NILE YEAR CALENDAR dating process, with relationship to the DYNASTIC CHRONOLOGY of the High-Culture that preceded the Macedonian-Greeks invasion and conquest of Ta-Merry and parts of LOWER Ta-Nehisi in c. 332 B.C.E. All of this preceded the occupation which brought about European imperial colonialism, the so-called "XXXIst Dynasty, for the FIRST TIME in North Alkebu-lan [Africa]. Moreover, the ECCLESIASTICAL YEAR CALENDAR contained two more pharaohs [kings] of Nile Valley High-Cultures than the others mentioned so far. These two pharaohs allegedly reigned between the rule of Pharaoh Artaxeres [Longimanus, Son of the Sun, Xerxes I] and Pharoah Darius Nothus [Son of the Sun, Ochus I or Darius II], c. 458.362 - 423.627 B.C.E.

At this juncture in our historical safari into the heritage of the Africans, African-Americans, and African-Caribbeans, we must take specific notation of the exact calculation for Alexander II [Son of the Sun, Philip of Macedonia] conquest of Ta-Merry; thus, we shall find that the actual NILE YEAR amounted to a period that was the total c. 331.628 B.C.E., which was rounded off to the whole number c. 332 B.C.E. This period in the DYNASTIC SEQUENCE of Ta-Merry's CHRONOLOGICAL CHART was called the "PERSIAN ERA" or "EPOCH" [Dynasty] by High-Priest Manetho. It began with Cyrus Husht-asp [Hystapes or Darius I; Son of the Sun, Xerxes or Aha-Suerus] in the NILE YEAR c. 535.750 or the equal of c. 525 B.C.E.
216

To make certain that the calculations of the NILE YEARS were kept in total accuracy Manetho, who had established "CHECK POINTS" for references where there
were no fractional parts of a NILE YEAR, noted the following phoenomena. During the
50th NILE YEAR of the reign of Cecrops I, c. 1596 - 1546, who reigned 26 NILE
YEARS in Athens, c. 1596 - 1570, and 24 NILE YEARS in Ta-Merry, c. 1570. 625 -
1546. 625, there was a calculation that resulted in a fractional part of a NILE YEAR.

The last reference to the calculations we have been so far engaged in can be best
observe in the records of the ARMENIAN ERA OF HAYGH, which was during the period
of time when the NILE YEAR calculations ran in fractional parts. But, this method of
calculating NILE YEARS was comprised of a conglamorate of FOUR [4] separate
schemes: Ist, the ERA beginning with the TROPICAL CYCLE - a year very much longer than that of the SOTHIS CALENDAR system used before the alleged "EXODUS OF
THE ISRAELITES FROM EGYPT" [Ta-Merry, Kimit, Sais, etc.], North Alkebu-lan;
IInd, the ERA of the alleged "EXODUS" itself; IIIrd, the ERA of the MENOPHREAN;
and IVth, the ERA of the proclamation of the "BIRTH OF JESUS CHRIST OF NAZARETH"
[the son of two Haribu or Israelites, Joseph and Mary]. The actual date given by MASONI-
FIED calculations for the HAYGHIDE DYNASTY of Armenia was c. 2492. 55 TROPICAL
YEARS, and for the ARSACIDE DYNASTY of Armenia - c. 577. 50 TROPICAL YEARS.
Both figures or dates calcualted gave the PERIOD or TIME-SPACE elapsed from the
beginning of the TROPICAL CYCLE up to the alleged "BIRTH OF THE CHRIST CHILD"
or "NATIVITY" adopted by the renegade Hebrew chronicler Luke - also known as the
"EVANGILIST." The calculation used to obtain said result was as follows:

$$1234.000 + 286 + 1460 = 2492.550 + 577.500.$$

The difference between LUNAR YEARS and NILE YEARS was arrived at by taking
away 340 YEARS from 1340 LUNAR YEARS = the equivalent in NILE YEARS. Using
said figures, we can establish the actual date of "JOSEPH'S SALE TO POTIPHER,
CAPTAIN OF THE GUARD OF EGYPT," if such did in fact occured other than in the
Haribu religious story in the Holy Torah [Five Books of Moses or Christian Old Tes-
tament], which is set at 430 LUNAR YEARS before the alleged "EXODUS" or c. 1298 -

---

0* Exodus, Chapter VI, Verses 16-20, for the birth of Joseph, etc. This event allegedly took place during the reign of Pharaoh Rameses II, XIXth Dynasty, c. 1298-1232
B.C.E., or that of his son and successor Merneptah, c. 1232 - 1224 B.C.E.

1232 B.C.E.

The following dates are only a few of the most important historical periods in
terms of NILE YEARS, were we still using the ancient indigenous Africans ["Negro,
Bantus," etc.] NILE YEAR CALENDAR on page 130 of this volume instead of the
JULIAN or GREGORIAN. This is equally true for the AFRICAN SOLAR YEAR
CALENDAR and STELAR CALENDAR, the latter having been developed sometime
during c. 10,000 B.C.E., which was approximately 6,800 years before the Ist Dynasty,
c. 3200 B.C.E.

NILE YEAR [N.Y] CALENDAR RELATED TO DATES OF THE CHRISTIAN ERA [C.E.]

N.Y. 138 = 1 C.E.   Christ's birth ["the nativity"] = 0 B.C.E. = 0 C.E. [The beginn-
    ing of the Christian Experience by African "Jews" of Ta-Merry, and matching
    dates from the Gregorian and Julian calendars [the so-called "Christian ca-
    lendars].

N.Y. 146 = 140 C.E. This period marked the reign of Atonius Pius.

N.Y. 338 = 284 C.E. This period marked the reign of Diocletian.

N.Y. 976 = 622 C.E. Year of the Hejire or Hagira = A.H. 1 = the year the Prophet
    of the Muslim Faith, Mohamet ibn Abdullah, fled the ancient Arab HOLY CITY
    of the worship of the Goddess AL'LAT to the Oasis of Yathrib around the 2nd
    HOLY CITY of Medina and founded the Religion and Nation of Islam. All of this
    took place in the year 622 C.E. or 1 A.H. From this period the Goddess AL'LAT
    gave way to the God AL'LAH; but, the KA'ABA [the "Black Stone" or "piece of
    fallen meteor from Ethiopia, East Africa] still remained one of the most sacred
    mentors of the Islamic World up to the present period in history.

SOLAR CALEDAR [S.Y.] RELATED TO DATES BEFORE THE CHRISTIAN ERA [BCE]

S.Y. 2010.00   The projected date of Joseph's ministry.
S.Y. 2005.10   The beginning of the SEVEN YEARS of extreme hunger and famine
    7.00   the Haribu suffered in the Asian desert before they were rescued by
the African people of Egypt [Ta-Merry].
S.Y. 1998.20   The period when the Haribu ["Hebrews, Israelites" or "Jews"] suf-
    6.9   fered the last stage of their famine in the Asian desert.
S.Y. 1996.10   The period Joseph's brothers arrived in Egypt to purchase wheat and
    2.10   corn from the Africans of Egypt who worshipped the GREAT I AM,
THE GREAT ONE, I, RA, to feed the starving fellow Haribu [nomads] who worshipped
another I AM, JEHOVAH, GOD OF THE [so-called] "CHOSEN PEOPLE".
S.Y. 1994.93   The projected period of Joseph's audience with his father.

LUNAR YEAR [L.Y.] CALENDAR RELATED TO DATES BEFORE THE CHRISTIAN ERA
[B.C.E. or B.C.]

L.Y. 430 = 1640 B.C.E. The beginning of the sojourn of the Haribu in Egypt, North
    Alkebu-lan; computed from the time of "JOSEPH'S SALE TO POTIPHER, CAP-

218

TAIN OF THE PALACE GUARD OF THE PHARAOH RAMESES I," c. 1230 - 1318 B.C.E.

L.Y. 400 = 1595 B.C.E. From the year of the alleged "BONDAGE OF THE HARIBU IN EGYPT" back to "THE ENTRY OF JACOB AND HIS FAMILY IN EGYPT," North Alkebu-lan [Africa].

In the above calculations under the heading of the "SOLAR YEAR CALENDAR," the figures : 7.00, 6.9, and 2.10 indicate the time-space elapsed between periods. The "LUNAR CALENDAR" related periods are supposed to have taken place between the Africans of Egypt and the Haribu or Asians of the area around ancient Palestine, or today's Israelis desert.

We can now move into another area of the much more complexly sophisticated MASONIFIED NUMEROLOGICAL CALCULATIONS related to the HOUSE OF THE NE-THER WORLD, errection of STELAE, development of ASTROLOGICAL and ASTRO-NOMICAL OBSERVATIONS, etc., all of which the indigenous Africans of the Nile Valleys and Great Lakes regions developed in order to deal with the sciences related to the RISE and FALL of the TIDE and FLOW of the Nile River, and the data related to the development of ASTROLOGY, MAGIC, RELIGION, PHILOSOPHY, and other disciplines of the SEVEN LIBERAL ARTS.

CHRONOLOGICAL NUMEROLOGY OF THE ALL-SEEING EYE, One, the GOD Ra. THE FORMULA FOR TIME-YEARS EXPRESSED IN THE ANCIENT MYSTERIES SYSTEM, LUXOR.

The formula for TIME-YEARS gives us the basic calculation for the equal length TRI-LEG OF THE POLE STARS or HOUSE OF FIRE (the Pyramid, or House of Amenta). Thus we have the PYRAMID IDEOGRAM and the "SACRED MAGICAL NUMBER" Seven [7]. We also have the MASONIFIED NUMBERS: b = 24 and c = 15. Using the TIME-YEAR formula, we have:

$$\text{Time times and a half} = \frac{b + b^2 + b + b^2}{2} - \frac{(c + c^2 + c + c^2)}{2} =$$

900 - 360 = 540 "SACRED YEARS" of 360 DAYS/YEAR = 532.238 JULIAN YEARS = D.

By substituting D in the formula, we then have:

$$D - \frac{7\text{days}}{365.25} = 532.238 - 0.459 = 531.778$$

This date relates back to the second of the four Persian Kings mentioned by the Haribu prophet, Daniel, in the Holy Torah [Five Books of Moses]. The kings referred to began

with Cambyses [Son of the Sun, Cyrus or Sirus]. The dates were between 1360 and
1365 LUNAR YEARS from the MENOPHREAN ERA, sometime around c. 525 B.C.E.
This calculation was identical with the formula used by Dionysius in his MASONIFIED
NUMEROLOGICAL CALCULATIONS OF THE ERA OF THE "BIRTH OF JESUS CHRIST"
[the nativity].

Using the same D above, but in its negative sense, we have the following:

$$D - 360c - 7b - c = 517.626 = \text{the date of the end of the}$$
SIXTH [6th] NILE YEAR, c. 365.25 or 365 1/4 DAYS/YEAR,

which is during the reign of Pharaoh Darius [Son of the Sun, Hystapes], the third
Persian King that ruled Ta-Merry [Egypt]. It is, also, equal to the date when the
building of the Israelites SECOND TEMPLE by Zerubabel and Joshua was completed -
c. 527 B.C.E. These dates were computed in accordance with the MASONIC ERA of
the "BIRTH OF JESUS CHRIST," [0] as proclaimed by certain Haribu ["Jews"], many of
whom became the originators of Christianity and the established Church of Christendom in North Africa, the first of which took place while they were still living in Ta-
Merry, Ta-Nehisi [Nubia or Zeti],and Itiopi [sometimes including Kush and Meroe].

There are certain other scatered data we can use here. However, we noticed,
or should have, that from the beginning of the SOTHIS PERIOD there were certain
established PATRIARCHIAL CHRONOLOGIES in the "ERA OF THE EXODUS" [pass-
over], which was also "the end of the Israelites NINETY-SEVENTH [97th] GENERA-
TION." Yet, only two [2] of the men listed were actually in existence by the "ERA OF
THE EXODUS;" they were Caleb and Joshua. In this CHRONOLOGY Moses was allegedly 80.00 years old, Joshua 48.031, and Caleb 38.01, all calculated on the principles
of LUNAR YEARS, at the "ERA OF THE EXODUS." It is also an indication that the
Haribu supposedly left Northeast Alkebu-lan, around the Sinai Desert of Ta-Merry -
to be exact, "...during the 20th DAY of the 2nd MONTH of the 1st YEAR of the
EXODUS, arriving in Kibroth-hataavah after a journey of 3 DAYS - where they remain-

---

*The author of this volume bears no responsibility for the validity of the Birth Of
The Christ Child mentioned above. The remarks relative to such a happening are
only repititions of Christian religious history and mythology. The author is very
much aware of the fact that the alleged "VIRGIN BIRTH" and "MIRACULOUS DEATH"
of Christ were established by men at the NICENE CONFERENCE OF BISHOPS ordered by Emperor Constantine ("the great") in 322 C.E. Only 219 Bishops (men)

ed for 40 DAYS." It must be noted that the date of the alleged "EXODUS" was MASONI-
FIED by Theophilus and Flavius Josephus in the variations they developed and introduced into the ANTE-MENOPHREAN SECTION of the African-European High-Priest,
Manetho, SECOND DIOSPOLITAN DYNASTY. The original African historical NUMER-
OLOGY was, never the less, sacrificed by Theophilus and Josephus in order to adopt
certain NUMBERS of their own calculations in many CHRONOLOGICAL SCHEMES for
recording dates of the events before the MEDIUS AEVORUM. Flavian, also known as
Flavianus, who we depend upon for the duplication of much of Manetho's original re -
cords that were otherwise destroyed by the invading Arab-Muslim armies during their
JIHADS [Holy Wars] as they swept across North and Northeast Alkebu-lan around the
year 640 C.E. or A.H., added one more name to his ANTE-MENOPHREAN SECTION
of Manetho's SECOND DIOSPOLITAN DYNASTY than did Josephus and Theophilus.

On pages xxx and xxx of this chapter the two MASONIC SCHEMES from Hekekyan
Bey's treatise, EGYPTIAN CHRONOLOGY, London, 1863, pp. 66-68, should aid us to
further understand the previous, and following, data. From them we should be able to
perceive certain pointers and cross-references with respect to many of the other CHRON-
OLOGIES in this volume, particularly in this chapter. Hopefully, they also serve to
show that the indigenous Africans, the so-called "NEGROES" or "BANTUS," of Ta-
Merry did not originate from any kind of "CAUCASIAN, INDO-EUROPEAN ARYAN," or
"SEMITIC" and "HAMITIC" ancestry in the mythical drama of the Holy Torah's story
about "NOAH'S SONS" and the matter of a "CURSE GOD" [the Haribu Yaweh] "PLACED
ON HAM" in one of his fits of anger.

The following CHRONOLOGIES will also show that the formulae for the MATHE-
MATICAL CALCULATIONS from the NUMEROLOGICAL SYSTEM of the Osirica were
first used in the planning of domestic buildings, pyramids, obelisks, stelae, layouts
and surveys for engineering projects of canals and dams that were used for irrigation
schemes dealing with the RISE and FALL of the Nile River, etc. They will also show
that from these MASONIFIED MATHEMATICAL FORMULAE the NUMEROLOGICAL sophistication developed by these ancestors of the Africans of the Harlems of the entire
world, the United States of America and "Western" Europe in particular, all other
MATHEMATICAL SYSTEMS known to "modern man" derived their origin.

The above developments preceded the Europeans in Ta-Merry by thousands of years;
but, such were equally true of the contributions made by the African-European High-

Priest, Manetho, of the Mysteries System, while he was under due res of the army
of the Macedonian general, Soter, who seized the reign of the Egyptian government at
the death of his King and military commander, Alexander II ["the great"],thereafter
taking upon himself the name Soter I, which he later changed to PTOLEMY I, all of
which he accomplished with the aide of Aristotle - who had already began to sack all of
the royal libraries and other repositories of all of their moveable documents and artifacts he could find, much of which he published as his own works and placed his name
upon them as author. Such was the conduct of the men who started what was to become
the XXXIInd DYNASTY OF EGYPT, the XXXIst being that of Alexander II ["the great"]
reign, c. 332 B.C.E. This, too, was the first time in the history of Ta-Merry of
period that finally developed into one of infamy.

We now approach the attempt at making "JUDAEO-CHRISTIAN HISTO-THEOLOGY
and MYTHOLOGY appear to have had very basic Nile Valley African heritage ancestry that was void of the so-called "NEGRO." The European and European-American
authors, "CAUCASIANS" or "SEMITES," writing in said vein, relate all the way back
to the Haribu God-head, YAWEH [Jehovah, Elohen, Adoni, etc.]. This we will certainly observe in the following materials your author have extracted from the published
treatise by Hakekyan Bey, EGYPTIAN CHRONOLOGY, which has been mentioned before.
Mr. Bey's treatise, a most enlightening insight into the machinations of the "WESTERN-
IZED VERSIONS" of the concepts developed by the ancient Africans and Asians High-
Cultures that predated the origin of Greek ["Western"] civilization by thousands of years,
developed various graphs and charts which he expected to validate the histo-theological
and mythological teachings in the so-called FIVE BOOKS OF MOSES ["Jewish Holy Torah,
and Christian Old Testament, any version]. He developed others for the so-called NEW
TESTAMENT [any version], but in so doing he tried to attribute them to the African-
European High-Priest, Manetho, who did not indicate any knowledge whatsoever with
respect to the Haribu ["Jewish" or Israelite] God - JEHOVAH, and could never have
written anything at all about JESUS CHRIST - the God of the Christians, as he died more
than 279 years before the proclaimed "BIRTH OF JESUS CHRIST."

The following CHRONOLOGICAL SCHEME by Mr. Bey should make the reader understand the extent to which certain writers have gone in order to make religious mythology appear to be HISTORY. They have distorted, and sometimes plagiarized, the
works of many who were anti-religious to appear religious; the reverse being also true.

222

MASONIC CHRONOLOGICAL SCHEME OF ISRAEL FROM THE EXODUS TO SOLOMON
IN LUNAR AND SOLAR YEARS
(By Hakekyan Bey)

	Lunar years.	Lunar years.	Solar years.
		B.C.	B.C.
Solomon { After the foundation of the Temple...........	36·63		
Solomon { Before the foundation of the Temple.........	3·360825		
David.. { In Jerusalem...............................	32·5		
David.. { In Hebron.................................	7·5		
Saul .. { After he selected a body-guard.............	38·		
Saul .. { When he selected a body-guard.............	2·		
Samuel..	23·350515		
Eli (Samson).....................................	40·		
Second Philistine servitude	40·		
Abdon	8·		
Elon	10·		
Ibzan	7·		
Jephthah	6·		
First Philistine servitude	18·		
Jair	22·		
Tola	23·		
Abimelech	3·		
Gideon	40·	1362·5	1321·625
Midianite servitude..............................	7·		
Deborah	40·		
Canaanitish servitude............................	20·		
Ehud (Shamgar)..................................	86·		
Moabitish servitude..............................	18·		
Othniel	40·		
Mesopotamian servitude..........................	8·		
The Elders	20·		
Joshua	21·845360		
The Exodus	40·	1657·345	1607·625

"The astrogeological Nile observations should extend
fifty-seven [57] centuries of Tropical Years anterior to
the Era of Christ Nativity and to the reign of a monarch
in whose time the valley of the Nile, down to those lati-
tudes in which the hippopotamus dwells, was under the
Egyptian rule, appears incredible to those who are familiar with the short chronology, and would remain incredible, in spite of the checking or proving numbers mentioned to have been inserted by Manetho [who died before the NATIVITY] if the Siriadic Monuments had not testified to the accuracy of his calculations."**

We must end this very short safari into this aspect of the CHRONOLOGICAL

NUMEROLOGY of the indigenous African Mysteries System of the OSIRICA with

the following from pages 36, 37 and 38 of Hakekyan Bey's EGYPTIAN CHRONO-

LOGY, showing the manner in which the JULIAN CALENDAR got its origin from

---

*Inserted by the author of this volume for clarity and documentary observations
words shown in brackets [ ].
**From H. Bey's, EGYPTIAN CHRONOLOGY.

the Nile Valley and Great Lakes regions African NILE YEAR CALENDAR; and, in the process how so much of Manetho's teachings and writings have been deliberately distorted by so many Europeans and European-Americans in their attempt to prove the validity of Judaism and Christianity over all other Nile Valley religious experiences, yet using the same Nile Valley Mysteries System teachings of the Osirica that were developed by "...THICK LIPS, BROAD NOSE, WOOLLY HAIR, AND BURNT SKIN..." Africans for support; and, even said Africans' CALENDAR CALCULATIONS have been utilized to prove that Jehovah and Jesus Christ, equally the "CHOSEN PEOPLE", are realities of an experience that started with so-called "CAUCASIANS" or "SEMITES" in North and East Africa [Alkkebu-lan] - in this particular case EGYPT [Ta-Merry, Kimit, Sais, Mirain, Mizrair, etc.].

Let us examine Mr. Bey's presentation of his JUDAEO-CHRISTIAN CHRONOLOGICAL GENEALOGY, which is very typical to that by thousands of other theologians and religious historians, especially those who are bent upon making the entire world accept EUROPEAN-STYLE "CHRISTIANITY" according to the KING JAMES version of the "OLD" and "NEW TESTAMENT." The following is his major attempt at creating for Judaism and Christianity a Nile Valley High-Culture basis of origin. According to Mr. Bey:

"This is the Samaritan record :—

B.C. 2280·135 . . . . . The birth of Abram.

2446·338 Sacred years of 360 days from the creation of Adam to the birth of Abram.

+22 . . Sacred years. The second complementary number in the Zootomic formula.

$2468\cdot338 \times \frac{360}{365\frac{1}{4}} = 2433\cdot11$ Nile years.

+2432·859

B.C. 4712·994 . . . . . Date of Julian period, and of the Great Sphinx of Suphis II.

+2432·859

+ 15·77 $= 16 \times \frac{360}{365\frac{1}{4}}$ The first complementary number in the Zootomic formula, reduced from sacred into Nile years.

————

B.C. 7161·623 . . . . . Epoch of the generation of the fourth Sothis period anterior to the Menophrean. It may be also designated the Samaritan Sothis period, and the Sesochrean.

The second record is the one in the Septuagint version of

224

the Patriarchal genealogies. It is the work of Manetho himself. Its accounts are in lunar years, and the supplementary
number is also in lunar years."

It is to be noted that Bey's JUDAEO-CHRISTIAN orientation totally influenced his

writings and calculations. The SEPTUGINT'S version of the OLD TESTAMENT [Holy

Torah or Five Books of Moses] upon which he relied made them no more authentic than

the original writers, YAWEH'S "INSPIRED SCRIBES," did. Manetho's works did not

validate Haribu MYTHOLOGY or RELIGIOUS HISTO-GENEALOGY either. His incident-

al references to what may have happened to appear as Haribu mythology and biblical

history were comparable only due to a remote chance or accident, but not by intent on

his part, as evidenced by the EIGHT [8] VOLUMES he wrote on many subjects, includ-

ing the major works on Ta-Merry. However, Mr. Bey continued in an area of even

greater impossibility when he connected "ABRAHAM," the Patriarch of the Haribu re-

ligion and High-Culture, with "ADAM - the first man" of Moses' Genesis. He used the

following CHRONOLOGICAL DEDUCTION:

> "B.C. 2280·135 Nile yrs.. The birth of Abram.
>
>   3651·691 Lunar years from creation of
>   Adam to birth of Abram.
>
>   —130   Lunar years of 354 days, the value
>   of the intercalation of Caïnan II.
>   in the Septuagint version.
>
> +3396·640 = 3501·691 Lunar years of 354 days.
> +   24·819 =   25·617 Lunar years of 354 days, the
>   third complementary number in the
>   Zootomic formula.
>
> B.C. 5701·625 = ... Epoch of the generation of the third
>
> Sothis period anterior to the Menophrean. It is the com-
> mencement of the Annus Magnus, and the zero of the
> Niloscopic accounts to our time. It may be designated
> the epoch of the Menaïc period of Sothis.
>
> But the record of the Hebrew version is in Nile years;
> thus :—
> B.C. 2280·135 . The birth of Abram.
>   2046 Nile years from creation of Adam
>   to birth of Abram."

If the above deduction are true, then the Haribu Patriarch, ABRAHAM, must have

entered Ta-Merry [Lower Egypt] sometime in the year c. 2185 B.C.E., which would

have been during the XIth Dynasty, or 509 years before the HYKSOS [the so-called "SE-

---

Note that One NILE YEAR = 365 1/4 days, as against 365 days for the Julian calendar.

MITIC SHEPHERD KINGS"] that invaded and conquered the Delta region of Lower Ta-
Merry in the year c. 1675 B.C.E. - which was during the end of the XIVth Dynasty.
Here, also, there is an assumption that "ADAM" was "CREATED BY YAWEH," the
Haribu God, at approximately:

$$2046.696 + 2280.135 = 4326.135 \text{ B.C.E. or } 4326.135 +$$
$$1972.000 = 6298.135 \text{ years ago.}$$

Thus, it is evident that the mythological and/or allegorical story of the "CREATION
OF ADAM AND EVE IN THE GARDEN OF EDEN," as shown in the FIRST BOOK OF
MOSES [Genesis],took place long after many Nile Valley and Great Lakes African High-
Cultures had already reached their zenith and passed away; yet, all of them had pro-
duced their own "CREATION" story, one of which can be observed in the BOOK OF
THE COMING FORTH BY DAY [The Egyptian Book Of The Dead, and the Papyrus Of
Ani, as translated into English by Sir E.A. Wallis Budge]. Not only did the Haribu's
"CREATION" myth follow that of many African High-Cultures, it also followed the Afri-
can creation and development of the FIRST CALENDAR ever made by man - the STELAR
CHRONOGEOLOGICAL OBSERVATORY CHART. They also developed many other Nile
Valley and Great Lakes MASONIFIED CALCULATED CHARTS, some dated back to ap-
proximately c. 10,000 B.C.E. But, the Sebilian SILT TERRACE High-Cultures of the
Nile Valley went back even further - to at least 250,000 B.C.E., which was more than
243,000 years before the "CREATION OF ADAM" by the Haribu God-head - Yaweh.
Never the less Mr. Bey continued on from "ADAM," and gave:

" —100	Nile years, the value of the inter-calation of Caïnan II. in the He-brew record.
———	
1945·5	Nile years.
+ 15·989 = .. 16	Egyptian years of 365 days, the first complementary number of the Zoo-tomic formula.
.B.C. 4241·625 Nile yrs.	Epoch of the generation of the se-cond Sothis period anterior to the Menophrean. It constitutes a mid-dle line between the Samaritan and the Menophrean epochs. It may be designated the Mencherean epoch, or that of the fourth pyramid of Gizeh."

Mr. Bey topped all of his previous hypotheses by comparing the Haribu Patriarchs'

HISTO-GENEALOGICAL CHARTS to the ASTROLOGICAL CALCULATIONS of the indigenous Nile Valley African GEOPHYSICAL CHARTS they were taught while they were
"SLAVES IN EGYPT" and Nubia. He continued further, trying desperately to find much
more common grounds between the so-called "SEMITES OF ISRAEL" and the "SEMITES
OF EGYPT" and Ta-Nehisi, equally being forgetful that the "SEMITES" of Egypt had
"...THICK LIPS, BROAD NOSE, WOOLLY HAIR, AND BURNT SKIN..." like those
described by Herodotus and other ancients who visited and lived among the Egyptians
and other indigenous African of the Nile Valley.

Mr. Bey summarized the entire Haribu histo-genealogy he tried to attached to
the Africans of Ta-Merry [Egypt and Ta-Nehisi] with the following comments:

> "We will now compare the Patriarchal genealogies of the
> three versions with the astrogeological Nile lists of Manetho.
> The Manethonian sections of Nile observations which are called
> "the dynasties" will be numbered in Roman numerals from
> the first, of Thinites, up to the nineteenth, of Diospolitans,
> inclusively. His nineteenth dynasty is the post-Menophrean
> section of cataclysm, which lasted 204 Nile years and mea-
> sured 209 noctas. The cepyrosal sections are marked with
> the letter B. The claim of the Samaritan to greater antiquity
> than the Hebrew rests only on the circumstance of its record-
> ing the epoch of the generation of the second Sothis period
> anterior to the one recorded by the Hebrew lawgiver, con-
> firming the Mosaïc graduation by making it occupy a middle
> line between the Menophrean epoch and the graduation
> pointed to by its own chronological scheme. We shall per-
> ceive that the authors of the Samaritan genealogies lived after
> B.C. 1118; and as the Hebrew text does not refer to the Nile
> lists posterior to the Section XVII., embracing only the cepy-
> rosal periods from Menes to the year of the Exodus, these
> Egyptian Nile lists strongly confirm the universal tradition
> that Moses, a man learned in the wisdom of the Egyptians,
> wrote the first books, and that he made use of copies of the
> historical Nile accounts to refer to when he devised the scheme
> of recording the generations of Sothis periods.*

It should be obvious that Mr. Bey failed to recognize the fact that "MOSES" was
not only...

"A MAN LEARNED IN THE WISDOM OF THE EGYPTIANS;"
MOSES, if in fact this biblical character did exist in reality other than in the Haribu
Holy Torah, was an indigenous African of Ta-Merry [Egypt] of the same type of phy-
sical characteristics as any other African we know today that carries the misnomer -

"NEGRO, BANTU, AFRICANS SOUTH OF THE SAHARA, PYGMY," and even "NIGGERS."
This, of course, was until European and European-American ["Jewish" and "Christian"]
ethnologists, anthropologists, palaeontologists, and other self-appointed "AUTHORITIES
ON AFRICA AND AFRICAN PEOPLES" made him a "WHITE SEMITE" of "INDO-
EUROPEAN ARYAN [Caucasian] STOCK." In Moses' own words, however, his fiancee
ZEPORAH [daughter of the High-Priest of Media] could not distinguish him from any
other African of Egypt, Ethiopia or Nubia. This was his own story he allegedly "PASS-
ED ON TO GOD'S HOLY SCRIBES," which they in turn allegedly wrote down in the FIVE
BOOKS OF MOSES - also known as the HOLY TORAH or OLD TESTAMENT [any ver-
sion].

All through this escapade of Mr. Bey the tampering with High-Priest Manetho's
original works can be distinctly observed. He tried to give the impression that Manetho,
himself, developed the above hypothesis on Judaeo-Christian and Islamic mythology and
allegory, when in TRUTH he knew very well that they were only attempts by certain
so-called Jewish, Christian, and Muslim OLD TESTAMENT scholars, theologians,
and writers like himself; their main objective was to establish a new sense of credibility and validity to Haribu histo-genealogical mythology in the "CREATION STORY" of
the Book Of Genesis - the FIRST BOOK OF MOSES. But, in so doing they have only established their own justification for certain European and European-American so-called
"SEMITIC PEOPLES" claim to the land presently occupied and controled by none-
African and none-Asian "ISRAELITES" [Hebrews or "Jews"]. Of course many of the
African-American "ISRAELITES" are being expelled from the same "PROMISSLAND"
today because of the BLACKNESS OF THEIR SKIN and the PHYSICAL CHARACTERIS-
TICS Herodotus used in describing their ancestors more than 2,422 years ago [c. 457 -
450 B.C.E.].

The ancient Africans of Egypt had no records whatsoever, and left none, relating
to the biblical stories about "ADAM AND EVE IN THE GARDEN, THE GREAT DELUGE"
[Flood], or the "EXODUS OF THE ISRAELITES FROM EGYPT WITH MOSES." Most of
these stories are nothing more, or less, than the historical glorification of one group
of people's histo-mythological experiences over another's, most of which they have expanded and blown totally out of perspective and normal rationalization, some of it being
actual distortions of theirs and other people's history and religion; the other portion
left from the whole can be attributed to no more than wishful thinking on what "GOD'S

228

CHOSEN PEOPLE" hoped human experiences would have had to begin - from a JUDAEO-CHRISTIAN, JEWISH, CHRISTIAN or MUSLIM point of view. Of course the BEGINNING must have had a "WHITE SEMITIC CAUCASIAN INDO-EUROPEAN ARYAN MALE in control of everything in site of his "CREATION" - the WORLD AND EVERYTHING IN IT.

The "QUEEN OF SHEBA [Makeda of Axum, Itiopi] - KING SOLOMON OF ISRAEL" episode in the Holy Torah [Old Testament] is quite typical of the same type of magnification that is way out of proportion to the reality of the FACTS relating to a Haribu personality of biblical histo-mythology. This indigenous African [Ethiopian or Black] Queen, MAKEDA, reigned over an empire at the time of her alleged meeting with the indigenous Asian King, SOLOMON. It was more than seventy-five [75] to one humdred [100] times larger than the tiny Kingdom of Israel, stretching all the way from Central East Africa to the Ganges River in India, Asia. Yet, this most beautiful and powerful African Queen and Empress, MAKEDA or QUEEN OF AXUM [Sheba], stately...

"THE MOST BEAUTIFUL WOMAN IN THE WORLD,"

is shown apologizing to a little kingdom monarch, SOLOMON, and the "DAUGHTERS OF ISRAEL", because of her BLACKNESS OF COLOR, in the Holy Bible [all versions]. This type of biblical RACISM and RELIGIOUS BIGOTRY still is not classified as such anywhere in "Western society's " educational system, religious or secular; for, even BLACK PEOPLE, especially those who refer to themselves as "NEGRO" and/or "COLORED," continue echoing that "...the Queen of Sheba told King Solomon of Israel;

"I AM BLACK, BUT COMELY."

What type of madness could have justified "...THE RICHEST, MOST BEAUTIFUL, MOST POWERFUL MONARCH IN THE ENTIRE [known] WORLD..."dehumanizing herself in the presence of a POWERLESS MAN and his TINY KINGDOM'S WOMEN FOLK like that, other than in the mythological Judaeo-Christian RELIGIOUS BIGOTRY and and the "CHOSEN PEOPLE" RACISM in the European and European-American [Semites or Caucasians] interpretation and translation of a historic incident which had no such experience? The MADNESS of "Western Civilization's GREAT WHITE RACE," which has become synonymous with Judaism, Chrisianity, and philosophy.

Another instance of the same type of RELIGIOUS BIGOTRY and SEMITIC RACISM is shown in the so-called "PROVERBS OF KING SOLOMON." In it, we have already observed the same type of distortions and plagiarisms as we did in the above story about the African Queen of Ethiopia [Sheba or Axum], East Africa or Alkebu-lan. We have also noted that the actual author was not KING SOLOMON OF THE KINGDOM OF IS-RAEL, but instead, an African of the Ta-Merrian [Egyptian] Empire, AMEN-EM-EOPE, who lived more than two [2] to three hundred [300] Years before SOLOMON. In order to refresh your memory on this point, the author refer you back to pages 102 - 103, Chapter III, of this volume, also to the bibliography that is specially given for this point in Judaeo-Christian and Islamic mythology and theology.

We have reached   another crossroad in our SAFARI into the HISTORY OF THE HERITAGE OF THE BLACK MAN AND HIS FAMILY HIGH-CULTURES he created and developed along the banks of the Nile Valleys, Great Lakes, Northern, Eastern, Western, Southern, and Central limits of Alkebu-lan, otherwise known as "MOTHER AFRICA." Thus, we now enter into the...

CHRONOLOGICAL COMMENTS ON HIGH-PRIEST MANETHO'S CLASSIFICATION OF THE TA-MERRIANS [Egyptians], TA-NEHISIANS [Nubians], MEROEANS, KUSHITES, ITIOPIANS [Ethiopians, sometimes the same as Kushites or Cushites], PUANITS, LEBUS [Libyans], AND OTHER INDIGENOUS AFRICANS AND FOREIGNERS FROM ASIA AND EUROPE, WHO DOMINATED THE "EGYPTIAN DYNASTIC PERIODS. [1-2]

Date: B.C.E. [3]   Description and Comments.

3200-2780   The Ist and IInd Dynasties; THINITE DYNASTIES:

Thinite because the Pharaohs of these two dynasties were buried at Abydos near Thinis. Their residences were at Nackhen. A few were built elsewhere along the Nile River. These dynasties were famous for their remarkable development of FINE ARTS, and for the production of PRECIOUS JEWELRY and various METALS. It was a Ist Dynasty pharaoh [king] who was tempted to regulate the waters of the Nile River around the Fayum region. This attempt to change the course and flow of the Nile River for agricultural purposes was the obsession of many of Egypt's ancient monarchs that preceded and followed this one.

2780-2270   The IIIrd and IVth Dynasties; MEMPHITE PERIOD:

Sometime between these two periods the Royal Residence of the Pharaohs was moved to Memphis. It was, also, within this era that the "ARCHITECTURAL LOVER " Pharaoh Djoser, whom Herodotus called "Zozer" or "Zoser," had the first STEP PYRAMID built at Sakhara [Saqqara]. The architect and builder of said structure was Imhotep, also known as Imhopteh [the Greeks renamed him "Aesculapius," etc.], who was before his death recognized and "DIEFIED" as the "GREAT GOD OF MEDICINE" by the Africans and Europeans of his lifetime, and after, because he was vastly superior as a phy-

230

sician than he was an architect. This was more than 1,500 years before the Europeans and European-Americans' "FATHER OF MEDICINE" - Hypocrates of Greece - was born. The time-period of the building of the first STEP PYRAMID proved that this was not one of those allegedly built by the Haribu ["Jews"], if in fact they did build any in Egypt. For, they did not arrive in Egypt [Ta-Merry, Kimit or Sais] until c. 1640 B.C.E. at the earliest with the "FIRST JEW" - the Haribu "Patriarch, ABRAHAM, " and seven others, according to the FIRST BOOK OF MOSES - Genesis.

2565-2420   The Vth Dynasty...was marked by the predominance of the RELIGION OF RA [The Sun, as the Great I Am]. Beginning from this period, and subsequent to the SOLITARY of Pharaoh Men-kau-Re [Herodotus' Mycerinus] of the IVth Dynasty, all of the pharaohs named themselves "SON OF RA" or "SON OF THE SUN." They also built their PYRAMID [House of Amenta of House of Heaven] TEMPLES at Abusir, near Sakhara [Saqqara]. The most peculiar of these temples was one built by Pharaoh Ne-user-Ra. It was the FIRST temple known to be built with red granite lotiform capitals, which in no way whatsoever resembled the pilars of previously built temples. It became the model for many more that followed its construction. During this Pharaoh's reign the planning and errection of the famous tomb by one of Ta-Merry's most famous architect, TI, was built at Sakhara. The completion of a "TREATISE ON PHILOSOPHICAL MAX-IMS" by Pharaoh Ptah-hotep and the building of the PYRAMID OF UNAS at Sakhara that contained the first of the world's most famous "PYRAMID TEXTS " were further accomplishments of this period. A composition of PRAYERS from the Book Of The Coming Forth By Day [Egyptian Book of the Dead] that adorn the walls of one of Pharaoh Unas' pyramids was also completed. This was one of the indigenous Nile Valley Africans of Egypt most creative periods in FINE ARTS, ARCHITECTURE, LITERATURE, RE-LIGION, PHILOSOPHY, and other disciplines in the social and physical sciences. It marked one of the highest artistic periods in the history of mankind all over the Planet Earth, all of which was completed before the first foreigner from Asia and Europe arrived in Alkebu-lan [Africa], Egypt in particular, other than as a visitor or student of learning in the Osirica that was centered at this period in Ta-Nehisi [Nubia or Zeti].

2270-2100   The VIIth to Xth Dynasties...started with varied political disorders, which were largely due to the incoming Asian foreigners that followed the reign of Pha-raoh Pepi II. It was, also, during the period of the transfer of POWER to the hands of Egypt's functionaries of the courts, followed by their abondonment of the OFFICIAL

ROYAL RESIDENCE at Memphis to establish themselves in the SOUTHERN [upper]
half of the nation as minor feudal kings [lords] - from whence they became regional
kings and lords, but of equally minor importance in the affairs of the government of
Egypt, which was still centered at Memphis. They were centered and assembled at
one court, which was more powerful than that of Memphis, however. Its residence was
at Herakleopolis [the Arabs renamed this area Ahmasis-el-Medina], the Africans Ahmasis. This court very soon after asserted itself as the rival of its counterpart centered
at the court of Memphis.

2100-1675   The XIth to XIVth Dynasties; THE MIDDLE KINGDOM:

The beginning of the Middle Kingdom Period was marked by a series of family wars between the minor kings [lords] of Ahmasis and those of Hermonthis [the Arabs renamed
this area Armant]. However, it was Pharaoh Mentu-hotep's Dynasty which became
authoritatively powerful, along with the supremacy of Luxor [Thebes according to the
Greeks and Romans]. From this point on the reunification of Egypt [Ta-Merry, etc.]
came under the sceptre of a unique and most mighty monarch - "THE MOST GLORIOUS
SON OF THE SUN, Pharaoh Amen-em-hat I, the so-called "NEGROID PHARAOH" - according to "Western modern man." Pharaoh Amen-em-hat I, upon taking command of
his throne, immediately established the worship of AMEN[0] as the OFFICIAL RELIGON
of the African people of Egypt. But, Amen-em-hat was unable to subdue all of the op-
posing nobles by force; because they had grown very strong in the localities they were
allowed to govern by previous pharaohs before his reign. Yet, he did win many others
over to his side by promising them glory and power under his rule. The others he could
not convince through military power or peaceful means remained forever afraid of him.
Amen-em-hat erected many temples in the main region of the Delta , Memphis, Fayum,
and in Ta-Nehisi [Nubia or Zeti]. He , also, established his Royal Residence at Itet-taui
[renamed "Lisht" by foreigners]. In order to secure his power Itet-taui was made a fortified city. For a very long time it was considered "...IMPREGNABLE...." This belief
did much to save it from its enemies attacking it on various occasions. The very mention of its name brought awe to his followers, and utter fear to his enemies.

The reign of Pharaoh Amen-em-hat III, whose likeness is shown on page 199 of

---

[0] It must be noted that the GOD the ancient Haribu [Hebrews or "Jews"] worshipped before YAWEH or JEHOVAH was "AMEN." The same "AMEN" appears at the end of
prayer, in every Christian Church, Jewish Synagouge, and Muslim Mosque.

this volume, completed the line of the "GRAND PHARAOHS [Kings] OF THE XIIth
DYNASTY." Pharaoh Amen-em-hat IVth and one of the very few QUEEN-PHARAOHS
[Monarchs] who actually ruled Egypt, Queen Skemiophris, preceded members of the
Sebek-hoteps family [the so-called "Dwarf Kings"]. But, all of them failed to maintain
the very high standards and strength in character set by their illustrious predecessors,
Pharaohs Amen-em-hat I and II. The lack of governmental skills and military "know-how"
caused their successors to fall into the military clutches of the invading Hyksos Asians
from the banks of the Oxus River. These Asians, the so-called "SEMITIC PEOPLES,"
were the first of the non-indigenous African peoples to invade, conquer, and rule over
Ta-Merry [Sais, Kimit, Cham, Mizrair, Mizrain, The Peral of the Nile, Egypt, etc.].
This took place between the years c. 1676 and c. 1675 B.C.E. [B.C.]. Until this era
[epoch] only indigenous Africans, the so-called "NEGROES, BANTUS, AFRICANS
SOUTH OF THE SAHARA, PYGMIES, BUSHMEN, HOTTENTOTS, BLACK AFRICANS,
DARKIES, COLOURED FOLKS, FOREST NEGROES," and even "NIGGERS," ruled
Ta-Merry [Egypt, Upper and Lower]. This fact brings back memory of the XIIIth Dy-
nasty Pharaoh, Neh-si-Ra, who was called "...THE BLACKEST OF THE PHARAOHS"
by "White liberal" and "Orthodox Africanists." This Pharaoh mounted the throne of
Ta-Merry when it was divided for the third time in its long and glorious history; and,
he reunited the "...DIVIDED KINGDOMS OF THE NORTH AND SOUTH." This is not
to say that other peoples did not come to Ta-Merry and other nations along the Nile
Valleys from Asia and Europe to live, work, learn, and even visit as tourists, just
as other Africans of Alkebu-lan throughout the continent - irrespective of the so-called
"BARRIERS" European and European-American "EDUCATORS" declared stoped the com-
merical and social intercourse between NORTHERN and SOUTHERN Africans. But, it
was the very FIRST TIME that non-indigenous people of the continent of Alkebu-lan
were able to seize control of any part of this continent which the ancient Greeks and
Romans renamed "AFRICA" and a host of other nomenclatures.

1676-1580   The XVth and XVIth Dynastues; The HYKSOS or "SHEPHERD KINGS
PERIOD: Sometime between c. 1676-1675 B.C.E. a rampaging army of nomadic people
under the command of their leader and general named Saltis, from Middle Asia, invaded and occupied the Nile Delta of Ta-Merry, in so doing overcame its indigenous African peoles. These invaders were given the name "HYKSOS SEMITES" or "CHIEFS OF
BEDUINA" [Shepherd Kings] by certain European academicians or scholars. They were

the same people the indigenous Africans of Ta-Merry called:

"PEOPLE OF AN IGNOBLE BIRTH,"

as recorded in the works of the African-European High-Priest who wrote the CHRON-OLOGY OF EGYPT [Egypt] these commentaries relate to. Their invasion was partly due to the effects of an enforced mass migration of Europeans fleeing East into Assyria [modern Syria] and Babylonia [Babylon] to escape persecution by their fellow Europeans, along with Asians who were at the time invaders of Europe. The vast majority of these very destitute nomadic Asian peoples, who amalgamated with the fleeing nomadic Europeans [the minority of the group][4], resulted in a Southerly push by Asians of the Oxus River to protect their homeland from the fleeing bands; thus, the people called "HYKSOS" or "SHEPHERD KINGS OF BEDUINA" continued their thrust until they overran the Delta region of Ta-Merry. But, in a very short time in the Delta the Hyksos became extremely powerful, as they joined in with other Asians and Europeans who were living as guests of the indigenous Africans to overthrow the existing government. The successful overthrow of the indigenous Africans gave control of Lower Ta-Merry - from Lebus [Libya] to the easternmost limits of the Sinai Peinsula. They also settled in parts of the Middle-Egyptian interior, and ruled supreme over the areas they occupied in great numbers. But, the Hyksos also destroyed vast amounts of the temples and other monuments they met when they arrived in Ta-Merry.[5] They subsequently forced their Egyptian captives into slavery.[6] Then, they established their own capital at Avaris - in the Delta. They, never the less, had already destroyed practically everything they touched in Ta-Merry. Why was this so? Because they did not understand the indigenous Africans of Ta-Merry's High-Culture [civilization] they had invaded and captured. This meant that they had to be constantly watchful, and did not relate sufficiently to assimilate with or contribute to the culture of the vanquished indigenous Africans.[7]

1600-1555   The XVIIth Dynasty: This period marked the beginning of the indigenous Africans of Ta-Merry's struggle for indpendence from the Asian Hyksos enslavement. Three Luxon [Theban] pharaohs - Seqen-en-Ra I, II, and III directed the drive for independence against the Asian foreigners. Pharaoh Seqen-en-Ra III died in one of the liberation battles with his weapons still clutched within his hands. The last of his three sons, Pharaoh Ahmose I, in c. 1580 B.C.E., succeded him in driving the Hyksos from Ta-Merry. Pharaoh Ahmose I followed the Hyksos in hot pursuit as far as the city of Sharuhen in Southern Palestine[8] [part of the modern state called Israel]. This famous vic-

234

tory by the indigenous African people of Ta-Merry over the mixed Asian-European invaders and colonialists is recorded on the equally famous INSCRIPTION OF EL-KAB.

1555-1090   The XVIIth to XIXth Dynasties; The NEW KINGDOM PERIOD:

Pharaoh Neb-pehti-Ra Ashmes [Amasis] founded the Mighty XVIIth Dynasty which ruled over Ta-Merry for more than two hundred [200] years. He occupied himself with the expansion of the Hyksos; but, in the meantime the Ta-Nehisians [Nubians], other indigenous Africans, were taking advantage of his preoccupation up North, and as a result the Ta-Nehisians were able to reconquer all of Ta-Merry's territories North of the Second Cataract which they had originally surrendered to the Ta-Merrians in the IInd and VIth Dynasties. Ashmes ruled in Ta-Merry extended for a little more than twenty-two [22] years, until his death. He was burried in the Luxor region, which the present rulers [Arabs and Africanized-Arabs] renamed "Dira-abu-n-Naga". His mummy is still in its originally preserved state in the Egyptian Museum, Cairo [Egypt, originally called the "United Arab Republic, " or "U.A.R."].[9] Ashmes was followed on the throne by his son Amen-hotep I.

The passing of Amen-hotep I and II was rather swift; thus, the last of the most honoured of the XVIIth Dynasty pharaohs, Amen-hotep III, was installed on the throne. One of his greatest accompl ishments was the conquest of Ta-Nehisi. During his reign, however, the world famous and most often quoted correspondence in Babylonian cuneiform writing - the "CORRESPONDENCE OF TELL - el - AMARNA" - was written. This "CORRESPONDENCE" dealt with marriages between the indigenous Africans of Ta-Merry [Egypt] and the so-called "ASIAN SEMITES" of Babylon. The proposed marriages were intended to cement political and economic relations between both nations, and the surrender of total military control to the Pharaoh of Ta-Merry over the countries surrounding Babylon and Ta-Merry. It also guaranteed Babylon's freedom from Ta-Merrian invasion. They were to be marriages of political expedience and convenience on the part of the Africans. Of course they, also, offered the militarily weak Babylonians some semblance of military protection from war and invasion by all foreigners, including the Africans.[10]

1580-1340   The XVIIIth Dynasty cannot be treated properly without mention of Pharaoh Tut-ankh-Amen. Yet, he was not a direct successor to the throne of Ta-Merry. He got there through one of Pharaoh Amenhotep IV [Akhenaten or Ikhnaten] seven daughters, the eldest, of whom he married.[11] Pharaoh Smenkh-ka-Ra, once a very much unknown prince, the predecessor of Tut-ankh-Amen, had remained hardly anytime on the throne after he inherited it. Following Pharaoh Tut-ankh-Amen's ["The Living Image of Atem" or "Beautiful is the Life of Aten"] marriage to Amen-hotep IV ["The God Aten is Content"][12] daughter, this name was given him. Akhenaten had made of Tut [the name many "Westerners" called this former commoner] a "ROYAL" figure in order to protect the honour of his daughter.[0]

According to a stelae unearthed at Karmak, it is written that Pharaoh Tut-ankh-Amen converted the LUXANS [later called Thebans] to the worship of the God - AMEN upon his return to Luxor [Thebes]; thus, the beginning of the worship of "AMEN" throughout Ta-Merry and all of her colonies in Asia and Europe during this period.

1340-1200   The XIXth Dynasty began with Pharaoh Her-em-heb [Herum-m-heb]. He was a general of the army and Regent during the reign of Pharaoh Tut-ankh-Amen, whom he eventually succeeded. After him came a very old man to sit on the throne, RAMESES, who was not related in anyway to Pharaoh Tut-ankh-Amen or Pharaoh Her-em-heb. But, for some unexplained circumstance he was able to take over the Empire of Ta-Merry [Egyptian Empire] and proclaim himself PHARAOH RAMESES I. He was subsequently forced, through old age, to share the throne with his only son - Pharaoh Seti I, who was also known as Sethos I. This same Pharaoh Seti I conquered Palestine before it was conquered and settled by the Haribus ["Hebrews, Israelites" or "Jews"]. He also restored many of the temples of AMEN,[13] most of which were later on destroyed during the reign of Amen-hotep IV [Akhenaten, Tut-ankh-Amen's father-in-law, the first of the "Trinitarians" and "Prince of Peace" known in history]. Pharaoh Seti I reigned for more than twenty [20] years before he died. He was followed on the throne by his son - Rameses II. [See pages 239 and 286 for two of the Rameses and other indigenous Africans of Ta-Merry. Note the varied facial characteristics of these African peoples; yet, not one was a "SEMITE" whatever this is].

Upon the death of Pharaoh Rameses II his thirteenth son, Pharaoh Meneptah, im-

---

[0] Review pictures of this entire family on pages 7, 203 and 290 of Chapter IV of this volume. There is no available picture or statue of Tut; the only impression of him is the "Death Mask" one constantly sees in most of the books on Ta-Merry [Egypt] written by European and European-American professionals in African affairs - "AFRICANISTS."

[00] The continuation of the worship of this African GOD is still common at the end of each prayer and each song in the Christian Church, Jewish Synagouge, and Muslim Mosque. AMEN is called "SO BE IT" by the Christians, Jews and Muslims, a far cry from "GOD."

mediately mounted the throne of the Ta-Merrian Empire and began to wage war against Lebu [Libya] and Palestine. He left an accounting of these wars on the famous so-called "ISRAEL STELE," where the name "ISRAEL" appear for the first time in Ta-Merrian [Egyptian] history, as written by the ancient African historians of Ta-Merry and Ta-Nehisi [Nubia or Zeti]. Even the so-called "EXODUS" drama in the SECOND BOOK OF MOSES [Holy Torah or Old Testament] was never mentioned in Ta-Merrian history by indigenous African scribes of Ta-Merry, who were as much "INSPIRED BY GOD" as those in the FIVE BOOKS OF MOSES [Old Testament] and NEW TESTAMENT. Yet, it was during the reign of Pharaoh Meneptah's father, Pharaoh Rameses II - c. 1298-1232 B.C.E., that the most publicized accounts of the Haribu mass migration ["EXODUS"] out of Ta-Merry [Egypt] allegedly took place under the leadership of an African named "MOSES." This was at a period when the Haribu ["Hebrews, Jews" or "Iaraelites"] were supposed to have...

"BROKEN THE BOND OF SLAVERY"...

under their fellow indigenous African worshippers of RA in Ta-Merry, and all of them migrated to Eastern Ta-Merry at Mount Sinai - following a forty [40] year journey from Middle Ta-Merry, at a place called "SUCCOTH." They were supposed to have travelled from Succoth, to Rameses, to Mount Sinai, and then to the "PROMISED LAND" which they took away from the Amalakites, Jebusites, Moabites, Pezzarites, and three other small kings of Asia-Minor [today's Middle East, where the modern nation of the Republic of Israel occupies]. Yet, this land was not the original area from whence the original Haribu came when they entered Ta-Merry [Egypt] with their first Patriarch - Abraham, nor with their second - Jacob, which had to be during the reign of the first foreigners from Europe and Asia to enter Alkebu-lan as invaders and conquerors - the so-called "HYKSOS SEMITES" in approximately c. 1675 B.C.E. However, the most recent excavations in the area of Ta-Merry, where the monumental drama of the "EXODUS" allegedly took place, have not proven that this major event ever occurred in the manner indicated in the FIVE BOOKS OF MOSES at any time in Ta-Merrian history, including the XVIIIth Dynasty. For, only in the XVIIIth Dynasty is there any INSCRIPTION whatsoever dealing with any form of migration of Haribu people from Ta-Merry. Moreover, the INSCRIPTION deals with the Haribu people, a very small group of them - but still nomadic, being expelled, not voluntarily leaving with any leader crossing the "RED SEA" that "...OPENED UP AND SWALLOWED THE ARMIES OF THE PHARAOH"

237

according to the SECOND BOOK OF MOSES [Exodus].

One should notice that it was contrary to common practice of the indigenous Africans of the High-Culture of Ta-Merry and other Nile Valley nations not to have recorded as significant an event as the Haribu ["Jews"][0] leaving Ta-Merry in such a mass migration ["EXODUS"] as dipicted in the SECOND BOOK OF MOSES, even when considerin the extreme projections of the national mythology that generally creeps into all religious history from secular events - of which the FIVE BOOKS OF MOSES [Holy Torah] is so well noted, equally works of all religions of an organized nature. For, if Moses [a fellow African of Ta-Merry like Pharaoh Rameses II] was not being pursued for the crime of "MURDER:" why was he sought after by Pharaoh Rameses, who charged him with "...KILLING" his "...SOLDIER." All of this took place long before Moses arrived at Mount Sinai [forty , 40 , years exactly] and "...received the laws...," one of which commanded him and all of the people of the entire Planet EARTH [at least that is what we were taught]:

"THOU SHALT NOT KILL."

A likeness of the PHARAOH, who allegedly chased Moses and the Haribu all over the North African Desert into the Asian Desert, is shown on the following page with other modern indigenous Africans of the same physical characteristics generally. Certainly he is a "SEMITE," bu not the other two. Why? RACISM and RELIGIOUS BIGOTRY is the answer.

1200-1085   The XXth Dynasty: Rameses III, the son of a commoner named Set-nekht [no relationship to Rameses II], mounted the throne of Ta-Merry. He too commanded Ta-Merrians in many successful battles against his fellow Africans of Lebu [Libya], and the Europeans off the banks of the Aegean Sea around Pyrrhus [later Hellas or Greece]. He followed these attacks with an invasion of Assyria and Palestine, thereby making them vasal states or kingdoms under the control of the indigenous Africans of the Ta-Merrian Empire of North Alkebu-lan [Egyptian Empire of North Africa]. This story is highlighted in the so-called "HARRIS PAPYRUS"[14] taken from Ta-Merry without the consent of any of its indigenous African owners - the descendants of the anicent Ta-Merrians.

The reigns of the so-called "RAMESIDE KINGS" followed Pharaoh Rameses III. Very little is known to date about them. Their successions were ended rather quickly, which

---

0• "JEWS" is used as a general classification for all of the "TRIBES". It is a misnomer, and as such it is rejected by miilions of Israelites the world over. It is not a "RACE."
238

SHILLUKS of Sudan (Ta-Nehisi, Zeti or Meroe). What is there that is "CAUCASOID" about either than Africans of the Congo.

Pharaoh Rameses II wearing the CROWN OF THE ROYAL THRONE.

Pharaoh Rameses II, with his Queen shown at his left foot standing.

The pictures above bear witness to the likeness of today's indigenous Africans of the Nile Valley nations in Ta-Merry, Ta-Nehisi, Kush, Itiopi, and other African High-Cultures [civilizations] such as Puanit, Zaire [formerly called Congo], Monomotapa, the Akan States and other West African, South African, Central African, and East African nations - to numerous to mention here. Yet, the features presented above are always called "CAUCASIAN, CAUCASOID, SEMITIC, HAMITIC," and a host of other RACIST and RELIGIOUSLY BIGOTED terms directed to create the impression that there were never Africans called "NEGROES, NEGROIDS, BANTUS, BLACK AFRICANS," etc. in any part of North Africa "...BEFORE THEY WERE BROUGHT THERE AS SLAVES FROM NUBIA...."

caused very little to be written of them by indigenous African scribes. Between the death of Rameses III and Rameses IX there was only an elapsed time of twenty-one [21] years. The "Rameside Kings" reign marked one of Ta-Merry's worst periods of decline. Looting was widespread, as many of the royal tombs and pyramids were looted and otherwise violated sacreligiously. It was under these pharaohs that the indigenous Ta-Merrian Empire began its first aspect of total decline - Egypt[15] was on her way to ruin.

1085-718   The XXIst to XXIIIrd Dynasties; The TANITE and BUBASITE PERIOD: Pharaoh Smedes and his son, Psusennes I, inaugarated the XXIst Dynasty at Tanis. The Libyan Chief, Shashanq [the Shishak of the FIVE BOOKS OF MOSES, Old Testament], who married a Royal Princess, became the first pharaoh of the Bubasite Dynasty - the XXIInd. Pharaoh Shashanq's reign came shortly after the death of King Solomon of Palestine [Israel, c. 976-936 B.C.E.].[16] The period of rivalry between King Solomon's successors - Rehoboan in Southern Palestine and the usurper Jeroboan in the North - encourage Pharaoh Shashanq to intervene in order to assert his control and re-establish "LAW AND ORDER" among the Haribu ["Jews"] of Palestine. This kind of revelation indicates very vividly why every attempt by "Western" [European, British, and European-American - Jewish, Christian and Muslim] historians and other "educators" who propagandize "WHITE RACIAL PURITY" must present the ancient Africans of Ta-Merry as anything other than "NEGROES" or "BANTUS." For, it is obvious, or should be, that the "INFERIOR NEGROES AND BANTUS," or whatever they may have been in ancient times, amalgamated sexually with everyone along the banks of the Mediterranean Sea - those who invaded, conquered, ruled, enslaved, and educated or civilized the "CAUCASIAN SEMITES" of "INDO-EUROPEAN ARYAN" origin. Pharaoh Shashanq responded by taking Jerusalem in 930 B.C.E., bringing back to Ta-Merry many treasures from his campaign, among which were...

"...THOSE OF THE TEMPLE OF KING SOLOMON."

Pharaoh Sheshanq died about five years later, and was succeded by his very weak son - Pharaoh Osorkon I, c. 925-893 B.C.E. Pharaoh Osorkon I did not accomplish very much. His son, Pharaoh Osorkon II, captured Ta-Nehisi [Nubia][17] and reduced the Africans of this nation to the state of vassals [serfs or slaves] for the Africans of the Lower Lands to the North, Ta-Merry, which at this time began at the FIRST CATARACT.[18] He also invaded and conquered much of Palestine beyond the territories he had inherited

240

from his father,[19] and equally reduced the Palestinians to the stage of serfs or slaves.

After Pharaoh Osorkon II certain Luxon [Theban] "PRIEST-KINGS"[20] began to dispute the title to the throne of Ta-Merry along with Lebus [Libyan] usurpers. This period was quite obscure in parts of its history - according to the available data.

Another Pharaoh named Piankhi, a Cushite [Kushite, Itiopian or Ethiopian] King, succeeded in unifying Ta-Nehisi [Nubia or Zeti], Meröe, Kush [Cush], and Ta-Merry [Egypt, Kimit, Sais, etc.] under one powerful empire once more with an indigenous African ["Negro"] control. On a most important stele, the top section which is shown on page xxx of this volume, presently housed in the Egyptian Museum, Cairo [Egypt or United Arab Republic - U.A.R.], is recorded the information of this great undertaking by Pharaoh Piankhi [Piankhy].

During this period Assyrian invaders, after their conquest of Palestine [Israel], arrived at the borders of Ta-Merry and demanded her surrender - to which the indigenous Africans refused.

718-525   The XXIVth to XXVIth Dynasties; THE SAITE AND ETHIOPIAN PERIODS: During the XXIVth Dynasty European foreigners, mostly from the ports of Hellades, flourished throughout Ta-Merry's Delta region. They choose Sais[*] [one of the names Ta-Merry was called] for their capital city. They re-established commerce with the Northern Mediterranean countries of Europe that later on flourished to suprising limits upon the training and "civilizing" efforts of the Africans and Europeans from Sais, who taught the Europeans in Alkebu-lan [Africa] and in Europe. But, the foreigners at Sais, mostly Greeks and Macedonians, attempted to seize Ta-Merry and establish European rule under two "SAITE KINGS" - Tefnekht and Bocchris. This treachery made the history of Ta-Merry appeared to have had two sets of Pharaohs during this period. However, before these two pretenders to the throne became entrenched another Ethiopian King named Shabaka [Sabacom] invaded Ta-Merry's Delta region and caused the establishment of the XXVth Dynasty over the entire Empire of Ta-Merry [Egypt]. Pharaoh Shabaka's military Chief of Staff, his nephew, was later defeated by the Assyrians under Sennacherib. Taherq [Taharqa, the Tirhakah of the FIVE BOOKS OF MOSES], the grandson of Pharaoh Piankhi, followed Pharaoh Shabaka and became "PHARAOH OF ALL EGYPT" [Ta-Merry,

---

[*] Renamed "Sa-el-Hager" by the current Arabian and Arabized-Africans in control of Ta-Merry as a whole, and what is left of Sais in partuclar.

Upper and Lower]. He established his ROYAL RESIDENCE at Tanis. This city was selected in order that his attention could be always centered on the Assyrians, who were
constantly growing stronger militarily all the time on Ta-Merry's frontier with Palestine [Israel] - which the Assyrians had already conquered and colonized. But, Esahad-
don - the son of Sennacherib - succeded in invading and capturing as far inland as Herakleopolis in Lower Ta-Merry. He captured the Princess [a so-called "NEGRESS"] of
Ta-Merry, and made her pay tribute to Assyria.

The Assyrian armies were finally expelled from Lower Ta-Merry during the reign
of Pharaoh Ashurbanipal of Assyria by Pharaoh Taherq of Ethiopia. But, two years
later, with the help of a Phoenician fleet at his command, Ashurbanipal reconquered
Ta-Merry and secured his soldiers at the Walls of Luxor [Thebes].

663-525   The XXVIth Dynasty; SAITE PERIOD:

This period was started by Pharaoh Psaemthek I. He established his ROYAL RESI-
DENCE at Sais, in the Delta, and reorganized the Ta-Merrian army with Carian, Ionian,
and Assyrian mercinaries as his CHIEF GENERALS and CONFIDANTS. Ta-Merrians of
indigenous Alkebu-lan [African] origin, the so-called "NEGROES," were generally excluded from top command posts. Mentu-em-hat was placed as Governor of the highly
mobilized fortresses on the Eastern frontiers at Luxor. He was later succeded by Necho
[Neku or Necku],[21] who is mentioned in the FIVE BOOKS OF MOSES as:

"...THE EGYPTIAN GENERAL OF THE BATTLE OF CARCHEMISH,

where he was defeated by Nebuchardrezzar. It was after this defeat that Nebuchardrezzar destroyed the Temple of Jerusalem. Again,we see the inter-relationship between
BLACK STUDIES or AFRICAN STUDIES with SEMITIC STUDIES or ASIAN STUDIES.

525-332   The XXVIII to XXXIst Dynasties; The OLD PERSIAN AND MENDESIAN
PERIOD: In this Period a Persian named Cambyses, who had become Pharaoh of Ta-
Merry by conquest. began the reconstruction of Ta-Merry. He immediately dropped all
of his foreign pretexes and reinstituted all forms of the traditional protocols and attributes of former indigenous African Pharaohs that preceded him on the throne of Ta-
Merry. He followed all of this by renaming himself accordingly - "SON OF THE SUN"
or "SON OF THE GOD RA," just as all of the ancient African Pharaohs called themselves. However, Cambyses conducted many unsuccessful military campaigns against
Ethiopia, which he considered the Upper part of Ta-Merry [Egypt] along with Nubia. He
also invaded the tiny Kingdom of the Oasis at Siqa, in the Oasis of the Libyan Desert. He

242

depended upon the indigenous Africans of Khart-Haddas [later called "Carthage"] for use of their fleet; but, they refused to fight against other indigenous Africans[22] for the benefit of the Asian foreigners from Persia. Cambyses, thereafter, started a most vicious campaign of destroying all of the Ta-Merrian DIETIES of Khart-Haddan influence. He destroyed statues of all sorts, demolished temples of evry kind; worst of all, he actually killed one of the most "Sacred APIS BULLS.[23] Cambyses was immediately re-called to his native country, Persia, because of his reckless conduct, and for political reasons. He departed from Ta-Merry during the year c. 521 B.C.E. Upon Cambyses removal Darius I, the Son of Hystaspes, was declared the new Persian "...PHARAOH OF ALL EGYPT...," etc.

404-394   The XXVIIIth Dynasty was founded by Amyrtaeos of Sais, its only Pha-raoh. Nothing of major significance happened during this period of Egyptian history. This was actually the period when the indigenous Africans began their withdrawal from Ta-Merry [Egypt] up to the Northern frontier of Ta-Nehisi [Nubia or Zeti, modern Sudan]. It also marked the beginning of their flight SOUTH and SOUTHWEST into the same interior territories of other nations of Alkebu-lan where they had originally comethousands of years prior to reaching their zenith at the end of the Nile River. They were reuniting with their kinfolks SOUTH OF THE SAHARA. It was during this period that the TUSI and TWA or BAHUTU [the so-called "Pygmies" and "Watusis"] peoples fled Ta-Merry and Ta-Nehisi in mass migrations, according to their own traditional history and that of other African peoples who came in direct contact with them. Like the indigenous Ta-Merrians and other North Africans, the Tutsi and Twa peoples original-ly came from the Great Lakes region of Uganda, Kenya, Tanzania, Eastern Zaire [Congo], Malawi, and other Alkebu-lan states around the general area, also from the Ethiopian-Highlands, all of this having taken place during the prehistoric migrations of the Blue and White Nile Valley peoples,[24] and of course those of the Great Lakes region. We will remember that all of the African peoples came from Central Alkebu-lan according to the latest archaeological findings shown in Chapter II of this volume.

394-378   The XXIXth Dynasty; of MENDESIAN ORIGIN:

King Hager, whom the Greeks renamed "ACHORIS," repulsed the Persian invaders after three years of resistance to protect his throne. Hager and Evagoras had formed a partnership and aided Cyrus against the Persians - his fellow countrymen. This Dy-nasty fell after twenty [20] short years of existence. It was just another one of the uneventful periods in Ta-Merrian history.

378-341   The XXXth Dynasty; The SEBENYTIC PERIOD:

This Dynasty was founded by Pharaoh Nectanebus I, last of the truly indigenous African ["Negroes", etc.] pharaohs. He restored most of the ancient monuments, and built new ones. He was intent on restoring Ta-Merry's [Egypt's] indigenous African GLORY, which had been destroyed by the many foreign invasions and colonial periods under Asians and Europeans. He also reorganized the government, and fortified the so-called "WHITE WALLS" of the City of Memphis. He defeated Pharnabazus, the Persian Satrap [Governor], who was being helped militarily by the much feared Greek general - Iphicrates. The Persians had hoped to defeat the Ta-Merrians [Africans of Egypt] one more time, and seize control of their government. Nectanebus' son and successor, Djed-her, whom the Greeks renamed "TACHOS," had conspired with many Asian princes against the King of Persia. Failure was his only reward, as he too fell victim to his fellow conspirators' treachery after the Persians recaptured Ta-Merry.

341-332   The XXXIst Dynasty was founded by Artaxerxes III and Darius [all of them renegade Persians]. It lasted until 332 B.C.E. The end came when Alexander II ["the great"] of Macedonia, Europe, defeated the Persian government of Ta-Merry, which was ruled by renegade Persians who had reduced the indigenous peoples to serfdom. This took place after Alexander II had defeated all of the other nations around Ta-Merry's North and Northeast borders. Alexander crushed the Poser of the Persians in Ta-Merry and ended Persian rule; but, he also introduced Macedonian-Greek colonial rule. He had forgotten that the indigenous Ta-Merrians supported his Macedonian and Greek army, making it possible for both groups to defeat their common enemy - the Persians. The indigenous Africans had, once again in their history, exchanged an Asian colonialist slave master for one from Europe. This was a pattern of behavior the Africans were to adopt, and project, up to the present - TRUSTING EVERYONE AS FRIENDS. This marked the first time in the thousands of years of Ta-Merrian history and High-Culture that they were to be ruled by solely Europeans ["Caucasians, Anglo-Saxons, Semites, Indo-Europeans, Master Race," or whatever]; yet, European and European-American "EDUCATORS" continue teaching that:

"THE EGYPTIANS WERE CAUCASIANS OF A SEMITIC LANGUAGE GROUP, BUT NEVER NEGROES."

Of course the facts revealed in this volume negate this RACIST proclamation totally.

244

332-30   The XXXIInd Dynasty: This was the so-called "GREEK EPOCH" [Era];

the PTOLEMAIC PERIOD - from Ptolemy I to XVth, including the Cleopatras - Ist-

VIIIth [some historians claimed there were only SIX , the last being the daughter of

Ptolemy XIIIth].

30 B.C.E.   The POST DYANSTIC PERIODS: These periods were divided were some-

times called erroneously the "XXXIIIrd and XXXIVth Dynasties". They ended with the

Greek Ptolemies and Roman Caesars. There is quite a lot of contention between Euro-

pean and European-American historians as to whether Rome conquered Ta-Merry

[Egypt] in c. 47 or c. 30 B.C.E.

30 B.C.E.   The last two Dynasties brought nothing but wars and general destruc-
to
640 C.E.   tion of the Ta-Merrian [Egyptian] Empire. They included numerous

palace intrigues, and wanton murder of members of the royal family. The sacred

temples, pyramids, libraries, and other repositories of learning were ravaged. The

indigenous Africans were enslaved and brutally persecuted, thousands having to flee

into Ta-Nehisi [Nubia] and points farther SOUTH. So was the ending of the FIRST PHASE

OF THE PEARL OF NORTHERN ALKEBU-LAN ["Mother Africa"]. The SECOND PHASE

has just began. The THIRD PHASE begins when the indigenous Africans regain their

rightful place at the BEGINNING AND THE END OF THE NILE RIVER WITH HAPI.

BIBLIOGRAPHY FOR THE NILE and GREAT LAKES NATIONS CHRONOLOGY
[The following list of works present the student, researcher, and general reader with
some of the Books, Magazines, Thesis - published and unpublished - used in the preparation of the Chronological Charts, Graphs, Mathematical and Masonified Calculations,
in this chapter. All of the works suffixed by an asterisk have been specifically mentioned
or quoted in the texts].

BOOKS

W.G. Waddell, MANETHO, Cambridge, Mass. [The LOeb Classical Library, 1940]
Wm. F. Petrie, A HISTORY OF EGYPT, London, 1923 [8 vols.]
W.S. Smith, ANCIENT EGYPT, Boston, 1952
W.C. Hayes, THE SCEPTRE OF EGYPT, New York, 1953
J.B. Hurry, IMHOTEP, THE VIZIER AND PHYSICIAN OF KING ZOSER, Oxford, 1926
H. Bey, EGYPTIAN CHRONOLOGY, London, 1863
C.M. Firth and J.E. Quibell, THE STEP PYRAMID, Cairo, 1963-69
H. Vyse, OPERATIONS CARRIED ON AT THE PYRAMIDS OF GIZEH IN 1873, London,
          1840 - 42 [3 vols.]
S. Hassan, EXCAVATIONS IN GIZA,
Wm. M. F. Petrie, THE PYRAMIDS AND TEMPLES OF GIZA, London, 1883

S. Clarke and R. Englebach, ANCIENT EGYPTIAN MASONRY: THE BUILDING CRAFT, London, 1930

G.A. Reisner, THE DEVELOPMENT OF THE EGYPTIAN TOMB DOWN TO THE ACCESSION OF CHEOPS, Cambridge, Mass., 1936

I.E.S. Edwards, THE PYRAMIDS OF EGYPT, London, 1947

L. Grinsell, EGYPTIAN PYRAMIDS, Gloucester, 1947

W.M. Petrie, MEYDUM AND MEMPHIS, London, 1910

----, MEYDUM, London, 1882

A. Fakhry, THE BENT PYRAMID OF DAHSHUR, Cairo, 1954

W. M. F. Petrie, Wainwright, and Mackay, THE LABYRINTH, GERZEH, AND MAZGHUMEH, London, 1902

D. Dunham, EL KURRU, Cambridge, Mass., 1950

D. V. Denon, TRAVELS IN UPPER AND LOWER EGYPT, [transl. by Authur Aikin], New York, 1803 [3 vols.]

A.B. Edwards, A THOUSAND MILES UP THE NILE, [2nd ed.], New York, 1988

S. Mercer, THE RELIGION OF EGYPT, London, 1949

W.S. Smith, ANCIENT EGYPT, Boston, 1952

Sir E.A. Wallis Budge, THE EGYPTIAN SUDAN, Philadelphia, 1907

A.J. Arkell, HISTORY OF THE SUDAN, London, 1955

W.C. Hayes, THE SCEPTER OF EGYPT, New York, 1953

J.L. Burckhardt, TRAVELS IN NUBIA, London, 1819

R. Lepsius, DENKMALER [text], I.

G. Belzoni, RESEARCHES AND OPERATIONS IN EGYPT, NUBIA, etc., London, 1843

P. Barquet, LA STELE DE LA FAMINE A SEHEL, Cairo, 1953

D. Dunham, ROYAL CEMETERIES OF KUSH, I: EL KURRU, Boston, 1950

J. Garstang, A.H. Sayce and F.L.Griffith, MEROE, THE CITY OF THE ETHIOPIANS, Oxford, 1911

S.H. Johnson, THE NICE QUEST, London, 1903

P. Thompkins, SECRETS OF THE GREAT PYRAMIDS, New York, 1971

L.Waddel, THE MAKERS OF CIVILIZATION IN RACE and HISTORY, Delhi, 1968

Polybius, THE HISTORIES OF POLYBIUS, vol. I and II [trans. from the text of F. Hultsch by Evelyn S. Schuckburg], Indiana, 1962

G.G. Starr, HISTORY OF THE ANCIENT WORLD, New York, 1965

C.A. Robinson, Jr., ANCIENT HISTORY FROM PREHISTORIC TIMES TO THE DEATH OF JUSTINIAN, New York, 1967

J.H. Breasted, ANCIENT TIMES: A HISTORY OF THE EARLY WORLD, New York, 1944

H. Vyse, OPERATIONS CARRIED ON AT THE PYRAMID OF GIZEH IN 1837, London, 1840-42 [3 vols.]

J.P. Lauer, La PYRAMIDE a DEGRES, Cairo, 1936-39 [3 vols.]

C.B. Moburney, THE STONE AGE OF NORTHERN AFRICA, Baltimore, Md., 1960

A.H. Gardiner, THE ADMONITIONS OF AN EGYPTIAN SAGE, Leipzig, 1909

--------, AN ANCIENT LIST OF THE FORTRESSES OF NUBIA, [In: Journal of Egyptian Archaeology, III], 1916

Maj. R.E. Chessman, LAKE TANA AND THE BLUE NILE, London, 1936

E.E. Evans-Pritchard, THE NVER, Oxford, 1940

K.S. Sandford and W.J. Arkell, "PALEOLITHIC MAN AND THE NILE VALLEY IN NUBIA AND UPPER EGYPT", [In: Oriental Institute Publications, XVII], Chicago, 1933

J.D. Clark, THE PREHISTORY OF SOUTHERN AFRICA, Baltimore, Md., 1959
246

Dr. J. Garstang, et al, MEROE, Oxford, 1911

W.B. Emery, NUBIAN TREASURE, London, 1948

H.A. MacMichael, A HISTORY OF THE ARABS IN THE SUDAN, Cambridge, 1922

I. Pallme, TRAVELS IN KORDOFAN, London, 1834

R.C. Slatin, FIRE AND SWORD IN THE SUDAN, London, 1898

G.W. Steevens, WITH KITCHENER TO KHARTUM, New York, 1898

G.A. Reisner, THE ARCHAEOLOGICAL SURVEY OF NUBIA, REPORT FOR 1907-08,
        Cairo, 1910

G. Caton-Thompson and E.W. Gardner, THE DESERT FAYUM, London, 1934

C.R. Lepsius, DISCOVERIES IN EGYPT, ETHIOPI AND THE PENINSULA OF SINAI,
        [2nd ed.], London, 1853

L. Lhote, THE SEARCH FOR THE TASSILI FRESCOES, New York, 1959

J.A. Wilson, THE CULTURE OF ANCIENT EGYPT, [First published as The Burden
        of Egypt], Chicago, 1956

W.H. Yales, MODERN HISTORY AND CONDITION OF EGYPT, London, 1843 [2 vols.]

G.M. Maspero, HISTORY OF EGYPT [8 vols. Ed. by A.H. Sayce; trans. to English
        by M.L. McLure], London, 1840

       -------, ANCIENT EGYPT AND ASSYRIA, New York, 1895 [2 vols.]

       -------, THE DAWN OF CIVILIZATION: EGYPT AND CHALDEA [Ed., Rev. and
        Enlrgd. Fourth Edition], London, 1901

       -------, ART IN EGYPT, New York, 1912

G. Massey ANCIENT EGYPT, THE LIGHT OF THE WORLD, New York, 1907 [2 vols.]

W.B. Emery, EGYPT IN NUBIA, London, 1965

W.A. Fairservis, Jr., THE ANCIENT KINGDOMS OF THE NILE, New York, 1962

ARTICLES

A. Butt, "The Nilotes of the Anglo-Egyptian Sudan and Uganda" [In: Ethnographic Survey
        of Africa, Ed. by D. Forde, East Central Africa, Part IV; London,
        International African Institute, 1952]

D. Dunham, "Outline of the Ancient History of the Sudan, V" [In: Sudan Notes and Records,
        XXVIII, 1947]

D. Dunham, and M.F.L. Macadam, "Names and Relationships of the Royal Family of
        Napata" [In: Journal of Egyptian Archaeology, XXXV, 1949]

E.E. Evans-Pritchard, "The Divine Kingship of the Shilluk of the Nilotic Sudan" [In: The
        Frazier Lecture, 1948, Cambridge, 1948]

L.P. Kirwan, "Note of the Topography of the Christian Nubian Kingdom", [In: Journal
        of Egyptian Archaeology, XXI, 1959]

G.A. Reisner, "The Merotic Kingdom of Ethiopia: Chronological Outline", [In: Journal
        of Egyptian Archaeology, IX, 1923]

       -------, "The Viceroys of Ethiopia," [In: Journal of Egyptian Archaeology, VI, 1920]

K.S. Sandford and A.W. Arkell, " Paleolithic Man and the Nile Valley in Nubia and Upper
        Egypt " [In: Oriental Institute Publications, XVII; Chicago, Univ. Of
        Chicago Press, 1933]

P.L. Shinnie, "The Fall of Merowe," [In: Kush, III, 1955]

E. Zyhlarz, "The Countries of the Ethiopian Empire of Kush and Egyptian Old Ethiopia in
        the New Kingdom," [In: Kush, VI, 1958]

Note: All of the above works are listed in the outline of the course on NILE VALLEY
HIGH-CULTURES PAST AND PRESENT - "NEGROID" OR "SEMITIC"?

SPECIAL SUPPLEMENTARY BIBLIOGRAPHY USED IN THE PRE-
PARATION OF THE CHRONOLOGIES THAT CROSS-REFERENCED
THE NILE VALLEY HIGH-CULTURES : TA-MERRY, TA-NEHISI,
MEROE, KUSH OR CUSH, ITIOPI, PUANIT OR PUNT, AND OTHERS.

F. Addison, "Fung Origins," [In: Sudan Notes and Records, XV, 201-50 [1952]

A. Amon, "A negro slave in neolithic Egypt? The Fayoum Skull," [In: Illustrated London
        News, 5 Feb., 1938]

A. J. Arkell, "Fung Origins," [In: Sudan Notes and Records, XV, 201-50 [1952]
        ------, "Dafur antiquities II, [In: Sudan Notes and Records, XX, 91-105 [1937]
        ------, "Dafur antiquities I," [In: Sudan Notes and Records, XXVII, 185-202 [1936]
        ------, "A Sudanese Abu Simbel," [In: Illustrated London News, pp. 214-15
        [15 Feb., 1947]

J. H. Breasted, ANCIENT RECORDS OF EGYPT, Chicago, 1906 [5 vols.]
        --------, A HISTORY OF EGYPT, [2nd ed.] , London, 1951

Sir E.A. Wallis Budge, THE EGYPTIAN SUDAN, London, 1907 [2 vols.]
        ------------, ANNALS OF NUBIANS KINGS, London, 1912

G. Caton-Tompson, KHARGA OASIS IN PREHISTORY, London, 1952

S.E. Chapman, Dows, and Dunham, THE ROYAL CEMETERIES OF KUSH III. DE-
        CORATED CHAPELS OF THE MEROITIC PYRAMIDS AT MEROE AND
        BARKAL, Boston, 1952

O.G.S. Crawford, THE FUNG KINGDOM OF SENNAR, Gloucester, 1951

S. Clarke, "Ancient Egyptian Frontier Fortresses,"   [In: Journal Of Egyptian Archae-
        ology, III, 155-79 [1961]

J.W. Crowfoot and F.L. Griffith, " The Land Of Meroe and Meroitic Inscriptions, I,"
        [In: Egyptian Exploration Fund, London, 1911]

D. Dunham, "Notes on the history of Kush," [In: American Journal of Archaeology, I,
        378-88 [1946]
        ------, "Outline of the ancient history of the Sudan, V.," [In: Sudan Notes and
        Records, XXVIII, 1-10 [1947]
        ------, ROYAL CEMETERIES OF KUSH, I: EL KURRU, Boston, Mass., 1950

W.B. Emery, NUBIAN TREASURE, London, 1948
        ------, THE ROYAL TOMBS OF BALLANA AND QUSTUL, Cairo, 1938

C.M. Firth, THE ARCHAEOLOGICAL SURVEY OF NUBIA. REPORT FOR 1908-9,
        Cairo, 1912
        ----, THE ARCHAEOLOGICAL SURVEY OF NUBIA, REPORT FOR 1909-10,
        Cairo, 1915
        ----, THE ARCHAEOLOGICAL SURVEY OF NUBIA. REPORT FOR 1910-11,
        Cairo, 1927

J. Garstang, A.H. Sayce and F.L. Griffith, MEROE, THE CITY OF THE ETHIOPIANS,
        Oxford, 1911

F.L. Griffith, KARANOG, THE MEROITIC INSCRIPTIONS OF SHABLUL KARANOG,
        Philadelphia, 1911
        ------, "Meroitic Inscriptions II," [In: Egyptian Exploration Fund, London, 1912]
        ------, "Meroitic studies I and II," [In: Journal of Egyptian Archaeology, 111, 22-
        30 and 111-24 [1916]
        ------, "Merotic studies III and IV," [In: Journal of Egyptian Archaeology, IV, 21-
        7, 159-73 [1917]
        ------, "Pakhoras - Bakharas-Faras in geography and history," [In: Journal of
        Egyptian Archaeology, XI, 259-68 [1925]

248

H.R. Hall, THE ANCIENT HISTORY OF THE NEAR EAST [8th Ed.], London, 1932

A.H.M. Jones and E. Monroe, A HISTORY OF ABYSSINIA, Oxford, 1935

H. Junker, "The first appearance of the negro in history," [In: Journal of Egyptian
    Archaeology, VII, 121-32 [1921]

L.P. Kirman, "A Survey of Nubian Origins," [In: Sudan Notes and Records, XX, 47-62
    [1937]

L.S.B. Leakey, ADAM'S ANCESTORS [2nd Ed.], London, 1953

C.R. Lepsius, DISCOVERIES IN EGYPT, ETHIOPIA AND THE PENINSULA OF SINAI,
    [2nd Ed.], London, 1853

Mf. L. Macadam, THE TEMPLES OF KAWA, I, Oxford, 1912

C.K. Meek, A SUDANESE KINGDOM, London, 1931

K.P. Oakley, MAN THE TOOL-MAKER [2nd Ed.], British Museum of Natural History,
    London, 1950

H.P. Palmer, SUDANESE MEMOIRS, Lagos, 1928 [3 vols.]

W.M.F. Petrie, "The Royal Tombs of the early Dynasties, II," [In: Egyptian Expedition
    Fund, London, 1901]

  -----, QURNEH, London, 1909

  -----, "Tools and weapons," [In: British School of Archaeology in Egypt,
    London, 1917]

  -----, PREHISTORIC EGYPT CORPUS, London, 1921

W.M.F. Petrie and R.L.B. Moss, TOPOGRAPHICAL BIBLIOGRAPHY OF ANCIENT
    EGYPTIAN HIEROGLYPHIC TEXTS RELIEFS AND PAINTINGS, VII.
    NUBIA, THE DESERTS, AND OUTSIDE EGYPT, Oxford, 1951

G. Posner [ed.], ENCYCLOPEDIA OF EGYPTIAN CIVILIZATION, New York, 1960

J.E. Quibell and W.F. Green, "Hierakonpolis, II," [In: Egyptian Research Account,
    London, 1902]

G.A. Reisner, "Outline of the Ancient History of the Sudan, IV. The first kingdom of
    Ethiopia," [In: Sudan Notes and Records, II, 32-67 [1919]

  -------, "Discovery of the Tombs of the Egyptian XXVth Dynasty at El-Kurru in
    Dongola Province," [In: Sudan Notes and Records, II, 237-54 [1919]

  -------, "The Viceroys of Ethiopia," [In: Journal of Egyptian Archaeology, VI,
    28-55 and 73-88 [1920]

  -------, "The Meroitic Kingdom of Ethiopia: a chronological outline," [In: Journal
    of Egyptian Archaeology, IX, 34-77 and 157-60 [1923]

A.H. Sayce, "The Karian and Lydian Inscriptions," [In: Proceedings for the Society of
    Biblical Archaeology, XVII, 39-41 [1895]

  -----, "A Greek Inscription of a King [?] of Axum found at Meroe," [In: Proceed-
    ings of the Society for Biblical Archaeology, XXXII, 261-2 [1910]

C.G. Seligman, EGYPT AND NEGRO AFRICA, London, 1934

C.G. Seligman and B.Z. Seligman, PAGAN TRIBES OF THE NILOTIC SUDAN,
    London, 1932

G.A. Wainright, "From the Napatan and Meritic ages," [In: Sudan Notes and Records,
    XXVI, 5-36 [1945]

  ---------, " The Ancient Records of Kordofan," [In: Sudan Notes and Records,
    XXVIII, 11-24 [1947]

H.E. Winlock, "Neb-hepet-Re-Mentu-hotep of the XXIst Dynasty," [In: Journal of Egyp-
    tian Archaeology, XXVI, 116-19 [1940]

The following books are either out of print or very rarely published, except for those written by the author of this volume. Most of them can be used in the Authur O. Schumburg Collection of the Cuntee Cullen Public Library, West 135th Street, Harlem, New York City, New York; the John Henrike Clark Collection, Harlem, New York; the Sieffert Collection, Harlem, New York; the Clarence Holt Collection, Harlem, New York; and the Y. ben-Jochannan Collection, Harlem, New York.

Sir E.A. Wallis Budge, BOOK OF THE DEAD and the PAPYRUS OF ANI, London, 1895
Y. ben-Jochannan, BLACK MAN OF THE NILE [Ist Ed. , 1st-5th impression], New
          York, 1970
          ---------, AFRICA: MOTHER OF WESTERN CIVLIZATION, New York, 1971
          ---------, AFRICAN ORIGINS OF THE MAJOR "WESTERN RELIGIONS, New
          York, 1971
Y. ben-Jochannan and G.E. Simmonds, THE BLACK MAN'S NORTH and EAST AFRICA,
          New York, 1971
B.D. Alexander, HISTORY OF PHILOSOPHY
E.B. Sandford THE MEDITERRANEAN WORLD
C.H. Vail, ANCIENT MYSTERIES
S.W. Clymer, FIRE PHILOSOPHY
J. Kendrick, HISTORY OF ANCIENT EGYPT
G.G.M. James, STOLEN LEGACY
A. Besant, ESOTORIC CHRISTIANITY
Herodotus, THE HISTORIES
Tyler and Sedgwick, HISTORY OF SCIENCE
Sir J. Frazier, THE GOLDEN BOUGH [13 vols.]
Count C.F. Volney, RUINS OF EMPIRES
M. Muller, EGYPTIAN MYTHOLOGY
S.R.K. Glanville [ed.], THE LEGACY OF EGYPT
W.M. Adams Marshan, BOOK OF THE MASTER
J.C. deGraft-Johnson, AFRICAN GLORY
Dr. A . Churchward, THE ORIGIN OF FREEMASONRY
          -----------, ARCANA OF FREEMASONRY
          -----------, SIGNS AND SYMBOLS OF PRIMORDIAL MAN
          -----------, THE ORIGIN AND EVOLUTION OF THE HUMAN RACE
THE AQUARIAN GOSPEL
LOST BOOKS OF THE BIBLE AND THE FORGOTTEN BOOKS OF EDEN
PALESTINE BEFORE THE JEWS

Note: Students of "BLACK" or "AFRICAN STUDIES" must use a very liberal selection of all of the above works listed. All references should be documented with at least 3 to 5 quotation in support of a particular position. Cross-referencing must be applied wherever controversies arise between sources. Use other references in the above works.

250

Date BCE   Description and Comments

10,000   Man's first CALENDAR was developed along the Nile River Valley and the
Great Lakes of Africa. The world's most ancient sculptured work of a human figure
was sculpted by indigenous Africans of Monomotapa [South Africa]. It is presently located in the Museum Of Vienna, and erroneously misnomered "VENUS OF DUSSEL-
DORF."[1]

5,000   The oldest and most noted statue of MAN AND BEAST combined was worshipp-
ed as the God - HORUS. It is presently designated as "ONE OF THE WONDERS OF
THE WORLD" or "SPHINX OF GHIZEH" [Giza or Gizeh]. It was also worshipped as
"HAMACHIS" - The Sun God Of Life And Light."[2] [See page iii of this volume].

4,100   The introduction of the first SOLAR CALENDAR ever made by man. It had
365 1/4 Days to One Year, Three seasons of Four months each. [See page 130]. It was
introduced by the indigenous Africans of the Nile Valley - those of Ta-Merry, Ta-
Nehisi, Merüe, Kush or Itiopi [Ethiopia], and others along the Central African Great
Lakes.

3,200   The Paleolithic Period [Old Stone Age]; Neolithic Period [Old Stone Age];
the Prehistoric Epoch [Era]; the Tasia Period; the Badavian Period; and the PreDynastic Period; all of them met at this juncture in Alkebu-lan's history.

2,900   The High-Culture [civilization] called "ELAM," a kingdom within the Persian
Empire, flourished during this period of time. On of its most famous kings was named
KUDAR NAKUNTAR, the conqueror of the Chaldeans. ELAM was predominantly populated with an indigenous African ["Black, Negro, Bantu," etc.] people, who were no different to those of Ta-Merry and Ta-Nehisi during this period in world history.[3]

2,780   Beginning of the GREAT PYRAMID AGE. This Period began with Pharaohs:
Khufu, Men-kau-Ra, and Khafra.[0] But the most ancient of the TRULY "GREAT PYRA-
MIDS" was built Pharaoh Djoser [Zozer or Zoser according to Herodotus and other ancients of Greece and Rome] during the IIIrd Dynasty.[4] Imhotep, whose statue is shown
on page 190 of this volume, was Chief Architect and Builder of this project - the "STEP
PYRAMID of Sakhara [Saqqara].[5] The stones used in the building on this structure were
taken from Quaries which were opened-up earlier by indigenous Africans at the easternmost point of North, Alkebu-lan [Africa], the Sinai Peninsula of Ta-Merry [Egypt]
during the reign of Pharaoh Semerkhet, and kept in service by following pharaohs from
c. 3200 to at least c. 2780 B.C.E.

2685   The GRAND LODGE OF LUXOR was built at Danderah by Pharaoh Khufu
during the IIIrd Dynasty. This area, which was part of Ta-Nehisi when the GRAND
LODGE was built, is prsently called "Upper Egypt." It is presently called "TEMPLE
OF THE CITY OF THEBES." It was originally 2,000 feet long and 1,000 feet wide at its
base. Its oblong shape is copied by all secret societies based upon Masonic principles.

---

[0] The Greek names for these pharaohs were "KHEOPS" or "Cheops" for Khufu; "MY-
CERINUS" for Men-kau-Re; and "CHEPHREN" for Khafra.

Here the fundamental basis for the rituals of FREE MASONRY and most of the 20th Century "Western" Secret Societies were established[6]by indigenous Africans whose descendants are now despised for their SABLE SKIN , WOOLLY HAIR, THICK LIPS, BROAD NOSE;" even rejected from the INNER CIRCLES for the same reason. The ancients, including the Greeks and Romans, visited this GRAND LODGE to obtain the "HIGHEST DEGREES" in human learning. Here they were introduced to PHILOSOPHY, LAW, RELIGION, SCIENCE, ENGINEERING, MATHEMATICS, ASTRONOMY, ASTROLOGY, MEDICINE, HISTORY, and all of the other sub-divisions of the "SEVEN LIBERAL ARTS. Even King Solomon Of Israel, Moses of the Haribu religion, Jesus Christ, and others of world fame, had to visit this Grand Lodge for their education in the MYSTERIES OF THE OSIRICA, which was centered here. [See THE AQUARIAN GOSPEL OF JESUS CHRIST; FIVE BOOKS OF MOSES; G.G.M. James, STOLEN LEGACY; C.H. Vail, ANCIENT MYSTERIES; G. Massey, EGYPT THE LIGHT OF THE WORLD; M. Muller, EGYPTIAN MYTHOLOGY; Plato, APOLOGY; E. B. Sandford, THE MEDITERRANEAN WORLD;[7] J.J. Jackson, INTRODUCTION TO AFRICAN CIVILIZATION; Y. ben-Jochannan, AFRICA: MOTHER OF "WESTERN CIVILIZATION"].

SUBORDINATE LODGES OF THE GRAND LODGE OF LUXOR[0]

1. Palestine [at Mt. Carmel][8]
2. Assyria [at Mt. Herman in Lebanon]
3. Babylon
4. Media [near the Red Sea]
5. India [at the banks of the Ganges River]
6. Burma
7. Athens
8. Rome [at Elea]
9. Croton
10. Rhodes
11. Delphi
12. Miletus
13. Cyprus
14. Corinth
15. Crete
16. Cush [Itiopi, Ethiopia]
17. Monomotapa [South Africa]
18. Zimbabwe [Rhodesia]

LUXOR was destroyed by fire, burnt to the ground, in the year c. 548 B.C.E. It was set aflame by foreigners, who were jealous of the indigenous Africans ["Negroes,"et al] knowledge of the "MYSTERIES" taught in the Osirica - which included all of the above mentioned disciplines. [See John Kendrick's, ANCIENT EGYPT, Book II, p. 363; Eva B. Sandford's, THE MEDITERRANEAN WORLD, pp. 135 - 139; Yosef ben-Jochannan's, AFRICA: MOTHER OF "WESTERN CIVILIZATION", Chapter IX].

2,400   The Temple of Kharnak, the most pompteous of the Chapters of the Grand Lodge of Luxor's Secret Society, where the Mysteries were taught, was built at a distance of 1/2 mile from the Grand Lodge. Separated each 12 feet on both sides of an isle   stood a double row of sphinxes. The width of the isle was 60 feet. When in its perfection this entrance presented one of the most magnificent walkways imaginable [See pictures of this structure's ruins on pages 252 and 280 of Chapter VI].

2,340   Four different expeditions of Egyptian Pharaohs who left Egypt for visits to

---

[0] Special information relative to the Lodges listed above can be found in the following works: James Hasting's, ENCYCLOPEDIA OF RELIGION AND ETHICS [8 vols]; Dr. A. Churchward's, THE ORIGIN AND EVOLUTION OF RELIGION; Thomas Stanley's, HISTORY OF PHILOSOPHY; Sir J. Frazier's, THE GOLDEN BOUGH [13 vols.]; G.G. M. James', STOLEN LEGACY; G. Massey's, EGYPT THE LIGHT OF THE WORLD.

The colossal Cippus of Horus, which is commonly known as the " Metternich stele " (Obverse).

The colossal Cippus of Horus, which is commonly known as the " Metternich stele " (Reverse).

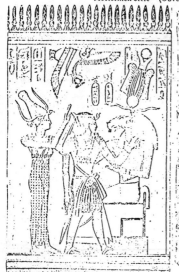

GRAND MASTER'S APRON AND COLLAR
Satit presents the Pharaoh Amenothes III. to Khnûmû.
Drawn by Faucher-Gudin, from one of the bas-reliefs of the Temple of Khnûmû at Elephantine. This bas-relief is now destroyed.

MASTER'S APRON AND COLLAR
The Pharaoh Menkauhoru.
Drawn by Boudier, from a photo-graph taken by Faucher-Gudin. The original is in the Louvre, Paris.

THE COMPANION'S (F.C.) APRON
Stele in the form of a door, and the Statue of the tomb of Mirruka.
Drawn by Boudier, from a photograph taken by M. de Morgan.

253

Nubia, Merŏe, Itiopi, and Puanit,[9] all of them to the SOUTH of Egypt [Ta-Merry, Sais, Kimit, etc.], which only adds proof to the fact that all of the Africans of Alkebu-lan [Africa], SOUTH to NORTH, had commercial, social, and sexual contact with each others for thousands of years before the arrival of the so-called "SEMITES" and "CAUCASIANS" to North and East Africa. Their exploits were revealed as part of the indigenous Africans of Ta-Merry's history in an INSCRIPTION in the tomb of a nobleman of Elephantine [Aswan of today]. With regards to some of the journeys the following was written:

"THE PHARAOH MENERE MADE THREE VOYAGES, AND PEPI II MADE ONE." [Arkell's, History Of The Sudan].

2,300 Imhotep of Ta-Merry [Egypt, Kimit, Sais, etc.], shown on page 190 of this volume, became known to the ancients as the :

"GOD OF MEDICINE."

This indigenous African was the FIRST MEDICAL MAN [physician] known to mankind, even preceding those mentioned in the Five Books Of Moses [Old Testament] and the New Testament. The Greeks, Romans, Chaldean, Babylonians, Sumerians, and others of the ancient world, learned their basic medicine from this African ["Negro"]. He was GRAND VIZIER, PRIME MINISTER, ARCHITECT, POET, and holder of many other positions during his lifetime while he served his Pharaoh, Djoser.[10] He was known to the Greeks as "PRINCE OF PEACE" over two-thousand [2,000] years before the Christians' JESUS CHRIST was born, muchless before Jesus was given said title. This is the man credited with the saying:

"EAT, DRINK, AND BE MERRY, FOR TOMORROW WE DIE."

Imhotep lived more than 2,000 years before the Europeans and European-Americans "FATHER OF MEDICINE" - Hippocrates of Greece - was born; yet, "Western" educators continue teaching that "HIPPOCRATES WAS THE FATHER OF MEDICINE"; whose "MEDICINE." On the following page we find the same "European Father Of Medicine," Hippocrates, paying homage to his teacher and God - IMHOTEP, whom the ancient Greeks and Romans called ..."AESCULAPIUS;" the "OATH" speaks for itself.

2,300   The oldest and first known records of a journey from Elephantine [today's Aswan], Ta-Nehisi or Nubia, to Memphis in Ta-Merry or Egypt, dealt with Pharaoh Mennere's ambassador - the son of the Ritual Priest named Iri - trip to the Kingdom of Yam. The purpose of the trip was to establish a highway between both cities. Here, again, the lies that there were natural barriers that separated the "Egyptian Semites" from the "Nubian Negroes" are exposed as RACIST hypotheses that have no foundation in fact or history.
       The second journey of King or Pharaoh Mennere's ambassador on the Elephantine Road, from Irthet to Mskhen, then to Tereres, and back to Isthet, was a trip that totaled eight [8] months duration. [See J.H. Breasted, ANCIENT RECORDS OF EGYPT, Chicago, vol. I, pp. 333-336 and 353 [1906].

1,555   Queen Hatshepsut [daughter of Thutmes I] was born.[11] She ruled as one of

254

The Oath

I SWEAR by Apollo the physician, and Æsculapius, and Health, and All-heal, and all the gods and goddesses, that, according to my ability and judgment, I will keep this Oath and this stipulation—to reckon him who taught me this Art equally dear to me as my parents, to share my substance with him, and relieve his necessities if required; to look upon his offspring in the same footing as my own brothers, and to teach them this art, if they shall wish to learn it, without fee or stipulation; and that by precept, lecture, and every other mode of instruction, I will impart a knowledge of the Art to my own sons, and those of my teachers, and to disciples bound by a stipulation and oath according to the law of medicine, but to none others. I will follow that system of regimen which, according to my ability and judgment, I consider for the benefit of my patients, and abstain from whatever is deleterious and mischievous. I will give no deadly medicine to any one if asked, nor suggest any such counsel; and in like manner I will not give to a woman a pessary to produce abortion. With purity and with holiness I will pass my life and practice my Art. I will not cut persons laboring under the stone, but will leave this to be done by men who are practitioners of this work. Into whatever houses I enter, I will go into them for the benefit of the sick, and will abstain from every voluntary act of mischief and corruption; and, further from the seduction of females or males, of freemen and slaves. Whatever, in connection with my professional practice or not, in connection with it, I see or hear, in the life of men, which ought not to be spoken of abroad, I will not divulge, as reckoning that all such should be kept secret. While I continue to keep this Oath unviolated, may it be granted to me to enjoy life and the practice of the art, respected by all men, in all times! But should I trespass and violate this Oath, may the reverse be my lot!

Aesculapius is the name the ancient Greeks gave to their AFRICAN GOD - Imhotep. This African, during his prominence as a philosopher, poet, architect, builder, physician, etc., predated the birth of the first European physician - Hippocrates - by more than two-thousand (2000) years - c2780-2680 B.C.E.
[From page 316 of Y. ben-Jochannan's AFRICA: MOTHER OF "WESTERN CIVILIZATION," New York, 1971].

Ta-Merry's most efficient monarchs. Her fame was known the world over during her lifetime. She too made a trip to PUNT [modern Somaliland], Cush, and Nubia in c. 1490 B.C.E.[12] [See page 283 for INSCRIPTION in Hieroglyph].

Amen-hotep IV, otherwise known as Akhenaten [Ikhnaten, etc.], was born.[13] He was known to the ancients of his lifetime as the "RELIGIOUS PHARAOH" [King]. Way back in the hundreds of years before the proclaimed "...BIRTH OF JESUS CHRIST...," the Christians' "GOD," Akhenaten taught his followers about a "TRINITARIAN GOD." He called his God "THE VIRTUES," or "GOD IN THREE VIRTUES." The "VIRTUES" were broken down into "LOVE, SOUL," and "BODY" or "Life". However, he was not much of a politician or administrator, not even a forceful man. This was at a period in the history of Ta-Merry [Kimit, Egytp] when a powerful leader was most needed, a man with both qualities. He made Ta-Merry weak militarily, and started her on her way down to her eventual downfall from:

"...THE MOST FEARFUL POWER OF HER TIME, AND LEADER
OF WORLD CIVILIZATIONS "

to a powerless second rate nation militarily. Akhenaten had reduced the army of Ta-Merry to a mere police force; thus, allowing Ta-Merry's enemies to constantly invade her border towns and other outposts. As such, Ta-Merry's trade was cut to a mere trickle; her treasury was almost broke; and, her generals were in total disunity.

The indigenous Africans of the Nile Valley - EGYPTIANS, NUBIANS, MERÖITES, ITIOPIANS, KUSHITES, PUANITS, and whatever else they were, discovered a "FERTILITY CONTROL RECIPE"[14] for Planned Parenthood [birth control]. This document is presently called the "EBERS PAPYRUS," and is presently held in London, Great Britain. For an English translation of this RECIPE and the original in Hieroglyph, see page 283 of this volume.

1,490   Queen Hatshepsut of Ta-Merry sent an expeditionary force to the land Southeast of Kush [Itiopi or Ethiopia] at the Red Sea - PUNT or PUANIT [Today's Somiland, part of Kenya, and possibly part of the mainland of Tanzania, formerly Tanganyika]. This journey is recorded on the walls of the Queen's Temple at Luxor [Thebes], at a place presently called "Deir-el-Bahri." The story in Hieroglyph appears on page of this volume. The Great Queen-King, Hat-shep-sut, died during this year, leaving the throne of Ta-Merry to her youngest brother - Thotmose III, of whom rumors have him causing her death by murder.

1,490   The Coeval of Queen Hatshepsut, Thotmose or Tuthmosis III [her brother,
1,436 to and possibly son, or stepson - the records are not clear as to which is cor -
rect], continued trading expeditions and diplomatic relations with all of the nations to the SOUTH of Ta-Merry his sister dealt with. See J.H. Breated, ANCIENT RECORDS OF EGYPT, Chicago, 1906, vol. II, pp. 486-487; G.G.M. James, STOLEN LEGACY; G. Maspero, A HISTORY OF EGYPT AND ASSYRIA, [8 vols.], London, 1898].

1,405   Pharaoh Amenothis III founded the "TEMPLE OF THE SECRET FIRE," a Chapter of the Grand Lodge of Luxor.[15] The latter was the "MOTHER" of all Grand Chapters and Secret Lodges of the ancient world. [See Swinburne Clymer, FIRE PHILOSOPHY; Max Muller, EGYPTIAN MYTHOLOGY; G.G.M. JAMES, STOLEN LEGACY; Yosef ben-Jochannan, AFRICA: MOTHER OF "WESTERN CIVILIZATION," Chapt. IX].

751   Pharaoh Kashta died. Pharaoh Piankhi took upon himself to carry on Kashta's rule over Ta-Merry. Earlier Ethiopian pharaohs had begun the seige of Egypt [Ta-Merry] from their own capital city - NAPATA. Pharaoh Taharka took over from Pharaoh Piankhi and made Cush, which at that period extended into Egypt, the world leading power of this era. Of the solely indigenous African ["Negro" or whatever] Pharanic Dynasties Piankhi's was one of the most powerful in Egyptian history.[16]

731   After approximately twenty-one [21] years of Pharoah Piankhi's reign over Egypt and Ethiopia he erected a STELE [tablet of stone with a flat surface] at Jebel Barkal, Ta-Nehisi [Nubia or Zeti, modern Sudan], a very short distance from the capital city of Kush - NAPATA. [See page 181 of this volume for the top section of the STELE erected by Pharaoh Piankhi].

718   Pharaoh Shabaka [Sabacom], the Cushite, invaded Lower Ta-Merry and captured it. He made his move from Ta-Nehisi, and followed it by annexing Ta-Merry, thus establishing the XXVth DYNASTY.

715   The Nubian Dynasty of Upper Egypt was founded.

700   The world's first religious principle was substantiated. It was verified when a slab of basalt was unearthed in Egypt bearing an INSCRIPTION with Cushitic script relating to a treatise on the moral concept of RIGHT and WRONG by King Ori in the year c. 3758 B.C.E. Ori declared that they are "MORAL FORCES OF GOD" [the Sun God - RA].[17]

670   Ionians and Carians were recruited for the first time to serve in Egyptian armies. During this period Greeks were used as translators in Egypt in matters relative to Europeans in Egypt. From this contact they begun receiving their first light into the mysteries of "PHILOSOPHY" and other aspects of the "SEVEN LIBERAL ARTS." This experience has been the basis for what was later called "GREEK PHILOSOPHY" by "Westerners". There is no record of anything resembling "GREEK PHILOSOPHY" before the Greeks arrival in Egypt and Nubia, or their arrival in Ionia where they studied under Egyptian teachers brought into Ionia - then an Egyptian colony. Later Greeks were brought into Egypt as students in the MYSTERIES SYSTEM to study the Osirica's "MYSTERIES" - the equivalent of today's universities. All of the works they studied were of the genius of the indigenous Africans of the Nile Valley High-Cultures, including those defined by Herodotus and Count Volney.

600   Pharaoh Neku [Necku, Nechu or Necho] II commissioned a fellow African to sail around [circumnavigate] the entire continent of ALKEBU-LAN [Africa]. The name of the African navigator was Hano [Hanno], a native of Khart-Haddas [also known later as Carthage]. This certainly assails the claim that:

"...VASCO daGAMA WAS THE FIRST TO SAIL AROUND THE COAST OF THE SOUTHERN TIP OF AFRICA..."

[Monomotapa] up to c. 1498 C.E. It is to be noted that the Portuguese, the first of the Western Europeans at Monomotapa - of whom daGama was one, were not the first people there. For, they, too, wrote about the "KAFFIR SAILORS AND PILOTS" they met "...AROUND THE COAST OF MONOMOTAPA...," etc. in their ship's logs. The first of the Portuguese at Monomotapa was Captain Bartolome Dias in c. 1488 C.E. This is certainly in conflict with the present WHITE RACIST POPULATION [English, Boers, Americans - Judaeo-Christian, Jew, and Christian] teaching that:

"...WHEN THE WHITE MAN ARRIVED IN SOUTH AFRICA THERE WAS NO AFRICAN THERE EXCEPT THE HOTTENTOTS AND BUSH-MEN. THE ZULUS WERE STILL PUSHING SOUTHWARDS...," etc.

They have conveniently forgotten that they arrived there in the latter part of the 17th century C.E. or A.D., which was more than 100 years following the Portuguese who met the Africans - the so-called "BANTUS", of which the "ZULUS" are a part.

548   DELFI, the "SECRET TEMPLE OF THE EGYPTIAN MYSTERIES SYSTEM" - a Chapter of the Grand Lodge of Luxor, was burnt to the ground. It was subsequently rebuilt by its "GRAND MASTER" - Pharaoh Amasis of Egypt, between c. 548 and 525 B.C.E. This pharaoh personally donated 1,000 talents and 50,000 pounds of alumn towards the rebuilding of the Temple for the FELLOW CRAFTSMEN, MASTERS, AND PASTMASTERS. The amount he donated was three times what was actually required. [See E.B. Sandford's, THE MEDITERRANEAN WORLD, p. 135 and 139; John Kendrick's, ANCIENT EGYPT, Book II, p. 363; G.G.M. James', STOLEN LEGACY; Y. ben-Jochannan's, AFRICA: MOTHER OF "WESTERN CIVILIZATION," Chapter IX].

525   Darius I, the Son of Hystapes, became ruler during the end of the XXVII th Dynasty. His ability as an administrator saved Egypt from the course of ruin it was taking under his predecessor - Pharaoh Cambyses, a fellow Persian. He introduced a new system of "MONEY EXCHANGE" to the Egyptians and other indigenous Africans in Egypt, which spread along the entire Nile Valley High-Cultures - Ta-Nehisi, Meröe, Kush and Itiopi, and even to Puanit at the extreme East Coast of Alkebu-lan.
      The genius of Greek englightenment into the "SEVEN LIBERAL ARTS," as it did in the field of "SCIENCE, LAW, ENGINEERING, MEDICINE, " etc., came about during many periods of their sojourn in Egypt, but mostly during this period; when, for the first time, immigration regulations barring them from Egypt was lifted by the Persians. This relaxation of the laws on immigration allowed the Greeks to settle in the town of Naacratis, where they met thousands of other foreigners from Asia. This took place during the reign of Pharaoh Amasis. Here at Naacratis, the Greeks were, for the first time, introduced into the full secrets of the Egyptian Mystereis System [Fraternal Brotherhood], and began their first contact in PHILOSOPHY and other disciplines which they been introduced before by much more indirect means. All of their teachers, up to the rank of "CHIEF PRIESTS," were indigenous Africans of the Nile Valley and Great Lakes. From this beginning the Greeks began to copy and otherwise aped the Nile Valley Africans concepts and teachings at their little settlement, many of them taking the same back to Greece where they returned frequently. [See Plutarch's, HISTORY, 380; Diogenes', BOOK IX, 49; OVID FASTI III, 338; Herodotus', HISTORIES; Y. ben-Jochannan's, AFRICA: MOTHER OF "WESTERN CIVILIZATION;" G.G.M. James', STOLEN LEGACY].
      Nectamebus I founded the last of the indigenous African Dynasties of UPPER and LOWER TA-MERRY [Kimit, Sais, Cham, Mizrain or Egypt] - the XXXth Dynasty, which was also known as the "SEBENYTIC DYNASTY" or "PERIOD."

525 to   Artaxarexes III ["the great"] formed the last Egyptian Dynasty before the de-

feat of the Persians in Egypt by the Macedonian-Greeks under the command of Alexander II ["the great"]. It was this event which started the rule of the Southern Europeans in Northeastern Alkebu-lan. This victory gave the Greeks their first run of their "STOLEN LEGACY" [Professor G.G.M. James' name for the so-called "Greek Philosophy"], as the indigenous Africans secrets of the Mysteries System's OSIRICA were totally seized, plagiarized, and co-opted by Aristotle and others under the leadership of General Soter, who had succeded Alexander II and took upon himself the title of "PHARAOH OF ALL EGYPT, SOTER I," and changed it to "PHARAOH OF ALL EGYPT, PTOLEMY I" later.

500   An African named Lochman, the "WORLD'S GREATEST FABLIST THAT EVER LIVED," was born in Itiopi [Ethiopia or Kush], East Africa - SOUTH OF THE SAHARA . The Greeks renamed him "AESOP." An ancient sketch, the only one ever made of Lochman, appears on page   of this volume.

500-   Herodotus, the "FATHER OF EUROPEAN AND EUROPEAN-AMERICAN HISTORIANS," established through his own writings that the basics of Greek High-Culture ["Western Civilization"] were copied from the teachings and developments of the Africans of the Nile Valleys and Great Lakes of Africa [Alkebu-lan]; also, from the Asians of the Tigris and Euphrates ; these Africans included Egyptians, Numidians, Khart-Haddans, Lebus, Nubians, Meroites, Kushites, Itiopians, Puanits, and many of the so-called "PYGMIES" of Central East Africa, and "AFRICANS SOUTH OF THE SAHARA" from Zimbabwe and the Empire of Monomotapa. This revelation by Herodotus has caused most European and European-American historians and other educators to establish their own COLOR and RACIAL distinction for each group or nation of the ancient Africans in contradiction to what Herodotus reported in his books in THE HISTORIES. They began by separating the indigenous Africans into "AFRICANS NORTH OF THE SAHARA" and those "SOUTH OF THE SAHARA." They also created NEW and "SEPARATE RACES" for Ethiopia, Egypt, Nubia, and other North and East African nations through the biblical mythology created by the Hebrews [Jews] and Christians of Europe, which was carried over to the Americas. Therefore, they introduced such characters as :

"BANTUS, HAMITES, SEMITES, NILOTICS, PYGMIES, BUSHMEN, HOTTENTOTS, NEGROES, NEGROIDS, CAUCASIANS, CAUCASOIDS,"

and a host of other SITES, OIDS, and TICS, claiming each as a...

"SEPARATE RACE."[18]

All of this they have done in order to camoflage the fact that the earliest Europeans [the Greeks and Romans included] were the recipients of the "CIVILIZING" efforts by indigenous African teachers like the so-called "NEGROES, BANTUS," and "AFRICANS SOUTH OF THE SAHARA " Herodotus described as the inhabitants of "EGYPT" and "NUBIA." Of course, hundreds of ancient Europeans also supported Herodotus' physical description of the North and East Africans; they, too, have been suppressed, that is - their works. It only shows that the prejudices of the European and European-American ["modern man" of the Jeffreys' and Breasteds," et al] are contaminated with an epidemic called "RACISM" and/or "RELIGIOUS BIGOTRY," the extent of which the forerunners of Herodotus, and his contemporaries, did not equally experienced. RACISM, obviously, did not cause Herodotus any trouble in writing that:

"...THE COLCHIANS, EGYPTIANS AND ETHIOPIANS HAVE
THICK LIPS, BROAD NOSE, WOOLLY HAIR, AND THEY
ARE BURNT OF SKIN",

in his major writings..., as it does "MODERN" or "WESTERN MAN " - the 'PROTEC-
TORS OF THE GREAT "WHITE RACE"; yet, Herodotus wrote his work between c. 457
and c. 450 B.C.E.

The fact that Herodotus described what is today called "NEGROES, ". and even

"NIGGERS," by certain groups of "MODERN" or "WESTERN MAN," as the ancient in-

digenous people of North and East Africa is further proof that the ancient Europeans,

Africans and Asians were not preoccupied with the same type of RACISM and RELIGIOUS

BIGOTRY, and the underlying concepts which flow from same causing certain professors

of history in the 20th century C.E. to color their interpretations to suit "modern" po-

litical, sociological, and ethnological needs, rather than the teaching of "TRUTH" as

found in research. But, in their RACIST hypotheses, which they have employed in their

attempt to separate the Africans into "PHYSICAL TYPES," they failed to recognize

that the people of Punt or Puanit [modern Somali Republic, part of Kenya, and part of

French colonial Somaliland] and Kush [Ethiopia] were as often ruled and occupied by the

indigenous Africans of Ta-Merry [modern Egypt], as Egypt was equally occupied by

these Africans when ruled by them. They also overlooked the fact that all of the people

and nations of the UPPER END OF THE NILE VALLEY ruled supremely at various times

over those at the LOWER END. By this factor alone, if for no other reason; how could

anyone, in good concience, still conclude that Egypt, Nubia, Meröe, Kush, Itiopi, Puanit,

Lebus, Numidia, Kharat-Haddas, and other nations of North and East Africa during an-

cient times ...

"...WERE ORIGINALLY SETTLED BY SEPARATE AND
DISTINCTLY DIFFERENT RACES...,"

that were eventually bastardized by the influx of :

"...NEGRO SLAVES THAT CAME INTO THE REGIONS
TO SERVE IN THE ARMIES OF THESE NATIONS...." ?

Of course the proposition is preposterous, particularly in face of the evidence presented

by Herodotus and other ancients in their firsthand testimonies that only ONE type of in-

digenous people occupied Egypt[19] during their visit there; this being further supported

very much later by Count C.F. Volney in his book - RUINS OF EMPIRE, and Baron V.

Denon's, JOURNEY AND TRAVELS IN EGYPT AND ASSYRIA, only to mention two more

of the thousands of Europeans who at one time spoke of the greatness of the so-called

260

"NEGROES." It is equally rediculous to speak of a...

"PURE WHITE RACE"

[Caucasian, Indo-European Aryan, Semitic or otherwise] following the invasions of
Southern Europe by indigenous Africans from Ethiopia, Egypt, Nubia, Khart-Haddas,
Mauretania [Morocco] and other parts of Alkebu-lan [Africa] who ran freely through
the lands bordering on the Mediterranean Sea - which included Turkey, Greece, Italy,
Portugal, Spain, and Southern France. It is equally as rediculous to speak about...

"PURE WHITE EUROPEAN AMERICANS,"

when almost every slavemaster had himself a least one [1] indigenous African ["NEGRO"
or "NIGGER"] MISTRESS - in many cases MANY MISTRESSES, most of whom bore
children who are today amongst the WHITEST OF THE WHITE EUROPEAN-AMERICANS;
some are even "BLONDE. " This fact is not solely related to the slavemaster, as many -
countless to be exact - slavemasters' DAUGHTERS, MOTHERS, SISTERS, COUSINS,
AUNTS, and other female relatives, became the mother of countless African-European-
Americans who are today passing as "WHITE AMERICANS." At the same time, most
of the Europeans who amalgamated with the indigenous African Moors [Mauretanians who
left Africa from Morocco] and Khart-Haddans [who were also called "Carthagenians]
are the ancestors of many millions of "WHITE EUROPEAN-AMERICANS;" one side of
their ancestors BLACK as the Ace of Spades, the other side WHITE as Sour Milk, the
end result is today called "MONGROLIZATION" - this being equally true for "SEMITES"
and "CAUCASIANS," JEWS AND GENTILES," and OTHERS.

One must conclude that the "LIGHT-SKINNED CAUCASIAN"...or..."MODERN
MAN" of professor Jeffreys and others [Greeks, Italians, French, Germans, etc.]
from Europe, SOUTH of Germany, and to its NORTH, remains "CAUCASIAN, INDO-
EUROPEAN ARYAN, SEMITIC," and even "DARK-SKINNED HAMITIC;"thus, Africans
NORTH and SOUTH of the Sahara must remain "AFRICANS," not "NEGROES, BANTUS,
HAMITES, SEMITES, NILOTS," or any other RACIAL or ETHNIC tag placed upon them
by their former and present colonialist and imperialist European and/or European-
American slave masters and overlords for over the last four hundred [400] years, from
c. 1500 or 1503 C.E. to the present - c. 1972 C.E. or A.D.

Herodotus expalined the North and East African NEGROMANIA and NEGROPHOBIA
which plague "MODERN MAN," when he wrote that:

"THE COLCHIANS, EGYPTIANS AND ETHIOPIANS HAVE BURNT SKIN. "

Herodotus was speaking of indigenous Africans, under many of whom he studied history and philosophy, two of the many disciplines they introduced to him. The vast majority of the indigenous people of the Nile River Valleys [both blue and white] he described in the same manner. [See Herodotus', HISTORIES, Book II, as translated from the original Greek text to English by different authors, much of which editing has plagiarized]. The Colchians were "MIDDLE" and "NEAR EASTERN" people from the area presently called the "MIDDLE EAST," formerly "ASIA-MINOR." Colchis, itself, was part of "modern" Turkey and the arc between the Eastern borders of the Mediterranean Sea. Herodotus went further in his HISTORIES to point out that:

"...AS THE BIRD BEING BLACK, THEY MERELY SIGNIFY THAT THE WOMAN WAS AN EGYPTIAN...."

Herodotus was expalining why the ORACLE OF DODOMA, Egypt, was called "BLACK." In a similar manner, he wrote of the Colchians' African ancestry:

"...my own idea on the subject was based first on the fact that they [the Colchians][0] have black skin and woolly hair, and secondly, and more especially, on the fact that the Colchians, the Egyptians, and the Ethiopians are the only peoples which from ancient times have practised circumcission...."

Could there be any further need for understanding just what Herodotus was saying, or who he was describing in terms of African peoples - the so-called "NEGROES"?

Herodotus lumped all Africans, NORTH and SOUTH OF THE SAHARA, in the same physical characteristics throughout his writings. Yet, today's recipients of Herodotus' works prefer to change his own first-hand account of what he actually saw and recorded in their own arrangements to suit their own "MODERN" RACIST DISTORTION and PLAGIARIZATION of world history with regards to the indigenous Africans of North and East Africa; thus, they make history what they want it to be, rather than leave it as IT IS. This type of behavior is commonly known as "RACISM." It is a disease which most so-called "ORTHODOX" and "LIBERAL" European and European-American historians and other writers [the so-called "AFRICANISTS"] on the subject of "AFRICA" [Alkebulan] and "AFRICAN PEOPLES," particularly those "SOUTH OF THE SAHARA" - the so-called "BLACK AFRICANS," appear to be unable to divorce themselves. Their "NEGROPHOBIA" prohibits them from seeing the indigenous African people [past or contemporary] as contributors to the world's HIGH-CULTURE, which they prefer to call

---

[0] The words in brackets [ ] are for clarity only; placed there by the author of this work.

"C-I-V-I-L-I-Z-A-T-I-O-N."

More than six-thousand [6,000] years after the historical recordings in hundreds of tombs [pyramids, etc.] of numerous pharaohs [kings], more than three thousand [3,000] years after the account of Queen-King Hatshepsut's expedition to Punt [c. 1515-1484 B.C.E.], and of course, long before the period relating to Herodotus's birth [c. 500 B.C.E.], the ancient indigenous Africans [Ethiopians or Blacks] along the entire Nile Valleys and Great Lakes, among other parts of Alkebu-lan, recorded their history on the inside and outside of their temples and other structures, many of which have survived the ages of time to substantiate the facts revealed in this volume. Herodotus, therefore, could not be :

"...THE FATHER OF HISTORY..."

in any sense of honesty; especially, when he admits in his own work that he learnt "HISTORY," among many other disciplines, from African HISTORIANS in school [the OSIRICA] at the Grand Lodge of Luxor [Thebes], Ta-Merry [Kimit, Sais, Egypt, etc.]. Yet, Herodotus could have been:

"...THE FATHER OF" [European] "HISTORY."[20]

Herodotus', HISTORIES, Book II, Chapter 57, states that "THE COLCHIANS, ETHIOPIANS AND EGYPTIANS"...are "BLACK...," as mentioned before. In the same Book II, Chapter 104, he wrote the following:

"...THEY ARE BLACK AND WOOLLY HAIRED...."

He did not call these indigenous Africans 'NEGROES, BANTUS, BLACK AFRICANS, AFRICANS SOUTH OF THE SAHARA,' nor anything similar. Yet, there could be no doubt that the majority of the EGYPTIANS, ETHIOPIANS, NUBIANS, LIBYANS, CUSH-ITES, MERÖITES,' and others of North and East Alkebu-lan [Africa] Herodotus met and lived with were similar to the Africans who were brought over to the Americas and the Caribbeans as slaves of the Europeans and European-Americans from c. 1503 to the latter part of the 19th century C.E., all of which began with the Most Right Reverend Bishop Bartoleme de LasCasas of the Island of Hispaniola [originally Hayte, presently called "Haiti"], the King and Queen of Spain, and the Roman Catholic Pope in Rome ordering Africans of Spain [Moors] to replace the exterminated Caribbean peoples ["Caribs" , between c. 1492 - 1500 C.E.], did not change them from "AFRICANS" to "NEGROES, NIGGERS" or "COLOURED PEOPLE;" nor did it changed the ancestors of said indigenous Africans of yesteryears - the EGYPTIANS, ETHIOPIANS, LIBYANS,

NUBIANS, CARTHAGENIANS, NIGERIANS, MEROITES, MONOMOTAPIANS, MOROC-
CANS, CONGOLESE, and countless others, to "SEMITES, HAMITES," or "CAUCA-
SIANS."

The maps on the following page by Eratosthenes and Herodotus leave no doubt that
the indigenous Africans they were relating too were those of North and East Africa; not
to "SLAVES FROM NUBIA IN THE EGYPTIAN ARMY," which is the usual claim by the
so-called "White LIBERAL" and "ORTHODOX AUTHORITIES ON AFRICA AND AFRICAN
PEOPLES" over the last two- hundred [200] or more years. The Africans, or "ETHI
PIANS" as the earliest Greeks and Romans called them, were from North and East
Alkebu-lan, as elsewhere; but, this was not known by either of these two men when
they drew their maps of the continent they called "AFRICA."

The man who made such an impact on the European and European-American world,
with respect to his PHYSICAL [racial] IDENTIFICATION of the North and East Africans,
Herodotus, an Ionian of the Egyptian colony by birth, Greek by citizenship, at the age
of 40 or 47, went to Egypt from Greece in the year c.457 or 450 B.C.E. to receive his
education, the same as all of the other Greeks of wealth before him, and many others
after him. He lived amongst the African [Ethiopian, Black, or "Negro"] "PRIEST OF
THE OSIRICA'S MYSTERIES SYSTEM," the intellectuals of Egyptian, Nubian, Ethiopian,
Meröite, and other Nile Valley and Great Lakes societies, "

> "...LEARNING AND COLLECTING CURIOUS INFORMATION...ON
> ALL THAT EGYPT COULD OFFER...,"

which he recorded scripulously, much of the same which he consigned to the Second
Book of the masterpiece he named EUTERPE. In it, he stated that which was coraborat-
ed in the African-European High-Priest, Manetho [who served under Ptolemy I - the
former general Soter of Alexander II -"the great" - army that conquered Egypt in c.
332 B.C.E.], book - HISTORY OF EGYPT. Unfortunately, Herodotus is still called:
"THE FATHER OF HISTORY," even though his works are loaded with the quoted data
of indigenous African HISTORIANS of the Nile Valley and Great Lakes regions of Alkebu-
lan [Africa]. Said information came from the very source Manetho used approximately
one hundred and seventy [170] years after Herodotus wrote his work on the Nile River
Valley, Egypt particularly, c. 450 - 280 B.C.E. Julius Africanus [Julius Afer or Julius
the African], Eusebius, and Josephus [all of them ancient historians of great distinction]
testified to the "GREATNESS OF MANTHO'S WORKS," and copied much of his data that

264

AFRICA ACCORDING TO ERATOSTHENES 200 B.C.E.

AFRICA ACCORDING TO HERODOTUS 450 B.C.E.

[The above maps were the most accurate of their era.]

It should be noted that Eratosthenes and Herodotus, as other Europeans of their era, believed that the Sahara was "A MAJOR BODY OF WATER" (ocean or lake). They had no conception of Africa "SOUTH OF THE SAHARA." And to date this general belief, though somewhat changed, still carries the same old stereo-type connotations. Yet, the Greeks had turned the "HORN" (at ancient Puanit, present day Somalia) of East Africa and entered the Indus River.

265

earlier Greek and Roman students had done but claimed AUTHORSHIP. Much of the
information all of them used are still to be seen on the various monuments, tombs,
walls of temples, etc., including the stolen works taken from the archives of the Grand
Lodge of Luxor and placed in the museums and private collections throughout Europe,
the United States of America, Great Britain, and other places without the consent of
the ligitimate African descendants - the so-called "NEGROES" and "AFRICANS SOUTH
OF THE SAHARA;" this being another reason why said AFRICANS had to be removed
from the history of North and East Africa.

430   Herodotus, the Ionian of Greek citizenship, arrived at Elephantine [modern
Aswan] in UPPER EGYPT[0] [previously a part of Lower Nubia]. He detailed this journey
in his book, EUTERPE. [See Herodotus' THE HISTORIES, as translated into English
by Aubrey deSelincourt, Penguin Books, 1954].

400-   Between c. 400 to c. 300 B.C.E. a Greek named Euthyminus sailed to West
300   Africa. Some historians claimed that he became: "...THE FIRST EURO-
PEAN TO DISCOVER" [reach] " THE SENEGAL RIVER...," " etc., which he called
"PHREMETES."[21] This is possible, his reaching, not discovering , since the only
other Europeans on record before the Christian Era [B.C.E. or B.C.] to arrive in
West Africa were two Romans - Seutimus Flaccus and Julius Maternus in c. 50 and c.
25 or 30 B.C.E. respectively; but, they wrote of the "NIGER RIVER," not the "SENE-
GAL RIVER."

345   The Khart-Haddans [later called "Carthagenians" by European and European-
American writers] established an EMBASSY in Rome. Many "Western" historians
claimed that it was at Fort Veii, which is located a few miles from Rome. They based
their contention upon the fact that the Etruscans, friends of the Khart-Haddans, were
already expelled from Rome in approximately c. 510 B.C.E.,or one hundred and sixty-
five [165] years before the establishment of the EMBASSY.

332   Alexander II ["the great"] of Macedonia entered Egypt under military power.
This conquest initiated the Europeans [Caucasians] control, or SPHERE OF INFLUENCE,
in the Eastern limits of North Africa for the first time in world history. Aristotle, the
so-called "GREEK PHILOSOPHER," and many of his fellow Greek cohorts, shortly thereafter, sacked the archives of Egypt, escpecially that of the Grand Lodge of Luxor
[Thebes]. They stole what they understood, and burned much of what they could not decipher from the insight they had received from other Greeks and Romans who studied
the Africans MYSTERIES of Egypt and other nations of the Nile Valley before their arrival. [See Professor George. G.M. James', STOLEN LEGACY, New York Philosophical Library, New York, 1954; Y. ben-Jochannan's, AFRICA: MOTHER OF "WESTERN
CIVILIZATION," Alkebu-lan Books Associates, New York, 1971; John J. Jackson's,
INTRODUCTION TO AFRICAN CIVILIZATION, New York, 1970; and J.A. Rogers',
WORLD'S GREAT MEN OF COLOR, Vol. I, New York, 1954].

0* The word inserted into the brackets [ ] is for the sake of clarity only. It was inserted
by the author of this volume.

323   Alexander II ["the great"] died in Egypt. His vast conquered Empire was divided among his top generals, all of whom refused to recognize the authority of King Philip IIIrd - Alexander's brother in Macedonia.

306   General Soter, Alexander's best general, the person Alexander assigned the post of GOVERNOR OF EGYPT, declared himself "SOTER I,PHARAOH OF ALL EGYPT," which he later changed to "PTOLEMY I, PHARAOH OF ALL EGYPT." He,too,was from Macedonia, but of Greek parentage. He brought the first Europeans in the history of the world to sit on the throne of the "STAR OF THE NILE," Egypt. All of the other foreign conquerors until the Macedonians and Greeks were from Asia, except fellow Africans that conquered the Africans of Egypt.

Under the reign of Ptolemy I the African-European High-Priest, Manetho, became the first historian to codify Egyptian Royal History based upon "DYNASTIC CLASSIFI-CATION."He also completed a compilation of Egypt's "HISTORY OF ANTIQUITY," and divided it into the first "THIRTY [30]" of the "THIRTY-FOUR [34] ROYAL DYNASTIES" shown on pages 158 - 159 of the CHRONOLOGY OF THE DYNASTIES [with the consecutive dates and ruling monarchs] of this volume. His works have been translated by such noted historians as Josephus, Leo Africanus, and Eusebius; the latter brought forward the most important translation of Manetho's great works to date. At this juncture, it must be noted that Leo Africanus was an indigenous African [a so-called "Negro"]. He was renamed by his Godfather, Pope Leo of the Roman Catholic Church in Rome, following his capture, enslavement, and conversion to Christianity. Josephus of the other hand, was a Hebrew [misnomered "Jew"][0]. Here it is seen once more that there is quite a lot to a name. Volumes upon volumes of Africa's sons and daughters teachings have been called "GREEK PHILOSOPHY" because of a name, or names, being changed from the original African works to Greek and Latin personalities; the African names removed and European names substituted for them. In the case of Aristotle, who did not write a single word in PHILOSOPHY until he allegedly wrote thousands of books in Egypt, his name appears on African works that preceded his own birth by thousands of years. [For the best expose on this aspect of so-called "GREEK PHILOSOPHY" see professor G.G. M. James', STOLEN LEGACY]. This practice reached its zenith when Alexander IInd died and General Soter set Aristotle loose to ravage the Royal Library of Alexandria, which was originally an extension branch of the Library of the Grand Lodge of Luxor. The majority of the indigenous African works therein were given Aristotle's and other Greek titles and/or names, most of them having been written hundreds, some even thousands, of years before the birth of Homer - the first known literate Greek. Many of such works are today part of what is still called "GREEK PHILOSOPHY, WESTERN HISTORY," and "GREAT WORKS OF WESTERN CIVILIZATION." However, the "BLACK CULTURAL REVOLUTION" is forcing much of these "TRUTHS" to the forefront daily. Thus, the age-old maxim that:

"THE TRUTH SHALL SET YOU FREE,"

now lives to haunt those who have been parroting it from their pulpit in synagogues, churches, and mosques. Why? Because of the "TRUTH" in the BLACK CONFRONTA-

---

[0] There is no available evidence if he was WHITE, BLACK, BROWN, YELLOW, RED, or whatever else there may be in huma color. However, it is important to remember that being a so-called "JEW" has nothing to do with color of skin or type of facial or physical characteristics. There are "JEWS" in this world of every COLOR and PHY-SICAL TYPE possible in the human "RACE."

TION, which includes the purging of WHITE RACISM and SEMITIC RELIGIOUS BIGOTRY inserted in Africa's history and High-Culture by European and European-American "educators."

280   A Merötic Script of Egypt was introduced. It was an indigenous form of communication in Hieroglyph through written words and pictorial definitions that were similar to Egyptian and other Nile Valley people's Demotic Script. Very little of this writing is understood or decoded to date.

260   The indigenous Africans of Khart-Haddas [Carthage] were defeated in the Battle for Mylae.

256   The Khart-Haddans were defeated at the Battle of Ecnomus.

200   Polybius,[22] a Greek historian and colonial explorer, visited the same ports established by Admiral Hano many hundreds of years before on the coast of West Africa. In his book, TRAVELOGUE, he described several West African rivers, such as THE GAMBIA - which he called "BAMBOTUS." Note that the present Mande Africans, the so-called "MANDINGOES" of the Gambia,[0] name for crocodile is still "BAMBO," which gave rise to the basis of the name used by Polybius.

190   Another Greek, Eudoseus of Cyzicus, sailed down the East Coast of Alkebu-lan [Africa] after leaving Arabia. He sailed around the Cape of Monomotapa [renamed "Good Hope", before that "Cabo de Tormentos" or "Cape of Storms" by the Portuguese] with African navigators and sailors, stopping at Ngola [Angola according to the Portuguese], and the Empire of Zaire [Congo according to the Portuguese], and continued up the Ethiopian [South Atlantic] Sea coast of West Alkebu-lan until he turned easterly on through the Pilar of Herculese [later the Straight of Tarikh or Straight of Gibral Tarikh, today's Straight of Gibraltar][00] along the Mediterranean Sea back to his native Greece.

50   Marcus Antonius [Marc Antonio or Mark Anthony] captured Egypt for the Caesar [King or Emperor] of Rome. There is quite a lot of confusion as to whether this date should be c. 47 or 30 B.C.E. He, through his Ceasar, forced Queen Cleopatra VIII to surrender Egypt and abdicate her throne. Egypt was made a "PROVINCE OF THE ROMAN EMPIRE" following the publication of a DECREE to that effect issued by

---

[0] Formerly part of the African nation called "SENEGAMBIA", a combination of French colonial Senegal and The Gambia of Great Britain. [See Sir Edward Hertslett, THE MAP OF AFRICA BY TREATY, London - 1886, 1889, 1900, 1905; J. Scott-Keltie, THE PARTITION OF AFRICA, London, 1926; George Padmore, AFRICA: BRITAIN'S THIRD EMPIRE, London, 1947].

[00] Note that there are no other records avaiable indicating any other European voyages along East and West Africa's coastline until 1,624 years later, c. 1444 C.E. Also, that Gibral Tarikh [Rock of Tarikh or Tarikh Rock] is now called "ROCK OF GIBRALTAR;" and that, Tarikh was the name of the African Moor who led the first African [Moroccan] military forces in the African-Muslims conquest of the Iberian Peninsula [Spain, Portugal, and part of Southern France] during c. 711 C.E. [See S. Lane-Poole, THE MOORS IN SPAIN; J. Soames, COAST OF BARBARY; J.C. deGraft-Johnson, AFRICAN GLORY; J.A. Rogers, WORLD'S GREAT MEN OF COLOR, vol. I].

268

Julius Caesar - The Holy Emperor of Rome and Colonial North Africa [the "Province"].

47   Julius Caesar reinstated Cleopatra VIII, daughter of Ptolemy XIII [son of African-European parentage], as Queen Of All Egypt. All of the Ptolemies, except Ptolemy I - the former General Soter from Macedonia, were from similar African-European parentage.

30   A Roman, Seutimus Flaccus, crossed the Sahara to reach the Kingdom of Niger, West Africa, around the regions of Lake Tchad [today's Chad]. The report he gave upon his return to his native Rome indicates that he actually saw ancient Ghana. "Western" historians have falsely assigned Ghana an origin of approximately "300 A.D." in their attempt to keep all of the African nations "SOUTH OF THE SAHARA" to a history without pre-Christian origin. Flaccus followed Paulinus, another Roman, who visited the Nothernmost reach of the Niger River in approximately c. 50 B.C.E. [See map of Greek and Roman colonial Africa on the following page].

0 B.C.E.   Roman rule continued in North Africa, Egypt in particular, during the
1 C.E.   Egyptian "Jews" proclamation of the "BIRTH OF JESUS CHRIST," which introduced the "CHRISTIAN ERA" or the "YEAR ONE" of the present calendar used officially by the United States of America. Some historians relate the YEAR ONE to the "BIRTH OF CHRIST," others to the "DEATH OF JESUS CHRIST."

332 B.C.E. – 30 C.E.

Greek and Roman Colonial Africa

From Alexander "The Great" to Julius Caesar

Roman generals Suetonius Paulinus (c50 B.C.E.) and Septimus Flaccus (c. 19 B.C.E.) reached the upper limits of the Niger River around Tombut (Timbuktu). Roman colonial explorer Julius Maternus, after 4 months journey, one more than the others, reached the northern Akan States and Kano (Nigeria)

270

BIBLIOGRAPHY FOR CHAPTER V

Wallis-Budge, Sir E. A., BOOK OF THE DEAD

Arkell, Dr. A., HISTORY OF THE SUDAN

James, G.G . M., STOLEN LEGACY

Muller, Max, EGYPTIAN MYTHOLOGY

ben-Jochannan, Y., AFRICA: MOTHER OF "WESTERN CIVILIZATIONS

ben-Jochannan, Y. and Simmonds, G. E., THE BLACK MAN'S NORTH AND EAST
    AFRICA

Vail, C. H., ANCIENT MYSTERIES

Clymer, S., THE PHILOSOPHY OF EGYPT

Breasted, ANCIENT RECORDS OF EGYPT

Sanford, E. B., MEDITERREAN WORLD

Kendrik, John, ANCIENT EGYPT, Book II

Diognes, BOOK IX, 49

Herodotus, HISTORIES, (as translated by Aubrey de Selincourt)

Hastings, James, ENCYCLOPEDIA OF RELIGION AND ETHICS

Stanley, Thomas, HISTORY OF PHILOSOPHY

Laertius, Diogenen, LIVES OF EMINENT PHILOSOPHERS

Turner, William, HISTORY OF PHILOSOPHY

Frankfurt, INTELLECTUAL ADVENTURE OF ANCIENT MAN

Alexander, D. B., HISTORY OF PHILOSOPHY

Bakewell, SOURCE BOOK OF PHILOSOPHY

Rogers, A. K., HISTORY OF PHILOSOPHY

Botsford and Robinson, HELLENIC HISTORY

Couch, HISTORY OF GREECE

Woodhouse, W. J., THE TUTORIAL HISTORY OF GREECE

Bury, T. B., HISTORY OF GREECE

Thilly, Frank, HISTORY OF PHILOSOPHY

Weber, Alfred, HISTORY OF PHILOSOPHY

Tenneman, W. G., HISTORY OF PHILOSOPHY

Frazier, Sir I., GOLDEN BOUGH (13 vols.)

Rogers, J. A., WORLD'S GREAT MEN OF COLOR (2 vols.)

Petrie, F., HISTORY OF EGYPT

Maspero, G., HISTORY OF EGYPT AND ASSYRIA

Chapter VI: A PICTORIAL REVIEW OF THE ANCIENT AFRICANS OF EGYPT [Ta-Merry] AND OTHER NILE VALLEY HIGH-CULTURES [Civilizations].

This chapter was organized with the objective of showing a PICTURE STORY of various aspect of African art-forms and inscriptions used in architecture, all of which one calls "PRIMITIVE" today in the "Western world." Another aspect is the presenta-tion of many examples of African peoples of the entire Nile Valley who are designated "CAUCASIANS, NEGROIDS, HAMITES, SEMITES, BANTUS, NEGROES, BUSHMEN, HOTTENTOTS, PYGMIES," etc. by certain "LIBERAL" and "ORTHODOX AFRICAN-IST AUTHORITIES ON AFRICA," but, with the expertise of comparative objectivity in order to show the RACIST basis behind these classifications.[1]

One will readily notice that the characteristics which allegedly distinguished one "RACE" from another are to be found in abundance in all of the other RACIAL groups. For example: The ancient indigenous Africans of Ta-Merry [Kimit, Sais, Egypt, etc.] have been,for the past one hundred [100] to two hundred [200] years,labeled "Caucasoid" and "Semitic" by European and European-American "orthodox" historians and other "educators." Ethiopians, on the other hand, are labeled "HAMITIC;" whereas, the Afri-- cans next door in Zaire [Kongo or Congo] are called "BANTU, PYGMY, FOREST NE-GRO," etc. Strange as it may seem, the Africans located between the Egyptians and the Ethiopians are called "NUBIAN NEGROES." But, the facial expressions in the many pictures and photographs of these Africans, that special SOMETHING which is supposed to make one "HAMITIC, SEMITIC" or "CAUCASOID " is equally as strong among the indigenous Africans who -allegedly - live remotely from each others[2] - the so-called "AFRICANS SOUTH OF THE SAHARA," NEGROES, NEGROIDS" and/or "BANTUS."

On page 291 Egyptians of royal lineage are compared with their fellow African peers of Nubia in the NORTH against their equal. in the Kingdom of Monomotapa [ne-fariously renamed "the Republic of South Africa"][3] at the SOUTHERN end of Alkebu-lan [Africa]. This was purposefully arranged, in order to see what is the "PRIMITIVENESS"[4] of the indigenous African SOUTHERNERS to those of the NORTH. However, the NORTH.-ERNERS are not generally shown in the same manner as the type of pictures selected in this volume. Only those who are descendants of the invaders from Europe and Asia are generally shown by "Western" historians and other educators. The purpose of this unusual arrangement of the pictures is to give the impression that the NORTHERNERS [Egyptians, Numidians, Libyans, Nubians, Khart-Haddans, Maueritanians] and SOUTH-

ERNERS were very much alike in physical appearance. On the other hand, the manner in which they are shown by "Western Africanist" historians is to give the impression that the NORTHERNERS never passed through the same stages of development the SOUTHERNERS of Zimbabwe and Bonyoro did, equally of their fellow Africans of Kush and Punt. These factors are also seen in the presentation of the different types of structures built by each group under different natural conditions.[5] One will also notice that the homes which the SOUTHERNERS are associated with are always called "HUTS" or "MUD HOVELS;" yet, they also developed the type of major structures seen in the "ZIMBABWE HOLY OF HOLIES" on page 287. There could be no doubt that this type of structure is equal in engineering and architectural greatness as the pyramid structures of Ta-Merry and Ta-Nehisi, also the City-State of Carthage shown on page 311.

It is readily seen that the indigenous African High-Cultures branched out from a central point along the Great Lakes,[6] where they built their first pyramids.[7] From this base outwards the pyramids, just as the temples and other structures shown in the Zimbabwe metropolis on page 289 of this volume, increased in size, quality, and quantity.[8] They also show signs of the Africans progressive development as they traveled in a NORTHERLY direction along the Nile Valley [from Uganda to Egypt], or SOUTHERLY along the Great Lakes and the rivers that connect them [from Uganda to Monomotapa].[9]

The only mark of SEPARATION, or DISTINCTION, between the indigenous Africans traveling NORTH to Ta-Merry [Egypt], and those traveling SOUTH to Monomotapa, is that the NORTHERNERS [thousands of years later] had been able to maintain much more successful armies against their natural enemies ; therefore, they had much more leisure for making their High-Cultures perfect. As such, the NORTHERNERS were able to force some of their fellow indigenous Africans to their SOUTH into servitude at various periods that amounted to a sort of "BRAIN DRAIN".[10] Yet, most of the NOTHERNERS craftsmen, natural resources, and manufactured goods came from the SOUTH, from as far SOUTH as Punt[11] [where today's Kenya, Somali Republic, and "French colonial Somaliland" are located].[12] The SOUTHERNERS growth was, therefore, stymied; but, they developed the necessary science, mathematics, engineering, architecture, religion, philosophy, and other disciplines which produced the "GREAT HOLY OF HOLIES" of Zimbabwe - with its cone-shaped tower and artistic excellence. The GREAT ZIMBABWE'S art and sculpture in some degree exceded that of Egypt, Ethiopia, Numidia, Nubia, and all other

African nations more commonly known to the average "Westerner," is not listed as one of the "WONDERS OF THE WORLD." Why? Because those who render such Kosher Seal Of Approval did not in the past, and do not now, consider this African High-Culture of antiquity the development from the genius of the African people they still consider less than human. Thus, they can only compromise that it was built by Africans "...WHO ARE DEAD...." But, at first they attributed it to "SHIP-WRECKED GREEKS," followed by "MAROONED CHINESE MARINERS," and "EARLY CAUCASIAN SETTLERS OF PRE-HISTORIC AFRICA."

Everywhere along the more than four thousand and one-hundred [4,100] miles long Nile Valley and River the indigenous African of antiquity ["Negro, Pygmy, Black" or Bantu"] built pyramids which remind mankind today of the common heritage of the in-digenous African population that produced them. As one travels from the same starting point [the Great Lakes] to the SOUTH similar types of reminders exist in the High-Cultures and Religions of these Africans. [14] This TRUTH was much more obvious even up to the arrival of the first so-called "EUROPEAN" and "EUROPEAN-AMERICAN CHRITIAN MISSIONARIES" and their "ASIAN MUSLIM" counterparts that preceded them in the destruction of most of the rich HERITAGE that was once a part of the "GREAT AND GLORIOUS ALKEBU-LAN" [15] [which the Greeks and Romans corrupted with the name "Africa"].

Why is that professor Jeffreys' "MODERN MAN" cannot see the obvious parallels among all of Alkebu-lan's HIGH-CULTURES? For the same reason that it took LIFE and LOOK magazines, along with hundreds of other American publications of similar projection, so many generations of continued existence to publish a few weeks of major articles on the contributions of African-Americans IN, and TO, the United Sattes of America. [16] For the same reason it was not told nationally and internationally that many indigenous Africans, like their European counterparts, came to the so-called "NEW WORLD"[0] ["Western Hemisphere] as explorers - such as Pietro Olonzo Niño [Capitain or Admirante Colon's flagship - the SANTA MARIA], when the first Europeans arrived [not discovered] in the Caribbean, which they misnamed "WEST INDIES" and willfully and maliciously called the people "INDIANS."[0] The Africans role in the Americas was

---

[0] Like the so-called "AMERICAN INDIANS," the "CARIBS" and other indigenous people of the Caribbean were virtually exterminated by European colonizers and slavers. This genocide was committed under the banner of "CIVILIZATION" and CHRISTIANITY."

equal in time [c. 1492 C.E.] to that of the Europeans, and before them.[17] It is equally the same reason Francesco Buwato,[18] the founder of the City of Brooklyn [presently a Borough of New York City], was not publicized, Henri Pointe du-Sable,[19] the founder of the City of Chicago, Illinois; both have been kept secret from America's school children, there being no difference in the fact that Phoebe Francus [or Frances],[20] daughter of the original proprietor of "FRANCUS TAVERN" of Lower Manhattan, New York City, New York, Samuel Francus [a black man from the caribbeans], who saved the "FATHER OF THE UNITED STATES OF AMERICA" - George Washington from being poisoned by Thomas Hickey,[21] Washington's most trusted body guard - an agent of the British army, and countless other historical fetes performed by other Africans who were still slaves to the European-Americans and Europeans in the British, French, and Spanish colonies that later became the "UNITED STATES OF AMERICA." What is it called? Everyone knows, or should know, that it is politely titled "...SELF-CENTERED EGOTISM" and friends; to the less sophisticated it is plain old "RELIGIOUS BIGOTRY" and "WHITE RACISM." This is the reason Africans with thin nose, thick lips and straight hair suddenly, for the past one-hundred [100] years, and moreso for the last fifty [50] years, have been made "CAUCASOIDS, HAMITES, SEMITES, NILOTS, BUSHMEN, HOTTENTOTS," and a host of other forms of special RACIAL stereotype characters to be preserved in the minds of "MODERN MAN'S" RACIST VOCABULARY.[22] Yet, at one time when the Tigris and the Eurphrates valleys[23] were still claimed as the "...ORIGINAL HOME" [Garden of Eden] "OF MANKIND," all of the Africans and their descendants - regardless of the shape of their NOSE, texture of HAIR, size of LIPS, and color of SKIN, and whatever else, were considered the same: "NEGROES" and/or "NIGGERS." At that period in history Europeans and European-Americans had no trouble in accepting Herodotus' description of the Africans; nor did they condem others who stated that the indigenous Egyptians were like any other African one could find in East, West, South or Central Africa [Alkebu-lan]. One must be reminded that "THICK LIPS, WOOLLY HAIR, BURNT SKIN" and "BROAD NOSE" were attributed to the Colchians, Egyptians, and Ethiopians by Herodotus[24] and other Greeks and Romans before and after him. Strange as it may seem, what had been established in history for over two thousand [2,000] years to be Egyptian physical ["RACIAL"] characteristics suddenly disappeared in the teachings of European and European-American educators of various disciplines having to do with "MANKIND" and "RACE" in the late 19th Century.

MAN, the habitually egotistical teacher, has taught himself certain basic philosophical concepts beyond his own physical power and capabilities.[25] That is, because he is a DREAMER who looks for solutions beyond the realities of his everyday being. One such teaching that came down to "MODERN MAN" [professor Jeffreys and others "CAUCASIAN MAN", the "GREAT WHITE RACE"] from the teachings of the ancient African philosophers of the Nile Valleys, Great Lakes regions, Southern and Western Alkebulan through their students [Hebrews, Christians, Judaeo-Christians, and Muslims], is:

"THE TRUTH SHALL SET YOU" [mankind] "FREE."

But the same "TRUTH" may not "SET YOU" [White man] "FREE" after "YOU" have already enslaved YOUR African fellow human being , who found out that his ancient African brothers coined the phrases:

"MAN KNOW YOURSELF" and also "EAT DRINK AND BE MERRY
FOR TOMORROW WE DIE."[26]

But, we will not "DIE" until "TOMORROW." Yet, "TOMORROW" may never come in time. It will come at time. TIME in this sense being the unmeasurable distance for the African, African-American, African-Caribbean, and all other peoples who have claimed African heritage; yet, more specifically those who have had to suffer the humiliation of the SLAVE TRADE, STUD FARM, COTTON FARM AND OTHER FORMS OF PLANTATION LIFE, RAPE BY THE SLAVEMASTERS, GENOCIDE, and worst of all - CULTURAL DEGRADATION OF BEING TOLD "YOU PEOPLE HAD NO HISTORY."

The following examples, just a drop in the bucket so to speak, of the contributions made by the indigenous African peoples to WORLD CIVILIZATION are basic to the original peep man took into the elementary concepts of life and the universe around. Yet, it is from these original concepts and precepts that the Africans developed in their CIVILIZING OF THE ENTIRE WORLD. CIVILIZING: Not in its typically perverted usage by so-called "MODERN MAN;" but, in the sense of the introduction of ALKEBU-LAN'S HIGH-CULTURE to Asians and Europeans who had other developments which were quite dissimilar. These works are from the genius of the ancestors of people who are rejected from human society [CIVILIZATION] because of their "THICK LIPS, WOOLLY HAIR, BROAD NOSE, AND BURNT SKIN" - people who are called "NEGROES, BANTUS, NEGROIDS, HOTTENTOTS, NILOTS, AFRICANS SOUTH OF THE SAHARA, NIGGERS, FORREST NEGROES, CRIME IN THE STREET, PRIMITIVES, SAVAGES, CANNIBALS, HEATHENS," etc., only to mention a few of the degrading names reserved for them.

276

ALPHABETIC SIGNS.
HIEROGLYPHS

a	á	ā	y	u	b	p	f	m	n	n	r	r, l	h	ḥ	kh

s	ś	sh	k	q	g	t	d	ṭä	ṭ	dj	i	ch	m	u

SYLLABIC SIGNS

au	ur	mer	āa	neter
ab	ba	mes	ua	ka
ānkh	gem	nu	pa	sha

Maāt-ka-Rā, Hat-shepsut-chnem-Āmen   (Hatshepsut).

Neb-peḥti-Ra, Āāḥ-mes I (Amasis).

Religious scenes and writing (1st Dynasty).

Note: Royal names (3rd set from the top) were placed in catouches. Try to decipher the names in the catouches from the above alphabet.

IRELAND AND GREAT BRITAIN	MAYAS CENTAMERs MEXICAN	EGYPTIAN		IRELAND AND GREAT BRITAIN	MAYAS CENTAMER & MEXICO	EGYPTIAN
			29			
			30			
			31			
			32			
			33			
			34			
			35			
			36			
			37			
			38			
			39			
			40			
			41			
			42			
			43			
			44			
			45			
			46			
			47			
			48			
			49			
			50			
			51			
			52			
			53			
			54			
			55			

Note: There is actually fifty-five different Hieroglyphic symbols, words, and/or letters above, all of which predated everyone related to Greece and Rome; yet, it is the Greeks and Romans "Westerners" give constant credit for being the "ORIGINATORS OF WESTERN CIVILIZATION." From the above roots much of what is loosely called "WESTERN CIVILIZATION" receive its origin. Needless to mention the role the Africans played.

278

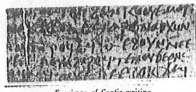

ግርማዊ፡ቀዳግዊ፡ኃይለ፡ሥላሴ፡ከቡር፡ሚስተር፡አርተ
ር፡ኤል፡ሪቻርድር ፡ላደረጉት፡ንግግር፡መልስ፡ሲጡ፡

His Imperial Majesty called H. M. S.
ETHIOPIA a sign of the continuing friendship
between the governments of Ethiopia and
the United States

Specimen of Coptic writing.

Specimen of Amheric writing.

Specimen of Demotic writing.

The different specimen of indigenous African writings shown on the two preceding pages are best demonstrated in inscriptions on the following page. Here
the Africans artistic creation in writing and architecture are harmoniously matched. The graphic presentation of history, philosophy, science, religion and other
disciplines related to many of the Pharaohs and Gods of the XVIIIth Dynasty are
meticulously recorded on the colums of the temple shown on the following page;
these being no different in quality or beauty than the inscription on the so-called "ROSETTA STONE" shown on page 281 following.

The Amheric characters shown above, equally those of the Coptic, are just
two more types of the writings created by the Nile Valley indigenous Africans
for communication between each others for the benifit of all. There are many
other forms of hieroglyphical scripts related to this area of Alkebu-lan which
this volume is not prepare to deal with at this edition; but,hopefully it will meet
this challenge in the following edition if such should be needed.

279

The HYPOSTYLE HALL of the TEMPLE OF AMON, at Karnak.
[A view looking to the southwest]

Built around c. 1555-1340 B.C.E., XVIIIth Dynasty, by the indigenous Africans
of the Nile Valley. Note scale of man to the colossal columns; also inscriptions.
280

The "ROSETTA STONE": The shape and description as it appears in its damaged condition in the British Museum, London, England. This STONE was seized from the French by the British, after the French had stollen it from its African land.

Graphic Reproduction of the "Rosetta Stone"

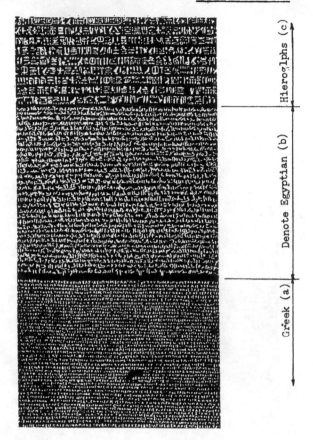

The "Rosetta Stone" was illegally taken from Egypt by one of Napoleon's army officers in 1799 C.E. during the French invasion of Egypt, Africa. It is presently located in the British Museum, London, England.

The inscriptions on the stone are divided into three different languages
- a) The lowest layer of the writings is in Greek.
- b) The middle layer of the writings is in a Demotic Script.
- c) The top layer of the writings is in Hieroglyphic (Egyptian).

In 1822 Jean Champollion, a Frenchman with an extensive knowledge of Greek, was able to read the lowest layer of the stone and compared it with the other two layers, thereby breaking the "mystery" of the language used in Egypt, North Africa, in which most of the history we know about ancient Egypt is written. This foundation laid the groundwork for what is today called "Egyptology" (the study of the ancient civilizations of Egypt).

282

The so-called "EBERS PAPYRUS" of 1550 B.C.E. The earliest known FERTILITY

CONTROL RECIPE. This is one of a compendium of medical inscriptions left by

the indigenous Africans of the Nile Valley, particularly of Ta-Merry, Ta-Nehisi,

Itiopi and Meroe. It is a prescription for a medicated tampon designed to prevent

pregnancy. It requires the following: A mixture of the tips of the shrub of accacia

and honey, made into a tampon and inserted into the vagina as a suppository.

The chemical reaction is that ACCACIA FERMENTATION BREAKS DOWN INTO LAC -

TIC ACID, ONE OF THE ACTIVE SPERMICIDAL AGENTS USED IN CONTRACEPTIVE

JELLIES TODAY.

283

A photographic view (from the north-east) of the ruins of Queen Hatshepsut's Funeary at Luxor [Thebes] or Deir el-Bahri

The splendor of Egypt's architecture is best exhibited in this structure. Modern public buildings fall short of its beauty and colossal magnitude.

HAT-SHEP-SUT, XVIIIth Dynasty, c. 1515 – 1484, the FIRST QUEEN in history to rule over a nation. Limestone statue, Museum of Art.

QUEEN HATSHEPSUT'S EXPEDITION TO THE LAND OF PUNT.[27]

Loading Egyptian boats in Punt.

Punt or Puanit was an indigenous African nation located where today's Somalia, parts of Kenya and Tanzania, also Ethiopia, are. There were many voyages between the Egyptians and the Puanits to each others homeland for various reasons

284

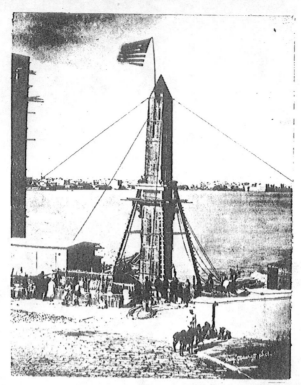

OBELISK OF PHARAOH THUTMOSE III, SUCCESSOR OF QUEEN HAT-SHEP-SUT
[The so-called "Cleopatra's Needle" in Central Park, New York City, N.Y.]

Reconstruction Of Queen Hat-shep-sut's Temple at Luxor (Thebes or Dier el-
Bahri) according to a drawing from G Steindorff and W Wolf 1936 The funerary
temple of Mentu-hotep Nebhepetre (pointed roof) is in the background plane.

Abu Simbel. XIXth Dynasty. Facade of the Great temple from the northeast.[22]

The Temple of Abu Simbel is one of the greatest masterpiece of the indigenous Africans of the Nile valleys (Blue and White). It demonstrates the professional artistry, architectural and engineering genius of the Ta-Nehisians (Nubians or Zetis) that designed and built it for Pharaoh Rameses II, c. 1298-1232 B C E

(6) Round massive tower

(1) Vulture's head; (2) Model of ruins; (3) Oxen; (4) Head of man;   29
(5) Hunt (the hunter is shown as suffering from steatopygia)

From J.C. deGraft-Johnson, AFRICAN GLORY, London,
1954, page 52, etc.

Note the majesty of the architectural beauty and astetic richness of the Africans of Monomotapa, Alkebu-lan. The engineering achievment demonstrated
in this structure has never been surpassed in any of ancient Ta-Merry, Ta-
Nehisi, Itiopi, Numidia, Khart-Haddas or Puanit, etc.

Cameos from the
Bibliotheque Nationale, Paris.

2.

ALESSANDRO DEI MEDICI, Duke of Florence,
Italy, son-in-law of Emperor Charles V of
Austria. Mother African "NEGRO;" father
Cardinal Medici (Medici Palace, Italy).

3

5

Ptolemy XIII (Neus Dionysius),
father of Cleopatra VIII. This
Pharaoh of African-European
origin called himself "THE NEW
NEW OSIRIS."

4

Bougeoir of Marie de Medici,
Queen of France (Lourve).
Descendant of Alessandro.

1

Emperor Lidj Yasu of Ethiopia,
deposed by Ras Tafari Makonnen
(Emperor Haile Selassie).

FIVE PEOPLE OF AFRICAN ORIGIN OR BIRTH
"Caucasian"? "Caucasoid"? "Hamitic"?
1, 2 & 3   4   5

Note: If any of the above was born in the U.S.A. he or she would have been designated a "NEGRO" or "NIGGER." Yet, they are all "CAUCASIAN, HAMITIC,
SEMITIC" or "CAUCASOID" because of their birth in Alkebu-lan or Europe. Why?

288

Right: ANN ZINGHA, Queen of Matamba.
Central African. "NEGRO" or "BANTU"?
Use European-American standard of RACE.

Below: LOCHMAN or LOQMAN, whom the
Greeks called "AESOP," from a print in
the Bibliotheque Nationale, Paris (France)
"Caucasoid", according to European-
American educators of ethnology, etc.

Aesopus Phrix gente. scriptor fabular,
floruit Olymp. 54.

Le R Pere Louis Molina
Jesuite natif de Cuenca en Castille
et decede a Madrid le 11 Octobre
1600. age de 65 ans.

Louis Molina, "great" Catholic reformer
(Bibliotheque Nationale, Paris)
A SPANIARD

Note: Strange as it may seem, only the Queen is called a "NEGRO." Why?

LONG BEFORE "JESUS CHRIST" WAS PRONOUNCED

TO HAVE BEEN BORN   THIS MAN SPOKE OF

A "GOD OF THE TRINITY IN ONE SPIRIT"

Djeser-ka-Rä, Amen-hotep (Amieno- phis) I. [30]

Amen-hotep IV (Akhenaten, Ikhnaten, " The
God Aten Is Content").Pharoah of the XIXth
Dynasty and family seated on their thrones.

    The father of the theory of the "HOLY TRINITY OF GOD" concept copied by the
Christian Church of North Africa, followed by the Christian Church as it established itself in Southern Europe - ROME - after more than one hundred and twenty-five [125]
years in North and East Africa [Egypt, Nubia, and Ethiopia]. The author of many of the
so-called "PSLAMS OF KING SOLOMON OF ISRAEL" written in the Five Books Of
Moses [or Holy Torah, Old Testament, any version]. He was called "THE CHAMPION OF
PEACE ON EARTH AND GOOD WILL TOWARDS MEN" over one thousand [1,000] years
before the birth of "JESUS CHRIST OF NAZARETH." In keeping with this title he reduced Egypt's army to the size of a police force, thereby making his nation the weakest
it had ever been up to his reign; which, eventually, caused Egypt to be invaded and conquered by the Assyrians at a later date during his reign. He preached "MONOTHEISM"
hundreds of years before the birth of another Egyptian African named "MOSES," whom
the Haribu ["Hebrews, Israelites" or "Jews"] adopted and attributed this philosophical
concept. Moses, the hero of the BOOK OF EXODUS - the Second Book Of Moses, was
taught this concept, and many others, at the Grand Lodge of Luxor - where he studied
the "MYSTERIES OF THE OSIRICA" with his other fellow Africans of the Nile Valleys.

290

Mangbetou   CongoQueen

The Congo and Bantu-type
Negroes of Africa are not
related to the Semites and
Hamites of North and East
Africa. They are of the
same racial type as the Forrest Negroes of the Savanah.

OF THE BLOOD ROYAL.
This sister of King Mwami
of Ruanda is a characteristic Watusi having little in
common with the negroid
peoples of Africa."
THE SPHERE February 13, 1937

AUGUST. 1928 THE NATIONAL
GEOGRAPHIC MAGAZINE

THE NATIONAL
GEOGRAPHIC MAGAZINE

The Hottentots, like
the woman above,
have no racial iden-
tity with the Bantus.

KINKY HAIR AND THICK LIPS.
BUT OTHERWISE NOT NEGROD.

THE ETHIOPIANS HAVE PRONOUNCED
SEMITIC FEATURES"

It should not suprise anyone familiar with Alkebu-lan's HISTORY and HIGH-
CULTURE, Particularly that of North and East, that two of the United States of America's most distinguished journals: NATIONAL GEOGRAPHIC MAGAZINE and THE
SPHERE, should overlook the fact that all of the indigenous Africans shown above have
THICK LIPS, BROAD NOSE, WOOLLY HAIR, and BURNT [black] SKIN like the Colchians, Egyptians, and Ethiopians described by Herodotus in c. 457 or 450 B.C.E. But,
since the entire basis of "WESTERN CIVILIZATION" rests upon its Greek and Roman
beginnings in North and East Alkebu-lan [Africa], only the African from "SOUTH OF
THE SAHARA" is called a "NEGRO" or "NEGRESS." The others are closely related to
the "CAUCASIAN, CAUCASOID, SEMITE, and/or "HAMITE" from Europe?

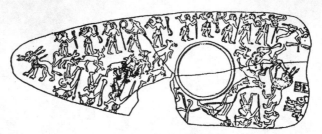

HUNTING SCENE

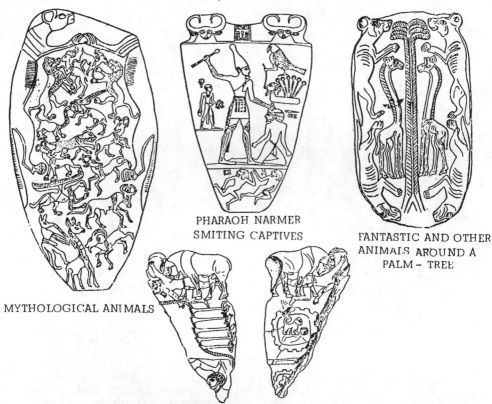

PHARAOH NARMER
SMITING CAPTIVES

FANTASTIC AND OTHER
ANIMALS AROUND A
PALM – TREE

MYTHOLOGICAL ANIMALS

THE PHARAOH AS A BULL TRAMPLING
ON HIS CAPTIVES OR ENEMIES

All of the above art-forms are housed in the Cairo Museum, Cairo, Egypt (UAR).
Just how many of their variations are today called "MODERN ART" is anyone's
rightful guess. They are "PRIMITIVE" when done by Africans, but "IMPRESSION-
ISTIC" when done by Europeans and European-Americans of various schools.

The ba bird
(attached to Royal mummies, represents the soul)

Mirror-case of Queen Hent-taui.

Eighteenth Dynasty inlaid with ivory and wooden, swivel-topped ointment container

Boys of Old Kingdom Egypt playing leapfrog

Note: It is commonly stated that the indigenous Africans of Sais (Egypt) did not understand the ratio and proportion of the human anatomy. Is that pronouncement self-evident in the above pictures.

293

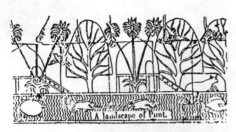

A landscape of Punt.

Symbolical demolition of towns.

Take note of the fact that the indigenous Africans of Punt
also drew their elevations and plans in single-plain projections as seen in the above HOUSE AND GARDEN PLAN.
This method is the same as that used by the Ta-Merrians.
The DEMOLITION scene of the section of the town at the
right is typical of the type of presentation Nile Valley engineers showed on their plans to enable the builders to
have a visual picture of the end result of the work to be
accomplished. Most of the plans and inscriptions followed
this method of Hieroglyphical witing and drawing.

A Nubian and Syrian
to Queen-Pharaoh Hat-shep-
c. 1515-1488 B.C.E. A com-

(king s both) paying homage
-sut during the XVIIIth Dynast
mon scene in Egypt.31

ORIENTAL INSTITUTE. UNIVERSITY OF CHICAGO

The above picture is a compliment of that on p.198 ,show-
ing both an AFRICAN (allegedly Ta-Nehisian or Nubian)
and an ASIAN king as slaves for an AFRICAN pharaoh of Ta-
Merry (Kimit, Sais or Egypt). In most "WESTERN EDUCA-
TORS'" writings and other works it is only the "NUBIANS"
who are always shown as the "SLAVES OF THE EGYPTIANS;"
never the so-called "SEMITE, HAMITE" or "CAUCASIAN;"
but history proved that everyone of the ancient known
WORLD suffered the same fate at the Ta-Merrians MERCY.

An Egyptian drawing water. Scene from a painting in the tomb of Ipui at Luxor (Thebes), XIXth Dynasty. Note so-called   CHARACTERISTICS" of Egyptian.

Egyptians of the NEW KINGDOM PERIOD harvesting with their ploughs and steeds. Note that these so-called "NEGROES" were ordinary Egyptian gardeners, Not SLAVES.

295

The above is a scene from the
BOOK OF THE COMING FORTH BY DAY.[52]
(Egyptian, Book of the Dead)

DEATH MASK of Pharaoh Tut-ankh-Amen with the Goddess of ALL EGYPT represented by the animal-bird and reptile figures. They are : Left, NEKHBET – the Vulture, and Right, WASET – the Cobra Snake. This MASK was made around c. 1349 B.C.E.

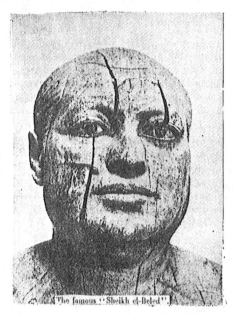

The famous "Sheikh el-Beled"

The famous "Sheikh el-Beled"

The term "Sheik el-Beled" is from the Arabic language meaning "MAYOR".

Note cracks developed in the wood statue over the years.

Ra-hotep and Nefert.

IVth Dynasty Pharaoh and Queen

What about the above Africans is SEMITIC, CAUCASIAN or HAMETIC that is not equally NEGRO, BANTU, NEGROID, PYGMY or AFRICAN SOUTH OF THE SAHARA?

Chapter VII : <u>THE AFRICANS OF KHART-HADDAS [Carthage] IN HISTORY; ITS FOUND-</u>
<u>ING AND ITS DESTRUCTION. A CHRONOLOGICAL OUTLINE AND DATA</u>

Date: B.C.E.   Description

1000   Princess Elissar [Dido][0] and a contingent of her Phoenician male subjects left
from the City of Tyre on the Western shore of Asia and sailed to Alkebu-lan [Africa].
They landed at many ports along the North Alkebu-lan coast with the Mediterranean
until they finally reached Khart-Haddas [The New Town], which was later condensed into what is today called "CARTHAGE."[1]This area of Alkebu-lan is presently the nations
of Algeria, Tunisia, and Morocco. The Phoenicians integrated with the indigenous "NE-
GROES" they met at Khart-Haddas; thus, the thousands upon thousands of Africans integrated the less than one thousand [1,000], at most, Phoenicians into their nation at
the very time when their nation was on its way to become the "MASTER OF THE ME-
DITERRANEAN WORLD." What started out to be a mission of mercy on the part of the
hand full of fleeing Asians with their princess seeking haven, following the death of the
princess' father - the King of Tyre- and control of the Kingdom by her ruthless and
greedy brother, turned out to become an experience in one of the world's most powerful nation of all times.

600   The Carthagenians [Khart-Haddans] established colonies along the coast of
North Africa [Alkebu-lan], Southeastern Spain [Iberian Peninsula], and Northwest
Africa.

500   Admiral Hano [Hanno] was commissioned by Pharaoh Necho [Necku, Neku]
II of Ta-Merry to sail around the continent of Alkebu-lan.[2]

522   Admiral Hano, a Carthagenian of mixed Phoenician [BROWN] and African
[BLACK] stock, with a fleet of Carthagenian ships sailed along the Northwestern coast
of West Africa. The fleet of approximately fifty [50] ships, over two thousand [2,000]
sailors, and a number of colonist settlers journeyed as far South as Rio de Oro [River
of Gold, Gold River], where Admiral Hano established a Carthagenian settlement. He
called this settlement "KERNE." It became Carthage's most important West African
trading post. KERNE is presently called "HERNE" by the Moors, an African people-
the vast majority of whom originated in the area which has been known for thousands of
years as "MAURITANIA."[3]

520   Admiral Hano left Herne for ports farther South, along the Ethiopian [North
and South Atlantic] Sea or Ocean coastline of Africa at what is today Ghana and Sierra
Leone. From this point he proceded to Wouri - today's KAMERUM, KAMEROON, or
CAMEROON.

518   Admiral Hano set sail for his return voyage to Carthage by way of Kerne,
with stops at the other settlements he had established before from c. 522 to c. 518
B.C.E.[4]

[0.] The name "DIDO" was given to Princess Elissar by Virgil in his writings about Carthage. [See Virgil's, STORY OF AENAS].
298

509   Carthage and Rome signed their first "TREATY OF FRIENDSHIP." The Etruscans [Tarquins, later on Romans] and Carthagenians were at this period in history very good friends, both of whom were plotted to conquer Hellas [Pyrrhus or Greece].

500   During the year 500 B.C.E. the Roman Republic was more-or-less established; in recognition Carthage set-up an embassy in Rome. [See account of this historical event in the works of the Roman poet, Livy]. Rome at this period occupied a minute enclave on the Italian Peninsula's West Coast - on the Etruscan Sea. By c. 300 B.C.E. Rome had expanded to at least four-times its original size.[5] It covered an area from the Etruscan Sea across Italy to the Eastern shores on the Adriatic Sea. This was Rome's size up to the beginning of the Samnite Wars. After the Samnite Wars, up to the late half of c. 290 B.C.E., the once tiny Rome occupied more than half of the Italian Peninsula. Rome's expansion was leaping without control, whatsoever. And, by the end of the War with Pyrrhus [Hellas orGreece] in c. 275 B.C.E., Rome had already taken over all of Italy. In other words the City of Rome, in Italy, had become the Nation and Empire of Rome.

What did Rome's expansion meant to North Africa, particularly Carthage [Khart-Haddas]? It meant that an eminent invasion from Rome was but a matter of time. This was obvious, because Sicily, which is a natural geographic part of Italy, was under the colonial control of Carthage.[6] Carthage at this period had become the most feared in Africa, just as Rome was equally feared in Europe. Of course Greece also remained a natural challenge to young Rome. Yet, the Carthagenians had already sent a fleet to help Rome against Greece[7] which held an enclave on Italy's East coast on the Adriatic Sea.

Why was the above true? Because Rome, after the defeat of Pyrrhus [Greece] , took on its victim's cultural, political, and commercial characteristics. The latter development forced Rome to challenge Carthage for mastery of the Mediterranean commercial trading posts around the Tryrrhenia Sea.[0] The area involved formed a triangular enclosure of the Mediterranean Sea that embraced both Rome and Carthage.

With the fast growing commercial expansion of Carthage on the North African coast, from the frontiers of the Greek City of Cyrene Westward to the Ethiopian [North Atlantic] Ocean, Carthage had become the dominant power of the "KNOWN WORLD." As a direct result of said power Carthage began to expand her empire to satisfy her trade needs. The following chronology deals with the periods and events of Carthage's expansion, contraction, and defeat.

Carthage, in approximately c. 600 B.C.E., established [annexed] trading posts in Southern Spain, and seized all of the Spanish silver mines.[8]

Carthage seized the British tin trade with Spain, also control of what is today called the "STRAIGHT OF GIBRALTAR."[9] The "STRAIGHT" and the ports of Southern Spain were closed to all shipping except Carthagenian. All ships not having Carthagenian clearance were rammed by Carthage's warships and sunked. Carthage also maintained her Spanish Zone control and "SPHERE OF INFLUENCE" until c. 550 B.C.E., at which

---

[0]See maps at rear of this volume with respect to the 3rd Century B.C.E.

time Rome signed a treaty with her, which excluded Rome's trading rights in the Carthagenian area. [See Polybius', HISTORY, 400 to 370 translated]. The "TREATY" regulations finally infuriated the Roman Senate, as Roman merchant ships passing the Straits of Messing to the City of Messina were forced to receive Carthagenian clearance. The Mediterranean Sea had became in reality, a kind of "CARTHAGENIAN SEA." The Romans, also, feared the Carthagenians closing the "Strait."

Rome attacked Carthage in c. 264 B.C.E. This was the beginning of the Sicilian War, for the attack had created an insurrection in Carthagenian controlled Sicily, the island being a colony of Carthage at the time. The Carthagenian garrison from Sicily followed the attack and invaded Rome in the latter part of c. 264 B.C.E., and also occupied the City of Messina. They took command of the Straits of Messina away from the Romans. The indigenous Africans had, for the first time, successfully invaded Southwestern Europe and occupied European territories as conquerors.[10] Rome had suffered her greatest defeat to date in history.

The first Roman army to cross over the Mediterranean Sea left Italy in November c. 264 B.C.E. to engage the Carthagenians, whom they had become to despise - for obvious reasons.

The "ROME-SYRACUSE ALLIANCE," in c. 260 B.C.E., had given Eastern Sicily to Rome because of the Roman invasion of the island in c. 264 B.C.E., just four short years before the "Alliance." It was the African colonizers first real setback at the hands of the Europeans. However, just one year later, c. 259 B.C.E., a much better prepared Carthagenian military force under the command of Hamalcair Barca[10] battered the Roman fleet attempting to expand Rome's control over the entire island of Sicily. This defeat had virtually ended Rome's mastery of European naval powers. The Africans had once again become masters of all of the European nations along the Mediterranean seaboard.

In c. 242 B.C.E. Roman donations to the treasury of Rome were speeded up. Rome hurriedly built a new and much more modern naval fleet than she originally had.[11] With a force of 200 battleships of 5 banks of oars each Rome's rebuilt navy met and defeated the Carthagenians in c. 242 B.C.E. This was, in fact, to become the most significant turning point of the Africans of Carthage [Khart-Haddans] military mastery over the Europeans of Rome.[12]

Between c. 242 and c. 241 B.C.E. a somewhat uneasy peace ensued between Car-

300

thage and Rome. This was only possible, because the Romans had forced certain restrictions on Carthage after the Africans were defeated.[13] For example: Rome compelled Carthage to surrender Sicily and other neighbouring islands; and, to pay an almost impossible sum of 3,200 tallents [over three and one/half million - 3,500,000 dollars] within a period of ten years - by c. 231 B.C.E. Thus, after more than twenty-three [23] years of fighting, from c. 259 to c. 241 B.C.E., the first battles of the struggle between Carthage and Rome were concluded. This victory gave Rome her first colony outside the Italian Peninsula. It was the beginning of a series of wars which were later to be called the "FIRST PUNIC WARS." Note that "PUNIC" is the Latin word for Phoenician, the name the Romans called the dominantly African-Asian mixed peoples of Carthage. One has to remember that the original group in the area came to Khart-Haddas and amalgamated with the thousands of indigenous Africans - the so-called "NEGROES" they met there; the Asians being less than 200 to 300 men, women, and children. However, in less than 100 years after the arrival of the Phoenicians with Princess Elissar [Dido], the two groups had become one African-Asian people, their African characteristics being most pronounced due to the overwhelming amount of the indigenous Africans against the Asian settlers. By any sense of RACIAL STANDARD in the United States of America, the Carthagenians[14] would have been classified as the BLACKS, AFRICAN-AMERICANS, who are otherwise called nefariously "NEGROES."

Rome invaded and annexed Corsica and Sardinia in c. 238 B.C.E., only a scant three years after she had made a "PEACE TREATY" with Carthage covering certain limitations which did not include these two territories [island outposts]. But, Rome had also seized Gaul [France] and the Po Valley. Roman power then extended from the Alps Mountain range at the North, and the entire Italian Peninsula down to the Mediterranean Sea at the South.

The Carthagenians, fearing Rome's expansion and new power, invaded Spain anew under the leadership of the world's youngest general in history, Hannibal Barca,[0] who was the son of an equally great Commander and General of Carthagenian military forces during the First Punic Wars, c. 262 B.C.E., named Hamalcair Barca. At this period of his life the younger Barca, Hannibal, was a mere twenty-four [24] years of age, hav-

---

[0] See C.T. Seltman, GREEK COINS: A HISTORY OF METALIC CURRENCY AND COINAGE DOWN TO THE FALL OF THE HELLENISTIC KINGDOMS, London, 1933; also, J. A. Rogers, SEX AND RACE, New York, 1967, vol. I.

ing been born in the year c. 262 B.C.E. He appeared like his image on the coins used in Carthage during his conquest of Iberia and Northern Italy.

In the year c. 220 or 218 B.C.E. General Hannibal Barca launched the first battle of the SECOND CARTHAGENIAN-ROMAN [Punic] WARS, when Roman and Carthagenian military forces clashed along the Spanish-Roman borders. The young African general marched with a combined force of only seventy thousand [70,000] men. Some historians claimed that they were one-hundred thousand [100,000] men, and a few hundred elephants, against Rome's more than three-hundred thousand [300,000] men army. He started in a direction which led him to the East coast of Spain, from whence he had planned to cross over into Gaul [France] at the South and invade Italy from the North.[15]

During the latter part of Autumn c. 218 B.C.E. General Hannibal Barca reached Europe's magnificent and most freightful mountain range - the ALPS. With his very small army having been forced to tackle vicious snow storms, avalanches, narrow precipices with rock-slides being everyday happenings, some with too narrow pathways for the passing of the elephants which required the soldiers to cut passages for them as he continued through the Alps. The savage fighting against the forces of nature and the hostile Europeans who inhabited the mountain ranges [people hardly removed from their cave-dwelling days], also, became part of the general's daily problems. The worse of these obstacles were the mountain dwellers, who were constantly hurling down monsterous boulders [giant stones] along the mountain-sides and pricipices on the passing Carthagenian soldiers and elephants, forcing the Africans to engage in numerous bitter battles with the European mountain peoples all along the way to the Po Valley.

One solid year of wretched calamities sapped General Hannibal Barca's forces of what was originally seventy to one-hundred thousand Africans. And, by the time of his arrival out of the Alpine Pass in c. 217 B.C.E. into the Po Valley, Italy, more than the astonishing figure of thirty-six thousand [36,000] of his best soldiers were killed through one mean or another, leaving him with a total striking force of thrity-four to seventy thousand half-starving, frost bitten, and weather-worn soldiers to face the world's most feared armies of mighty Rome.[16]

After one year of exhaustive preparations [from c. 217 to c. 216 B.C.E.] the young general, Hannibal, was ready for the big push into the heart of Rome with many of the pacified Romans. He attacked Rome's greatest general, Flamius, who lost his fortresses and the Apennines. Hannibal followed the defeat of Flaminus by systematically cutting the Roman Legions into pieces at the shores of Lake Trasimene. The entire Roman army suffered its most humiliating defeat in this battle. The Consul was himself killed in the battle. Hannibal was now only a few days march from the "GATES OF ROME." But, his army was too weak to begin the seige of the Roman fortresses guarding the Eternal City. He was forced to fight a few other battles to create some diversionary moves to incduce further desertions from the Romans to his side; at the same time, giving his men and animals [elephants mostly] chance to recuperate while expected supplies from Spain could arrive for the big push.

Rome got its first real dictator in c. 217 B.C.E.,[17] when the Roman Senate appointed Fabius "MARSHALL OF ALL FORCES" to stop the indigenous African invaders and their commander General Hannibal Barca. Fabius engaged Hannibal in a few small delaying battles. However, in the meantime Rome was also rebuilding her new army and extending her naval fleet. The people of Rome, in the meantime, was growing angry with the tactics of Fabius - who they mockingly gave the name "THE CUNTATOR" [laggard].[18]

By the year c. 216 B.C.E. the Roman consuls had organized a new and modern army of more than two hundred thousand [200,000] men from all over their colonies, a striking force of more than four-times the size of Hannibal's total army. The Romans had taken advantage of the fact that Hannibal could not secure supplies or replacements for his army. On the otherhand, the Romans were able to secure as many men as they needed, along with the fact that they had on their side the strategic factor of being on their own territory. Also, in their favor was the fact that all around the Africans there were hostile European captives from various battles General Hannibal Barca was forced to engage with them during his crossing of the Alps. Thus, in c. 216 B.C.E. Rome hurled her newly built army of the North of seventy thousand [70,000] men against the Carthagenian army of a little less than thirty thousand [30,000] men; this started the "BATTLE FOR CANNAE," at the "gates of Rome."

During the Battle for Cannae in c. 216 B.C.E. Hannibal's cavalry chased the Roman horsemen into hasty retreat, which caused the main Roman army to be caught in the center of the two main columns of the Carthagenians on each side, and the Carthagenian elephants [fully equipped] with other members of the cavalry at the rear. Two units of Carthagenian reserves had been held in the rear by the general. These two "FORCES OF DEATH," as they were called by many historians, closed in on approximately fifty-five thousand [55,000] Roman soldiers caught in the trap. By nightfall of the same day the Africans closed in, and every last Roman soldier was annihilated. Historians of this era claimed that:

"ROMAN BLOOD FLOWED LIKE A RIVER..."[19]

during this battle as the Africans slaughtered their trapped adversaries.

Shortly after the Battle for Cannae [c. 216 B.C.E.] Macedonia signed a "TREATY OF ALLIANCE" with Carthage.

General Hannibal Barca [the greatest African general of his era, and reputedly the world's greatest military strategist to date], at age thirty, had made Carthage:

"THE GREATEST SINGLE MILITARY POWER OF THE KNOWN WORLD."

He had defeated the world's greatest military power in many battles, and taken that honour for Carthage from Rome, having destroyed three Roman armies within less than two short years [c. 216 - 214 B.C.E.]. The Africans were again masters of the Mediterranean World; and now, they were masters of Northern Italy. [See map of the Carthagenian [Khart-Haddan] Empire on the following page].

Hannibal had established his mastery as a statesman over all of Northern Italy, as was his military genius, causing most of the allies of the Romans to desert in panic in c. 213 B.C.E. First to desert to Hannibal and the Carthagenians was Northern Italy's entire population. They were followed by many Greek "CITY-STATES" which were under the "sphere of influence" of the Romans. Even Syracuse [in Sicily] forsook Rome and joined Hannibal. Only one Roman State in Southern Italy remained loyal to Rome; Central Italy, which became the core of Rome's nationalism, her senators standing their ground after the most disasterous defeat at that time ever suffered by the Roman armies. Yet, it was not the first time that indigenous Africans had defeated the Europeans in battle. However, it was their worse defeat in their history to date.

By c. 207 B.C.E., after ten [10] long years of African rule over Northern Italy, General Hannibal Barca's core of African invaders and conquerors started to dwindle; for, he was unable to reinforce them with newly seasoned soldiers from Africa.[20] As such, he was forced to use deserting Romans and other captured Europeans to supple-
304

ment his African "CRACK-SHOT" elite troops. But, the captured Europeans could not take the rigorous training with the elephants and other military techniques which were employed by the African general.

In c. 207 B.C.E. Hastrubal, Hannibal's brother, was in Southern Spain gathering-up a relief army for Hannibal. He had set forth in the early part of the year with a relief column to link up with the battle-weary Carthagenians. But, Hastrubal's column marched between a Roman army on both sides of a mountain pass which was twice the size of his relief column. The Romans swooped down upon the Spaniards and annihilated every man, including Hastrubal. This defeat was the final turning point of the Africans ["NEGROES" or whatever else] rule over Roman territory in Northern Italy. This marked the beginning of the end of African rule over any other part of Europe until c. 711 C.E., at which time another group of Africans ["Negroes", etc.] invaded and annexed the Iberian Peninsula [Spain and parts of Southern France] under the command of General Tarikh - the African for whom the ROCK OF GIBRALTAR is named - GIBRAL TARIKH or ROCK OF TARIKH, TARIKH ROCK, etc.

During the year c. 203 B.C.E. the Romans finally found a hero in a general who was born, raised, and studied in Carthage. He was trained as an officer in the Carthagenian military school in Carthage, North Africa [Alkebu-lan], the same school from which Hannibal also graduated. This man was the renowned General Scipio [Africanus] Nasica. The same Scipio, who had defeated Carthagenian military forces twice before, having been sent earlier to Spain by the Roman Senate to cut off the chief supply of money and men from Carthage passing through the Iberian Peninsula to Hannibal at the "gates of Rome." Scipio was very much aware of Hannibal's predictment. Most damaging of all; he, also, knew Carthagenian military strategy.

Having convinced the Roman Senate in c. 203 B.C.E. not to attack Hannibal in Northern Italy, where he still remained in total control, Scipio was allowed to invade Carthage instead, which he did with the greatest of success. This forced Hannibal to hurriedly retreat from all of Northern Italy to his native Carthage in North Africa for its defense. His African and European troops in Italy were left there; for, it would have taken at least one year to retreat the entire army through the same route from whence they had come originally. It was the only way opened to them which they would not have had to fight inch by inch to the Mediterranean Sea and across its waters to Carthage - at the shores of North Africa.

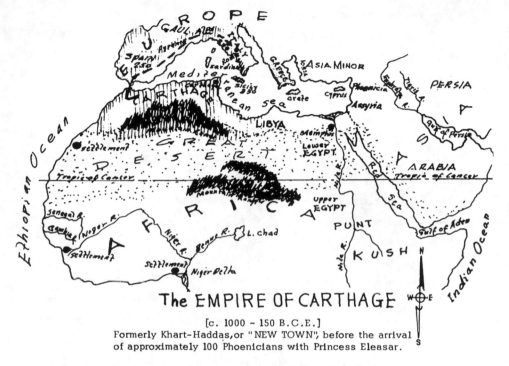

The EMPIRE OF CARTHAGE

[c. 1000 - 150 B.C.E.]
Formerly Khart-Haddas,or "NEW TOWN", before the arrival
of approximately 100 Phoenicians with Princess Eleasar.

● Carthaginian settlements in other parts of Alkebu-lan (Africa).
1. Carthage founded by indigenous Africans of Khart Haddas and incoming mi-
   grants from Phoenicia, Asia (todays Middle East) in c. 1000 B.C.E.
2. Khart Haddas became independent under the name of Carthage with a population of African-Asians in c. 850 B.C.F., Africans being the dominant numbers.
3. Carthage considered a "Phoenician Tributary," Sidom and Tyre also; all to be
   ruled by the Assyrians and Chaldeans. The African-Asian population of Carthage rejected proposal and was never ruled by either Asian nation, 700-650.
4. Carthaginian fleet defeated by Greek fleet,causing subsequent wars, 450-410.
5. Carthaginians conquered Sicily in c. 350 B.C.E. Phoenicia captured by the
   Greeks and made a PROVINCE OF GREECE up to fifty years later.
6. Spain became a PROVINCE OF CARTHAGE under Hamilcar Barca (father of Hastrubal and Hannibal). The beginning of the FIRST PUNIC WAR or Carthaginian-
   Roman War, c. 250 B.C.E.
7. General Hannibal Barca and his African and African-Asian military troops,
   along with several hundred elephants, entered Europe through Spain, and
   crossed the Alps Mountain in his vain attempt at conquering Rome.
8. Carthaginians expelled from Spain after Hastrubal's defeat. Carthaginians
   annexed Sardinia after treaty with Rome and caused the SECOND PUNIC WAR
   in c. 200 B.C.E.

In c. 202 B.C.E. the big "SHOW DOWN" finally came. But, General Hannibal Barca had returned to a Carthage [Khart-Haddas] whose army was allowed to carouse and grow fat and lazay while he was still fighting at the "gates of Rome" with haggard-out troops. His only experienced and battle-ready troops were all "striking at the gates of Rome" in the presence of equally prepared Roman troops, all of whom he was in need of in Carthage, not one of whom it was possible to bring back with him.

Hannibal Barca, determined as ever to defeat Rome after he had taken care of the war at home, met Scipio Nasica and the most powerful Roman military striking force ever assembled up until that date; they were also joined by an almost as powerful force of fellow Africans from the neighbouring state of Carthage - NUMIDIA, Carthage's historical enemy. This was the historic beginning of the BATTLE OF ZANA. It was yet to become the final battle between the Carthagenians and Romans...,

"THE BATTLE FOR THE SUPREMACY OF THE MEDITERRANEAN," the battle in which the Romans and Numidians under the command of General Scipio Nasica [an indigenous African, "NEGRO," etc.] fought solely indigenous Africans of Carthage under the command of General Hannibal Barca [an indigenous African, "NEGRO," etc.]. Over one-hundred thousand [100,000] men died in this military engagement, most of them unseasoned Carthagenian trainees - the core of the Carthagenian army having become aged, overstuffed, and unable to give leadership to the young recruits.

Just before the final surrender ultimatum was rendered to the Carthagenians General Hannibal Barca escaped a trap set for him by General Scipio Nasica. But, the old and 'FOXY" general, Hannibal, was set on regrouping for another try at the overwhelming joint military combine of Rome and Numidia, an impossible task. However, by c. 201 B.C.E. all of Carthage's ability to defend itself was already depleted. Carthage was compelled to come to the PEACE TABLE. The Carthagenians were forced to pay Rome "TEN THOUSAND TALENTS," a little better than eleven million [11,000,000] dollars in a period of approximately fifty [50] years. By c. 151 B.C.E. Carthage was forced to surrender all ships of war, except for ten triremes.[21]

The worse of Carthage's humiliation was that she could not wage war in her defense against any nation, even her traditional enemy - her sister state Numidia, without the consent of Rome; nor was she allowed to conduct any foreign trade without first obtaining sanction from Rome. In other words, Carthage had no independence in anything;

for all practical purposes she had become a COLONY of the Roman Empire. Carthage
had become the new "GATEWAY" for the Roman Empire in North Africa [Alkebu-lan].
Northwest Africa had become the victim of it's first European invaders. And, thousands
of Carthage's sons were left at the "GATES OF ROME" in middle Italy to do the best
they could for their own survival.[22] Survived they did, as they abondoned their futile
mission and amalgamated into the general Italian or Roman population.

During the year c. 201 B.C.E. the Romans demanded that their African COLONY,
Carthage, must expell General Hannibal Barca, a constant threat to the Roman High
Command in North Africa. He was at this period of time at the ripe old age of fifty [50].
He was deported, reluctantly so, to the East - somewhere around Egypt and Libya.
From his exile, however, he continued his fight against Rome by stirring up the suc-
cessors of the Macedonian Alexander II ["the great"], rulers of Egypt [Ta-Merry, Kimit,
Sais, etc.], in a plan for a combined invasion on Rome with Greek and Egyptian forces.[23]

"CARTHAGE MUST BE DESTROYED." This was the persistent cry of Senator Cato
at the end of each and every speech he ever made following Carthage challenge of Roman
domination of Mediterranean trade. It was the same manner in which he ended the last
one during c. 146 B.C.E., some fifty-five [55] years after Carthage's surrender to
Rome. WHY? Because Carthage had prospered back into a powerful nation, inspite of
the extra heavy burden of the tributes which was placed upon her by Rome. Cato and
many more Roman senators, business entreprenuers, and others, were afraid of the
Carthagenians recapturing Rome's dominance over the Mediterranean Sea. At the same
time Carthage was also in fear of Numidia, her historical enemy in North Africa, joining once more with Rome against her, she knowing very well her plans for challenging
Rome; as, the Numidians had for more than twenty [20] years out of the fifty-five [55]
years of Roman subjugation of Carthage attacked Carthagenian merchant ships, a condition which Rome condoned and in some instances supported. The Carthagenians had
to invade Numidia anyhow, which was in direct violation of their treaty agreement with
Rome after their defeat during the Battle of Zana. The provision of the "TREATY OF
THE BATTLE OF ZANA," at least one of them, was that:

> "CARTHAGE SHALL MAKE NO WAR AGAINST ANY OF HER
> NEIGHBOURS WITHOUT THE SANCTION OF ROME...," etc.

But, it was impossible for the Carthagenians not to have attacked the Numidians, regardless of the "TREATY" agreements, especially since the Romans encouraged the Numi-

308

dians to violate the same provisions.

In the year c. 149 B.C.E., after Carthage had attacked Numidia, the Roman Senators [many of whom had encouraged Numidia's attacks on Carthagenian shipping] decided to once and for all times "DESTROY CARTHAGE," following the lead of their elder statesman - Senator Cato, the arch exponent of the "CARTHAGE MUST BE DESTROYED" syndrome which had finally become a common cry throughout all of Rome. Rome called Carthage to task for the "TREATY VIOLATION." Carthage refused to be a willing party to her own destruction and further colonization at the hands of the Europeans from Rome and the Africans from Numidia. The Carthagenians defiance was met with a monst rous attack on Carthage by the Europeans and the African allies in c. 146 B.C.E. The Beginning of the THIRD PUNIC [Carthagenian-Roman-Numidian] WARS were launched in full force. These wars, or battles, were fought in the most vicious forms of man's hatred for his fellowmen for three most horrible years [c. 149-146 B.C.E.]. The atrocities were equal on both sides. For the Africans the war meant GENOCIDE. For the Europeans and the other Africans it meant their military integrity and commercial dominance over the Mediterranean Sea and all of its trading ports.

By the end of c. 146 B.C.E. Rome and Numidia had sufficiently destroyed Carthage's man-power and cut off her trading routes, to the extent that the Carthagenians could not secure basically needed supplies from the "outside world." Cut off from the "outside world," the Carthagenians made their last stand. Reduced to a mere police force, the fearless Carthagenian army [what was left of it] fought the Romans and Numidians until the battleground became the public streets of the City of Carthage, where the struggle took place from house to house. But, the ill-armed, ill-fed, and ill-clothed Carthagenians, with no place to gain added supplies, found it impossible to stop the combined African-European forces of Rome and Numidia. The end of the once great "PEARL OF THE MEDITERRANEAN" was about to become a reality.

The time had come, the year c. 146 B.C.E., the Romans finally set fire to Carthage [Khart-Haddas], destroying all that physically remained which were combustible. But the passion and loyalty of the Carthagenians for their beloved City caused thousands upon thousands of them to toss themselves in the firery grave of the burning city, rather than submit to Roman mercy and live under foreign rule [colonialism].

During c. 146 B.C.E., following the end to the smoldering smoke from the furnace which Carthage became, the Europeans annexed what was left of the nation, thereby reducing it to a mere "ROMAN PROVINCE." So ended the only true rival Rome had in the Western Mediterranean world until the Arab Muslims chased the Romans out of North Africa. It was a struggle which lasted for approximately one hundred and twenty [120] years - c.266-c.146 B.C.E. Senator Cato's fanatical cry that echoed in the halls of the Roman Senate year after year,

"CARTHAGE MUST BE DESTROYED, CARTHAGE MUST
BE DESTROYED, CARTHAGE MUST BE DESTROYED."

had become a historic reality. Carthage [Khart-Haddas, The New Town] was in fact "DESTROYED." Senator Cato was satisfied. The beginning of the end to indigenous African ["NEGRO" or whatever else one desires to call them] rule in North Africa had been placed in motion. It proved to be the beginning of the end to indigenous African rule over the entire continent the Europeans of Rome and Greece give the name "AFRI-CA", which other ancient peoples called "ETHIOPIA, LIBYA, ORTYGIA, HESPERIA, OCEANIA," and a host of other names, each forgetting that the indigenous people - MOORS and ETHIOPIANS - called it "ALKEBU-LAN.

If one is to read other works on this and other African subjects, such as the author's unpublished single volume manuscript titled AFRICA [Alkebu-lan], HER PEOPLES, AND EVER CHANGING MAP, currently being edited for publication, they will show, Chrono-logically, that from the destruction of Carthage in c. 146 B.C.E. the end to indigenous African rule in all of Africa began. This is not to overlook the fact that other groups of Europeans, the Greeks particularly, had already invaded and occupied another African land - Ta-Merry [Egypt] in c. 332 B.C.E. However, the Macedonian-Greeks had de-monstrated in their conquest of the indigenous Africans of Ta-Merry they had also ex-hausted the capabilities of their own war machinery.[24] On the other hand Roman power, at the end of the so-called "Third Punic War," was growing like a monster, destined to devour everything within its path. And, from this juncture [c. 146 B.C.E.] onward, it was all Europeans over Africans until c. 640 C.E. [or 18 A.H.], at which time the Arab Muslims [Moselems or Moslems, sometimes Musselmen] from the Arabian Pen-insula and other points East [Asia] invaded and conqured North Africa to become the new colonizers and slavemasters of both the European slavemasters and their indige-nous African victims. The Arabs did not only turned the tide of European rule in North Africa, but created the avenue by which they and the indigenous Africans ["NEGROES"] were able to become the slavemasters of the Europeans in Spain, Portugal, and parts

310

of Southern France from c. 711 B.C.E. until the 11th Century C.E., some of the African Moors remaining the major power in Iberia [Spain] until the latter part of 1485 C.E. The last of the African Moors were not driven out until seven [7] short years before Admirante Cristobal Colon [Admiral Christopher Colombus] and his Moorish Chief Navigator - the Captain of the Flagship Santa Maria, Don Pietro Olonzo Niño [a native of Morocco or Mauritania, North Africa], set sail to find a shorter route to India and wound up in the Caribbean Sea, which the Europeans have since renamed the "WEST INDIES." The final expulsions of the Moors - Africans, Asians, and African-Asians from Granada, Spain [Southwestern Europe], in 1485 C.E. initiated another chain of victories by the Europeans over the Africans until they were partially checked in 1957 C.E., at which time Dr. Kwame Nkrumah led the African peoples of the so-called "GOLD COAST CROWN COLONY OF GREAT BRITAIN" to a semblance of political freedom under the name of "GHANA," or "COMMONWEALTH OF GHANA," which was later on changed to the "REPUBLIC OF GHANA" in 1958 C.E. Due to the fact that the European imperialist and colonialist North Atlantic Treaty [N.A.T.O.] powers, backed by the United States of America's military might, do not surrender ECONOMIC CONTROL to their former POLITICAL colonies when "INDEPENDENCE" is negotiated, Ghana's attempt at seizing such ECONOMIC CONTROL met with the joint N.A.T.O. powers undermining of her political entity; and finally, they arranged the overthrow of Ghana's most noted PATRIOT and FATHER OF THE COUNTRY - the former Prime Minister and President Dr. Kwame Nkrumah ["the Osagyefo", Savior] by indigenous traitors to Pan-Africanism, many of whom have been forced to flee Ghana already; others are pending in jails for double-crossing their double-crossing compartiots who sold Ghana to the British and American neo-colonialists.

The end of CARTHAGE, formerly the indigenous Africans or "NEGROES" Khart-Haddas or New Town, came to pass; Rome came to pass; the Vandals followed the Romans and passed; but, the present Arabs from Asia came to Carthage and all of North Africa, equally parts of East Africa, and still remain there. WHY? Is it not time for the indigenous Africans to control all of ALKEBU-LAN [Africa] - from North to South, East to West, and Central? If man, "MODERN MAN" that is, claim's land because of biblical and traditional occupancy; WHY NOT THE AFRICAN ["Negro, Bantu, Black African, African South of the Sahara, Hottentot, Pygmy, Bushman, Forrest Negro, Nilot, or whatever else they may be called]? ONE DAY THEY WILL.

311

The GLORY OF CARTHAGE is seen in the artist RECONSTRUCTION of what was once "THE WORLD'S GREATEST METROPOLIS EVER CREATED BY MAN". This was the CITY and CITY-STATE of Carthage [Khart-Haddas] during c. 600-350 B.C.E.

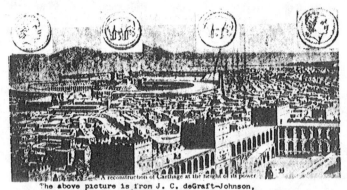

The above picture is from J. C. deGraft-Johnson, "African Glory", p. 68, Watts & Co., London, 1954.
The above likeness of General Hannibal Barca was photographed from one side of the coins used in Carthage during his lifetime. The elephant is on the other side. Why is he projected as a "Caucasian" by European-American educators? Are they not aware of this coin?

BIBLIOGRAPHY FOR CHAPTER VIII

(Use jointly with Chapter VII Bibliography)

Sandford, E. B., THE MEDITERRANEAN WORLD

Virgil, STORY OF AENEAS

Wells, H. G., A SHORT HISTORY OF THE WORLD

de Graft-Johnson, J. C., AFRICAN GLORY

Rogers, J. A., WORLD'S GREAT MEN OF COLOR

ben-Jochannan, Y., AFRICA (Alkebu-lan): HER PEOPLES AND EVER CHANGING MAP

--------------, AFRICAN ORIGINS OF THE MAJOR RELIGIONS ADOPTED BY THE WESTERN WORLD, (Manuscript being edited for publication).

--------------, AFRICA: LAND, PEOPLE, CULTURE (co-author Hugh Brooks and Kempton Webb)

Lane-Poole, S., THE MOORS IN SPAIN

Erskine, Mrs. Stewart, VANISHED CITIES OF NORTH AFRICA.

Soames, Jane, COAST OF THE BARBARY

Chapter VIII: <u>AFRICAN ORIGINS OF "GREEK PHILOSOPHY" [The Myth]</u>??????????

To speak of a "PHILOSOPHY" that is solely the development of one <u>High-Culture</u> or <u>Civilization</u> is to be totally IGNORANT of human migrations and amalgamation down through the centuries. This is especially true in the case of what is being misnomered for over two hundred [200] years "GREEK PHILOSOPHY," particularly when those who created the term, and those that continue its usage, knew or know, that it is without validity - as the Greeks or peoples of Hellades [Pyrrhus, Athens, Macedonia, etc.] were not in existence as a national entity before c. 600 to c. 1000 B.C.E. And, this was thousands of years following the end and beginning of countless African and Asian High-Cultures from whom most of what is called "GREEK PHILOSOPHY" originated. However it is the ORIGINS, at least some of it, from the continent of AFRICA [correctly Alkebu-lan], and by its indigenous sons and daughters - AFRICANS, NEGROES, BANTUS, and even "NIGGERS," found in so-called "GREEK PHILOSOPHY", that this writer examine and point out to his students, researches, and general public which is of the gravest importance at this time. WHY? Because it is the AFRICAN and his AFRICAN-AMERICAN, AFRICAN-CARIBBEAN, and other descendants who are made to feel that they had nothing whatsoever to do with the development of "GREEK PHI - LOSOHY" - "WESTERN CIVILIZATION" except the role of "INDENT"RED" or "CHATEL SLAVES." Thus the following, which is but a very short INTRODUCTION into the contributions of the AFRICAN ["Negro, Ethiopian, Black???]ORIGINS OF GREEK PHILO LOSOHY"?

"THE BASIC THEORY OF PHILOSOPHY IS SALVATION." This was the foundation upon which Egyptian [Ta-Merrian] PHILOSOPHY, as taught in the Osirica's MYSTERIES SYSTEM of the Nile Valley and Great Lakes, was ORIGINATED. "GREEK PHILOSOPHY" [whatever it means], which receive much, if not most, of its concepts from the Africans ["NEGROES, ETHIOPIANS, BLACKS, etc.] of Egypt, Nubia, Meroe, Ethiopia, Puanit, Numidia, Khart-Haddas, and countless other nations from one end of the Nile River to the other, North and East Alkebu-lan [Africa], along with nations of Asia, follows the same FUNDAMENTAL TEACHINGS OF "SALVATION." The Africans of Egypt's Mysteries System [common among all Nile Valley and Great Lakes High-Cultures] most important objective was the ...

"DEIFICATION OF MAN."[1]

Teaching that the "SOUL OF MAN, if liberated from its bodily abode, could enable him

313

to be in reality GOD-LIKE." As such,

> "...MAN WOULD BE AMONG THE GODS IN HIS LIFETIME
> ON EARTH AND ATTAIN VISION IN HOLY COMMUNION
> WITH THE IMMORTALS...," etc.

[See C.H. Vail, ANCIENT MYSTERIES, p. 25; G.G.M. James, STOLEN LEGACY; Sir
J. Frazier, THE GOLDEN BOUGH, 13 vols.; H.W. Smith, MAN AND HIS GODS; S.
Clymer, FIRE PHILOSOPHY; G.K. Massey, EGYPT THE LIGHT OF THE WORLD; Y.
ben-Jochannan, AFRICA: MOTHER OF "WESTERN CIVILIZATION"]. We have noted
that the Judaeo-Christian and Islamic ethics in religion and High-Culture adopted this
very basic of all teachings dealing with "PHILOSOPHY" and/or "RELIGION." It is best
demonstrated in Christendom's "BEATIFIC" customs in "SAINTS, VIRGIN BIRTHS,
RESURRECTIONS, CRUCIFIXION," etc., all of which the indigenous Africans of the
Mysteries System practiced and recorded in their various works thousands of years
before the existence of the first Hebrew or Jew - ABRAHAM, and equally the same
amount of time before Abraham's God-head - "YWEH" or "JEHOVAH."

It was of course Plotinus the Greek, who was first among Europeans to state that:

> "...THE LIBERATION OF THE MIND FROM ITS FINITE CON-
> CIOUSNESS IS SALVATION...," etc.

Yet, this PHILOSOPHICAL concept was nothing new when he uttered it to his fellow
Europeans of Greece, and they to others, as; the "HIGHEST STEP" in the attainment of
KNOWLEDGE in the Mysteries System[2] was the THIRD STEP, defined as the...

> "CREATORS" or "THE SONS OF LIGHT."

This means that the respective candidate reached the point where he could have...

> "IDENTIFY HIMSELF WITH [unite] THE LIGHT'S [wa's] TRUE
> SPIRITUAL CONCIOUSNESS...," etc.[0]

[See W. Marsham Adams, BOOK OF THE MASTER; Sir E.A. Wallis Budge, BOOK OF
THE DEAD AND THE PAPYRUS OF ANI; F. Pete, HISTORY OF PHILOSOPY; Erdman,
HISTORY OF PHILOSOPHY; G.G.M. James, STOLEN LEGACY; Y. ben-Jochannan,
AFRICA: MOTHER OF "WESTERN CIVILIZATION;" AFRICAN ORIGINS OF THE MAJOR
"WESTERN RELIGIONS" - Judaism, Christianity, and Islam].[3]

According to the noted professor on "Greek Philosophy" and history Pietchmann;
the Egyptian "Mysteries System" had "...THREE DISTINCT GRADES OF STUDENTS,"
the THIRD or HIGHEST GRADE have been cited in the previous paragraph. They were

---

[0] Words in brackets [ ] by the author of this volume for clarity only.

as follows:

1.   THE MORTALS: Students on probation under instruction, who had
     not yet achieved experience into the "inner vision."

2.   THE INTELLIGENCES: Students who had attained the "inner vision,"
     and also received "mind" or "Nous."

3.   THE CREATORS or SONS OF LIGHT: Students who became a part
     of the "spiritual consiousness."

In the Osirica's Masonified Mysteries System structure the THREE STEPS were listed
in the following order:

1. INITIATION; 2. ILLUMINATION; 3. PERFECTION. [All of which contained]

"...THE TEN VIRTUES OF ETERNAL HAPPINESS...," etc.[4]

These "THREE STEPS" were not the end to the teachings of the Osirica ; for, beyond
this reach every student had to excell in the "SEVEN LIBERAL ARTS"[5] which were intended to "LIBERATE THEIR SOUL." Above this limit the students were ready to enter
into the "GREATER MYSTERIES " where ESOTERIC PHILOSOPHY[6] was taught to the
THIRD STAGE students, those who had demonstrated a deep sense of proficiency. [See
C.H.Vail, ANCIENT MYSTERIES; G.G.M. James, STOLEN LEGACY; Sir E.A. Wallis
Budge, BOOK OF THE DEAD; OSIRIS; G. Massey, EGYPT THE LIGHT OF THE WORLD;
H. Frankfurt; HISTORY OF PHILOSOPHY; Sir J. Frazier, THE GOLDEN BOUGH , 13
vols.; H. Hastings, THE ENCYCLOPEDIA OF RELIGION AND ETHICS, 8 vols.].[7]

The attainment of the witnessing of the "DIVINE LOGOS" was open to the student
through his[*] proficiency in GRAMMAR [Hieroglyph], LOGIC, and RHETORIC, among
many other disciplines. These three were disciplines of a "MORAL NATURE" by which

"...MAN'S [the student's] IRRATIONAL TENDENCIES OF BE-
HAVIOR WERE CLEANSED OR OTHERWISE PURGED...," etc.

according to the teachings of the Osirica's Mysteries.

All of the values so far cited were adopted into what is today called "GREEK PHI-
LOSOPHY, JUDAISM, CHRISTIANITY, ISLAM, WESTERN CIVILIZATION," and a host
of other misnomers which allegedly contain nothing that the ancestors of the African-
Americans, African-Caribbeans, and even the so-called "BLACK AFRICANS" or AFRI-
CANS SOUTH OF THE SAHARA", contributed. For "GREEK PHILOSOPHY," as it is
today, was allegedly the development and creation of the Greeks and Ionians. The ad-

---

[*] HIS, because the Mysteries System only allowed male students within its societies.

vocates of such a ridiculous claim have carefully removed most of the historical evidence which shows the contrary. Yet, that which remains clearly demonstrates its outgrowth of the teachings Greeks and Ionians learnt while they were students in Egypt, Nubia, and other parts of Alkebu-lan, or while they were taught by students who studied in Egypt and/or by others who taught them outside of Egypt. Said Egyptian professors were not necessarily from Egypt, as many of the teachers and priests of Egypt [Ta-Merry] - equally the Egyptians themselves - they said came from points "FARTHER SOUTH." The Greek students in this case included Herodotus - "FATHER OF EURO-PEAN HISTORY, Hippocrates - "FATHER OF EUROPEAN MEDICINE, Anaxagoras, Aristophanes, Plato, Aristotle, and other so-called "GREEK PHILOSOPHERS" that studied for years in Egypt under African professors and priests. Even the greatest of the so-called "GREEK PHILOSOPHERS," Socrates, studied under African PHILOSO - PHERS that entered Greece from Ionia - at the time an Egyptian colony of the Egyptian Empire.[See page 396 for a partial map of the Egyptian Empire before this period]. But, the ancient Greeks did not label the teachings they learnt from the indigenous Africans and Asians,"GREEK PHILOSOPHY;" such is of very recent origin. [8]

What is the difference between "GREEK" and "EGYPTIAN PHILOSOPHY"? Or; at what point does "GREEK PHILOSOPHY" differ from "EGYPTIAN" or other "AFRICAN PHILOSOPHY" [the philosophical mysteries]? These are only a very few of the questions to be answered "objectively" in this chapter by the rigorous investigation into the following facts which have been carefully edited-out of the United States of America's educational system [public, private, religious: Judaic, Christian, Islamic, Ethical Culture, etc.], in order to maintain the alleged "RACIAL INFERIORITY OF THE NEGRO" and the KOSHER endorsement of the RELIGIOUSLY BIGOTED myth of a "GOD'S CHOSEN PEOPLE;" not one of whom could have possibly fit Herodotus' physical description of the people of Africa [Alkebu-lan] that was mostly responsible for the ORIGINS OF GREEK PHILOSOPHY, those with:

"THICK LIPS, BROAD NOSE, WOOLLY HAIR, AND BURNT OF SKIN."

The answers could not be definitive enough to create a TRUE separation between what is being called "GREEK PHILOSOPHY" and its original sources of origin in Africa [basically among the Nile Valley and Great Lakes Africans] and Asia [with the Tigris and Euphrates Valley peoples that also migrated from as far East as China and Japan]. This fact is very easy to observe, providing a sensible person can look for the second

316

time at the TRIAL and SUICIDE or MURDER of Socrates in a perspective other than
the RACIST and RELIGIOUSLY BIGOTED manner in which it has been, and still is,
presented to all of us within the educational system throughout the "Western World."
In the experience of Socrates, the same being true for many of his other so-called
"GREEK PHILOSOPHERS"- contemporaries,predecessors, and followers, we find him
PERSECUTED and PROSECUTED by the Athenian [his] Government for teaching "GREEK
[Athenian] PHILOSOPHY." One of Socrates' own fellow Greek Philosphers, a contempor-
ary of his, stated, with regards to this point, the following:

> "...SOCRATES IS AN EVIL DOER, WHO BUSIES HIMSELF WITH
> INVESTIGATING THINGS BENEATH THE EARTH AND IN THE
> SKY, AND WHO MAKES THE WORSE APPEAR THE BETTER
> REASON, AND WHO TEACHES OTHERS THESE SAME THINGS...."

The above is clearly documented in the following works: Plato's, APOLOGY, C. 1 - 10,
18, 19C, and 24 B; Aristophanes', FROG;[9] all of which can be had in many translations.
The charge against Socrates was made by Aristophanes around c. 423 B.C.E. However,
Socrates was officially charged by the Athenian [Greek] Government as follows:

> "SOCRATES COMMITS A CRIME BY NOT BELIEVING IN THE GODS
> OF THE CITY [Athens],[10] AND BY INTRODUCING OTHER NEW
> [Egyptian or African][11] DIVINITIES. HE ALSO COMMITS A CRIME
> BY CORRUPTING THE YOUTH...," etc.[0]

Of course, we are to believe that the Athenian Government was trying Socrates for
teaching its own "GREEK PHILOSOPHY," just as we arc to assume that the United
States of America's "PROSECUTION" or PERSECUTION of the Communists during the
1940's through 1960's was due to the Communist Philosophers teaching "CAPITALISM"
and "...CORRUPTING THE YOUTH..." of America with such an AMERICAN PHILOSO-
PHY!

We have noted, those who have studied or in any manner whatsoever dealt with so-
called "GREEK PHILOSOPHY," that Anaxagoras and Aristotle were similarly charged
by the Athenian Government during different periods to Socrates.[12] It is equally note-
worthy that most of them got their basic [elementary] education in Egypt [Ta-Merry,
Kimit, Sais, etc.] and Nubia [Ta-Nehisi, Zeti, etc.] and other Nile Valley High-Cultures,
or from other Africans and Asians, including Europeans, who studied in these nations or
their colonies. In the case of Aristotle, he did not only study in Egypt and Nubia; he

---

[0] Words in brackets [ ] are inserted by the author of this volume for clarity only.

SACKED the libraries and other repositories of the Osirica's Mysteries System and stole an entire collection of works, all of which were/are the properties of the indigenous Africans of the Nile Valley [Egyptian] Mysteries System, and the common heritage of the Africans, African-Americans, African-Caribbeans, and others who are today kept in ignorance of this African contribution to European-America and Europe. Aristotle stole these works after he had entered Egypt with Alexander II ["the great"] in the year c. 332 B.C.E. The fact that he signed his name to many of them as the author, most of which he kept in his own private collection, while others he sent to friends in Greece [Athens] - to which they too claimed "AUTHORSHIP," does not make Aristotle a "GREEK" or anyother type of "PHILOSOPHER." One must also understand that the many works of the Africans he put to the torch or otherwise destroyed[15] would have easily shown that he could not have possibly written the first one, as they would have been in total conflict with the temper of Greek High-Culture during the periods all of the so-called "GREEK PHILOSOPHERS" lived.

The act which Socrates [the only one of the four so-called "PHILOSOPHERS" named who did not go to Egypt to study, but received his education from professors and priests in Ionia and Greece], Aristotle, Anaxagoras, Plato, and others in Hellas [Pyrrhus or Greece] were in fact guilty of doing was the...

"FURTHERING OF THE STUDY AND INVESTIGATION INTO ASTRONOMY AND GEOMETRY...,"

etc., all of which they had to learn during their INTRODUCTION to the Mysteries while they were students in Egypt,[14] or students of others who had been trained in Egypt. These subjects were very basic requirements for students in the FIRST STAGE of learning of the African [Egyptian] Mysteries System. But, such disciplines were foreign to the people of Hellas [Greece] and their government during the era of the so-called "GREEK PHILOSOPHERS." As such, they were very DANGEROUS to the Greek State. And, the State moved against these "FIFTH COLUMINISTS" [as they would be called today] to protect itself by "PROSECUTING" and PERSECUTING those who it felt used said FOREIGN knowledge to undermine its own LAWS, ORDER, and RELIGION.[15]

"SEAUTON GNOTHI" [Man Know Yourself] is an inscription which appeared on the interior walls of temples and pyramids, also on papyri, thousands of years before the birth of Thales, muchless Socrates. Yet, most of the so-called "Western" historians and teachers of philosophy [Greek and others] have willfully attributed its origin to

Socrates who, obviously, copied it directly, or indirectly, from its original source. The works of the following people have clearly pointed out the distortion of the historical origin of this PHILOSOPHICAL CONCEPT with repect to any Greek, Socrates not excluded: F. Heller, HISTORY OF PHILOSOPHY, p. 105; S. Clymer, FIRE PHILOSOPHY; Max Muller, EGYPTIAN MYTHOLOGY; G.G.M. James, STOLEN LEGACY; G. Massey, EGYPT THE LIGHT OF THE WORLD; Sir J. Frazier, THE GOLDEN BOUGH; Y. ben-Jochannan, AFRICA: MOTHER OF "WESTERN CIVILIZATION," Chapter IX; Sir G. Higgins, ANACALYPSIS, 2 vols. But, the depth of this willful DISTORTION was achieved when certain of the "AUTHORITIES" on Africa, particularly Egypt, began to suppress certain documents and artifacts relating to "THE DIAGRAM OF THE FOUR QUALITIES AND FOUR ELEMENTS" [16] in order to attribute it to Heracleitus and a few "IONIC PHILOSOPHERS." These educators, or MISEDUCATORS, know very well that it appeared in the various Nile Valley inscriptions housed in Egypt more than one thousand [1,000] years, at least, before the birth of Heracleitus, and equally as long before the Ionians became literate under the tutelage they received from the Africans of Egypt, Nubia, and Ethiopia. They are well aware that the same "DIAGRAM" shown on the following page was a part of the GRAPHICAL CHARTS used in the Osirica's Mysteries System throughout Egypt and her colonies in Asia-Minor [today's Middle-East] and points farther East - all the way to India. This fact is best demonstrated in the pages of C.H. Vail, ANCIENT MYSTERIES, p. 61; H. Frankfurt, CREATION STORY OF THE MEMPHITE THEOLOGY; THE ROSICRUCIAN DIGEST, May 1952, p. 175; G.G.M. James, STOLEN LEGACY; H. Bagsby, AFRICA BEFORE THE EURO-PEANS; Y. ben-Jochannan and G.E. Simmonds, THE BLACK MAN'S NORTH and EAST AFRICA; Sir J. Frazier, THE GOLDEN BOUGH, 13 vols.

After the indigenous Africans of Egypt and other Nile Valley High-Cultures developed the fundamental "PRINCIPLES OF THE LAW OF OPPOSITES" as "THE UNDERLYING FACTOR OF LIFE IN THE UNIVERSE and applied it to natural phenomena Plato, another so-called "GREEK PHILOSOPHER," came forth with his alleged "THEORY OF IDEAS," which he culminated with "THE REPUBLIC: THE IDEAL STATE." However, this work, allegedly written by Plato himself, is still being disputed as to its authorship, just as it was with Plato's contemporaries when he first published it. The evidence of Plato's PLAGIARISM in "THE REPUBLIC.." etc. is best observed in the references to the "...CHARIOTEERS..." and "...WINGED STEEDS...," all of which were already

DIAGRAM OF THE PRINCIPLE OF OPPOSITES

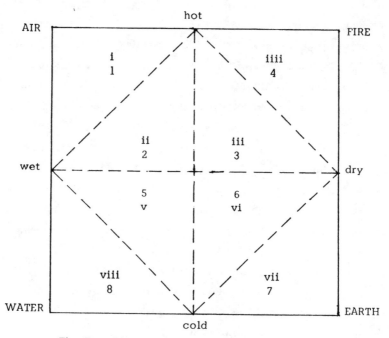

The Four Elements: AIR, FIRE; WATER, EARTH.

The Four Qualities: HOT, DRY; WET, COLD.

THE 8 EQUAL △ POLE STARS

dramatized thousands of years before the birth of Plato in the "Judgement Scene" of
the BOOK OF THE COMING FORTH BY DAY [Egyptian Book Of the Dead and the Papyrus of Ani],[17] where its Egyptian and other Nile Valley Africans origin is obvious. Therefore , when Plato referred to these in his "...ALLEGORY OF THE CHARIOTEER..."
and "...WINGED STEED...", they only gave support to the proof that he copied the
Africans of Egypt works, since neither "...CHARIOTS..." nor "...WINGED STEEDS"
were a part of Greek cultural patterns of development before or during Plato's lifetime;
neither were they a part of the Greeks war machinery, as the Greeks fought their wars
with the Persians and Peloponnesians on the Mediterranean Sea. During this same
period the indigenous Africans of Egypt [Ta-Merry, Kimit, Sais, Mizrain, etc.],
Nubia [Ta-Nehis, Zeti, etc.], Puanit [Punt, Somaliland, etc], Ethiopia [Kush, Meroe,
etc.], and other Nile Valley High-Cultures were the main manufactures of "CHARIOTS,"
and were also known to be...

"THE MOST PROFICIENT OF THE STEED [horse] BREEDERS;"
this the ancients even recorded in the so-called First Book of Moses, GENESIS, Chapter 45, verse 27; Chapter 47, verse 17; also the Book of DEUTERONOMY, Chapter 17,
verse 16; and the Book of KINGS I, Chapter 10, verse 28; in any version of the Old Testament Bible or Holy Torah.[18]

Diogenes Laertius, Favotinus, and Aristoxenus [all of them Greeks] claimed that
Plato's alleged discoveries in his "REPUBLIC" were all to be found in the "CONTRO-
VERSIES" written by Protagoras [c. 481 - 411 B.C.E.], which was during Plato's boy-
hood. These facts are further dramatized in the following works: Diogenes Laertius,
HISTORY OF THE PHILOSOPHERS, p. 311-327; Sir E. A. Wallis Budge, BOOK OF
THE DEAD, Chapter 17; Plato, THE REPUBLIC, III, 415, V. 478, and VI, 490 sqq.;
G.G.M. James, STOLEN LEGACY; Erdman, HISTORY OF PHILOSOPHY; J. Kendrick,
HISTORY OF PHILOSOPHY; and, H. Hastings, ENCYCLOPEDIA OF RELIGION AND
ETHICS, 8 vols.

The last example of the STOLEN AFRICAN SECRETS co-opted by the Greeks from
the indigenous Africans of Egypt and other Nile Valley and Great Lakes High-Cultures,
otherwise called "GREEK PHILOSOPHY," appears in Aristotle's alleged "DOCTRINE
OF THE SOUL...," etc. It must be noted that this PHILOSOPHICAL goal and/or concept is also found in the BOOK OF THE COMING FORTH BY DAY [Sir E.A. Wallis
Budge's English translation is called "The Egyptian Book Of The Dead and Papyrus Of

Ani. See pages 29 - 64 of Budge's works]. In the BOOK OF THE COMING FORTH BY DAY[0]the Africans dramatized the principle and concept of the "DOCTRINE OF THE SOUL" throughout the journey of Ani in his quest for "DIVINE LIFE" and "IMMORTAL-ITY," which he eventually found in AMENTA after his "RESURRECTION FROM THE DEAD;" whereas, in Aristotle's plagiarized work the use of the material is extremely sketchy at most. This of course, did not stop Aristotle's attempt to steal the author-ship of Pharaoh Akhenaten's [Amenhotep IV , XIIIth Dynasty - c. 1373-1357 B.C.E.] "DOCTRINE OF THE UNMOVED MOVER" [Proton Kinoun Akhneton], which came di-rectly from the Memphite Theology's "ATOM", the teachings of the Egyptian SUN GOD another name for "RA."[19] For a more extensive look at this area in African PHILOSO-PHY consult the following works: H. Frankfurt's, "Memphite Theology," in ANCIENT EGYPTIAN RELIGION, C. 20 and 23, also pages 102 - 103; William Turner, HISTORY OF PHILOSOPHY, pp. 141-143; and George G.M. James, STOLEN LEGACY [the entire book].

The preceding revelations are but a very few of the pertinent examples that divulge what is today confidently being sold as "GREEK PHILOSOPHY." Yet, there seems to be no better source of exposure, in many respects, than Sir E.A. Wallis Budge's BOOK OF THE DEAD and THE PAPYRUS OF ANI, equally his OSIRIS and GODS OF THE EGYP-TIANS, along with professor George G. M. James' STOLEN LEGACY.[20] There is no doubt that there are thousands of other major works dealing with this subject which also show the plagiarization of the Greeks with repect to what "WESTERN" educators have been calling "GREEK PHILOSOPHY." However, it is professor George G.M. James, of all of the educators' works which point out the fallacy of a separate body of concepts and principles developed by the Greeks independent of Africans and Asians, who was the only one willing to state flatly [on the title page of his work, "Stolen Legacy"], that:

> THE GREEKS WERE NOT THE AUTHORS OF GREEK
> PHILOSOPHY, BUT THE PEOPLE OF NORTH AFRICA, COM-
> MONLY CALLED THE "EGYPTIANS."

It is understandable, though not at all acceptable, why most "Western" [European and European-American, White "Orthodox" or "Liberal"] historians and pfrofessors of

---

[0] This work by the ancient Africans of the Nile Valley and Great Lakes regions was used by them approximately about 4,11 B.C.E. at least. Certain editing in the work indicates an origin of much greater age than its Ist Dynasty, c. 3200 B.C.E. teachings. Its cor-rect name is "THE BOOK OF THE COMING FORTH BY DAY."

philosophy had to deny the existence of the origin of PHILOSOPHY and other CON -
CEPTS OF HUMAN SALVATION origination by the Egyptians and other indigenous Africans of the Nile Valleys and the Great Lakes regions which they have for so long called
"NEGROES, BANTUS, AFRICANS SOUTH OF THE SAHARA, BLACK AFRICANS," and
even "NIGGERS," or any other group of Africans indigenous of the continent the Greeks
and Romans named "AFRICA," which the Moors and Ethiopians named "ALKEBU-LAN."
This had to be done, that is if the theory of the "...INFERIORITY OF THE NIGGERS"
[indigenous Africans, their ancestors, and their descendants], with respect to their
WHITE EUROPEAN and EUROPEAN-AMERICAN CAUCASIAN-SEMITIC-INDO-
EUROPEAN PURITY image is to be maintaied without blemish of their ever having to
learn anything whatsoever from anyone other than their fellow RACIALLY PURE and
RELIGIOUSLY CHOSEN people of the one and only God that annointed them to take control of the world and all of its peoples. For, to admit that the Egyptians, Ethiopians,
Nubians, Carthagenians, Zairians, Ghanaians, Bantus, Negroes, and others indigenous
to Alkebu-lan [Africa] were responsible for teaching the ancient Greeks and Romans,
the forerunners to European-Americans of the United States of America, would be ad-
mitting that the ancient Europeans were to a major extent "CIVILIZED" [cultured] by
the ancestors of the "NIGGERS" of the United States of America and elsewhere. Upon
such an admission all of the textbooks currently in use throughout Europe, European-
America, Great Britain, and all of the colonies controlled by the masters of the continents and nations mentioned, educational institutions dealing with the origin of SCIENCE,
LAW, RELIGION, PHILOSOPHY, HISTORY, ENGINEERING, MEDICINE, AGRICUL-
TURE, PHARMACOLOGY, and all of the other disciplines not mentioned here, would
have to be totally revised, the vast majority totally discarded. Next to follow would be
the RE-EDUCATION of the entire nation, including most of the "EDUCATORS" who have
willingly and knowingly PLAGIARIZED, DISTORTED, SUPPRESSED, and otherwise
made every contribution by none-European-Americans and Europeans appear to have
been created, developed, or advanced solely by the genius of SEMITES, CAUCASIANS,
INDO-EUROPEAN ARYANS of the Jewish or Christian religions; all, to the glory of
RACIAL PURITY and RELIGIOUS BIGOTRY exhibited in the "CHOSEN PEOPLE" myth.

The following steps must be taken for the re-establishment of the ancient indigenous Africans to take their rightful place in WORLD HISTORY as the contributors who
made what is today called "GREEK PHILOSOPHY" a part of MANKIND'S SALVATION.

This the indigenous Africans and their descendants must do; and thus their role as the

original contributors to the World's High-Culture, which is presently misnomered

"CIVILIZATION,"[21]

will be deservingly and properly recognized. It is only in this "LIGHT" this work continue

The following data denotes a chronological order in which the ancient Greeks were

influenced by the indigenous Africans of the North, South, East, West, and Central

Alkebu-lan [AFRICA]. All of the following has been documented.

ALKEBU-LAN [Africa]: MOTHER OF GREEK PHILOSOHPY
A CHRONOLOGY

Date B.C.E.   Description

640   Thales received all of his basic education in Egypt along with his associates
Anaximender and Anaximenes. They were natives of Ionia - Asia Minor, which was at
that time one of the colonial strongholds of the Egyptian Mysteries System Schools.
However they, like all other foreigners in the Mysteries, had to come to Egypt for extended and/or final studies. [See E.B. Sandford's THE MEDITERRANEAN WORLD, pp.
195-205].

576   Xenophanes, Parenides, Zeno, and Melissus [all of them natives of Ionia -
the Egyptian colony] migrated to Elea, Italy, after completing their education in Egypt.
They established themselves, while spreading the teachings of the Africans of the
Egyptian Mysteries as taught to them in the Osirica. From Italy they journeyed into
Greece [formerly called Hellas, Pyrrhus, Athens, etc.] where they continued their
proscelytization of the teachings of the Mysteries, of which "PHILOSOPHY" was one of
the major disciplines.[22]

540   Pythagoras finished his education in Egypt[23] and migrated to Croton in Southern Italy, which was following his return to his native island of Samos. He later returned to Greece to teach and experiment on the fundamentals he received while a
student studying the African Mysteries in the Osirica of Egypt.[0]

530   Heraclitus, Empedocles, Anaxagoras, and Democritus were also natives of
Ionia [at the time of their birth a colony of the Africans of Egypt, North Alkebu-lan].
They all became interested in the study of PHYSICS. And, they too went to Greece to
live and teach at the end of their studies in the Subordinate Lodges established in their
native island, and advanced studies in Egypt's and Nubia's Secret Temples of the Grand
Lodge's Osirica. At the Temples they were given advanced training and insight into the
SECRET SOCIETIES and DEGREES. But, not one of them reached the completion of the

_____

[0] One must remember that the Mysteries System of Egypt and Nubia had its origin at
Central Alkebu-lan's [Africa] Great Lakes regions - the home of the oldest "HUMAN
BEINGS" or "HUMANOIDS" known to man, vie. Zinjanthropus boisie, Boskop Man, Zim-
babwe ["Rhodesia"] Man, et al. The following works verify this fact: A. Churchward's
THE ORIGIN AND EVOLUTION OF THE HUMAN RACE; A. Churchward's SIGNS AND
SYMBOLS OF PRIMORDIAL MAN; Sir E.A.W. Budge's AMULETS AND TALISMAN;
Sir J. Frazier's THE GOLDEN BOUGH [13 vols.]; S. Cole's PREHISTORIC EAST AFRICA
324

studies all of the students had to attain in order to become a HIGH PRIEST in the Mysteries System.[24]

457?   Herodotus arrived in Egypt for the purpose of receiving his education. He was entered into the Mysteries System and "...PLACED IN SECRET ISOLATION, WHERE HE STUDIED HISTORY, SCIENCE, PHILOSOPHY, RELIGION, MAGIC, MEDICINE, LAW, GOVERNMENT...," etc. as all other "ENTERED APPRENTICES" had to do, including all of the other Greeks who came to Egypt and Nubia before and after him.

399   Socrates was sentenced to death for "...THE TEACHING OF A PHILOSOPHY WHICH IS ALIEN TO OUR" [Greek, Athenian, Hellenistic][0] "TEACHINGS."[25] It was a "PHILOSOPHY" which Socrates[00] and all of the other Greeks preceding him learned in the Egyptian colony of Ionia, or in Egypt and Nubia, under indigenous African teachers who had ...
         "THICK LIPS, BROAD NOSE, WOOLLY HAIR, AND BURNT
         OF SKIN...," etc.
according to Herodotus' own writing in his book - THE HISTORIES. These teachers came from as far SOUTH as Central Africa, beyond the beginning of Hapi [the Nile]. These facts are corraborated in Zeller's HISTORY OF PHILOSOPHY, pp. 112, 127, 170-172.[26] In this sense Plato and Aristotle had to flee Greece to protect their own life; for, they too were found GUILTY by the Greek [Athenian] government for teaching the same "PHILOSOPHY" Socrates and Herodotus learnt in Ionia and Egypt.[27]

Digressing somewhat from the chronological order of the so-called Greek and Ionian "PHILOSOPHERS" at this juncture for a few brief comments on the above listings so far; it must be remembered that the periods mentioned in the history of the ancient Greeks, from THALES [c.640 B.C.E.] to ARISTOTLE [c. 332 B.C.E.], the Ionians were not Greek citizens, but instead EGYPTIANS, and later PERSIAN subjects. The following writers and their works are very clear on this latter point: Zeller's HISTORY OF PHILOSOPHY, pp. 37, 46, 66-83, 112, 127, 170-172; W. Turner's HISTORY OF PHILOSOPHY, pp. 34, 45, 53; Rogers' STUDENT HISTORY OF PHILOSOPHY, p.15; D.B. Alexander's HISTORY OF PHILOSOPHY, pp. 13, 21; E.B. Sandford's THE MEDITERRANEAN WORLD, pp. 157, 195-205.

What they are all saying? That "GREEK PHILOSOPHY" is merely the continuation of the Africans of the Nile Valley and Great Lakes, especially Egypt and Nubia, PHILOSOPHICAL TEACHINGS, which were first carried into Ionia when said country was a colony of Egypt, Nubia, and Ethiopia; to Italy; and, finally to Greece or Athens.[28]

---

[0] Words in brackets [ ] by the author of this volume for the sake of clarity only.
[00] At this juncture one must be reminded that Socrates, like Herodotes, was not a Greek by birth, only through citizenship. He too was of Ionian birth; and, at the time of his birth Ionia was a colony of Egypt.

Diodorus - the Greek scholar and Manetho - the African-Europen High Priest of
Egypt during the so-called "XXXIInd DYNASTY" - recorded that African [Egyptian]

"...COLUMNS WERE FOUND AS FAR OFF AS NYASA, ARABIA."

And, that the inscription on the "COLUMNS" showed that "ISIS" [Egyptian Goddess] and
"OSIRIS" [Egyptian God] declared that they...

"LED AN ARMY INTO INDIA, TO THE SOURCE OF THE GANGES,
AND AS FAR AS THE INDUS OCEAN. [29]

There could be no doubt that the Egyptian Empire, part of which is shown on page 396
of this volume, and its African Mysteries System [at a very early date in ancient
history] included not only the islands off the Aegean Sea and Ionia, but it also stretched
to certain extremities of the Asian "FAR EAST," which included the homeland of the so-
called "INDO-EUROPEAN ARYANS" - otherwise called "CAUCASIANS" [light-skinned
and dark-skinned] and "SEMITES."

The above account was not the only one in which the indigenous Africans of Egypt
are shown to have conquered all the way to India, and probably much farther EAST.
Pharaoh Senusert I, who reigned over Egypt during the XIIth Dynasty, c. 1970-1936
B.C.E., conquered the entire coastline of India up to, and beyond, the Ganges River, [30]
and to the Eastern Ocean [Indus or Indian Ocean]. There, in India, he left thousands of
indigenous African soldiers, the same as General Ganges of Ethiopia [for whom the
Ganges River is named] did. The descendants of the offsprings of the soldiers left by
both of these African commanders, and others since, are just another segment of the
present population of India - notably those of Madras. During the same period he conquered India   Pharaoh Senurest I also captured Cyclades and a large part of the territory of Southeastern Europe.[31] Here too there were thousands of indigenous African
["NEGRO, BANTU, NIGGER," etc.] soldiers, who along with their offsprings, and
their offsprings descendants, amalgamated freely with the indigenous European population[32] - members of the "SUPERIOR GREAT WHITE RACE," the same as they did in
Asia.

The 1500 B.C.E. "AMARNA LETTERS" [found in the ruins of the government
offices of Pharaoh Amenhotep IV, otherwise known as Akhenaten, [33] XVIIIth Dynasty]
show that the Egyptian Empire extended to Western Asia, which included Assyria and
Palestine; and, that for centuries the Africans of Egypt and other Nile Valley High-
Cultures power had been supreme throughout the continent of Alkebu-lan, Asia, Europe,

326

and these three continents neighbouring islands.[34] Therefore, the Africans of Egypt and Nubia ["BLACKS, ETHIOPIANS, NEGROES, BANTUS," or whatever else] High-Culture or "CIVILIZATION," with all of its ramifications, became LAW AND ORDER in every colony within the EGYPTIAN [Africans of many nations of the Nile Valley and Great Lakes regions] EMPIRE. Proof of the preceding facts can be easily found in the following works: J. H. Breasted's CONQUEST OF CIVILIZATION, p. 84; DIODORUS, p. 128; Manetho's HISTORY OF EGYPT; Strabo's DICAERCHUS; J. Kendrick's, ANCIENT EGYPT, vol. I; J.J. Jackson's INTRODUCTION TO AFRICAN CIVILIZATION; Eva B. Sandford's THE MEDITERRANEAN WORLD; G.G.M. James' STOLEN LEGACY; Sir E.A. Wallis Budge's HISTORY OF EGYPT, 8 vols.; and, G. Massey's EGYPT THE LIGHT OF THE WORLD.

AN EXAMINATION OF CERTAIN MISCONCEPTIONS OF THE EXISTENCE
OF A BODY OF PHILOSOPHICAL THOUGHTS OF THE ANCIENT AFRICANS
OF TA-MERRY [Egypt] and TA-NEHISI [Nubia] MISNOMERED.............
"Greek Philosophy"

The BOOK ON NATURE, renamed "PERI PHYSEOS" by so-called "Greek Philoso-phers," was used by Greek students who were interested in the study of NATURE. This same work these students were supposed to have written. But, the earliest copies of said work are dated no farther back into antiquity than the 16th Century B.C.E. Yet, "PERI PHYSEOS" is written in a style that indicates an origin which had to have existed at least around c. 2000 B.C.E. or earlier, at which time the people of Hellas [Pyrrhus or Greece] were not engaged in this height of High-Culture or civilization, nor in such intellectual advancement, because they were not yet a nation until approximately c. 1000 B.C.E. at the earliest. However, within the pages of "PERI PHYSEOS" most of the doctrinal basis of the PHILOSOPHICAL CONCEPTS it teaches are plagiarized versions from the works of the Egyptian and Nubian Mysteries System; the source from whence the forerunners of so-called "Greek Philosophy" got their education. [See William Turner's HISTORY OF PHILOSOPHY, p. 62].[35] The teachings in this work remained the exclusive domain of "...THE CENTER OF CULTURE OF THE ANCIENT WORLD...," which was Egypt and Nubia - up until Egypt's conquest by Alexander II ["the great"] in c. 332 B.C.E. This was equally true until Aristotle and his school of Greek students compiled the indigenous African works of Egypt they found in the Mysteries System's libraries of the Osirica and claimed to be their own. [See C.H. Vail's ANCIENT MYS-TERIES, p. 16].[36] Some of the Greeks accredited with the origin of said works, such as

327

Heraclitus, Anaximandes, Anaxagoras, and Parmenides - were all students of Egyptian [African] Philosophy, as well as other disciplines; and, most of them were not in fact Greeks, but instead Ionians of Greek citizenship.

The "SCHOOLS OF PHILOSOPHY" of the ancient Chaldeans, Greeks, Ionians, Persians, and others of the ancient world, were extensions of the Africans of the Nile Valleys and Great Lakes Mysteries System that included PHILOSOPHICAL THOUGHTS which were common among the teachings of the so-called PYGMIES and BANTUS. This is mainly the reason why in Greece, Chaldea, and Persia "...THE STUDENTS OF THE MYSTERIES SCHOOLS WERE REPEATEDLY PERSECUTED AND PROSECUTED, AND MANY MURDERED," because of their "...ALIEN" [African] "TEACHINGS."[37] In only one place were their "...TEACHINGS..." unchallenged, and that was in the homeland of the Mysteries System or Osirica - ALKEBU-LAN [Africa].[38] Yet, all of the instructions were given in "STRICT SECRET BY WORD OF MOUTH," nothing whatsoever in WRITING, according to the demands of the Osirica, whose teachings were common among all of the Subordinate Schools or Lodges of the colonies [39] which had their "MOTHER" [Grand] "LODGE OF LUXOR" [Thebes later].[40] WHY? Because all colonial [Subordinate] GRAND LODGES were chartered by the ONE, and ONLY, "Mother Lodge" at LUXOR.

The reliance upon Aristotle to establish the authorship of the indigenous Africans of Egypt and Nubia's works, which when compiled into a single unit is called "GREEK PHILOSOPHY," is by any stretch of the imagination incredulous. For, no where in history is Aristotle accredited with a singulatory writing of any sort whatsoever before he had totally sacked the Temples, Pyramids, and Lodges of the Africans ["Negroes, Bantus," etc.] Mysteries System in Egypt and Nubia following his arrival with Alexander II ["the great"] in c. 332 B.C.E.[41] as conquerors. After that time the African works Aristotle did not place under his own name he attributed to his fellow Greek colleagues, most of whom there are no records of their existence except for their alleged authorship of the African works they stole, works that relate in too many ways to secrets of Egypt and other Nile Valley High-Cultures which they could not have possibly known unless they too were part and parcel of the Egyptian and Nubian [African] Mysteries System from its origin at the Great Lakes regions of Central Alkebu-lan [Africa].[42] For further information on this area of Nile Valley history see the following works: Alfred Weber's HISTORY OF PHILOSOPHY, p. 16; Theophratus' FRAGMENT 2 APUD DIELS; and G.

328

Massey's EGYPT THE LIGHT OF THE WORLD.

There is in existence a list of alleged "GREEK PHILOSOPHERS" who were "per-
sonae non gratas [undesirables] within the Hellenic [Greek] State. Yet, they continued
accepting their source of wisdom and knowledge from Egypt and Nubia. They were
men who kept their records in their head and operated in the deepest secrecy in fear
of the Greek State persecuting and prosecuting them for...

"TEACHING AN ALIEN PHILOSOPHY...," etc. ,

which was solely the Nile Valley Africans Mysteries.

A CHRONOLOGICAL LIST OF THE GREEKS WHOM THE PHI-
LOSOPHICAL TEACHINGS OF THE NILE VALLEY AFRICANS
OF EGYPT, NUBIA, MERÖE, KUSH, ETHIOPIA, ETC. ARE
ATTRIBUTED AND GIVEN THE MISNOMER: "Greek Philosophy."
[According to European and European-American "authorities"]

Date B.C.E.   Description

325   Aristotle, with the aid of Alexander's Chief General - who had by now declared himself "PHAROAH OF ALL EGYPT, SOTER I" [later "PTOLEMY I"] - soldiers,
sacked the Library and other repositories of the Mysteries System of Egypt and Nubia,
removed and destroyed most of its invaluable works, and proclaimed many of the remaining ones to be of his own genius - the "AUTHOR."

274 or   Eratosthenes, a stoic, compiled a chronology of his countrymen he called
194   "PHILOSOPHERS." They were the copiers, who copied word for word the
teachings of the Africans of Nubia and Egypt's Mysteries System Osirica secrets - all
of which later Europeans, Britons, and European-Americans have given the name
"GREEK PHILOSOPHY."

140   Apollodorus, who drew another chronology of sort - similar to that of Eratosthenes during c. 274-194 B.C.E., was equally guilty of perpetuating the listing of
his fellow Greeks as originators of the African philosophical concepts which are today
misnomered "GREEK PHILOSOPHY."

60-70   Adronicus, the eleventh Head of the Peripatic School, drew the third list of
so-called "GREEK PHILOSOPHERS" up to his era, and before, which included Ionians,
Cretians, Samosans, and Africans. [See the "Introduction" to Zeller's HISTORY OF
PHILOSOPHY].

Another major observation of the so-called "GREEK PHILOSOPHERS" and "GREEK
PHILOSOPHY" must be made at this juncture in the chronological order in which the
alleged "PHILOSOPHERS" followed each other. That is, only three of the Athenians
[Greeks] given said lable date of birth could be confirmed without any question of their
ever having lived at all. They are: "SOCRATES" [whose place of birth is questionable],

329

"PLATO, " and "ARISTOTLE. " Orthodox European and European-American historians and other educators generally agree to the certainty of these three date of birth. For all of the others this type of information is non-existant, or purely speculative. Many are only traditional in the mythology of Greek history; no history of their existence is available other than the references to them in the chronologies which each chronicler copied from the original and otherwise edited to suit his or her prejudice. In this context the so-called "PRE-SOCRATIC GREEK PHILOSOPHERS" are listed according to the speculative chronology by Diogenes Laentius, himself quite indefinite on their date of birth and/or origin. Most of them, as mentioned before, have questionable existence.[4] But, the guessing game continues from the original Greek chroniclers to the current philosophers, professors of philosophy, historians, and other educators of WHITE STUDIES in the United States of America, Great Britain, and Europe. All of the above mentioned Greek personalities, and those to follow, have been presented by the European and European-American "AUTHORITIES" in every major institution of learning, as well as in elementary schools [private, public, religious, and parochial] as the originators of every concept in so-called "GREEK PHILOSOPHY;" and, not one of them has given credit to the first African, Egyptian or not, for one concept within "GREEK PHILOSOPHY, " which even include that which Aristotle stole out of the Lodges, Pyramids, and Temples of Egypt and Nubia. In this light, it is equally noted that none of the personalities misnomered "GREEK PHILOSOPHERS" was in existence within one-thousand [1, 000] years after the Africans of Egypt [Egyptians] published their last set of PHILOSOPHICAL CONCEPTS shown in their Book Of The Coming Forth By Day [the so-called Egyptian Book of the Dead and the Papyrus of Ani, as translated into English by Sir Ernest A. Wallis Budge in 1895 C. E.], The Pyramid Texts, The Coffin Texts, The Negative Confessions, and/or The Osirian Drama. Not one of them lived during the IIIrd Dynasty, c. 2780-2680 B. C. E. , at which time Imhotep ["the Great God of Medicine, " whom the Greeks called "Aescalapius" etc.] wrote PHILOSOPHICALLY; neither was any of them in existence when countless numbers of the indigenous Africans of Ta-Merry [later called Kimit, Sais, Cham, etc.],Ethiopia, Carthage, Nubia, Merĕe, Puanit, Numidia, and other nations along the more than 4,100 miles Nile River and the Great Lakes regions were teaching and preaching their PHILOSOPHICAL CONCEPTS which later became the basis for the Mysteries System of the Osirica in the Grand Lodge of Luxor [Thebes] where most of the Greeks came for their education in Philoso-

PHY and other disciplines. Yet, we are taught by the so-called "AUTHORITIES" in
WHITE STUDIES setting that most of the so-called "GREEK PHILOSOPHERS" reached
the same conclusions, and wrote on the same subjects, before the indigenous Africans
of North and East Alkebu-lan [Africa]. This had to be done, as the plagiarized versions
of the Africans works in PHILOSOPHY by their European students from Greece, Rome,
and other lands were proven to be in some instances WORD FOR WORD dialogues of the
Africans works - which are otherwise labeled now "GREEK PHILOSOPHY." They WERE,
and still ARE, and will forever BE, African PHILOSOPHICAL CONCEPTS and TEACH-
INGS, all of which were foreign to the Greeks, and for which many of the Greeks that
eventually learned them were "PERSECUTED, PROSECUTED, TORTURED," and even
"MURDERED" by the Greek [Athenian] Government - including the star of them all:
S-O-C-R-A-T-E-S. As we return to Diogenes Lentius chronology we find the others
listed after Heraclitus were:

500   Anaxagoras. Diogenes confidence was manifested in this date. He was very
certain that the date of birth was 500 B.C.E. However, Turner, Rogers, and Alexander [all European-American "authorities"] elected to remain mute on this persoanlity's
existence, place of origin, and/or date of birth.

    Parmenides. Diogenes accredited his birth at approximately c. 500 B.C.E. Rogers,
Fuller, and Thilly said that no date whatsoever for this man's birth can be found in any
available records.

484   Empedocles. Diogenes placed his birth at 484 B.C.E. Rogers, Thilly, Turner, Windelbrand, Fuller, and Alexander calculated that it was c. 490 B.C.E.

464 to   Xeno. Diogenes found it impossible to established any date whatsoever for
460   this man's existence, nor his date of birth , or his ever being a "PHILOSO-
PHER" of any sort. However, he specualtively concluded that his date of birth must
have been sometime within c. 464 or 460 B.C.E. B.D. Alexander, Frank Tilly, and
William Turner, in their respective works titled - "HISTORY OF PHILOSOPHY" -
placed the date of birth at c. 490 B.C.E.; whereas, A.K. Rogers, Fuller, and W.G.
Tennermann declared that the date is definitely unknown.

    As we have completed Diogenes Laentius' list of so-called "GREEK PHILOSO-
PHERS;" it becomes very much necessary that we also give an extensive examination
to the available records which show that "GREEK PHILOSOPHY" has been proven to be
nothing more than a plagiarized extension of AFRICAN [Egyptian] PHILOSOPHY, and
of course very much ASIAN also. At best, with some stretch of the imagination, it could
be called:

GREEK INTERPRETATION OF AFRICAN AND ASIAN PHILOSOPHY.

Emperor Justinian's EDICT closing the Egyptian Mysteries System Lodges and Philosophical Schools of the Osirica in Egypt and Nubia, also the extension of these two bulwarks of man's original look into science, mathematics, the Seven Liberal Arts - of which Philosphy is included, religion, medicine, magic, astronoy, astrology, etc. in Greece and Rome, simultaneously plunged Europe [including the British Isle] into a world of utter IGNORANCE, SUSPICION, and FEAR for more than ten centuries [1,000 years]. At the same instance it allowed the Greeks to maintain control of the data their forebearers confiscated from the repositories of Egypt and Nubia, which also gave them the opportunity to rewrite and otherwise plagiarized the entire works of the Africans of the Nile Valley and Great Lakes regions of Alkebu-lan. Meanwhile, during said period of the EDICT, systemized learning in Egypt and Nubia was forced to disappear. But, the Greeks showed no creative understanding or imagination in perpetuatiing farther the information and documents within their control, as their African priests and other teachers were no longer available to them. Thus, they were not able to improve upon what they were taught by their African teachers. In other words, the Greeks could go no farther with their own alleged "GREEK PHILOSOPHY," even though they were in total control of it. The following works should assist the student, researcher, and general reader on this latter point: Sedgwick and Tyler's HISTORY OF SCIENCE, pp. 141, 163; Zeller's HISTORY OF PHILOSOPHY [the Introduction], p. 31; George G. M. James' STOLEN LEGACY; and Eva B. Sandford's THE MEDITERRANEAN WORLD.

In analyzing this aspect of the indigenous Africans of North and East Africa's HIGH-CULTURE, particular its zenith, one has to remember that a later group of indigenous Africans of Northwest Alekebu-lan [Afrika] called "MOORS" have preserved much of their ancestors teachings in the works confiscated by the Greeks and Romans from the Egyptian and Nubian Mysteries System - which European and European-American educators and others very much later have notoriously misnomered "GREEK PHILOSOPHY." Unfortunately, most of the Moors works remain untranslated in the Arabic language which they used. The very few works translated into the English are mostly out of the reach of the average student, and most ceratainly beyond the reach of the general public. These works include: MEDICINE, SCIENCE, PHARMACOLOGY, ASTROLOGY, NUMEROLOGY, ASTRONOMY, RELIGION, ART, MUSIC, MAGIC, HISTORY, LAW, and other branches of the arts and sciences. However, the English translations of Leo-

332

nardo Pisano's works in Arabic, on mathematical science are just a few of those available now. There are other works of his on PHILOSOPHY and MORALS, the NATURAL SCIENCES, and METAPHYSICS, which may be found at tremendous cost. Equally, there are available English translations of Gideo the Monk from Arezzo's musical notations in Arabic which were copied from Nile Valley African treatises and other works; some of these are also available in the English language, but equally as expensive. Of course there are countless others, many of which are visible in the works of Tyler and Sedgwick, particularly in their book HISTORY OF SCIENCE, Chapter IX.

The African Moors, not Arab Moors, extensive knowledge of ancient Egypt and Nubia was due to their constant cultural exchanges with their Northeast African brothers and sisters through the diplomatic relationship which existed between both groups. Many of the works the Moors recorded were unknown to the Greeks and Romans; most of them were stolen from Egypt and Nubia by Arab Muslim invaders who also sacked the depositories of learning of the Nile Valley High-Cultures as did their predecessors from Persia, Assyria, Greece, and Rome. A very good example of the type of works being mentioned could be seen in Ault's EUROPE IN THE MIDDLE AGES, pp. 216-219. It should be also noted that a number of medieval European scientists and members of other disciplines, such as Copernicus, Roger Bacon, and Johann Kepler received much of their basic understanding from the researches they made when they became in contact with the original treatises on science which the Africans of Northeast and North Africa originated and developed, and from works which the Moors introduced to the Europeans when they entered the Iberian Peninsula [Spain, Portugal, and Southern France] in c. 711 C.E. under the command of the African general - Tarikh [for whom the Rock of Gibraltar is named]. True the Arab-Moors and Berber-Moors also contributed in this respect to the Europeans, but they followed the African-Moors. The following works are testimonials to the above: C.H. Vail, ANCIENT MYSTERIES, pp. 59, 61, 75; F.H. Hitti, HISTORY OF THE ARABS, pp. 370, 629, 572; A. Besant, ESOTERIC CHRISTIANITY, pp. 107, 128-129; Copernicus and Kepler's writings shown in GREAT BOOKS OF THE WESTERN WORLD, vol. 16 [Encyclopedia Britanica]; S. Lane-Poole, THE MOORS IN SPAIN; J.A. Rogers, WORLD'S GREAT MEN OF COLOR, vol. I; Herodotus, HISTORIES, Book III, p. 124; Pliny, N.H. 35, 9; Diogenes VII, 3; Porphyry, ANTIPHO. It must be noted that these works also show that Pythagoras, a native son of Samos, secured the necessary consent of the indigenous Africans of Egypt and

Nubia[0] [particularly the High-Priests] before he was allowed to enter the Mysteries System to learn some of the secrets of the Osirica which the African-Moors[00] also alluded to. Accordingly, Diogenes Laentius stated that Pharaoh Amasis and Polycrates of Samos developed a friendship with Pythagoras, whom they introduced to the...

"PRIESTS FOR HIS INITIATION INTO THE EGYPTIAN MYSTERIES;" first to the priests of ON [Heliopolis], and next to the others in Memphis and Luxor. It is written that:

"EACH OF THEM RECEIVED A GIFT OF A SILVER GOBLET FROM PYTHAGORAS.

The presents were tokens of appreciation for his pending schooling he was to receive from them, which included "MEASUREMENTS;" the same "MEASUREMENTS" which European and European-American educators have attributed their origin to something they have labeled "PYTHGORAN THEOREM."

Pliny, Herodotus, and Jablonsk, all three of them, stated that Pythagoras was subsequently...

"INITIATED AND RECEIVED ALL OF THE SECRETS OF THE MYSTERIES...,"

which included PHILOSOPHY, from the African priests. They also stated that his lessons followed his "CIRCUMCISION" and other severe trials imposed upon him. And, that the disciplines he learnt included...

"MEDICINE, THE DOCTRINE OF METAPSYCHOSIS, GEOMETRY," etc.

which there were no presence of before in Greek learning. John Kendrick in his own work, HISTORY OF ANCIENT EGYPT, vol. I, p. 234, with respect to the disciplines Pythagoras learnt from the Africans of the Nile Valley Mysteries System, states that he also "...LEARNT MUSIC."

Demetrius, Anthisthenes, and Plutarch wrote in their works that:

"...PYTHAGORAS ESTABLISHED THE TEACHINGS OF SCIENCE

---

[0] Nubia must be emphasized at this point, as most European and European-Americans have carefully omitted the fact that Luxor [later called Thebes by the Greeks], the center of the Osirica's Mysteries System was located in Nubian territory; and, most of the African priests [professors] were from the Upper Nile Valley.

[00] Many have confused the MOORS' religion - "ISLAM", as being synanymous to Arab people as a physical group. They were two groupings of MOORS. The Africans, who were the first to conquer the Iberian Peninsula in c. 711 C.E. or A.D. [89 A.H.] with General Tarikh, and the Asian MOORS who followed them twelve [12] years later in c. 723 C.E. or 101 A.H. [the Year after the Hegira or Hejira].

AND MATHEMATICS AMONG THE GREEKS...," etc.

That he also:

> "...SACRIFICED TO MUSES AFTER THE PRIEST OF THE EGYP-
> TIANS MYSTERIES EXPLAINED TO HIM THE PROPERTIES OF
> THE RIGHT TRIANGLE...," etc.

The above information is further corroborated in the works of the following persons: Demetrius, PHILARCH DE REPUGN STOIC, II, p. 1089; Cicero, DE NATURA DEORUN, III, p. 36; and Antistehes, SUCCESSION.

Democritus, a native of Abdera in Miletus, was also educated in Egypt and Nubia - according to Demetrius' PEOPLE OF THE SAME NAME, and Anthisthenes' SUCCES-SION. They also wrote that he received his education from the Egyptian priests of the "Mysteries." Diogenes Laentius and Herodotus verified the fact that Democitus spent five [5] years in learning all phases of Egyptian and Nubian disciplines after his submission to the same rites Pythagoras underwent. Origen, an Egyptian national residing in Greece, in support of this contention, noted that:

> "Apud Aegyptios nullus aut geometrica studebat, aut astronomine
> secreta remabatur, nisi circumcisione suscepta."

The above translated into English reads:

> "NO ONE AMONG THE EGYPTIANS EITHER STUDIED GEOMETRY,
> OR INVESTIGATED THE SECRETS OF ASTRONOMY, UNLESS CIR-
> CUMCISSION HAD BEEN UNDERTAKEN."

Plato received his final training in Egypt after visiting with Euclid at Megara, along with other students of Socrates - who was also a product of Egyptian and Nubian PHILOSOPHICAL and SCIENTIFIC teachings of the Osirica. In this regards we find Hermodorus saying that:

> "...PLATO WAS TWENTY-EIGHT YEARS OF AGE WHEN HE LEFT
> FOR SCHOOL IN EGYPT...," etc.

Although history does not mention that Socrates and the so-called "PRE-SOCRATIC PHILOSOPHERS" did not specifically travel to Egypt and Nubia for their respective education as the others had, their teachings were wrought with the basic disciplines of the Africans of Egypt and Nubia Mysteries they learned from others who studied there. As a result, it was so similar that many of them, besides Socrates, were equally...

> "TRIED AND FOUND GUILTY....," etc.

by the Greek [Athenian] Government for...

> "TEACHING A FOREIGN PHILOSOPHY."

The above quotations are further supported in William Turner's HISTORY OF PHILOSO-
PHY, pp. 62, 126; Zeller's HISTORY OF PHILOSOPHY, p. 84; Plato's PHAEDO; and
W. Rogers' HISTORY OF PHILOSOPHY, p. 76.

Max Muller's EGYPTIAN MYTHOLOGY, pp. 187-189; John Kendrick's ANCIENT
EGYPT, vol. II, pp. 56, 432; and Diodorus' 16 and 51, should have laid the misnomer -
"GREEK PHILOSOPHY" - in its final resting place when they so adequatelt recalled,
in the works already stated, that:

> THE GREEKS RECEIVED MOST OF THEIR EARLIEST EDUCATION
> FROM LOOTING THE CENTRAL LIBRARIES OF ALEXANDRIA,
> THEBES, AND THE MENEPHTHEION.

The latter library, The Menephtheion, from which Euclid[0]received much of the data he
used in his mathematical calculations, was founded by Pharoah Seti I - who reigned
during the XIXth Dynasty, c. 1318-1298 B.C.E. It was the most important of all Royal
Libraries of Egypt and Nubia. It was completed by Pharaoh Seti I son, Pharaoh Rameses II - who reigned over Egypt and Nubia from c. 1298 to 1232 B.C.E.,[44] having succeded his father.[Rameses II was the same Pharaoh Of Egypt and Nubia the Haribus or
"JEWS" charged with chasing Moses and his followers out of North Africa to Northeast
Africa - from Succoth to Mount Sinai]. Although this Library was the finest of all, very
little has been written about the works it contained after the Greeks sacked it during
Alexander II ["the great"] and Ptolemy I tyranical rule over Egypt and Nubia, which began in c. 332 B.C.E.

One must remember that Aristotle had full run of all educational insitutions throughout Egypt, Nubia, and Merüe as a reseult of Alexander and Ptolemy's control of these
nations. He was given full power by Alexander when he entered Egypt as conqueror. Following Alexander's death in c. 327 B.C.E., his power was extended by General Soter -
who had become Pharaoh. But Alexander, who was much more interested in meeting
the African "ORACLE OF ANMON."[45][in many books called a "Negro"], he did not care
what action Ptolemy and Aristotle took in respect to the destruction and co-option of the
Mysteries System's libraries packed with all sorts of written materials by the indigenous
Africans of the entire Nile Valley and Great Lakes High-Cultures. This point has been
carefully suppressed by European and European-American writers. Yet, to many Afri-

---

[0]Wilson Amistead, in his book - A TRIBUTE TO THE NEGRO, London, 1840, p. 121,
was quite forceful when he reminded his readers that EUCLID was an African from Me-
gera in Lebu [Libya], a tiny town on the Mediterranean Sea of North Alkebu-lan [Africa]

can, African-American, and African-Caribbean educators who have written on North and East Africa's history have also ignored ; thus, they avoid any conflict with the self-appointed "AUTHORITIES" on everything African. But, it is at this point that the crucial understanding why this work is brought into fruition. It is not to lead anyone into a "MILITANT" path; for, such is a direction that is as negative as the term itself is. It is not to present a masterpiece of literary work. It is, however, an opening of the doors to much of the information which have been willfully an maliciously withheld, suppressed, and sometimes destroyed, in order to keep the African, African-American, and African-Caribbean peoples SOMEWHAT, if not TOTALLY, ignorant of their most glorious HERITAGE and HIGH-CULTURES of the entire continent of ALKEBU-LAN.

The fact that the Greeks swarmed into Ta-Merry [Egypt] and Ta-Nehisi [Nubia] for their most basic and earliest education during the reign of Alexander II and Ptolemy I is added proof that they were leaving their own schools in Greece for first hand, person to person, learning from the Africans of the Mysteries System - PHILOSOPHY included, though the indigenous Africans' educational system had already suffered extreme corruption after falling into the hands of Alexander II, General Soter [Ptolemy], and Aristotle. The Africans' educational system, the greatest of which was symbolized by the Osirica, was a major part of the bounty or loot the Greeks and Romans got for their conquest of Egypt, Nubia, and Meröe. From these loathsome beginnings on the part of the Greeks with Alexander, but mainly with Soter and Aristotle, much of what was later on unjustifiably called "GREEK PHILOSOPHY" had their latest plagiaristic origin in ancient times, which of course does not take into account the further plagiarization which took place during the Christian Era and the Christian Emperors of Rome - such as Justinian and Gregory.

From that which history reveals is the origin of "GREEK PHILOSOPHY;" it should be of no supprise to anyone that the practise of denying African peoples everywhere this aspect of their rich and glorious heritage in PHILOSOPHY will continue to greater heights by the same "AUTHORITIES" who now control the writing of textbooks and other materials used in AFRICAN and BLACK STUDIES courses throughout the United States of America. WHY? Because such behaviour among "Western educators" , all of whom call themselves "ORTHODOX" or "LIBERAL AFRICANIST HISTORIAN," etc., is the only method available to them in their perpetuation of the BIG LIE PROPAGANDA that:

"...NORTH AFRICA'S HISTORY IS CAUCASIAN AND SEMITIC.[46]

Yet, history will continue proving that ALKEBU-LAN [Africa] IS THE CRADLE OF MAN'S CIVILIZATION;[47] a sort of "GARDEN OF EDEN." And, that TA-MERRY and TA-NEHISI were the places where the ancient Nile Valley Africans from the Great Lakes region of Uganda, Kenya, Tanzania, and Zaire, etc. reached the zenith of their High-Cultures. Also, that the indigenous African most advanced High-Cultures travel-ed with the flow of the Nile River [Blue and White], from Uganda to the Egyptian [Me-diterranean] Sea,[48] from SOUTH to NORTH and into the sea; not up hill against gravity in the opposite direction, from Egypt's Delta [Lower Egypt] to Uganda.

The maps of the Nile Valley shown in Chapter III of this volume outline the contour of the three bodies of water which comprise the Nile River after it leaves its main sources of the Great Lakes and Lake Tana. Thus; the WHITE NILE, BLUE NILE, and ATBARA rivers.The modern maps on the continent of Alkebu-lan [Africa] présent boudaries established at the Berlin Conference of 1884-85 C.E., and recorded in the Berlin ACT, which has been adopted by the countries whose territories they enclosed following the colonial enslavement to European and British nations with the close co-operation of the United States of America. As to the RAPE of Africa, otherwise called "THE PARTITION OF AFRICA," the following works must be read: Sir Edward Herts-lett, THE MAP OF AFRICA BY TREATY, 3 vols.; J. Scott-Keltie, THE PARTITION OF AFRICA; Parker T. Moon, IMPERIALISM AND WORLD POLITICS; George Pad-more, AFRICA:BRITAIN'S THIRD EMPIRE; and Sir E. Hertslett, THE BERLIN CON-FERENCE.

One must conclude after reading the above, equally all that preceded the above in the other chapters, that:

"GREEK PHILOSOPHY" IS NOT ONLY A MISNOMER; IT IS A LIE.

Bibliography For Chapter IX

Plato, APOLOGY

Aristophanes, FROG

Frankfurt, H., CREATION STORY OF THE MEMPHITE THEOLOGY

Muller, Max, EGYPTIAN MYTHOLOGY

Heller, P., HISTORY OF PHILOSOPHY

Clymer, S., FIRE PHILOSOPHY

338

Plato, REPUBLIC

Turner, William, HISTORY OF PHILOSOPHY

Alexander, D. B., HISTORY OF PHILOSOPHY

Snadford, E. B., THE MEDITERRANEAN WORLD

Rogers, A. K., STUDENTS HISTORY OF PHILOSOPHY

Breasted, J. H., CONQUEST OF CIVILIZATION

Weber, A., HISTORY OF PHILOSOPHY

POLYBIUS HISTORY, C. 400—370

Coprenicus and Kepler, GREAT BOOKS OF THE WESTERN WORLD, Vol. 16

ben-Jochannan, Y., AFRICA: MOTHER OF "WESTERN CIVILIZATION"

ben-Jochannan, Y. and Simmonds, G. E., THE BLACK MAN'S NORTH and EAST
        AFRICA

Petrie, F., PREHISTORIC EGYPT

-----, ANCIENT EGYPT

Maspero, G., HISTORY OF EGYPT AND ASSYRIA (8 Vols.)

Massey, G., EGYPT THE LIGHT OF THE WORLD

deGraft-Johnson, J. C., AFRICAN GLORY

Glanville, S. R. K., THE LEGACY OF EGYPT

Breasted, J. H., ANCIENT RECORDS OF EGYPT

Montet, P., ETERNAL EGYPT

Casson, L., (ed.) ANCIENT EGYPT

Bessant, Annie., ESOTERIC CHRISTIANITY

Tyler and Sedgwick, HISTORY OF SCIENCE

Ault, B., EUROPE IN THE MIDDLE AGES

Hitti, P., HISTORY OF THE ARABS

Herodotus, THE HISTORIES

Porphyry, ANTIPHO

Diogenes VIII

Cicero, DE NATURA DEORUM, III

Plato, PHADEO

James, G. G. M., STOLEN LEGACY

Wallis Budge, Sir E. A., BOOK OF THE DEAD

Vail, C. H., ANCIENT MYSTERIES

HOLY BIBLE (Christian, King James Version)

HEBREW TORAH (Five Books of Moses)

The following Questions and Answers are directly related to the general texts of the four [4] books of this series, but more specifically to:

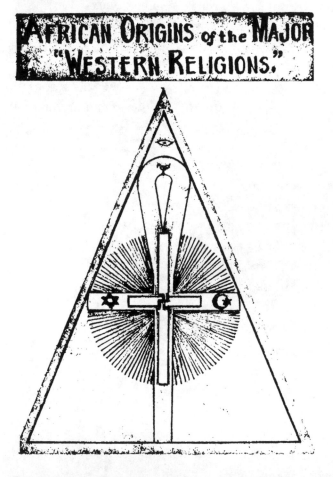

However, being that they also encompass a much broader secular scope than is generally associated with things religious in the European-American system of WHITE STUDIES, otherwise called "WESTERN CIVILIZATION" or "DEMOCRACY," it became very much necessary to add them to the expansion of this section of the BLACK EXPERIENCE of the NILE VALLEYS, the GREAT LAKES, and the GENERAL AREAS of Alkebu-lan's most glorious past.

Notably the last QUESTION will be treated independently, due to the extent to which African peoples have become so much engulfed in their every act related to their daily life with "Jesus Christ;" and, moreso, due to its control over the African peoples in their INTRA and INTER relationship with each others, not even to mention its effects in the present MUSLIM-CHRISTIAN-CHRISTIAN-ISRAELITE feud within the African-American communities [definitely not ghettos] throughout the United States of America, South and Central America, the Caribbean Islands, and of course in "MOTHER ALKEBU-LAN [Africa]" herself.

In dealing with the last QUESTION, it is paramount that we realize there could have been no MOSES, JESUS CHRIST, or ALLAH without the teachings of the Africans of the Africans of the Nile Valleys and Great Lakes High-Cultures that produced the original foundation upon which they rest. For, it is from the great writings and oral teachings of the Africans of these areas, all of whom are now only a memory, that the so-called "TEN COMMANDMENTS" of Judaism, Christianity, and Islam are based; these alleged "COMMANDMENTS" that preceded the African - Moses, who introduced them to Judaism, Christianity, and Islam - each following the order in which they are listed here; all three of them being offsprings of the religion of the "GREAT I AM, RA, THE SUN - the first of the "GOD OF ALL GODS" commonly mentioned in all of the so-called "WESTERN RELIGIONS'" teachings - Judaism, Christianity, and Islam.

The QUESTIONS relating to a much more common understanding of just what is "SECULAR" and what is "RELIGIOUS," from a "Western" point of view or reference, are answered in the same light as the text of the general work of this entire volume; thus, from an African or BLACK perspective and interpretation as the events that brought them about affected the African peoples and their continent - ALKEBU-LAN, otherwise known as "MOTHER AFRICA." Certainly these questions, as others, will generate lots of objections to the type of projection they serve; moreso than in the case of the approved type of "NEGRO HISTORY" books written upon the strength and endorsement of "WHITE LIBERAL AUTHORITIES ON AFRICA AND AFRICAN PEOPLES." But, this is to be expected. WHY? Because the major premise of this work, as all the others by this author, is to expose to the general reader, student, and researcher, the Africans involvement in this aspect of WORLD HIGH-CULTURE. In so doing, there is bound to be conflict with WHITE STUDIES that presented, and still present, that which the Africans have contributed to the WORLD as being the works of "SEMITES, HAMITES, CAUCA-

SIANS, INDO-EUROPEAN ARYANS," and a host of other names for members of the "GREAT WHITE RACE" developed in disciplines which are designed to accomplish the isolation of the so-called "AFRICANS SOUTH OF THE SAHARA, NEGROES," and "BANTUS," from the general body of African peoples who resided in NORTH and EAST AFRICA [Alkebu-lan] after their migrations from the central regions of the continent where the most ancient proof of the true "GARDEN OF EDEN" [Olduvai Gorge], ZINJANTHROPUS BOISE, was unearthed by Drs. Louis and Mary Leakey.

There is hardly any of the data presented in which the author of this volume can verify as an actual FACT by virtue of his living through the experience or experiences which brought it or them into being, the same being equally true for all of the authors writing during the 20th century C. E. and before - back to the beginning of the so-called "Christian Era." Thus, it is necessary for documentation; and such must be presented in the form of BIBLIOGRAPHICAL RECORDS and ARTIFACTS or other forms of evidence common to "ACADEMIC RESEARCH" and "SCHOLARSHIP", and totally free to the examination of the reading public. But "SCHOLARSHIP," in this light, should not be something that is lacking of human emotions, as so many "SCHOLARS" are trying to make of it toda' The presentation of HISTORICAL DATA should show in every manner the position of the author politically, socially, economically, and otherwise, and not in the realm of the HIPOCRACY OF NEUTRALITY which is the common order of the so-called "WHITE LIBERAL AFRICANIST HISTORIANS."

The following Questions and Answers are not given for the sole purpose of information relative to facts and figures of a chronological nature. They are given, in the main, for the purpose of letting the student, researcher, teacher, and general reader know that much of what they have been taught as FACTS and the "INSPIRED WORDS OF GOD" are not necessarily so, and in many cases they are complete DISTORTIONS of the truth and/or down right LIES. Also, that such DISTORTIONS and LIES are specifically geared to perpetuate the myth of the "SUPERIORITY OF THE GREAT WHITE RACE OVER THE INFERIOR BLACK RACE," etc. In other cases it is to perpetuate the RELIGIOUSLY BIGOTED idea of a "ONE AND ONLY TRUE GOD" of the Caucasians and/or "Semites" which no other people on the face of the earth had anything to do with its concepts, philosophically, spiritually, or otherwise.

The following should be compared to the works of "WHITE" historians, egyptologists, and other educators, if only to see how they have DISTORTED World History.

342

Q. Is it true that Queen Hatshepsut was murdered by her brother - Thutmosis III?

A. The prevailing hypothesis by certain European and European-American "egyptologists" is that Queen-King Hatshep-sut was murdered by her brother Thutmosis III in order that he could reign over Egypt as sole ruler is without any historical proof whatsoever. Their entire hypothesis is based solely upon the fact that certain erased cartouches and recut ones in her temple at Deir el Bahri show her name removed. This practice, the removal of certain pharaohs names from their personal effects after their death, was common throughout Egyptian history, such being especially true when the successor's rule was in disagreement with the Gods of the departed pharaoh that was succeded.

Q. Who started the profession known as "ARCHAEOLOGY"?

A. Professor W.M.Flanders Petrie's statistcal recording of "... SEQUENTIAL DATINGS", one of the recognized methods in archaeology today, became the earliest established data processing norm in the discipline called "ARCHAEOLOGY". He divided the prehistory of Egypt into five [5] separate periods: 1] TASIAN, 2] BADARIAN, 3] AMRATEAN, 4] GERZEAN, and 5] SEMAINIAN; all from names of villages located near the place where each major find was unearthed [discovered]. This was the manner in which the discipline was actually started. The beginning of Professor Petrie's work rested upon his AMRATEAN and GERZEAN pottery finds. During his lifetime they were the oldest known to him and his contemporaries. See F.Petrie, DIOSPOLIS PARVA, where he established his dating system process by arbitrarily giving them numbers, beginning with 30 and ending with 80; thus, 39 is lower than/or before 49-s39 or s49.

Q. Which one of these cultures is the older: the TASIAN PERIOD, or the BADARIAN PERIOD?

A. There is as much evidence that the TASIAN PERIOD was a different culture to the BADARIAN PERIOD as night is to day. However, there is also an abundance of evidence that the former may have predated the latter, instead of just being its contemporary culture. "Tasian potery", the main artifacts which W.M.Flanders Petrie and others used for establishing the five [5] periods above, was in many respects equal in refinement to that of the Badarian Period. Some historians and archaeologists even claimed that the Tasian Period, in fact, belongs to the NEOLITHIC AGE. Upon this flimsy basis the entire area of "EGYPTOLOGY" and "ARCHAEOLOGY" rest, with respects to the elements of "TRUTH" and "FALSEHOOD" of North and East Africa's prehistory; also, upon them much of the current racist theories and hypotheses about these areas are based.

Q. Is it true that "FLINT STONES were once used for CIRCUMCIZING PEOPLE"?

A. It is often mentioned by certain European and European -American historians that a " BADARIAN-type FLINT STONE KNIFE OF EGYPT" was used on Moses of the Hebrew Holy Torah [Five Books of Moses or Old Testament] when he was circumsized as an African boy in Egypt. The same is said to have been true of Joshua. See EXODUS

343

IV: 25, also JOSHUA, V: 2 and 3.

Q. How did the ancient Africans of Egypt write "JEHOVAH" ?

A. The strangest chain of events in Egyptian religious history is topped by the XXVIth Dynasty's divine emblem of the figure of one of the Gods named " YWH, YAHWA, YAWHE ..'ect., written in Hieroglyph   The first FOUR [4] letters mean "DIVINITY"; the last is a pic-   ture of the God himself. Note that this Egyptian God was adopted   by the Haribu [Hebrews, colloquially " Jews "] in their own mythology about the " CREATION OF THE WORLD." YWH was the name of a very minor God; equally AMON, who later became the"AMEN" at the end of most Jewish and Christian prayers and hymns. "Modern Theologians " have claimed that the word "AMEN" means "...SO BE IT," thereby ignoring the "AMEN-RE" and "AMEN-RA" the Haribu African, Moses, also worshipped in the lodges of the Mysteries System of Egypt.

Q. What period is said to have been the " mother of the Dynasties of Ancient Egypt"?

A. The GERZEAN CULTURE is said to have been "... THE ANCESTOR OF THE DYNASTIC CIVILIZATION OF ANCIENT EGYPT." Also,that the SEMARIAN PERIOD was in many ways merely a continuation of the GERZEAN PERIOD, but with many characteristics quite dissimilar.

Q. What specific characteristics distinguish the SEMIANIAN PERIOD from all others?

A. European and European-American anthropologists, archaeologists, and egyptologists have constantly claimed that:"... THE INTRODUCTION OF COPPER, IVORY, AND CLAY STATUES DISTINGUISHED THE SEMIANIAN PERIOD FROM THE FIRST DYNASTY OF EGYPT..."c. 3200 B.C.E. [according to High-Priest Manetho's Chronological Dating of the Dynastic Periods].

Q. Is it true that armies of Muslim-Arabs from the Arabian Penninsula of Southwestern Asia invaded Egypt and destroyed much of the Africans' works of history they met there?

A. In the year 640 C.E. [or 18 A.H.] two waves of Arab-Muslim invaders from the Arabian Peninsula destroyed untold amounts of the most important scrolls, books, and other works of the African scribes and scholars of ancient Egypt. One set of such works included volumes written by Manetho - the African-European High-Priest of Sebenmytus, who at the command of Ptolemy Philadelpheus [c. 270 B.C.E.] was forced to "WRITE A COMPLETE HISTORY OF EGYPT." Manetho's "HISTORY" was the first to divide Egyptian experiences into "DYNASTIES," all of which he placed securely in the Great Library of Alexandria, Egypt. Never-the-less, some of Manetho's writings were saved through the writings of ancient historians who had copied from him, and by many others who copied from them. The most important ancient off-shoot from Manetho's works is called the "PALERMO STONE" [mentioned dramatically in the works of Breasted and others quoted in this volume]. It is an engraved "STONE", showing records of pharaohs [kings] of the first FIVE [5] DYNASTIES: Ist - IIIrd Proto-Dynastic c. 4777 - 3998 B.C.E. and IVth - Vth Old Kingdom c. 3998 - ? B.C.E. [See Schaefer's, "Ein Bruchstuck altaegyptischer Konigsannalen" [In: Anhang zu den Abhandlungen der

344

Koniglichen Precussischen Akademie, 1902].

Q. What is meant by the Chronological Listing Of Dynastic Egypt as described by High-Priest Manetho; and, what is it like?

A. The following is an exact facimile of the Dynastic Divisions or Periods of Egyptian prehistory and history according to High-Priest Manetho. The original was written in Hieratic and/or Demotic script - HIEROGLYPHICS. Note that most of the so-called European and European-American "AFRICANISTS" follow Dr. Burgsch's version, which he presented in his book - EGYPTIAN DOCUMENTARY HISTORY.

MANETHO'S CHRONOLOGY
[All periods BCE]

Division or Period.	Dynasty
Proto-Dynastic c. 4777-3998	I- II
Old Kingdom c. 3998-3335	IV - VI
First Intermediate Period c. 3335-3005	VII- X
Middle Kingdom c. 3005-2112	XI - XIII
Second Intermediate Period c. 2112-1738	XIV- XVI
New Kingdom c. 1738-1102	XVII- XX
Late Period c. 1102-525	XXI- XXVI
Persian Period c. 525-332	XXVII- XXX

The so-called "Ptolemaic Period", c. 327-47 or 30 B.C.E., which followed the death of Alexander II ["the great"] in c. 327 B.C.E., is not listed above. Yet, it was during said "Period" that the African-European High-Priest Manetho composed his listing of the "Pharaohs" and "Dynasties of Egypt." The term B.C.E. and C.E. are used here in the same context as in all other areas of the general text of this volume; but, it must be remembered that the ancients of the above "periods' were not aware of any GOD-HEAD by the name of "JESUS CHRIST," thus they could not have refered to any dating process relating to him. The dating of the above can be traslated into SOLAR and LUNAR CALENDAR years of the Nile Valley and Great Lakes African Mysteries System, which was convereted to the so-called "JUSTINIAN CALENDAR" and "GREGORIAN CALENDAR" of the Europeans and European-Americans.

Q. Before the onset of European imperialism and colonialism in Africa during c. 332 B.C.E., which culminated with the 1884-1885 C.E. Berlin Conference and/or "ACT;" what type of COLONIAL CHRONOLOGY Egypt had following the death of High-Priest Manetho?

A.   THE CHRONOLOGY OF FOREIGN CONQUESTS OF EGYPT
            FOLLOWING THE DEATH OF MANETHO - c. 270 B.C.E.
                       [All periods B.C.E.]

Division or Period	Dynasty
Ptolemaic Period, c. 270 [Manetho died]	"XXXIIIrd"
Ptolemaic Period, c. 270-30 [Post-Manetho]	"XXXIIIrd"
Roman Occupation [incl. Byzantine], c. 30 B.C.E. - 640 C.E.	"XXXIV th"

Arab Conquest, c. 640 C.E. or 18 A.H.
Ottoman Turks and Manelukes
French, c. 1789-1792 C.E.
British, c. 1792-

Special attention must be given to the fact that all of the PERIODS of conquest following the death of High-Priest Manetho are not considered "DYNASTIES." On the other hand, many "Western" historians and egyptologists have used the Macedonian invasion and conquest of Egypt and part of Nubia as a "DYNASTIC PERIOD." They also include the Greeks rebelion against the Macedonians with the Ptolemies as another "PERIOD." The latter reasoning is the factor which created the so-called "THIRTY-TWO" [xxxii] DY-NASTIES" we so often see in history books of the past and present. Even Manetho did not refer to the "GREEK PERIOD" as a "DYNASTY." The so-called "XXXIIIrd" and "XXXIVth" are only for conjecture; but, they are sometimes seriously mentioned as the "ROMAN" and "ARAB DYNASTY."

Q. Did Manetho separate the Africans of Nubia and Egypt into "DIFFERENT RACES?"

A. There is no historical record written by High-Priest Manetho in which he referred to any of the other Nile Valley Africans as members of a "DIFFERENT RACE" to his fellow Egyptians or Nubians. Manetho, himself, was of African [BLACK] and European [WHITE] parentage. He saw the nation of the Egyptians, Nubians, Kushites, Meröites, and Puanits as political entities, but, never as NATIONS OF "DIFFERENT RACES" as shown in the distorted pages of history by European-American historians, egyptologists, and other educators of WHITE STUDIES. No where in the CHRONICLES of the ancient Africans of the Nile Valleys and Great Lakes High-Cultures have they ever used any word with the same meaning as the bigoted term "RACE." This expression is of Euro-pean and European-American origin. Its ugliest and earliest form is still in practice in the "CHOSEN PEOPLE" myth of the so-called "JEWISH" or "SEMITIC RACE" inserted into the texts of the Five Books Of Moses [Holy Torah or Old Testament] by some of the most degenerate RACISTS and RELIGIOUS BIGOTS, all of whom continue to hide behind a God-head by the name of "JEHOVAH" as a cloak of respectability.

Q. Which noted Greek historical figures perpetuated Manetho's works the most?

A. Eusebius and Syncellus stated that "...MANETHO BEGAN HIS [Egyptian] HISTORY WITH DYNASTIC GODS AND DEMI-GODS..." who reigned for very long periods of time. They also stated that he referred said history to about "...36,525 years..." before the period c. 280 B.C.E., when he began his own work; the latter figure representing the period marked by "...THE FIRST DYNASTY OF THE GODS." He connected "...THE REIGN OF THE GODS" as "THIRTY [30] DYNASTIES," and said of them:

> "...which number of years, resolved and divided into its consistuent
> parts, that is to say, 25 times 1461 years, shows that is related to
> the fabled periodical revolution of the Zodiac among the Egyptians
> and Greeks; that is, its revolution from a particular point to the same
> again, which point is the first Ram, as it is explained in the Genesis
> of Hermes and in the Cyrannian Books."

Q. Can you define what is meant by the "Egyptian Calendar-Year Corrections"?

346

A. The "EGYPTIAN CALENDAR-YEAR" [forerunner of the present so-called "Western Calendar" in use], which was created and developed by indigenous African ASTRONOMERS, was as follows:

One [1] CALENDAR YEAR = 365 days; minus one [1] day each fourth [4th] year. The result of these differences caused the Egyptians and other Nile Valley Africans to employ two [2] CALENDARS. Thus:

No. 1. The OFFICIAL CALENDAR, which began with the month of THOTH, having no CORRECTION for a LEAP YEAR [fourth year].

No. 2. The SOLAR CALENDAR, which was based upon "...the rising of the Dog-Star at the dawn." This was the truly astronomically correct calendar with the Fourth [4th] Year having a One [1] Full Day CORRECTION.

It must be noted that the true EGYPTIAN and NUBIAN CALENDAR YEAR had 365 1/4 DAYS, 12 MONTHS, and 3 SEASONS, as shown in Chapter IV of this volume. Although both CALENDARS began at the month of THOTH, the OFFICIAL lost ONE FULL DAY in FOUR YEARS; thus, "...the helical rising of Sirus..." took place on the 2nd DAY of THOTH, instead of the Ist DAY as the SOLAR CALENDAR. Also, in the TWENTY-EIGHT [28th] YEAR the OFFICIAL CALENDAR was short ONE [1] FULL WEEK. In a span of ONE HUNDRED-TWENTY [120] YEARS the loss was ONE [1] COMPLETE MONTH; and, in ONE THOUSAND FOUR-HUNDRED AND SIXTY [1,460] SOLAR YEARS both CALENDARS [Official and Solar] returned to the FIRST DAY OF THOTH ; thus, "...THE 360^0 CIRCLE..." was complete. c. 139 C.E. or A.D. was the last YEAR in which the coincidence of the OFFICIAL and SOLAR Egyptian [African] CALENDARS had their FULL 360^0 CIRCLE or "WHEEL MEETING." From this latter date, c. 139 C.E., modern chronographers have established calculations for the "SOTHIC CYCLE." In the reign of Pharaoh Thotmes III of the XVIIIth Dynasty there was a period when the "HELICAL RISING OF SIRUS" was mentioned in the inscriptions of the Africans of Egypt and Nubia, this being the earliest period known that the Egyptian records showed an exact DATE or DAY and MONTH when it was first calculated from a known "SOTHIC CYCLE." The following works contain said calculation: E. Meyer's "Aegyptische Chronologie" [in: ABHANDLUGEN der KONIGLICHEN PREUSSISCHEN AKADEMIE, 1905]; and S. Smith's ALALAKH. Before this period all calculations appeared to have been approximated. However, the calculated CALENDARS [Official and Solar] were used by the Africans along the entire Nile Rivers [blue and white], such as the Nubians, Meröites, Ethiopians, and Kushites, equally among their fellow Africans of Puanit - at the HORN of East Africa where the present nations of Kenya and Somali occupy, and Tanzania. Many South, Central, and West African nations' oral and traditional history also indicate that said CALENDARS were in use among their indigenous peoples.

Q. Who did Manetho called the "FIRST MORTAL PHARAOH"?

A. Manetho stated that AHA, MENA or NARMER" [whom the Greeks renamed "Menes] was the "FIRST MORTAL PHARAOH OF EGYPT BORN OF MAN." Herodotus wrote in his HISTORIES, Book II, p. 99 the following about him:

"...Menes, the first ruler of Egypt, in the first place protected Memphis by a mound... Beginning about a hundred stades above Memphis, he filled in the elbow towards the south, dried up the old chann-

el, and conducted the river by a canal so as to make
it flow between the mountains: this bend of the Nile
which flows excluded from its ancient course, is
still carefully upheld by the Persians.... When the
part cut off had been made firm land by this Menes,
who was the first king, he in the first place built
on it the city that is now called Memphis; for Memphis is situated in the narrow part of Egypt; and
outside it he excavated a lake from the river towards
the north and west; for the Nile itself bounds
it towards the east. "

The above comments by Herodotus bear witness to the magnitude of the major engineering achievements of the ancient African engineers and mathematicians of the
entire Nile Valley High-Cultures; especially when one considers the early period in
human history the indigenous Africans were able to change the direction of the Nile's
flow – this about c. 3200 B.C.E. One has to remember that this fete was accomplished

more than one thousand nine-hundred and sixty-eight [1,968] years before the theory
of "ADAM AND EVE IN THE GARDEN OF EDEN" was advanced by an African of the
Haribu [Hebrew, Israelite or "Jewish"] religion wrote of such in his books of history,
mythology, theology, and allegory; particularly in the first of his five books, which he
is alleged to have called "GENESIS." This African, MOSES, allegedly published his
plagiarized version of the BOOK OF THE COMING FORTH BY DAY, the so-called
"Book Of The Dead and Papyrus Of Ani" as translated from its original Hieroglyph into the English language by Sir Ernest A. Wallis Budge; works which Moses stole from
his fellow Africans of Egypt and Nubia's Secret Societies which belong to the Mysteries
System OSIRICA. For another side of the story see the so-called "SECOND BOOK OF
MOSES", otherwise called "EXODUS," in the Hebrew or Jewish HOLY TORAH [Chris-
tian Old Testament].

Q. What is meant by "...THE HIERAKANPOLIS MURDERS..."?

A. This question calls for no submission of proof that there were other Africans in
Egypt before the arrival of Asian and European conquerors from c. 1675 to 30 B.C.E.;
from the so-called "HYKSOS SEMITES" to the ROMANS. F. Quibell writing in his book,
HIERAKANPOLIS, I, plates xxix and xl, described the massacre of the Africans from
the SOUTH OF EGYPT by the pharaohs of the IInd Dynasty, those following the death of
Pharaoh Perabsen. Other European and European-American historians and egyptologists
wrote that "...THERE WERE AT LEAST 47,000 OR MORE MASSACRED." [See W.M.
Flanders Petrie's RESEARCHES IN SINAI, plate xlvii, in which he depicted trading expeditions of all kind by Africans beyond the Sinai Peninsula of Northeast Africa in search
of copper].

Q. Did the ancient Africans of Egypt, Nubia, and Ethiopia engaged themselves in the
writing of what is today called "LITERATURE"?

A. The earliest known "...PATRON OF LITERATURE..." in recorded history anywhere was an Egyptian - PHARAOH DJOSER [Herodotus called him "Zoser" and "Zozer"].
Many "Western" anthropologists, historians, egyptologists, and other educators have purposefully suppressed the fact of said African achievement in order to discredit the so-

called "NEGROES OF NUBIA," whom they alleged had no existence in Egypt of antiquity before they were brought in as "...SLAVES OF THE EGYPTIANS...," etc. Since
most of them have conceded that this pharaoh of Egypt was originally from the SOUTH,
Nubia; thus a "NEGRO," it was only natural that they would have had to suppress his
contributions in this area of academic discipline, or at least attribute it to the Greeks,
Romans, and/or "Semites" of Egyptian origin. But, the Egyptian High-Priest Manetho
wrote the following about Pharaoh Djoser's reign:

> "...CALLED AESCALIPIUS BY HIS FELLOWMEN FOR HIS MEDICAL
> KNOWLEDGE. HE BUILT A HOUSE OF HEWN STONES, AND GREAT-
> LY PATRONIZED LITERATURE...," etc.

It is to be noted that "AESCALIPIUS" was in fact IMHOTEP the architect, philosopher,
Grand Vizer, Prime Minister, physician, etc. for Pharaoh Djoser. He was the same
African or "NEGRO" Hippocrates called the "...GOD OF MEDICINE..." in the so-
called "HIPPOCRATIC OATH" shown on page 316 of Y. ben-Jochannan's AFRICA:
MOTHER OF "WESTERN CIVILIZATION," Alkebu-lan Books Associates, New York,
1971. It must be noted, also, that many historians claimed that DJOSER and/or IM-
HOTEP was in fact "TOSOTHROS," such as M. A. Murray's THE SPLENDOUR THAT
WAS EGYPT: A GENERAL SURVEY OF EGYPTIAN CULTURE AND CIVILIZATION,
1949, plate xlv.

Q. Who built the first PYRAMID of the so-called "GREAT PYRAMIDS"?

A. The first of the "GREAT PYRAMIDS" was built for Pharaoh Djoser by his architect
and builder - IMHOTEP [see page 190] around c. 2780-2680 B.C.E. It was also the
first structure of its kind, and known as the "STEP PYRAMID OF SAKHARA [Saqqara].
Yet, so-called "modern liberal White Africanists" have only assigned the term "GREAT
PYRAMIDS" to a few of the IVth through VIth Dynasties pyramids built after this one.

Q. Who built the "GREAT PYRAMIDS"?

A. The builders of the so-called "GREAT PYRAMIDS" of the IVth through VIth Dynasties [c. 2680-2270 B.C.E.] were the following:
> KHUFU, KHAFRA, and MEN-KAU-RE; the Greeks called them:
> CHEOPS, CHEPHREN, and MYCERINUS.

Khufu [Herodotus' Cheops] was the first of the "MAJOR" or true "GREAT PYRAMID
BUILDERS" of the IVth Dynasty. He, also, was the first man in history to decry the
custom of "...HUMAN SACRIFICES," which is quite to the contrary of the teachings
of Judaeo-Chritianity. For, it is stated that "...ABRAHAM'S REFUSAL TO SACRI-
FICE HIS OWN SON WAS THE FIRST TIME SUCH AN ANCIENT CUSTOM CEASED IN
ANY NATION OF ANTIQUITY...," etc. But, Pharaoh Khufu died more than one thousand years before the birth of ABRAHAM - the first of the Haribu people. The ancient
records of the Africans of Egypt and other Nile Valley nations said the following about
Pharaoh Khufu:

> [He] "...SHUT UP ALL THE TEMPLES AND FORBADE THE
> SACRIFICES...," etc.

Pharaoh Khufu did this more than one thousand three hundred [1,300] years before an African named Moses told anyone there was an ADAM and the story about the "CREATION OF THE WORLD BY JEHOVAH," as stated in the Holy Torah or Old Testament BOOK OF GENESIS. The above quotation is taken from Herodotus' HISTORIES, Book II, p. 124. Herodotus also wrote the following about King Cheops [Pharaoh Khufu] and the workmen he hired for the building of the PYRAMID:

> "...WORKED TO THE NUMBER OF A HUNDRED THOUSAND MEN
> AT A TIME, EACH PARTY DURING THREE MONTHS PERIOD. THE
> TIME DURING WHICH THEY WERE THUS HARASSED BY TOIL,
> LASTED TEN YEARS ON THE ROAD WHICH THEY CONSTRUCTED.
> TWENTY YEARS WERE SPENT ERRECTING THE PYRAMID ITSELF."

Sketches, drawings, pictures, etc. of Pharaoh Khufu and his PYRAMID can be seen in Chapter IV of this volume.

Q. Who built the second of the GREAT PYRAMIDS?

A. Pharaoh Men-kau-Re [Herodotus' Mycerinius]. He was the son of the first of the MAJOR PYRAMID BUILDERS of the IIIrd DYNASTY. His father was Pharaoh Khufu, whom Herodotus and other Greeks called "CHEOPS." Herodotus wrote the following about him in his HISTORIES:

> "...MYCERINUS, THE SON OF CHEOPS, REIGNED OVER EGYPT.
> HE OPENED THE TEMPLES AND ALLOWED THE PEOPLE, WHO
> WERE WORN DOWN TO THE LAST EXTREMITY, TO TURN THEIR
> EMPLOYMENTS AND TO SACRIFICES; AND HE MADE THE MOST
> JUST DECISIONS OF ALL THEIR KINGS."

Pictures of this pharaoh's PYRAMID and his statue are shown in Chapter IV of this volume.

Q. What did Flavius Josephus say about the HYKSOS from Asia, who invaded Egypt in approximately c. 1675 B.C.E.?

A. Josephus, the Hebrew or Jewish historian, paraphrased High-Priest Manetho's depiction of the "...PEOPLE OF AN IGNOBLE BIRTH....,"[the Hyksos, so-called "Semitic peoples"] as "...A DIFFERENT RACE TO THE EGYPTIANS." He left us the proof in his work, AGAINST APION, as he quoted the following from Manetho's HISTORY OF EGYPT:

> "We had formerly a king whose name was Amenophis. In his time
> it came to pass, I know not how, that God was displeased with us,
> and there came up from the East in a strange manner men of an
> ignoble race, who had the confidence to invade our country, and
> easily subdued it by their power without a battle. And when they
> had our rulers in their hands they burnt our cities, and demolish-
> ed our temples to the Gods, and inflicted every kind of barbarity
> upon the inhabitants, slaying some, and reducing the wives and
> children of others to a state of slavery. At length they made one of

themselves king, whose name was Salatis; he lived at Memphis and rendered both Upper and Lower regions of Egypt tributary, and stationed garrisons in places which were best adopted for the purpose. But he directed his attention principally to the Eastern frontier, for he regarded with suspicion the increasing power of the Assyrians, who he foresaw would one day undertake an invasion of his kingdom. And observing in the Saite nome, upon the East of the Bubasite channel, a city which from some theological reference was called Avaris; and finding it admirably adapted to his purpose, he built it, and strongly fortified it with walls, and garrisoned it with a force of two hundred and fifty thousand men completely armed. To this city Salatis repaired in summertime, to collect his tribute, and pay his troops, and exercise his soldiers in order to strike terror into foreigners. Some say they were Arabians. This people who were thus demoninated Shepherd Shepherd Kings, and their descendants, retained possession of Egypt during the period of five hundred and eleven years."

It is to be noted that the Hyksos was called an "...IGNOBLE RACE..." by the Africans of Egypt; not a "SEMITIC RACE" as implied and also taught by European-American professors. Also, that they were totally ILLITERATE and INTOLERANT of the indigenous African people and High-Culture of the Nile Valley, Egypt in particular. Equally, they had no appearent understanding of the philosophical concepts taught in the African RELIGION of the Osirica the found when they arrived in Egypt. Yet, we are made to believe that the indigenous Africans the Hyksos met in Egypt were of the same "SEMITIC RACE AND CIVILIZATION." At least, this is what we have been taught by most of the so-called "ORTHODOX" and "LIBERAL" White Africanists. Secondly; the ancient indigenous Africans spoke of the "INVADERS" as "ARABIANS," not as "SEMITIC PEOPLES" from the "EAST." Of course, not even CAUCASIANS or INDO-EUROPEAN ARYANS was mentioned. But, our textbooks on this period of African history continue projecting the RACIST LINE of North and East African SEMITISM and CAUCASIANISM, using for a base the alleged "SEMITIC RACE OF EGYPTIAN ORIGIN." These facts bear further witness to the reason why most so-called "modern [European and European-American] writers have condemned Herodotus' HISTORIES, paticularly Book II, in which he described the physical chracteristics of the indigenous Egyptians, Colchians, and Ethiopians, as shown elsewhere in this volume - "...THICK LIPS,..."etc.

Q. What did the "Jewish" historian, Flavius Josephus, said about Manetho's references to Pharaoh Amenophis and the "...UNCLEAN PEOPLE..." [the Hyksos]?

A. Josephus quoted Manetho's HISTORY OF EGYPT in one passage of his own book, AGAINST APION, as follows:

"[Manetho again says]: After this Amenophis returned from Ethiopia with a great force, and Rameses also, his son, with other forces, and encountering the Shepherds and the unclean people, they defeated them and slew multitudes of them, and pursued them to the bounds of Syria.

351

What we have just read in the remarks of Flavius Josephus is rather startling evidence; in fact, evidence that incriminates each and every "MODERN AFRICANIST." Here is more than ample proof that the indigenous Africans of Egypt and those of Ethiopia [Egyptians and Ethiopians] maintained very close ties in every respect, even to the point of being united allies against all foreigners from Asia and Europe. Also, it was impossible for these two African national groupings to keep such contact across Nubia, the so-called "...ONLY LAND OF THE NEGROES IN NORTH AFRICA...", without equally being amalgamated with their fellow Africans of Nubia in every human endeavour possible. Records such as this expose the lies of the so-called "SEMITISTS" and "CAUCASIANISTS", who domminate AFRICAN and BLACK STUDIES courses throughout the United States of America and write most of the textbooks used in these courses and WHITE STUDIES.

Q. Who initiated the insurrection against the Hyksos in Egypt?

A. The following quotation was extracted from the testimony of Aahmes the son of Abana, a descendant of Sequenen-Ra [Prince of Thebes], who started the nationalist uprising against the Hyksos during the XVIIIth Dynasty.

> "...I will tell you, O all ye people, I will inform
> you of all the honours which came to me. I was pre-
> sented with gold seven times in the presence of the
> whole land, male and female slaves likewise. I was
> endowed with many fields. The fame of a man valiant
> in his deeds shall not perish in this land for ever."

Note that the presentation of "GOLD" to a soldier in ancient Egypt was one of the highest of honours the state could have paid. It was higher than awarding the Congressional Medal of Honour to an American soldier. Aahmes the son of Abana fought in all of Pharaoh [King] Aahmes' military campaigns as a naval man. He also served under pharaohs Amenhotep I and Thothmes I. His service record caused him to reach the rank of "COMMANDER" of a Nile fleet, where many of his greatest naval fetes were made, including the capture of one of the Hyksos "CHIEFS" during the "BATTLE OF TYNT-TO-ANU" [located a little beyond the south of the first Cataract]. One can also observe that the Christian teachings about "...JESUS CHRIST JOINING ...GOD THE FATHER IN HEAVEN..." was nothing new, as seen in the above declaration. [See Lepsius, DEMKMALER II].

Q. Which other pharaoh built a structure comparative to that of Pharaoh Narmer?

A. The engineering fete of Pharaoh Amenemhat's reign compared to that of Pharaoh Narmer's. He built the greatest structure and largest engineering project since the reign of Pharaoh Narmer [Mena or Aha] of the Ist Dynasty, who altered the course of the Nile River's natural flow. The DAM Amenemhat I built on the same Nile River was at least twenty-five[25] miles long, and reclaimed forty-two [42] square miles of the best fertile land. He turned the lake created by the DAM into a reservoir to retain the annual flood water [innundation] until the arrival of dry season, thus releasing the much needed water all year around for irrigational purposes. Herodotus, who witnessed the many sluces and canals built by Pharaoh Amenemhat for the DAM's operation,wrote the following about them in his book, HISTORIES:

"...the water in lakes does not spring from the
soil, for these parts are excessively dry, but
it is conveyed through a channel from the Nile,
and for six months it flows into the lake, and
for six months out again into the Nile.
The above quotation was taken from Lepsius' DEMKMALER.

Q. Can you mention some of the names the indigenous Africans of what is today called
"EGYPT" used for their nation before the arrival of the Haribu [Hebrews or "Jews"],
who renamed it such according to the "Noah and the Flood" story in their HOLY TORAH?

A. Egypt was called many names by the indigenous Africans of the WHITE and BLUE
Nile Valley and elsewhere. Which of the many names was the first cannot be documented
at the present time, as there is not sufficient evidence to warrant such a conclusion.
However, some of them are as follows: "TA-MERRY, TETY-MERY, KIMIT, SAIS,
PEARL OF THE LOWER NILE, FLOWER OF THE NILE, THE LOWER NILE, LAND
OF THE GODS, LAND OF RA or LOWER NUBIA, LOWER ETHIOPI [Ethiopia], the
Haribu's CHAM and MIZRAIN , and finally their "Egypt." Today it is also called
THE UNITED ARAB REPUBLIC [U.A.R.] by descendants of Arab Muslim invaders who
came there in approximately 640 C.E.-18 A.H. from the Arabian Peninsula of Asia.

Q. Was Herodotus [the 5th century B.C.E. Greek citizen] the "FATHER OF HISTORY"?

A. The following facts disproved Herodotus' fatherhood of any "HISTORY" other than
that of the Europeans and European-Americans. We note that Aahmes, the son of
Abana, while reporting to Pharaoh Thothmes I XVIIIth DYNASTY [c. 1580-1558 BCE]
about his conquest of Palestine [the land of the "Jews"] and Assyria recorded said
events historically. He wrote:
"...I was at the head of our soldiers,[0] and his majesty saw my valour when I seized upon a chariot,
its horses and those who were in it, as living captives."
A later report, also written in the disciplinary manner we now call "HISTORY", by
the same Aahmes at the age of ninety[90] follows:
"...I have reached old age, and I shall rest in the
tomb which I myself have made."
He was a "CAPTAIN-GENERAL" of the sailors, the equivalent of a 20th century C.E.
naval commander or admiral of a fleet.

Q. Who was the first and only "QUEEN-KING" or "WOMEN PHARAOH" of Egypt?

A. HATSHEP-SUT, the so-called "QUEEN-KING" of the XVIIIth Dynasty, became
Egypt's first and only "WOMAN PHARAOH" in the year c. 1515 B.C.E. She succeeded
her father, Pharaoh Thothmes I, with whom she had ruled as co-regent until his death.
She stated in her inscriptions on the walls of her tomb that she was "...THE PHARAOH
..." during the reign of her illustrious father and his two sons - Thothmes I and II.
European and European-American historians and egyptologists, most of them, have
distorted this aspect of indigenous African history and disclaimed the "Queen-King's
historical recordings of these events in her own reign, which she personally experi-

enced thousands of years before their own birth. The fact is that Thothmes I, her
father and co-Regent, died when Hatshep-sut was still very young. Her oldest brother,
Thothmes II, ruled for thirteen [13] years. The younger brother, Thothmes III, was an
infant at the time of his father's death, and only a little boy at the death of his older
brother; thus it was that Hatshep-sut was able to usurp her younger brother's authority as sole ruler of the Egyptian Empire by right of her inheritance. The reign of Queen-
King Hatshep-sut was not only distorted by so-called "Western historians" and "egyptologists," but equally her death, which they have theorized was caused by her brother,
Thothmes III, after he had reached the age of maturity and wanted to exercise his legal
right of succession as the sole ruler and hier to Egypt's throne. They have cited the
following as proof of her murder by her brother:

> "...SHE WAS NOT BURRIED AMONG THE ORDINARY QUEENS OF
> EGYPT, BUT THROUGH HER POWER OF ROYAL RULE HAD HER-
> SELF BURRIED IN THE VALLEY OF THE TOMBS OF THE KINGS."

Of course there is no justifiable basis upon which this distortion has been alleged other
than to make the so-called "SEMITIC RULE" in Egypt, and the Mosaic violence that occurred earlier. appear to have been the works of some God named Jehovah, thus belittling
the indigenous God of the Africans of Egypt as a DEVILISH character. [See Marietta's
ABYDOS; Piehl's INSCRIPTIONS; Sethe's UNTERERSUCHUNGEN; J. J. Jackson's IN-
TRODUCTION TO AFRICAN HISTORY; G. G. M. James' STOLEN LEGACY; F. B.
Sandford's THE MEDITERRANEAN WORLD; Lepsius' DENKMALER, III, pp 22-24].

Q.   What Pharaoh adopted ATEN as the God of Egypt?

A.   Pharaoh Amenhotep IV, commonly known as "AKHENATEN, the son of Pharaoh
Amorphis or Amenhotep III and Queen Tiyi [Tyi - of commoner birth], was the first to
adopt ATEN as the national God of the Africans of Egypt above all other Gods. Note
that his mother's "COMMONER" status or "LOW BIRTH" caused Akhenaten's name to
be unlisted among the "PHARAOHS OF ROYAL BIRTH;" this was in accordance with
Egyptian law. For further detail see the TELL-el-AMARNA ROYALTIES list.
   Akhenaten adopted the worship of ATEN in the Fourth Nile Year of his reign, c.
1366 B.C.E. He devoted the rest of his life to the perpetuation of the teachings of this
Diety and neglected all other duties of his office. ATEN [the Sun Disc] was different to
the God RE or RA [The Divine Spirit In The Sun]. Along with ATEN, he also worshiped
RE, HOROUS, and the MENEVIS BULL. He challenged the priests and their worship of
the God AMON; and, he moved the capital of Egypt from LUXOR [later called Thebes]
to his own city that he named "AKHENATEN" - which the Arab invaders and conquerors of Egypt renamed "TEL-el-AMARNA," thus removing the commercial control of
the priests over the religious life of Egypt. He also spent most of the treasury's money
on the building of new temples to ATEN, with the wealthy and the nobility following his
lead. Using most of his time, while in isolation for the most part, for the composition
of hymns and prayers to ATEN; thus, he allowed Egypt to sink into economic disaster;
all of which he did in consort of his declared belief that he was "...A PRIVATE PRISON-
ER OF MY OWN CITY FOR ATEN. He did not leave the CITY OF AKHENATEN from the
time of his conversion to ATEN to the end of his natural life on earth in c. 1352 B.C.E.
He had also established the "TRINITARIAN SOLAR DIETY" concept more than one thousand three hundred and fifty-two [1,352] years before the birth of the Christians' God -

354

"JESUS CHRIST" - was proclaimed. Following the birth of his sixth child with his wife, Queen Nefet-yti [Nefer-ti-ti], she was forced to live apart from Akhenaten - who had declared himself "CELEBATE" in order to give full and undivided attention to the worship of ATEN. By so relieving himself of his wife; he then proceded to make his teenage son-in-law, Tut-ankh-aten [later Tut-ankh-amon affectionately "TUT"], his co-Regent.

The downfall of Pharoah Akhenaten's Egypt, the destruction of the religious temples of ATEN, and the stomping-out of other religion's GOD, according to a story about "...THE COLLAPSE OF EGYPT UNDER THE RULE OF AKHENATEN...," by one Ribaddi of Gebal, which the Tell-el-Amarna Letters allegedly revealed, Pharoah Akhenaten supposedly made the following statement in concern with the preceding conditions of Egypt:

"...IF NO HELP COMES, THEN I AM A DEAD MAN...."

The above quotation was allegedly taken from the most basic message of Pharoah Akhenaten's last words before the armies of the foreign invaders attacking Egypt closed-in on his capital city while he still knelt in silent prayers to ATEN.

There is no other pharaoh of Egypt, except possibly Rameses II, who have suffered as much character assassination as Akhenaten. Why? Because he was the first person in history to teach much of what European-American and European Christians teach as the original contributions of their God "JESUS CHRIST" to mankind before anyone else. A footnote to the above follows: Akhenaten had eight daughters, no sons, and one son-in-law of record up to his death - Tut-ankh-amon. But the latter is mistaken as the co-Regent with Akhenaten; "Western" historians and egyptologists have erred significantly by attributing such to this period of Africa's history. For, Tut followed Pharoah Senenkh-ka-Re on the throne - the successor of Akhenaten, who equally carried on the worship of ATEN. The second reason for this author's contention is that the teenager, TUT, returned the Africans of Egypt to the worship of AMON, taking on the God-head name for himself - "TUT-ANKH-AMON," and dropped the "ATEN" his father-in-law gave him. TUT lived to the ripe old age of nineteen [19] before he died.

Q. Can you give a few details about Pharaoh Rameses II and the Hittites?

A. After twenty [20] long years of continuous wars Egypt and the Land of the Hittites peace treaty was negotiated as a result of the easy demands Pharaoh Rameses II placed upon his Asian neighbours. The following are some of the demands:
    1. Preparation of mutual plans for the conquest of Assyria by Egypt and the Kingdom of the Hittites;
    2. Establishment of a common defence alliance against all foreigners purported to be the enemies of either of our nations;
    3. Sharing of the mutual expenses for the suppression of Assyria's threat of war against Egypt at the present;
    4. The immediate exchange of political refugees and fugitives on a mutual basis; and
    5. Economic assistance and trade relations to be established immediately between both of our nations according to established needs.
To make certain that the above provisions, and all of the others within the treaty agreement, were observed to the letter of each word invocations of the GODS of the Hittites

and those of the Egyptians were included as part of the text of the treaty agreement.
Part of one of the many invocations as translated by Lepsius in his book, DENKMAL-
ER, III, 146, read as follows:

> "...that a thousand dieties of the male Gods and female Gods
> of the Hittites, and a thousand dieties of the male Gods and
> the female Gods of the land of Egypt sanction this treaty...."

Q. Is it true that Pharaoh Rameses II was married to a Hittite princess?

A. Reigning on the throne of Egypt for a little more than sixty-four [64] years,
Pharaoh Rameses II of the XIXth Dynasty, c. 1298-1232 B.C.E., married one of the
princesses of the Land of the Kingdom of the Hittites to cement further political and
economic ties between both his nation and that of his Hittite wife. The security and
peace between both nations that resulted from this marriage allowed Pharaoh Rameses
II to move his capital city from LUXOR to MEMPHIS, then finally to TANIS in the Delta
region, in order to keep a constant vigilance over the Assyrian and Palestinian wars;
thus, he was able engage himself in the expansion of new metropolitan centers - towns
and cities - all over the Delta; but, not one of these major monuments he had con-
structed equalled the greatness of the masterpiece of his entire career or reign -
ABU SIMBEL - in Nubia, which he built in cooperation with the nobilities of Nubia and
Ethiopia. At Luxor his second greatest accomplishment in the form of construction of
buildings or monuments was realized. The works of this pharaoh are further proof
that the indigenous Africans of the Nile Valleys [Blue and White] were the originators,
or of the same "RACIAL STOCK," in every manner imaginable, particularly before
the entrance of the "...PEOPLE OF AN IGNOBLE RACE..." - the "HYKSOS" - in
approximately c. 1675 B.C.E. The priests of Nubia, during this period, had already
gained very much sway over those of the Lower Lands around the Delta region. The
comparative peace in Egypt had removed her from an imperial and colonialist power;
thus, it was possible to re-introduce another cultural renaissance throughout the entire
land. Pharaoh Rameses II death caused his historic mantle to pass on to his oldest
son, Pharaoh Mer-en-Ptah [The Beloved of the God Ptah],in c. 1232 B.C.E.

European-American historians and egyptologists, as other writers, who call themselves "AFRICANIST " and "AUTHORITY ON AFRICA," among many other such names,
constantly distort this period of Africa's glorious history and High-Culture in order to
attribute all of the developments and creations of the Nile Valley Africans, Egypt in
particular, to some sort of people they have given the name "SEMITES" and/or "CAU-
CASIANS OF NORTH AND EAST AFRICA;" all of this is in keeping with the RACIST
and RELIGIOUS BIGOTRY of the "CHOSEN PEOPLE" myth and the "NEGRO-LESS
NORTH AND EAST AFRICA" syndrome. Why? Because Rameses II was the reigning
Pharaoh of all Egypt and Nubia when the Haribu [the so-called "JEWS"] were allegedly
driven out of Egypt and Nubia with an African they called "MOSES." Also, without the
Africans of the Nile Valleys, particularly those of Egypt and Nubia, there is no FIVE
BOOKS OF MOSES, and more specifically the FIRST and SECOND - otherwise called
"GENESIS" and "EXODUS;" thus, there would have been no "ADAM AND EVE, GARDEN
OF EDEN, EXODUS OF THE ISRAELITES FROM EGYPT [Africa]," and/or "JEHOVAH"
and "JESUS CHRIST," equally AL'LAH."

Q. What was objectionable about Pharaoh Rameses II reign in Egypt?
356

A.   The attempt to discredit the name and honour of Pharaoh Rameses II is not coincidental or unintentional on the part of his modern RACIST and RELIGIOUSLY BIGOTED
distractors - both "Jewish" and "Christian." Many so-called "SEMITIC" historians
and egyptologists, and other forms of "educators', have established among themselves
all sorts of theories and hypotheses about the alleged "DEGENERACY" of Pharaoh
Rameses II, as projected in the first chapter of this volume; the same being equally
true for Pharaoh Akhenaten; all of this in keeping with the RACIST manner in which
WHITE STUDIES have been perpetuating the CAUCASIAN-SEMITIC syndrome of a North
and East Africa that was free of "NEGROES UNTIL THEY WERE BROUGHT INTO
EGYPT FROM NUBIA AS SLAVES FOR THE EGYPTIANS," each of them forgetting that
NUBIA is in North Africa. For example: Margaret A. Murray wrote in her book, THE
SPLENDOUR THAT WAS EGYPT, New York, 1949, pp. 59-60, the following comments
with respect to Pharaoh Rameses II:

> "...As often happened in Egypt when there was to much peace and
> prosperity, the country degenerated, the pharaoh became slothful,
> the officials neglectfull, and the peasants unhappy. Foreigners be-
> gan to flock in and settle in Egypt, pushing out the rightful inhabi-
> tants, and when Rameses died his son and successor, Meren-Ptah,
> was faced with a perilous situation."

The mere fact that the above conditioned may have occurred before in Egypt is no indication that it happened during the reign of Rameses II. Murray did not submit a single
word of evidence to prove this allegation. However, in order to maintain the lies told
about the Egyptians and other Africans in the Holy Torah [Old Testament], allegedly
written or handed down from Moses - another African, it is always necessary to perpetuate the myth of the "...INHUMANITY OF THE EGYPTIANS...," particularly
those who had anything whatsoever to do with the alleged "...EXPULSION OF THE
JEWS" [God's Chosen peoples] "FROM EGYPT" [Northeast Africa].

Q.   Give some particulars on the attempt to disspoil the good name of Pharaoh Rameses
II of Egypt, North Africa, with respect to the "PASSOVER STORY OF THE JEWS."

A.   The major cause for trying to disspoil Pharaoh Rameses II great and glorious
name and contributions to Egypt and other Nile Valley High-Cultures, which in turn influenced the Europeans [Greeks and Romans], as Asians who benefited from what he
left when they arrived in Egypt and Nubia for their earliest of education into the Seven
Liberal Arts, the sciences, etc., both by the so-called "SEMITISTS" and "CAUCASIAN-
ISTS," which began sometime around the latter part of the 18th to early part of the 19th
century C.E., is his alleged role as the main Egyptian personality in the EXODUS
drama of the Hebrew Holy Torah [Old Testament of the Christians]. Rameses allegedly
chased "...MOSES FROM THE CITY OF SOCCOTH TO RAMESES...," etc.; then "...
ACROSS THE RED SEA AND INTO THE SINAI DESERT...," etc. All of these were supposed to have taken place around c. 1298-1232 B.C.E., during the XIXth Dynsty, the
period when Pharaoh Rameses II reigned over Egypt and other nations of the Nile Valleys. One must remember that there is no other records than the Hebrew or Jewish
Holy Torah to justify the existence of the biblical figure named "MOSES," and/or the
sto·ies attributed to him. The EXODUS, or PASSOVER STORY, created much of the
current and past myths with respect to the Africans of Egypt's history, moreso than

ADAM AND EVE IN THE GARDEN OF EDEN myth in the Holy Torah - a hypothetical drama by Moses in tne BOOK OF GENESIS, one of the so-called "FIVE BOOKS OF MOSES." Moreso, many European and European-American, as Europeanized African and African-American, theologians and other RELIGIOUS BIGOTS who decry the religions of those who are Christians or Jews, held, and still hold, that it was during the reign of Pharaoh Rameses II son's, Mer-en-Ptah, the entire drama took place - from c. 1232 to about c. 1224 B.C.E. Others have decided that it was during the reign of Rameses II father's , Seti I, reign, who ruled over Egypt from approximately c. 1318 to c. 1298 B.C.E. The sole source of the EXODUS, the so-called "FIVE BOOKS OF MOSES" or "HOLY TORAH," by the Hebrews or Jews [also Israelites later], is without any corraboration of any of the writers who lived in Egypt and all other nations bordering on Egypt during the period this alleged historical drama took place. Yet, it must be noted that there are as many diviations to the story as there are translations and members of the clergy of Judaeo-Christian and Islamic institutions who perpetuate the histo-religious mythology of the Holy Torah, Holy Bible, and Holy Quran.

Q.   What about the Africans invasion of Palestine stated in II CHRONICLES, xvii, 2, of the Hebrew Torah or Old Testament of the Christians?

A.   In Hebrew or Jewish mythology there is a story of an African invasion of Palestine from Egypt. This is best observed in II Chronicles, xii, 2-4, 9. The following came from the stylus or pen of one Haribu historian and mythologist. It alludes to an African invasion of Palestine in the "FIFTH YEAR OF REHOBOAN'S RULE" over Palestine from his throne in Jerusalem. Exaggarating the historical facts totally out proportion and the slightest possibility of its truthfullness, the Hebrew historian-mythologist wrote that Pharaoh "SHESHANQ:"

> "...came up against Jerusalem with twelve hundred chariots, and
> three score thousand horsemen, and the people were without numb-
> er that came with him. And he took away the treasuries of the house
> of the Lord, and the treasurers of the King's house, he took away all."

Needless to say that the Africans of the Egyptian and Nubian empire at this time in history did not need one-tenth of the soldiers and chariots mentioned by the writer in order to take tiny Palestine as their colony; muchless to march on such a little nothing of a country with "...PEOPLE... " who "...WERE WITHOUT NUMBER...," etc. One must concede that the ancient Hebrews were some of the best dramatists.

Q.   Was the God AMON also from Ethiopia [Itiopi or Kush]?

A.   The home of the Egyptian God AMON was said to be in "ETHIOPIA." During the reign of the so-called "RAMESIDE KINGS" - Rameses III to Rameses XIII, c. 1168 - 1085 B.C.E., a calamity of palace intrigues supposedly took place in Egypt. By the year c. 950 B.C.E. the Africans from Lebu [later Libya], who had migrated into the Delta region of Egypt and had already began usurping the power of the Egyptian throne and rule over parts of Egypt until Sheshanq II, c. 823-774 B.C.E., seized power over the entire land. Yet, it was not until Kashta, c. 772 B.C.E., followed by his successor Piankhy, c. 751 B.C.E., that the Ethiopians from the SOUTH were able to stabalized Egypt once again, which included bringing in new GODS and GODDESSES into Egyptian

High-Culture and religion. However, AMON preceded the latter three Pharaohs as GOD OF EGYPT, equally many others. In taking control of Egypt, we find Pharaoh Piankhy giving the following instruction to the invading armies from Ethiopia who were about to destroy the armies of their fellow Africans of Egypt:

> "...Delay not, day or night, as if at a game of chess, fight at sight. Force the battle from a distance. Yoke the war-horses! Draw up the line of Battle! Amon is the God who sent us! He makes the weak strong, so that a multitude flees before the feeble, and one man takes a thousand captives. Say to Him, give us the way that we may fight under the shadow of YOUR sword. When the young men whom YOU have sent out make their attack, let multitudes flee before them."

The words underscored above are for the purpose of dramtizing the manner in which all of the ancient recorders dramatized and mythologized historical events. It must be noted that the Hebrew text in the BOOK OF ISAIAH, xxx, 17 coopted the teachings of the Africans of Egypt, Nubia, Ethiopia, and other High-Cultures of the Nile Valleys' national God-head - "AMON." It reads:

> "ONE THOUSAND SHALL FLEE AT THE REBUKE OF ONE."

Note that the ancient value of the game of chess was as much for war as for pleasure, and as such held in greater esteem than it is today. AMON was the "GOD ABOVE ALL GODS" many pharaohs and kings of Egypt and other North and East African High-Cultures worshipped in their temples, and for whom many temples were built. For further reading in this area see Marriette's MONUMENTS DIVERS, plates 1-6; also, the recording of the above battle on the Piankhi Stele in the Temple of Napata [Barkal] shown in this volume.

Q. What was Pharaoh Piankhi's remarks to the Egyptian and their fellow Africans from Ethiopia?

A. The generousity and hospitality, if either term is applicable in situations such as this, of an African pharaoh from Ethiopia was extold in Pharaoh Piankhi's order to his fellow Africans just prior to his final thrust into Egypt and the grand entry that followed. This African King or Pharaoh, and general of the Ethiopian armies, had issued the following warning to his brother Africans of Egypt who were fighting a losing battle:

> "Do not shut up!Do not fight! Those who wish to enter, let them enter in; those who leave, let them leave. The people of Memphis will be safe and protected, not even an infant shall weep! Look at the provinces at the South, not a single person has been killed, except those who were slain for rebel activities."

Even when the Egyptians at Memphis refused to heed Piankhi's warning to surrender; he was moved to swear the following to the GODS:

> "As RE loves me, as AMON favours me, this shall happen. I shall

take Memphis by a flood of water!"

Before he ordered the final command to take action on the final attack Piankhi still reminded his fellow Africans that his power was like "...the flood waters of the Nile...."
The Egyptians, stubornly refusing to surrender to the Ethiopians and their commanders
beseeching commands, heard General Piankhi ordered his fellow Ethiopians:

> "Forward against Memphis! Mount the walls! Penetrate into the
> fortresses across the river Nile."

Pharaoh Tafnekhet and his defenders of Memphis were handily defeated. Thousands
were dead at the end of the battle by "...the flood waters..." of Piankhi's troops, up
to that period in Nile Valley history the most powerful army ever assembled along the
more than 1,400 miles long waterway. Brought to his knees Pharaoh Tafnekhet felt
obliged to enter the temple, and he was heard uttering the following to his fellow African conqueror, Piankhi, who had become the new master of all Egypt - the PHARAOH:

> "I will never transgress the command of the Pharaoh; I will not violate
> the Pharaoh's orders; I will not commit any hostile act against any of
> the other princes without Your knowledge; I will submit to all of the
> Pharaoh's orders; I will not disobey any of the Pharaoh's commands."

The above CONFESSIONS, very similar in many respect to the NEGATIVE CONFESSION
Moses used in copying his so-called "TEN COMMANDMENTS," should not be taken as a
sign of weakness on the part of the African commanders from the SOUTH of Egypt; for
Pharaoh Shabacon [Sabacon], another of the Ethiopian Pharaohs of Egypt, who succeded
in c. 716 B.C.E., was not as obliging when he destroyed Pharaoh Bocchoris' army.

Q.   What is it about Pharaoh Piankhi that the so-called "SEMITES" resent even today
in the 20th century C.E. ?

A.   Another reason to suppress AFRICAN and BLACK STUDIES in the educational institutions of the United States of America. Because Pharaoh Taharqa [the Hebrew
Holy Torah's Tirhakah - c. 690-664 B.C.E.], the second to the last of the Ethiopian
Pharaohs that ruled over Egypt, Nubia, Meröe, and Kush - c. 751-653 B.C.E., joined forces with the so-called "SEMITES" [Jews] OF PALESTINE" under the reign of
King Hezekiah of Judah [Judaea] against Sennacherib and the Assyrians and turned the
tide of the war in saving both Palestine and Egypt from the invading Assyrians. This
story is mentioned the BOOK OF ISAIAH, xxxvii, 36; also, Herodotus' HISTORIES,
Book II, p. 141. There is an obvious fact here; that is, the "NEGROES" had to save
the "SEMITES" from anihilation by the Assyrians. Yet, the treachery of the Jewish
King, Hezekiah of Judah, forced his "NEGRO" allies and their commander, Pharaoh
Taharqa [sometimes mistaken for Pharaoh Piankhi], to withdraw in haste from Palestine when the Jews failed to hold back the Assyrians on their side of the military line;
thus. allowing Ashurbanipal, who had replaced the defeated Sennacherib as leader of the
Assyrians. The following maliciously false statement about the Africans were written
by modern so-called "SEMITIC SCHOLARS" in many textbooks:

> "Taharqa fled south to Ethiopia, the mighty soldiers of my Lord

Aushur having overwhelmed him, as he went to his place at night."

Tne mighty forces of the Africans of Ethiopia and other Nile Valley countries had counter-attacked under the command of the last of tne Ethiopian pharaohs, Tanutemun, who reigned from c. 664 to 653 B.C.E., only to be eventually overthrown by a reinforced and much more powerful army under tne command of Ashurbanipal - which included turn-coat Jews that deserted to the Assyrians for protection after they country was threatened of being over-run. This was the beginning of the end of another of the African national groupings that invaded, captured, and ruled over their fellow Africans - the so-called "NEGROES" - of Egypt.

Q. How old is the symbol we call the "CHRISTIAN CROSS"?

A. In fact, there is no such thing as a "CHRISTIAN CROSS." The oldest amulitic sign known to man is probably the "CROSS;" that is to say, the common figure made by two [2] straight lines bisecting each other at midpoint and at right angles ✚ is typically the original CROSS. This "CRUX SIMPLEX" or "SIMPLE CROSS" predated all of the SAVIORS and/or CHRISTS adopted by African or European Christendom by thousands of years; going back all the way before historic man - which included the mythical "ADAM AND EVE IN THE GARDEN OF EDEN" we were forced to believe in as we were brain-washed by our parents and their so-called "RELIGIOUS LEADERS."

The first "CROSS" used by the earliest Christians of North Africa, those who predated the Europeans of Rome and Greece by over two hundred [200] years, so far as our records have been documented with the Christian experiences down through the past nineteen hundred and seventy-one [1,971] years and a few months, is one of pre-Christian origin which the Kassites used. These were the same people whose kingdom began around c. 1746 B.C.E. with King Gandash, and came to its end in c. 1171 B.C.E. with King Ellil-nandir-ahi. This CROSS had a cylindrical-seal around it, bearing an inscription to the Sun God, RA or RE; and, it displayed an image of said God in a seated position holding an object of undetermined character in His right hand. Tne latter position is typical of the more recent teachings by so-called "CHRISTIAN THEOLOGIANS" with respect to the myth about "JESUS CHRIST AROSE FROM THE DEAD AND ASCENDED INTO HEAVEN, WHERE HE SITS AT THE RIGHT HAND OF GOD THE FATHER...," etc. The so-called "KASSITE CROSS" can be found on artifacts, and in tombs, all along the Nile Valleys [Blue and White] and Great Lakes regions area of Alkebu-lan [Africa]; some dating back to thousands of years before the Kassite Kingdom came into existence. Today the TWA people - tne so-called "PYGMIES" of central East Africa - around Zaire [Congo] and Burundi, still use various prehistoric forms of this type of "CROSS." The various types of said "CROSS" are to numerous to list here. However, the following works can further your knowledge and interest in much more details than is possible in this volume: Rosellini, MONUMENTI STOR; Gabriel de Nortillett, Le SIGNE de la CROIX, Paris, 1866; A. Churchward, THE ORIGIN AND EVOLUTION OF RELIGION; A. Churchward, SIGNS AND SYMBOLS OF PRIMORDIAL MAN, London, 1920; Sir E.A. Wallis Budge, AMULETS AND TAILSMANS, London, 1920 [first published in the United States of America in 1961]. Special exhibits of all manner of CROSSES can be seen in the British Museum of London, England, where they have been kept since they were confiscated from their rightful owners in Africa and Asia; many from the Americas, the Caribbeans, and the Pacific.

The following "KASSITE CROSSES" ▨ ✛ were copied from a wall-painting in an African tomb at Luxor, Egypt, North Africa. They show the height of sophistication the prehistoric Africans or "NEGROES" reached in perfecting their CROSSES.

History tells us that Admirante Cristobal Colon [Christopher Colombus] "...FOUND A CROSS IN THE AMERICAS WHEN HE ARRIVED THERE IN 1492 A.D.;" but, in his amazement at finding it there, he still attributed its origin to "...THE TEACHINGS OF THE APOSTLE THOMAS." Of course Colombus could not explain what "THOMAS" was doing in the "AMERICAS," or how he got there before he did in 1492 A.D. Quite naturally Colombus could never have believed that the indigenous peoples, the so-called "CARIBS," could have developed it independently of his own God-head's, JESUS CHRIST, aid; not even without the help of his "CHOSEN CAUCASIANS" from Europe - at this period ROMAN CATHOLICS from Spain. But, Colon believed he was in INDIA, where "...THOMAS WENT TO WORK AS A CARPENTER...," etc.; Thus, the logic of Colon's conclusion. On the other hand Mexican, Brazilian, Peruvian, and Caribbean islanders of the indigenous soil claimed that their CROSS represents "THE DIRECTIONS OF THE WIND-GODS;" and, it possesses the "SOLAR" and/or "STELAR ASTROLOGICAL NATURE OF THE UNIVERSE."

Another of the earliest known CROSSES is the indigenous African ANKH ♀ of Ta-Meri [Kimit, Sais, or Egypt] and other Nile Valleys High-Cultures. The earliest European Christian writers refer to the ANKH as:

"THE SYMBOL OF ETERNAL LIFE OF THE EGYPTIANS."

Of course they were as wrong as they had been in most of everything they had ever written before about the religions of the indigenous Africans of the Nile Valleys and everywhere else in Alkebu-lan [Africa]. And, since they did not ask any of the indigenous Africans for any information about their ANKH, none was given them.

The so-called "OLD TESTAMENT CROSS", otherwise known as the "SAINT ANTHONY CROSS," was used by the earliest European Christians of Rome in the Catacombs under the name of "CRUX COMMISSA" or "TAU CROSS." Most of the 18th through 20th century C.E. European and European-American "Christian" theologians refer to this CROSS as the "TYPE CROSS" T. The "TAU CROSS" received its name from the erroneous translation by European scholars who believed that the Africans' ANKH was equivalent in value to their fellow Europeans of Greece's letter of the alphabet - TAU. This error was no different to what they had done with respect to the musical sign of the same Africans of Egypt and Nubia's NEFER ♂ or ♂ , which they held represented a "...LATIN CROSS..." or "...UPSIDE-DOWN ANKH..." with the meaning of "SORROW."[See Schliemann, MYCENAE AND TIRYNS, p. 66; Baring-Gould, MYTHS OF THE MIDDLE AGES, p. 358; Payne Knight, SYMBOL LANGUAGE, p. 238; Wilkerson, ANCIENT EGYPT, iii, p. 362; Munter, RELIGION der BABYLONIER, Kopenhagen, 1827; Louisa Twining, SYMBOLS OF EARLY AND MEDIAEVAL CHRISTIAN ARTS].

Some historians of "SEMITIC ORIGIN" even refer to their own books of religious mythology and quote from EZEKIEL, ix, 14, where it is stated that their God, YAWEH or JEHOVAH, etc., sent Ezekiel to Jerusalem "...TO SET A MARK UPON THE FOREHEADS..." of certain males [Jews] as a sign of their "...RIGHTEOUSNESS AND EXCEPTION FROM JOHOVAH'S WRATH...," etc. This gave rise to their translation of the word "MARK" in Hebrew to be the equivalent of the Greek "TAU" or hithwitha tau; thus, their association of it to the so-called "TAU CROSS."

One of the most noted of the African Fathers of the Christian Church of North Africa and Rome, Tertullian of Khart-Haddas [Cartnage] held that the "TAU CROSS" was the same CROSS spoken of in EZEKIEL, ix, 4. He wrote:

"...ipsa enim litera Graecorum Tau, notra autem species crucis."

Tertullian comments were written in his ADVERSUS MARCIANI, iii, 22. However, in EXODUS, iii, 7 references are also made with respect to the same CROSS, with respect to the "...BLOOD OF THE PASCHAL..." painted on "...THE HOUSES OF THE ISRAELITES...," etc., prior to their allegedly enforced departure from central Egypt sometime between c. 1298 and 1232 B.C.E. when they were chased by the "NEGROES" of North Africa - the Egyptians or Romiti.

The NEW TESTAMENT or Christian HOLY BIBLE confessants claimed that :

"JESUS CHRIST WAS CRUCIFIED ON A CROSS MADE OF TWO
PIECES OF WOOD, EACH NAILED TO THE OTHER...," etc. †

The fact that there exist very deep controversies over whether "CHRIST" was

"...NAILED TO THE CROSS WHILE IT LAID ON THE GROUND...,"

etc., or

"...WHILE IT WAS PLANTED ERRECT FOR THE CRUCIFIXION,"

etc., is not challenged here. The medieval presentation of a "LADDER" against the "CROSS" which "CHRIST" allegedly used to "MOUNT" said "CROSS" does not change the symbol, and should not be conceded as an integral part of the "CROSS."

The four [4] forms of the so-called "CHRISTIAN CROSS" used by the early European Christians are as follow:

1. The "GREEK CROSS" with four equal arms ✚ ;
2. The "LATIN CROSS" or "Crux Capitala, also Crux Immissa, the most commonly used today, having at its top three extensions of equal length, the bottom extension of a much greater length ✝;
3. The "SAINT ANDREWS CROSS" or Crux Decussata, with two arms of equal length crossing each other diagonally at mid-point ✗ ; and
4. The "TAU CROSS" or Crux Commissa ⊤ .

The CROSS generally seen on the garment of priests is called the "MONOGRAM OF CHRIST" ☧ . It represent an attempt to incorporate the so-called "PASSION CROSS" with the "SAINT ANDREWS CROSS" and "LATIN CROSS" [Calvary Cross] versions into one symbol. The last CROSS, that generally shown "...IN THE HANDS OF CHRIST... " with a banner or pennant attached thereto, is called the "CROSS OF THE RESURRECTION."

Less we arrive at some kind of a distorted conclusion about Jesus Christ and the so-called "CHRISTIAN CROSS," as we have so often done in so many other areas dealing with tne Christian Church and its history down through the ages; for, it must be remembered that not one of the four CROSSES mentioned with respect to Cnristendom existed as any kind of a symbol of CHRISTIANITY or CHRISTENDOM before the Fourth [4th] Century following the "DEATH OF CHRIST." The preceding remarks have been contingent upon the finding of a CROSS,called the "CHRISTIAN CROSS", by Empress Helena on 3 May 328 C.E. It is alleged that it was...

"THE CROSS UPON WHICH CRIST WAS CRUCIFIED...,"

etc. The conflict which arose from this alleged find by Empress Helena is that the same "CROSS" was supposedly "...FOUND... during the reign of Emperor Tiberius by a member of Saint James' staff when he was Bishop of Jerusalem." But, the "CROSS" Empress Helena "FOUND" was supposed to have had "...TWO [2] CROSS PIECES" ✝, with the top member longer than the bottom, somewhat like the so-called "CROSS OF LORRAINE." It must be noted however, that the "SAINT HELENA CROSS" and the "SCROLL" found attached thereto were lossed, only to be "...REDISCOVERED IN THE CHURCH OF SAINT GROCE AT ROME IN THE YEAR 1492 A.D....," etc. Finally, it was allegedly "...AUTHENTICATED BY POPE ALEXANDER III..." in one of his many "...PAPAL BULL..." dealing with this same subject matter.

There are numerous variations of the so-called "CONSECRATED CROSS," the last one in question, with all forms of inscriptions and carvings imaginable; but, not one of them is that much more AUTHENTIC than any of the others with respect to its "CHRISTIAN ORIGIN," irrespective of that which "...POPE ALEXANDER III PAPAL BULL..." declared to be "...AUTHENTICATED...," etc.

The author of this volume suggest that the student who is disireous of further inquiry into this symbol of man's PRIMODIAL SIGNS AND SYMBOLS should read a book by Dr. Albert Churchward, M.D. of said name, published in London, 1924; equally: W. Wilson Blaike, THE CROSS ANCIENT AND MODERN, New York, 1888; Yosef ben-Jochannan, AFRICA: MOTHER OF "WESTERN CIVILIZATION," New York, 1971; G. De Mortillet. La SIGNE de la CROIX AVANT le CHRISTIANISME, Paris, 1866; Sir Godfrey Higgins, ANACALYPSIS [2 vols.], London, 1840; F.E. Hulme, SYMBOLISM IN CHRISTIAN ART, London, 1908; Lepsius, De CRUCE CHRISTI; Albert Churchward, ORIGIN AND EVOLUTION OF RELIGION, London, 1920; Sir E.A. Wallis Budge, EGYPTIAN BOOK OF THE DEAD, London, 1885; Sir E.A. Wallis Budge, GUIDE TO THE EGYPTIAN COLLECTIONS IN THE BRITISH MUSEUM, London, 1909; Sir E.A. Wallis Budge, HISTORY OF ETHIOPIA, London, 1924; Sir E.A. Wallis Budge, BANDLET OF RIGHTEOUSNESS, London, 1929; ETHIOPIAN BOOK OF THE DEAD [Lefâtâ Sedek]; George Gerster, CHURCHES IN ROCK: EARLY CHRISTIAN ART IN ETHIOPIA, London, 1970; Prof. William Wright, CATALOGUE OF THE ETHIOPIC MSS., London, 1877; Prof. James A. Montgomery, ARAMAIC INCANTATION TEXTS FROM NIPPUR, Philadelphia, 1913; Dr. M. Gaster, "Proceedings of the Society of Biblical Archaeology" [in: March, May and June, 1915, Feb. 1916, and Feb. 1917, STUDIES AND TEXTS, 3 vols.], London, 1925-28; Max Muller, HISTORY OF PHILOSOPHY; Gregg, ARCHAEOLOGIA, vol. xlviii, London, 1885; T. Wilson, OTHER FORMS OF THE SWASTIKA, Washinton, 1896.

ADDED PRE-CHRISTIAN CROSSES ꞩ ✗

The "FYOT, GRAMMADION, CROIX PATTEE," and "SASTKA," or whatever else the "CROSS" is called, all of them are represented in the artifacts of Alkebu-lan [Africa], Asia, the Americas, and the Islands of the Caribbeans and the Pacific. The Chinese refer to their Buddhist-type as the "THUNDER-SCROLL" or "LEI WEN": 버 ꭓ ꭐ 도 ꭗ

As an end to this chapter the question is, to this author, very significant. It can only add to remind African people everywhere that, even the symbol of the Europeans and

364

European-Americans - the so-called "CAUCASIANS, SEMITES, INDO-EUROPEAN ARYANS," etc. God-head [Jehovah and/or Jesus Christ] they are willing to distort in order to suppress any possibility of its African origin being exposed.

One can only imagine what will happen when "ACADEMIC SCHOLARSHIP" and "ACADEMIC FREEDOM" in the United States of America's institutions of learning, secular, religious, and otherwise, become truly NONE-RACIST and free of RELIGIOUS BIGOTRY. The following CROSSES and SWASTIKAS and other symbols related to the ancient religions and secret societies of Alkebu-lan, Asia, Europe, and the Americas, will be openly examined for their religious significance that predated Judaism, Christianity, and Islam. This, however, would mean that Judaism and Christianity must be treated with the same respect, no more, as all other religions of the peoples of the entire world. It would also mean that JEHOVAH, JESUS CHRIST, AL'LAH, and any-other God-head of the "Western World" will not find special favor in the universities and colleges as they now enjoy over all other Gods and Goddesses.

Pages 365 to 371 following are presented for the purpose of showing the student, researcher, educator, and general reader that there are literally thousands of CROSS-ES and other symbols related to Christianity which the general parishoners are kept ignorant of; the same being very much true for the SWASTIKAS. All of these symbols have been used before the origin of Christianity in North Africa, EGYPT; all of them predated the proclaimed "BIRTH OF JESUS CHRIST OF NAZARETH" and all of the other sixteen "SAVIORS" who came to "SAVE THE WORLD" after Pharaoh Akhenaten taught the same teachings to the Africans of the Nile River Valley High-Cultures over two thousand [2,000] years before the Cnristian HOLY BIBLE was written.

Like the following chapter on the various "MOTHERS" who had "VIRGIN BIRTHS" before the "VIRGIN MARY" had hers with the "BIRTH OF JESUS CHRIST," the symbols shown in tnis chapter are totally new to most of us. Yet, many of us will insist that we know everything to be known dealing with the origin and evolution of religion tnroughout the entire world. When we are confronted that we have been total fools for those who are aware of our ignorance in this area of human High-Culture.

Osiris

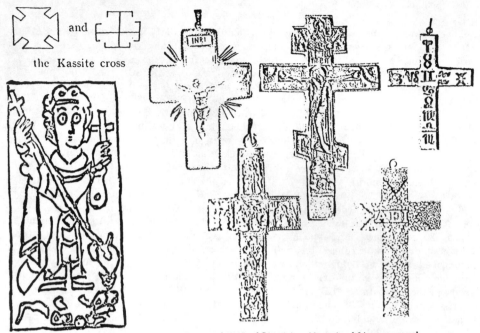

and

the Kassite cross

Saint George of Lydda.

A group of Crosses in gold, steel and Limoges enamel.

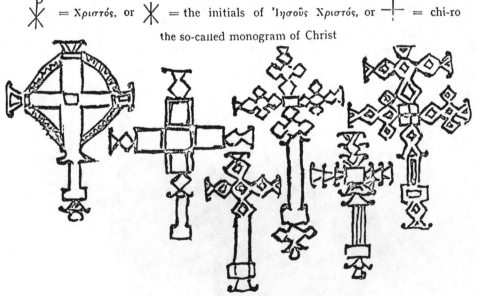

☧ = Χριστός, or ✗ = the initials of Ἰησοῦς Χριστός, or ☧ = chi-ro

the so-called monogram of Christ

Tracings of the magical forms of the Cross found in an Ethiopian Book of
the Dead called " Lefâfâ Ṣedḳ " (Brit. Mus. MS. Add. 16204).

366   ETHIOPIAN AMULETS

COPTIC AMULETS   On the stele of ABRAHAM

(B.M., No. 1257) we have it in this form

with the letters ⳗ and Ω.   On the stele of PLÊINÔS
(B.M., No. 679) we have the ordinary Greek cross

, the ⳨ and two *ānkh* crosses

On the stele of SABINOS (B.M. 1352) we have ⳨

and ⳗ and Ω.   On another stele are cut

figures of doves holding ⳿ (B.M., 1327).   NAVILLE

found a mummy with the *suwastika* drawn on
the left shoulder (see *Deir el-Bahari*, ii, p. 5), but
there is no proof that the mummy was that of a
Christian. There is in the British Museum (No. 54051)
a mummy of a child of the early Christian or late
Roman period ; the hands are crossed over the breast,

and in one he holds a cross   and in the other

a flower (lotus (?) which suggests that the mummy
is that of a girl).   On a portion of a mummy swathing
found at LYCOPOLIS is painted a Christian cross
(No. 55056).   On a very rare amulet which
was given to the British Museum by Sir RIDER
HAGGARD, the Birth of Christ is represented

[The above was extracted from Sir E.A. Wallis Budge,
TALLISMAN AND AMULETS, p. 129. See next page also]

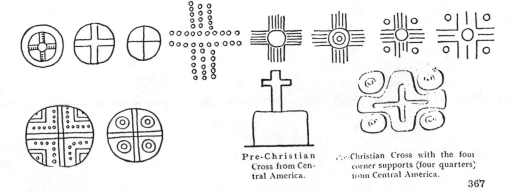

Pre-Christian
Cross from Cen-
tral America.

Christian Cross with the four
corner supports (four quarters)
from Central America.

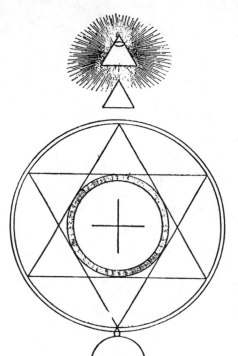

From Egypt

"The Tuat and the Twelve Hours of the Night," hewn in stone in the Great Pyramid of Gizeh. In the Christian doctrine the twelve gates of heaven were taken from this.

The converted Amsu into

to represent Jesus Christ, and have given his age as thirty-three at time of resurrection and fourteen as the Child Jesus.

33 —  — 14

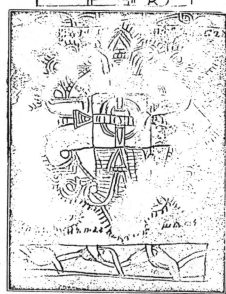

The Cross of 'Abû Fara.
(From the amulet of Batra Gîwârgîs.)

Sacred Triangle of West African

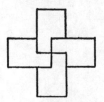

The St Andrew's Cross—the Red Cross or Fiery Cross a very important one to Freemasons of the 18°

368

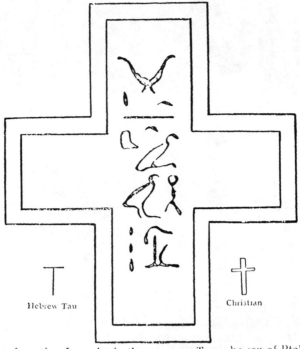

Hebrew Tau

Christian

way of writing I-u, who is the same as Tem, the son of Ptah.
Tem, Temu or Atem, son of Ptah, was Heru-Khuti—*i.e.*
Horus I. Heru-Khuti (Egyptian) "Light of the World,"

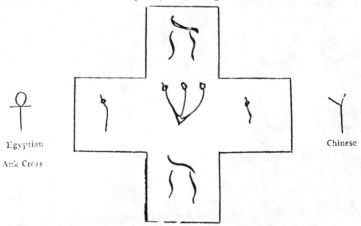

Egyptian

Ank Cross

Chinese

She-en or Se-en, the initial standing for The Al-
mighty in Hebrew Shadai.

Note.—Readers must not confound the "Great Serpent fiend Apepi or Sui" with
the "Holy Serpent" representing Tem. In the Egyptian Mythology there were
many serpents, some types of "good" and some "evil."

369

SYMBOLS OF THE DIVISION OF HEAVEN, REPRESENTING HORUS AND SET AND HORUS, SET AND SHU WITH SWASTIKA OF THE FOUR QUARTERS.

Egyptian Swastika

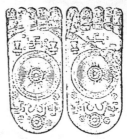

The Two Feet of Buddha.

On a Sepulchral Stone at Meigle, in Perth- shire, there are four human figures in the form of the Swastika.

Feet of Horus from MEXI- CAN CODICES, with the three Rods or Rays of Light symbol.

Two feet of Horus I., as shown in the Vignette—Plate ii., " Book the Dead "—Renouf's.

" Druids " Swastika from Egypt

Swastikas from Schliemann's, TROY AND ITS REMAINS, (1876). They are shown on Trojan spin- dle whorls of pre-Christian era.

Solar mythos Cross, the 4 quart- ers is depicted as Atum-Ra

Swastika, brought on in the Roman Catholic religion as a symbol representing the Trinity, which dates about A.D. 100–200. But it was an Egyptian Symbol for the same, 300,000 years at least, before that date.

Swastika from a Cross at St Vigeans, in Forfarshire

old Mahometan Swastika

МЕΣ (PERCY GARDNER, in *Numismatic Chronicle*, Part I, 1880).

Rough for, Latin Cross

Lanteglos Churchyard, Cornwall Ank Cross

It is an old Druid ot the Dolmens of Brittany.

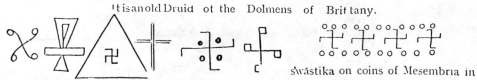

swastika on coins of Mesembria in Thrace This group shows that the swastika and the cross were entirely different signs; the second sign represents the Egyptian sign for "life," ☥.

Swastica Totem of North America.

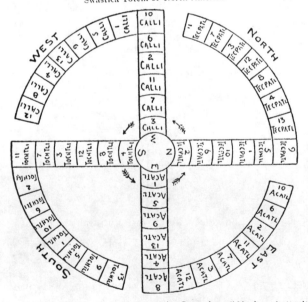

The Mexican Calendar in form of Swastica Cross, from "Mexican Antiquities,"
p. 29, with the names of the Four Children of Horus as gods of the four corners, at
N. S. E. and W.

MOTHER AND CHILD

Middle Kingdom Period, c. 2100 - 1675 B. C. E. [Bronze H, 5"]
Berlin-Charlottenburg, Staaliche Museen der Stiftung PreuBisher
Kulturbesitz, Egyptian Department.

    In describing the above BLACK MADONNA AND CHILD statue the Museum
writers stated that "...BOTH HAVE TYPICAL NEGROID CHARACTERISTICS...," etc.

Drawn by K. Watkins

MERSEKERT SUCKLING HORUS

A type of Hathor in the Lunar Cult.

374

Q.   Is it true that JESUS CHRIST and his mother, MARY, were presented to the early Christians as two BLACK people?

A.   Yes. The early Christian Church, which had its beginning in North Africa [Egypt] more than one hundred [100] years before it reached Europe [Rome and Greece] in its organized institutional form, presented artifacts, drawings, statues, documents, and other artifacts in evidence which depicted the MADONNA AND CHRIST CHILD [Mary and Jesus Christ] as a BLACK woman and her BLACK child. The image of a BLACK MADONNA AND CHILD was nothing more or less than the adoptation of the FERTILITY symbol of Egypt's and Nubia's ISIS [the Mother or Madonna] and HORUS [the Child]. The extent to which this statue was held in very high esteem in the eyes of the ancient Christians is best demonstrated by the SCALA SANTA in Rome, Italy; a figure of the "BLACK VIRGIN" with an auroa of light that engulfs her and the "BLACK CHRIST CHILD" she holds in her arms. [See Pigmorius, "Exposito Mensae Isiacae," in: VETUSTISSIMAE TA TABULAE; and, Wilkinson, ANCIENT EGYPT, Vol. III].

The figure at the right side of this page shows the infant HORUS just completed nursing on his mother's, ISIS, breast. In most of the ancient statues and paintings HORUS is shown sucking ISIS breast; this was also true for the child JESUS CHRIST sucking MARY'S breast. In the latter case it was before European "PURITANISM" entered Christianity along with "SEXUAL ABSTINANCE" as the "...TEACHINGS OF JESUS CHRIST." This was equally before the biological function of "BREAST FEEDING" became "DIRTY" in the eyes of the self-proclaimed PROTECTORS OF HUMAN MORALS.

One has to take note of the fact that ISIS and HORUS, or the BLACK MADONNA and CHILD, symbol was copied by religious figures and dieties of many ancient and current religions other than Christianity. DIANA OF EPHESUS was always presented as a "BLACK WOMAN," equally CHRISTNA - a God-head of the Hindus. At corinth VENUS was also BLACK, and so were: CERES, METIS, JUNO, CYBELE, JUPITER, APOLO, BACCHUS, ADONIS, AMMON, and others, according to the ancient pictures and statues presented of them. [See Inman, ANCIENT FAITHS EMBODIED IN AN- CIENT NAMES, Vol. I; and, Sir G. Higgins, ANACALYPSIS, Vol. I].

The BLACK Goddess - ISHTAR - was called "THE MOTHER OF THE GODS" according to Rawlinson's ANCIENT MONARCHIES, Vol. I. The MOON was called the same name in ancient Egypt, Nubia, Meroe, Ethiopia, etc. when it represented ISIS, according to Plutarch's De ISIS et OSIR, p. 48. The BLACKNESS OF ISHTAR caused Lieutenant Wilford to write the following comment in an article titled, "On Egypt and the Nile, from the ancient Books of the Hindus'[ASIATIC RESEARCHES, Vol. iii, pp. 399, 406], that:

"IT CANNOT REASONABLY BE DOUBTED THAT A RACE OF
NEGROES HAD FORMERLY PREEMINENCE IN INDIA."

The above statement has been substantiated in many other early works at the turn of the 20th century C.E., such as Layard's MINEVEH AND BABYLON.

In Moor's HINDOO PATHEON, plate lix, the figure depicting India's "Holy Family" - DENAKI holding the infant child CHRISHNA - is another example of the BLACK MADONNA AND CHILD of the ancient world. CHRISHNA [the Hindus "Incarnate Diety"] is not only shown BLACK; he is also shown with WOOLLY or KINKY HAIR - the texture of which is always called "NEGRO HAIR" in everyone of the commonwealths

within the borders of the United States of America. This picture of the child -CHRISH-
NA, and his mother - DENAKI, as extracted from Frederick T.
Elsworthy's THE EVIL EYE: THE ORIGIN AND PRACTICES OF
SUPERSTITION, London, 1895, p. 190, as shown at the right
side of this page. Very serious attention is given this MA-
DONNA AND CHILD; for, it is not very rear that one could
have find a picture or statue in India of God-heads who
had, or have, BLACK SKIN and WOOLLY HAIR.

Dramatizing the type of shock modern European
and European-American "Christians" and Jews receive
when they discover that the original MADONNA AND
CHILD - Mary and the infant Jesus Christ - were
BLACK is best told in a short story about an Italian woman from Florence, who had just arrived in Rome for a
pilgrimage to the world renown SCALA SANTA. As she
knelt before the massive, but asthetically beautiful, image,
she was overheard saying the following:

"MA! NON HO CAPITO MAI CHE FU MORO"!

The old lady was completely astonished that her God - JESUS CHRIST" - was a "MORO
"MORO" or MOOR like Shakespeare's Othelo. [See F.T. Elworthy's THE EVIL EYE:
THE ORIGIN AND PRACTICES OF SUPERSTITION, p. 190, footnote 312]. It should be
noted that the word "MORO" is used in many Latin-based languages in the same manner
the word "NEGRO" is used in the United States of America; excluding, of course, the
derogatory intent in the English or American languages. Also, that is was the Portuguese colonialists who introduced this digusting term, along with its companion word
"NEGROLAND," to discribe West Africa's Guinea Coast and the inhabitants the Portuguese met there in about c. 1430 C.E. But, these terms were not given any wide
usage, even among the Portuguese, until the 16th or 17th century C.E., as shown on
pp. xxvi - 402 of this volume. [See Richard B. Moore's THE WORD NEGRO, ITS
ORIGIN AND EVIL USE, New York, 1954]. Continuing in the same footnote above, F.T.
Worthy wrote:

> "Upon the remarkable halo surrounding the heads of both the
> Indian mother and child one might almost say that it belonged
> to a Christian work and not a heathen. The mimbus is, however,
> far older than the nineteen centuries of Christendom. Rays were
> said to have proceeded from the head of Isis; and they have been
> called the proper attributes of Juno, of Isis, or the "Mother of
> the Gods." [Pigmorious, VETUSTISSIMAE TABULAE, p. 16].

Although Elworthy was trying to be as objective as he possibly could, this writer is
convinced, never the less, that his own Western European religious bigotry forced
him to become amazed that the work could have been done by people that presented its
"...HEATHEN CHARACTERIZATION...," etc. Of course any person who is not a Jew
or Christian is a "HEATHEN."

It would have been totally impossible for this writer not to have detailed some of

376

the "CHRISTIAN HOLY FAMILY" myth with respect to the BLACKNESS of the Christ
Child and Mother developed from Isis and Horus "FERTILITY SYMBOL that became
the "BLACK MADONNA AND CHILD, after having given such an extensive analysis of
the so-called "CHRISTIAN CROSS" and/or "CROSSES". For, not only has the "HOLY
FAMILY" myth permeated the thinking of millions of African peoples almost everywhere; it has been presented to them as a LILY-WHITE, BLONDE, BLUE-EYED, and
.GOLDEN-HAIR "FAMILY" of INDO-EUROPEAN SEMITIC and/or "CAUCASIAN God-
head which had no "NEGRO" or "NEGROID" heritage whatsoever. Whenever this type
of RACIST and RELIGIOUSLY BIGOTED presentation is seriously challenged with evidence, such as we have just examined, Judae-Christian "THEOLOGIANS" and other
defenders of WHITE and SEMITIC BIGOTRY and RACISM in religion, particularly the
so-called "Western Religions" related to the OLD and NEW TESTAMENT personalities,
are very quick to admit that the "HOLY FAMIL'S" origin in Egyptian, Nubian, and
Meroite mythology from ISIS and HORUS - the BLACK MADONNA AND CHILD FER-
TILITY SYMBOL - was African, but not of "NEGROID STOCK" - although it was
"BLACK." However, such European and European-American "EDUCATORS", who are
so very astute in their understanding of the BLACK-WHITE confrontation in this area,
cannot explain why the characterization of the "HOLY FAMILY" has turned from solely
"BLACK" in its earliest presentation to solely "WHITE" following its Europeanization
in the picture drawn by Michaelangelo for the Pope of the Roman Catholic Church a few
centuries ago. Equally; Why would PURE WHITE MEMBERS OF THE MASTER RACE
paint their God-Head - JESUS CHRIST and His mother - MARY - "BLACK" in the
first place? This should be the question those who now present the "HOLY FAMILY" as
WHITE SEMITES, CAUCASIANS," and/or "CAUCASOIDS" should be asking themselves.
But, each of the self-proclaimed "AUTHORITY ON CHRISTIANITY, JUDAISM, NORTH
AND EAST AFRICA, forget, quite conveniently, that the BLACK MADONNA or "HOLY
FAMILY'S MOTHER" symbol of FERTILITY was, and still is, common among all of
the indigenous African High-Cultures of the Nile Valleys and Great Lakes regions of
North, Northeast, East, and Central Alkebu-lan [Africa] for thousands of years before
the creation of the theory of "ADAM AND EVE IN THE GARDEN OF EDEN" by an indigenous BLACK AFRICAN named "MOSES," much less before the proclaimed "BIRTH'
of his much more recent descendant - "JESUS CHRIST OF NAZARETH."

The extent to which this revelation, or any of the others mentioned before, may cause the student, researcher, and general reading public to investigate further into these areas and other related fields; it should also lead one to take a second look at the FALSE presentations one had to accept as the "GOSPEL TRUTH" written by "GOD INSPIRED MEN." But, anyone can open his or her own mind to a TRUTHFUL examination of this type of Judaeo-Christian theology being expounded by European and European-American "EDUCATORS", whose basic interest seems to be the further perpetuation of WHITE RACISM and JUDAEO-CHRISTIAN RELIGIOUS BIGOTRY under the disguise of "SCHOLARLY INVESTIGATION" and/or "ACADEMIC AUTHORITY."

But; what king of "TRUTH" and/or "AUTHORITY" are we talking about throughout these last two chapters? Are they UNIVERSAL to all of mankind? If they are, why were they not revealed simultaneously to each and every living SOUL at the period of understanding by the same God-head or God-Heads responsible for the "CREATION OF THE WORLD," rather than to the Europeans and European-Americans through African and Asian national [ethnic or racial] groupings in their BOOK OF THE COMING FORTH BY DAY, PAPYRUS OF ANI, NEGATIVE CONFESSIONS, COFFIN TEXTS, PYRAMID TEXTS, OSIRIAN DRAMA, HANURABI CODE, PROVERBS OF THE TEACHINGS OF AMEN-EM-EOPE," and hundreds of others to many to be listed here?

Students and professors engaged in A FRICAN, AFRICAN-AMERICAN, AFRICAN-CARIBBEAN [otherwise "BLACK"] STUDIES courses must, also, find it basically necessary to equally engage in limitless re-examination and re-evaluation when WRITING about the contributions made by the indigenous Africans and their descendants everywhere to the WORLD'S HIGH-CULTURES , "Western Civilization" definitely included, from a BLACK PERSPECTIVE, irrespective of the European and European-American "A UTHORITIES" who stand in the gateway of ACADEMIC DISCIPLINES for the purpose of discrediting all who differ with JUDAEO-CHRISTIAN religious BIGOTRY and CAU-CASIANISM, also SEMI TISM, under the disguise of advancing "DEMOCRACY" and "ACADEMIC FREEDOM." But most of all, the Africans experience in WORLD HISTORY and PREHISTORY must be told once more from an AFRICAN POINT OF VIEW, from an AFRICAN INTERPRETATION, and for an AFRICAN READING PUBLIC; as, ONLY AN AFRICAN CAN BE AN AUTHORITY ON AFRICA AND HER SONS AND DAUGHTERS TO THE SATISFACTION OF SELF-RESPECTIN AFRICAN PEOPLE EVERYWHERE.

ANOTHER BLACK MADONNA AND CHILD

WHO ARE THEY?

Conclusion: ORTHODOX AND LIBERAL AFRICAN HISTORY AND THE HISTORIANS

This writer has tried to maintain a third-party role in the presentation of AN aspect of the GLORIOUS HISTORY of the High-Cultures of North, East, and Central-East Alkebu-lan [Africa] which the so-called "NEGROES" created and developed before, and since, the appearance of the earliest Europeans [CAUCASIANS or SEMITES] arrived on the scene of WORLD HISTORY. But, in so doing, the consistent memory of certain other African, African-American, and African-Caribbean professors of history and other related disciplines, who have demanded that my style and approach in this and other works I have written be drastically change to conform with "...STANDARDS ESTABLISHED BY LIBERAL" and/or "ORTHODOX" chronological history, as taught by European and European-American "AUTHORITIES" on African, African-American, and African-Caribbean history, irked me to conclude that:

> I WILL NEVER SUCCUMB TO THE STYLE OF THE WORKS OF
> THE PAST OR CURRENT RACIST AND RELIGIOUSLY BIGOTED
> TACTICS OF EUROPEAN AND EUROPEAN-AMERICAN [Cau-
> casian or Semitic] HISTORIANS AND OTHER "EDUCATORS",
> NOR THEIR NEGRO AND/OR COLOURED UNDERSTUDIES,
> WHO PRESENT EUROPEAN VALUES INTO AFRICAN EXPERI-
> ENCES THEY CANNOT POSSIBLY KNOW...................

Very few Africans, African-Americans, or African-Caribbeans are aware that most European and European-American historians of every religious, political, or economic persuasion have, from just prior to the turn of the 20th century C.E., patterned their total approach to world history, with particular emphasis on the so-called "NEGROES," after the works of RACIST STALWARTS such as Madison Grant, John Ambrose Price, A. Gobineau, James Henry Breasted, C.P. Groves, and Lothrop S. Stoddard. Yet, it is the latter's works, particularly the following: THE RISING TIDE OF COLOR AGAINST WHITE WORLD SUPREMACY [1920]; RACIAL REALITIES IN EUROPE [1924] - including its serialized version in the Saturday Evening Post; THE CLASHING TIDES OF COLOR [1935] - an extension of Madison Grant's book, The Passing Of The Great Race, Or The Racial Basis Of European History [1916], which provided the thrust of so-called "NORDIC CAUCASIAN SUPERIORITY" and "NEGRO INFERIORITY" as the foundation for the later works by so-called "WHITE LIBERAL AFRICANIST HISTORIANS" etc. up to the present 1970's.

Educated at Harvard University, Cambridge, Massachusettes, where he earned a Ph.D. degree in 1905 C.E., and of New England birth, Dr. Lothrop S. Stoddard be-

380

gan his career catering to the historical theories of RACISM and RELIGIOUS BIGOTRY in the "Jewish" and "Christian" bibles [Old and New Testament], also from the existing so-called "SCIENTIFIC BOOKS ON THE INFERIORITY OF THE NEGRO RACE" of his era, all of which were written by European and European-American "EDUCATORS" before and during his lifetime. One of the historians whom he most idolized, John Ambrose Price, and whose works he relied upon most heavily as the fundamental basis for his own RACISM and RELIGIOUS BIGOTRY, was the author of the following statement written in the year 1907 C.E.:

> "I LOVE THE OLD SOUTH OF THE DAYS OF MY YOUTH, THE LAND OF PEACE AND PLENTY, OF BLUE BLOOD, ARISTO-CRACY, AND HAPPY NIGGERS."

It was this type of RACIST rationale by Price which "...The 20th century's most prolific American writer and historian...," Dr. Lothrop S. Stoddard, was to make the standard for each and every European-American "AUTHORITY" on history that followed him. His articulate sophistry in the manipulation and perpetuation of the RACISM in the Jewish and Christian Holy Bibles [Old and New Testament], which he carefully amalgamated with the teachings of the anti-African ["anti-Negro"] propaganda of the era prior to his own involvement as "...one of the United States of America's greatest historians...," eventually made him the recognized "AUTHORITY ON RACIAL ORIGINS" within the continental borders of North America, and gave him great influence over the RACIAL and RELIGIOUS thinking of his European and British counterparts. His appeal to NATIONAL RACISM and RELIGIOUS BIGOTRY in the United States of America, which of course he did not create, but instead over-stimulated, was best highlighted in the following statement from one of the many articles he contributed to the Saturday Evening Post in 1924, in which he warned his fellow European-Americans of "White Nordic Caucasian Stock:"

> "...the relative strength and importance of the different racial elements in a nation will largely determine every phase of that nation's life, from its manners, customs, and ideas to its government and its relations with other nations."

The above warning served more than to suggest the historical minimization of the role of the so-called "NEGRO AMERICANS" contribution to the development of European-America from their entrance in the original "THIRTEEN [13] COLONIES OF GREAT BRITAIN," and including the "COLONIES" independence as the United States of America. It was in essence the beginning of the role each succeeding generation of "MODERN

381

WHITE LIBERAL" and "ORTHODOX HISTORIANS" were to employ in the suppression
of the so-called "NEGROES" contribution to any and all aspects of the world's HISTORY
and HIGH-CULTURE, and more specifically to the origin and development of the myth
called "WESTERN CIVILIZATION." The warning also failed to recognize that "WEST-
ERN CIVILIZATION" or "HIGH-CULTURE" began with the philosophical concepts the
ancient indigenous peoples of Africa and Asia taught the Europeans [or Caucasians] of
Hellas and Rome, which was long before Homer wrote his ILIAD and ODESSY in approximately c. 600 B.C.E.

Stoddard's popularization of "MODERN [20th century] RACISM," though almost
without any historical foundation whatsoever, was never the less the "AUTHORITY" for
most of his fellow academicians and historians of his era, most of whom were the
teachers of the current ones. For example, he wrote that:

> "The age of Pericles and Alexander, with its grand achievements
> in molding the destinies of the civilized world" [was a] "striking
> illustration of the supreme mission of the civilized white race."

Appearently Dr. Lothrop S. Stoddard must not have read or heard about the Greeks
and Romans who, at the pain of great economic expense to themselves, journeyed all
the way to Alkebu-lan [North Africa] and Asia to receive their earliest peek into the
disciplines which later became the basis for the establishment of their own "CIVILI-
ZATION." Dramatically, it was this same experience the Romans and Greeks gained
from the Africans of North and East Africa, equally as well of West Africa, which
caused many of them to be murdered by their respective state upon their return home
when they began spreading the PHILOSOPHICAL CONCEPTS, MATHEMATICAL and
SCIENTIFIC THEORIES, among other disciplines introduced to them for the first time
in Alkebu-lan by their so-called "NEGRO" teachers. Along with his shortness of memory
seems to have been his ignorance of the fact that the HANURABI CODE of the Asians,
from whence the ancient Greeks and Romans drew heavily upon for much of their own PHI-
LOSOPHICAL insights in their MORAL CODE OF ETHICS, needless to mention what they
adopted from the indigenous North and East Africans ["NEGROES"] of Ta-Merry [Egypt],
Ta-Nehisi [Nubia], Kush, Meröe, Ethiopia, Puanit, Lebu, Numidia, Khart-Haddas, and
other High-Cultures of Alkebu-lan. Stoddard, equally as Jeffreys, Wiedner, Junod, et
al, had carefully overlooked the fact that the same "INFERIOR NEGROES" of North
and East Alkebu-lan taught the beginners of the "GREAT WHITE RACE" science, phi-

losophy, history, medicine, civics, astronomy, only to mention a few of the disciplines to which they were introduced along the Nile. These African and Asian peoples who were the teachers of the original founders of "WESTERN CIVILIZATION" came from nations whose HIGH-CULTURE [civilization] preceded those of Greece and Rome by many thousands of years, much less before their teachings were made common knowledge for the intelligencia of Greece and Rome following the conquest of said nations by Alexander II ["the great," son of Philip of Macedon] and the subsequent plundering of the repositories of learning in such countries by his fellow Macedonian-Greeks from c. 332 to 47 or 30 B.C.E. Thus, when Dr. Stoddard held that the beginning of the Africans and Asians SEXUAL COHABITATION or AMALGAMATION with the first of his "CIVILIZED GREAT WHITE CAUCASIAN RACE" of Europe caused the...

> "RAPID, ALMOST SUDDEN DECLINE IN THE INTELECTUAL
> PRODUCTIVITY OF THE GREEK PEOPLE...," etc.,

he equally failed to take note of the history of his "INFERIOR NEGROES" that built the COLLOSSUS OF RAMESES II [Abu Simbel] more than six hundred and fifty [650] years before the first of his NORDIC CAUCASIANS of Scandanavia and MEDITERRANEAN CAUCASIANS of Greece were part of the history of the known world; and, that the building of said "INFERIOR NEGROES" first stone house - THE STEP PYRAMID OF SAKHARA [Saqqara] - took place more than 2,200 years before the first Greek appeared on the scene of world history.

The RACIST and RELIGIOUSLY BIGOTED projection of the Stoddards, Breasteds, Jeffreys, Amisteds, Junods, Groves, Johnstons, and others of the late 19th and early 20th century bred the current Wiedners, Seligmans, Fages, Galleghers, Olivers, et al, of the modern vintage of so-called "WHITE LIBERAL AFRICANIST HISTORIANS, EGYPTOLOGISTS, ANTHROPOLOGISTS, PALAEONTOLOGISTS," and others of disciplines which are to many to list here. For, it is not only those older ORTHODOX HISTORIANS and other educators, who have written in total contempt for the indigenous peoples of Africa and their descendants everywhere, that African peoples of today must refute; it is , equally, those like the Basil Davidsons, who seem to believe that platitudinous presentations of the HISTORY of the African peoples that occupied, and still do, the areas of ALKEBU-LAN [Africa] just above the equator, and below said line, works we must also scrutinize, challenge, and expose for their "HISTORY OF AFRICA SOUTH OF THE SAHARA," which excludes the indigenous so-called "BANTUS, NEGROES," and others from the history and heritage of nations "NORTH OF THE SAHARA." One must also remember that it is the same Stoddard's, Jeffreys', Junod's, Breasted's,

et al, RACIST NEGROPHOBIA which caused Davidson and others to down-grade Herodotus' physical description of the Colchians, Egyptians, and Ethiopians, whom he stated:

"...HAVE THICK LIPS, BROAD NOSE, WOOLLY HAIR, AND
THEY ARE BURNT OF SKIN...," etc.

This we can plainly observe in Basil Davidson's THE AFRICAN PAST, page 46, as
he dismissed the importance Herodotus placed upon the value of the physical characteristics of the North and East Africans he met and lived with during his stay in Egypt and
Nubia.

Besides the obsessive anti-NEGRO, anti-AFRICAN, and anti-AFRICAN-AMERICAN
RACISM in all of the European and European-American volumes of history dealing with
peoples of African origin and/or birth which caused this writer's refusal to accept the
recordings of the "WHITE ORTHODOX" and "LIBERAL HISTORIANS," all of whom declared themselves "AUTHORITY ON AFRICA" and "THINGS AFRICAN," it is equally
the dull and boring chronological manner in which kings, queens, and other members
of the royal classes in general are presented as the only important people ever involved in mankind's experiences throughout the hundreds of centuries that it becomes impossible to relate to. For, this writer is convinced by the records of the HISTORY of mankind that the ancient past is as much of the present and the future, just as a tree is to
the fruit it produced and the by-product from said fruit. Thus, then HISTORY, particularly that of the African peoples everywhere, must be written as an INTRA and INTER-
CULTURAL and CROSS - REFERENCE projection of the past and current socio-
political and economic upsurge of the African peoples total experience, rather than from
the point of the vacumatic slave syndrome in which it is now taught in all of the educational institutions of every dimension in the United States of America, Great Britain, Europe,
and wherever else European-American and European colonialism and imperialism, also
neo-colonialism have dominated, or still dominate.

There is not a single aspect of European or European-American ORTHODOX HISTORY
intended in this work, for such an approach has never been contemplated. And, the manner
of moving from the PAST to the PRESENT, also from the PRESENT back to the PAST,
with projections for the FUTURE from events of the PAST and PRESENT, consistently and
persistently, is intentionally done. By so doing this writer, who is equally of African origin, is able to interpret the PAST and PRESENT from an African, African-American, and
African-Caribbean perspective. For, he is convinced that it is completely IMPOSSIBLE for

384

any White man, woman, or child [Jewish or Christian], irrespective of "GOOD INTENT, LIBERALISM" and/or "HUMANITARIANISM," in this RACIST and RELIGIOUSLY BIGOT-ED Greek and Nordic Anglo-Saxon Caucasian and Semitic oriented conflagration, other-wise called "WESTERN SOCIETY" and "JUDAEO-CHRISTIAN SOCIETY," to write with any sense of UNBIAS and HONEST perspectives about the African peoples view of their involvement in world history - "THE BLACK EXPERIENCE." It is needless to remind this author of isolated and specific incidents in which Europeans and European-Americans have acted humanely towards Africans and African-Americans as justification for their being allowed to teach BLACK or AFRICAN STUDIES courses, or to have their works ac-cepted as the standard "AUTHORITY" for African and African-American HISTORY, PHI-LOSOPHY, and MORALITY. This attitude stems from the PATERNALISM of the slave and master relationship between the Africans and Europeans. The height of this deceptive machination was reached in the claim that Lord Chief Justice Mansfield was humane with respect to the African people when he ordered the halt to the further enslavement of Afri-can peoples on British soil, each person claiming such have forgotten that his decision was not based upon any humane consideration, but on the fact that the AFRICAN SLAVES were no longer economical for English capitalism. These people are fooled by the 1847 C.E. decision, which they have labeled "...A MAJOR BREAK-THROUGH IN HUMAN RE-LATIONS," basing much of their own conclusion on some of the comments the Lord Chief Justice made with respect to his findings in the case of the slave he set free - "Sommer-set." The major comment was as follows:

"...THE AIR IN ENGLAND HAS LONG BEEN TOO PURE FOR A
SLAVE, AND EVERY MAN IS FREE WHO BREATHES IT...,"

as reported in Campbell's LIVES OF THE CHIEF-JUSTICES OF ENGLAND, vol. ii, p. 321. However, one should equally take note of the fact that even in England the case Sommerset only caused the removal of the physical shackels that bounded the African peoples in England, and later her colonies, but to the present time did not remove one shackle from the European-American, European, and British peoples' mind with respect to the so-called "INFERIORITY" status of their so-called "NEGROES." Thus, they have never once ceased to write "ORTHODOX" and/or "LIBERAL HISTORY" about their "NE-GROES" in the same light, even to the point where it even forced the "conservative" pro-fessor Albert Barnes to write the following in the "Prefatory Note" of his book, THE CHURCH AND SLAVERY, Parry and McMillan, Philadelphia, 1857, p. ii:

385

"It opens, too, a wider field of inquiry in regard to the foundation of our faith in the Bible,
than could be occupied in the argument pursued
in this book, - a field which I hope to enter in
another form. The language which I used in these
extracts is not material to any argument, and I
do not know that it essentially aids it. In this
edition I have, therefore, so modified it as to express the idea which it was only intended to illustrate, - that a book defending slavery as on
the same basis as the relation of parent and child,
husband and wife, guardian and ward, CANNOT be
made to commend itself to the mass of mankind as
a revelation from God, and, THEREFORE, that all
attempts to show that the Bible does thus authorize
and sanction slavery, contribute, to just that extent,
to sustain and diffuse infidelity in the world. This I
maturely and firmly believe."
Philadelphia, March 26, 1857   ALBERT BARNES

Professor Barnes declaration, obviously, if at all representative of the conduct of
today's priests, rabbis, ministers, inmans, and other members connected with the
clergy - JEWISH, CHRISTIAN, MUSLIM, etc. were never heeded in the SYNAGOUGE,
CHURCH, TEMPLE, MOSQUE, or ETHICAL CULTURE SOCIETY. For the preaching
of a "LILY-WHITE HEAVEN" or "HEREAFTER" and "GOD" where there is not a single
"NEGRO," except as a PORTER or SLAVE for the WHITE ANGLES, continues almost
unchallenged and totally unchecked in the published ORTHODOX historical works of
these so-called "WESTERN RELIGIONS - Judaism, Christianity, and Islam.

In Chancellor Harper, Governor Hammond, Dr. Simms, and Professor Dew's
book, THE PRO-SLAVERY ARGUMENT...," etc., Walker, Richards and Co., 1852,
pp. 67-70, under the sub-title "Harper's Memoir On Slavery," the following appears:

I have before said that free labor is cheaper than the labor
of slaves, and so far as it is so the condition of the free laborer
is worse. But I think President Dew has sufficiently shown
that this is only true of Northern countries. It is matter of
familiar remark that the tendency of warm climates is to relax
the human constitution and indispose to labor. The earth
yields abundantly—in some regions almost spontaneously—
under the influence of the sun, and the means of supporting
life are obtained with but slight exertion; and men will use
no greater exertion than is necessary to the purpose. This
very luxuriance of vegetation, where no other cause concurs,

renders the air less salubrious, and even when positive malady does not exist, the health is habitually impaired. Indolence renders the constitution more liable to these effects of the atmosphere, and these again aggravate the indolence. Nothing but the coercion of Slavery can overcome the repugnance to labor under these circumstances, and by subduing the soil, improve and render wholesome the climate.

It is worthy of remark, that there does not now exist on the face of the earth, a people in a tropical climate, or one approaching to it, where Slavery does not exist, that is in a state of high civilization, or exhibits the energies which mark the progress towards it. Mexico and the South American Republics,* starting on their new career of independence, and having gone through a farce of abolishing slavery, are rapidly degenerating, even from semi barbarism. The only portion of the South American continent which seems to be making any favorable progress, in spite of a weak and arbitrary civil government, is Brazil, in which slavery has been retained. Cuba, of the same race with the continental republics, is daily and rapidly advancing in industry and civilization; and this is owing exclusively to her slaves. St. Domingo is struck out of the map of civilized existence, and the British West Indies will shortly be so. On the other continent, Spain and Portugal are degenerate, and their rapid progress is downward.

On page 70 of the same book Chancellor Harper, dealing with the "degenerate" Portugal and Spain - which they allegedly became due to their heavy concentration of indigenous "NEGROES" in their populations, continued on by noting:

I will venture to say that nothing has dealt upon it more heavily than the loss of domestic slavery. Is not this evident? If they had slaves, with an energetic civil government, would the deadly miasma be permitted to overspread the Campagna, and invade Rome herself? Would not the soil be cultivated, and the wastes reclaimed? A late traveller* mentions a canal, cut for miles through rock and mountain, for the purpose of carrying off the waters of the lake of Celano, on which thirty thousand Roman slaves were employed for eleven years, and which remains almost perfect to the present day. This, the government of Naples was ten years in repairing with an hundred workmen. The imperishable works of Rome which remain to the present day were, for the most part, executed by slaves.

* Eight days in the Abruzzi.—*Blackwood's Magazine, November,* 1868.

If an African, African-American, or African-Caribbean "HISTORIAN" can still contain himself or herself to accept this form of "ORTHODOX" European and European-American "HISTORICAL AUTHORITY" today [in the latter half of the 20th century C.E.],

it can only stem from said African [turned "Negro"] total stupidity and utter ignorance
of world history, fear of economic reprisal against approval of his or her tenure, or
fear of possible rejection from a particular integrated academic society, and possibly
fear of not being able to secure a publisher for his or her manuscript.

The state of the NATIONAL RACIST MENTALITY in the United States of America
that provided the air of ease in which the above was written has changed very little philosophically, spiritually, socially, politically, or economically, with respect to the
MASTER-SLAVE [White-Black, Caucasian-Negro] attitudes up to the present time in
the latter part of the 20th century C. E. - 1972. The "PURITY" of the "GREAT WHITE
RACE" [Nordic, Alpine or Mediterranean] President Dew and others of the past wanted
to preserve is the same as that which the "MODERN WHITE LIBERAL AUTHORITIES
ON AFRICA AND AFRICAN PEOPLES" have been trying to protect today by editing-
out their "NEGROES" and "BANTUS," also their "AFRICANS SOUTH OF THE SAHARA,"
from North and East Africa's "ORTHODOX HISTORY" - through a process of systematic CULTURAL GENOCIDE. Governor Hammond summoned it best when he wrote the
following with regard to the "ORTHODOX HISTORICAL" justification of the enslavement
of the African ["NEGRO"] peoples from a biblical point of view, under the sub-title -
"Hammond's Letters On Slavery," pp. 105-107:

> Nay more,
> that every attempt which has been made by fallible man to
> extort from the world obedience to his "abstract" notions of
> right and wrong, has been invariably attended with calamities
> dire, and extended just in proportion to the breadth and vigor
> of the movement. On Slavery in the abstract, then, it would
> not be amiss to have as little as possible to say. Let us con-
> template it as it is. And thus contemplating it, the first
> question we have to ask ourselves is, whether it is contrary to
> the will of God, as revealed to us in his Holy Scriptures—
> the only certain means given us to ascertain his will. If it
> is, then Slavery is a sin. And I admit at once that every
> man is bound to set his face against it, and to emancipate his
> slaves, should he hold any.
> Let us open these Holy Scriptures. In the twentieth chap-
> ter of Exodus, seventeenth verse, I find the following words :
> "Thou shalt not covet thy neighbor's house, thou shalt not
> covet thy neighbor's wife, nor his man-servant, nor his maid-
> servant, nor his ox, nor his ass, nor anything that is thy neigh-
> bor's"—which is the tenth of those commandments that de-
> clare the essential principles of the great moral law delivered
> to Moses by God himself. Now, discarding all technical and

verbal quibbling as wholly unworthy to be used in interpreting the Word of God, what is the plain meaning, undoubted intent, and true spirit of this commandment? Does it not emphatically and explicitly forbid you to disturb your neighbor in the enjoyment of his property; and more especially of that which is here specifically mentioned as being lawfully, and by this commandment made sacredly his? Prominent in the catalogue stands his "man-servant and his maid-servant," who are thus distinctly *consecrated as his property*, and guaranteed to him for his exclusive benefit, in the most solemn manner. You attempt to avert the otherwise irresistible conclusion, that Slavery was thus ordained by God, by declaring that the word "slave" is not used here, and is not to be found in the Bible.

Raving and ranting further, still confused by his own illogical deductions of the Hebrew scripture, he stated:

You cannot deny that there were among the Hebrews "bondmen forever." You cannot deny that God especially authorized his chosen people to purchase "bondmen forever" from the heathen, as recorded in the twenty-fifth chapter of Leviticus, and that they are there designated by the very Hebrew word used in the tenth commandment. Nor can you deny that a "BONDMAN FOREVER" is a "SLAVE;" yet you endeavor to hang an argument of immortal consequence upon the wretched subterfuge, that the precise word "slave" is not to be found in the *translation* of the Bible. As if the translators were canonical expounders of the Holy Scriptures, and *their words*, not *God's meaning*, must be regarded as his revelation.

Hammond touched the basic area of SEMITIC RACISM in the Holy Torah [Five Books of Moses or Old Testament] when he reminded his audience of "CHOSEN PEOPLE," whom the same WHITE RACISTS were also discriminating against in Europe, Great Britain, and the United States of America. But, he continued saying:

It is vain to look to Christ or any of his Apostles to justify such blasphemous perversions of the word of God. Although Slavery in its most revolting form was everywhere visible around them, no visionary notions of piety or philanthropy ever tempted them to gainsay the LAW, even to mitigate the cruel severity of the existing system. On the contrary, regarding Slavery as an *established*, as well as *inevitable condition of human society*, they never hinted at such a thing as its termination on earth. any more than that "the poor may cease out of the land," which God affirms to Moses shall never be: and they exhort "all servants under the yoke" to "count their masters as worthy of all honor;" "to obey them in all things according to the flesh; not with eye-service as men-pleasers, but in singleness of heart, fearing God;" "not only the good and gentle, but also the froward;" "for what glory is it if when ye are buffetted for your faults ye shall take it patiently? but if when ye do well and suffer for it ye take it patiently, this is acceptable of God." St. Paul actually apprehended a runaway slave, and sent him to his master! Instead of deriving from the Gospel any sanction for the work you have undertaken, it would be difficult to imagine sentiments and conduct more strikingly in contrast, than those of the Apostles and the abolitionists.

It is impossible, therefore, to suppose that Slavery is contrary to the will of God.

The ORTHODOX HISTORICAL argument of the "...SUPERIORITY OF WHITES OVER BLACKS...," etc. can be best seen at the height of its ignorance in the following remarks from Governor Hammond's pen on pages 131 and 132 of the same book, as he wrote:

I cannot go into a detailed comparison between the penalties inflicted on a slave in our patriarchal courts, and those of the Courts of Sessions, to which freemen are sentenced in all civilized nations; but I know well that if there is any fault in our criminal code, it is that of excessive mildness.

Perhaps a few general facts will best illustrate the treatment this race receives at our hands. It is acknowledged that it increases at least as rapidly as the white. I believe it is an established law, that population thrives in proportion to its comforts. But when it is considered that these people are not recruited by immigration from abroad, as the whites are, and that they are usually settled on our richest and least healthy lands, the fact of their equal comparative increase and greater longevity, outweighs a thousand abolition falsehoods, in favor of the leniency and providence of our management of them. It is also admitted that there are incomparably fewer cases of insanity and suicide among them than among the whites. The fact is, that among the slaves of the African race these things are almost wholly unknown. However frequent suicide may have been among those brought from Africa, I can say that in my time I cannot remember to have known or heard of a single instance of deliberate self-destruction, and but of one of suicide at all. As to insanity, I have seen but one permanent case of it, and that twenty years ago. It cannot be doubted that among three millions of people there must be some insane and some suicides: but I will venture to say that more cases of both occur annually among every hundred thousand of the population of Great Britain, than among all our slaves. Can it be possible, then, that they exist in that state of abject misery, goaded by constant injuries, outraged in their affections, and worn down with hardships,

390

which the abolitionists depict, and so many ignorant and
thoughtless persons religiously believe?

With regard to the separation of husbands and wives, parents and children, nothing can be more untrue than the
inferences drawn from what is so constantly harped on by
abolitionists. Some painful instances perhaps may occur.
Very few that can be prevented. It is, and it always has been,
an object of prime consideration with our slaveholders, to keep
families together. Negroes are themselves both perverse and
comparatively indifferent about this matter. It is a singular
trait, that they almost invariably prefer forming connexions
with slaves belonging to other masters, and at some distance.
It is, therefore, impossible to prevent separations sometimes,
by the removal of one owner, his death, or failure, and dis-
persion of his property. In all such cases, however, every
reasonable effort is made to keep the parties together, if they
desire it. And the negroes forming these connexions, knowing the chances of their premature dissolution, rarely com-
plain more than we all do of the inevitable strokes of fate.
Sometimes it happens that a negro prefers to give up his
family rather than separate from his master.

Hammond's citation that there were "...FEWER CASES OF INSANITY AND SUICIDE
AMONG THEM [his "Negro" slaves] THAN AMONG WHITES..." failed to demonstrate
to himself that maybe the "NEGRO SLAVES" were a "SUPERIOR STOCK" to his "GREAT
WHITE RACE" he mentioned throughout his book. This type of rationalization the Ham-
monds of the past, and these of the present used is not condusive to the alleged "COM-
MAND OF GOD TO MOSES" to keep his fellow African peoples in perpetual slavery. Hammond's hypothesis was hardly any different than that of the Stoddards, Wiedners, Jeffreys,
Seligmans, and many others; the slight variation being that he was able to write down his
own RACIST and RELIGIOUS BIGOTRY without hiding under the cover of ACADEMIC
LICENSE as the so-called "MODERN WHITE LIBERAL AFRICANIST HISTORIANS" of
the present.

Within the past three hundred to four hundred years or more of depicting the African
peoples everywhere as SLAVES for the Europeans and European-Americans, and as such
their "INFERIOR," it becomes virtually impossible at this late date for the inheritors of
such an "ORTHODOX HISTORICAL TRADITION" and its related SOCIO-POLITICAL and
ECONOMIC rewards to abandon it solely on the basis that BLACK and AFRICAN STUDIES
have began to reveal formerly suppressed documents and other data that prove the heights
and glory of the African peoples who once served as the "CHATTEL SLAVES" for their
former "SLAVES" from Europe and Great Britain. This tradition, or ORTHODOXY, built-
up from the repository of RACIST recordings, will not suffer any meaningful updating or

revamping by the so-called "AUTHORITIES ON HISTORY," who have constantly refer to themselves as the only source of reference to the HISTORY and HIGH-CULTURE [civilization] of all of the peoples of the entire world. Needless to say that African, African-American, and African-Caribbean PROFESSORS and WRITERS of HISTORY, "ORTHODOX" or not, on the average, can do that much less in this respect. Thus, the "ORTHODOX HISTORIANS," those who have established themselves as the sole "AU-THORITY" on anything and everything African and about Africa [Alkebu-lan], must be disregarded in their interpretation of African peoples' HISTORY and HIGH-CULTURE whenever they are in conflict with that of African, African-American, and African-Caribbean scholars, particularly those in the area of NORTH and EAST AFRICAN HIS-TORY - where the "CAUCASIANS" and "SEMITES" have been substituted for the so-called "NEGROES" - the INDIGENOUS AFRICANS.

This CONCLUSION is not one of the typical variety normally used by African people in their dealing with WHITE or BLACK studies, most of whom believe that they have to constantly apologize for their own enslavement by the European and European-American physical and mental slavemasters who have kept them in said condition for the past four hundred years. Most certainly this work is defiant of said mentality; and, most certain-ly such defiance in no way whatsoever is accidental. It stems from the TOTAL CON-TEMPT which European and European-American "ORTHODOX HISTORIANS," past and present, have treated the legacy that WAS, and still IS, the heritage of Africans and their descendants everywehere - both deceased and alive. This LEGACY and HERITAGE cannot be abrogated, though at times it had been STOLEN and SUPPRESSED. The fact that part of its teaching is presently called "GREEK PHILOSOPHY, WESTERN CIVILI-ZATION, JUDAEO-CHRISTIANITY, ISLAM," and whatever else "ORTHODOX" or "LIBERAL HISTORIANS" termed it, never the less it remains the "LEGACY and HERITAGE of the indigenous African peoples and their descendants the world over.

Hopefully this work has reached the goal of presenting this aspect of AFRICAN HISTORY from an AFRICAN INTERPRETATION and POINT OF VIEW, which is no way manner or form dependent upon what any European or European-American think about it. The author has tried very hard indeed to accomplish such an end. He has carefully used only those TERMS and NAMES of people, place, and thing, which the indigenous Africans have used in all cases known to him. He has rejected, and will continue re-jecting, any and all attempts to remove the so-called "NEGROES" from EAST and

NORTH AFRICA'S [Alkebu-lan's] ANCIENT HISTORY and HIGH-CULTURE, all of which is the special area of consentration of this volume. This the author strongly suggests will be the projection which following young AFRICAN, AFRICAN-AMERICAN and AFRICAN-CARIBBEAN students and scholars of the future will take; and, probably from a very much greater dimension in the RECREATION and RECONSTRUCTION of the GLORY that was once "MOTHER AFRICA" [Alkebu-lan] and her equally GLORIOUS SONS and DAUGHTERS of the past and present, and most certainly of the FUTURE.

A TYPICAL DAUGHTER OF THE NILE[0]

It is truly written that:

IN ONE SPADE OF THE EARTH OF AFRICA THERE IS TEN-FOLDS OF TRUTH MORE THAN IN ALL OF THE WRITTEN WORKS BY THE AUTHORITIES ON AFRICA AND AFRICAN PEOPLE. THE HISTORY OF AFRICA COMES ONLY FROM THE PEOPLE OF AFRICA.

From Yosef ben-Jochannan's book,
WE THE BLACK JEWS, Madrid, 1949

---

[0]. Deceased daughter of Emperor Haile Selasie of Ethiopia, East Alkebu-lan [Africa].

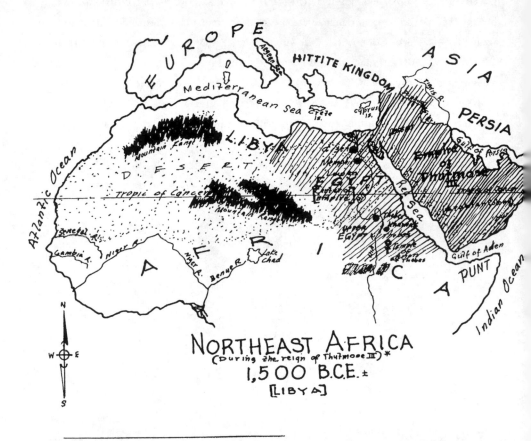

NORTHEAST AFRICA
(During the reign of Thutmose III) *
1,500 B.C.E. ±
[LIBYA]

Note that there was no nation called "ISRAEL" during this period in World History
[c. 1500 B.C.E.]. Thotmes III was a XVIIIth Dynasty pharaoh, who was instrumental
in driving the Hyksos invaders and imperialist colonizers out of Ta-Merry and into
Palestine.

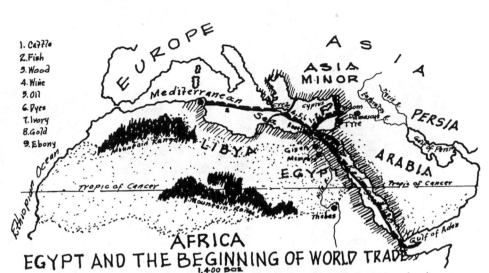

1. Cattle
2. Fish
3. Wood
4. Wine
5. Oil
6. Dyes
7. Ivory
8. Gold
9. Ebony

EGYPT AND THE BEGINNING OF WORLD TRADE
1,400 BCE

The ancient Africans of Egypt (Ta-Merrians or Egyptians) began world trade when
they journeyed to Crete for products needed in their economy. There is sufficient
evidence that they journeyed as far West as Khart Haddas (Carthage) and around
the turn at the Pillars of Herculese or Straights of Gibraltar.

PHOENICIAN TRADE ROUTES
TO EUROPE, ASIA MINOR & AFRICA
± 1,000 - 700 BCE

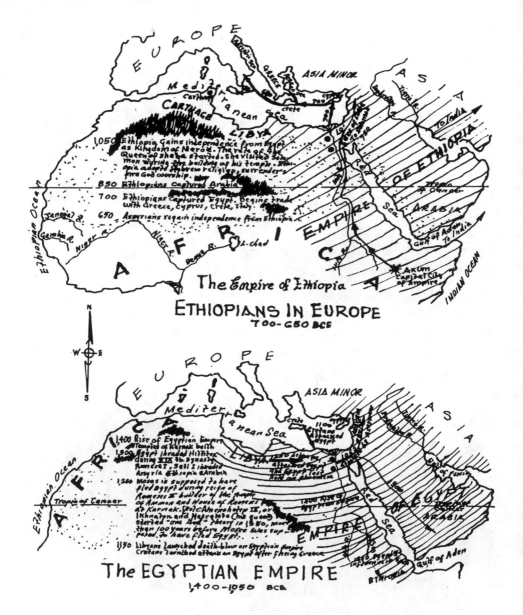

The *Empire* of *Ethiopia*

ETHIOPIANS IN EUROPE
700-650 BCE

The EGYPTIAN EMPIRE
1,400-1,050 BCE

EGYPTIAN COLONY
OF ASSYRIA
[PERSIA]
450 BCE

1. Persians under Cyrus deposed Astyages (last of the Median Kings) in 550 and started the Persian Empire.

2. Darius expanded empire to Indus in 500, and pharoah Psamtik III was defeated by Cambyses.

3. Egypt became Persian province (colony) in 450, Greeks defeated Persians under Miltiades, and Hano (the Phoenician) was defeated by Greece.

4. Persian driven from Egypt in 400 under Darius II.

5. Persians recapture Egypt in 350 under Atraxerxes III.

The PERSIAN EMPIRE
550-300 BCE

6. The Persians were driven from Egypt by Alexander II ("the great") in 332 BCE, as Alexander established the first European ("Caucasian") control of Egypt. Ptolemy I, formerly Genearal Soter or Soter I, established the line of the Ptolemies.

397

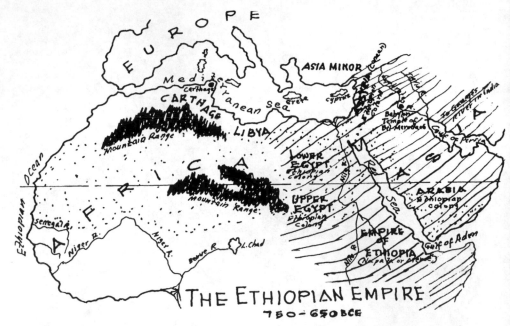

THE ETHIOPIAN EMPIRE
750-650 BCE

The conquest of Egypt by the Ethiopians in 750 B.C.E. during the reign of Pharaoh Sheshonk or Oroskon III was not the first time Ethiopians ruled Egypt.

Pharaoh Psamthik I of the XXVIth Dynasty forced the Ethiopians out of Egypt in 650 B.C.E. after they were already withdrawing to the SOUTH, this due to the Israelites failing to fight the Assyrians as agreed in their treaty with the Ethiopians. King Essarhadden drove them from Assyria and restored the Temple of Bel-Merodach at Babylon as Assyria's second capital.

The ETHIOPIAN EMPIRE
850 BCE

The Ethiopians captured all of Arabia an Persia in 850 B.C.E., and up to india.

EMPIRE OF THE MOORS
(The Moors: Africans, Arabs, Persians, Berbers)
700 C.E. - 1500 C.E.

1. Moors invaded Spain in 711 C.E. under the leadership of Gibra Tarik (an African Moslem) of Morocco.
2. African Sultan establish control of North Africa. Yusuf I, 1080 C.E.
3. Moors driven from all parts of Spain except Granada in 1250±.
4. Moors driven out of Granada in 1500±C.E. during reign of Ferdinand and Isabela.

Area of MALI EMPIRE: —
Songhai Empire formerly Ghana

The ROMAN and/or BYZANTINE EMPIRE
150 BCE - 700 C.E.

1. Roman Empire came into being 156 B.C.E.
2. Romans and Greeks defeated Hannibal, under the Command of Scipio in 150 at the Battle of Zama (the Third Punic War); Carthage Roman Province.
3. Romans burned Carthage burned 100BCE
4. Byzantine period of Roman Empire began in 500CE under Emperor Zeno. Nestorian Church established under Emperor Anastsius.
5. Arabs and other Moslems fleet defeated Byzantine fleet in 700C.E.; Siege of Constantinople by Moslems.
6. Moslem hordes (Arabs and Persians) invaded and captured North Africa, ending the Byzantine period in North Africa in 700 C.E.

by: J. Ben-Jochannan

399

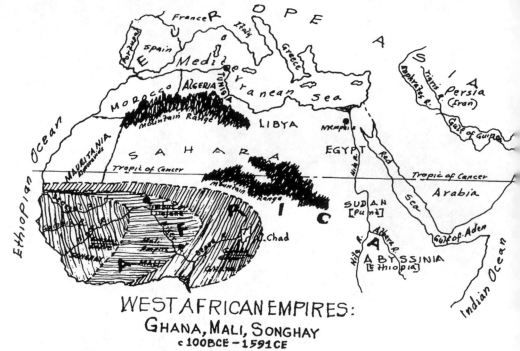

WEST AFRICAN EMPIRES:
GHANA, MALI, SONGHAY
c 100 BCE – 1591 CE

1. The Ghana Empire was established between 50 B.C.E. and 100 C.E. The exact time is debated daily. However, there are sufficient fossils and artifacts unearthed in the area to concretize the fact that it was in existence before the Christian Era. Take note of the Roman travelers who reached the Niger River and Lake Chad areas about as early as 50 B.C.E.; and those who arrived later.

2. Ancient Ghana was destroyed by the Almahodes (Almoravids) around 1076 C.E. They had destroyed the capital, Dejene or Ghana City earlier in 1070 C.E.

3. The Mali Kingdom, which was under the Ghana Empire, was established by Sundiata (Mari Jata) in 1230 C.E.

4. The Mali Kingdom became an Empire under Sundiata in 1238 C.E.

5. The Mali (Mele) Empire ended in 1390 C.E. when it was attacked and invaded by Turaegs from the North. Mansa Musa II was king at the destruction of Mali.

6. The Songhai (Songhay) Kingdom was established in 1464 C.E. by Sonni Ali Ber.

7. The Songhai Kingdom became an Empire in 1488 C.E. under Sonni Ali Ber (the former Ali Kolon).

8. The Songhai Empire was destroyed in 1592 C.E. by African Moors from the North. The invasion from Mauritania (Morocco's original empire) started in 1582 C.E. at the end of King Askia Ishak II reign.

Note: Tombut (Timbuktu, Timbuctoo, Timbuctu, etc) was the capital city of the Mali Kingdom and Empire; in the same area of the Ghana capital Djene.

400

The extent of Europeans knowledge about North Africa around 1651
C.E. is clearly indicated on the maps of said area shown below
on this page. The Nile Delta is very well detailed; also the
various pyramids and landmarks which they knew, even though
there were grave inaccuracies in terms of scaling. Note the location of the City of Carthage and different viaducts, mountains
and rivers shown. For the period these maps were made to cover
they are about the most accurate of all that one can find to
date.

Note: The student should observe that the early Europeans along
the northern coast of Africa believed that there were numerous
rivers that came from the Sahara and emptied into the Mediterranean Sea. The nations along the Barbary Coast were were not outlined as yet, they are shown as cities or settlements without
any distinct boundaries. At the head of each river penetrating
the Sahara there is shown a lake. Most of the maps of ancient
history, drawn by the Europeans, reflect these erroneous conclusions but the history connected thereto were never updated.

401

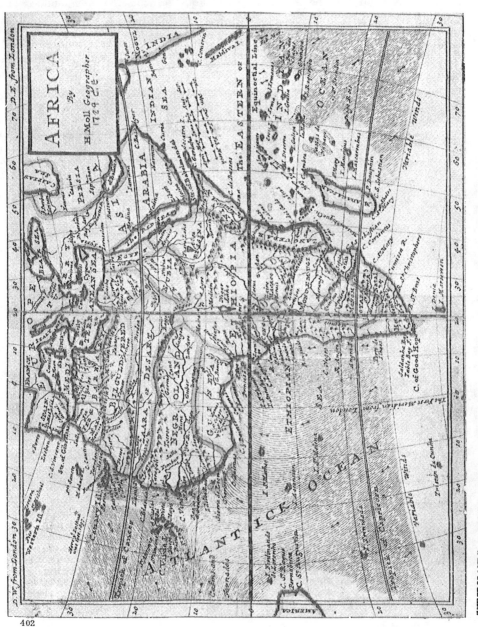

402

"NEGROLAND" on this map hightlights the usual distortion of Africa's geography. This map is representative of the Europeans attempt to be "AUTHORITIES" on Africa and its people, though they were not knowledgeable of most of the continent's landmass or cultural groupings.

Added Bibliography and Supportive Documentation

General

Botsford, G. W., "A History of the Ancient World, New York, 1911

Breasted, J. H., "Ancient Times," New York, 1935

Bury, J. B., S. A. Cook, F. E. Adcock, and M. P. Charlesworth, "Cambridge Ancient History, 12 Vols., 5 Vols. of plates, New York, 1923.

Bury, J. B., "A History of Greece to the Death of Alexander the Great," London, 1951

Hall, H. R. H., "Ancient History of the Near East, 9th ed., London, 1936

Marrou, H. I., "A History of Education in Antiquity," New York, 1956

Newbigin, M. A., "The Mediterranean Lands," London, 1924

Rostortzeff, M. A., "A History of the Ancient World (transl. by J. D. Duff) 2 Vols. 2nd ed., Oxford, 1933

Sandys, J. E., "History of Classical Scholarship" 2 Vols. 3rd ed., New York, 1921

Starr, G. G., "A History of the Ancient World," New York, 1965

Thomson, J. G., "History of Ancient Geography, Cambridge, 1948

Ullman, B. L., "Ancient Writing and Its Influence," New York, 1932

Prehistory

Braidwood, R. J., "Prehistoric Men," Chicago, 1948

Burkitt, M. C., "The Old Stone Age." 2nd. ed., New York, 1949

Childe, V. G., "The Dawn of European Civilization," 4th ed., New York, 1948

------, "New Light on the Most Ancient East," New York, 1934

------, "What Happened in History," Hammondsworth, 1948

Coon, C. S., "The Origin of Races," New York, 1962

-----, "The Races of Europe," New York, 1939

Hooton, E. A., "Up from the Ape." Rev. ed., New York, 1946.

Houalls, W., "Mankind so Far," New York, 1945

Radin, P., "Primitive Religion," New York, 1937

Raphael, M., "Prehistoric Cave Paintings." (transl. by N. Guterman), New York, 1946

Vendryes, J., "Language, A Linguistic Introduction to History," (transl. by P. Radin), New York, 1931

Weidenrich, F., "Apes, Giants and Men," Chicago, 1946

Philosophy and Religion

Frankfort, H., "Kingship and the Gods." Chicago, 1948

Frankfort, H. et al, "Before Philosophy," New York, 1949

————————, "Intellectual Adventure of Ancient Man," Chicago, 1946

Gadd, C. J., "History and Monuments of Ur," New York, 1929

Egypt and the Nile

Alfred, C., "Old Kingdom Art in Ancient Egypt, London, 1946

Breasted, J. H., "Ancient Records of Egypt." 5 Vols., Chicago, 1906—07

————————, "A History of Egypt," 2nd ed., New York, 1935

Clarke, S. and R. Englebach, "Ancient Egyptian Masonry," Oxford, 1930

Drioton, E. and J. P. Lauer, "Sakkarah," Cairo, 1939

Edwards, I. E. S., "The Pyramids of Egypt," New York, 1947

Engleback, R., "Introduction to Egyptian Archaeology with special Reference to the Egyptian Museum, Cairo," Cairo, 1946

Erman, A., "The Literature of the Ancient Egyptians," (transl. by A. M. Blackman) London, 1927

Gardiner, A. H., "The Attitudes of the Ancient Egyptians to Death and the Dead," Cambridge, 1935

Glanville, S. R. K., "The Egyptians," London, 1933

————————, "Daily Life in Ancient Egypt," London, 1930

Peet, T. E., "A Comparative Study of the Literature of Egypt, Palestine, and Mesopotama," London, 1931

Pendleburry, J. D., "Tell-el-amarna," London, 1935

Petrie, W. M. F., "Seventy Years in Archaeology," New York, 1932

—————, "Arts and Crafts of Ancient Egypt," 2nd ed., London, 1910

Shorter, A. W., "An Introduction to Egyptian Religion," New York, 1939

——————, "The Egyptian Gods," London, 1937

Winlock, H. E., "The Rise and Fall of the Middle Kingdom in Thebes," New York, 1947

Bell, H. I., "Egypt from Alexander to the Arab Conquest," Oxford, 1948

The Middle-East (Asia Minor)

Albright, W. F., "From Stone Age to Christianity," Baltimore, 1940

Albright, W. F., "The Archaeology of Palestine," London, 1949

Bertholet, A., "A History of Hebrew Civilization," (transl. by A. K. Dallas), London, 1926

Bevan, E. R. and C. Singer (editors), "The Legacy of Israel," Oxford, 1927

Delaporte, L., "Los Hittites," Paris, 1936

Diringer, D., "The Alphabet," New York, 1948

Finegan, J., "Light from the Ancient Past," Princeton, 1946

Gurney, O. R., "The Hittites," Harmondsworth, 1964

Meek, T. J., "Hebrew Origins," New York, 1936

Moore, G. F., "History of Religions," 2 Vols., New York, 1937

Mendelsohn, I., "Slavery in the Ancient Near East," New York, 1949

Olmstead, A. T., "A History of the Persian Empire," Chicago, 1948

Rogers, R. W., "A History of Ancient Persia," New York, 1929

Sykes, P. M., "A History of Persia," 2 Vols, 3rd ed., London, 1930

North of the Mediterranean

Glotz, G., "The Aegean Civilization," (transl. by M. R. Dobie and E. M. Riley), New York, 1927

Hall, H. R., "The Civilization of Greece in the Bronze Age." London, 1928

Hutchinson, R. W., "Prehistoric Crete," Baltimore, 1963

Huxley, G. L., "Achaeans and Hittites," Oxford, 1960

------, "Crete and the Luwians," Oxford, 1961

Myres, J. L., "Who Were the Greeks?" Berkeley, 1930

Nilsson, M. P., "Homer and Mycenae," London, 1933

Page, D., "History and the Homeric Illiad," Berkeley, 1959

Person, A. W., "The Religion of Greece in Prehistoric Times," Berkeley, 1942

Starr, C. G., "The Origins of Greek Civilization," New York, 1961

Thomson, G., "Studies in Ancient Greek Society: The Prehistoric Agean," London, 1949

Young, A. M., "Troy and Her Legend," Pittsburgh, 1948

Botsford, G. W. and E. G. Sihler, "Hellenic Civilization," New York, 1920

Gary, M., "The Documentary Sources of Greek History," Oxford, 1927

Ferguson, W. S., "Greek Imperialism," New York, 1913

Grote, G., "A History of Greece," New ed. 12 vols., New York, 1906

Pritchett, W. K., "Studies in Ancient Greek Topography," Berkeley and Los Angeles, 1965, Part I.

Robinson, C. A. Jr., "Alexander the Great," New York, 1949

Tarn, W. W., "Alexander the Great," 2 vols., Cambridge, 1948

Snowden, F. W., "Blacks in Antiquity: A Greco-Roman Experience," Cambridge, 1970

Milne, J. G., "Greek and Roman Coins and the Study of History," London, 1939

Seltman, C. T., "Greek Coins," London, 1933

Seltman, C., "Masterpieces of Greek Coinage," London, 1949

Black, R. S., "Plato's Life and Thought," London, 1949

Field, G. C., "The Philosophy of Plato," London, 1949

Kirk, G. S. and Raven, J. E., "Presocratic Philosophers," Cambridge, 1960

Nilsson, M. P., "A History of Greek Religion," Oxford, 1925

Pearson, L., "Early Ionian Historians," Oxford, 1939

Wells, J., "Studies in Herodotus," Oxford, 1923

Jouquet, P., "Macedonian Imperialism and the Hellenization of the East," (transl. by M. R. Dohie), New York, 1928

McEwan, C. W., "The Oriental Origin of Hellenistic Kingship," Chicago, 1934

Block, R., "The Origins of Rome," New York, 1960

Homo, L., "Primitive Italy and the Beginnings of Roman Imperialism," (transl. by V. G. Childe), New York, 1927

Randall-MacIver, D., "The Etruscans," Oxford, 1927

Baker, G. P., "Hannibal," London, 1930

Boak, A. E. R., "A History of Rome to A. D. 565," 5th ed., New York, 1965

Chapot, V., "The Roman World," New York, 1928

Frank, T., "Roman Imperialism," 2nd ed., New York, 1914

-----, "A History of Rome," New York, 1923

Liddell-Hart, B. H., "A Greater than Napoleon, Scipio Africanus," London, 1927

Mommsen, T., "The History of Rome," 5 vols. new ed., New York, 1903—05

Ormerod, H. A., "Piracy in the Ancient World," Liverpool, 1924

Sculland, H. H., "Scipio Africanus in the Second Punic War," Cambridge, 1930

Thiel, J. H., "Studies in the History of Roman Sea-Power," Amsterdam, 1946

FORWARD NOTES
[1st Edition]

Note No.   Description

1. These names are not African. They were assigned to the Africans by their
   European colonizers as names of contempt and ridicule.

2. See Parker T. Moon, IMPERIALISM AND WORLD POLITICS; Sir Edward Hertslett, THE MAP OF AFRICA BY TREATY; Henry Nevinson, A MODERN SLAVERY,
   and E. D. Morel, BLACK MAN'S BURDEN.

3. "Race" is a concept that is foreign to the peoples of Alkebu-lan (Africa). European colonialist used it to the extent of making short people of a different "race"
   to tall people; Christians of a different "race" to Hebrews (Jews), etc; even the
   languages spoken by people are classified into "RACIAL GROUPS."

4. This word comes from the mythical "Negroland" European colonialists invented
   for an area of West Africa. See the following maps on pages xxvi and 401...,
   R. Morden, AFRICA, 1688; and H. Moll, AFRICA, 1729.

5. Note that the inter-relationship and kinship feelings between Europeans and European Americans were encouraged; whereas such feelings and contacts were de-
   nied the Africans and African-Americans by their European and European-
   American slave masters and owners. To date such relationship between Blacks
   of Africa and the U. S. A. are frowned upon and openly discouraged.

6. Professor Jeffreys is a common symbol of a particular stereotype characteristic
   in "Western" society. For this reason his symbolic utterances have been used
   to highlight certain aspects of the basic behavior patterns and "Negrophobic
   delusions" so common among White America today.

7. The recorded history of Egypt began thousands of years before the birth of
   Abraham—"the father of the Hebrew peoples" (Jews); muchless before he gave
   up his Chaldean religion, as stated in the Hebrew Torah. And, whereas the
   Hebrews only record less than six-thousand (6000) years of history, the indigenous
   Africans of Egypt relate back at least twenty-five-thousand (25,000) years.

8. This is the usual RACIST interpretation of the allegedly "biblical story" about
   Noah and the flood by many "White" and "Black" ministers; both indicating that
   their "God" initiated "color prejudice." This concept is most common in the
   teachings of Mormon and Calvinist Christian sects. It is to be found in the written
   words of many of the Sixth Century C. E. Babylonian Talmudist scholars. (See
   R. Graves and R. Patai, HEBREW MYTHS, p. 121, New York, 1964; Y. ben-
   Jochannan, AFRICA: MOTHER OF "WESTERN CIVILIZATION," p. 599, New
   York, 1971; and Y. ben-Jochannan and G. E. Simmonds, THE BLACK MAN'S
   NORTH AND EAST AFRICA, p. 29, New York, 1971).

9. See story of the Passover. Moses marriage to the daughter of the High Priest
   of Kush (Ethiopia)—according to NUMBERS XII, I, of the Hebrew Torah.

10. A mythical country placed on maps alleged to be Africa during the 16th through
    18th centuries C. E. See map by H. Moll, AFRICA, 1729, at the rear of this

volume. Note that this area was covered during much of this period by the Songhai Empire; before that by the Ghana and Melle empires. [See page 402].

11. See maps on pages 395 to 403.

12. Africa is a whole continent and must be treated in its entirety. This is strictly a "racist" term.

CHAPTER I NOTES

1. This area of Africa was invaded in the late 19th century and conquered by British imperialist military forces of the colonial office in the early 20th century C. E. Britain was forced out in 1957. Ghana was the first of the indigenous African-controlled country in Africa to win its political freedom after World War II. Ghana's "Father of Independence," first Prime Minister and President was Dr. Kwame Nkrumah—otherwise known as "OSAGYEFO" (the Redeemer or Savior of his people).

2. The TWI people, for centuries, had their own written language and alphabet. Wars with the various European colonial powers destroyed their culture, including their educators and educational system. This is typical of what happened to the indigenous Africans of Egypt by the Arab invaders in 640 C. E. It is to be noted that the Arabs also aided in the destruction of many West African cultures, including the TWI'S.

3. The Nile is comprised of the "WHITE" and "BLUE" bodies of water, also the ATBARA RIVER. The Blue Nile starts at Lake Tana in the Ethiopian High-lands, and ends at Khartoun, Sudan. The White Nile starts at Mwanza Nyanza (also called "Lake Victoria" by the British colonialists), Uganda, and ends at Khartoun. Above this tangent point the Nile continues northwards to Atbara, Sudan—where it is joined by the Atbara River. It then flows through Sudan and Egypt into the Mediterranean Sea. Note that the Nile River flows from south to north; not east to west as Herodotus and other early Europeans believed. (See map of Africa by Herodotus).

4. Monomotapa was the indigenous name of the entire southern limits of Africa—according to ships' logs of the first Europeans to arrive there and meet the Africans—Captain Bartolome Dias (a Portuguese), 1488 C. E., and Captain Vasco da-Gama (another Portuguese), 1499. This vast empire extended as far North as Zimbabwe (Zimboae according to the Portuguese)—presently called "Rhodesia" by the European colonialists that control it in honor of Cecil Rhodes—one of the world's master at genocide during the 19th century C. E. It ended as far south as the Cape of Storms (Cabo de Tormentos—according to the Portuguese).

5. Herodotus' description of the indigenous Africans of Egypt in 450 B. C. E. is shown in this volume. [See Herodotus, HISTORIES, Book II, Chapter 57].

6. Practically every European and European-American historian start European and European-American history from the earliest Greeks (Pyrrhus) and Romans (Etruscans); the assumption being that "...from the Greeks all knowledge originated."

7. See G. G. M. James, STOLEN LEGACY; Sir E. A. Wallis Budge, BOOK OF THE

408

DEAD; J. Kendrick, THE HISTORY OF PHILOSOPHY; and, Pliny, HISTORY.

8. This is a common theory among European and European-American historians and others of disciplines related to history. No proof to justify this conclusion has ever been submitted, however. It is all conjecture.

9. This revelation completely refutes Professor Jeffreys' statement in Chapter II of this volume. (See Professor Jeffreys, "The Negro Enigma," in the September, 1951 issue of the WEST AFRICAN REVIEW).

10. Note that the usage of the word "primitive" by H. G. Wells is no longer tolerated when applied to people of Caucasian origin. Such reference is generally used, currently, to Africans, Asians and indigenous Americans, almost exclusively; the assumption being the same for the word "tribe."

11. See J. A. Rogers, SEX AND RACE, Vol. I, II and III; and, WORLD'S GREAT MEN OF COLOR, Vol. I and II.

12. The Africans of the Kingdom of Elam, in Persia, were also described in the same manner that Herodotus described the indigenous Africans of Egypt, Ethiopia, and Colchis. Note that the Ethiopians who invaded India and settled there were equally described.

13. This struggle had its zenith in the successful revolution in Haiti against the French; and the frustrating defeat of "Queen Mary, Bottom Belly" and "Ellen Fire-bun" in their attempt to seize the Danish Virgin Islands during the 19th century C. E. (These three African women led an independence struggle that almost toppled Danish colonialism in the Caribbean).

14. Sabacom, Piankhi and others from Nubia (Sudan) and Kush (Ethiopia) ruled Egypt as Pharaohs (Kings). See pp 160-164 chronologies. Note that the Nubians [Zetis] ruled Egypt from approximately 775 B. C. E. until 653 B. C. E.

15. The Moors introduced the "common bath" to the Europeans of southern France, Spain and Portugal. They also introduced the use of "undergarment" and linen wear from 711 C. E. (See Jane Soames, THE COAST OF THE BARBARY; J. C. deGraft-Johnson, AFRICAN GLORY; and Stanley Lane-Poole, THE MOORS IN SPAIN).

16. Note Herodotus' description of the Egyptians he saw and met when he attended school in Egypt. (See also, E. A. Wallis Budge, BOOK OF THE DEAD; Count C. Volney, RUINS OF EMPIRE; G. C. M. James, STOLEN LEGACY; H. G. Wells, A SHORT HISTORY OF THE WORLD; J. A. Rogers, WORLD'S GREAT MEN OF COLOR, Vol. I; J. Dorsey, CIVILIZATION MAN'S OWN SHOW).

17. Ibid. Also, Sir J. Frazier, THE GOLDEN BOUGH; H. W. Smith, MAN AND HIS GODS; and, Eva B. Sandford, THE MEDITERRANEAN WORLD.

18. The Hyksos invaded Egypt in 1675 B. C. E.; the Persians in 616 B. C. E.; the Greeks in 332 B. C. E.; and the Romans in 47 B. C. E. (See pages 140 - 157 in this volume).

19. The Nile River in this case is from (about), the Second CATARACT to the Mediterranean Sea.

20. The Arabs came to North Africa as invaders in 640 C. E. Their zeal, under the sword and Islam, raised as much havoc against the indigenous Africans as did the Europeans with their guns and Christianity. Both of them brought their own God, in their own likeness, and imposed them upon the indigenous Africans through Holy Wars (Jihads).

21. "AFRICAN GLORY" was universally considered among Europeans as one of the major books on African High-Cultures, especially West and North African history.

22. The word "Negro" came from the Portuguese. It was also placed on maps of the 17th century C. E. by other colonialist-minded Europeans in West Africa to coincide with the mythical "Negroland" they had already established. See the following maps on pages 402 and xxvi:.....H. Moll, AFRICA, 1729, R. Norden, AFRICA, 1688; also R. Moore's THE WORD NEGRO, ITS ORIGIN AND EVIL USE, N.Y.,1955.

23. See note No. 22 of this chapter.

24. See note No. 5 of this chapter.

25. Note that he is also known as Orsokon II. (See pages 158 - 159. He reigned from 870 to 847 B. C. E.

26. The U. S. A.'s "racial" scale is the best example. A person can be blonde with golden hair and still be a "Negro" according to the U. S. A.'s census standard. "Negro," like "Caucasian," is not a definite measurement, and is not scientific.

27. This type of propaganda is still being preached inside and outside of Africa by "Christian missionaries" from Europe, Britain,and the United States of America.

28. See "Liber Pontificals" (Book of the Popes), p. 17, for Pope Victor's birth; for Melchiades'(also known as Miltiades) p. 40; for Galasius, p. 110, [as translated by L. R. Loomis, New York, 1916). See also: J. C. deGraft-Johnson, AFRICAN GLORY; A Weisberger, LES BLANCS d'AFRIQUE (The Whites of Africa), p. 83, Paris, 1910. He detailed the peoples of the area these popes came from.

29. Count C. Volney, RUINS OF EMPIRES, described the indigenous Africans he met in Egypt back in the 18th century C. E. as being similar to the "Negroes" of the United States of America. Baron Denon made the same observations in describing the Sphinx of Ghizeh in his works and painting of this monument. (See pages 111 and 192 in this volume).

30. Some European and European-American historians have tried to claim that the Hyksos were from Europe. In their hypotheses they have failed to show any evidence of the Hyksos civilization in Europe. The most accurate location of their civilization before entering Egypt is to date (currently) called the "Middle-East" (Asia-Minor).

31. See Manetho's, "History of Egypt" (A chronological history of dynastic Egypt).

32. The current reckless usage of the term "RACE" is much worse than it was in H. G. Wells' lifetime. Today's usage makes every national grouping a "race of people," etc.

33. See Adolph Hitler's "Mein Kampf, or South Africa's "apartheid." In the case of the latter, "God (the White Man's God) made the Bantu Negroes to serve the white man," etc. The former placed anyone who was not an "Aryan" as a slave,

making millions of Europeans similar to "Negroes" they considered inferior.

34. See, H. Nevins, "A Modern Slavery;" H. Stanley, "The Dark Continent;" C. P. Graves, "The Planting of Christianity in Africa;" Eric Williams, "Capitalism and Slavery;" and L. Stoddard, "The Rising Tide of Colour;" and E. D. Morel, "Black Man's Burden."

35. Herein lies the basis for most of the lynchings of "Negro" males in the U. S. A.; for the mere staring at "Caucasian" females.

36. The reaction to the "brutish sexual potentials" which the "Negro" males are supposed to have in "abundance" brings forward the usual White American query: ..."would you like your daughter to marry a Nigger." The word "Nigger" would be "Negro," depending upon which section of the U. S. A. the question is asked.

37. The word "Jews" stems from the word "Judah," one of the Hebrew tribes— according to the Hebrew Torah—(the Christian Old Testament). Thus: the Hebrew People, or the Tribe of Judah (Jewish Tribe).

38. See statements by both men in previous pages of this work.

39. He has been credited with many other racist remarks in his alleged works, many of which predates him.

40. The "American Negroes" were properties (chattel slaves) at the time of the framing and adoption of the U. S. A.'s Federal Constitution. Most of the signators of this document were slave holders, including America's first President—George Washington. The Fourteenth Amendment of said document made the "Negro" human; at least this is what the amenders felt.

41. This statement completely refutes the positions of Professor Jeffreys, Dr. L. Stoddard, and others who claimed "no Negro" [African] "lived in the Stone Age era."

42. Sir E. A. Wallis Budge's conclusion has been stated for hundreds of years by African writers and traditionalists. Current archaeological findings, other existing artifacts, and structures along the 4,100 miles (plus) Nile Valley have proven this point. These facts are common knowledge to "educators" in this field; but politics and prejudice caused many of these truths to be smothered. Punt was where the Somalis and parts of eastern Ethiopia now occupy.

43. To what degree can the Europeans and European-Americans prove that there are no Moors, Carthaginians or Egyptians in their ancestral lineage after having been subjugated by these Africans. Obviously no more so than the African-Americans can now prove the absence of European lineage in their families.

44. Those who claim that "Caucasians occupied the Nile Valley before the present Africans" (not Arabs) have submitted only theories, no facts whatsoever.

45. Taken from the Africans of the Nile Valley who worshipped Ra.

46. See: Sir E. A. Wallis Budge's, "Osiris"; J. A. Rogers', "World's Great Men of Color," Vol. I; also statues of same in Rome, Madrid and other capitals in Europe.

47. See: J. C. deGraft-Johnson's, "African Glory;" J. A. Rogers', "Africa's Gift

to America;" Carter B. Woodson's, "The Negro In Our History;" Basil Davidson's "The African Past;" and Y. ben-Jochannan, "Africa (Alkebu-lan): Her Peoples and Ever Changing Map;" and "Africa: The Land, the People and Culture," W. H. Sadlier, Inc., New York, 1968.

48. Ibid. 45.

49. The concentration camps, for indigenous Africans only, are called "Native Reserves" by the Afrikaners and other Whites of the world. They reflect certain vivid similarities to the "Indian Reservations" in the U. S. A.

50. Typical orthodox "Christian" Missionary teachings and practices.

51. Sir Harry must not have read Herodotus' description of the Africans of North Africa. In order to call any African "Hamitic," he or she must have followed "Ham's" lineage. What color or physical characteristics does he claim for Ham? Where does the line between "Negro" and "Negroid" begin and end? Who decides the standards to be used?

52. See: J. C. deGraft-Johnson's, "African Glory;" J. A. Rogers', "World's Great Men of Color."

53. Septimus Severus and his son Carracalla. (See: J. C. deGraft-Johnson's, "African Glory;" Jane Soames', "The Coast of Barbary;" J. A. Rogers,' "World's Great Men of Color").

54. He was born in Lipsus Magna, North Africa.

55. Swarthy color, thick lips, broad nose, etc., usually assigned to Africans.

56. See: J. C. deGraft-Johnson, "African Glory;" Jane Soames, "The Coast of Barbary;" J. A. Rogers, "World's Great Men of Color;" Raymond Lull's, Lull Reports; Mrs. Stewart Erskine, "The Vanished Cities of Northern Africa."

57. Augustine was born in Numidia; Cyprian and Tertullian in Carthage (all in North Africa). These names were the so-called "Christian (European) titles" given to them when they became converts to the religion.

58. The current teaching in "Christian" Churches credits the Romans for this accomplishment.

59. Who can tell what color or feature all of their ancestors had?

60. The Vatican in Rome, Italy; the Church of England (Anglican) in England; the Methodist, Baptist and other White Protestant groups in the U. S. A.

61. The reference to "Jesus Christ" does not endorse his existence, nor deny it. It is only used in this manner as a frame of reference in history.

62. These wars are detailed in Chapter VII, including the 3rd Punic War.

63. Coptic (Koptic) Christians from Egypt and Ethiopis carried Christianity to these parts of Africa before the arrival of the first Europeans (the Portuguese) in West Africa during the mid-Fifteenth Century C. E.

64. Pope Martin V was given the first Africans enslaved by the slavers of Prince Henry (the so-called "Navigator") and some of the gold they stole from the Africans. The Church in Rome also sanctioned the importation of slaves from

Africa into the Caribbeans upon request of Bishop Bartolome de LasCasas on the Island of Hispaniola (Haiti and Santo Domingo) in the early 16th Century (c. 1503) C. E.

65. Leopold was awarded the entire Congo nation as his personal estate by the Berlin Conference in 1884—1885. The U. S. A. took part in this "Act," even though it refused to sign the final document—called ..."The Berlin Act." The lack of signature was only a formality, as the U. S. A. took part in bringing about all of the repressive measures within this infamous document that later became the nucleus of what is today called "International Law." (See Sir Edward Hertslett, "The Map of Africa By Treaty," Vol. 2, Africa in General).

66. China, Viet Nam, Congo, Sudan, etc.

67. Before Dr. Gertrude Gaton-Thompson published her outstanding work the Africans who spoke of Zimbabwe's existence were scorned by their European conquerors as being "...all hearsay nonsense..." This was also true after some European prospectors visited Zimbabwe's holy places.

68. The Moors (Africans) wore baggy pants that were wide at the knees and narrow at the ankles, of course picturesque in color.

69. J. A. Rogers, "Nature Knows No Colour Line;" J. C. deGraft-Johnson's, "African Glory;" B. Davidson, "The African Past;" Stanley Lane-Poole, "The Moors in Spain;" Jane Soames, "The Coast of Barbary,"

70. See J. C. deGraft-Johnson's, "African Glory;" J. A. Rogers, "World's Great Men of Color."

71. J. C. deGraft-Johnson's, "African Glory;" Jane Soames, "The Coast of Barbary."

72. The term "Negroid" has no definite scientific basis; the same for "Caucasoid" and "Mongoloid." One can see any of these alleged "racial traits" in any group of people.

Chief among those who continue to perpetuate certain ethnic slurs against Blacks ("Negroes"), yet claiming leadership of the same people—are the N. A. A. C. P., Urban League, National Association of Colored Women, etc. For example: Can anyone see anything which does not have a color? What then is meant by "Colored Women?" Continued usage does not by itself make anything right; proof by facts, through evidence, does.

73. Jane Soames, "The Coast of Barbary;" J. C. deGraft-Johnson's, "African Glory;' J. A. Rogers, "World's Great Men of Colour;" B. Davidson's, "The African Past."

74. Prof. Breasted wisely hid his distinction between the Africans of Egypt and those of (his) "South of the Sahara" by means of the quotation signs. But the result is the same if he had not placed this common connotation in quotes. He too attempted to prove that the Africans from North of the Sahara to be of a different "race" than those South of the Sahara. What was there among the ancient Egyptians (North Africans) one could not find among those of Central and

75. See page 395 of this work.

South Africa except for a greater development of common cultures, all of which
is evidenced around the African Great Lakes near the Congo, Uganda, Ethiopia,
Tanzania, Tchaᶰ (Chad) etc.

76. Herodotus used the word "ETHIOPIAN" to describe Africans, not "NEGRO."

77. Common Orthodox Christian teachings on the first "martyrs of Christendom."

78. Those who agree with the "martyrdoms," but differ between father and son's
responsibility for the acts.

79. "Modern Man" (whatever this is) claims to have become wiser than his more
ancient brother. Maybe the fact that the ancients lacked color prejudice is a
sign of their so-called "primitive mentality." That is, if the prevailing racism
of modern educators is to prevail.

80. All Roman Catholic Church history known to the author has established this date.

81. He mounted the Roman throne in 193 C. E. (See Jane Soames, "The Coast of
Barbary;" J. C. deGraft-Johnson's, "African Glory;" J. A. Rogers, "World's
Great Men of Color").

82. The church was involved with dividing the world between Spain and Portugal
during the 15th Century. It was involved with the first Africans enslaved in
Europe; when Pope Martin V accepted a present of 5 Africans—as slaves—from
Prince Henry of Portugal. The church was once the biggest slave owner in the
world. One of its Bishops, Bartolome de LasCasas, introduced Africans into
slavery in the Western Hemisphere. This does not exclude the Protestants, who
followed the lead of Rome.

83. This does not mean that today's Roman Catholics are to be persecuted for the
wrongs of their forerunners.

84. General pulpit lectures by the clergy against all who had to fight the early
Christians and were defeated are said to have been defeated by "Jesus Christ"
(or "God"). They see professing "Christianity" tantamount to "righteousness"
and "Godliness." That they are the "representatives of God (Jesus Christ) on
earth." Yet they do not see the same God that crushed the Crusaders. Of course
this is not considered a failure of God to help his "onward Christian Soldiers"
defeat the "pagan Moslems" and others.

85. Some "Negro preachers" still claim, in their pulpits, that their own Black
people are paying a price because of "God's curse against Ham." They have
accepted the mythical story of "Ham" of the Hebrew Torah (Bible) as being...
"the source from whence black people originated." Fortunately most Black
clergymen from seminaries have refused to prattle this stereotype gospel; but
the so-called "Store Front Churches" continue its perpetuation.

86. There are thousands of clergymen whose only knowledge of their religion is
through one version of the Christian "Holy Bible" or another. They have never
received any form of secular teachings of the history within the same book. Some
actually believe that ..."God wrote the Bible." Some even claim that ..."the
Christian Religion was the first religion known to man," and other such beliefs;
yet these "Men of God" are responsible for most of the religious prejudice and
stereotype amongst mankind today, just as they were in yester-years.

87. These questions represent real existing conditions. Shrugging them off, as was

the case for the last four-hundred years, will not make them go away. They **are** basic to world peace. Certainly they are direct, and maybe prickle some puritans; that is good. Maybe someone who can change these things may move towards change by this open and frank dialogue.

CHAPTER II NOTES

1. All sorts of attempts are being made to reconstruct ancient man, which is in itself laudable. However, the attempt to reconstruct the African fossils along European (Caucasian) standards indicate the extent to which "racism" interferes with scientific research. It is as unlikely for **Neanderthal** man to have been an African, as much as **Zinjanthropus boisie** being a European.

2. There are literally thousands of Africa's art treasures and artifacts in Museums and private collections throughout Europe, Britain and the Americas. Most of them have been taken out of Africa without the permission of the Africans to whom they belong.

3. The hypothetical maps indicate how much the **"authorities"** differ on ancient man's history. Note the "racial" conflict within the author's mind on who settled Central Africa in pre-historic times.

4. Because of the usage of the word "primates," and other similar connotations, the author of this work has refused to use the word "primitive" to living people.

5. This was true in the U. S. A. until the **Fourteenth Amendment** of the Federal Constitution changed the "Negro" status from "slave" to citizen."

6. Some historians relate the indigenous Australians ("Aboriginees") to East Africa and Southeast Africa; others refute it.

7. Huxley-Wilberforce debate of 1861, presided over by John Steven Henslow.

8. Theologians willfully distort Darwin's pronouncement on earliest man in order to prejudice their followers against any attempt to prove any origin of mankind other than "Adam and Eve in the Garden of Eden."

9. The Christian Church was the prosecutor and persecutor of many leading palaeontologists of 19th century C. E.

10. The Hyksos were the first non-African invaders of Egypt. They captured Lower Egypt in c. 1675 B. C. E.

11. **Monomotapa** was the name the Africans gave to this area of their continent before it was called "**Union of South Africa**" and "**Republic of South Africa**" by European colonialist invaders and settlers. See reports of Bartholemew Dias (a Portuguese—the first European to visit the area, in 1488 C. E. This was later corroborated by Vasco daGama's subsequent trip in 1496 on his way to India).

12. Most books on Africa's **prehistoric fossils** will reveal others not listed here. Unfortunately no book (to date) published lists all of the fossils or artifacts. This is, because of the frequency of the finds, also the hardship of dating them and making certain other classifications are met.

13 Louis B. Leakey is the husband of Dr. Mary Leakey. They work as a team on most excavations and other work.

14. There are many more modern methods of dating prehistoric materials at present than were available when Zinjanthropus boisie was dated. He was updated from the original figure of 600,000 years old to the current 1,750,000 (1.8 million).

15. Tanganyika joined with Zanzibar in 1964 to form the "Republic of Tanzania." The Island of Zanzibar and the Island of Pemba were called the Republic of Zanzibar. The Republic of Tanganyika was on mainland Africa. The two islands are approximately forty miles off the east coast of Tanganyika in the Indian Ocean.

16. This conclusion is, of course, quite speculative. There is no hard-fast fact that every animal with smaller brain than man have to be less intelligent. Since there is no prehistoric man's brain to be examined at present one can only speculate.

17. The question of what color the prehistoric men found in Africa were is only ful-filling to those who need such support. To intelligent humans the import is that there could be a link found between man as he is today and as he was yester-year. Would it make a difference if the people on the Moon were technicolored? If they are Black should all effort to make contact with them cease? One has to re-member that the same Africa that was rejected proved to be the best possibility of the true "Garden of Eden" (Original Home of Man).

CHAPTER III NOTES

1. DuBois was himself of African and European origin.

2. See Note No. 22 of Chapter I Notes.

3. The old English translation is from the original work. The "f" was used as "s" in old English.

4. Translations into English by Griffith, Ranke (in: Gressmann, Lange, "Das Weisbertsbuch des Amen-em-eope," 1925).

5. See Story of Moses' birth, upbringing, charge of crime, etc., in the Hebrew Torah's SECOND BOOK OF MOSES (Exodus).

6. Although Sir John Harris was supposedly criticizing his fellow colonialist, Rhodes, he too shows contempt for the African peoples when he refers to them as "back-ward peoples."

7. Rhodesia is a colonialist name, in honor of the Hitler of South Africa—Cecil Rhodes. The proper African name for this land is "Zimbabwe."

8. What is meant by the "Dark Continent"? There is no precise established mean-ing for this phrase. For each writer this term means something different. In general it is degrading.

9. Volney spoke from first hand experiences; yet those who followed him by over 100 years give the impression that the opposite is fact.

10. One marvels how "modern" historians make the **Sphinx of Ghizeh** and other major African statues European ("Caucasian"). It is obvious that these facts have been known to "western" educators from the late 18th Century C. E. Why, then, were the facts held in secret from Black and White alike?

CHAPTER IV NOTES

1. The foundation for most of what every Egyptologist knows about the Africans of Egypt came from Manetho's masterful works, "The History of Egypt."

2. **High-Culture** is used in place of "Civilization"—which has no set or detailed standard. The word implies that there are people who are "not civilized" (uncivilized). Yet experience has shown that where more than two people live together for the common good of each other a **civil compact** exists. This is regardless of what their values may be.

3. Though the actual text does not relate much beyond the 1st Century C. E. the Chronology is brought up to date for current reference in the **preceding pages.**

4. This word—"**tribe,**" only meaning, when used by the author of this work, is similar to the word "ethnic" (a group of similar appearance and/or similar culture). The manner of its usage to non-European peoples by people of European origin is derogatory in every aspect.

5. Thebes was the center (nervous system) of the Africans government. Here **lies the** answer to the "mysteries" (See Sir E. A. Wallis Budge, "Book of the Dead;" and his "Osiris", for English translations of the Mysteries from its original language, **hieroglyph**). There were two other reasons why the Hyksos could not penetrate Upper Egypt: 1) To small an army for so large a territory. 2) Upon arrival in Africa they were not organized under a central figure.

6. At this juncture the indigenous Africans (Egyptians) began amalgamating with Asians and Europeans. At least the proof is recorded. Since man is but human everywhere, one can assume that there was always human amalgamation. (The word "amalgamation" is used herein in the sense of human group identity (geo-political compact). Thus: The **amalgamation of Africans with Europeans**— people with other people from different lands). In this work mankind is in itself a "race," irrespective of color, feature, hair, sex or size. When enslavement arrives to any national group of people their women's integrity is violated by the enslavers; this happened to all of mankind, including the present enslavers.

7. Defeated peoples; not exterminated.

8. The Hebrews (mis-nomered "Jews") were being subjected by the Africans of Egypt for the third time in their history. Egypt and Israel (Palestine) are again fighting each other for the last two generations. Yet neither of their peoples are of continuous lineage to the lands for which they fight. The Israelis are from Europe; the Egyptians from Asia (mostly Arabia). The ruling power in Israel comes from "Jews" in America.

9. The U. A. R. does not in fact exist any longer. The second partner of the "Unity," Syria, withdrew unilaterally from the Union in 1961 C. E. The establishment of the "Union" was to create an Arab-based tie between Egypt and the rest of the Arab world, as Arabs. Egypt's African geography was not considered.

10. The marriages never took place. One can only wonder if the Babylonians would have been better off with them. Of course students of this area of study verbally fight among themselves in academic calisthenics without any possible solution ever.

11. There is not sufficient proof of this pharaoh even being a distant relative of the Royal Families of Egypt. Some historians believe he was.

12. A picture of Akhenaten and family appears on pages 203 and 290 of this work. Examine the comments in relation to present Christian teachings about the life and origin of the concepts of a Trinitarian God-Head, etc.

13. The worship of the God Amen was being revived for the 4th time in Egypt. Note that striking similarities exist between the Egyptians worship of Amen and many West Africans worship of Orishas.

14. Like Aristotle, and other Greeks of his era, falsely naming the African mysteries, so are the many remaining Papri given names that are not related in anyway whatsoever to the contents. Moreso, these documents are the properties of Africa and her peoples.

15. Physically Egypt, as an empire, lingered on; but the moral fibre of the nation was already destroyed under this regime.

16. Solomon's reign is to be reckoned with his alleged authorship of the "Proverbs."

17. See pages 00 and 000 of this work relating to his capture of Nubia and the stele he had erected. Note that Osorkon II and Usertsen II are the same person. There is conflict in the translation of this name from Hieroglyph to English.

18. See page 197 of this work.

19. Ibid.

20. See page 150 for dates and names of these kings or pharaohs.

21. He commissioned Admiral Hanno of Carthage to circumvent Alkebu-lan (Africa) in 600 B. C. E. During this commission Hanno established Carthaginian colonies along West Africa's coastline. [See page 159 for order of his reign].

22. Note that the Phoenicians power declined due to political reasons. Some historians imply certain racial conclusions without submitting any data to support same.

23. This act was tantamount to spitting on a Christian Crucifix or blowing one's nose on a Hebrew Scroll. The effects of either of these today would have brought on the same-reactions as killing an Apis Bull in ancient Egypt.

24. Biblical and traditional history are also parts of the Africans heritage. Of course mythology plays its role, as it does in all other people religious and traditional histories.

CHAPTER V NOTES

1. There is no record of this statue ever being sold by any African. It was taken out of Africa illegally, the same as the overwhelming majority of other African properties in private art collections and public museums throughout Europe, Great Britain and the United States of America.

2. See page 111 middle and bottom pictures.

3. See J. A. Rogers' "World's Great Men of Color." Vol. I; J. C. deGraft-Johnson's "African Glory."

4. See page 193.

5. See pages 186 and 187.

6. Richards' "Freemasonry;" Dr. Albert Churchward's "Origin and Evolution of Free Masonry;" J. A. Rogers' "World's Great Men of Color."

7. All of these authors attested to the African origin of "Free Masonry." [See A. Churchward's "Arcana of Free Masonry." 1915].

8. G. G. M. James' "Stolen Legacy" claimed that "Jesus Christ" and "King Solomon" visited and took instructions from the Lodge at Mt. Carmel. This is supported by most of the researchers on secret societies.

9. The most publicized trip to Punt by Egyptian royalty was the trip of Queen Hatshepsut. [See page 284 for the story in Egyptian script - Hieroglyph].

10. Khafa or Djoser was renamed "ZOSER" or "ZOZER" by the early Greeks. who found it difficult to pronounce the African names.

11. See page 284 for picture of her statue.

12. See page 284 for story in Hieroglyphics.

13. See page 2. Unitarianism as a religious force. is built upon the philosophical teachings and concepts of Akhenaten and many other pharaohs of Ta-Merry.

14. Note that the Africans had developed this science beyond the current methods, since the average housewife could have made her own compound from the ingredients mentioned. [See page 283].

15. See also G G. M. James' "Stolen Legacy;" Frankfurt's "History of Philosophy;" Kendrick's "History of Philosophy."

16. See "The Legacy of Egypt" [ed. by S. R. K. Glanville]; J. A. Rogers' "World's Great Men of Color;" G. G. M. James' "Stolen Legacy." [See page 159].

17. This occurred before there was a Moses of the Hebrew Torah. Everyone of the laws in the Hebrew "Ten Commandments" God was supposed to have given Moses at Mount Sinai were in effect in Kush under King Ori. and in Egypt for over three-thousand [3000] years before Moses was born in Africa [Egypt] about c. 1338 B. C. E.

18. This is the old "DIVIDE AND CONQUER" technique of Napoleon and other colonialists of Europe Great Britain, and the United States of America.

19. See the writings of Herodotus in his major work - "THE HISTORIES."

20. Herodotus cannot be accepted as the "Father of African History;" only European.

21. Like the Columbus-Lief Ericson fiasco, the Portuguese got credit above the Greeks as being the first Europeans to sail along the coast of West Africa because they too failed to record their voyage as well as the Portuguese did. And because of the small area of communication during B. C. E. as against C. E.

22. Polybius in his "HISTORIES" Book III. 59 mentioned his visit to the West Coast of Africa [Alkebu-lan].

419

CHAPTER VI NOTES

1. This is common in most textbooks in the Americas and Europe on the subject of Africa and the indigenous African peoples.

2. This type of "historical writing" found its beginning in the Henry Morton Stanley and Dr. David Livingstone "DARK CONTINENT" episodes; needless to mention **Tarzan and Jane**, also the Christian Missionary canibal tales.

3. Today's European-Africans of the Union? or Republic? of South Africa exclude all **"non-white"** peoples from the government. Therefore, the Africans have refused to recognize that it has any legitimacy from their point of view.

4. The word "PRIMITIVE" is generally used in a contemptuous manner; mostly in relationship to the peoples of Africa, Asia, South America, Australia and the indigenous of North America.

5. This is due to the fact that Europeans and European-Americans have tied their beginnings to ancient Egypt and other parts of North and East Africa.

6. The home of **Zinjanthropus boisie**: The oldest manlike (probably man) animal found to date—1,750,000 years old. Also, refer back to Chapter I of this volume.

7. Most people believe that only in Egypt there are pyramids, because of their mis - education in current "educational systems" which are designed to promote policies of the national culture of "white supremacy"—which makes Egypt "**Semitic, Caucasoid, or Hamitic**", and mentally stop the Nile River from flowing out of Uganda (Central East Africa).

8. See the "PYRAMID FIELD" on pages 195, 206, also on other pages in this chapter dealing with the structures of all forms, etc.

9. From Uganda, Kenya, Congo, Tanzania, Burundi, Rwanda and other areas around Mwanza Nyanza (colonial Lake Victoria), Lake Ituri (colonial Lake Albert), Lake Tanganyika, Lake Malawi (colonial Lake Nyasa) through Zimbabwe (colonialist Southern Rhodesia), to the tip of the once powerful and most expansive Monomotapa Empire (renamed "Union of South Africa," then "Republic of South Africa," by the minority "for whites only" racist government of European descendants— mostly from the Netherlands and England). This former empire's seat of government was in the Kingdom of Monomotapa (presently misnamed "Mozambique" by the present Portuguese colonialist and slave masters who still illegally occupy it). The religious capital was in Zimbabwe (today's white dominated colony of Rhodesia).

10. This is typical of the story on Osorkon IInd's stele, in which he recited his conquest of Nubia (at times part of Upper Egypt, Kush or Meröwe) and his attack on Kush (Ethiopia), etc.

11. See maps at the rear of this volume, beginning on page 394.

12. As recorded in Queen Hatshepsut's account of her Royal voyage to Punt (around the area of today's Republic of Somalia and the present "French colony of Somali land) and other events in the history of Upper Egypt. See page 284 also.

13. This structure is one of a series of buildings and wall enclosures within the com-

plex of the once powerful Rozwis High-Culture (civilization).

14. Note that the design of its structure was in such a manner as to induce the sunlight and sunrays always to shine on the altar of the Holy of Holies.

   The basic value of the Sun as God, or Godlike figure, is maintained.

15. ALKEBU-LAN is the ancient name of the continent which the Greeks and Romans renamed "AFRICA." The Ethiopians and Moors called their continent by the name "ALKEBU-LAN."

16. **Life Magazine** issues of November 22 and 29; also December 6 and 13 (1968). Look Magazine issue of January 7 (1969).

17. Books on **Pietro Olonzo Niño** are to be found in abundance in the Arthur Olonzo Schomburg Collection of the Countee Cullen Branch of the New York City Public Library, Harlem, New York City, New York.

18. See: J. A. Rogers, AFRICA'S GIFT TO AMERICA; and C. G. Woodson, THE NEGRO IN OUR HISTORY.

19. Ibid.

20. Ibid.

21. Ibid.

22. Every facet of "Western society" reflects the division of mankind into something which no one can tell where it begins or ends—called "RACE."

23. Previous to the discovery of "BOSKOP MAN" in Monomotapa (South Africa) these two valleys were considered to be "...the original home of man" (the biblical "Garden of Eden").

24. Herodotus saw the **Colchians, Egyptians and Ethiopians**, whom he described to be the same as the Africans and African-Americans currently being called "BANTUS" and "NEGROES"—among other things much worse. Herodotus was the "**...father of European history.**" The impression is given that he was '**...the father and originator of all history up to his era.**'

25. He has established "**heavens**" and "**hells**" with **reward and punishment** concepts to suit each, none of which he can truly prove exist or do not exist in fact.

26. Sir E. A. Wallis Budge, BOOK OF THE DEAD; J. A. Rogers, WORLD'S GREAT MEN OF COLOR, Vol. II; J. C. deGraft-Johnson, AFRICAN GLORY; and G. G. M. James, STOLEN LEGACY.

27. Punt occupied the area now called "**Somali Republic**," "**French**" **Somaliland** and (parts of) **Kenya**. Like Kush (Ethiopia), it supplied much of the wealth Egypt displayed. This **Royal Visit** was in response to a visit from the Royal Family of Punt to Egypt. Trade between all of the Nile Valley High-Cultures were extensive. It was a 4,100 miles long trade route, and approximately 1,000 miles wide (from Congo the the Mediterranean Sea; from the Libyan Desert to the Indian Ocean and Red Sea).

28. This Temple has been removed in sections to higher ground than its original location to make way for the flood waters of Egypt's new **Aswan Dam**. An inter-

national team of all disciplines in science and social studies was retained to accomplish this feat. The original location was of solid stone, from whence the temple was sculptured by the Africans of the Nile Valley.

29. There is no special pattern to the arrangement. The selection, as well as their placement, is just a matter of asthetic taste of the author. The same is true for all of the other plates, except in cases where they are specifically tied to a particular reference in the texts.

30. Refer to pages 2, 7, 199 and 203 of this work for historical reflections on this unusual man of "Peace on Earth Good Will Towards All."

31. Is it not strange that the only pictures usually displayed of Nubians with regard to Egypt are those depicting them as slaves to the Egyptians? Is there much difference between these two nobles in respect to their obligations to Egypt? Yet both of these two nobles ancestors ruled Egypt. Note the varied degrees of sophistication in the Africans art in Egypt. What is "primitive" about it that is not considered "Modern" today?

32. The "Book of the Dead" is an English translation of the Africans of Egypt sacred Texts, religious ceremonies and philosophical beliefs. It is taken from countless Papyri, slabs of stone and stele of which the Egyptians wrote. It is written in three scholarly volumes. However it may be had in One Volume (condensed) from which beginners in Egyptology or other related disciplines can readily find to be adaptable to their needs.

CHAPTER VII NOTES

1. Carthage was both a City-State and Empire.

2. See Jane Soames, "The Coast of the Barbary;" J. A. Rogers, "World's Great Men of Colour," Vol. I.; J. C. deGraft-Johnson, "African Glory."

3. Arabs (Asian 640 C. E.), Berbers (European 150—146 B. C. E.), Africans (indigenous people). The dates indicate arrival of groups to the area. The Berbers are remnants of the Etruscans (Romans, etc.) who conquered Carthage and traded with North African peoples. The Arabs came to North Africa spreading the gospel of Islam in two Jihads (waves of religious wars, similar to the Christian Crusades.)

4. See Jane Soames, "The Barbary Coast;" J. C. deGraft-Johnson, "African Glory;" J. A. Rogers, "World's Great Men of Colour."

5. Rome's expansion was due to her conquest over less powerful states of the Italian peninsula.

6. Carthage was using Sicily as a military outpost.

7. Pyrrhus is the Greek name for Greece. The latter is an English word.

8. Carthage at this period had established settlements along Africa's west coast for trading purposes.

9. **Gibraltar** is named in honor of the African who invaded and conquered Southern Spain in 711 C. E.—General Tarikh. See J. A. Rogers, "World's Great Men of Colour"; J. C. deGraft-Johnson, "African Glory;" Jane Soames, "The Coast of Barbary;" C. P. Groves, "The Planting of Christianity in Africa;" H. Leclercq, "L' Afrique Chritienne," 1904.

10. General Hamilcar Barca, Hannibal's father, was commander of Carthaginian forces.

11. During this period the Carthaginians were enjoying their defeat of Rome, and failed to rebuild their damaged naval vessels.

12. This was the beginning of Carthage downfall.

13. None of these restrictions had anything to do with the Africans' "color" or "race," as some historians implied. Jane Soames in her work, "The Barbary Coast," made certain to mention that Rome was not a homogeneous society of one ethnic group.

14. Most historians carefully ignore the African peoples of Carthage, and give the

    impression that the Carthaginians were "**Caucasians**." There is no difference between the Africans of Carthage experiences with the Phoenecians and what the West Africans experienced with the colonialist powers of Europe from 1830 C. E. to the present. For regardless of the role of the conqueror and the conquered, carnal intercourse between both will inevitably take place.

15. **Hannibal Barca** was forced to make this decision, as the Carthaginian naval fleet was all but destroyed in the latter part of the "1st Punic War" (Rome vs. Carthage).

16. Hannibal did try to recruit Europeans along the way, but most of them were not trainable to meet the standards set for his army. They were only suitable for labor details. It would have taken months to get them acquainted with the elephants that terrified them.

17. Rome had appointed many dictators for periods of a few months during crisis, but this was the first time that no time limit was established by the Senate for the end of Fabius' dictatorial rule.

18. Fabius was obviously only holding Hannibal's forces until the new Roman army could complete its training; and until the navy could be rebuilt.

19. S. Selincourt, "The Carthaginians in Europe."

20. His supply line could not meet his war demands without a full-size sea power which was at this time impossible, being that the fleet had been destroyed.

21. A **trireme** (tri-rēm) is a vessel with three benches or banks of oars on each side; or a galley.

22. These Africans were eventually forced into the Roman army and became Roman citizens.

23. This plan was never tried. Hannibal tried many other places, but was always turned down.

24. Upon Alexander "the great" untimely death the Greeks fought among themselves over who was going to rule what captured land and people. Soter I (or Ptolemy I), Alexander's Macedonian general, took Egypt.

CHAPTER VIII NOTES

1. The making of Jesus Christ a God-Head figure was done by man in the First Century of the Christian Era. Similarly, it is man who said that "God inspired" those they called "prophets" to speak about each particular religious philosophy; and of course the same applied to those who wrote the "Christian New Testament Bible," Hebrew Torah, Muslim Quoran (Koran) and all other religious rule books. All of them based upon the same theory of the Africans view of "Salvation."

2. "Mysteries System" is a name established by egyptologist for the system of order that existed in ancient Egypt with regards to religion and education in all disciplines.

3. See, also, G. G. M. James, "Stolen Legacy."

4. Note that these 3 Stations in man's experiences are also fundamental principles in practically all religious and secret societies (such as the Free Masons, Knights of Columbus, Elks, Druids, Odd Fellows, etc.) in Europe and the Americas.

5. All western higher institutions of learning still cling to the African values.

6. "Esoteric Philosophy" is claimed to be part of the development of "Greek Philosophy" in most universities in Europe and the Americas, yet the ancient Africans used it long before the first European (the Greeks) philosophers had schools of learning.

7. Prof. G. G. M. James in his book, "Stolen Legacy," also made extensive researches and conclusions on these points.

8. The Greeks themselves did not call their development "Greek Philosophy," as they did not claim to have had anything new or different in philosophic ideals to that which they had learned from their African teachers in Egypt.

9. It is strange that Greek officials would have challenged the teachings of Socrates in this manner if it was the official "philosophy" of Greece (Pyrrhus) he was spreading.

10. Word in brackets by your author.

11. Ibid.

12. If Aristotle and the Greek students he had migrated to Egypt to be taught by African teachers (such as the High Priest Manetho) did in fact develop a Greek-based "philosophy," as most Western educators claimed; why did he also suffer rejection by his fellow Greeks? Because the new "philosophy," he taught, he learned from his African professors of/and in Egypt; Professors who came from the length and breadth of the Nile Valley High-Cultures. Some from as far south as Zimbabwe. (See Dr. Churchward, "The Origin of Free Masonry"; G. G. M. James, "Stolen Legacy").

424

13. See G. G. M. James, "Stolen Legacy"; S. Clymer, "Fire Philosophy"; Kendrick's, "History of Philosophy"; William Turner, "History of Philosophy."

14. There are no records of these men ever being engaged in these pursuits prior to their education in them while studying in Egypt. And there are no justifiable reasons to assume that such was the case.

15. Refer back to the charges against Socrates on page 317 of this work for observation of the depth to which the state felt it was being undermined by the introduction of the Africans philosophic concepts brought back by the Europeans (Greeks).

16. These two concepts (the last paragraph on page 318 and this), like the others, are teachings that preceeded the birth of all of the so-called "Greek Philosophers."

17. Religious recordings and beliefs of the Africans of Egypt as translated into English from its original Hieroglyph by Sir Ernest A. Wallis Budge.

18. Is it not strange that one continues hearing educators claim that ..."The Africans knew nothing of the wheel before the Europeans introduced it to them." Yet one finds that the Africans were the master chariot builders of ancient days. The

    question is; Were these facts not known to the educators in Western institutions of higher learning? If yes; Why was the opposite taught?

19. Note that Akhnaten wrote his works more than one thousand (1000) years before the birth of Aristotle.

20. To date these three works are the most descriptive on the subject matter in discussion.

21. This negative term, like the word "race," is used to degrade those who do not meet certain standards established by the user. Of course the user is the "civilized" one.

22. Note that the period involved is more than one-hundred (100) years before any knowledge of Socrates is recorded, and more than two-hundred (200) years before Aristotle.

23. Here in Egypt, amongst the Africans, Pythagoras learnt the fundamentals for what is now called the "Pythagorum Theorem."

24. Use the following bibliography on Socrates.

25. These references are also applicable to Heraclitus and others in Note 24; and Herodotus, in the preceeding paragraph.

26. See page 317 for review on the official charge and its analysis.

27. See pages 317 and 318 for review.

28. It was also carried eastward into Asia. Thus; in Babylonia, Asyria, Persia and other parts along the Tigris and Euphrates Valleys.

29. See ancient maps on the Egyptian Empire on page 396 of this volume.

30. Note that the name "Ganges" itself came from the famous Kushite (Ethiopian) General Ganges, who led African forces into this area of Asia.

31. This historical fact should answer much of professor Jeffreys' dilemma, which has been shown throughout the first section of this volume.

32. With this background in mind, how is it possible to claim this area of Europe as "pure white" or "pure Caucasian" today, if at all? These facts are widely known to academicians in the various institutions of "higher learning"; yet they continue to be hidden from students of social subjects.

33. Also Ikhnaton, Akhnaten, Akhenaten, Amen-hotep IV, etc.

34. "Black power, Negro power, Bantu power" etc.; either name. It all means that at one time in history the indigenous African ancestors of the African peoples in Africa, Europe and the Caribbeans were powerful enough to have been rulers over the Europeans and Asians (Professor Jeffreys' "light-skinned" and "dark-skinned" Caucasians"). It also shows that man, be he black, white, yellow, red, brown, or even technicolor, has ruled others as he is, or was, ruled by them.

35. See G. G. M. James, "Stolen Legacy"; and John Kendrick, "Ancient Egypt," for more critical analysis of a detailed discipline. (Although the former is very hard to be had, there are existing copies available. This book is particularly

    recommended for students wanting to examine these facts further).

36. Other works should be consulted. The specific reference to this work is due to the exact wording on that page.

37. The suicide of Socrates and exile of Aristotle and others are marked examples.

38. Because of its Egyptian origin, it is only logical that Egypt would be the last place to expect persecutions and prosecutions for its teachings.

39. A Lodge or School of the ancient Nile Valley High-Cultures, especially in Egypt, was the equivalent in value (somewhat) of a college of university of the 20th century C. E.

40. This Lodge is the "Mother Lodge" of all existing Masonic orders in the world.

41. 323 or 325 B. C. E. Historians vary on these two dates.

42. Some of the African works attributed to Aristotle did not claim for himself were claimed for him by "scholars" and "educators" who followed him over one-thousand (1000) years later.

43. Most of these men's biography began after their education in Egypt. The average one was more than forty (40) years old when history first referred to them. Many of them were not even Greek nationals.

44. From approximately 1318—1232 B. C. E. These figures represent the beginning of Pharaoh Seti I reign to the end of Rameses II reign. See page 159 of this work for chronological review.

45. The Oracle was a man "who could tell the future." During this period the Oracle of Anmon, in Egypt, was considered the greatest; not only in Africa, but of the known world.

46. The prevailing teaching in all Western institutions of higher learning follow this concept.

47. See materials on Dr. L. S. B. Leakey's "Zinjanthropus boisei." A 1,750,000 year old fossil-man of Africa's middle-eastern region. Also known as "Nut-cracker Man." Zinjanthropus boisei was discovered on July 17, 1959 in the Olduvai Gorge, Tanganyika [Tanzania]. East Africa. His age was determined by the process called "POTASSIUM-ARGON TEST" [a scientific process of dating matter through measuring its carbon or atom c contents. It is popularly known as the "ATOM CHANGE TEST."

48. See maps on the Egyptian and Libyan Sea.

SPECIAL PAGE FOR NOTATIONS AND INDEX

Page No.   Remark   Date

SELECT BIBLIOGRAPHY

Adams, Walter M. *The Book of the Master*. New York: Putnam, 1898.

Albright, William F. *From the Stone Age to Christianity*. Baltimore: The Johns Hopkins Press, 1940.

Armistead, Wilson. *A Tribute for the Negro*. Manchester: W. Irwin, 1848.

Arkell, Anthony J. *A History of the Sudan: From the Earliest Times to 1821*. London: University of London, Athlone Press, 1955.

Augustine, Aurelius. *Confessions*. Translated by Edward B. Pusey. New York: Dutton, 1950.

_____ *On Christian Doctrine*. Edinburgh: T. and T. Clark, 1892.

Ault, Warren O. *Europe in the Middle Ages*. Boston: D.C. Heath and Co., 1932.

Baker, George P. *Hannibal*. London: Grayson and Grayson, 1930.

Bakewell, Charles M. *Source Book in Ancient Philosophy*. New York: Charles Scribner's Sons, 1909.

Barnes, Albert. *The Church and Slavery*. Philadelphia: Parry and McMillan, 1857.

Ben-Jochannan, Yosef. *Africa: Mother of Western Civilization*. New York: Alkebu-lan Books Associates, 1971.*

_____ *African Origins of the Major Western Religions*. New York: Alkebu-lan Books Associates, 1970.

_____ *We the Black Jews*. Spain: N.P., 1949.

Ben-Jochannan, Yosef, Hugh Brooks, and Kempton Webb. *Africa: Land, People and Cultures of the World*. New York: W.H. Sadlier, 1970.

Ben-Jochannan, Yosef and George E. Simmonds. *The Black Man's North and East Africa*. New York: Alkebu-lan Books Associates, 1971.

Besant, Annie. *Esoteric Christianity; or, the Lesser Mysteries*. New York: J. Lane, 1902.

Blake, Wilson W. *The Cross, Ancient and Modern*. New York: A.D.F. Randolph and Co., 1888.

Bloch, Raymond. *The Origins of Rome*. London: Thames and Hudson, 1960.

Bovill, E. W. *Caravans of the Old Sahara*. London: Oxford University Press, 1933.

Braidwood, Robert J. *Prehistoric Men*. Chicago: Chicago Natural History Museum, 1948.

Breasted, James H. *Ancient Records of Egypt*. Vols. 1-5. Chicago: The University of Chicago Press, 1906-1907.

_____ *Ancient Times: A History of the Early World*. New York: Ginn and Co., 1944.

_____ *The Conquest of Civilization*. London: Harper and Brothers, 1926.

_____ *A History of Egypt from the Earliest Times to the Persian Conquest*. New York: Scribner, 1937.

Budge, Ernest A. *Amulets and Talismans*. New Hyde Park: University Books, 1961.

_____ *Annals of Nubian Kings*. London: Kegan Paul, 1912.

_____ *The Bandlet of Righteousness, an Ethiopian Book of the Dead*. London: Luzac and Co., 1929.

_____ *The Book of the Dead. The Papyrus of Ani in the British Museum*. London: British Museum, Longmans and Co., 1895.

_____ *Egypt*. Vols. 1-6. New York: Frowde, 1902.

_____ *The Egyptian Sudan; Its History and Monuments*. Vols. 1-2. London: K. Paul, Trench, Trubner and Co., 1907.

_____ *A History of Ethiopia, Nubia and Abyssinia*. Vols. 1-2. London: Methuen and Co., 1928.

_____ *The Negative Confession*. New York: Bell Publishing Co., 1960.

_____ *Osiris and the Egyptian Resurrection*. Vols. 1-2. London: P. L. Warner, 1911.

_____ *The Papyrus of Ani*. Vols. 1-3. New York: G. P. Putnam's Sons, 1913.

Burckhardt, John L. *Travels in Nubia*. London: J. Murray, 1819.

Caton-Thompson, Gertrude. *The Zimbabwe Culture*. Oxford: The Clarendon Press, 1931.

Childe, Vere G. *The Dawn of European Civilization*. London: K. Paul, Trench, Trubner, 1947.

_____ *New Light on the Most Ancient East*. London: K. Paul, Trench, Trubner, 1934.

_____ *Man Makes Himself*. London: Watts and Co., 1936.

Select Bibliography

Churchward, Albert. *The Arcana of Freemasonry.* New York: Macoy Pub. and Masonic Supply Co., 1915.

_____ *Origin and Evolution of the Human Race.* London: G. Allen and Unwin, 1921.

_____ *The Origin and Evolution of Freemasonry Connected With the Origin and Evolution of the Human Race.* London: G. Allen and Unwin, 1920.

_____ *The Signs and Symbols of Primordial Man.* New York: E. P. Dutton and Co., 1910.

Clark, John D. *The Prehistory of Southern Africa.* Middlesex: Penguin Books, 1959.

Clymer, Reuben S. *The Philosophy of Fire.* Quakertown: The Philosophical Publishing Co., 1942.

Cole, Sonia M. *The Prehistory of East Africa.* New York: Macmillan, 1963.

Collingwood, Robin G. *Roman Britain.* Oxford: The Clarendon Press, 1932.

Cook, Stanley A. *The Religion of Ancient Palestine in the Light of Archaeology.* London: Oxford University Press, 1930.

Coon, Carleton S. *The Origin of Races.* New York: Knopf, 1962.

Couch, Herbert N. *Greece.* New York: Prentice-Hall, 1940.

Dalzel, Archibald. *The History of Dahomey, an Inland Kingdom of Africa.* London: The Author, 1793.

Darwin, Charles G. *The Next Million Years.* London: R. Hart-Davis, 1952.

Darwin, Charles R. *The Origin of Species.* London: J. M. Dent and Sons, 1934.

Davidson, Basil. *The African Past.* Boston: Little, Brown, 1964.

DeBuck, Adriaan and Alan H. Gardiner, eds. *The Egyptian Coffin Texts.* Vols. 1-7. Chicago: University of Chicago Press, 1935-1961.

DeGraft-Johnson, John C. *African Glory.* London: Watts, 1954.*

Denon, Dominique V. *Travels in Upper and Lower Egypt.* Vols. 1-2. London: B. Crosby and Co., 1802.

Diogenes Laertius. *Lives of Eminent Philosophers.* Translated by R. D. Hicks. Vols. 1-2. London: W. Heinemann, 1925.

Dorsey, George A. *Man's Own Show: Civilization.* New York: Harper and Brothers, 1931.

Dowling, Levi H. *The Aquarian Gospel of Jesus the Christ.* Tucson: Omen Press, 1972.

Drioton, Etienne and Jean-Philippe Lauer. *Sakkarah, The Monuments of Zoser.* Cairo: Impr. de L'Institut Francais D'Archeologie Orientale, 1939.

Dubois, Felix. *Timbuctoo the Mysterious.* New York: Longmans, Green and Co., 1896.

Elworthy, Frederic T. *The Evil Eye. An Account of this Ancient and Widespread Superstition.* London: J. Murray, 1895.

Emery, Walter B. *Nubian Treasure.* London: Methuen, 1948.

Erman, Adolf. *The Literature of the Ancient Egyptians.* Translated by Aylward M. Blackman. London: Methuen and Co., 1927.

Erskine, Beatrice Steuart. *Vanished Cities of Northern Africa.* London: Hutchinson and Co., 1927.

Frankfort, Henri. *The Intellectual Adventure of Ancient Man.* Chicago: The University of Chicago Press, 1946.

_____ *Kinship and the Gods.* Chicago: The University of Chicago Press, 1948.

Frazer, James G. *The Golden Bough; A Study in Magic and Religion.* Vols. 1-13. London: Macmillan, 1911-1936.

Frobenius, Leo. *The Voice of Africa.* Vols. 1-2. London: Hutchinson and Co., 1913.

Garstang, John, A. H. Sayce and Francis L. Griffith. *Meroe, The City of the Ethiopians.* Oxford: Clarendon Press, 1911.

Glanville, Stephen R., ed. *The Legacy of Egypt.* Oxford: The Clarendon Press, 1942.

Graves, Robert and Raphael Patai. *Hebrew Myths; The Book of Genesis.* Garden City: Doubleday, 1964.

Groves, Charles P. *The Planting of Christianity in Africa.* Vols. 1-4. London: Lutterworth Press, 1964.

Hall, Harry R. *The Ancient History of the Near East.* London: Methuen and Co., 1913.

Harris, John H. *Slavery or "Sacred Trust".* New York: Negro Universities Press, 1969.

Hastings, James, ed. *Encyclopedia of Religion and Ethics.* Vols. 1-13. New York: C. Scribner's Sons, 1908-1926.

Herodotus. *The Histories.* Translated by Aubrey DeSelincourt. Baltimore: Penguin Books, 1955.

Hertslet, Edward. *The Map of Africa by Treaty.* Vols. 1-3. London: Harrison and Sons, 1896.

Higgins, Godfrey. *Anacalypsis.* Vols. 1-2. London: Longman, 1836.

Select Bibliography

Hitti, Philip K. *History of the Arabs*. London: Macmillan and Co., 1937.

The Holy Bible. Authorized King James Version. New York: Oxford University Press, 1963.

The Holy Qur'an. Translation and Commentary by Maulana Muhammad Ali. Lahore: The Ahmadiyyah Anjuman Isha'at Islam, 1963.

Hooke, Samuel H. *Myth and Ritual*. London: Oxford University Press, 1933.

Huggins, Willis N. and John G. Jackson. *An Introduction to African Civilizations, with Main Currents in Ethiopian History*. New York: Avon House, 1937.

Hulme, Frederick E. *The History, Principle and Practice of Symbolism in Christian Art*. London: Sonnenschein and Co., 1908.

Hurry, Jamieson B. *Imhotep, the Vizier and Physician of King Zoser and Afterwards the Egyptian God of Medicine*. London: Oxford University Press, 1926.

Hutchins, Robert M., ed. *Great Books of the Western World*. Vols. 1-54. Chicago: Encyclopedia Britannica, 1955.

Inman, Thomas. *Ancient Faiths Embodied in Ancient Names*. Vols. 1-2. London: Printed for the Author, 1868-1869.

James, George G.M. *Stolen Legacy*. New York: Philosophical Library, 1954.

Johnston, Harry H. *A History of the Colonization of Africa by Alien Races*. Cambridge: Cambridge University Press, 1899.

Keltie, John S. *The Partition of Africa*. London: E. Stanford, 1895.

Kenrick, John. *Ancient Egypt Under the Pharaohs*. Vols. 1-2. London: B. Fellowes, 1850.

Knight, Richard P. *The Symbolical Language of Ancient Art and Mythology*. New York: J.W. Bouton, 1876.

Lane-Poole, Stanley. *The Moors in Spain*. London: T. Fisher Unwin, 1887.*

Leakey, Louis S. *Adam's Ancestors*. London: Methuen, 1953.

_____ *The Stone Age Races of Kenya*. London: Oxford University Press, 1935.

Leo Africanus, Joannes. *The History and Description of Africa*. Vols. 1-3. London: Hakluyt Society, 1896.

Lepsius, Richard. *Discoveries in Egypt, Ethiopia, and the Peninsula of Sinai*. London: R. Bentley, 1852.

The Lost Books of the Bible and the Forgotten Books of Eden. New York: The World Publishing Co., 1963.

McGlinchey, James M. *The Teaching of Amen-Em-Ope and the Book of Proverbs.* Washington:The Catholic University of America, 1939.

MacMichael, Harold A. *A History of the Arabs in the Sudan.* Vols. 1-2. Cambridge: Cambridge University Press, 1922.

Manetho. *Manetho.* Translated by William G. Waddell. London: W. Heinemann, 1940.

Maspero, Gaston C. *The Dawn of Civilization; Egypt and Chaldea.* New York: Appleton, 1901.

_____ *History of Egypt, Chaldea, Syria, Babylonia, and Assyria.* Edited by A. H. Sayce. Vols. 1-9. London: The Grolier Society, 1901.

_____ *Life in Ancient Egypt and Assyria.* London: Chapman and Hall, 1892.

Massey, Gerald. *Ancient Egypt, the Light of the World.* Vols. 1-2. New York: S. Weiser, 1970.

Meek, Theophile J. *Hebrew Origins.* New York: Harper and Brothers, 1936.

Montet, Pierre. *Eternal Egypt.* Translated by Doreen Weightman. London: Weidenfeld and Nicolson, 1954.

Moon, Parker T. *Imperialism and World Politics.* New York: The Macmillan Co., 1926.

Moore, Richard B. *The Word "Negro", its Origin and Evil Use.* New York: Afroamerican Publishers, 1960.

Murray, Margaret A. *The Splendour That Was Egypt.* New York: Philosophical Library, 1949.

Padmore, George. *Africa: Britain's Third Empire.* London: D. Dobson, 1949.

Palmer, Herbert R. *Sudanese Memoirs.* Vols. 1-3. Lagos: The Government Printer, 1928.

Peet, Thomas E. *Egypt and the Old Testament.* Liverpool: University Press of Liverpool, 1922.

Petrie, William M. *A History of Egypt.* Vols. 1-6. London: Methuen, 1898-1924.

_____ *The Pyramids and Temples of Gizeh.* London: Field and Tuer, 1885.

Plato. *The Apology of Plato.* Oxford: The Clarendon Press, 1877.

_____ *The Republic.* Vols. 1-2. New York: G.P. Putnam's Sons, 1930-1935.

Polybius. *The Histories.* Translated by W. R. Paton. London: W. Heinemann, 1922-1927.

Select Bibliography

Posener, Georges. *A Dictionary of Egyptian Civilization*. New York: Tudor Pub. Co., 1962.

Pyramid Texts. Vols. 1-4. New York: Longmans, Green, 1952.

Rawlinson, George. *The Five Great Monarchies of the Ancient Eastern World*. Vols. 1-4. London: J. Murray, 1862-1867.

Robinson, Ronald E. and John Gallagher. *Africa and the Victorians; the Climax of Imperialism*. Garden City: Doubleday, 1968.

Robinson, Theodore H. and William O. Oesterley. *A History of Israel*. Vols. 1-2. Oxford: Clarendon Press, 1932.

Rogers, Joel A. *Africa's Gift to America*. New York: J.A. Rogers Publications, 1959.

_____ *Nature Knows No Color-Line*. New York: J.A. Rogers Publications, 1952.

_____ *Sex and Race*. Vols. 1-3. New York: J. A. Rogers Publications, 1940-1944.

_____ *World's Great Men of Color*. Vols. 1-2. New York: J.A. Rogers Publications, 1946-1947.

Sanford, Eva M. *The Mediterranean World in Ancient Times*. New York: The Ronald Press Co., 1938.

Santos, Joao dos. "Ethiopia Oriental." In: George M. Theal, *Records of South - Eastern Africa*. Vol. 7. London: Printed for the Government of the Cape Colony, 1898-1903.

Sedgwick, William T. and Harry W. Tyler. *A Short History of Science*. New York: The Macmillan Co., 1927.

Seligman, Charles G. *Races of Africa*. New York: Henry Holt and Co., 1930.

Slatin, Rudolf C. *Fire and Sword in the Sudan*. Translated by Francis R. Wingate. New York: E. Arnold, 1898.

Smith, Homer W. *Man and His Gods*. London: Cape, 1953.

Snowden, Frank M. *Blacks in Antiquity; Ethiopians in the Greco - Roman Experience*. Cambridge: Belknap Press of Harvard University Press, 1970.

Soames, Jane. *The Coast of Barbary*. London: J. Cape, 1938.

Stanley, Thomas. *History of Philosophy*. Vols. 1-3. London: H. Moseley and T. Dring, 1655-1660.

Stoddard, Theodore Lothrop. *Racial Realities in Europe*. New York: C. Scribner's Sons, 1924.

_____ *The Rising Tide of Color Against White World - Supremacy.* New York: C. Scribner's Sons, 1920.

Tertullian, Quintus S. *De Anima.* Amsterdam: Holland Pub. Co., 1947.

Thilly, Frank. *A History of Philosophy.* New York: H. Holt and Co., 1922.

The Torah: The Five Books of Moses. Philadelphia: Jewish Publication Society of America, 1967.

Turner, William. *History of Philosophy.* London: Ginn and Co., 1903.

Vail, Charles H. *Ancient Mysteries and Modern Masonry.* New York: Macoy Publishing and Masonic Supply Co., 1909.

Volney, Constantin F. *The Ruins: Or, A Survey of the Revolutions of Empires.* London: Printed for J. Johnson, 1795.

Waddell, Laurence A. *The Makers of Civilization in Race and History.* London: Luzac and Co., 1929.

Weber, Alfred. *History of Philosophy.* New York: Charles Scribner's Sons, 1899.

Wells, Herbert G. *A Short History of the World.* London: Heinemann, 1927.

Wiedner, Donald L. *A History of Africa South of the Sahara.* New York: Random House, 1962.

Williams, Eric E. *Capitalism and Slavery.* Chapel Hill: University of North Carolina Press, 1944.

Woodson, Carter G. *The Negro in Our History.* Washington: The Associated Publishers, 1922.

PERIODICALS, JOURNALS AND NEWSPAPERS

Arkell, Anthony J. "A Sudanese Abu Simbel." *The Illustrated London News,* Saturday, Vol. 210, No. 5626, February 15, 1947, pp. 214-215.

Dunham, Dows. "Notes on the History of Kush, 850 B.C.-A.D. 350." *American Journal of Archaeology,* Vol. 50, No. 3, July - Sept. 1946, pp. 378-388.

_____ "Outline of the Ancient History of the Sudan." *Sudan Notes and Records,* Vol. 28, pt. 5, 1947, pp. 1-10.

Gilroy, Harry. "Falasha Jews From Ethiopia Studying in Israel: Their Tribe Practices Judaism According to Law of Moses." *The New York Times,* Friday, March 4, 1955, p.3.

Select Bibliography

Harvey, Steve. "Nefertiti Ruled in Her Digs." *New York Post,* Wednesday, January 26, 1972, p. 21.

Hodgkin, Thomas. "National Movements In West Africa." *The Highway,* Vol. 43, February 1952, pp. 169-174.

Kirwan, L. P. "Notes on the Topography of the Christian Nubian Kingdoms." *The Journal of Egyptian Archaeology,* Vol. 21, Pt. I, Sept. 1935, pp. 57-62.

Read, John. "Alchemy and Alchemists." *The Rosicrucian Digest,* May 1952, pp. 174-177 and 195-196.

Reisner, G.A. "The Meroitic Kingdom of Ethiopia: A Chronological Outline." *The Journal of Egyptian Archaeology,* Vol. 9, Pts. 1-2, April 1923, pp. 34-77.

Wilford, Francis. "On Egypt and the Nile; From the Ancient Books of the Hindus." *Asiatic Researches,* Vol. 3, pt. 13, 1792, pp. 295-468.

Zyhlarz, Ernest. "The Countries of the Ethiopia Empire of Kash (Kush) and Egyptian Old Ethiopia in the New Kingdom." *Kush,* Vol. 6, 1958, pp. 7-38.

"Fossils Trace Man Back 600,000 Years in Gorge in Africa." *The New York Times,* Monday, August 24, 1959, p. 23.

"43,000 Year Old Mine Discovered in Swaziland." *The New York Times,* Sunday, February 8, 1970, p. 6.

* Titles available through *Black Classic Press.*

Name Index

Name Index

Subject Index

Subject Index

Rosetta Stone, 279, 281-82

S

Saite period, 241-43
Semianian period, 344
Semitic, 14, 30-31
Seven Liberal Arts, 257-58
Solar Calendar, 251
Sphinx of Gizeh
    features of, 109-11
    maimed by Napoleon's officers, 194
    wonder of the world, 251
    world's largest statue, 201
Swastika, 370-72

T

Tanite period, 240-41
Tasian period, 343
Thinite dynasties, 230-31
Trinitarian concept, 256, 290, 354-55

V

Venus of Dusseldorf, 251

W

Women
    Monomotapa's army, 112
    pharaohs, 233, 353-54
Writing
    Egyptian, 277-83
    literature, 348-349

Z

Zinjanthropus boisie
    characteristics, 23, 83-84
    location, 47
    oldest fossilman, 43, 91, 94-95